PORNOGRAPHY
Women, Violence
and Civil Liberties

Catherine Itzin is an Honorary Research Fellow in the
Violence, Abuse and Gender Relations Research Unit in The
Department of Applied Social Studies at the University of
Bradford. From 1985 she was a Senior Research Officer and
subsequently Research Fellow in the Department of Sociology
at the University of Essex. She is a member of the Executive
Committee of the National Council for Civil Liberties.

D0024229

PORNOGRAPHY

Women, Violence and Civil Liberties

Edited by CATHERINE ITZIN

OXFORD UNIVERSITY PRESS

Oxford University Press, Walton Street, Oxford OX2 6DP
Oxford New York Toronto
Delhi Bombay Calcutta Madras Karachi
Kuala Lumpur Singapore Hong Kong Tokyo
Nairobi Dar es Salaam Cape Town
Melbourne Auckland Madrid
and associated companies in
Berlin Ibadan

Oxford is a trade mark of Oxford University Press

Published in the United States
by Oxford University Press Inc., New York

See p. 636 for copyright details

First published 1992
Reprinted (new as paperback, with corrections) 1993 (twice)

British Library Cataloguing in Publication Data
Data available

Library of Congress Cataloging in Publication Data
Pornography : Women, Violence and Civil Liberties / edited
by Catherine Itzin.
Includes bibliographical references and index.
1. Pornography – Social aspects.   2. Pornography – Social aspects –
– Great Britain.   3. Censorship.   I. Itzin, Catherine, 1944–
HQ471.C377   1991   363.4'7 – dc20   91–22575
ISBN 0–19–825755–4 (pbk)

Printed and bound in Great Britain by
Biddles Ltd
Guildford and King's Lynn

To my parents, Neva and Frank,
with thanks,
without whom this work would not
have been possible

ACKNOWLEDGEMENTS

I want to thank the many women and men whose lives and work have contributed to the contents of this book, and those who have read and commented on the manuscript or parts of it. In particular I want to thank the eight lawyers who read – and re-read – the legislation chapters through their many drafts. I also want to thank my friends, family and colleagues who have recognized the mental, physical, emotional and spiritual exhaustion sustained by working on pornography over a long period of time and who have given me encouragement to continue.

I want to thank all of these people, but I do not want to name any of them, because it is not safe to do so.

One of the women who launched the Irish Campaign Against Pornography and Censorship lost her job two weeks later. One of the lawyers who worked over a period of years to draft sex discrimination legislation against pornography lost her job because of this work. Another of these lawyers asked not to be mentioned in the knowledge that her job would be in jeopardy if this work were acknowledged. An eminent barrister read the manuscript and made invaluable comments, but asked not to be included in the acknowledgements. In the USA for a long time, and now in the UK, women who have researched and written about the negative effects of pornography have encountered barriers to advancement in their academic careers.

The sad reality is that legitimate legal and academic, as well as campaign, work on pornography is a personal and a professional liability. Just as pornography has damaged and destroyed the lives of those who have been victims of it, the reputations, careers and livelihoods of those whose work documents this damage suffers as a consequence.

The work in this book has been produced at great cost by many people and I thank them for it, both the named and the unnamed.

CONTENTS

CONTENTS

INTRODUCTION: FACT, FICTION AND FACTION

Why make a fuss about pornography? Men seem to like it.[1] It's a very profitable industry.[2] It offers women employment and some women a 'glamorous' career. It's said to be just a bit of harmless fun: entertainment for men. So what if it does degrade women; aren't there more important issues to do with women's equality? After all, it's only images. Isn't there a big difference between fantasy and reality? Also, the problems inherent in pornography are small compared with the problem of trying to tackle them. What about the censorship of art and literature? Or the desire of right-wing moralists to suppress anything to do with sex and sexuality? Why bother?

The short answer is because pornography plays an important part in contributing to sexual violence against women and to sex discrimination and sexual inequality. And this must matter at least as much as men's pleasure, as much as art and literature, more than the profits of the pornography industry. The long answer is to be found in the pages of this book: in the descriptions of what pornography actually is, in the evidence of harm it does to women, in the links between pornography and rape, in the accounts of the connections between child pornography and child sexual abuse, in how women really feel about it, in what it does to men, how it reinforces racism, infringes the civil liberties of women.

My interest in pornography dates from an article by Polly Toynbee published in the *Guardian* on 30 October 1981, describing what she had seen as a member of the Williams Committee on Obscenity and Film Censorship. 'These included scenes of castration, cannibalism, flaying, the crushing of breasts in vices, exploding vaginas packed with hand grenades, eyes gouged out, beatings, dismembering, burnings, multiple rape and every other horror that could befall the human body.' She had also witnessed 'women engaged in sexual intercourse with pigs and dogs' and heard of women killed on screen in snuff movies. However, she, together with the other members of the Williams Committee, concluded that there was no evidence that pornography harmed people, except in a few cases where participants in the photos might have come to harm: 'the poor, unhealthy, unhappy, many Third World children' or the 'South American prostitutes who were actually sexually murdered in films'. The Williams Committee recommended making 'most pornography freely available to adults and to remove all controls from the printed word'.[3] In Polly Toynbee's words, they recommended 'the greatest possible freedom from censorship combined with rather stringent restrictions on the open display of material'.

What she described was burned into my brain. I was completely bewildered as to how anyone could look at that material and not see that the 'people' in the pictures were real women who were actually harmed, and that what was being witnessed was unadulterated misogyny: hatred and violence against women.

I, then, like the members of the Williams Committee, was also concerned about the 'greatest possible freedom from censorship'. As a student in the 1960s I had been active in the efforts to end official state censorship in the theatre: laws which dated back 400 years, being used then to censor the plays of Edward Bond, but abolished in the Theatres Act 1968.[4] In the 1970s, I had campaigned on the left against censorship and for freedom of speech, production and publication in the theatre in my capacity as drama critic for *Tribune* and editor of *Theatre Quarterly*, and in my book *Stages in the Revolution*, on political theatre in Britain from 1968.[5] In 1981, the year of Polly Toynbee's article on the Williams Committee, I had been defending Howard Brenton's play *The Romans in Britain* against a prosecution attempted by Mary Whitehouse.[6] As with Bond's plays, I believed that sexual immorality was a pretext for the censorship of 'dissident' social and political comment.

Although I was deeply concerned then about threats to free speech in the theatre, and absolutely opposed to censorship in any form, I knew in my bones that the publication of the pictures described by Polly Toynbee could not constitute a freedom that had any meaning or value, and that, in spite of apparent contradictions, it would be quite compatible to campaign against censorship and for civil liberties, and also against pornography – that being opposed to pornography does not mean being in favour of censorship.[7]

For the past ten years I have worked to translate my 'intuition' about the meaning of pornography and freedom into a form that could be understood by other people who are also committed both to civil liberties and freedom of expression, and to freedom and equality for women. This book is the outcome of that process. It is also the result of the work of many individuals and organizations campaigning against pornography as a women's issue for two decades in the USA and in the UK (see Appendix 1).

Our case against pornography is based on what it means and what it does to women: the part played by pornography in contributing to sexual inequality, sex discrimination and to sexual violence. The story starts in the section on the pornography industry and its product, with a chapter drawing on a number of sources to describe the content of the pornography available in the USA and the UK. This chapter covers everything from legal, mass-marketed, so-called soft-core pornography to illegal snuff films, and explains exactly what this 'entertainment for men' actually does to and communicates about women.

One major argument in the case against pornography is its function in creating inequality and maintaining oppression. The nine chapters in Part II therefore address the issue of pornography and power in all its different guises. In Chapter 2, I describe how inequality is institutionalized in the structures of society and internalized in the attitudes and behaviour of individuals: how it is socially constructed and conditioned, not biologically determined, and how pornography contributes to sexual violence and sexual inequality. Just as low pay is a key factor in the economic subordination of women, pornography is central to the sexual subordination of women, and, like low pay, is itself a form of sex discrimination. Susanne Kappeler, in Chapter 4, explains how the power of men to represent women *as sex* in pornography is a means of subjugation and shows how pornography is a collective enactment of male power. She compares the commonplace of sexual violence in a male supremacist society with the commonplace of racial violence in a white supremacist society, and challenges claims that the feminist critique of pornography in any way constitutes censorship.

Kappeler reminds us that pornography is a product of capitalism as well as patriarchy: a multi-billion-dollar international industry, largely controlled by organized crime in the USA,[8] and in the UK, as Chapter 3 demonstrates, increasingly a part of   **3** mainstream printing, publishing and magazine business. Aminatta Forna, in Chapter 5, argues that pornography is a practice of racism and anti-Semitism as well as sexism, exploiting black and Third World women, and trading in racist stereotypes. She compares the women's suffrage and anti-pornography movements with the black civil rights movement and argues that pornography, like race hatred literature, incites hatred and violence.

Liz Kelly (in Chapter 6) discusses child pornography as a product of the power of adults over children, as well as of male power and racism and imperialism. She describes the connections between the use of child and adult pornography, and child sexual abuse. She argues that child pornography is a record of the sexual abuse of children: its very existence evidence of harm. The multiple connections between pornography and abuse are also discussed by Corinne Sweet, Ray Wyre and Peter Baker.

In Chapter 7, Peter Baker looks at male power from the point of view of heterosexual men and shows that while men may benefit from its privileges, they are also hurt by the effects of male conditioning and the constraints of male sexuality as it is currently socially constructed. He explains the damage that pornography does to men and to relationships between men and women, as well as the harm it does to women through men.

Then in Chapter 8 John Stoltenberg describes the damage that pornography does to gay men. He argues that pornography is central to creating and maintaining gay oppression: that homophobia is integral to sexualized male supremacy, a by-product of misogyny, both a consequence of and an enforcer of sex discrimination. Homophobia won't end, he says, until male supremacy ends, and this means there should be a natural alliance between gay men and women against pornography. In Chapter 9, Janice Raymond discusses the alliance between lesbian sado-masochists and libertarians in defending pornography. She challenges the view that women's sexual liberation should be modelled on male sexuality, and that objectification, subordination or violence are in any way progressive or liberating.

Deborah Cameron and Elizabeth Frazer are critical (in Chapter 19) of what they call the 'addiction model' of pornography as depoliticizing male power and open to abuse: permitting individual men and the criminal justice system to 'personalize' the problem of pornography and to rationalize or justify crimes of violence. But in Chapter 10 Corinne Sweet provides a new perspective: a political analysis of pornography as addiction. She shows how all addictions are a product of capitalism and oppression; how addiction itself is conditioned and socially constructed. She explains the origins of addiction to pornography in relation to normal childhood socialization for all people, and for some people in relation to child sexual abuse; and she challenges the traditional view of addiction as deviance.

The other major argument in the case against pornography is the evidence of sexual violence experienced by women and children as a result of the manufacture and use of pornography. The eight chapters of Part III cover the evidence of harm. In Chapter 11, Tim Tate describes the growth of the international trade in child pornography following the liberalization of the law in Denmark in 1969. He also documents the cottage industry in child pornography produced by paedophiles as part of their practice of child sexual abuse, and demonstrates the need to criminalize possession of child pornography in order to deal effectively with the abuse of children. In Chapter 12 Michele Elliott describes the sexualizing of children in advertising, the process of normalizing children as erotic objects and desensitizing people to child abuse.

A major source of evidence of women's experience of harm caused by pornography has come from public hearings held in the USA. The National Organization of Women (NOW) held hearings in four major US cities in 1984, and the US Senate subsequently held hearings when considering legislation for victims of pornography. But the first hearings were held in Minneapolis in 1983, when the city council heard evidence of harm in considering civil rights legislation against pornography. There, for the first time, women spoke in public about the damage pornography had done to them and their lives. In Chapter 23 Catharine A. MacKinnon quotes in considerable detail from the evidence of harm presented to the Minneapolis hearings.[9] Chapter 13 provides data on women's experience of pornography-related sexual violence collected from surveys in women's magazines in the UK and compares these with data from surveys of women in the USA.

In Chapter 14, Ray Wyre describes the stages in the 'cycle of abuse' that he has identified in his work with sex offenders, and the part that pornography plays in predisposing men to abuse, in reducing internal and external inhibitions to abuse, and in legitimizing and initiating abuse. His clinical experience **5** challenges the myth that sexual fantasy and sexual acts are separate and unconnected, and he argues that pornography is particularly dangerous in conditioning and reinforcing male orgasm to sexual violence and child sexual abuse.

In 1986 Edna F. Einsiedel produced a report entitled 'Social and Behavioral Science Research Analysis' for the US Attorney General's Commission on Pornography Final Report which included a brief review of the research evidence examined by the 1970 US Pornography Commission, a description of American public opinion on pornography based on data from several public opinion polls, and a summary of clinical studies on sex offenders and pornography. Her report – regarded by experts in the field of pornography research as a 'state of the art' review of the academic research prior to 1986 on the effects of pornography – has received limited publication. Einsiedel's review of the experimental research is reproduced in Chapter 15. It establishes correlations between sexually violent pornography, acceptance of sexual violence, laboratory aggression against women, and self-reported sexually aggressive behaviour. It explains the theoretical approaches used in the research, and provides answers to questions that are commonly raised about methodological issues.

The chapters by James Weaver and Diana E. H. Russell update Einsiedel's review, covering the experimental research carried out after 1986 and the research on pornography and sex offenders over the past twenty years. In Chapter 26 I discuss the attempts to discredit this scientific evidence, and in response to claims that it is inconclusive and unreliable, James Weaver (Chapter 16) evaluates the key research and its methodologies, provides accurate information and explanation about issues of controversy in this field, and shows the social science and psychological research evidence to be both reliable and conclusive in establishing the negative effects on attitudes and behaviour of both sexually violent and 'standard' non-violent pornography.

Diana Russell (Chapter 17) specifically reviews over fifty social science research studies which provide evidence of male proclivity to rape and to sexually abuse children, and of the function of pornography in the cycle of abuse described by Wyre. The research leads Russell to propose a model of the causal links between pornography and rape – in which pornography is identified as one of several causes of sexual violence.

6   In Chapter 18 James Check discusses the status of the social

science and psychological research and explains how it has been used to influence social policy and the law on obscenity in the USA, Australia, and Canada. In particular he describes how Canadian courts have used the research evidence of harm in decisions to convict material which is violent or subordinating, but to acquit sexually explicit material which does not fall into these categories (what he calls erotica).

In Chapter 19, Deborah Cameron and Elizabeth Frazer are critical of basing the case against pornography solely on causal links between pornography and specific instances of sexual violence. They acknowledge that these links exist, but believe that causal links account for only a small part of the harm caused by pornography. Like others in the book they believe that pornography accounts for only part of the problem of male power and male violence (and also that there are other factors in addition to pornography that contribute to it). They are particularly concerned with other 'causal factors' such as the function of pornography in the 'construction of desire', and in its cultural influences on the imagination: in order, they argue, for something (like sexual murder) to be possible and put into action, it has to be imagined. They see pornography as telling men what can be done to women, thereby creating the possibility for sexual violence to be carried out. They see the problem of pornography as firmly located within the social construction of masculinity, male sexuality and male power as it affects all men.[10]

In Chapter 20, Patricia Hynes compares environmental pollution with the harm caused by pornography. She identifies male social and sexual dominance as a common factor in both. She finds some revealing similarities in the arguments used to defend environmental pollution and pornography, but a difference in attitude: more concern about what is metaphorically called the rape of the planet than the real rape of women.

How pornography subordinates women, and infringes women's civil rights and civil liberties, how it limits the freedom of movement and safety of women, and functions to deny women freedom of speech and equality in society, is described in different ways by Catharine A. MacKinnon, Andrea Dworkin, Michael Moorcock and myself in Chapters 23 to 26. Contributors to this book describe the problem of pornography as they see it from the 'new' perspective of women's oppression, and thereby arrive at an entirely 'new' perspective on the problems of censorship and free speech and the possibilities of personal and political change.   **7**

Part IV deals with legislation. In Chapter 21 I review the rationale behind and the history of obscenity legislation, explaining how and why it fails to deal with the problem of pornography. This chapter shows how, with an understanding of the function of pornography in constructing and maintaining sexual inequality, it is possible to legislate against pornography *without censorship*, on grounds of sex discrimination, enabling women to seek remedy for the harm or injury caused by pornography. In Chapter 22, I discuss ways of defining pornography concretely and specifically for what it is and what it does to women, so that only pornography is targeted, not art or literature or sex education or sexually explicit materials which are not pornography (erotica). This chapter also deals with issues of child pornography, gay and lesbian pornography, erotica and eroticized violence. In Chapter 5, Aminatta Forna argues the case for using the Race Relations Act 1976 as a model for legislating against pornography as incitement to sexual hatred and violence.

There was a major breakthrough in the USA in the early 1980s with the civil rights legislation against pornography drafted by Andrea Dworkin and Catharine A. MacKinnon. In Chapter 23, Catharine MacKinnon explains the reasoning behind the civil rights ordinance, and what it means to legislate against pornography on grounds of gender and harm rather than morality. She also explains the advantages of civil law, the injuries for which women could seek remedy, and the grounds on which action could be taken.

Part V concludes the book with chapters on pornography, censorship and civil liberties, getting behind the rhetoric to look afresh at what freedom and censorship really mean. Andrea Dworkin, in Chapter 24, puts censorship and obscenity into a concrete historical perspective, describes what pornography is and does to women, and who the pornographers are. She defines subordination, discusses the meaning of 'speech' and 'equality' for women, and demonstrates how civil rights legislation could empower women to deal with the pornography industry. In Chapter 25, Michael Moorcock compares contemporary Britain to Orwell's *Nineteen Eighty-Four*, in which pornography was used cynically to control the masses as part of the apparatus of state censorship. He describes the bankrupt politics of the left, how in spite of its feminist rhetoric its real alliance is with the right in defending pornography and thus reinforcing the sexist status quo. He argues that abolishing the obscenity legislation and replacing it with sex discrimination legislation against pornography, specifically defined, would actually give him *greater freedom* from censorship as a writer about sexually explicit matters. The case against pornography is concluded in the final chapter, where I discuss the position taken by the American Civil Liberties Union in the USA and the National Council for Civil Liberties in the UK on the matter of pornography, summarize the different kinds of evidence of different kinds of harm caused by pornography, and suggest that there is sufficient evidence by civil liberties standards to give the human rights and civil liberties of women precedence over pornography.

I am tempted to apologize for the size of this book, but I believed it was necessary to be comprehensive and exhaustive in covering all of the issues, and meticulous in documenting the evidence of harm. This evidence is frequently denied or discredited, and accurate information about the evidence of harm and the feminist anti-pornography arguments do not often get published to a wide audience. The reality as far as free speech is concerned is that pornographers and pro-pornography interests have the money and the power in society and much greater freedom to publish pornography and to defend its publication. In the USA it is the speech of women injured by pornography and the voice of the feminist anti-pornography movement which is suppressed. The transcript of the Minneapolis Hearings, for example, has never found a publisher in the USA.[11] And as Susanne Kappeler points out, the women who attempt to speak about the harm of pornography are themselves called censors at the same time as their speech is being suppressed.

This book has been inspired by and built on the achievements of the many women – and some men – who have committed themselves to eliminating pornography, often at considerable personal cost; and the achievement of organizations like Women Against Pornography (WAP), Organizing Against Pornography (OAP), National Anti-Pornography Civil Rights Organization (NAPCRO), and Men Against Pornography (MAP) in the USA, the Campaign Against Pornography and Censorship (CPC), the Campaign for Press and Broadcasting Freedom (CPBF) and the Campaign Against Pornography (CAP) in the UK, the Irish Campaign Against Pornography and Censorship (ICPC) in Ireland, and Women Against Violence Against Women (WAVAW) on both sides of the Atlantic. In Appendix 1, there is a chronology of women's anti-pornography initiatives in the UK from the 1970s.

The success of these developments has provoked fierce opposition from pro-pornography interests in the USA, and now increasingly in the UK. In the absence of arguments that stand up to the mounting evidence of harm, or which deal with the increasingly apparent role of pornography in the subordination of women, the strategies of the pro-pornographers are often based on personal attack and intellectual dishonesty: attempts to stereotype, ridicule, trivialize and discredit individuals, and to distort and misrepresent the evidence and arguments against pornography. Indeed, a major reason for publishing this book is to counter this misinformation with accurate information.

Attempts to distort and misrepresent the evidence that exists of the harm caused by pornography range from denying that it exists to claiming that it does but that it is inconclusive. The Williams Committee, for example, came to the conclusion that the evidence of harm was inconclusive, but the review of the evidence which they commissioned has subsequently been shown to have been incomplete, failing to include the research that existed at that time showing links between pornography and sexual violence.[12] This kind of misrepresentation is not uncommon; it creates doubt and confusion. Denying or discrediting the evidence of harm is an essential strategy of pro-pornography interests because it is on the basis of this evidence that action is most likely to be taken against pornography. This book therefore provides a comprehensive record of evidence of harm.

In the USA the pornography industry has, in fact, been instrumental in originating much of the misrepresentation. One outstanding example of this concerns the US Attorney General's Commission on Pornography in 1985, which was unanimous in its finding of a causal link between pornography and sexual violence. It has been accused of both right-wing and left-wing bias, and even of feminist bias. I have heard many people, civil libertarians in particular, refer to the unreliability of its results.

Then it is revealed, in a leaked letter, that a major Washington D.C. PR company produced a tender for members of the Media Coalition (which included the Council for Periodical Distributors Associations and the International Periodical Distributors Association) following a meeting with them setting forth 'strategy recommendations for dealing with . . . the problems raised by the work of the Attorney General's Commission on Pornography' at a proposed charge of nearly a million dollars. The letter 'proposed a strategy designed' to 'discredit the Commission on Pornography, the manner in which its members were chosen,' and 'the way in which it has conducted its deliberations,' to create 'doubts . . . about the objectivity and validity of the Commission's findings and recommendations', to make it 'more difficult . . . to use the report as an effective tool . . .' against pornography.

The letter (excerpts from which are published in Appendix 2) proposed the 'creation of a broad coalition of . . . academicians, civil libertarians, religious leaders, civic and community leaders, politicians, business and foundation executives, authors and editors, columnists, commentators and entertainers' using a 'program of print and broadcast activities, creation of a national information center and speakers' bureau, development of a grass roots membership base, publication of a newsletter and a special book or collection of essays on the subject, an annual conference and regional seminars and symposia . . . to dispel the notion that opponents of the Commission's work are only interested in protecting their own financial interests or are somehow "pro-pornography".'

In the event a new organization was created, called Americans for Constitutional Freedom, which also included the American Booksellers Association and the Magazine Publishers of America (representing trade and pornography publishers and distributors). A PR campaign 'to discredit the Commission' and its findings did take place (along the lines outlined in the letter) and a belief was fostered that 'there is no factual or scientific basis for the exaggerated and unfounded allegations that sexually oriented content . . . is in any way a cause of violent or criminal behaviour'.[13] This belief is frequently repeated as fact, even by serious and respectable academics and journalists who are not easily able to verify the facts of the Commission's findings because the only publisher the report could find was an obscure press in Tennessee and it is therefore virtually unavailable.[14]

There have been two government commissions on pornography in the USA in the past twenty years. The 1970 Commission found 'no evidence of harm.'[15] This was in part because its terms of reference excluded consideration of sexually violent materials which were being evaluated at that time by a separate government commission on media violence.[16] Flaws in the research and the conclusions of the 1970 Commission were subsequently **11** identified by the social science research establishment and acknowledged by conservatives and liberals alike.[17] An enormous amount of new, and far more rigorous research was carried out in the fifteen years following the 1970 Commission.

This research was reviewed by Professor Edna F. Einsiedel for the US Attorney General's Commission in 1985 (see Chapter 15 for excerpts from this review, which for the reasons described above, has received limited publication). The Commission also heard evidence from all sources for and against pornography: from academics, from victims, from the pornography industry and from 'every qualified libertarian and First Amendment advocate . . . requesting the right to testify'.[18] Its conclusions about the link between pornography and sexual violence were, according to a leading researcher in the field of pornography, 'correctly drawn and correct, based upon a narrow reading of the totality of the available evidence'.[19] Furthermore, there was no evidence that pornography did *not* contribute to sexual violence.

The Commission concluded that pornography harmed women (and children), and the report made 87 recommendations for federal, state and local government action. One of these was, in fact, for civil rights legislation giving women the right to sue for injury proveably caused by pornography. But the majority of its recommendations relied on the use of the obscenity legislation the Commission itself had discredited and demonstrated to be ineffective.

The power of pornography and of the pornography industry is not to be underestimated. It has exercised its influence on the American Civil Liberties Union (ACLU) in the USA, which not only defends pornographers but receives subsidy from the pornography industry and includes pornographers on the Board of Directors of one of its state affiliates.[20]

Women in the USA who have promoted civil rights legislation against pornography have been the target of vicious attack by the pornography industry. This book has been inspired by the work of some of those women: by Kathleen Barry, Robin Morgan, Gloria Steinem, Andrea Dworkin and Catharine A. MacKinnon. It has also been inspired by the work of Susan Griffin and Susan Brownmiller in the USA, and by Susanne Kappeler, Deborah Cameron and Elizabeth Frazer in the UK. Many of these women are familiar with attack and misrepresentation, as is the MP Clare Short, who has been vilified in the tabloid press in response to her proposals to legislate against Page 3 photographs. She has been both sexualized and presented as a prude or a moralist. In the USA a major pornography magazine published a purported interview with Gloria Steinem's clitoris (illustrated and virulently anti-feminist); portrayed Susan Brownmiller as sexually insatiable, a 'thrilling cock-fondler'; caricatured *Cosmopolitan* editor Helen Gurley-Brown as a man-hating, ball-breaking 'bitch'; and represented Andrea Dworkin as a 'Jewish pimp' of black children in a racist and anti-Semitic cartoon.[21]

The material is misogynist in the extreme, full of hate and violence and intended to incite contempt, disgust and hatred against 'independent' women generally and feminists in particular. The American writer Andrea Dworkin has been particularly vulnerable to attack, often of a vicious and personal nature. That she has been targeted by the pornography industry is perhaps not surprising. The civil rights legislation she advocates poses the only real threat the industry has ever faced. But the extent to which she and her work have been misrepresented and/or misunderstood more widely is slightly more perplexing.

She is represented as being an essentialist and a biological determinist, but in fact she has written of biological determinism as the 'world's most dangerous and deadly idea'.[22] What she does not find acceptable is male power and masculinity as constructed in a male supremacist society. She has been eloquent in exposing the structures and practices of male power and explaining the system of sexual inequality as it affects both women and men on a personal as well as a political level. Pornography is one part of that system.

Inherent in her theories is the possibility of change. Male power, male dominance, masculinity, male sexuality, male aggression are not biologically determined. They are conditioned. Pornography plays a part in this. What is conditioned can be deconditioned. Men can change. The structures of male power can be dismantled. Men have the power to make these changes if they choose.

Attempts by pro-pornography interests to degrade and discredit, to trivialize and monsterize anti-pornography feminists, have also been translated into statements (often by respectable academics and journalists) that these women have 'split the women's movement in the USA'.[23] The allegations are absurd, yet quoted as fact. The alleged 'split' is itself a fiction. A **13** difference in viewpoint is exaggerated into a division in a way that rarely happens when there is disagreement on other issues of women's oppression. There are, however, two feminist organizations which have – like the pornography industry and the liberal and libertarian left – promoted and participated in misrepresentation of the feminist anti-pornography movement.

In the USA, FACT (Feminists Against Censorship Taskforce) was set up in conjunction with the American Civil Liberties Union and has campaigned to discredit and to defeat the civil rights ordinance. FACT filed a legal 'Brief' in the US courts which incredibly attempted to invest the civil rights legislation *against* pornography with all the properties of pornography itself: characterizing it as 'detrimental to women', as 'discriminating against women', not only 'reinforcing sexist stereotypes' but 'creating them', creating sexual double standards and a sexist definition of pornography (which FACT, like the pornography industry, prefers to call 'sexually explicit speech').

A similar organization called FAC (Feminists Against Censorship) was set up in the UK in 1990, in response to the campaigns against pornography as a women's issue which had emerged – to the CPC, CAP, CPBF, NCCL and trade union initiatives described above and in Chapters 18 and 23 and Appendix 1. FAC's policy leaflet also includes examples of the kind of distortion and misrepresentation which this book aims to correct.

Although it claims to oppose censorship, the FAC policy leaflet is largely concerned to discredit women who resist pornography with allegations that they present a false picture of women's oppression by 'reducing all oppression to pornography' and 'ignore the real violence and real causes of women's oppression.'[24] No such beliefs are held and no such claims are made. On the contrary, it is claimed by those women who oppose the sexual subordination of women in pornography that 'pornography is central to women's oppression', *together with* discrimination in 'employment, education, property and public services' and with 'rape, battery, sexual abuse of children and prostitution' which are also central to women's oppression.[25]

The feminists who campaign against pornography have been for many years at the forefront of efforts to end the economic subordination of women. They have worked for equal pay and conditions of employment, pension rights, positive action and childcare. They have worked against rape, domestic violence, sexual harassment, child sexual abuse. They have worked for the end of prostitution and the international traffic in women, and for reproductive rights, especially the right to abortion.[26] They have also 'tackled issues of class and race' and age and disability and sexuality, and have been at the cutting edge of lesbian liberation work. To represent any of them as 'single-mindedly focusing on pornography' and 'ignoring the fundamental causes of cultural and social oppression' is, as FAC does, a lie.[27] The truth is that they have recognized that ending women's economic subordination is not possible without also ending women's sexual subordination: that women's oppression needs to be tackled on all fronts simultaneously – including pornography.

Women who campaign against pornography as a women's issue are also often characterized as sexually repressed and repressive, as puritanical, anti-sex and censorious. Some of us have been stereotyped as 'Ms Grundy': out to spoil everyone's fun.[28] And FAC have invented a 'belief' which they describe as 'common among anti-pornography campaigners, that women do not really like sex'.[29] The truth is quite the opposite: an ability to like sex and to hate pornography, and the capacity to distinguish between the two.

Another strategy adopted by pro-pornography interests attempting to discredit campaigns against pornography as a women's issue is to claim alliances with right-wing moral crusades and religious fundamentalism. FAC, for example, describe anti-pornography feminists as 'authoritarian', suggesting a linguistic link with the 'moral majority', and claim that they 'collaborate with the religious right' to give the state power to censor all forms of sexual expression.[30] Two recent FAC publications rely heavily on slurring anti-pornography campaigns by making spurious right wing associations: that 'whatever they allege to the contrary, their view of pornography is identical to that of traditional conservatism', that they have done nothing but 'give undeserved respectability to the beliefs of the moral right and the fundamentalist lobby' and even that the campaigns themselves 'constitute a form of secular fundamentalism' – like religious fundamentalism.[31] This is, quite frankly, rubbish.

No such alliances exist or have ever been made, either in the USA or in the UK.[32] Furthermore, the analysis of pornography as a practice of sex discrimination and the international movement for women's liberation, of which feminist anti-pornography campaigns are a part, are fundamentally incompatible with the ideology of the religious right with its repressive views on sex, sexuality and the role of women.

On the other hand, there *is* evidence of an 'alliance' (e.g. working together, sharing the same views about pornography) between FAC and the pornography industry illustrated, for example, in the FAC membership of the editor of *Penthouse* and FAC's own campaign to promote pornography generally and sexually violent pornography in particular.[33] FAC delegates to the National Council for Civil Liberties AGM in 1990 lobbied to overturn the NCCL's then anti-pornography policy, speaking in defence of sadistic pornography which was the only material covered by the narrow definition of the policy.[34] One of the pro-pornography speakers at the meeting was an editor of *Quim*, the British lesbian pornographic magazine, the first issue of which in July 1989 contained 'a piece of writing which described the sexual abuse of young boys by a group of women and a misogynist account of the sexual assault of an injured and helpless woman by a nun'.[35]

The FACT Brief also appears to include a defence of sexually violent pornography, euphemistically described as 'rough sex': arguing that 'women need the socially recognized space to appropriate for themselves the robustness of what traditionally has been male language'. 'Danger' as a euphemism for sexual violence is also favoured by the libertarian left.[36] In Chapter 20, Patricia Hynes notes that the pornography industry, like industries involved in environmental pollution, is partial to the use of such euphemisms to obscure and to legitimate practices which are damaging and destructive.

Janice Raymond – and John Stoltenberg in Chapter 8 – discuss the sexualized woman-hatred at the heart of sado-masochism whether heterosexual, lesbian or gay. The sado-masochist position – which defines liberation in terms of violence, and regards sadistic pornography as representing sexual freedom – has been decisively challenged by lesbian feminists, the majority of whom oppose this inversion of the fundamental values of freedom, who see the small but vocal lobby of sado-masochists in the libertarian and lesbian communities as a serious threat to women's liberation generally and to lesbian liberation specifically, and who have themselves conducted major campaigns against sado-masochism.[37] 'From a feminist perspective,' writes Sheila Jeffreys, for example, 'there are all kinds of difficulties in accepting sado-masochism as a revolutionary practice for lesbians and other women.' She argues that the libertarian and lesbian sado-masochist attack on anti-pornography feminism shows 'a callous disregard for the abuse of women', and finds it 'difficult to see pornography, which is a mainstream massive industry, as radical' or progressive.[38]

Janice Raymond also questions the politics of the alliance between lesbian sado-masochists, libertarians and the pornography industry, and between 'liberal patriarchal men' and 'FACT feminism.' The alleged alliance between anti-pornography feminism and the religious right is in fact, a fiction, the propaganda of 'sexual liberals' which, according to Dorchen Leidholdt, has served to divert attention from the 'actual alliance that has long existed between pornographers and civil libertarians'.[39] The ultimate irony in the alliance of women with the sexual libertarians is, as Sheila Jeffreys points out, that they are 'not simply involved in a massive defence of pornography', but using 'gross . . . distortion . . . they attack the basic premises of feminism'.[40] To the extent that there *is* any 'split' in the women's movement, responsibility must lie with the tactics of pro-pornography feminists and the alliance between sado-masochists, libertarians and pornographers.

Furthermore, as Patricia Hynes points out in Chapter 20, most defenders of pornography are defending it not just because they are protecting profit or free speech, but because they use it and they like it and they want to protect 'sex based on dominance, degradation and humiliation'. Amy Elman has suggested that it is FACT's strategy to play down their defence of pornography because they understand that it is 'politically more acceptable to object to the legislation by alleging that it constitutes an assault on speech more generally than to assert that they simply derive pleasure from pornography. They therefore attempt to cast the discussion of pornography in terms of censorship and away from notions of harm.'[41] The FACT Brief – an apologia in effect, I think, for the pornography industry – actually called for *less* restriction on pornography as a 'category of speech from which women have been excluded'.

In the UK, the underlying strategy of the FAC campaign has been to equate feminist anti-pornography campaigns with 'campaigns for censorship', and the FAC rhetoric frequently attaches the epithet 'pro-censorship' to feminists who campaign against pornography, thereby entirely falsely presenting women who are against pornography as being de facto in favour of censorship,   **17** and wholly misrepresenting the civil rights approach to legislating against pornography.

This strategy creates confusion. There are many women and men who have supported FACT in the USA (and now FAC in the UK) because they are genuinely and justifiably worried about censorship. They do not like pornography, but they do not want to appear to be 'illiberal' and censorious – or to be called 'censors'. They have been misinformed and misled about the civil rights ordinance (which, as this book demonstrates, has nothing to do with censorship) and they are unaware of FACT's pro-pornography 'politics'. The use of intellectual sophistry and politically correct rhetoric exacerbates the confusion.

From other quarters, attempts are made to discredit antipornography campaigns – or research on pornography and sexual violence – because it is, or is labelled, feminist.[42] But what is feminism, and who are feminists, but women (and men) who are aware of the economic and sexual subordination of women in society and who wish to achieve sexual and social equality? Why, therefore, should this (surely not unreasonable, even worthy) objective be the basis for denigration?

Proposals to legislate against pornography as a civil rights or a sex discrimination issue lead some people to assume that all 'sexually explicit' material would disappear. Proponents of this approach are accused of wanting to ban sex and to deny women the freedom to explore their sexuality. Fears about sexual repression are well-founded, given the history of obscenity legislation, but they are unfounded with respect to this new form of legislation. The fears in this case are based on another fundamental misrepresentation by the pornography industry: that its product is 'just sex' or 'pro-women'. As Chapter 1, 'Entertainment for Men: What It Is and What It Means', clearly shows, pornography is much more than sex: sexual explicitness is just one characteristic of pornography.

Definitions of pornography for purposes of civil rights legislation in the USA and sex discrimination legislation in the UK define pornography not just in terms of sexual explicitness, but also in terms of subordination *and* sexual violence *and* sexual objectification. Legal definitions of pornography also distinguish between pornography and erotica (i.e. sex and sexually explicit material which is non-objectifying, non-violent and non-subordinating). The scientific evidence shows that this kind of material (referred to in this book as erotica) is not linked with the harm caused by sexually violent or subordinating and dehumanizing pornography. In a recent study, James Check and Ted Guloien found that 'exposure to non-violent, erotica materials did not have any demonstrated anti-social impact' and that 'this was in contrast to sexually violent and dehumanizing pornography, where such effects were found'.[43] Canadian courts are now using the results of this research as a basis for convicting harmful material and acquitting erotica (see Chapter 18 and Appendix 3). And the Canadian Supreme Court in a recent (February 1992) landmark decision has accepted the link between certain kinds of pornography and sexual violence *and* sexual inequality, with a unanimous ruling that depictions of degrading and dehumanizing sex and sex with violence are harmful to women. Sexual explicitness *per se* is not a problem: the sexualized and sexually explicit dominance, subordination and violence of pornography are the problem.

One purpose of this book is to illustrate some of the differences between pornography and sexually explicit materials which are not pornography, and to suggest that in an environment of social equality, free from the influence of pornography, sex might be experienced and presented differently: not in terms of male definition, or of male dominance and female subordination or power and powerlessness, but based on reciprocity, mutuality and equality. The nature of sex and sexuality premised on equality is a discovery denied and arguably suppressed by pornography, with its false premises about women, its false promises for men, and its power as a form of sex discrimination to 'pornographize' women in all aspects of their lives. Given the cultural dominance of male power and pornography, erotica is not as common as pornography, but it does exist, and when viewed alongside pornography is quite distinguishable from it. In this book Janice Raymond, Diana Russell, John Stoltenberg and Gloria Steinem (within Chapter 21) all describe sex and sexual explicitness which is not subordinating, objectifying or violent – and not pornography. To assume that sex and sexuality are only what pornography says they are is a tacit and perverse acceptance of the power of pornography and of sex as determined by sexual inequality.

The genuine concerns from which the lies, distortions, misrepresentation and confusion detract are political and sexual freedom, women's liberation, lesbian and gay liberation and censorship. This book seeks to address all of the interests and all of the issues that matter: persistent in pursuit of liberation on all fronts. This means acknowledging that pornography *is* a problem, that censorship *and* sexual repression *and* sexual violence *and* sex discrimination *and* discrimination against lesbians and gay men *all* matter. And conversely that free speech *and* sexual freedom *and* lesbian and gay liberation, *and* women's safety, freedom of movement and equality *all* matter.

Contributors to this book include lesbians and gay men as well as heterosexual women and men. Everyone who writes here is personally and professionally, publicly and privately, committed to free speech and freedom of expression. Many are long-standing anti-censorship and civil liberties activists. When they talk about censorship, they speak with authority. But they are also committed to freedom and equality for women, and many are also long-standing women's rights campaigners. For them pornography and the freedom of women are incompatible. They do not accept the harm to women and children to which pornography contributes, but equally, in seeking remedies for the harm of pornography, they can be relied upon not to tolerate the oppression of others in the process. They define freedom in terms of equality, and civil liberties in terms of liberation: for everyone.

It took women in the UK and the USA more than fifty years to win the right to vote.[44] In their campaign for electoral equality women were ridiculed, trivialized, stereotyped and vilified. They went to prison. They were subjected to force feeding and other forms of violence. Some died. But women won the vote, and it is difficult to imagine now the time when they did not have it. Women who campaign now for freedom from pornography also face hostility, contempt, hatred and outrage: for daring to want to be *that* free from discrimination, and *that* equal.

But imagine a time, fifty years from now if need be or more, when we will all look back with horror and dismay on that period in history when women were reduced to their sexual and excretory organs for the entertainment of men, and sold for profit, or hung by their breasts from meat hooks for someone's sexual pleasure. When this will look like a phenomenon so at odds with human dignity and justice that it will be almost unimaginable. When women are so highly valued and pornography such a thing of the past, we will hardly be able to believe it ever existed at all.

When this 'fantasy' becomes a reality, the work in this book will have helped to make it happen. The ideas in this book represent a sea-change in understanding both of sex and of sexual equality: a new way of looking at the world, a new way of seeing, a new way of being.[45] These ideas give new meaning to liberty and to liberation. They are ideas whose time will come.

Catherine Itzin
London, June 1992

Notes

1. Nick Cohen, 'Reaping Rich Rewards from the Profits of Pornography', *Independent*, 19 December 1989. Cohen put monthly sales at 2.25 million copies.
2. Mike Baxter, 'Flesh and Blood: Does Pornography Lead to Sexual Violence?', *New Scientist*, 5 May 1990.
3. A. W. B. Simpson, *Pornography and Politics* (London: Waterlow, 1983), p. 49.
4. Richard Findlater, *Banned: A Review of Theatrical Censorship in Britain* (London: MacGibbon and Kee, 1967).
5. Catherine Itzin, *Stages in the Revolution: Political Theatre in Britain since 1968* (London: Methuen, 1980).
6. Catherine Itzin, 'Sex and Censorship: The Political Implications', *Red Letters* 13, Spring 1982, pp. 5–12, reprinted in Gail Chester and Julienne Dickey (eds.), *Feminism and Censorship: The Current Debate* (Dorset: Prism Press, 1988), pp. 36–48.
7. This I have done: as a member of the Women's Rights and Executive Committees of the National Council for Civil Liberties since 1986 and co-ordinator of the Campaign Against Pornography and Censorship (CPC) since 1989.
8. According to the US Attorney General's Commission Report (1986), 85 per cent of the US pornography industry is controlled by organized crime.
9. The full transcript of the Minneapolis Hearings has been published in the UK under the title *Pornography and Sexual Violence: Evidence of the Links* (London: Everywoman, 1988).
10. Some readers may find this chapter contradictory in acknowledging the causal links, but arguing against causal links as the 'problem' of pornography. But the contradictions, in my view, are only apparent and designed to underline the authors' point that pornography functions in different ways to influence attitudes and behaviour: that in order for its influence to be translated into action, it must operate on the imagination and the intellect and the emotions, and that in none of its forms do causal influences absolve individuals of responsibility for their actions.
11. *Pornography and Sexual Violence*, op. cit.
12. J. H. Court, (1984) 'Sex and Violence: A Ripple Effect' in *Pornography and Sexual Aggression*, ed. Neil M. Malumuth, and Edward Donnerstein. (New York: Academic Press), p.144
13. A letter from Frank Mankiewicz, Vice Chairman of Hill and Knowlton (who acquired Gray and Company in 1986) to Catherine Itzin (dated 7 July 1992) confirmed that 'Gray and Company did indeed represent the coalition of magazine publishers variously

called The Media Coalition and Americans for Constitutional Freedom, in response to the Attorney-General's Commission Report on Pornography.' A letter from Christopher Finan, Executive Director of The Media Coalition, Inc. (dated 21 July 1992) explained that the 'Media Coalition itself was not directly involved in the effort to craft a response to the Meese Commission report. Two members of Media Coalition – the Council for Periodical Distributors Associations and the International Periodical Distrubtors Association – joined forced in 1986 to create Americans for Constitutional Freedom, an organization whose purpose was to refute the unsubstantiated and misleading assertions of the Meese Commission. They decided to organize a new group because Media Coalition had always fought censorship in the legislative and legal arenas and lacked expertise in putting its case to the public. ACF, whose members came to include the American Booksellers Association and the Magazine Publishers of American, operated independently from Media Coalition from 1986 through 1989; the two organizations merged in 1990.

Even in its most active years, ACF never had the resources attributed to it in the news accounts at the time of its organization. It was reported that its initial budget was almost $1 million. This estimate was based on a memo by Gray and Company, which helped set up ACF. However, the memo was not an outline of an agreed upon plan but a proposal that Gray and Company was attempting to 'sell' to the members of ACF. Ultimately, a much more modest plan was approved. Among other things, it involved the hiring of a full-time executive director and the dissolution of the tie with Gray and Company.'

14. *Final Report of the Attorney General's Commission on Pornography* (Nashville TN: Rutledge Hill Press, 1986).
15. *The Report of the Commission on Obscenity and Pornography*, September 1970, US Government Printing Office, pp. 23–7.
16. US Commission on the Causes and Prevention of Violence, 1969, *Violence in the Media*, US Government Printing Office.
17. See Catharine A. MacKinnon, Chapter 19.
18. *Report of the US Attorney General's Commission on Pornography*, 1986, op. cit.
19. D. E. H. Russell (1989), Declaration in the US District Court for the Western District of Washington, p. 5.
20. Dworkin and MacKinnon, op. cit., pp. 83–4. Personal letter from the ACLU's Public Education Officer, 18 April 1991.
21. Evidence submitted to the United States District Court for the Western District of Washington, 1989.
22 Andrea Dworkin (1978), 'Biological Superiority: The World's Most Dangerous and Deadly Idea', *Heresies: Issue on Women and Violence*. No. 6, Summer, p. 50.
23. Feminists Against Censorship, 'Do You Really Want More Censorship?' (Leaflet) (London: FAC, 1989). Feminists Against Censorship, *Pornography and Feminism*, ed. Gillian Rodgerson and Elizabeth Wilson (London: Lawrence & Wishart Ltd, 1991). Lynne Segal and

Mary McIntosh (eds.), *Sex Exposed: Sexuality and the Pornography Debate* (London: Virago Press, 1992). See also Melissa Benn, 'Adventures in the Soho Skin Trade', *New Statesman*, 11 December 1987. Carol Smart, 'Theory into Practice: The Problem of Pornography' in *Feminism and the Power of Law*, (London: Routledge, 1989). Kate Ellis et al., *Caught Looking: Feminism, Pornography and Censorship* (Seattle, Washington: The Real Comet Press, 1988).

24. FAC leaflet *Pornography and Feminism* op. cit.
25. Preamble to the Model Civil Rights Ordinance, in Andrea Dworkin and Catharine A. MacKinnon, *Pornography and Civil Rights: A New Day for Women's Equality* (Minneapolis MN: Organizing Against Pornography, 1988, p.138).
26. My work for women's rights dates from the 1970s: campaigning for subsidy for feminist theatre and promoting women's writing, campaigning for childcare, and tax allowance for childcare; writing on marriage, divorce and single parents. In the 1980s my work was concerned with ageism, sexism, social class, and discrimination against women in employment. See Catherine Itzin, 'The Art of Non-fiction' in Gail Chester (ed.), *In Other Words* (London: Hutchinson, 1987); 'Head, Hand, Heart – and the Writing of Wrongs' in Lesley Saunders (ed.), *Glancing Fires* (London: Women's Press, 1987); *Tax Law and Child Care: The Case for Reform* (London: One Parent Families, 1980); *Splitting Up* (London: Virago, 1985); 'Media Images of Women: The Social Construction of Ageism and Sexism' in Sue Wilkinson (ed.), *Feminist Social Psychology* (Milton Keynes; Open University Press, 1985); with Paul Thompson and Michele Abendstern, *I Don't Feel Old* (Oxford: Oxford University Press, 1990).
27. FAC Leaflet, op. cit. pp. 1, 3.
28. Paul Ferris, 'The Onward March of Ms. Grundy', *Observer*, 6 May 1990, pp. 47–8. Elizabeth Wilson, 'Against Feminist Fundamentalism', *New Statesman*, 23 June 1989. Kate Ellis *et al.*, op. cit. Gillian Rodgerson and Elizabeth Wilson, op. cit. Lynne Segal and Mary McIntosh, op. cit.
29. Gillian Rodgerson and Elizabeth Wilson, op. cit., p. 58.
30. Ferris, op. cit. A FAC press release dated 29 December 1990 'calls on the government to resist the anti-porn lobbies of moral majority and authoritarian feminists'.
31. Gillian Rodgerson and Elizabeth Wilson, op. cit., p. 39. Lynne Segal and Mary McIntosh, op. cit, p. 27.
32. The fact that conservative elements may choose to support feminist anti-pornography legislation does not make the legislation conservative, either in ideology, design or effect.
33. Mary McIntosh and Isobel Koprowski on *Woman's Hour*, 29 April 1992.
34. The NCCL's anti-pornography policy was overturned at that meeting. See Appendix 1 and Chapter 24.
35. Liz Kelly and Maureen O'Hara observed that 'presumably boys were used because the producers assumed that the outrage caused among lesbians by the piece would be greater had the children been

girls'. 'The Making of Pornography: An Act of Sexual Violence', *Spare Rib*, Issue 213, June 1990, p. 19. According to Gillian Rodgerson, the editor of *Quim* told her 'that the personal element in the writing is what makes *Quim* so special'. In Lynne Segal and Mary McIntosh, op. cit., p. 276.

36. Carole S. Vance (ed.), *Pleasure and Danger: Exploring Female Sexuality*: (London: Routledge & Kegan Paul, 1984).
37. R. R. Linden, D. R. Pagano, D. E. H. Russell, S. L. Star, *Against Sado-Masochism: A Radical Feminist Analysis* (San Francisco: Frog in the Well Press, 1982); Dorchen Leidholdt, Janice Raymond, *The Sexual Liberals and the Attack on Feminism* (New York: Pergamon Press, 1990).
38. Sheila Jeffreys, *Anticlimax: A Feminist Perspective on the Sexual Revolution* (London: The Women's Press, 1990), pp. 275, 266, 267.
39. D. Leidholdt and J. Raymond, op. cit., p. xv.
40. S. Jeffreys, op. cit., p. 281.
41. R. Amy Elman (1989), 'Sexual Subordination and State Intervention: Lessons for Feminists from the Nazi State; *Trivia*, Fall, p. 57.
42. Dennis Howitt and Guy Cumberbatch, *Pornography – Impacts and Influences: A Review of Available Research Evidence on the Effects of Pornography* (London: Home Office Research and Planning Unit, 1990); Guy Cumberbatch and Dennis Howitt, *A Measure of Uncertainty: The Effects of Mass Media* (London: Broadcasting Standards Council/John Libbey, 1989), p. 65.
43. James V. P. Check and Ted H. Guloien, 'Reported Proclivity for Coercive Sex Following Repeated Exposure to Sexually Violent Pornography, Nonviolent Dehumanizing Pornography, and Erotica', in *Pornography: Research Advances and Policy Considerations* (Hillsdale, NJ: Erlbaum, 1989), p. 178. Most of the social science research, when it distinguishes between categories of sexually explicit material, suggests that non-violent, non-abusive, non-sexist sexually explicit material is not harmful. See, for example, James V. P. Check, 'The Effects of Violent and Non-Violent Pornography', Final Report, Department of Justice for Canada, 1985, pp. 97–155. This report includes detailed descriptions of the materials used in each stimulus category: sexually violent material, non-violent dehumanizing material and non-violent erotic material. Erotica are sexually explicit, but do not appear to have the negative effects of the violent and dehumanizing categories. See Appendix 3 for an illustration of how the distinctions between different kinds of pornography have been operationalized in Canadian courts.
44. Thanks to Corinne Sweet for this analogy.
45. Liz Stanley and Sue Wise, *Breaking Out: Feminist Consciousness and Feminist Research* (London: Routledge & Kegan Paul, 1983), p. 54.

PART ONE

The Pornography Industry
and Its Product

1   'Entertainment for Men': What It Is and What It Means

PORNOGRAPHY IN THE USA

In the USA in 1984 the pornography industry grossed $8 billion,[1] said to be more than the music and the movie industry combined.[2] Six of the ten most profitable newsstand monthlies were 'male entertainment magazines' and the combined circulation of *Playboy* and *Penthouse* was greater than *Time* and *Newsweek*.[3] Pornography is an international industry with an estimated worldwide value of several billion pounds.[4]

Midwest Content Analysis: *Playboy, Penthouse, Hustler*
In 1985 an organization in the USA called Organizing Against Pornography put together an educational slide show entitled *Pornography: A Practice of Inequality*. It aimed to inform people about what pornography was available, what it communicated about women: to explain its meaning.

The research for the slide show was carried out in Minneapolis, Minnesota, a mid-western city with a strong liberal tradition. Two years earlier its city council had made an historic decision to enact legislation against pornography defined as a 'violation of the civil rights of women', a central practice in the inequality of the sexes and the subordination of women.

The slide-show research involved reviewing every issue in the previous two years of *Playboy, Penthouse* and *Hustler* – the most 'popular' and widely available pornography magazines in the USA. Selected issues of *Newlook, Gallery* and *Gentlemen's Companion* were reviewed, together with materials purchased on several visits to Minneapolis 'adult' bookstores. Pictures were sought that provided the most representative samples over a broad range of pornography – from what is called 'soft porn' to hard-core pornography. But it aimed to show that distinctions between soft and hard pornography are misleading: the messages about women are similarly misogynist regardless of the degree of sexual violence. The following extracts from the slide-show text written by Jeanne Barkey and J. Koplin provide examples of the kind of pornography available in the USA.[5] It starts, however, with an advertisement from a mainstream women's magazine, not pornography but an illustration of the influence of pornography on other representations of women.

SLIDE 1: *Self*, April 1984, p. 128
This is an advertisement from Self, *a women's magazine. Most people wouldn't consider this pornography, but themes of violence and sex are combined here. A man's fist, globbed with make-up, is striking a woman's face. The woman looks both surprised and frightened. The title of the article is 'Make-up with Knockout Ease'. Note the words, 'Colour that has knockout punch'. This ad glamorizes battery for the sake of selling make-up, which supposedly enhances women's sexual attractiveness.*

SLIDE 2: *Penthouse*, December 1984, p. 118
The next three slides are from a series appearing in the December 1984 'Holiday Issue' of Penthouse *magazine. A classic Japanese poetry form, the haiku, accompanies the photos in an attempt to gain artistic credibility. Here, we see a Japanese woman flung on to a rocky coastal bluff, with one ankle bound, the rope held taut by an unseen captor. The woman is motionless, she seems to be unconscious. Unconsciousness becomes an erotic event in pornography, a way to show the power men wield over women. Some call this art.[6]*

SLIDE 3: *Penthouse*, December 1984, p. 127
In another photo from the Penthouse *series, a woman is bound in an elaborate rope interlacing, especially around. her crotch and breasts, to accentuate them. Her arms are tied close to her body and a mask hides her face, rendering her less-than-human . . . thus, more available for harsh treatment and degradation.*

Some of the most brutal, racist pornography in our country uses Asian women. This corresponds with the huge traffic of Asian women into the United States for prostitution and sale as mail-order brides.[7] Targeting Asian women also resonates from US soldiers' experiences of fighting wars in Asian countries.

SLIDE 4: *Penthouse*, December 1984, p. 126
Hanging commonly is seen in pornography. In the third slide from Penthouse, *a woman is bound into a harness and suspended by a rope from a tree. Her breasts are squashed by the harness. She seems to be*

unconscious, her body limp, her head slumped forward. Remember, a real woman is experiencing this torture!

SLIDE 5: *Playboy,* January 1985, p. 104
Playboy *is available in bookstores, drugstores, convenience stores . . . almost anywhere.*[8] *This photo once again features bondage paraphernalia. Note the leather harness. The bullets on the model's leather belt point downward, suggesting penetration. Her mouth is open and legs spread, also inviting penetration. Notice the shadow cast by a chain link fence across her body implying that she is imprisoned and vulnerable. In* Playboy, *restraint and immobility are subtle, but unmistakable.*

SLIDE 6: *Shackled,* vol. 1, no. 1
This photograph was taken from a hard-core pornography magazine called Shackled. *This man's power over the woman is raw and clear. Real bruises are visible on the woman's thigh, stomach and breast. Her face is red as she struggles to remove a chain tightened around her neck. She is being kicked in the crotch by a man wearing boots – genital torture and penetration are common themes in pornography. This material looks as if it were made in a garage, basement, or bedroom.*

SLIDE 7: *The Best of Hustler,* 1979, p. 30
The next three slides come from The Best of Hustler. *The story is called, 'The Naked and the Dead'. In the first scene, a nude woman is being led from a cell by fully dressed guards, one of whom is a woman.*

SLIDE 8: *The Best of Hustler,* 1979, p. 35
Here, the woman's head has been shaved, concentration-camp style. Her pubic hair is being shaved, a standard theme used in pornography to make women appear as hairless young girls. Entire magazines are devoted to shaving and showing pictures of shaved genitals. The prisoner is naked, vulnerable, imprisoned, handcuffed, powerless. The male guard rapes her in the next page of the series.

SLIDE 9: *The Best of Hustler,* 1979, p. 38
And finally in the last photo, Poof! Closed eyes suggest unconsciousness and death . . . the mouth and the vagina gape open. Even in death, women are sexually inviting. This sequence mimics 'snuff' pornography, where a woman's murder is the ultimate sexual turn-on. Of all the kinds of power one may wield over another, the ultimate control one can have is the power of life and death. And here it is . . . eroticized.

SLIDE 10: *Hustler*, January 1983
The next three slides appeared in the January 1983 issue of Hustler, *about two months before the highly publicized New Bedford, Massachusetts, pool-hall rape. In case you don't remember, several men in a New Bedford bar gang-raped a woman on a pool table as onlookers cheered.*

This story is called 'Dirty Pool'. It begins with an apprehensive waitress being pinched by a lecherous male pool player. His buddies are giving him silent, yet obvious, approval. Note the contrast between the waitress's skimpy uniform and the men's black leather and chains.

SLIDE 11: *Hustler*, January 1983
As the story unfolds, the text reads: 'Watching the muscular young men at play is too much for the excitable young waitress. Though she pretends to ignore them, these men know when they see an easy lay. She is thrown on the felt table, and one manly hand after another probes her private areas. Completely vulnerable, she feels one after another enter her fiercely. As the three violators explode in a shower of climaxes, she comes to a shuddering orgasm . . .' The message is that while she says 'no' at first, she really means 'yes' for once the men touch her, she immediately gives way to the 'ecstasy' of gang-rape.

Think about this casual portrayal of rape. Anyone who has survived a rape can't forget the terror, trauma and lasting psychological effects. This kind of material trains men to see rape as something women really want, as something casual and fun.

SLIDE 12: *Hustler*, August 1983, p. 21
Hustler *printed this postcard following the actual New Bedford pool-hall rape. It shows a nude woman lying on a pool table waving and it reads, 'Greetings from New Bedford, Massachusetts, the Portuguese Gang-Rape Capital of America'. Along with trivializing the woman's rape,* Hustler *makes an ethnic slur against Portuguese people, as did much of the media attention on the incident.*

The tragic reality is that a woman is raped every three minutes in this country.[9] *Pornography and rape are interconnected. Rape victims' testimonies reveal that men often refer to pornographic material during the rape itself. Also, filming street rapes and distributing them on the pornography market has become a profitable business.*

SLIDE 13: *Penthouse*, December 1984, p. 111
This picture is from Penthouse's *Pet of the Month series titled 'Angela: Puppy Love'. The message? If no man is around to meet a woman's insatiable desire for pain, penetration and force, she'll meet them herself*

. . . in this case, with the help of a high-heeled shoe. Remember, this is the pornographer's and consumer's fantasy about women's sexuality. Some pornography shows even more extreme masochism, such as a woman cutting her breasts or inserting scissors into her vagina.

SLIDE 14: *Hustler Kinky Sex*, vol. 1, 1984, p. 70
Penetration by animals is another way women are shown satisfying their sexual urges. This slide is from a ten-page photo-essay in Hustler *called 'Danielle: the Bear Facts'. A bear is licking the woman's stomach; by the story's end, he is licking her genitals. The woman's sexual parts are completely exposed to the bear and to the camera. No matter how tame the bear, this is dangerous for the woman.*

SLIDE 15: *Playboy*, September 1981, p. 145
The caption of this cartoon from Playboy *reads: 'Your dog is the first basset hound I've ever seen that doesn't look sad.' While* Playboy *does not show explicit photographs like the previous one from* Hustler, *it would suggest the same thing through cartoons.*

SLIDE 16: *Hustler*, April 1985, p. 94
Women often are coupled with other women in pornography, but only for the pleasure of the male viewer. This photo from Hustler *is called 'Eve/ Ebony: Mixed Doubles'. Two young women are engaging in sexual play on the tennis court. One woman is exposing her vagina to the camera. Remember, the intent here is to stimulate males.*

SLIDE 17: *Knotty*, vol. IV, no. 1, p. 23
This is from a bondage magazine called Knotty, *which features women with women. However, gender is less important here than the eroticized power imbalance between these two.*

SLIDE 18: *Hustler*, January 1985, p. 124
Pornography is also available by telephone. One phone number can generate up to $30,000 in profit daily. And you can pay for the call by credit card. This is a page of phone sex ads from the January 1985 issue of Hustler. *Aside from the small snapshot of her face, this woman is shown as no more than a glued-open vagina and anus.*

Throughout pornography, women's bodies, and genitals in particular, are manipulated to look a certain way. The labia are often trussed up, tied open, painted, or brushed with eggwhite. And the pornographers tell us this is the way women look naturally.

31

SLIDE 19: *Young Love*, no. 1 (cover)
Using children under eighteen in pornography is illegal, yet this does not stop youth from being sexualized. In the magazine Young Love, *women are made to look like girls – notice the pigtails and knee socks. The cover tells what's inside, 'Tender lovelies open for your enjoyment. Any which way she can. When you're balling Oona, no hole's barred. And four more hot and sexy stories.' The disclaimer at the bottom reads, 'All models are eighteen years or older. Proof on file. Adults only.' The model may in fact be over eighteen but she is presented as a vulnerable young girl to satisfy the customer.*

SLIDE 20: *Hustler*, May 1984, p. 15
This Hustler *cartoon shows a father being sexual with his daughter while she turns down a date with a friend. 'Gee . . . I'd love to go to the drive-in, Tommy, but my dad has some, uh, extra household chores for me tonight.' The father–child relationship is one of the most frequently abused in our society. One in four female children is sexually abused before she turns eighteen. By making light of incest, pornography condones this crime.*

SLIDE 21: *Playboy*, 1976
In this cartoon from Playboy, *a girl is shown leaving an older man's house after a sexual encounter. She says, 'You call* that *being molested,' implying that she seduced him and didn't get enough. This reinforces two harmful myths: young girls are actively seeking sex, thus, appropriate sex objects for men; and that youngsters possess the real power in adult/child relationships.*[10]

SLIDE 22: *Latin Babes*, vol. II, no. 1 (cover)
The cover of Latin Babes, *an adult-only publication featuring Latin women. The text inside plays off the stereotype that Latinas have an exotic sexual drive. 'Hot Salsa or Sweet Salsa, however you like your Latino babes, we've got 'em. These cuties are so sweet to look at, so soft to touch, but so-so hot to fuck.' The cover uses another trend – infantilizing women by making them look like girls. The pose, munching candy – even the word 'Babes' – reminds one of a youngster.*

SLIDE 23: *Custer's Revenge* (X-rated videocassette cover)
Custer's Revenge *is an X-rated video game for home use. Male figures with erections move through a maze scoring points by raping the Native American women. The player scoring the most rapes wins the game. In December 1983, hearings were held before the Minneapolis City Council regarding the effects of pornography on women's lives. An American Indian woman told of being gang-raped by white men who made constant reference to this so-called game. The following is part of the testimony:*

'I was attacked by two white men, and from the beginning they let me know they hated my people, even though it was obvious from their remarks they knew little about us. They screamed in my face as they threw me on the ground, "This is more fun than Custer's [Revenge]!" They held me down and said, "Do you want to play Custer's [Revenge]? It's great – you lose but you don't care, do you? A squaw out alone deserves to be raped." '

SLIDE 24: *Auschwitz Bitch – Hitler's Sex Doctor Exposé! Nazi Sex Cult Bared* (paperback covers)
We usually think of pornography as pictures; however, written material is a significant part of the pornography market. The stories in these paperbacks sexualize atrocities during the Nazi era. Adult bookstores contain racks and racks of these inexpensive paperbacks on a wide range of pornographic themes.

Just as there are books of anti-Semitic pornography, there are books legitimating incest. Indeed, one publisher's series title is 'Incest Library' with book titles such as *Already Wet for Daddy, Hot for Her Dad, Harry's Trained Daughter, Kneeling for Daddy, Son, Dad and Daughter,* and *The Lustful Stepdaughter* with images of intercourse, oral sex and bondage on the covers.

SLIDE 25: *Hard Boss* (cover)
This is the cover of an 'adults only' publication called Hard Boss. *The magazine sexualizes the boss/secretary relationship – one of great power disparity. The secretary, complete with high heels, stockings and garter belt, is shown as a willing participant. On the inside cover she reveals: 'I was in love with my boss. I wanted so badly for him to fuck me that my pussy ached with desire whenever he came within ten feet of me. At last I decided to make a move, knowing in my heart he couldn't refuse to let me suck his cock.'*
This type of material teaches male supervisors that their female employees want to be sexual with them. In reality, women often are abused and sexually harassed on the job and forced to perform sexually or risk being fired or physically harmed.[11]

SLIDE 26: *Playboy*, November 1984, pp. 100 and 101
Here are the opening pages to the centrefold story, 'Playmate on Patrol'. The woman is shown at work as a highway patrol officer. On the opposite page, she is undressed and posing provocatively. In other words she may hold a post in a respected, male-dominated occupation, but like all women, her real desire is sexual servitude.

33

SLIDE 27: *Hustler*, December 1982, p. 37
In this Hustler *cartoon a canvasser for the National Organization of Women is greeted at the door by a husband holding his battered wife by the hair saying, 'We don't believe in that feminist shit, do we, Marge?' This attempt at humour trivializes wife-beating and ridicules those who are leading the fight against it.*

SLIDE 28: *Penthouse*, January 1985, p. 184
This Penthouse *cartoon is another emphatic example of woman-hating. The butler, having just torched the woman, asks the man of the house, 'Will that be all, sir?' Thus, murder is used to rid the man of a 'nagging wife'.*

Woman-hatred underlies all pornography. In a *Hustler* cartoon a woman is stripped and tied to a chair which is tipped over so her legs are in the air, her genitals where her face would be, and her face smashed against the floor. A man with a large erect penis is dressing. He says to her: 'You're really sick! You could have told me you were on your period before I raped you.' Another *Hustler* 'rape cartoon' shows a woman with blouse ripped open dragged down an alley by a man with a knife who says: 'I am not a rapist . . . I'm a sexual adviser. I advise you to give me sex.'

A *Hustler* cartoon, shows a woman naked and spreadeagled, tied to bed posts, a shadow of a man with a knife hovering over her. The caption reads: 'It felt good hitting her around, stripping her, ripping her clothes off while she screamed. I held her mouth and stuck my knife into her chest. Yeah, that made me very hot – watching her reaction to being stabbed like that and cutting her breasts open.'

Misogyny is taken to extremes in US magazines entitled *Tit and Body Torture, Corporal Quarterly, Captured, Uptight, Kinky Girls, Big Tits in Bondage* and *Star*. In these magazines women are bound and gagged, trussed up with ropes and chains, tortured; anuses and vaginas penetrated by nails, knives, bottles, broom handles, pokers; breasts clamped with vices, clothes pegs, mouse traps, electrodes. Real women are being hurt; they are in visible pain. The ultimate misogyny is sexual murder.

SLIDE 29: *Snuff*, 1979 (poster)
This leads us to the subject of snuff films where the death of a woman is viewed as the ultimate sexual turn-on. This poster advertises a film called Snuff. *It reads: 'The film that could only be made in South America, where life is cheap!' In the final scene of* Snuff, *a woman is killed, her uterus*

ripped out of her body and held up in the air, while the man reaches orgasm. Although the murder is a hoax simulated through trick photography, this movie conveys the essence of actual snuff films.

In real snuff films, women are actually murdered in front of the cameras.[12]

East Coast Cover Analysis: A Random Sample of 5,132 Covers

In 1985 and 1986 in the USA a survey of 5,132 books, magazines and films was carried out in four American cities (New York, Washington, DC, Baltimore and Boston), based on a random sample sold in thirteen adult book stores. The aim of the survey was to identify what pornography was available and what its images communicated in order to evaluate the evidence being submitted to the US Attorney General's Commission on Pornography and to 'provide a comprehensive description of the merchandise available'. The researchers coded cover images only (not content) of every fifth title and therefore covered 20 per cent of the estimated 1,000 titles in each shop. There were forty-eight images categorized. The table reproduced below shows the percentage of each image discovered on covers of books, magazines and films.[13]

Table 1: Frequency and Percentage of Magazines, Books and Films Visually Depicting Particular Images on Their Covers

Image	Magazines		Books		Films		Total'	
	N	(%)	N	(%)	N	(%)	N	(%)
Gag	140	(3.8)	32	(4.4)	13	(1.8)	185	(3.6)
Blindfold	36	(1.0)	7	(1.0)	5	(0.7)	48	(0.9)
Hood or mask worn by person in submissive position	38	(1.0)	9	(1.2)	2	(0.3)	49	(1.0)
Hood or mask worn by person in dominant position	17	(0.5)	1	(0.1)	3	(0.4)	21	(0.4)
Neck restraint held or fixed to another point	76	(2.1)	11	(1.5)	9	(1.2)	96	(1.9)
Handcuffs	40	(1.1)	12	(1.6)	5	(0.7)	57	(1.1)
Leg irons	24	(0.7)	8	(1.1)	4	(0.6)	37	(0.7)
Restraint of body other than mentioned above	237	(6.5)	87	(11.8)	28	(3.8)	352	(6.9)

35

Table 1: (*cont.*)

Image	Magazines N	(%)	Books N	(%)	Films N	(%)	Total[a] N	(%)
Whip, gun, knife, or other weapon	123	(3.4)	34	(4.6)	21	(2.9)	179	(3.5)
Hoist or rack	66	(1.8)	14	(1.9)	7	(1.0)	88	(1.7)
Forcible rape	12	(0.3)	13	(1.8)	2	(0.3)	28	(0.6)
Whipping[b]	26	(0.7)	8	(1.1)	3	(0.4)	37	(0.7)
Piercing[c] (other than ears)	7	(0.2)	4	(0.5)	3	(0.4)	14	(0.3)
Bruise(s)	13	(0.4)	0	(0.0)	4	(0.6)	18	(0.4)
Blood	11	(0.3)	2	(0.3)	0	(0.0)	13	(0.2)
Other bondage or sado-masochistic imagery (excluding spanking and women fighting)	161	(4.4)	23	(3.1)	24	(3.3)	208	(4.0)
Spanking	64	(1.8)	11	(1.5)	4	(0.6)	80	(1.6)
Women fighting with one another	16	(0.4)	10	(1.4)	0	(0.0)	26	(0.5)
Corpse[d]	4	(0.1)	2	(0.3)	1	(0.1)	8	(0.2)
Fisting[e]	4	(0.1)	1	(0.1)	3	(0.4)	8	(0.2)
Enema	11	(0.3)	3	(0.4)	3	(0.4)	17	(0.3)
Urine or urination	2	(0.05)	1	(0.1)	12	(1.6)	15	(0.3)
Faeces and defecation	2	(0.05)	1	(0.1)	4	(0.6)	7	(0.1)
Diapers and diapering	8	(0.2)	1	(0.1)	0	(0.0)	9	(0.2)
Bestiality[f]	8	(0.2)	16	(2.2)	33	(4.5)	57	(1.1)
Person with breasts and penis ('He/She')[g]	101	(2.8)	16	(2.2)	6	(0.8)	123	(2.4)
Anatomically normal man wearing female clothing	17	(0.5)	3	(0.4)	1	(0.1)	21	(0.4)
Leather	202	(5.5)	19	(2.6)	28	(3.8)	249	(4.8)
Rubber or latex	59	(1.6)	7	(1.0)	6	(0.8)	72	(1.4)
Exaggerated shoes or boots	109	(3.0)	7	(1.0)	9	(1.2)	125	(2.4)
Childlike clothing, props, or setting	112	(3.1)	69	(9.4)	11	(1.5)	192	(3.7)
Shaved pubic area	68	(1.9)	5	(0.7)	7	(1.0)	81	(1.6)
Pregnancy	57	(1.6)	1	(0.1)	2	(0.3)	61	(1.2)
Engorged breasts with depiction of milk production	54	(1.5)	1	(0.1)	1	(0.1)	56	(1.1)
Extremely large breasts	224	(6.1)	24	(3.3)	28	(3.8)	277	(5.4)
Anal insertion of penis	536	(14.7)	27	(3.7)	37	(5.1)	601	(11.7)
Three or more persons engaged in sexual activity	432	(11.8)	70	(9.5)	56	(7.7)	558	(10.9)

Image	Magazines		Books		Films		Total[a]	
	N	(%)	N	(%)	N	(%)	N	(%)
Woman dealing with more than one penis	133	(3.6)	5	(0.7)	9	(1.2)	147	(2.9)
Sex between two women, regardless of others present	227	(6.2)	32	(4.4)	43	(5.9)	304	(5.9)
Sex between two men, regardless of others present	376	(10.3)	39	(5.3)	12	(1.6)	428	(8.3)
Man and woman shown with none of the above	320	(8.8)	103	(14.0)	70	(9.6)	493	(9.6)
Woman or man posed alone with none of the above	730	(20.0)	165	(22.5)	387	(53.2)	1288	(25.0)
Vaginal intercourse	397	(8.4)	18	(2.4)	35	(4.8)	362	(7.0)
Fellatio	1005	(27.5)	46	(6.3)	71	(9.8)	1122	(21.9)
Cunnilingus	307	(8.4)	20	(2.7)	28	(3.8)	356	(6.9)
Masturbation[h]	190	(5.2)	24	(3.3)	16	(2.2)	230	(4.5)
Penetration by inanimate objects	119	(3.2)	19	(2.6)	9	(1.2)	147	(2.9)
Homosexual material[i]	640	(17.5)	110	(15.0)	39	(5.4)	790	(15.4)
Anorectal eroticism[j]	552	(15.1)	32	(4.4)	47	(6.5)	632	(12.3)

[a] A few row totals exceed the sum of other frequencies in the row because of missing data on whether particular items were magazines, or books, or films.
[b] Does not include spanking.
[c] Includes rings, pins, hooks or other items inserted through or into the labia, nipples, foreskin, penis, scrotum or other body parts or demonstrations of the process of infibulation through which a channel is made to allow the passage of such items through the skin.
[d] Images of motionless individual with closed eyes were not coded as positive on this item, regardless of apparent injury or torture, unless a coffin, grave site or other imagery of death was also present.
[e] Insertion of the entire hand (and sometimes the wrist, forearm and arm) through the anus of another person into the rectum (and sometimes into the large intestine).
[f] Sexual contact between a human and another species (e.g. horses, ponies, dogs, pigs, sheep and chickens).
[g] Partial transsexuals, i.e. former anatomical males who have developed breasts through hormonal treatment with or without surgery but who have not had any surgical alteration of the male genitalia.
[h] Coded as positive only if an individual is depicted stimulating his or her own genitals with his or her hand(s) and without the use of any foreign object.
[i] Includes items depicting 'sex between two men, regardless of others present' as well as items obviously meant to appeal to homosexual men that do not depict sex between two men on the cover.
[j] Depicts one or more of the following: fisting, enema, faeces and defecation, or anal insertion of penis.

Sado-masochistic images were depicted in 11.6 per cent of the total. In addition to the sado-masochism, a further 12.7 per cent depicted violence such as bondage, spanking, whipping and 'fisting'. A quarter of the covers therefore depicted violence. According to the authors: 'Bondage, sadism, sado-masochistic themes and violence were each significantly more likely to appear in materials in which females appear. This finding is consistent with the view that violent pornography typically depicts violence towards women.' Nearly 10 per cent depicted 'pseudo-child pornography' – adult models portrayed to look like children – and another 10 per cent focused on pregnancy, breasts engorged with milk or extra-large breasts.

The authors thought their categorization underestimated the quantity of sexual acts portrayed and minimized the extent of sexualized violence in the materials surveyed. They pointed out that the category of 'women posed alone' included:

> . . . the videotape, *Forgive Me I Have Sinned*, which included vaginal intercourse, anal penetration by the penis, restraint of the body (including stocks, locks, and chains); a preview of another title that includes the actual piercing of the labia; *Pregnant Dildo Bondage*, which includes numerous depictions of one or more females posed alone, in an advanced stage of pregnancy, fettered in ropes or ball gags, with dildos and other objects penetrating the vagina or anus or both.[14]

The authors concluded: 'The data can be interpreted as providing *minimum* estimates of the proportion of materials depicting deviant sexual conduct and *minimum* estimates of the number and variety of sexual acts explicitly depicted within the merchandise sold in commercial pornography outlets.' In addition it represented what was *marketed*, what was available on open display to all persons who entered the outlet. It represented only what was sold 'over the counter', not the under-the-counter commercial pornography – the 'most heinous torture and mutilation materials and child pornography'.

In a statement to the US Commission on Pornography, Park Elliott Dietz, professor of law, behavioural medicine and psychiatry at the University of Virginia and one of the authors of the research, summed up the messages of the materials surveyed and described what someone seeing it would have learned from it:

A person who learned about human sexuality in the 'adults only' pornography outlets in America would be a person who had learned that sex at home meant sex with one's children, stepchildren, parents, stepparents, siblings, cousins, nephews, nieces, aunts, uncles, and pets, and with neighbours, milkmen, plumbers, salesmen, burglars, and peepers, who had learned that people take off their clothes and have sex within the first five minutes of meeting one another, who had learned to misjudge the percentage of women who prepare for sex by shaving their pubic hair, having their nipples or labia pierced, or donning leather, latex, rubber, or child-like costumes, who had learned to misjudge the proportion of men who prepare for sex by having their genitals or nipples pierced, wearing women's clothing, or growing breasts, who had learned that about one out of every five sexual encounters involves spanking, whipping, fighting, wrestling, tying, chaining, gagging, or torture, who had learned that more than one in ten sexual acts involves a party of more than two, who had learned that the purpose of ejaculation is that of soiling the mouths, faces, breasts, abdomens, backs, and food at which it is always aimed, who had learned that body cavities were designed for the insertion of foreign objects, who had learned that the anus was a genital to be licked and penetrated, who had learned that urine and excrement are erotic materials, who had learned that the instruments of sex are chemicals, handcuffs, gags, hoods, restraints, harnesses, police badges, knives, guns, whips, paddles, toilets, diapers, enema bags, inflatable rubber women, and disembodied vaginas, breasts, and penises, and who had learned that except with the children, where secrecy was required, photographers and cameras were supposed to be present to capture the action so that it could be spread abroad.[15]

PORNOGRAPHY IN THE UK

In the UK, as in the USA, pornography is 'big business'. It was estimated that the so-called 'top shelf soft porn' magazines would sell 'over 20 million copies' in 1990 and be read by about '5 million people' – mostly men.[16] Another source put the total sales of British monthly pornography magazines at 2.25 million copies, pointing out that these were only estimates 'because large parts of the industry . . . do not release figures'.[17] It was also estimated that several companies in Europe would 'secure multi-million-pound turnovers on pornographic magazines and videos' in 1990.[18]

Some people have argued and many assumed that the   **39**

pornography market in the UK is different – that there is much more and much worse pornography in the USA. But until 1989 the major difference was that there had been no similar surveys or documentation of pornography in the UK looked at from the perspective of women. This began to change in response to various campaign initiatives. What follows is information about some of the magazine and video pornography available legally in local newsagents and video shops, on the telephone, in hotels, at 'tupperware-type' parties, and illegally from 'under the counter' in Soho.

Legal High Street Magazine Pornography

In 1989 Catherine Itzin and Corinne Sweet conducted a survey of the pornography available for sale from newsagents in the High Street of a mixed-race, mixed-class neighbourhood in south London. The aim of their small-scale study was to quantify this sector of the pornography market by buying one of every title available from every newsagent within the specified area and then to carry out a qualitative analysis of the contents, providing both a descriptive and interpretive account of the material. The initial results of this research were published in the *Independent* newspaper (17 April 1989).

We visited four shops, buying twenty-four titles for £51.65 at the first, another thirty-nine for £108.25 at the second, eight more for £27 at the third and two for £5 at the last: seventy-three titles costing nearly £200.

We categorized systematically according to cover information. Sat side-by-side at the Amstrad taking turns typing and turning the pages, putting into words this degradation of women. We were shocked by what appeared to be a new development (volume 1, number 1), of titles like Shaven Ravers *and* Shaving Special. *Could it be true that there were four whole magazines devoted to women with their pubic hair shaved?*

Child pornography is illegal in the UK, but we found teenage women made to look like little girls. Young, flat-chested, posed with legs tight together wearing white socks and sandals. Photographed headless from the waist down or posed to look child-like, pouting, fingers in mouth, wearing gingham dresses and straw hats – with vaginas exposed to the camera.

What is represented are female children inviting sexual accesss and what is being engineered is the sexual arousal of adult males from

*female children. Cover text quote: 'Totally bare and naked, bare as
the day they were born, the young ladies within these pages bring new
meaning to the word shameless as they pose and cavort showing
absolutely all they've got just for you.'*

*Our notes: 'Close-up shots of genitals stretched, gaping or posed
with inner labia pulled grotesquely far-out projecting or hanging.
Woman on her knees like an animal pulling her anus wide-open to the
camera.'*

*Photos of women shaving themselves or being shaved by a man. An
'after the Op' photo where she is lying like a Barbie doll. 'Feel
sickened by the sight of this. Know the part that pornography plays
in child sexual abuse, know the appeal and the sexual arousal in this
for both women and men who were sexually abused themselves as
children. Know this is dangerous. Is it really legal?'*

*Struck by the images of violence in this 'child pornography': 'close-
up of knives and scissors, poised with points over clitoris or entrance
to vagina . . . overt sadism'. We found the same overt sadism in a
group of very expensive magazines: innocuous outside, violent inside.*

*In one, the black-and-white photo-story of a young Portuguese
woman submitting to 'punishment' on threat of losing her passport. A
dingy warehouse set, an older man in overalls forces the frightened
girl to strip. Text reads: 'I climb onto the blanket crying inside,
loathing this man, and hating everything about him. His voice is
harsh, he's a revolting man, "Up on the couch, slut," he sneers. I
cringe with horror.' He rubs her with motor-oil and beats her with a
leather whip.*

*She is described as liking the assault, becoming sexually aroused
and wanting more of it. So apparently do the readers: 'let's have more
open-legged photos revealing the woman's reluctant excitement in
pitiless detail' (S. B., Guildford).*

*Four pages at the end of this magazine listing words to describe
'the bottom, the punished bottom, the punishments, the weapons, the
positions, the bottom-coverings, effects of impact, sounds of impact,
marks of impact and the cries'.*

*Another magazine featured military uniforms, schoolgirls, images
of punishment and interrogation with Nazi overtones, young girls in
the power of men, presented as willing victims begging to be beaten,
humiliated and penetrated. Advertisements in this magazine for whips
and torture equipment.*

*Pornography often portrays women as enjoying violation and
violence. There is evidence to show men find this sexually arousing and
are erroneously led to believe that women enjoy being sexually abused.*

41

Expected the 'popular' titles to be 'softer', but found to our dismay and distress they communicated the same messages and more. Our notes on Penthouse Collection, *vol. 5, no. 2, 'child pornography images invading the mainstream . . . most models partially-shaved, genitals looking child-like, one model in noose-like ropes, chains and studs, woman shown as desperate for sex, fondling own breasts, open-legged lasciviousness, fingers buried in crotch, masturbatory'.*

In Mayfair *(vol. 24, no. 3), more child-porn themes, ads for hard-core videos.* Penthouse *photo-features of 'named women' (e.g. Gaynor Goodman from Dudley). 'Designed to create the impression that ordinary women want to be treated like this.'* Fiesta *features, 'Wife of the Month', and invites male readers to submit open-genital shots of wives and girlfriends and 'bag a £100'. 'One harm caused by pornography is that women are forced by partners to mimic the sexual acts and postures they see in the magazines.'*

Competition in Men Only: *headless photos 'guess the models' identity from genital close-ups'. Frequent image: stiletto heel pointed at entrance to vagina. Our note: 'Totally dehumanizing. Complete obsession with the inside of women's genitals and anuses.'*

Features on women together creating the impression of 'lesbian sex' for the male eye. Women editing or presenting magazines ('Miss Sadie Stern's Specials') creating the impression that women approve of the contents. Women's liberation harnessed: 'on the move' (i.e. driving cars, flying planes) naked. Black women depicted as animalistic and exotic: the racist message being they are more sexual. Overt violence: woman in leather and chains trussed-up like a chicken, straps hooked to a dog-collar, pulling her legs up and apart, forcing her breasts to balloon grotesquely. Harmless? These are real women. The message? Women are pieces of meat. This is how men who use pornography learn to see and treat women.

More specialist magazines. Particularly shocked by the 'big boobs' magazines (discovered that 50+ meant breast size, not age). Women with large breasts posed in clothes and positions which squeeze, contort and often painfully distort their breasts to appear even larger. One feature was entitled 'Mammary masochism'. Also many magazines with bare buttocks on the outside, anuses inside.

Using Women to Legitimate Pornography

By 1989 the pornography industry was increasingly using women to legitimate its products. A new pornography magazine launched on to the market by the directors of a successful pornography video company used women to 'front' the magazine as editor and 'presenter'. This magazine launched a 'Wife of the Month' feature, with a model to demonstrate how it should be done, and instructions on how readers' wives and girlfriends should pose their vaginas and anuses wide open to the camera in future issues.

The legitimating function carried through to the letters page where editor Marie (whose own genitals are photographed on the contents page) extends a personal invitation to male readers: 'I hope you will all be encouraged to come out of the closet and tell me what gets your prick up in the air and looking for a silky slot to pop it into.'[19] Women are reduced to their genital organs, to holes, slots, sluts, pieces of meat. Men can walk the streets looking for 'slots', look at their wives as 'slots'. And indeed letters from male readers describe their wives in such dehumanized and derogatory terms: as 'groaning and moaning like a stuck pig', with 'gushing fannies' and 'sopping cunts'. A letter from a woman (it is often alleged that letters in these magazines are written by the staff) described how she used her breasts as 'a weapon at work' and increased her salary by £3,000 by performing fellatio on her sixty-year-old boss. The message here – that women are seeking sexual harassment. The reality is that sexual harassment is a violation of women's bodies and rights and, as a form of sex discrimination, unlawful.

For individual women, promotion from model to managing director can be seen as a good career move, but the interests of the pornography industry are served by reinforcing for men the misinformation that most women want to be sexually objectified, sexualized and violated. The pornography industry's use of 'front women' seems to have been developed as a deliberate strategy in response to campaigns by women against pornography: an attempt to fight women with women, to use women to discredit and to divide women and to create confusion in the minds of both women and men.

Marketing Pornography to 'Housewives'

The pornography industry has devised schemes to market pornography direct to women. One such venture is to encourage women to perform in their own pornography video. According to the promoters of one company:

Last year against a background of extensive publicity, 'XXXXX' launched their very own 10-minute customized film service: 'XXXXX'. **43**

> *Picking her own fantasy setting, any secretary or housewife can become*
> *a star for a day and present the results to a dumbfounded husband,*
> *lover, or local MP . . . At £1,000, it's a snatch.*[20]

One of the tabloid newspapers advertised a competition for
women to pose in their own personal pornography.[21]

Another way of marketing pornography to women is the
'Tupperware Party Model': get women to sell it to each other in
'the comfort of their own homes'. Quinton Bradley and Michelle
Foster described the 'DIY Porn Parties' in the *Leeds Other Paper*
(April 1989).

> *Holding an Ann Summers party brings rewards of 10 per cent*
> *commission on all goods sold. Selling over £80 brings two free gifts.*
> *Bringing in more sales demonstrators pays off in further rewards.*
> *Leaflets stuck up in pubs around the city show a network of women*
> *Ann Summers homeworkers is spreading through Leeds and the*
> *surrounding region.*
>
> *Adele Lodge likes Ann Summers parties. She goes regularly. She's*
> *been to parties of twenty women in friends' houses or in nurses' homes.*
> *'We have a laugh, have some wine and a look at the products. Pass*
> *vibrators around, have a look at everything – duo balls, lager flavoured*
> *booby drops.' Ann Summers publicity advertises a fun evening. Games,*
> *gifts, prizes and raffles in the comfort of your own home.*
>
> *The biggest part of the products are 100 per cent nylon versions of*
> *Janet Reger-style underwear. These baby dolls, waspies, teddies and*
> *playsuits go by names like Tiger, Linzi, Suki and Lola. Adele says*
> *they're 'cheap and nasty'. But she's more interested in the Ann*
> *Summers sex aids. A bewildering variety of vibrators are displayed in*
> *the catalogue. Phallic contraptions are shaped like gnomes and dwarfs,*
> *pink and covered with glitter. They're called girls' 'joy kits', 'stallion'*
> *or 'moulded in lifelike latex', the 'bully boy vibrator'.*
>
> *The women modelling Ann Summers underwear are posed in front*
> *of machine-guns and revolvers. Among pages of penis-fixated novelties*
> *are a set of plastic handcuffs. Also advertised is an inflatable woman.*
> *'Open mouth, plus two openings, silky realistic hair' reads the*
> *packaging.*
>
> *Their branch in Charing Cross Road also boasts a lifesize female*
> *dummy, trussed up and ready for torture, with masked eyes and*
> *manacled hands and feet, wearing a spiked dog collar, leather knickers*
> *and suspenders, her mouth gagged by a horse bit.*

Telephone Pornography

Telephone pornography is also a relatively new market in the UK. The I Spy Collective monitored telephone lines advertised in the tabloid press for three months between April and June 1989 for an article in the *Leeds Other Paper* (July 1989).

> *British Telecom is directly profiting from pornography which describes women getting sexual pleasure out of violence and enjoyment out of receiving obscene phone calls.*
>
> *The privatized telephone company takes a cut on each call received by firms running a dial-up pornography service. Advertising in the tabloid newspapers, these 0898 numbers promise daytime recordings full of double meanings and night-time telephone lines for 'adults only'.*
>
> *There's no pretence in these telephone lines that they are providing pornography for both sexes – the caller is always assumed to be male. Firms have over twenty lines, each giving access to a recorded story; one line is an index to all the others. The different recordings, each with their own telephone line, are likened to women sexually available to the man who dials them. 'Why not have all of us?' asks the woman's voice on the introduction to one number.*
>
> *The night-time recordings of one company called Northglow recount stories of women enjoying pain, women being tied-up, chained and getting sexual pleasure from rape. Another company called Bestrich uses violent sex done to a submissive woman as a common story-line.*
>
> *One of the standard themes of the pornography lines is the obscene phone call. To the silent male listener, the recordings describe women using obscene phone calls to recount sexual fantasies.*
>
> *Over two million women a year receive obscene phone calls, many are persecuted by callers who appear to know details of their lives and threaten them with violence. They have been called 'a form of mental rape' by one survivor.*
>
> *Telephone pornography lines encourage men to believe that women enjoy rape and violence and get pleasure from receiving threatening phone calls.*

Computer Pornography

The following are excerpts from an article in *Time Out* by Richard Pendry (25 October–1 November 1989).

> *It is now possible, using the sort of home computer already owned by thousands of Londoners, to get hold of pornography as strong or*

45

stronger than you would find on a newsagent's top shelf. You can do this without stirring from the privacy of your bedroom. And most novel of all, the service is free.

So-called 'adult material' is now easily within the reach of any computer user. It ranges from computer sex games like 'Astrotit', modelled on the classic Space Invaders series, to startlingly realistic state-of-the-art computer porn, consisting of digitalized excerpts from American 'fucking and sucking' movies. London, which has more computers per head than anywhere in Europe, is particularly well placed to take advantage of the boom.

The technology is not difficult to master, and the price of the hardware has fallen spectacularly over the last few years. Apart from a computer, all that is needed is a modem, a communications device which sends files down the phone lines, costing around £100. The most basic set-up starts at around £400, but for an outlay of £1,500, computer porn addicts can access moving graphics and enjoy the results in full colour. But while British controls are even slacker for computer-based porn than for traditional under-the-counter magazines, domestic control of foreign hard-core porn is practically impossible. Many of the computer graphics imported into this country arrive in the most direct way possible, straight down British Telecom's own international phone lines, from France, Italy or America, places where pornography laws are few and far between.

New York is reputed to be the source of the 'Maxine Headboom' program, featuring a little less than two minutes of nonchalant cocksucking. The image – originally from a porn movie and then digitalized so that it could be stored in a computer file – is extremely realistic, rather like watching a slightly grainy black-and-white television picture. 'Maxine Headboom' has now spread all over the world via computer bulletin board clubs.

But much of the milder sort of material – games such as computer strip poker, whose aim is to divest women of their clothes, and images of naked Page 3-type girls – is aimed very much at the rather naff tastes of fifteen-year-old boys. One recent program for the Apple Mackintosh, for instance, draws an erect penis, and then invites the user to masturbate it using the 'mouse', the attached pointing device usually used for 'click and point' control of graphics programs.

Video Pornography

The following is an edited version of an article, 'What Should We Do about Pornography?', written for *Cosmopolitan* magazine by Catherine Itzin and Corinne Sweet (November 1989) based on a survey of video pornography available in local video shops and in hotels.

> Surveying what are called 'adult' videos for Cosmopolitan we found themes similar to those in the top shelf magazines: nymphomania, women sexually insatiable, desperate for 'it', constantly available for sex, either voracious or passive, always sex objects, humiliated, enjoying 'rough' sex and attempted rape, enacting 'lesbian' scenarios specifically for male voyeurs, dressed as lusting and rapacious 'schoolgirls'.

> Titles included Vices in the Family, More Desires within Young Girls, Killer Bimbos, Secrets of the Bitch, Nympho Girls, Sexual Deviants, The Best of the Big Boobs. One 'family' video shop alone produced eighty-one titles. Cover blurbs included: wife's 'steamy night of lust with lusty lesbian who is later raped by her husband', 'young housewife becomes prostitute', 'life story of the world's most over-sexed woman who just can't seem to get enough', and 'subjected to abuse, rape and fears for her life, will the girl manage to escape – does she want to?'

> Night Pleasures, a poorly-made dubbed French film, is the story of an 'innocent virgin who falls downstairs, is concussed and in a Jekyll and Hyde transformation becomes a neurotic and insatiable nymphomaniac'. In Nothing to Hide the dialogue is typically misogynist. 'I'd like to beat the shit out of you . . . you're a whore, a bitch', as sexual intercourse starts. He's mean and he makes her 'beg for it'.

> Teenager, another dubbed French film, portrays 'randy' schoolgirls in uniform depicted as eagerly participating in group sex with older men, with caning, prostitution and paedophilia. Dirty Love exploits feminism by portraying an 'independent' woman as really just a willing sex object. The Trap stirs up woman-hatred by presenting women as vile, neurotic temptresses.

> The pornographic videos we surveyed are currently available in local video shops and newsagents. They are increasingly available in hotels. Crest Hotels, who promote facilities for executive women, screen 'adult' videos in 50 per cent of their premises; Holiday Inns claim 70 per cent of their viewers choose to watch adult movies; Copthorne Hotels called it their 'most popular channel'. According to the Business Woman's Travel Club 'hotels stressed that they make no money out of showing these films, but it is enormously profitable to the supplier'.

> Bytex International, who supply hotels with an 'adult' channel   **47**

showing the kind of 'soft porn' titles available in local video shops (Going Down on the Girls from Oz, Fatal Attraction Nude, Into the Tunnel of Love) *did a hard sell to us of how 'humorous and harmless' it all was. Their Executive Chairman said 'they preferred not to use the term pornography' and talked about providing what their 'defined target' (95 per cent businessmen) wanted – 'escape and relaxation, harmless, normal sex in a humorous environment'.*

But is it really harmless? The messages are the same in magazines and videos, communicating to men that women are 'asking for it', that women mean 'yes' when they say 'no', that women want to be touched up, ogled and abused.

The videos surveyed here were all '18-rated' and therefore legally available in unlicensed video shops. 'R-rated' videos, which can only be bought in a sex shop licensed by a local authority, are much more sexually explicit, and violent. In 1989, the Campaign Against Pornography and Censorship (CPC) carried out an investigation into the legal soft-core (R-rated), and the illegal hard-core video pornography available in a licensed sex shop. This is what they found:

We decided to take a sample of one legal video on public sale and one illegal video sold under the counter. They were both available from one Soho shop which does a tourist and 'regular' trade, primarily in new and recent major movies, but it also sells a good many soft-core porn movies.

Staff are regularly asked by casual customers for 'stuff with youngsters', bondage or urination/coprophilia. This shop had about ten hard-core videos under the counter, mostly German, some American, a few Scandinavian. They are always pirate copies, generally of poor quality. The shop's soft-core videos, on open sale, are frequently the same videos with the penetration, cunnilingus, fellatio, erect penises etc. removed altogether or just 'glimpsed'. The message of these movies is identical, of course, and very little imagination is required to know what's going on.

The legal 'soft-core' video was in a box marked HOT RACKETS (although there was no such title on the tape itself) and is an American hard-core tape edited for UK legal consumption. It included buggery, 'lesbian' sex, group sex, voyeurism, oral sex and gang-rape which the woman is shown as enjoying. In one scene a woman is fucked on a pool table while men casually play pool around her. Erect

*penises are not shown to conform with the Obscene Publications Act,
but it's always clear what's happening.*

The hard-core video is called Home Bodies *and is German,
apparently one of at least a hundred from the same producer. The
German movie was in German but with an English credit suggesting
it was retitled for the UK market. The retitling was done at source
(i.e. not by the pirate himself) and suggests it was prepared for the
British under-the-counter market.*

*The illegal hard-core video included: various men and women
fucking, sucking and buggering one another, some using dildos. One
loops chains through her labia rings. Most are shaven. All show
women enjoying being fist-fucked, buggered, casually fucked, used as
animals and/or objects of lust and enjoying humiliation, including
having other women urinate in their mouths.*

Other hard-core videos included Animal Frolics, *in which women
seek out various farmyard animals to have intercourse with (Shetland
pony, collie dog, etc.). An untitled compendium shows a familiar
sampling of a white woman being roughly fucked and buggered by
two black men (in 'voodoo' necklaces) at the same time, reinforcing
racist stereotypes of black men's sexuality.*[22]

In Ireland it is possible to obtain extreme forms of sexualized
violence from the same shelves in video shops which display
Mickey Mouse cartoons. *Driller Killer*, for example, tells the story
of a man who, irritated with his partner, dismembers her with a
Black-and-Decker-type drill/saw, having first sexually abused
her. In *I Spit on Your Grave*, a young woman, living alone, becomes
the victim of gang-rape by a group of youths from the village.
The rapes are depicted in graphic detail, including buggering,
amid scenes of utter degradation and violence.

Snuff Films

Are snuff films available in the UK? A male reader responding
to an article by Catherine Itzin in the *London Daily News* (24 April
1987) wrote:

*I saw a 'snuff' movie some years back in the company of a male
friend and his fiancée. We'd been drinking, and as there was nothing
on the box, we fancied a video. I must confess I thought it was a plain
old hump 'n' bump, but then after a rather brutal rape, a young
woman was tied to a table, and a hand was amputated with a Black-
and-Decker type saw. Then she was raped again, and in the course of*

it her guts were spilled out by the rapist using a great butcher's knife. That was nearly four years ago. I've never forgotten that horror and the certainty that it was all too real – that the budget did not cover the movie special effects required to make it a 'set-up'. In itself that would hardly be defensible, but at least it would have convinced me the girl survived the film. I didn't sleep the night I saw that video, and poorly for weeks afterwards. It still fills me with horror. Some people will switch off, some like me will cry, some, like my friends, will be dismissive and think it all movie-tricks, but some bastard will go out and do it to somebody's wife or daughter.

Clodagh Corcoran, co-ordinator of the Irish Campaign Against Pornography and Censorship (ICPC) launched in October 1989, and author of *Pornography: The New Terrorism*, described the snuff film she obtained in Dublin without any difficulty:

I was sitting alone in a friend's home, in front of a television, waiting for this video to begin. I want to describe it to you in detail. But I cannot, because my mind won't let me. What I can tell you is that on that night I watched a man participate in the act of sex with a woman, and during that act he plunged a large hunting knife into her stomach and cut her open from vagina to breast. He then withdrew the knife and stuck it into her left hand, removing the first joints from three fingers, which fell from the bed. The woman's eyes remained open, she looked at the knife and said 'Oh, God not me.' It took her approximately three minutes to die. The camera was left running. The film was then canned and put on the commercial market as entertainment.

I left the house that night in an apparently calm state, although with hindsight, I realized I had gone into shock. Shock dissolved into terror and I didn't sleep for many weeks. I was grateful for the temporary loan of a stun gun to keep beside my bed.

I have lived in fear ever since, knowing that while the rape, degradation and dehumanization of women is filmed and sold as entertainment, women's status in society is worthless, and our lives within and outside our homes are also without value.[23]

Obscene Publications Branch Seizures

In April 1990 Catherine Itzin visited the Obscene Publications Branch at Scotland Yard (with the MP Clare Short and Ray Wyre, Director of the Gracewell Clinic for sex offenders in

Birmingham), where they were shown items of illegal child and adult pornography which had been seized by the police. These included:

Child Pornography

1. A cartoon about little Red Riding Hood who is gang-raped by several hunters and shown to enjoy it.
2. A boy of about eleven being buggered, forced to sit on top of an erect penis, visibly in discomfort and pain, but positioned to show as much of the genitals as possible to the camera.
3. A woman placing a female child (aged about eight) on top of a man's erect penis.
4. Portuguese boys masturbating and having oral sex.
5. A female child (aged about four or five) being forced to perform fellatio on an adult male.
6. Several children of both sexes lying together being urinated on by an adult male.

Adult Pornography

1. Fist-fucking – one woman with different men's arms up to the elbow in her vagina and anus at the same time.
2. Fist-fucking – a man pounding his arm up to the elbow repeatedly in the anus of another male.
3. Women being penetrated by a dog, a donkey and a pig (while she kisses the pig's snout).
4. A man putting a cigarette out on a woman's breast.
5. A close-up shot of a woman emptying her bowels into the mouth of a man who was chewing and swallowing her excrement.
6. A woman having her labia nailed to the top of a table.
7. A man urinating into the open mouth of women.
8. Women hung by their breasts from meat hooks.
9. A woman being eviscerated and sexually murdered.

These acts of coercion and violence, if they came to light as cases of ill-treatment in prisons, for example, as reported by Amnesty International, would be seen as torture. In pornography these acts of subordination, coercion, degradation and violence are, apparently seen as sex.

Notes

1. 'The Place of Pornography', *Harper's*, November 1985, p. 31. See note 39, Chapter 21.
2. Van E. White, 'Pornography and Pride', *Essence*, September 1984, p. 186. Van White was an original co-sponsor of the Minneapolis civil rights pornography ordinance.
3. *Pornography: A Practice of Sex Discrimination* (Minneapolis, Minnesota: Organizing Against Pornography, 1985), p. 17.
4. Mike Baxter, 'Flesh and Blood: Does Pornography Lead to Sexual Violence?', *New Scientist*, 5 May 1990, p. 37.
5. *Pornography: A Practice of Inequality*, developed by Organizing Against Pornography (OAP), a Resource Centre for Education and Action, Minneapolis, Minnesota, USA. OAP closed down in February 1990 after six years of operation due to 'a long-term lack of success in securing a stable financial base'.
6. Pornographers call this art and defend their pornography on aesthetic grounds. Pornographers have successfully used aesthetic value as a defence in court when prosecuted under obscenity legislation which permits publication of obscene material for the 'public good': for aesthetic, educational or scientific purposes.
7. Filipino brides by mail order is a multi-million pound business in Britain. 26 agencies operate and advertise to arrange contacts. *Daily Mirror* 27 November 1991.
8. In the USA *Penthouse* and *Hustler* are also widely available from the same outlets.
9. According to FBI statistics a woman is raped every seven minutes. Rape Crisis Centre statistics put the figure at every three minutes. This includes rapes which are not reported to the police.
10. The cartoon also implied that the child 'enjoyed' the sexual encounter, reinforcing yet another myth – that women and children enjoy being sexually abused.
11. This scenario represents sexual harassment, a form of sex discrimination which is illegal. According to the *Cosmopolitan* magazine survey (March 1990) 60 per cent of respondents said they had been sexually harassed. Polls in the USA put the figure at 80 per cent.
12. Sexual murder in snuff films involves the torture and evisceration of the woman while she is alive and after she is dead. The sexual turn-on is sadistic murder and dismemberment.
13. Dietz, Paul Elliott and Alan E. Sears, 'Pornography and Obscenity Sold in "Adult Bookstores": A Survey of 5132 Books, Magazines and Films in Four American Cities', *University of Michigan Journal of Law Reform* 21 (1 and 2) Fall 1987 and Winter 1988, p. 11. 'The study was limited to the imagery found on the front covers of magazines and books and the front packaging material for video tape cassettes and films' (p. 12). As covers tend to be composed so as not to provoke arrest or prosecution under obscenity law, the cover images will be less sexually explicit and less sexually violent than the content of the publications. The results of this study will therefore 'under-represent' the nature of the material sold. Covers

are coded communications to the consumers about what is inside, which is always worse. (Reprinted with permission.)

14. Ibid. p. 13.
15. Ibid. pp. 42–3.
16. Baxter, op cit.
17. Nick Cohen, 'Reaping Rich Rewards from the Profits of Pornography', *Independent*, 19 December 1989.
18. Baxter, op. cit.
19. *Electric Blue*, August 1989.
20. *Electric Blue*, promotion pack, 1989.
21. 'Give Your Fella a Sexy View of You', *Sun*, 20 October 1989.
22. Michael Moorcock, CPC Field Report 1, 1989.
23. Clodagh Corcoran, *Pornography: The New Terrorism* (Dublin: Attic Press, 1989), p. 4.

PART TWO
Pornography and Power

2 Pornography and the Social Construction of Sexual Inequality

CATHERINE ITZIN

This chapter is based on the assumptions:
1. That sexual inequality exists.
2. That it is institutionalized in social structures and internalized in the attitudes, beliefs and behaviour of individuals.
3. That sexual inequality is 'socially constructed', not 'biologically determined'.
4. That pornography plays a part in the social construction of sexual inequality.

What follows is an account of what this means in practice in the lives of women and men.

SEXISM

In all societies women as women are oppressed on the basis of gender. This takes different forms in different cultures, but however power is defined and valued in any culture, women do not have it.[1] In Western societies, women are additionally oppressed on the basis of race and class and sexuality and disability. Within this system of sexism, male power – or male supremacy – is institutionalized so that men as a group have access to economic, social, sexual and political power and privilege that women do not have. On the basis of gender, women are subordinated economically (in the labour market, in marriage and motherhood) and sexually (in reproduction, in sexual objectification and sexual violence). Women are oppressed in every aspect of their public and private lives. Women as a group are poor, and the 1980s saw an increase in the 'feminization of poverty'.[2]

Women are discriminated against in employment. The majority of women are located in low-paid, low-status sex-segregated work or the caring professions. The majority of women work part-time, and the majority of part-time workers are women – on the lowest pay with the least job security and frequently ineligible for statutory employment rights. Women are still a minority in senior positions of power and influence. They do not have equal pay or the same prospects of promotion as men. They have not had the same pension or taxation rights.[3] Men experience preferential treatment in sports and social clubs, in restaurants, and in access to credit and mortgage facilities.[4]

Women also suffer discrimination in their exclusion from employment, as wives and mothers. Most women are usually either economically dependent in marriage (particularly during the child-rearing years) or, because of low pay, partially economically dependent in marriage, expected to carry out both paid employment and unpaid work in the home. Even when they are in paid employment, the majority of women carry out the majority of housework.[5] Women do double shifts. Although motherhood is very much sentimentalized, the work of mothering is also unpaid, unsupported and carried out in isolation. There are very few childcare provisions to enable women to combine marriage, motherhood and paid employment, so when it is done, it is done under a maximum of stress and exhaustion.[6] The situation of single parents is even more oppressive.

Women are also vulnerable to and victims of physical and sexual violence. While other crime rates have fallen in recent years, reported rape and other sexual offences have increased.[7] Women experience sexual harassment at work, on the streets and in public places.[8] Women are not safe in their own homes, and they do not have freedom of movement in public safe from physical and sexual violence.[9]

Women have not been free to express their sexuality in the manner of their choosing, either as lesbians or as heterosexuals. Women's reproductive freedom has been restricted historically and increases in freedom are constantly being eroded. Before 1967 abortion in the UK was illegal and access to contraception was limited. This is still true in Ireland. In the USA women's right to abortion is under serious threat from the religious right. In the UK there have been many political moves to make abortion illegal again, or to lower the time limit and restrict women's freedom to control their own bodies and fertility.[10] Although other forms of discrimination will operate in addition to gender, in all these areas and aspects of their lives women are discriminated against on grounds of gender.

The oppression of women is both institutionalized and internalized. Discrimination is institutionalized in practices, procedures and behaviour, and it is internalized in attitudes, beliefs and feelings. Women are regarded as inferior – as less intelligent, less able, less important. On the one hand, women are trivialized and treated with contempt, while on the other hand they are idealized and sentimentalized. These attitudes and beliefs are then translated into discriminatory behaviour. Discrimination against women is underpinned and perpetuated by the negative attitudes held about women by men and also, to some extent, held by women about themselves and each other. Sexual inequality is a combination of the attitudes, beliefs and behaviour of individuals and the practices that are institutionalized in social structures: in law, education, politics, medicine, the health and social services, in the media and their representations.

THE SOCIAL CONSTRUCTION OF SEXUAL INEQUALITY

It used to be widely believed that sexual inequality was biologically determined. Eastern and Western fundamentalist religions like to believe this still: reducing women to their sexual and reproductive functions and subordinating them utterly to the will of their fathers and husbands, the patriarchs. But with the new enlightenment of liberation ideology over the past twenty years, derived largely from the black and women's liberation movements, has come the understanding that inferiority is not in the genes. The subordinate social status of black people and of women is not inherent in their skin colour or reproductive functions: rather, these physical characteristics have been used as an excuse for systematic discrimination.

There is no biologically inherent reason why women should be paid less than men or why black people should do the 'slave' labour and live in poverty. No biologically inherent reason why whites or males should be dominant and blacks or females should be subordinate. No genetic reason why sexual differences should become sexual divisions of labour, sex discrimination and sexual inequality. These systems of inequality and discrimination are *socially constructed* for the benefit of certain groups and to the disadvantage of others. Sexism and racism are institutionalized in the structures of society and individuals are systematically conditioned for their participation within these systems.

The ideology and practices of sexual inequality are pervasive within the culture. Both women and men are conditioned by them, and acquire many of the attitudes, beliefs and behaviour   **59** of the conditioning they are intended to acquire.[11] Within the system of sexism, women and men are conditioned to their positions of dominance and subordination. From birth, or before, males and females are socialized according to their gender roles within the gender hierarchy. Children's clothes, toys and books (with their 'cult of the apron') are gendered, and research has shown consistently that male and female infants are treated differently and gender–specifically: the attitudes embodied in the pink for a girl and blue for a boy infant sex stereotypes translated into discriminating behaviour.[12] This process of sex-role stereotyping and gender conditioning is continued in the education system which itself is entirely based on the premise that ideas, attitudes, beliefs and behaviour can be *learned*.[13]

As the oppression is internalized, significant aspects of identity are socialized and socially constructed. Oppression is generally internalized through a combination of misinformation, mistreatment and intimidation during childhood, when females are socialized into femininity and males are socialized into masculinity. Other forms of socialization (e.g. race and social class) also take place at the same time.[14] Sex-role stereotypes and sexual objectification are central to the social construction of identity for both women and men, and representations are instrumental in the process.[15]

Even desire itself is arguably a social construction influenced by representation, as Deborah Cameron and Elizabeth Frazer point out: 'Representations help construct and shape people's desires by offering them certain objects, certain channels, certain meanings. What aspirations and pleasures are available, what practices, identities and dreams are even thinkable is determined to a very large extent by our culture.'[16]

Women and men feel, think, believe and behave as they do as a result both of the institutionalized oppression which determines their opportunities and the internalized oppression which influences their identity: their attitudes, beliefs and behaviour. The lives of women and men are as they are for economic and political reasons, and also for psychological and emotional reasons. Both the system of sexism and sexist conditioning are damaging to women – and to men.

Of course, people are not mere victims of their conditioning. All human beings are unique and uniquely themselves and will always resist, sometimes successfully, adopting the attitudes, beliefs and behaviour of oppression, whether in the position of oppressor or oppressed. There are many individual variations in the process of conditioning. It is an imperfect process, but systems of inequality are very resilient and the process of gender (or race or disability or social class) conditioning is remarkably successful.

At the same time, it can be and constantly is being subverted. For implicit in the process of the social construction of identity or institution is the possibility of deconstruction and the potential for reconstruction. What is learned can be unlearned. What is institutionalized can be changed.

FEMALE SUBORDINATION AND FEMININITY

Women are coercively and painfully socialized into femininity. The main goals of successfully heterosexual females are held to be male approval, marriage and motherhood. Attracting and keeping a man is an essential part of this process.[17] To a certain extent – in so far as women are forced by sex discrimination in the labour market and by motherhood to be economically dependent on men in marriage – a woman's livelihood can depend on how successfully feminine she can make herself.[18] To some extent women's survival and to a great extent women's status depend on it.

Creating competition between women is part of female socialization. Women learn that in order to get and to keep men it is necessary to compete with other women. Women are encouraged to compare themselves with each other – and to evaluate themselves competitively. Men are encouraged to compare one woman with another. Men's status is enhanced by being attached to women who most successfully fit the standards of sex objectification and sex-role stereotypes.

One of the main ways in which women know what is required of them to be successfully feminine – a successful sex object, a successful wife or girlfriend, a successful mother – is through representations. Images which represent women in sex-stereotyped ways are a fundamental part of the conditioning. These include the 'Janet and John' type of children's books, soap-powder housewives, Oxo mums, the Mills and Boon books and *Jackie* magazine romantic heroines. ' "Gender advertisements" which represent "male dominance" and "female subordination" affirm the place that persons of the female sex-class have in the social structure . . . not merely expressing subordination, but in   **61** part constituting it.'[19] Women's magazines are an important source of images and information on femininity, acting as 'agents of socialization with implications for how the gender character-istics of females are acquired and how the position of women in society is determined'.[20] 'Women's magazines provide what can be described as "mirror images" for women, i.e. public images of femininity against which women measure themselves, men judge women, and which are, therefore, formative in actually shaping women's experience.'[21]

Whatever their employment (paid or otherwise), the pursuit of male approval is a constant occupation.[22] Women invest a lot of time and money in making themselves successfully feminine, and sometimes go to extremes of self-abuse to achieve and maintain the required appearance: wearing foot-deforming shoes and dieting or resorting to cosmetic surgery to fit themselves to the stereotyped images of successful femininity.[23] The sexual objecti-fication of women in advertisements and other representations reinforces women's subordinate status in society.

Women are conditioned to conform to the stereotyped images of femininity and womanhood in such a way that they are often unaware that they are misrepresented and mistreated. They often, apparently willingly, agree to participate in misrepresen-tation and mistreatment, and can even feel that they 'enjoy it'. This is because one characteristic of internalized oppression is to function as a form of self-oppression.[24] Structures of inequality are maintained by the extent to which people are forced to agree to their own oppression: in the acquired belief that they *are* less able, less intelligent, less important and that, on some level, they deserve to be oppressed. Thus if a person is either forced to and/ or agrees to participate in their own mistreatment, it will be a mechanism of survival and an assertion of self-respect and dignity to defend the position: 'I do this. I like it. I don't dislike it. I don't like it, but it's harmless. There's nothing wrong with it. I can cope. I'm good at it. Why shouldn't I do it? I am rewarded for it.' To maintain the pretence that there is value in what one does, however damaging it may be, can be one way to survive. This also has a positive function in offering protection from the pain of exploitation and abuse.[25]

Some women who work in the pornography industry argue in its favour.[26] Some women who were formerly workers in the sex industry subsequently explain why they had previously defended themselves and their work in this way: until they had the economic alternatives and therefore the emotional resources, they were unable to acknowledge the exploitation and hurt they had endured in that work.[27] Toby Summer, a lesbian, wrote thus about her life as a prostitute:

> Oppressed people develop a sixth sense with which we anticipate the next move of an enemy in order to try to be successfully out of the way or in the most acceptable pose ... This strategic lie attempted to turn my degradation into something more human ... Confronting how I've been hurt is the hardest thing that I've had to do in my life.[28]

MALE CONDITIONING AND MASCULINITY

Masculinity in men is also coercively conditioned. Social construction theory rejects biological determinism for men as well as women. Men are not naturally superior or aggressive any more than women are naturally passive and inferior. The characteristics of masculinity, both positive (independence, courage, logic, rationality) and negative (isolation, competition, aggression) are conditioned.[29] Male identity and masculinity is constructed: it is learned and can be unlearned.

Men as a group have power and privilege, and benefit from their dominant position in the social structures of inequality. Male power is a reality and individual men benefit from it. But masculinity is very damaging to men. It requires the construction of their identity primarily as workers, cuts them off from their feelings of vulnerability and pain, from showing emotion, and from participating in nurturing and caring relationships. It cuts them off from closeness and emotional intimacy with each other: this is a function of homophobia, the product of gay and lesbian oppression. It leaves men isolated from each other and emotionally disconnected from women. The only permissible place to be close and intimate and to reveal such 'feminine' feelings as tenderness is usually through sex, and even here men are under pressure to function and perform to standards of masculinity.[30]

In spite of the social, political and economic power held by men as a group and from which individual men benefit, masculinity and male sexuality is as unattractive from a human point of view as femininity is for women. Men are also forced to compete with each other for the most successfully feminine females. Their masculinity depends on it. They are measured by and measure each other not just by the size of their pay packets but the size of their penises. They are forced to judge themselves and each other by successful performance economically and sexually. They are only really permitted to feel passionate about cars, football – and pictures of women in pornography. This – masculinity and male sexuality – is not enviable.

THE SUBORDINATION AND SOCIALIZATION OF CHILDREN

In addition to learning through misinformation, itself a source of unacknowledged pain, childhood socialization is instilled through more overt mistreatment, including violence or threats of violence, but also including many practices which are regarded as normal, reasonable and even good child-rearing. According to Stevi Jackson, 'Childhood is not merely a natural state, for as well as being a stage of physical development, it is also a social institution' in which 'children are a subordinate social group'.[31] In the normal course of child-rearing, children are:

> dressed to please adults, their activities are regulated by adults. They are expected to please others, to play cute, to show off their accomplishments as if they were a dog's new tricks. Adults discuss them in their presence as if they were not there, laugh at them when they are doing something they take quite seriously, talk down to them and pat them on the head or chuck them under the chin, just as if they are stroking an animal. All this is seen as being perfectly acceptable, even as being kind to children. If a child shows resentment at treatment that most adults would find thoroughly humiliating, then she or he is cheeky, sulky or insolent.[32]

In the words of Alice Miller: 'the fountain-head of all . . . discrimination is the . . . exercise of power over the child by the adult which is tolerated by society (except in the case of murder or serious bodily harm)'.[33] In fact, parents do have the legal right to inflict bodily harm on their children, as long as it is not excessive or at least not excessively visible. 'Smacking' (which is a form of physical abuse) is regarded as a perfectly acceptable (even necessary) way to 'teach' a child to behave,[34] and forms of emotional abuse (threats, withdrawal of love) are so socially accepted that they are not even recognized as abuse: 'Child abuse is still sanctioned – indeed held in high regard in our society as long as it is defined as child-rearing.'[35] The belief is still widespread that these kinds of child abuse are somehow necessary to raising 'good' children, and also for the child's own good.[36]

Childhood socialization includes the learning of sexual scripts, the conditioning of sexual identity, the social construction of sexuality: 'a cumulative process of learning to become sexual'.[37] Cultural attitudes towards sex and sexuality are generally repressive: with a minimum of positive information and a maximum of negative attitudes. Sexual learning is part of gender learning.[38] Sexual abuse is also part of childhood socialization for many people. There is evidence, for example, that one in four children are sexually abused by the age of sixteen.[39] 'Children have to make their way in a society where adults' power over them is inescapable and where aggression and sexuality are hopelessly entangled.'[40]

THE ROLE OF PORNOGRAPHY

What part does pornography play in sex discrimination? In the conditioning of internalized oppression? And in constructing and maintaining the structures of sexual inequality?

Pornography is an industry in which women and children are exploited economically and sexually and which trades on women's and children's economic subordination. It is – like catering, cleaning and factory work – one of the traditional areas of women's work. It can be the only available way of making a living for some women. The pornography industry exploits the poorest and most vulnerable women, whose opportunities to earn a living are also limited by sexism and sex discrimination.[41] It particularly exploits black and 'Third World' women and children, trading on race discrimination and perpetuating racist as well as sexist stereotypes. There is the glamour end of the market, but a great deal of pornography is the recorded physical and sexual abuse of women. Some women are coerced into pornography and in the manufacture of some pornography women are hurt, physically and sexually.

Pornography and prostitution can look like some of the more attractive opportunities for working-class women who are the majority of sex-industry workers: more interesting, glamorous and sometimes better paid than factory work. In the words of Yasmin, 'a prostitute woman':

> Basically, I think you are pushed into prostitution . . . because if
> you come from a working-class background, and your father's
> worked in the mill all his life, and put in twenty-two hours'
> overtime to keep a large family, and you're the eldest, you then
> find that you leave school early, as quick as you can, to earn money
> to help the family. So then you've got no education behind you.
> What sort of job can you do? Go in a factory . . . who wants to go
> in a factory? If you like wearing nice clothes, being feminine . . .[42]

Or in the words of 'Anita, another prostitute woman': 'As for
me, if I hadn't done this, I'd be stuck in a house now, with about
ten kids. I'd've been married to some big, fat bum, I know I
would; but I'm not.'[43]

Women will also be drawn to exploit the natural gift of their
good looks. If society values and rewards a certain kind of
femininity and female attractiveness, then it is understandable
that women take advantage of the opportunities these provide for
male approval and employment. In addition it has been shown
that many women who participate in pornography and/or prostitution are in fact themselves survivors of child sexual abuse.[44]
The female editor of a UK pornography magazine, for example,
mentioned her own childhood abuse in a women's magazine
interview.[45] Statistics in the USA indicate that 75 per cent of
women involved in pornography are incest survivors.[46] The
pattern of repetition of childhood abuse in adulthood, either in
the position of abuser or abused (discussed in Chapters 7, 10,
and 13), may attract women to pornography.[47]

In pornography women are sexual objects for the titillation
and sexual gratification of men: objects of men's lust and desire.
Women in pornography are presented as sexually voracious and
sexually insatiable, seeking and enjoying sexual violence and
humiliation. Through the pornographic convention of 'the smile',
women are shown as enjoying their sexual objectification or
sexual assault. Women in pornography are often reduced to their
sexual body parts, completely dehumanized, pieces of meat.
Women are even reduced to animals, in sex with animals, and
women are often 'animalized' – and thereby dehumanized – in
the language of pornography (as pets, or bunnies, for example).
What does this say about the status and value of women in
society?

Sexual objectification in pornography is an act which subordinates women, as is the presentation of women as, passive, servile,
servicing men sexually, violated, victims of violence. In pornog-

raphy, women's subordination is sexually explicit and it is sexualized. Pornography conditions male sexual arousal and orgasm to sexual objectification and sexual violence: to women's subordination. Through pornography men experience the sexual subordination of women as sex and they experience sexual inequality and sexual violence as sexually exciting and sexually arousing.[48] According to Catharine A. MacKinnon, 'Pornography makes hierarchy sexy,'[49] or in the words of John Stoltenberg: 'Pornography is what makes subordination sexy.'[50] By establishing a physical and emotional association between sexual inequality or sexual violence and sexual arousal, and by communicating that 'women's worth is their sexual value alone',[51] pornography sexualizes women's social value.

Pornography also sexualizes violence, connects violence with sex and sexual arousal, makes violence sexy. It legitimates violence against women. It is used in the sexual abuse of some women. It stimulates some men to commit specific acts of sexual violence against some women. It is used in the sexual abuse of children: to legitimate sexual acts, to sexually arouse, to seduce. It is part of a continuing cycle of sexual abuse.[52] Pornography is one of the factors contributing to sexual violence, and there is an abundance of evidence of harm, both correlational and causal, of links between pornography and rape and child sexual abuse. Women are therefore subordinated in pornography, and women are subordinated as a result of the use of pornography.

Pornography also plays a part, together with other forms of sex-objectified, sex-stereotyped presentations, in the social and psychological conditioning of all men – in constructing *normal* masculinity *as the norm* and maintaining the whole system of male power.[53] Pornography presents to men how it is permissible to look at and to see women. It relentlessly communicates: this is what women are, this is what women want, this is how women deserve to be treated. It educates men in what it communicates. Men learn to see women in terms of their sexuality and sexual inequality as presented by pornography. In Susanne Kappeler's view:

> The fundamental problem at the root of men's behaviour in the world, including sexual assault, rape, wife battering, sexual harassment, keeping women in the home and in unequal opportunities and conditions, treating them as objects for conquest and protection – the root problem behind the reality of men's relations with women, is the way men see women, is Seeing.[54]

67

Pornography, according to Catharine A. MacKinnon, is 'a way of seeing and using women' and 'the viewing is an act . . . an act of male supremacy'.[55] The seeing is not passive: it is itself an act. As a result of viewing, looking and seeing, the ideas of pornography enter the imagination and are transformed into attitudes and behaviour: into actions. The underlying message of all pornography – whether it is sexually objectifying or sexually violent or both – is the misogyny which underpins the oppression of all women.

Although pornography oppresses women and contributes to sexual inequality it is only one part of the oppression of women, one of a number of factors that contribute to the subordination of women in society. The economic subordination of women has been the subject of extensive study, and strategies (including legislation against sex discrimination in employment) have been devised in attempts to eliminate the discriminatory practices, and to increase equality. The part played by pornography in the subordination of women has been unacknowledged, under-estimated or ignored. But it is part of the picture, part of the apparatus of oppression which contributes to constructing and maintaining the sexual subordination of women. Although there has been considerable effort invested in eliminating women's economic subordination, and some definite gains made in the past twenty years, women's *economic* position has not changed fundamentally in relation to men. Almost certainly, progress in creating economic equality for women has been limited because women's sexual subordination (including the sexual sub-ordination of women in pornography) has not been addressed, or remedies (legal or otherwise) found to redress this aspect of sexual inequality.

ENDING VICTIMIZATION

Social construction theory is sometimes criticized for 'turning women into victims'. In truth, it does imply that women – and men too – are victims of oppression: they are. That does not mean they are willing or even helpless victims. There is evidence to suggest that people resist the 'learning of oppression' and have to be quite systematically misinformed and/or mistreated before 'giving in' and 'taking on' the oppression, in either a position of dominance or subordination.[56] Nor does being victimized by an oppressive society absolve anyone from taking responsibility for their actions. Indeed, having been victimized can be viewed as grounds for taking full responsibility and in the process ceasing to be a victim. This is, in fact, the gift the women's movement has given to women: the insights and resources to assist women to give up being victimized, to give up conditioned passivity and to reclaim power.

Men are, of course, also in a position to give up being victims of *the system*: to give up pornography, to give up power. If women can liberate themselves from the shackles of femininity and sexist conditioning (and there is evidence that, influenced by feminism, many women have done this), then men can arguably likewise free themselves from the bonds of masculinity and male conditioning. In Chapter 7 Peter Baker explains how heterosexual men can give up pornography, and why it is in their interests that they should. What is learned can be unlearned. What is constructed can be deconstructed and reconstructed.

Can men give up pornography as they might give up cigarettes? Is pornography an addiction as is often claimed? If so, what are the implications? In the traditional view of addiction, addicts have been regarded as a special, separate category of people who are deviant from the 'norm', or from the majority of people who aren't addicts. Addiction to pornography has been used to legitimate sexual violence and to exonerate sexual offenders in courts of law. Being 'victims' of the addiction has been used to absolve them from personal responsibility for their actions: 'I couldn't help myself, your honour, when I raped her.'

However a new theory discussed by Corinne Sweet in Chapter 10 suggests that addictions too are socially constructed and conditioned as a *normal* product of early childhood socialization, and that the majority of people have serious, albeit socially acceptable, chemical addictions (alcohol, sugar, nicotine, chocolate, caffeine) and also behavioural addictions (to work, to television, to talking, to listening, to sex and/or specific sexual practices). There is also evidence now that sexual addictions are linked to sexual abuse. Adult addiction to sexually violent pornography is one legacy of child sexual abuse and, according to Ray Wyre, women who have been raped can become addicted to pornography and to sexual arousal through fantasy which replicates the rape (which he regards as another kind of unacknowledged harm caused by pornography).

Understanding the nature of addictions and the addictive nature of pornography, together with an understanding of the **69** social construction of identity and opportunity, provides a new perspective and possibilities for change for women and men. Acknowledging addiction as a normal, and inevitable, legacy of childhood socialization is not a cop-out: it provides a way out. If one is addicted, it is possible to detoxify, to give it up, withdraw, cure. If addictions are conditioned, they can be deconditioned. There are already effective models for giving up both chemical and behavioural addictions.[57]

Women have the right to be free from discrimination, to be treated equally in education, training and employment, and in every other aspect of their lives. Their work as wives, mothers and carers should be valued, rewarded and supported. Women should have freedom of movement without danger of violence or harassment. And women should be regarded, represented and treated with complete respect as human beings.

Pornography is completely incompatible with these rights. Pornography is propaganda against women. It is a practice which perpetuates sexism, sex discrimination and sexual violence. It is therefore one of the basic means of maintaining the sexual status quo. Sexual equality depends on the elimination of pornography as part of the elimination of sex discrimination. The two must go hand in hand. The elimination of pornography is an essential part of the creation of genuine equality for women – and for men.

Notes

1. There appears to be little evidence of matriarchal (i.e. female-dominated) societies (see J. Bamburger, 'The Myth of Matriarchy', in M. Rosaldo and L. Lamphere, eds, *Women, Culture and Society* (California: Stanford University Press, 1974). There appears to be some evidence of matrilocal societies in pre-state kinship societies, but since the rise of the nation state, women appear to have been systematically subordinated by patriarchy. This kind of subordination appears to be a cross-cultural phenomenon. The fact that the subordination has taken different and sometimes contradictory concrete forms in different societies has served to disguise the practices of male dominance which exist and therefore to obscure, the systematic pattern that whatever women do, its value is lower. See S. Ortner, 'Is Female to Male as Nature Is to Culture?', in Rosaldo and Lamphere, op. cit.; 'The Virgin and the State', *Feminist Studies*, Vol. 4 No. 3, October 1978; N. C. Mathieu, 'Man Culture and Woman Nature', *Women's Studies 1*, pp. 55–65; Ruby Rohrlich-Leavitt, 'State Formation in Sumer and the Subjugation of Women', *Feminist Studies*, 6/1, Spring 1980; Stephanie Koontz and Peter Henderson, eds, *The Origins of Gender and Class* (London: Verso,

1986); Gayle Rubin, 'The Traffic in Women: Notes on the "Political Economy of Sex"' in Rayna R. Reiter, *Towards an Anthropology of Women* (New York: Monthly Review Press, 1975); Heidi Hartmann *et al.*, *The Unhappy Marriage of Marxism and Feminism: A Debate on Class and Patriarchy* (London: Pluto Press, 1981).

2. Mary Daly, *Women and Poverty* (Dublin: Attic Press, 1989). Beatrix Campbell, *The Road to Wigan Pier* (London: Virago, 1987).

3. In 1990 in the UK women still earned less than three-quarters of what men earned, and there had been very little change in this earnings gap between 1975 when women's earnings were 72.1 per cent of men's (when the Sex Discrimination Act came into effect) and 1990 when women's earning were 76.9 per cent of men's based on average gross *hourly* earnings. When *weekly* earnings are considered, there is an earnings gap of more than a third between female and male full-time earnings (from *Women and Men in Britain: A Research Profile* [London: HMSO, 1988], pp. 45–7 and *New Earnings Survey*, 1991.) The position of women part-time workers is even worse, particularly when considering that the majority of women work part-time and the majority of part-time workers are women. In 1989, 93 per cent of men worked full-time as compared with 45 per cent of married women and 71 per cent of unmarried women. About three-quarters of part-time workers were married women (OPCS Labour Force Survey, 1989). 'The presence of dependent children and in particular young children has a major effect on the economic activity of women' (Jean Martin and Ceridwen Roberts *Women and Employment: A Lifetime Perspective* [London: Department of Employment and OPCS, HMSO, 1984]). Two-thirds of married women with children work part-time (EOC, 1985). See Ann Sedley, *Part-time Workers Need Full-time Rights*. (London: NCCL, 1983) In 1989 only 1 per cent of women workers were in professional occupations compared with 7 per cent of men (OPCS Labour Force Survey, 1989). Because of sex-segregated work, women constitute three-quarters of catering and clerical workers, but only 14 per cent of managers (EOC, 1987). In 1987 70 per cent of women worked part-time in manual trades (V. Beechey and T. Perkins, *A Matter of Hours: Women, Part-time Work and the Labour Market* [Cambridge: Polity Press, 1987]). Sex discrimination in the age of compulsory retirement was removed in the Sex Discrimination Act 1986, but women have remained disadvantaged in their pension rights. See Hilary Land, and Sue Ward, *Women Won't Benefit: The Impact of the Social Security Bill on Women's Rights* (London: NCCL, 1986).

4. Barbara Rogers, *Men Only* (London: Pandora, 1988).

5. Martin and Roberts, op. cit., found that 54 per cent of wives who worked full-time and 77 per cent of wives who worked part-time did all or most of the housework (p. 114). See also HMSO, op. cit., p. 5.

6. Ibid., pp. 96–115. See also M. G. Boulton, *On Being a Mother* (London: Tavistock, 1983); and Sheila Cunnison, 'Women's Three Working Lives and Trade Union Participation' in Allatt *et al.*, *Women and the Life Cycle: Transitions and Turning Points* (London:

Macmillan, 1987); Ann Oakley, *Housewife* (Harmondsworth: Allen Lane, 1974); Ellen Malos, ed., *The Politics of Housework* (London: Allison and Busby Ltd, 1980). Adrienne Rich, *Of Woman Born: Motherhood as Experience and Institution* (London: Virago, 1977); G. W. Brown and T. Harris, *Social Origins of Depression: A Study of Psychiatric Disorders in Women* (London: Tavistock, 1978); C. Itzin, *Splitting Up* (London: Virago, 1980).

7. Home Office Criminal Statistics 1985–1989 (London: HMSO). Reported rape increased by 29 per cent in 1985, 24 per cent in 1986, 8 per cent in 1987, 16 per cent in 1988, 16 per cent in 1989, 21 per cent in 1990 and 18 per cent in 1991. Indecent assaults on women on the London underground went up by 50 per cent between 1989 and 1990.

8. Sixty per cent of the 4,000 women in the UK who replied to the *Cosmopolitan* survey in 1990 said they had been sexually harassed. Pornography was *known* to have been used in 12 per cent of the sexual harassment incidents. See Ann Sedley and Melissa Benn, *Sexual Harassment at Work* (London: National Council for Civil Liberties, 1984); Natalie Hadjifotiou, *Women and Harassment at Work* (London: Pluto Press, 1983); Sue Wise and Liz Stanley, *Georgie Porgie: Sexual Harassment in Everyday Life* (London: Women's Press, 1987).

9. *Inside Story*, BBC documentary, 31 May 1989. There were over 1 million incidents of reported domestic violence in 1988. Reports to police of domestic violence increased by 54 per cent in 1991.

10. In April 1990 there was a vote in the House of Commons on whether to reduce the time in which abortions could be legally carried out as part of the Human Fertilization and Embryology Bill. R. Arditti, R. Klein and S. Minden, *Test Tube Women* (London: Pandora, 1984). Also G. Corea *et al. Man-Made Women: How New Reproductive Technologies Affect Women* (London: Hutchinson, 1985).

11. Jane Chetwynd and Oonagh Hartnett, *The Sex Role System: Psychological and Sociological Perspectives* (London: Routledge Kegan Paul, 1978); John Archer and Barbara Lloyd, *Sex and Gender* (London: Penguin, 1982); Oonagh Hartnett *et al.*, *Sex-Role Stereotyping* (London: Tavistock, 1979).

12. E. G. Belotti, *Little Girls* (London: Writers and Readers, 1975), p. 31; Sue Sharpe, *Just Like a Girl* (London: Penguin, 1976).

13. Ann Oakley, *Sex, Gender and Society* (London: Penguin, 1972); Dale Spender and Elizabeth Sarah, *Learning to Lose* (London: Women's Press, 1980); Pat Mahony, *School for the Boys* (London: Hutchinson, 1985); Sara Delamont, *Sex Roles and the School* (London: Methuen, 1980).

14. Stevi Jackson, *The Social Construction of Female Sexuality* (London: WRRCP, 1980); *Childhood and Sexuality* (Oxford: Basil Blackwell, 1982), pp. 22–6.

15. Marjorie Ferguson, *Forever Feminine: Women's Magazines and the Cult of Femininity* (London: Heinemann, 1983), pp. 39–77; Janice Winship, *Femininity and Women's Magazines* (Milton Keynes: Open University Press, 1983), p. 6.

16. Deborah Cameron and Elizabeth Frazer, *The Lust to Kill* (Cambridge: Polity Press, 1987), p. 143; Susanne Kappeler, *The Pornography of Representation* (Cambridge: Polity Press, 1986), pp. 196–211.

17. T. Sommers, 'The Compounding Impact of Age and Sex', *Civil Rights Digest*, 1974, pp. 2–9; C. Adams and R. Laurikietis, *The Gender Trap: Book III Messages and Images* (London: Virago, 1976); Shulamith Firestone, *The Dialectic of Sex* (London: Women's Press, 1979).

18. Christine Delphy, *Close to Home: A Materialist Analysis of Women's Oppression* (London: Hutchinson, 1984).

19. Erving Goffman, *Gender Advertisements* (London: Macmillan, 1979), p. 8.

20. Ferguson, op. cit., p. 6.

21. Winship, op. cit.

22. J. Hogstan, *Cosmetic and Toiletry Preparations Review*, June 1979; Catherine Itzin, 'Media Images of Women: The Social Construction of Ageism and Sexism' in Sue Wilkinson (ed.), *Feminist Social Psychology* (Milton Keynes: Open University Press, 1985).

23. Mary Daly, *Gyn/Ecology* (London: Women's Press, 1979).

24. Delphy, op. cit. Also 'A Materialist Feminism is Possible', *Feminist Review* 4, 1980, pp. 79–105.

25. Ibid.

26. Isabel Koprowski, 'Isabel Koprowski on Porn', *Company*, November 1988; Nigel Duckens, 'Formula in Flesh', *Guardian*, 18–19 November 1989; interview with Linzi Drew, editor of *Penthouse* who 'worked as a cigarette packer, as a barmaid at a football ground and as a Page 3 girl'.

27. Nickie Roberts, *The Front Line: Women in the Sex Industry Speak* (London: Grafton Books, 1986).

28. Toby Summer, 'Women, Lesbians and Prostitution: A Working Class Dyke Speaks Out Against Buying Women for Sex', *Lesbian Ethics* 2 (3), Summer 1987, p. 37.

29. Jon Snodgrass, *For Men Against Sexism: A Book of Readings* (California: Times Change Press, 1977); Jeff Hearn and David H. J. Morgan, *Men, Masculinities and Social Theory* (London: Unwin Hyman, 1990); L. Coveney et al., *The Sexuality Papers: Male Sexuality and the Social Control of Women* (London: Hutchinson, 1984); John Stoltenberg, *Refusing to be a Man* (London: Fontana,1990).

30. A. Ford, *Men: A Documentary* (London: Weidenfeld and Nicolson, 1985).

31. Jackson (1982), op. cit., pp. 22, 26.

32. Ibid., p. 25.

33. Alice Miller, *For Your Own Good: The Roots of Violence in Childrearing* (London: Virago, 1987), p. 70.

34. At the 1989 AGM of the Health Visitors Association a motion to support a new organization EPPOC (Elimination of Parental Punishment of Children), campaigning against physical abuse of children, was defeated. The view was expressed that there was nothing wrong with smacking children (Jean Rowe, General Secretary HVA, 1990, personal interview).

35 Miller, op. cit., p. 283.

36. Miller, op. cit., p. 283.
37. Jackson (1980), op. cit., p. 69. See also J. H. Gagnon and W. Simon, *Sexual Conduct: Social Sources of Human Sexuality* (Chicago: Aldine, 1973); Judith Laws and Penny Schwartz, *Sexual Scripts: The Social Construction of Female Sexuality* (New York: Dryden Press, 1977).
38. Jackson (1982), op. cit., p. 83.
39. Clodagh Corcoran, *Take Care: Preventing Child Sexual Abuse* (Dublin: Poolbeg Press, 1987), p. 14. Thirteen per cent of the 4,000 respondents to the *Cosmopolitan* survey said they had been sexually abused as children. See also Emily Driver and Audrey Droisen, *Child Sexual Abuse: Feminist Perspectives* (London: Macmillan, 1989).
40. Jackson (1982), op. cit., p. 63.
41. Roberts, op. cit., pp. 129, 191.
42. Ibid., p. 135.
43. Ibid., p. 175.
44. M. H. Silbert and A. M. Pines, 'Pornography and Sexual Abuse of Women', *Sex Roles*, 10, (11/12), 1984. In a sample of 200 prostitutes in San Francisco, 60 per cent reported juvenile sexual abuse and 73 per cent reported having been raped. Pornography played a part in 24 per cent of the rapes and 22 per cent of the child sexual abuse.
45. Koprowski, op. cit.
46. *Pornography: A Practice of Sex Discrimination* (Minneapolis, MN: Organizing Against Pornography, 1986), p. 13.
47. Diana E. H. Russell identifies child sexual abuse as one of the factors that predispose men to rape. It is now becoming known that male children as well as females are victims of child sexual abuse, though females appear to be more frequently abused than males. See Clodagh Corcoran, *The Rape of Childhood* (forthcoming, Virago.) Anyone who is abused – female or male – will be predisposed to repeat the abuse unless they can free themselves from its effects. Repetition can take the form of abusive behaviour (the role of oppressor) or becoming again a victim of abuse. Self-abuse is another legacy of child sexual abuse. (See Miller, op. cit., p. 281.)
48. Sexual arousal can also be conditioned to fear or violence as a result of early sexual abuse. See Ray Wyre, Chapter 13. Russell in Chapter 14 refers to research on 'masturbatory conditioning' and the reinforcement of orgasm.
49. Catharine A. MacKinnon, 'Pornography, Civil Rights and Speech', *Harvard Civil Rights – Civil Liberties Law Review*, 1985, p. 17. Also Andrea Dworkin, *Pornography: Men Possessing Women* (London: Women's Press, 1981). See Peter Baker, Chapter 7 and Ray Wyre, Chapter 13.
50. John Stoltenberg, 'Gays and the Pornography Movement: Having the Hots for Sex Discrimination' in *Men Confronting Pornography*, Michael S. Kimmel, ed. (New York: Crown Publishers, Inc., 1990), p. 260.
51. Susan Cole, *Pornography and the Sex Crisis* (Toronto: Amanita Publications, 1989), p. 67.
52. Gilbert and Pines, op. cit., p. 865. See Peter Baker, Chapter 7; Corinne Sweet, Chapter 10; Ray Wyre, Chapter 13.

53. Deborah Cameron and Elizabeth Frazer, op. cit., p. 143.
54. Kappeler, op. cit., p. 61.
55. Catharine A. MacKinnon, *Feminism Unmodified: Discourses on Life and Law* (Cambridge, Mass. and London: Harvard University Press, 1987), p. 130.
56. Miller, op. cit., pp. 281–3.
57. TRANX is an organization that helps people to give up their addictions to tranquillizers. Alcoholics Anonymous (AA) deals with alcohol addiction. See Robin Norwood, *Women Who Love Too Much* (London: Arrow, 1986) for information about relationship addictions.

3 Pornography and Capitalism: The UK Pornography Industry

The pornography on the shelves of nearly every corner newsagent is produced by respected members of the publishing industry. These are not backstreet merchants. Their companies trade with multi-million-pound publishing empires. The men who produce pornography publish newspapers and hobby magazines, speculate in property and run advertising companies.

Pornography gains maximum distribution because it is accepted by the business world. It is recognized as an important and profitable section of the publishing industry. Pornography is bread and butter to the commercial printers, the magazine distributers and wholesalers. It has acquired a strategic significance for tabloid newspaper barons and go-getting magazine companies. (See Diagram)

Most of the women's magazine companies deal with the pornography trade. Some other businesses take on the pornography market as a sideline, like the clothing firms who advertise in pornography magazines. The pornographers have been allowed to reach a position where their product is inescapable because of the profit they bring into mainstream companies.

The major pornography firms rake in total gross profits of £23 million each year. Pornography makes up 2 per cent of the profits of the UK publishing industry. Nearly all these firms have spread their business away from their roots as pornographic magazine and film producers. To guard against a sudden fall in profits from the porn market they have ventured into property and other publishing enterprises. On the figures registered it is impossible to break down just how much they gain from pornography dealings although they are estimated to sell 2.25 million pornographic magazines a month.

PAUL RAYMOND

Diversification away from pornography gives the business respectability. Pornographer Paul Raymond could afford to give

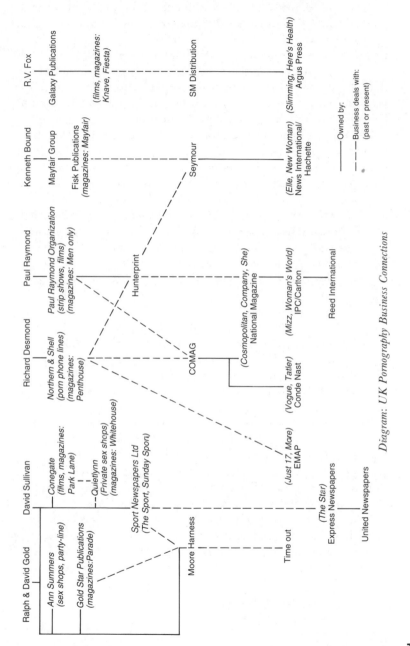

Diagram: UK Pornography Business Connections

support to attempts to shut down sex shops and strip shows because he is also the biggest landlord in Soho. Raymond produces *Men Only* and six other magazines in Britain. He owns the well-known strip club Raymond's Revue Bar. And his Soho Estates property company owns the freehold of whole West End streets – about £12 million in fixed assets. Paul Raymond knew that the clean-up Soho campaign could bring him more rent from up-market tenants than the money he was making from being landlord to the pornography underworld.

Raymond's is the respectable face of pornography. His strip club is on the tourist itinerary of foreign businessmen. He owns four West End theatres – none of them doing well these days. The Whitehall used to put on performances of *Deep Throat* but Raymond was also invited to a Downing Street drinks party after a Prime Ministerial visit to *Anyone for Dennis*. Raymond turned the Whitehall into a museum of World War II memorabilia and accrued patriotic kudos from shipping 30,000 copies of his pornography to troops in the Falklands.

Things weren't always so good for the Paul Raymond Organization. Three years after he opened his strip club Revue Bar in 1958, Raymond was fined for keeping a 'disorderly house'. One year after he bought his first pornographic magazine *Men Only* in 1971, his headquarters was raided by police and 300,000 copies seized. Two issues of the magazine were judged 'obscene' by the High Court and production of *Men Only* was suspended for six months. All Raymond's plans for launching a property development company on the stock exchange collapsed.

The *Sunday Times* Insight team revealed in 1983 that the managing director of Paul Raymond's organization was employing women to work as prostitutes in one of the Soho clubs which paid rent to the organization. The managing director, Carl Snitcher, was running a cross-over of models who posed for Raymond magazines and worked in the hostess clubs.

When the story got out, Raymond claimed, not for the first time, that the activities of his tenants weren't his responsibility and he threatened to sack his managing director. But Snitcher, a former South African barrister, is still at the top of the Paul Raymond Organization. Raymond continues to rake in huge rents while the porn trade creeps back into Soho.

PENTHOUSE

Princess Anne opened the headquarters of Richard Desmond's company, Northern & Shell – the UK publishers of *Penthouse*. Docklands-based Northern & Shell has added other magazine titles and a thriving advertising business on to its pornography base. They publish the health magazine *Fitness*, the ecology title *Green Magazine* and hobby titles like *Stamps* and *Bicycle*. Their other title *Video World* gives the game away by advertising pages of pornographic videos. At the core of Northern & Shell are the profits of pornography. *Penthouse* and *Forum* and the 'adult' phone-lines made about 50 per cent of their money.

Despite this, Richard Desmond was able to attract reputable City firms when he announced his intention to float Northern & Shell on the stock market. Only one merchant bank refused to touch the pornography firm. The public relations company Drew Rogerson, fresh from their 'Tell Sid' British Gas campaign, prepared to sign-up Northern & Shell, calling them a 'well-run and legitimate business'. But press criticism forced them to pull out in case their BP share issue contract was harmed.

WOMEN'S MAGAZINES

Paul Raymond's string of magazines make a lucrative contract for the printing company, Hunterprint. This Northampton-based leading colour printer turns out his *Escort* and *Club International* on the same presses that print the young women's magazine *Mizz* and Rupert Murdoch's *New Woman*. Hunterprint has contracts from IPC magazines and Argus Press as well as its pornography customer.

Paul Raymond's *Men Only* is printed by Hunterprint and distributed by COMAG, a subsidiary of Condé Nast and National Magazine – two of the biggest women's magazine publishers. Their titles include *Vogue*, *Tatler* and *Cosmopolitan*.

COMAG also distribute *Penthouse* and *Forum* for Northern & Shell. They handle as many as twelve pornography titles a month. COMAG market pornography with the same efficiency they apply to a new issue of National Magazine's *Company* or the leading feminist magazine *Spare Rib*, which they now also handle. They persuade wholesalers to handle pornography and arrange displays and promotional events with newsagents.

The magazine company Argus Press, publisher of the success- **79** ful title *Slimming*, distributes pornography through its SM Distribution subsidiary. It handles *Fiesta* and *Knave*, the money-spinners for the pornography company Galaxy Publications. They meet with the pornographers regularly – 'we are personally committed to the individual exploitation of every title' says the manager of SM Distribution.

Seymour Press, part of the French magazine group Hachette, publishers of *Elle* and *New Woman*, in partnership with Murdoch, have the distribution contract for the pornographic magazine *Mayfair*. Seymour supported the pornographers in their enterprise by lending Kenneth Bound's Mayfair Group £180,000 to buy out his partners. They also handle the international sales of *Penthouse*.

Wholesalers W. H. Smith and Menzies have taken head office decisions to handle pornography. W. H. Smith refuse to reveal their policy on so called 'men's magazines', although it is known that they wholesale many more titles than are stocked in their high street shops. Menzies handle titles from Gold Star and Quietlynn.

GOLD BROTHERS

Two brothers in pornography control magazine distribution throughout London. They have distributed the radical magazine *City Limits*. The feminist monthly *Spare Rib* used to reach newsagents through their fleet of vans.

Ralph and David Gold cornered the London distribution market when they bought-up Moore Harness and Ve-Line Publications to provide outlets for their pornography. The Gold brothers publish *Parade*, *Rustler* and a legion of similar magazines through their company Gold Star Publications. They also own the Ann Summers organization, the most profitable pornography company in Britain. Its shops in London and Bristol sell pornographic magazines and videos while a nationwide team of women party organizers and demonstrators sell underwear and vibrators on the Ann Summers Partyline.

Moore Harness was set up to distribute 1960s underground magazines including the London listings magazine *Time Out*. The Gold brothers continued this lucrative distribution contract. Getting *Time Out* into the shops made the Gold brothers financially secure.

When *City Limits* needed to expand their circulation, they had little choice but to sign up with the pornographers who have a stranglehold on the London market, although the alliance didn't last long.

PRIVATE SHOPS

Pornography gained its widest circulation when the *Star*, the daily tabloid owned by United Newspapers, joined forces with the Gold brothers and their partner, David Sullivan.

Sullivan set up the national chain of *Private* sex shops which brought copied and edited pornography imports to hundreds of towns throughout Britain. He launched dozens of magazine titles and pornography films through his companies Roldvale and Conegate. In an attempt to make it easier for the Private shops to be licensed by local authorities, David Sullivan leased them to his former managing director, Brian Richards, who took over a new company called Quietlynn.

Sullivan had been imprisoned on charges of living off immoral earnings after advertising massage parlours in his magazines. The sentence was overturned on appeal by which time Sullivan had handed his empire over to Richards. Quietlynn's directors were then arrested under the same charges – after advertising prostitutes in the same magazines, although they were later released without charge.

Sullivan then teamed up with the Gold brothers and is still publishing pornography through his Conegate company while indulging in a side line of property speculation.

Quietlynn, headed by Brian Richards, produces titles like *Whitehouse* and runs around 140 *Private* and other sex shops, many of them stocking other products as well as pornography, and thereby managing to avoid licensing restrictions. Quietlynn has been raided by the obscene publications squad three times in recent years. Many of its shops have been attacked by anti-pornography campaigners *Angry Women*.

Quietlynn shops are kept under tight control by the East End organization. Supervised by regional managers and subject to spot checks by head office, the shop keepers have to send their till rolls down to London at the end of every week. Sex shops are estimated to gross £4,000 a week; profit on videos alone is put at around £1,500 a week per shop.

David Sullivan has claimed he has no link of ownership with his former sex shop empire. His company Conegate and its director,

Sullivan's brother, both use Quietlynn offices as contact addresses. Quietlynn adverts filled the pages of Sullivan's *Sunday Sport*.

THE *SPORT*

The *Sport*, Sullivan's joint project with the Gold brothers, aimed to launch pornography into the tabloid market created by the *Sun* and the *Star*.

Although they are now trying to get a reputation for US-style far-fetched tabloid stories, the core content of both the *Sunday* and the daily *Sport* is degrading pin-ups, sex stories and pages of adverts for telephone pornography.

Set up in summer 1986, the *Sport's* publishing company Apollo is administered by the Golds and the *Sport* is distributed by their business Moore Harness. But the Gold brothers take a back seat. Sullivan is the public face of the *Sport* and he has seized publicity for the paper with all the tricks he learnt in the advertising trade.

The *Sport* only reaches an audience of about 400,000 – not much more than a monthly pornography magazine – but it is profitable. This is more than can be said for the *Star*. When Sullivan made out that he was going to start a daily tabloid, the *Star*'s owners flew into a panic. The *Sport's* style of pornographic paper seemed a likely success. Other publishers were interested in cashing in on it. A leading women's magazine company and two national newspaper chains held secret meetings with the pornographers to discuss joint ventures.

In an astounding deal, Lord Stevens of United Newspapers merged the *Star* with the *Sunday Sport*, giving the pornographers free rein over the daily tabloid. The deal with the *Star* was limited by strict financial controls – the pornographers had to make the circulation leap – but United gave their new editors carte blanche to turn the tabloid into the first daily pornographic magazine.

The number of topless pin-ups trebled. The *Star* ran a tale of a fifteen year-old girl who enjoyed a sexual assault next to a picture of her half-undressed. They promised a topless picture of her as soon as she was sixteen. A front-page story headlined how a woman had consented to rape. The problem page became the readers' letters of a pornographic magazine. Many of the *Star*'s reporters quit or were sacked.

The alliance between the *Star* and *Sport* lasted only eight weeks. Supermarket chains Tesco and the Co-op withdrew their advertising contracts because of the *Star*'s 'attitude to and treatment to women'. A hidden opposition to pornography gained strength and attacked the newspaper alliance, spurred on by Murdoch's papers.

Falling sales were the last straw for United Newspapers, forcing them to give the pornographers the push. Sullivan complained bitterly that he'd only been doing what the press barons had told him to do. The venture into pornography wasn't profitable enough for Lord Stevens.

The *Sport* continues to occupy a wedge on the borders of the pornography market, issuing magazines like *Sunday Sport Girls* to keep its feet among its competitors. The *Penthouse* team at Northern & Shell joined the tabloid scene for a short shift with a pin-up sheet *Call In*. They lost £126,000 on it.

PAGE 3

Although the pornography tabloids aimed to exploit a market created by Murdoch's *Sun* and *News of the World*, Rupert Murdoch's papers were the first to lash out at them.

Since Murdoch pushed the Page 3 institution to *Sun* readers, he has successfully denied that the topless pictures have any relation to pornography. *Sun* photographers say 'It's just a bit of fun.' Phrases repeat themselves every time Clare Short raises the issue in the Commons – 'a nice thing to look at . . . just the girl next door.' *Sun* model Linda Lusardi went as far as to say the pictures had nothing to do with sex, accusing her young audience on the BBC's Open to Question of all having dirty minds.

But Page 3 transformed the British pornography industry. It set up a new generation of porn stars whose careers span both tabloid and top shelf magazine.

Page 3 models, pored over by thirteen million *Sun* readers, became household names. Samantha Fox and Linda Lusardi were only the first to be eagerly bid for by other tabloids and find themselves on TV game shows.

Declining sales figures made the pornography industry look to create a similar star system among its own models and set up personalities to front its magazines.

For Paul Raymond it was just a matter of introducing his daughter and heiress Debbie into the credits of his pornography business. Becoming the deputy editor of *Men Only* and editor of the French export *Club pour Hommes*, she was soon getting interviews in mainstream magazines and featuring in sponsored sports events.

Richard Desmond, publisher of *Penthouse*, set up his own pin-up star. He made model, Linzi Drew, editor in name. Next she was on TV chat shows, with presenter Jonathan Ross asking questions about violence against women. Her inability to answer didn't damage her publicity.

Another *Penthouse* model, Fiona Wright, leapt to stardom when Burton's boss, Ralph Halpern, admitted an affair with her. She was immediately snapped up by the tabloids, the pornography model becoming a Page 3 feature.

Northern & Shell's tabloid *Call In* got *Sun* model Linda Lusardi to pose for its first issue, blurring the distinctions still further.

Gold Star Publications, Sullivan and the Golds' enterprise, appointed their own woman editor-in-name for their magazine stable. The model Suzanne Mitzi was set up to give a personal touch to the ramblings of the company's porn writers.

Mitzi soon found her way on to Saturday evening TV game shows in the company of other Page 3 models.

PORN PHONE LINES

The biggest part in the unification of tabloid and pornography was played by the 0898 telephone adverts, the new outlet for pornographers created by British Telecom. The phone lines offered expensive recordings of Page 3 models and pornography stars alike. Lusardi, Fox and McKenna were mixed haphazardly with Wright, Mitzi and Drew as the phone line companies – many of them owned by Sullivan and Richard Desmond – tried to tap the market for all it was worth.

Forty-five million calls were made to pornography phone lines in 1987. Pornographers get 50 per cent of peak time 35p a minute charges and 75 per cent of the off-peak 25p a minute, making an estimated £35 million a year. *Penthouse* publishers Northern & Shell run pornography telephone lines through their Communications and Media department, bringing in one third of the group's total profits of £3,911,355.

Sullivan and the Gold brothers' *Sport* tabloid gives several pages over to adverts for the phone lines. The *Sport* runs its own lines as does Sullivan's former company Quietlynn.

Two companies producing the most explicitly violent telephone pornography take elaborate precautions to keep the identity of their owners secret. A search of the company records of Northglow and Bestrich, two frequent tabloid advertisers who operated 'after 9' pornography on 0836 vodaphone lines, revealed a network of interlocking companies which served to obscure the ultimate owners. Using accommodation agencies as their registered office and company registration services to file returns, these anonymous companies were allowed to pump out recordings of women enjoying pain without any interference from the industry watchdog.

Since British Telecom opened up the 0898 lines their gross revenue has soared from £2 million in 1984 to £3 billion this year. The profits of pornography have been recognized by the business world. The collaboration of the mainstream media has increased the visibility and sales of the pornography companies.

The bigger profits coming this year to Gold Star Publications and Northern & Shell owe much to Rupert Murdoch and his Page 3 formula, to British Telecom and their 0898 lines, to the television appearances of Mitzi and Drew, and the companies which print and distribute major women's magazines.

Links between the business community and the pornography trade have increased the accessibility of pornography, have given it an aura of acceptability, and made the industry virtually unassailable.

But this collaboration may soon begin to hurt the profits of mainstream companies. Investors and consumers are beginning to avoid companies who have links with pornography on ethical grounds. The Ethical Investment Research Service (EIRIS) provides services to investors who want to make sure there is no inconsistency between their convictions or their objectives and the companies whose shares they own. EIRIS has advised investors who wished to invest in green initiatives or who wanted to avoid companies linked to South Africa.

Now EIRIS offers investors a service which enables them to exlude shareholdings in companies which are involved in pornography or violence. Investors are able to avoid firms who produce, distribute or retail videos and magazines with a violent or pornographic content or companies which have had relevant complaints to the Press Council or Advertising Standards Authority upheld against them.

Consumer boycotts and pressure from investors can be directed at companies linked to the pornography trade, as the *Daily Star*'s owner Lord Stevens found to his cost. When the business establishment begins to lose profits because of its association with pornography, this can operate as a powerful disincentive to their continuing the kind of business links with pornography that have been uncovered in this chapter.

PORNOGRAPHY FIRMS

Mayfair Publishing Group
Owned by Kenneth Bound
Publish *Mayfair*.
Distributed by Seymour Press which is owned by the publishers of *New Woman*.
1989 turnover £3.7m, pre-tax profit £0.9m.
Address: second & third floor
95A Chancery Lane, London WC2.

Galaxy Publications
Owned by Europress Overseas Ltd. Beneficial owner of shares R. U. Fox.
Publish *Fiesta, Knave* and *XS*.
Distributed by Argus Press, publishers of *Slimming*.
Group also makes films.
1989 turnover £4.4m, pre-tax profit £1.2m.
Address: 252 Belsize Rd, Swiss Cottage, NW6.

Northern & Shell
Owned by Old Court Ltd (Guernsey). Last registered owner Richard Desmond.
Publish *Penthouse* and *Forum*.
Distributed by COMAG, owned by the publishers of *Cosmopolitan* and *Vogue*. Also own Power Radio Ltd., publishes *Electric Blue*.
Also publish other titles, e.g. *Green Magazine*.
Manage 'adult' phone lines of *Call In*. Run advertising agency.
1990 turnover £5.8m, pre-tax profit £1.3m.
Address: N&S Building, Mill Harbour, Isle of Dogs, London.

Ann Summers Sales
Owned by Ralph and David Gold
Owns chain of sex shops, pays agents to sell underwear, vibrators, etc., to women.
1987 gross profits: £5,105,727
Address: see below

Gold Star Publications
Publish *Parade, Shaven Ravers, Miss Sadie Stern's Monthly, Rustler, Bottoms Up, Megaboobs, Park Lane, Shaving Special* , etc.
1987 gross profit: £2,185,197

Address: Gadoline House,
2 Godstone Rd, Whyteleafe, Surrey.

A & P Roberts (Holdings) Ltd
Gold Brothers holding company.
1989 turnover £45.3m, pre-tax profit £4.1m.
Ralph and David Gold also own magazine distribution companies Moore Harness and Ve Line Publications.

Quietlynn
Owned by Brian Richards
Publish *Whitehouse, Playbirds, Shaven Models, Lovebirds*, etc.
1986 gross profits: £3,943,352.
Address: warehouse at 34 Faraday Rd, Stratford, London E15.
Administration: first floor, 182 Cranbrook Rd, Ilford, Essex.
Also runs pornography phone lines.

Conegate
Owned by David Sullivan
Distribute *Park Lane*.
1989 turnover £7m, pre-tax profit £4.4m.
Address: warehouse at 2a Percy Rd, Leytonstone, London E11.
Also involved in property dealings.

Roldvale
Owned by David Sullivan
Pornography films, race horses, property.
1989 turnover £2.9m, pre-tax profit £3.1m.

Paul Raymond Organization
Owned by Paul Raymond
Publish *Men Only, Escort*, etc. Printed by Hunterprint – who also print *Mizz* – and distributed by COMAG.
Also runs strip clubs, as well as theatres and property company.
1989 turnover £16m, pre-tax profit £5.8m.
Property assets worth £12m
Address: 2 Archer St, Soho, London W1.

Sport Newspapers
Owned by Gold Brothers and David Sullivan.
Publish *Sport* and *Sunday Sport*.
1989 turnover £15.3m, pre-tax profit £0.5m.

4 Pornography: The Representation of Power

SUSANNE KAPPELER

The debate about pornography which feminists opened in the 1970s seems to have ended in stalemate as most advocates in the public domain begin and end with the 'conclusion' – that censorship is out of the question. Hardly anyone in fact engages with the analysis which feminists put forward about what exactly is the problem with pornography. Instead, the merest mention of 'pornography' is followed like a Pavlovian reflex by the word 'censorship', as if there was no context other than that of censorship and the law in which the problem of pornography could be raised. Although feminists have reopened the debate about pornography in a radically new context – the context of the civil rights of women and the context of a *gender* analysis of pornography[1] – the arguments invariably revert to the old and familiar playground of repression and taboo, liberation and permissiveness, where old certainties rule: since it used to be prigs and prudes who opposed pornography, we as sexual radicals must defend it (and since we are for it, those against it must be prudes); since pornography is a right-wing issue, as liberals or lefties we are against it being an issue at all; since those against pornography are for censorship, we as opponents of censorship must be for pornography. The *feminist* perspective on the problem of pornography has been well and truly buried again, as the old ghosts of church fathers and forbidding parents are invoked once more. Despite the protestations of a permissive society, these ghosts continue to haunt the collective consciousness of the left and the media public.

While it is true that censorship destroys freedom of expression, it is not true that the absence of censorship does anything like establish or guarantee freedom of expression. The absence of censorship, like the absence of a policy of protectionism, leaves 'expression' to the turmoil of market forces in a free market economy. The freedom our society protects is not the freedom of expression, but the freedom of the market.

Expression in the context of pornography concerns *published* expression – the sale and consumption of images, films, texts and tapes which have been industrially produced and commercially distributed. Censorship affects the circulation of those goods, their sale, import and transportation. It regulates the market. The individual, even under increased censorship laws, would remain free to doodle mutilated women on his notepad.

Censorship, in other words, does not abolish the private expression of pornography, the practice of and belief in a misogynist dogma, just as 'freedom of expression' does not seem to raise the 'private' objection of women to pornography to a sufficiently public level of expression. As feminists, we cannot be content with banishing pornography from the supermarket to the black market or shutting it behind shuttered establishments, since as women we are concerned about the opinions and beliefs expressed in pornography rather than the paper on which it is printed. That is, we are concerned with the beliefs and opinions so freely held and expressed by pornographers and by consumers of pornography, i.e. men in our society, a society which we know to be male-dominated and in which women are oppressed. And we cannot be content with a so-called 'freedom of expression' which means the simple non-interference in the trade of the pornographers, leaving 'expression' to be ruled by market forces, or in other words, the powerful and the rich.

The area of concern is one of ideas, ideology and culture where these are expressed and circulated through an industry and a market, both of which involve and affect real women. Feminist critics are engaged in a *critique* – of pornography and of culture – which is the necessary theoretical basis for the positing of any practical measures. Yet the intellectual debate about pornography has tended to elide any difference between critique and censorship: if you speak or write against pornography you are accused of 'censorship'[2] or of being an intellectual police force. We would do well to remember the difference between a police force with the *power* to intervene in the material reality and practices in society on the one hand, and a published opinion of oppositional critique on the other. Liberals and the left would have us believe that they oppose censorship precisely in order to enable critique to go on and opinions, even if feminist ones, to be mooted occasionally. Yet if they were serious about this, they would need to do more than sit back and be against censorship.

In the present political climate, the expression of political **89** opinion is in the process of falling prey to the dangerous simplification that it is equivalent to some quite different practice in society: if you are engaged in a critique of the state, you are accused of being an enemy of the state ('against' it) and should therefore be censored, i.e. surveilled, silenced and probably locked up – inside a shuttered establishment. In West Germany, the feminist critic and journalist Dr Ingrid Strobl has been sentenced to five years' imprisonment for her oppositional views to state practices (e.g. the treatment of political prisoners), new reproductive technologies and prostitution tourism. Since the targets of her political critique coincide with the targets of terrorist bomb attacks, her opinions are considered sufficient evidence that she might herself carry out terrorist attacks. Having identified 'themes relevant to terrorist attacks', the public prosecution could content itself with a public reading of Strobl's work as a recitation of 'evidence'.[3] With the prospect of 1992 – a Single Market which will require shared legislation to ensure its 'freedom' and its 'security' – we should not be indifferent to these issues of civil rights in a part of the free market zone. Let alone use the same form of argument: that speaking up against pornography makes you an enemy of the freedom of expression who should (be) shut up, that speaking against pornography is the same as censoring pornography is the same as acting as a police force or throwing a bomb.

A multinational industry and its output are called the 'expression of an idea', warehouses full of magazines, films and videocassettes are called specimens of 'speech'. Where dominant ideas have material reality in the form of industries, markets, institutions and the state they are seen as disembodied ideas; where an oppositional idea is expressed in print, it is equated with a guerrilla force, a terrorist army or a police squad. Being against pornography is not being against expression, much less the freedom thereof. And to be 'for freedom of expression', when that means being for the status quo of the market and the pornography industry, can by no stretch of the imagination be seen as being for freedom. Nor can it be said to be taking action to ensure, protect or guarantee the freedom of expression. It is to hold a political opinion in favour of preserving the status quo.

The debate for or against censorship delegates responsibility for the existence, circulation and consumption of pornography to the wrong place: the state, the law, the police. While advocates of censorship invoke the superior authority of the state and its apparatuses to take responsibility for our culture and society, the liberal opposition to censorship merely advocates continued irresponsibility with respect to pornography: permission for the maintenance of the status quo, and hence legitimation of pornography. Liberal protestations to the contrary, the 'no censorship' position does not mean a shift of responsibility from the state to the individual, but a shirking of all responsibility – in the name of the freedom of those individuals who stand to gain from it: pornographers and their clientele. It is freedom in the original sense of 'liberal': 'fit for a gentleman' (*OED*), and it is a liberty taken at the expense of women, the *objects* of pornography.

By contrast, the feminist critique of pornography and a pornographic culture is an invitation to collective social self-criticism, a process of consciousness-raising that, if taken seriously, would lead to the assumption of social responsibility in the interest of social change. Pornography is a feature of our culture, not just the business of pornographers, as the virulent attempts to define it or define it out of existence make plain. Nobody knows where to draw the line, where pornography stops – because it does not stop anywhere. There is a smooth transition from the hard-core to the soft-core to the photographic magazine to the advertisement to literature and the arts. And it is rarely pornographers themselves who leap to its public defence: a great many other people seem to have a vital stake in it.

Feminists have radically redefined what is problematical about pornography. And we have radically redefined what constitutes the harm of pornography. Whereas traditional censorship laws were concerned about the possible harm of pornography to its voluntary consumers (i.e. the vast army of men who choose to consume it), to involuntary consumers (called 'reasonable people') who have pornography foisted upon them through public displays, and to children (who are presumed to be too young to consume pornography), feminists identify the gendered relationships in pornography and the gendered pattern of its damaging effects: the harm and damage to women and children who are used in the production of pornography, the damage women and children suffer when pornographic products are used against them in a variety of forms of sexual violence, from sexual harassment through child sexual abuse, coerced sex, rape and prostitution to sex murder; and the damaging effect of such a vast cultural apparatus on the already discriminated position of women in society.

Unlike traditional definitions of pornography, feminist analysis does not locate the pornographic exclusively in the content of representation, but in the whole system of representation within a social, cultural and economic context. Key factors are the power relations between men and women in society, and the industrial production and commercial distribution of pornography as part of the culture and entertainment industry. A critique of pornography therefore is less a critique of the freedom of expression than of a particular industry and its output. In order to deal with it we do not need censorship, but first of all an educational campaign about the damage this industry creates, both through its production processes and through its products.[4]

Industrially, the women who model in the production of visual pornography are a group of non-organized, non-unionized casual workers with bad pay and worse working conditions, and without a share in the massive profits of the industry. This male industry for a male clientele makes its profits within a social order where men own over 99 per cent of the global wealth; that is, where women own less than 1 per cent collectively and have the worst opportunities for employment and income. This is the gendered *economic* context of the business with pornography, as with the prostitution of women.

Cultural history shows that cultural products – the expression of ideas and opinions circulated in a society – have been produced by a particular minority of race, class, gender and wealth, and reflect the interests of that minority. In the case of pornography, it has emerged and thrived in a patriarchal culture in which men have social, political and economic supremacy. The power arising from this social organization has enabled men to suppress the ideas and opinions of women (and other groups) without the help of a political instrument such as state censorship. The instrument of suppression lies in the control of access to the means of production, the market, and the 'ideological state apparatuses' where ideas and opinions are produced as public and disseminated in society, i.e. published, publicized and broadcast.

Women, typically, have not been involved in the production of public ideas, just as black people and the poor have not. Pornography as the expression of a particular set of ideas and opinions centres on women, a class of people who have no access to the means of production of public ideas: they are the *objects* about whom those ideas are formed.

The history of representation is the history of the male gender representing itself to itself, representing its power and supremacy. Culture as we know it is patriarchy's self-image. As the authors of culture men assume the voice, compose the picture, write the story, for themselves and other men, and *about* women. The pornographic scenario is but a stark representation of the social relationship between the genders. It is extremely limited in scope, devoid of any action or plot besides the act of sexual subordination. Yet this plot can be read and understood only in the context of a society based on the very same plot: the sadistic act of sex and violence, the power and domination of men and their sexual subordination of women.

There is power on the side of the (optionally) represented hero, and there is powerlessness embodied in the victim-object. But there is power, also, on the side of the subject of representation: the producer of pornography, and the consumer of pornography – the author and the reader. And there is powerlessness embodied in the class or gender being represented without access to the means of production of representation.

The necessary ingredient of a pornographic image or representation is neither 'sex' nor 'violence': it is the victim-object. In our society, a woman on view means 'sex', a leg means 'sex', a breast means 'sex', a mouth means 'sex', simply because the body is the body of a woman. In our culture, women *are* 'the sex'. This historical social subordination of women to the status of 'sex' as a gender ensures the cultural 'meaning' of a woman's body as 'sex', ensures the objectification of women in representation. The pornographic plot does not require explicit sex: the presence of a woman objectified, in the context of women's powerlessness as a gender, supplies the implicit action.

The sliding scale of representations from hard-core to soft-core to advertising to the aesthetic shows one and only one constant element of representational content: the woman-object. But there is another constant factor: the male subject, producer and consumer of representation. In the case of soft-core pornography, the 'sexual' plot lies between the viewer and the woman on display: the viewer plays the imaginary hero in relation to the woman-'object'. Striptease and the peep show exemplify this structure, where the action extends to the solitary booths with bucket. The woman objectified implies a subject, a hero of her degradation.

What women find objectionable in pornography, they have

learned to accept in 'high' art and literature. What feminist analysis identifies as the pornographic structure of representation – not the variable quality of 'sex' and violence, but the systematic objectification of women in the interest of the exclusive subjectivity of men – is a commonplace of art and literature as well as of conventional pornography. Moreover, it is the experts in art and literature who conduct the argument in the defence of pornography (under the guise of a defence of the freedom of expression). And as the 'high' culture is fighting for its right to include ever more pornography, the arguments become clearer and the message is spelt out.

Thus one literary critic explains to us the 'meaning' of the 'meaninglessness' of *The Story of O*: 'O progresses simultaneously towards her own extinction as a human being and her fulfillment as a sexual being.' And here is what 'sexual being' means for a woman: 'O does not simply become identical with her sexual availability, but wants to reach the perfection of becoming an object.'[5] It is 'perfection' for her to lose her identity, her self, her subjectivity, to be extinct and progress to the status of someone else's object, someone obviously still very much a subject himself.

Selflessness, the definition of perfect femininity in high cultural representation, the goal and virtue for wife and mother, for womanhood: today the double-bind for every mother in the country. This virtue is the prerogative of women, men being content with less than sainthood for themselves, encouraging women to find their salvation in the extinction of self, the evacuation of selfhood, taking upon themselves the risk of a slower salvation in the hereafter and the privilege of a selfish existence in the here and now.

This spiritual altruism, this material egotism, preaches to woman that 'her own extinction as a human being' means her fulfilment as a 'woman' in the nineteenth century – the angel in the house; her fulfilment as a 'sexual being' in the twentieth – the angel in bed. The message is not about sex, but about subjugation. Sex is the means of subjugation in the case of gender, sex is the generic violence of men against women.

Physical violence is the means of subjugation in the case of 'humans', that is, other men. A news story entitled 'Murder in Namibia' tells of the torture and eventual murder of Thomas Kasire, a black worker on the farm of the white van Rooyen.[6] Racist violence, of course, is an everyday occurrence in a society based on white supremacy and privilege and the lack of civil rights of black people. It is as everyday as sexual violence in our society. What is striking about the murder of Thomas Kasire is the additional pornographic pleasure the white murderer devised for himself: the torture, begun by van Rooyen on his own, was continued, and eventually led to murder, when white guests were visiting. Van Rooyen, the owner of the farm, wants to entertain his guests in a special fashion. Kasire, who has spent two days and nights chained in the backyard without food or water, is fetched and forced to pose while van Rooyen's guests take photographs and applaud. Shortly after the taking of the pictures, Kasire dies. Pictures accompany the article, taken by the murderer and his guests: one a close-up of Kasire's head, bleeding, mutilated, a heavy iron chain around his neck, with the white left arm of his murderer reaching into the middle foreground of the picture, holding on to the chain. Another picture has the caption: 'The victim is forced to pose with a clenched fist (SWAPO salute), while a friend of the murderer takes photos.' The murderer himself is in the picture, towering over the young black man whom he holds by the chain, smiling into the camera.

This is not just a racist murder, it is also a cultural event. There is a producer of the event, a director of the play, and there is an audience, applauding. Nor is it just a 'live' performance, it is also a production process which yields cultural products: pictures, careful compositions, deliberate representations, conforming to a genre. The victim is forced to pose for sheer display; in another picture, the torturer positions himself with respect to the camera, like a fisher with his catch. Another white man is behind the camera, framing the pictures.

With an audience, torture becomes an art, the torturer an author, the onlookers an audience of connoisseurs. Van Rooyen, the master of ceremonies, also acts as torturer-hero in the one picture. Another white man, behind the camera, is acting in the production of the picture. The two white men look at each other. The one in the picture will come out of the picture, joining the one behind the camera to look at the scene they have framed. The host mingles with his guests in the audience, becomes one with the audience. The victim does not come out of the picture, the victim is dead. In this case literally, in the general case of representation usually only symbolically and functionally, as there is no further role for the victim to play in the continued life of the picture. Kasire is dead, but the picture of Kasire lives on, **95** takes its place in society. It is not a fantasy, but a product. In the United States it is protected as 'free speech'.

The product reflects the conditions of its production, epitomized by the two white men. The one behind the camera has framed a vision and engendered an audience, a viewing public of white men in general. And the white man in the picture is still at large, has merged with the audience, has become interchangeable with it. Between the two white men there is collusion – they look at each other. One is the host, the other his guest. There is a sense of identification between them, a solidarity, a common purpose, a shared understanding, a communicated pleasure – the binding force of a culture.

On the evidence of the pictures, van Rooyen is brought to trial. 'Without them', the report continues, 'the court would in all probability have acquitted him. The explanations given by him and his white friends would have outweighed the statements of black witnesses. So safe are the whites in their dominant position within the apartheid system that, incredibly, the whole event was photographed at van Rooyen's request.' But the sentence is mild: van Rooyen gets only six years and moreover is secretly freed shortly after his prison sentence has begun.

Experts of art and pornography do not feel competent in a case like this, since the victim really died. They pass on the case to the courts so that these may punish the crime of murder. But the white men's party, their performance of the torture and murder of Thomas Kasire and their production of the pictures, are overlooked at the trial, where the pictures simply serve as evidence, a fortuitous aid in the hands of the prosecutor. The posing for pictures, however, was a central part in the torture of Kasire – finally the cause of his death. And taking the pictures, shooting on location, acting in the live performance of a drama of their design was an essential part of the white men's pleasure in the torturing and murdering of Thomas Kasire.

In our society, men are the owners of the farm and the employers who hand out the work. And they also host a party: the culture of our society, the entertainment produced for their pleasure. There is a shared understanding, a common purpose, a solidarity of vision and a shared enjoyment exchanged in their looks across the bodies of women. Solidified in images and exchanged as products, their glances engender a community, an audience of men, in which these products have their function. Men direct the poses of women, shape the plots of the action, tell the story and paint the picture, and occasionally they even play a part themselves. The woman, if she is lucky, is paid and dismissed once the show is over or the production completed. But she has no say and no role to play in the future life of the product. Unlike the cameraman and the *metteur-en-scène* who have a continued existence in the audience, she has neither function nor rights.

In the case of snuff films, increasingly popular as videos in the American home, the woman does not get paid and dismissed. She is, like Thomas Kasire, dead. Or like Linda Marciano, better known as Linda Lovelace, who played her notorious role in the film *Deep Throat* at gun point but survived, she is powerless to remove the film from circulation. She has no claim on the film and no stake in the further means of production – the cinemas and video shops the world over which day after day and year after year play her degradation to rapt audiences and full houses. For *Deep Throat* enjoys the protection of the law, as an example of 'free speech'.[7]

Nor is it just a matter of those products like *Deep Throat* or snuff films or videos of filmed 'live' rape where a recognized and punishable crime could be handed over to the courts for prosecution. My concern is with the white man's party, his celebration of his power. Had Thomas Kasire not died, had he ultimately been dismissed and sent back to work, there would have been no court case, and in the eyes of the dominant society of Namibia, there would have been no crime. In the event of death, the torture is overshadowed by the murder; in the event of survival, torture becomes invisible, insignificant, not worth talking about (in the eyes of the dominant white society). Without the corroborating evidence of a corpse, the pictures would not be evidence, but culture, fantasy, fiction.

Making pictures is itself an action in the world, not just an airy inspiration of the creative imagination. It is an action which has consequences for the so-called 'object' of representation, an action involving another subject. This action consists of humiliation, degradation, objectification. Thomas Kasire is made to feel his powerlessness in his own body; van Rooyen enacts his power. Nor is this just a personal matter between van Rooyen and Thomas Kasire. Van Rooyen's power is based on the collective power which whites have over blacks. This is evidenced by van Rooyen's white guests who are busy partying. Not one of them comes to Kasire's aid. Kasire's degradation, his reduction to a mere object, plaything of the white man, is meant not just for him personally, but for black people generally. It has less to do with Kasire's personality than with his 'race'.

Feminists recognize in pornography the collective enactment of male power and the collective degradation of women as a gender. It is not a personal matter between a specific pornographer and his allegedly willing female model; the whole thing has nothing to do with her personal attitudes, but everything with her gender. The power of pornographers is based on the collective power of men over women, evidenced by the existence of pornography in our society, the size of its edition and the scope of its circulation. The male consumers, like van Rooyen's guests, are busy partying. It does not seem to occur to one of them to take the side of the victim and to stop the host. Just as in Namibia the torture and humiliation of a black person is not an issue unless he dies, so the collective humiliation of women, their degradation to mere object and sexual plaything of men, is not an issue in our society. So safe are men in their dominant position within the patriarchal social system that, incredibly, the whole event is continually represented at men's own request.

In the current pornography debate, women are increasingly being invited to take the role of spectator of pornography or to become pornographers, in turn to objectify men and women. But even if more and more women today have the 'opportunity' (imposed or sought) to view pornography, this hardly affects the fundamentally sexist structure of pornography: its production by and for men, and about women. Just as a black man looking on at the picture of Thomas Kasire does nothing to change the racist nature of those pictures.

Rather, we might argue that since the legal emancipation of women in our society, culture – the white man's party – has acquired a new importance. When men are no longer entitled by law to do violence to women (other than their wives and daughters), when women's new status as citizens of the state theoretically gives them access to the law in their own right, culture has become the principal means in the struggle to maintain male supremacy. Where white men prior to the emancipation of black people, women and colonized peoples were free to subject their subjects by means of force, today's ruling groups are obliged to persuade their ex-slaves, ex-colonial subjects and ex-sexual chattels of their inferiority without the overt use of physical violence. Should the subjects of their education prove to be good pupils, they will soon agree with their taskmasters of their own free will. Frantz Fanon analysed this process of post-colonial cultural imperialism and its product: 'internalized colonization'.[8] We can see it at work in the explosive expansion of pornography since the legal emancipation of women, and we can see its results in the gradual emergence of eager women advocates of pornography, the good pupils of our culture's teaching. In that sense, we might say that men's exercise of *structural* violence against women in the form of their continued control of the cultural institutions has paid off. The tireless representation of men's superiority and women's willing sexual submission is having its educational and cultural influence also on women.

For the chief message of contemporary pornography is the lusty smile of the woman object, is the suggestion that women seek, endorse and enjoy their degradation and violation. Where simple sadism ignored the feelings of its victims, indeed presupposed their opposition and resistance, the advanced sadism of contemporary Western culture specializes in the violation not only of the victim's body, but also of her mind. The domination of her mind, however, is attainable only through the continued control over representation, where the author not only controls the plot, but also invents, dramatizes and produces the victim's 'will'. And as the supreme cultural Author, he has also himself named the phenomenon, as the 'masochism' complementing his own sadism. If he wishes moreover to extend the influence of his representation beyond the single and specific victim to a whole class of potential victims, his representation must become a cultural textbook. That is, he must control the cultural industry at large. Which is the situation we have today, the status quo of our much vaunted 'freedom of expression'.

On 12 March 1988 a plastic bag with the arms and legs of a murdered woman was deposited outside a London Refuge for Battered Women. The murderer has not only murdered: he also wants to be a cultural producer. He wants to represent himself and his power; and he has an audience in mind which he has carefully chosen. It is not an audience like the guests of the white van Rooyen, whose agreement and shared understanding he can presuppose. It is an audience which consists of the class of his victim, the class of potential victims, whom he wishes to teach a lesson. To him, it is abundantly clear that there is a connection between the women of his chosen audience and the woman who fell victim to his violent crime: he has not murdered a human being, he has murdered a woman. It is his cultural deed, not his single murdering deed, which shows the unity of a class which we call gender. And it is this cultural deed which shows up another connection: the link between the structural violence of a culture which teaches the subordination of women, apparently harmlessly, and the physical sexual violence which has been lurking behind it since the beginning of patriarchal history.

Notes

1. Andrea Dworkin and Catharine A. MacKinnon, *Pornography and Civil Rights: A New Day for Women's Equality* (Minneapolis, MN: Organizing Against Pornography, 1988); Andrea Dworkin, *Pornography: Men Possessing Women* (London: Women's Press, 1981); Catharine A. MacKinnon, *Feminism Unmodified: Discourses on Life and Law* (Cambridge, Mass. and London: Harvard University Press, 1987); Laura Lederer (ed.), *Take Back the Night: Women on Pornography* (Toronto, New York, London and Sydney: Bantam Books, 1982); Dusty Rhodes and Sandra McNeill (eds), *Women Against Violence Against Women* (London: Onlywomen Press, 1985); *Pornography and Sexual Violence: Evidence of the Links* (Minneapolis Hearings) (London: Everywoman, 1988); Margaret A. Baldwin, 'Pornography and the Traffic in Women', *Yale Journal of Law and Feminism* 1 (1), Spring 1989; Susanne Kappeler, *The Pornography of Representation* (Cambridge: Polity Press, 1986).

2. See Ian Vine's letter, 'Feminist Censors Won't Further Porn Debate', *New Socialist* 37, April 1986; or Simon Watney, 'Babbling at the Barricades of Pornography', *New Socialist* 39, June 1986, p. 21, for a couple of fairly typical examples. Vine feels 'silenced' by the 'repressive' arguments of anti-porn feminism, which in his view forms the 'new hegemony', intimidating and forbidding: 'Who will then dare to defend such representations of women as "victim-objects"?' Watney: 'We should therefore be *profoundly* suspicious of anyone EMPLOYING THE WORD "PORNOGRAPHY" IN ANY CONTEXT WHATSOEVER' (my capitals).

3. Ingrid Strobl, 'Prozesserklärung', in *Frausein allein ist kein Programm* (Freiburg i. Br.: Kore Verlag, 1989), p.33; Rolf Gössner, 'Die Offenkundigkeit von Vorurteilen: Beweiskonstrukte und "Gerichtskundigkeit" im 129a-Verfahren gegen Ingrid Strobl', *Clockwork 129a* 8, April 1989, p. 2.

4. Patricia Hynes, 'Matters of Life and Death', *Trouble & Strife* 15, Spring 1989.

5. Susan Sontag, 'The Pornographic Imagination', in *The Susan Sontag Reader* (New York: Farrar, Straus and Giroux, 1982), pp. 222 and 220.

6. Aslak Aarhus and Ole Bernt Froshaug, 'A Murder in Namibia', *Guardian Weekly*, 8 January 1984, p.7.

7. MacKinnon, op. cit., p. 11; pp. 234–5, n. 30 and n. 31.

8. Frantz Fanon, *Peau noire, masques blancs* (Paris: Edition du Seuil,

1952). See also Kate Millet's 'interior colonization', *Sexual Politics* (London: Virago, 1977), p. 25; or Andrea Dworkin's 'submission' as a result of subordination in 'Against the Male Flood', *Trivia: A Journal of Ideas* 7, Summer 1985, pp. 22–3.

5　Pornography and Racism: Sexualizing Oppression and Inciting Hatred

AMINATTA FORNA

SOME FACTS ABOUT RACISM AND PORNOGRAPHY

FACT: In Bombay, the production cost of a blue movie is around 28,000 rupees (around £1,000). The female model used is paid around £30. As many as 20,000 copies of the video will be produced and circulated to markets in India, the Middle East and Europe.

FACT: In Nazi Germany, Hitler's regime disseminated anti-Semitic propaganda depicting Jews as sexually voracious, Jewish men as rapists and Jewish women as sexually insatiable.

FACT: In the 1989 US presidential elections, a television advertisement for the Republican party accused the Democratic candidate Michael Dukakis of being soft on crime. The advertisement focused on the case of Willie Horton, a black prisoner released under the Dukakis rehabilitation programme who raped a white woman while on weekend leave. This campaign advertisement (based on the stereotype of black males as sexually dangerous) is generally credited with having ensured a Republican victory.

FACT: 'Some Girls' a song performed by the band the Rolling Stones contains the following lyrics: 'Black girls just want to get fucked all night. I don't have that much jam.'

FACT: When the Nazis took over the government of Poland, they flooded the Polish bookstalls with pornography – on the theory that to make the individual conscious only of the need for personal sensation will make the chances of unifying the people in rebellion more difficult.[1]

FACT: In her book *The Pornography of Representation*, Susanne Kappeler reproduced a newspaper account of the torture and murder of Thomas Kasire, a black Namibian, by his white employer, photographed by the murderer's friends. Substitute a young woman for Thomas, writes Kappeler, and you have the 'perfect scenario' of sadistic pornography.

At first, the notion of racism in pornography comes as no surprise. There is racism in schools, work, literature and language. There is racism in every aspect of life, why not in pornography? Only an unthinking person would fail to acknowledge the double burden of racial and sexual oppression which black women must bear. It is known, for example, that black women suffer more sexual harassment from both black and white men on the street. Being both black and female they are seen as having the least power. Sexual harassment is nothing if not the exercise of power over women, and black women are vulnerable targets for reasons of race as well as gender. Women are treated differently and less favourably than men: in employment, health, housing, in private and public. But black women are often treated differently and even less favourably than white women, not just in the marketplace, but even in the most mundane settings.

A black woman and a white woman enter an Indian restaurant late one evening. Unused to seeing women out alone so late – and perhaps disapproving – the waiters are impudent, slow and over-familiar in their treatment of the women. When the white woman asserts herself, they are subdued. Yet when the black woman does the same, she is treated with less respect, more insinuation, unconcealed contempt. Both women are certain that the difference in their treatment is due to race. That the waiter, having internalized the message of white superiority and black inferiority, will take rebuke from a white woman – whom he sees at least as his equal, perhaps superior. But he will not accord the same respect to the black woman.

Given the combination of racism and sexism that operates always in the lives of black women, what then is there that is in any way remarkable about the knowledge of the exploitation of black women in pornography? What makes racism in pornography different from racism in any other aspect of life?

This chapter will show how black women are injured by pornography, both by the perpetuation and exploitation of racial stereotypes, and through the actual harm that is done to them in the name of pornography. It will also explore the similarities and **103** differences between racism and sexism as systems of oppression and, where there are parallels, the relevance of existing race relations legislation as a model for legislation against pornography.

IMAGES OF BLACK PEOPLE IN PORNOGRAPHY

Black women as represented in pornography are synonymous with deep carnality, animal desires and uncontrolled lust. The black woman is portrayed as the most sexually voracious, the most wanton of all females. 'Naturally' less civilized than her white counterpart, she exists solely for sex and is even more sexually insatiable. The words and adjectives which caption pictures of naked black women are the same words used over and over again. The black woman is described as being 'panther-like', possessing 'animal grace'. She is photographed caged, chained and naked. Hers is a savage, wild and primitive, exotic sexuality: a less than human sexuality.

Black men are portrayed in the same way. Almost always they are the possessors of enormous penises, outsize to the point of absurdity. They are super-sexualized studs, members of a lower caste without the natural inhibitions of civilized whites. Sex between two blacks is a steamy, savage affair. Sex between a black and a white person is abnormal, freakish and kinky.

The idea of black people as sexually uncontrollable derives from the days of slavery in the USA. White slave masters were expected to, and did, exercise their power of sexual access to their property, their black women slaves. This was in practice the socially and legally sanctioned rape of black women by their white male owners. Black men, since the days of slavery, have been regarded as the rapists of white women. In the Deep South just looking at a white woman could result in the lynching of a black man. Rape was used to subordinate the black female population and castration and lynching to subjugate and control the black male population. Black men were usually charged with the rape or attempted rape of white women. In this way, black people have been sexualized and stereotyped as less than human: sexually dangerous and threatening. This myth is used to fuel white fears about black people and stir up racial hatred, which in turn perpetuates and justifies the inequality of blacks in American society.

104   The same ideas, in various forms, are still with us. From

Othello and Desdemona ('against all the rules of nature') to the 1980s film *Angel Heart*, with Mickey Rourke and Lisa Bonet, black/white sexual relations are portrayed as odd and the subject of licentious curiosity. The idea of black people as sexually primitive and voracious has transcended time and geography. In Great Britain now, there is a prevalent belief that black men have much larger penises than white men, a notion propounded as casually as if it were accepted fact. There is also an entrenched belief that sex with a black woman or a black man is different, more physical but less emotional and spiritual: less human. The myths and misunderstandings about black sexuality result in a fear and hatred of black people. Mere references to that fear in the Republican advertisement for George Bush is credited with swinging the tide of the 1988 presidential election in his favour.

At the Minneapolis City Council public hearings on pornography in 1983, a Native American woman gave evidence of how she was raped by two white men who were enacting scenes from a pornographic video game *Custer's Revenge*. That act of rape was a combination, and culmination, of racial and sexual hatred. She was made a victim simply for being a female member of that racial group, and the set of ideas which her attackers held about her were generated and reiterated through pornography.[2]

In pre-war Germany, Hitler's propaganda machine used the same notion of animal sexuality against German Jews, with great effect. Jewish men were accused of raping Aryan women: the Jewish female was an insatiable, licentious temptress of the German male. Anti-Semitism was sexualized. This preceded the systematic slaughter of 6 million Jews. It not only helped create the climate of opinion which made people accept and even take part in the murders, it was designed to have that effect. The Nazis also deliberately disseminated pornography in Poland to desensitize the Poles and to make their conquest and subjugation easier to carry out.[3]

Images of black women are exploited by pornography and black women are exploited by pornographers. Slavery was abolished, but black people still suffer economic discrimination and the disadvantage created by low pay and poverty. Because of their lower economic status and limited opportunities, black and 'Third World' women are economically and sexually exploited by the international pornography market.

Snuff movies in the United States are believed to be flourishing with the use of untraceable illegal immigrants and Latin **105**

American women and children as their victims. The pornographers will force their victims to make several blue movies before they are killed as the grand finale to the last. In Thailand and throughout South East Asia, an acknowledged international slave trade in women exists for the purposes of pornography and prostitution, exploiting the poverty of the black women and children in those countries.

Pornography exploits and regenerates the derogatory racist sexualized stereotypes of black people, continually reworking them so that they enter the reader's subconscious. The images may be subtle or blatant, but they exist in an historical context which makes every depiction of Nazi concentration camp sex, or black rape or nymphomania, a powerful racist and sexist weapon. Racism like sexism is sexualized in pornography: the inequality is sexualized. In their day-to-day lives, black women and men have to live with this kind of racism. For black women the pressure is acute. Ideas that originated in slavery are not being allowed to die, but are being retrieved and reworked into a nation's sexuality through pornography.

SEXISM AND RACISM – DIFFERENCES AND PARALLELS

Imagine if you walked into your high street newsagent and saw that one of the shelves was taken up with magazines devoted to racist pictures. Each magazine showed black men and women being tied up, gagged, bound and humiliated. Inside, advertisements urged the reader to send off for violent videos, in which black people were shown being tortured by whites. People browsing in the shop select copies and flick through the photographs, deciding which to buy. Some of the magazines are specially tailored to the views of the readers – specifically anti-Semitic, or Oriental, or Asian for example. All advocate white supremacy. There are black people in the shop but, humiliated and intimidated, they merely avert their eyes. The black shop assistant rings up the total on the cash till without comment.

People would be outraged. It would not be allowed. No one would expect black people to stand for it. Even if, for some reason, they could not assert their own rights, we would expect them to be able to seek protection in the law. Our expectations would be correct. To publish and distribute magazines like that is not only unthinkable for most people, it is an offence under the Race Relations Act 1976.

Racist literature is certainly not the only form or cause of racism, but it is one effective way of transmitting racist messages and 'inciting racial hatred and violence'. The power of the printed word and image cannot be overestimated, and the British law recognizes and upholds that fact. Material referred to the Attorney General for prosecution under the Race Relations Act 1976 (and the Public Order Act of 1936 which preceded it) illustrates the kind of racist literature targeted by the legislation.

The first prosecution under the Public Order Act 1936 was of an anti-Semitic speaker who had said at a public meeting that 'Jews are the lice of the earth and must be exterminated from national life'. Colin Jordan, the leader of the National Socialist Movement, was charged following a meeting in Trafalgar Square in 1962 for having said: 'Hitler was right . . . our real enemies . . . were not Hitler . . . but world Jewry and its associates in this country.' Jordan was charged again in 1967 for a pamphlet entitled *The Coloured Invasion* about 'the menace to the nation' of the 'coloured million'. John Kingsley Read, chairman of the British National Party, was charged in 1976 for referring to 'niggers, wogs and coons' but the jury failed to agree on a verdict. In 1977 a man was convicted for posting stickers reading 'Keep Britain White' and 'Niggers Go Back to Africa': he was wearing a Klu Klux Klan cowl when he was arrested.[4]

In the late 1970s the Commission for Racial Equality referred a booklet of photographs by Ian Newport, a National Front photographer, to the Attorney General. Captions in the book included: 'Asian thugs', 'Black savages', and 'Ape Rape – the wrong one is behind bars'. Under a photograph of a concentration camp survivor were the words: 'I am a death camp survivor. I was nearly exterminated 5, no 6 million times in my life.' A 1981 issue of *The Stormer* – published by the Nationalist Socialist Party of the UK – contained cartoons depicting black people caricatured as apes, a classroom of black people being blown up by skinheads captioned: 'The first lesson is white supremacy' and a 'Focus on Fact' showing 'Jewish ritual murder' with Jews drinking the blood of murdered children.[5]

Just as all black people are, or are potentially, victims of racism in a white society, all women, by dint of their sex alone, are potential victims of sexism. Both are relegated to a secondary status in a white, male-dominated society. Even the words used **107** to describe the oppression is the same in both cases: second-class, unequal, subjugation, prejudice, domination, chattel, subservient, powerless, subordination, discrimination. There are similarities between the oppression of blacks and women, particularly with respect to economic discrimination and subordination. But there is also a significant difference: where racism has kept blacks segregated from whites, sexism has kept women 'intimately integrated . . . in the common fabric of everyday life'.[6]

Representation of black people and women as race or sex-stereotyped and sexualized is part of the apparatus of oppression, influencing both the oppressors and the oppressed. For women, pornography represents a clear statement of their sexualized and subordinate status in society. The images intimidate, the images are internalized and women and black people are intimidated. When a racist attack takes place, the reason for that otherwise meaningless attack is the colour of that person's skin. The victim of a racist attack is chosen because of his/her race. Rape is a crime of violence, not an act of sex, but the target of that violence is chosen for her sex alone. Both forms of violence are perpetrated against an object of hatred, whether because of skin colour or sex. The hatred is not inherent, it is acquired and it is incited. The violence is then one form that discrimination takes.

The understanding of civil liberties that we, as a generation, now have derives from the struggle of two groups for a measure of equality in the law: the women's suffrage movement in Britain and the USA, and the black civil rights movement in the United States. In both cases women and black people fought a white, male-dominated establishment and forced themselves to be heard. In both cases it was a fight for power. In England women fought for years to obtain equal access with men to the ballot box, facing prison, forced feeding, humiliation and death for the right to vote and an equal share in the political power of the country. In the United States, the white Southern segregationists argued that the demands of blacks to have equal access to buses, eating places and educational establishments violated their own right to 'freedom of association', but they were in fact deprived of their 'right' so that the same right could be extended to blacks:

> The mathematics of the situation are clear: as long as whites count as the humans who have a right to rights, making them integrate means taking away their absolute control of association in public and in private. As soon as Blacks count as humans who also have rights, freedom of association is in fact extended,

increased, significantly multiplied, because Blacks can exercise it by going to the places whites had been able to forbid them to go.[7]

Eventually, after persistent challenges to this social inequality in a 'social conflict in which many were hurt and some were killed', the US government gave precedence to the civil rights of the black population to freedom of movement and association (1964) and to vote (1965).

Just as the white Southern segregationists used their right to associate with whom they pleased in order to block the moves of the black populace to establish their own rights of associations and freedom of movement, pornographers and the consumers of pornography try to claim similar refuge in their right to 'freedom of expression'.

> Women, who have lived in social, political, and legal silence, are told that freedom of speech is a sacrosanct right, and that any effort to diminish it for anyone diminishes it for women . . . women are supposed to value speech rights by valuing the rights of those who have excluded them.[8]

Pro-pornographers argue their inviolate right to portray women as they wish. Their right to portray women as sexually demeaned supersedes the rights of those women, collective or individual, who do not wish to be portrayed in such a way, or who live with the fear or the resulting consequences of such a portrayal. In *Pornography and Civil Rights* Andrea Dworkin and Catharine A. MacKinnon explain that the battle is not over rights, but power:

> He has the power disguised as rights protected by law that fosters inequality. The mathematics are simple: his diminished power will lead to an increase in her rights. Because the establishment of equality means taking power from those who have it, power protected by law, those who have wrongful power hate equality and resist it. They defend the status quo through bigotry and violence or sophistication and intellect. They find high and mighty principles and say how important rights are. They say that rights will be lost if society changes. They mean that power will be lost, by them. This is true.[9]

Free speech is regarded as the hallmark of a civilized and democratic society. But women, like black people, do not have access to power or the means of production or the 'platforms' from which to speak. Free speech is a right which they, as a **109** group, have had little opportunity to exercise because of their subordinate and unequal status in society.

THE RACE RELATIONS ACT AS A LEGISLATIVE MODEL FOR PORNOGRAPHY

The law of the United Kingdom has, since 1965, recognized the actual harm that is done to black people and all those who are members of an ethnic minority as a result of racism. In support of the rights of members of these groups, Parliament has passed legislation which gives members of these groups some measure of equality under the law and a basis from which to set about achieving actual equality. The legislation was designed to redress racial discrimination. The Race Relations Act 1976, which provides the weight of legislation against racial discrimination, was modelled on the 1975 Sex Discrimination Act. The Acts were drafted on similar lines to deal primarily with discrimination in employment practices, and to provide similar machinery for enforcement.

The sex and race discrimination legislation, although broadly similar in principle, differ in one particular way. The Race Relations Act, by amending the Public Order Act of 1936, broadened the protection extended to ethnic minorities to cover the incitement of racial hatred by the spoken or written word or image. By so doing, Parliament recognized the harm which could be caused to certain groups in a climate of racial intolerance, and the need for racial harmony as part of the process of eliminating racial discrimination.

The Public Order Act 1936 was passed to help combat a growing climate of anti-Semitism and the public activities of the British Union of Fascists in attempting to incite hatred against Jews. Section 5 of the Act made it an offence for any person in a public place or meeting to 'use threatening, abusive or insulting words and behaviour, with intent to provoke a breach of the peace'. In response to the increase in immigration of black Afro-Caribbeans in the 1950s, and early '60s (to meet the economic needs of the country for cheap labour), and the race attacks and riots which followed, there was pressure on government to make incitement to racial hatred a punishable offence. In 1965, the Labour government passed the first Race Relations Act, with a section (6) dealing with 'incitement to racial hatred'.

110   The Race Relations Act, by making it an offence to 'publish or distribute written matter which is threatening or abusive or insulting', is technically an act of censorship. But the 'censorship' of race hatred and anti-Semitic literature is regarded by our society as justifiable censorship. The harm that is caused to black people who experience systematic social discrimination is not regarded as a justifiable consequence of the freedom to 'speak, publish and distribute materials that are likely to incite racial hatred'. The right of black people to be free of the racial violence and the racism promoted and caused by race hatred literature takes precedence in the UK over the right of racists' freedom of speech.

If we weigh the balance of two apparently conflicting freedoms – individual free speech and racial equality – we put the freedom of black people first. If we weigh the balance of two censorships, which takes precedence – the censorship of black people as a result of race hatred or the censorship of race hatred? Black people do not regard the restriction of race hatred literature as censorship. They regard it as increasing their opportunity for a measure of freedom and equality.

Racist words and literature are accepted as a threat to the civil liberties of black people. There is evidence to show that pornography poses at least an equivalent threat to women. Pornographic images of women bound, gagged, raped or sodomized; women subjected to humiliation and torture for the reader's pleasure, and shown to enjoy what is being done to them; women posed in a sexually demeaning way – these must be recognized as doing the same harm as pictures or words which treat black people in a similarly subordinate or violent way. If those pictures were of blacks, Asians or Jews, they would be recognized as constituting 'an incitement to racial hatred'. Because they are of women, and women are regarded *as* sex in the way that pornography presents women as sex, the hatred is harder to recognize. But when women rather than blacks are the target, the material could constitute 'an incitement to sexual hatred'.

Some argue that banning pornography is a curtailment of the right to freedom of speech as exercised by pornographers. But pornography denies women their freedom of speech and freedom of movement and safety. With women as with race, it is a matter of weighing the balance of two censorships and two freedoms – the pornographers' right to publish pornography and women's right to be free of the sexual violence and sex discrimination to which pornography contributes. The 'incitement' part of the **111**

Race Relations Act provides a model for legislation against pornography on grounds of incitement to sexual hatred and violence. If such legislation is censorship then it is arguably, as with incitement to racial hatred, justifiable censorship. The Race Relations Act has been effective in restricting race hatred literature without censoring material which is not race hatred. It has prohibited white supremacist propaganda while preserving *Othello*. Banning incitement to racial hatred has not meant that black people can never be portrayed negatively. The film-maker, the writer, the journalist and the artist are still free to portray black people in all the ways they would portray any people.

Pornography contributes to sexual violence and sex discrimination, just as racist propaganda contributes to racial violence and race discrimination. What would happen if the legislative protection afforded to blacks were removed tomorrow, and racist literature was not only freely available but sanctioned by law? The Race Relations Act is, at the very least, an expression of the desire for equality, and a basis from which black people can work to achieve equality. While no one would pretend that racism has suddenly disappeared, there are few who would publicly defend it. Legislation against pornography modelled on the Race Relations Act, introducing 'incitement to sexual hatred' as an offence, would have a similar effect. Then through a process of education and information, as well as legislation, the climate of racial and sexual intolerance could be changed and the practice of discrimination in and through pornography could be ended.

Notes

1. R. Amy Elman, 'Sexual Subordination and State Intervention: Lessons for Feminists from the Nazi State', *Trivia*, 1989, p. 59.
2. *Pornography and Sexual Violence: Evidence of the Links* (Minneapolis Hearings) (London: Everywoman, 1988), p, 100.
3. Elman, op. cit.
4. Paul Gordon, *Incitement to Racial Hatred* (London: Runnymede Trust, 1982), pp. 2, 6, 9, 14.
5. Ibid., pp. 18, 22.
6. Andrea Dworkin and Catharine A. MacKinnon, *Pornography and Civil Rights: A New Day for Women's Equality* (Minneapolis, MN: Organizing Against Pornography, 1988), p. 15.
7. Ibid., p. 21.
8. Ibid.
9. Ibid., p. 22.

6 Pornography and Child Sexual Abuse

LIZ KELLY

The sex industry relies upon, and trades in, all forms of inequality; children's powerlessness makes them a particular target. Yet in feminist analyses of, and campaigning against, pornography relatively little attention has been paid to child pornography. For example, in a recent British publication, *Feminism and Censorship*,[1] not one of the pieces (including my own) mentions children or child pornography. The only explicit attempt to explain this absence which I have encountered was made by Susan Cole.[2] She argued that focusing on child pornography was too easy, since there was a general consensus about the harm involved, and our task was to demonstrate that there was a problem in relation to adult women. But is it really that simple?

Having shifted my work focus from all forms of sexual violence to child abuse I now suspect that part of the explanation as to why child pornography has not been a central concern lies in the way many feminists simplistically elide children's interests with those of adult women. Two other examples illustrate this tendency. Child sexual abuse was a relatively late arrival in contemporary feminist opposition to sexual violence, despite Florence Rush drawing our attention to it in 1974.[3] It is even more recently that feminists have begun publicly to address the physical abuse of children. It is also the case that while feminist theory, research and practical politics have directed much attention to motherhood, little addresses childhood directly.

Although there are historical and practical reasons for connecting the interests of women and children, some of these, certainly in the West, no longer hold true. There was a time when both women and children had no independent legal status. Women in many countries have achieved formal equality with men, while children retain the status of 'non-persons'. Failure to recognize that children's oppression has an independent structure can result in feminists not challenging the general resistance to seeing and knowing what adults do to children. I use 'adults' here deliberately, since part of what must be recognized is that women too have power over children by virtue of being adults, which in turn requires that we develop a more complex analysis of the relationships between men, women and children.[4]

In the 1980s the sexual abuse of children became a public issue in many Western societies. Yet what we witnessed was a growing willingness of adults to believe the testimony of children and adult survivors in general and in the abstract, while at the same time retaining the power to disbelieve in the particular. Individuals who accept that child sexual abuse exists and is much more prevalent than previously thought, none the less resist the fact that young children are anally abused (one of the key issues at stake in the so-called 'Cleveland crisis').[5] They also resist the fact that young children were abused while in day-care,[6] and the fact that groups of children are subjected to cult ritualistic abuse.[7]

This double-think provides a slightly different angle from which to view the fantasy versus reality issue of the pornography debate. Some of the very forms of sexual abuse which are contested appear as themes in general release horror films, others in under-the-counter porn videos, short stories and novels. It seems that a percentage of the general public finds these forms of sexual violence plausible enough for 'fiction', but unbelievable and unacceptable in reality, regardless of the testimony of child and adult survivors.

Accounts by social workers of how they came to believe the stories of children who had been sexually abused as part of 'satanic' rituals further illustrate this point. Most social workers could not initially accept that the children were describing real events, and attributed references to the devil, torture and ritual killings to the children having been allowed to watch 'video nasties': the stories were plausible as fiction but not as descriptions of reality. When some social workers courageously began to believe that the children were talking from personal experience, many of their colleagues challenged their belief. At least one case in Britain was not prosecuted because the police and Crown Prosecution Service felt that the jury would not believe the children's accounts. The willingness of adults to 'listen to children' (the slogan for a recent NSPCC campaign) and to believe them when they report abuse (the first principle recommended in most child protection guidelines) is all too frequently withdrawn.

114   The many ways in which children are abused and exploited raise uncomfortable issues about adult power and responsibility, the structure of the Western nuclear family, fatherhood, motherhood, male sexuality and Western imperialism. They, furthermore, challenge the Western fiction that childhood is 'a time of play, an asexual and peaceful existence'.[8] The power of this ideology is evident in the repeated use of emotive pictures of children by charities – Western child protection agencies using pictures of (usually) white children bearing the signs of abuse, Western aid agencies using pictures of starving black children. The momentary compassion and responsibility which may prompt a financial donation permits individuals both to acknowledge misery and oppression for what are seen to be the exceptions, while avoiding the fundamental issues at stake.

Many of us would rather not look too closely at the reality of childhood. If we did, we would discover, among many other things, that large numbers of children in our own countries and internationally are caught up in the sex industry, used in the production of pornography, used in prostitution. As both child pornography and child prostitution are illegal in most countries, both tend to be seen as relatively small and unimportant sectors of the sex industry. But as we know from our work on sexual violence, the fact that an act is illegal does not prevent it from being prevalent.

It is not so much that focusing on child pornography is too easy, but rather that it is too revealing. When we see or hear about children being used in this way we find ourselves asking 'Who is this child?', 'How did they get there?' – questions which are seldom asked about adult women in pornography. Child pornography forces us to face the issue of how pornography is produced, undercutting the safer terrain on which most discussion takes place about women's consent and participation in the sex industry. Since children have no legal status, limited access to knowledge and experience, they cannot meaningfully be held to have consented, or to have entered into any form of legal contract with the pornographer. The very existence of child pornography, therefore, undermines the distinction we are usually asked to make between acts of sexual violence and representations of them.

Libby Kroon was abused as a child by an adult male member of her family, and forced to act out violent pornography with other children. She makes this point with revealing clarity: 'Because of my experiences I believe that the real crux of the pornography **115** issue is not whether the national crime rate rises or falls, but what is actually done to the person or persons involved.'[9]

In exploring how the connections between child sexual abuse and child pornography reinforce each other I want first to address the concrete harm individual children experience in the production and use of pornography. I also want to examine the more generalized consequences of the existence and availability of child pornography and the sexualization of children in the Western media. In doing this I am not suggesting that child pornography is a 'new' form, but that like other forms of pornography its availability and acceptability have increased significantly in the latter part of the twentieth century. What twenty years ago would have been defined as pornography is now commonplace, seen every day in our newspapers, magazines and on our television screens.

THE PRODUCTION OF CHILD PORNOGRAPHY

The most obvious point about the production of child pornography is that pictures or films depicting adult sexual interactions with children cannot be produced without an act which is defined in law as illegal taking place. Each piece of child porn involving adults (or in some cases animals) is a document of the sexual abuse of the child who was required for its production. Not all child porn involves adults in the picture, but photographs and films which include only children in the frame involve adults outside it who control the situation and children's behaviour within it: demanding of and/or instructing the children in what the photographer requires from them. This too is a form of sexual abuse. Every piece of child pornography, therefore, is a record of the sexual use/abuse of the children involved. The connections are not mediated by abstract discussions about cause and effect, since the mere existence of the product is evidence of the fact of sexual abuse.

Investigating how child pornography is produced, who the children in the pictures are and how they got there, reveals further connections. While there are continuing debates about the scale of commercially produced child pornography,[10] there is agreement about who the children are. Much child pornography uses children from poor and, often but not exclusively, black countries. What connects these children with children used from rich Western countries is that they are trying to find ways to ensure their own physical survival. Children and young people in desperate circumstances, like many women, learn fairly quickly that if they have nothing else to sell they can sell their bodies – in more than one way.

Gitta Sereny, in her study of child prostitution in three of the richest countries in the world, discovered that every one of the young people she spoke to had been also asked at some point to pose for porn photos or appear in films.[11] In the UK, a spokesperson for the National Association for Young People in Care, appearing in a BBC *Newsnight* feature on child pornography in January 1990, revealed that 70–80 per cent of the young people contacting the organization (many of whom were on the run from local authority care) had had some involvement in the production of pornography.

Many studies of street children and runaways in the West have shown that a high proportion of these children had escaped from abuse at home. For example, in Mimi Silbert and Ayala Pines' study of 200 American street prostitutes,[12] 60 per cent of whom were under sixteen, over 60 per cent had been sexually abused as children and this was the single most important factor accounting for running away from home and having to fend for themselves when under sixteen. It is a bitter irony that one of the few ways to survive in Western countries for runaways is selling their bodies to men. For many of these children, getting paid and having some limited control is clearly preferable to remaining where sexual abuse is justified through references to 'love' and duty.

The use of black children from the 'Third World' in commercially produced child pornography also demands further investigation. Is it only that children are easier to procure where physical survival is a daily struggle, where children have to work from an early age? What role do racism and Western economic and cultural imperialism play in this particular form of sexploitation? Since child pornography is not officially acceptable in Western values, the sexualizing of black children is probably more acceptable to white supremacist male producers and consumers. While the picture of a white child might induce momentary guilt in the white Western consumer through a connection to his own children, this possibility is removed when the children are black. Even the outrage of white non-consumers of pornography often turns on what is being done to 'our' children, i.e. white children. Black children are thus not only 'non-persons' to   **117** the white Western consumer (and some of their critics), but also 'non-children'. At the same time child pornography using black children reproduces and reinforces white supremacist stereotypes of black people, and black women and girls in particular, as 'erotically exotic'.

For the same reasons South East Asia, Latin America and increasingly Africa have become the favourite destination for sex tourists, including those seeking sex with children. Tourism in general, and sex tourism in particular, are part of economic, political and cultural international relations. Is there not something which we should call obscene ('highly offensive, morally repugnant, repulsive, loathsome') in the fact that while Western-produced economic necessity forces 'Third World' people to seek low-paid employment in the West, Westerners travel to their countries to consume their 'unspoilt beauty' and white men travel there to consume sex with impoverished women and children? The sexual abuse of these children is the outcome of the conjunction of sexism, racism, imperialism and children's powerlessness in relation to adults.

As Tim Tate demonstrates in Chapter 11, though, it would be a mistake to think of child pornography as only commercially produced. The bulk of child pornography is produced in a 'cottage industry' run by abusers. They record their own abuse of children and/or train children they are abusing to pose or act out scenes. This pornography may simply be kept as part of a private 'collection' (the *Newsnight* feature revealed that an average police seizure would include 200 videos and thousands of slides and photographs, all of which are often minutely catalogued by the owner), shared/swopped with other abusers, or reproduced and sold.

While some commentators maintain that this division between commercial and 'cottage industry' production marks a crucial difference between child pornography and pornography involving adult women, the testimony of women in studies of sexual violence and in the hearings for the US ordinance[13] demonstrates that there is a similar process involving different levels of production in relation to adult women. I have heard from three different sources recently that about 40 per cent of the throughput of one of Britain's largest mail film-processing businesses is pornography and although a proportion is photos of children, much involves adult women.

118   It is also a mistake to see child pornography as a separate and distinct genre. Part of the appeal of Page 3 is that the pictures are of young women, and a number of the papers which publish such pictures tantalize their male readers with promises of 'future attractions' – i.e. young women they cannot show topless as they are not yet sixteen. *Playboy* developed a particularly devious way of publishing pictures of children: including photos of the centre-fold 'Playmate' as a child, with captions like 'Age one – *Playboy* material already', 'Age two – boy chasing already', 'Age three – anytime Dad'. Judith Reisman in a content analysis of 683 issues of *Playboy*, *Penthouse* and *Hustler* found 6,004 photographs, illustrations and cartoons depicting children, just under a thousand of which involved a sexual association with an adult.[14] She also noted the ways in which adult women are 'childified' through the removal of their pubic hair and/or being made to appear as if they are children.

THE USE OF CHILD PORNOGRAPHY

The emerging evidence of the connections between child sexual abuse and the use of pornography comes from two main sources: survivors and offenders. Mimi Silbert and Ayala Pines' study of women working as prostitutes did not include specific questions on pornography, but many of the women spontaneously mentioned it in their accounts of the sexual violence they had experienced as children and adults: it was mentioned in relation to 24 per cent of the instances of rape and 22 per cent of instances of sexual exploitation in childhood. Moreover, 10 per cent of the women had been used in porn videos and 38 per cent had had sexual photographs taken of them when they were children. The fact that there was no explicit question means that we have to take these responses as underestimates.

The women's accounts revealed three ways in which men used pornography in connection with sexual abuse. First, they would show it to children in order to persuade them that they would enjoy certain sexual acts. With younger children this would usually consist of pointing out the smiles on the faces of the children in the pictures. With older children, porn would be shown in the hope of getting them sexually aroused/excited. In this second instance the pornography shown would not always, or exclusively, depict children. Secondly, abusers show children child pornography to convince them that what they are being asked to do is all right. Being able to show a picture legitimizes the abuser's requests. **119**

Thirdly, some abusers use child pornography for their own arousal before abusing a child.

Another American study revealed that child pornography is a core part of most sex rings – where an individual or group of adults abuse large numbers of children.[15] Again both child and adult pornography may be used to 'normalize' the abuse and/or as a form of instruction. Most sex rings are also involved in producing child pornography. Production within the ring serves both to make profit through sale and establish links with other rings through exchange. It also helps to entrap children further within the ring since it increases the penalties for telling anyone about the abuse. Children are threatened that their parents will be sent the pictures and/or made to feel responsible for the consequences for the other children in the ring of discovery.

Some sex offenders are beginning to talk about the role porn played in their offending. Ray Wyre in a presentation to a House of Commons committee based on his work with offenders stated that commercial pornography, and representations in newspapers and the media generally, 'are all involved in maintaining offending behaviour'. His work has established that child abusers' initial use of child pornography is to legitimize their behaviour to themselves. Their own accounts should put paid once and for all to the view that abusers are unaware of what they are doing. It is precisely because they know that what they are doing, or wanting to do, is wrong that they 'need' to use child pornography to rationalize it. It enables them to construct a different version of reality – one in which they continually reinterpret the actions and responses of their victims.

One offender on the BBC programme 'Sex Offenders: A Suitable Case for Treatment' stated: 'I do know that it is abuse, but if I listen to that too much then I'd have to stop.' Abusers use child pornography in order to override their own knowledge that what they are doing is abusive. Child pornography 'normalizes' abuse by suggesting that it is the children who want it, and that they get pleasure from it. As Ray Wyre has pointed out, every time a professional or High Court judge suggests that a child was 'seductive', they reinforce both the messages of child pornography and the rationalizations which the abusers themselves use to justify their behaviour.

What emerges from examining the production and use of child pornography is a pattern of mutually reinforcing connections.

Child pornography is itself a document of abuse of one child. It is then used by abusers to reinforce their will to abuse. They may in turn show it to children they wish to abuse to secure their co-operation. Some of these children may, in turn, be photographed or filmed while being abused and/or trained to pose for pictures. The process then begins anew. An offender (quoted by Ray Wyre), who went on to produce pornography of the girls he was abusing, said:

> I used the pornographic films in actual fact to reinforce my belief that what I was doing wasn't wrong. I did show these porn films to underage schoolgirls and after they had seen them we many times copied what was going on ... I had a vast pile in my bedroom of pornographic literature, books, papers, cutouts and all this sort of thing and this was used in my seduction techniques ... I used that as an excuse to get them to do exactly the same.

Child sexual abuse is not 'caused' by child pornography, rather the pornography is the record of abuse which has already taken place. It may then be used to justify and/or facilitate further abuse which in turn may result in the production of more child pornography.

THE WIDER INFLUENCE OF CHILD PORNOGRAPHY ON CULTURE

The production and circulation of child pornography has a more general impact on our culture, and in this context too cannot be easily separated from adult pornography. The last two decades in the West have witnessed an increasing sexualization of culture, especially the media. This sexualization of culture has been most obvious, and most directly and creatively challenged by women, in the area of advertising. Not only have women been used with repetitive monotony to sell consumer products, but the stylization of mainstream photography has drawn from that used in pornography. Clothes features in *Tatler* depicting models in bondage and with 'designer bruises' are just one example of the way in which attempts have been made to transform porn into 'arty' fashion photography. At the same time, advertising has increasingly sexualized children: use of children in advertising is often a mirror of images in pornography.

At the same time as we have this preoccupation with, and exploitation of, sexuality in our culture, children are increasingly denied access to sex education. The same politicians who   **121** removed sex education from the core curriculum in Britain could be heard guffawing in the House of Commons when MP Clare Short introduced her Bill to ban Page 3 pictures in newspapers. Our children are denied knowledge about sex, but have the 'right' to see pictures of naked women in their homes, on the bus, at school. Many primary schools rely on parents sending in old newspapers to cover paint tables or use for other activities. Small children see Page 3 pictures in the classroom every day, and taking the enterprise culture to heart, some boys rip them out and sell them to others in the playground for 10p. It is increasingly the case that all children, not just boys, learn more about sex and sexuality from pornography than they do from accurate information and sex education.

Pornography reinforces the cultural mythology about sexual violence: it redefines assault and harm as normal behaviour and pleasure. The insistence that rape is really sex, that women enjoy coercion and even torture, that children are the tempters and want sex with adults, reflects and reproduces belief systems which permit judges to make outrageous statements in their summing up, and encourage jurors to acquit rapists and child abusers, thereby directly encouraging others, or would-be abusers. The attitudes of some High Court judges are not that different from those of men who produce and/or consume child pornography.

Lord Lane called a paediatrician's procuring and sale of child porn 'puerile' and compared it to schoolboys collecting cigarette cards. How could Lord Lane be so certain that this man's sexual interest in children had no impact on his work: work which required that he physically examine children, that gave him daily access to vulnerable children? Another judge in 1989 stated that since 900 photos of a man's child were for his own consumption, and were no worse than a lot of advertising, the offence was not a serious one. Seriousness for this judge related only to the content and use of the pictures: the fact that the child had been repeatedly used, what the impact of this had been on the child, was clearly of minimal concern.

Comments like these merely reproduce the central message in child pornography: that there is not that much wrong with adult men having sex with children. They should also challenge complacency about child pornography. Neither moral outrage nor the fact of illegality have been effective in halting the production or use of child pornography.

Notes

1. Gail Chester and Julienne Dickey (eds), *Feminism and Censorship* (Dorset: Prism Press, 1988).
2. Susan Cole in a keynote speech on child pornography at the 'No More Secrets' conference, Toronto, May 1988.
3. Florence Rush, 'The Sexual Abuse of Children: A Feminist Point of View', in Maureen Connell and Cassandra Wilson (eds), *Rape: The First Sourcebook for Women* (New York: Plume Books, 1974).
4. Liz Kelly, 'Gender and Power in the Family: A Feminist Approach to Child Abuse' (unpublished paper, 1989).
5. Bea Campbell, *Unofficial Secrets – Child Sexual Abuse: The Cleveland Case* (London: Virago, 1989).
6. David Finkelhor, *Nursery Crimes: Sexual Abuse of Children in Day Care* (London: Sage, 1988).
7. Anonymous (group of social workers), 'Networks of Fear', *Social Work Today*, 28 October 1989, pp. 14–16.
8. Jenny Kitzinger, 'Defending Innocence: Ideologies of Childhood', *Family Secrets: Child Sexual Abuse – Feminist Review* 28, 1988, p. 78.
9. Libby Kroon, 'Personal Experiences in the Pornography Industry', Women Against Violence in Pornography and Media *Newspage* IV(8), 1980.
10. Judith Ennew, *The Sexual Exploitation of Children* (Cambridge: Polity Press, 1986).
11. Gitta Sereny, *Invisible Children: The Shattering Tragedy of Runaways on Our Streets* (London: Pan, 1986).
12. Mimi Silbert and Ayala Pines, 'Pornography and Sexual Abuse of Women', *Sex Roles* 10 (11/12), 1984, pp. 857–68.
13. See, for example, Diana E. H. Russell, *Sexual Exploitation* (London: Sage, 1984); and *Pornography and Sexual Violence: Evidence of the Links* (Minneapolis Hearings) (London: Everywoman, 1988).
14. Judith Reisman, 'Children in Playboy, Penthouse and Hustler – Research Report', *Preventing Sexual Abuse*, Summer 1986, p. 4.
15. Ann Burgess *et al.*, 'Response Patterns in Children and Adolescents Exploited through Sex Rings and Pornography', *American Journal of Psychiatry* 141(5), 1984, pp. 656–62.

7 Maintaining Male Power: Why Heterosexual Men Use Pornography

PETER BAKER

I have probably seen about as much pornography as any other average heterosexual man in the UK. I first stumbled across it when I was nine – a copy of *Playboy* in a barber's shop, available on a table with the daily newspapers. I can remember that the pictures I saw left me feeling confused and disturbed, but also curious and a little excited. When I was eleven, a friend gave me a copy of a magazine called *Parade* which I hid at home in the middle of a pile of children's educational magazines called, ironically perhaps, *Look and Learn*.

I saw most pornography when I was a student, although I never actually bought it. I did not need to. My Cambridge college junior common room subscribed to *Penthouse*, one of the most popular UK pornographic magazines. Later, while on a teacher-training course in Nottingham, I lived in a house with two other men who, between them, had literally hundreds of pornographic magazines. I was by now aware that pornography was sexist and wrong – I would even vote against it at student union meetings – but I still looked at it and masturbated with its images in my mind.

I became much more concerned about some of the effects of pornography when I started to have a long-term relationship with a woman. I realized that sexual fantasies based on pornography I had seen and read were intruding into our relationship, affecting my sexuality – and my view of my partner's sexuality – and distancing me from her. It created expectations that could not possibly be fulfilled. I realized, too, that pornography could result in real harm being done to women. I felt that I should do something about what I came to recognize as a serious social (and, for me, personal) problem and, for the last three years, I have been active in anti-pornography politics.

It has become clear to me that, in order to eliminate pornography, it is essential first to understand why men seek out, purchase and consume it. While effective and appropriate legal measures against pornography could be an important means of limiting its distribution, the current widespread availability of both legal and illegal (so-called 'hard-core') pornography in Britain suggests that pornography will never disappear until men decide for themselves to give it up. This will involve men choosing to throw off the effects of their conditioning as men, relinquishing their power over women, embracing equality between the sexes and redefining their own sexuality as well as revising their currently flawed perception of the sexuality of women.

My own experience of pornography, as well as that of other men, suggests that it is highly likely that most men (gay and heterosexual) in the UK have seen at least some pornography. Certainly, pornography is not simply seen and used by a relatively small number of men with 'special' problems. Men usually first see pornography when they are quite young: it is clandestinely circulated on the way home from school or, increasingly, watched on parents' videocassette players. Many young men see pornography belonging to their fathers or other, older male relatives and friends. One childhood friend of mine found a box of pornography in a tree in his local park; he then kept it hidden in a locked suitcase at the back of his wardrobe.

Among adult men, pornography is more widely consumed and is sometimes available in the places where they work or take their leisure, sometimes circulated surreptitiously, sometimes openly displayed in the form of 'pin-ups'. At one local authority I worked for, imported 'hard-core' pornography was passed around the male section of the workforce; and, at a local council-run steam baths I used to visit, pornographic magazines were made available to male customers in the rest room. Many gay men also use pornography; this is discussed by John Stoltenberg in Chapter 8. This chapter is concerned with heterosexual pornography.

It is not possible to say exactly how many men use pornography or how often. One crude indication is the estimated circulation figures of the major legal and widely available 'men's magazines'. Almost 300,000 copies of *Mayfair* are sold each month in Britain. *Penthouse* has a circulation of 113,000 per month; *Escort*, 250,000; *Men Only*, 291,000; *Knave*, 134,900; *Fiesta*, 289,000; and *Club International*, 228,000. The total monthly circulation of these seven magazines alone is over 1.6 million.[1] It is **125**

estimated that the total monthly sales of all Britain's pornographic magazines is about 2.25 million.[2]

These figures are likely to represent only a small proportion of
the numbers of men using pornography. The magazines listed
above are printed on good quality, durable paper and may be
used repeatedly over a long period of time. Moreover, some
leisure magazines which are mainly read by men, particularly
those about photography, often contain pornographic images of
women. There are also videos, each of which can be rented scores
of times. There are films and books. Newspapers like the *Sun* and
Sunday Sport also contain pornographic images of women. (The
Sun alone has a daily circulation of 4 million and is estimated to
be read by over 11 million people each day;[3] *Sunday Sport* has an
average circulation of 460,000.)[4] Many magazines, videos and
books are shared among groups of men. Further, even if men are
not currently purchasing or consuming pornography, they
remain affected by the pornography they have seen and its
powerful images may often be recalled.

The attraction of pornography for men is neither accidental
nor a consequence of some innate male characteristic. Men's use
of pornography is closely related to the power that men exercise
over women in all aspects of our society – economic, social, legal,
political and sexual – and to the ways in which men have been
conditioned and socialized into a particular form of masculinity.

While feminists have revealed much about the nature of male
power, relatively little is known about the social construction of
male gender. Comparatively few books have been written on the
subject. Hardly any British men meet in consciousness-raising or
support groups to try and work out why they are as they are and
how they can change. Much of this chapter is therefore speculative, based on my own experiences as both a man and a counsellor
of men, on the experiences of other men I have talked to, as well
as the available literature. From all these sources there is enough
material to make possible a general assessment of pornography
and masculinity, why men are attracted to pornography and
what effects it has on them.

WHAT HAS HAPPENED TO MEN?

Every man is different, shaped and influenced by his unique
experiences. Some of these different experiences relate to class,
race, age, physical ability and region. Nevertheless, men in

British society behave in ways which are similar enough for it to be possible to describe, in broad terms, their common characteristics, their 'gender identity' as men, their 'masculinity'.

Boys grow up in a culture and society which appear to give them every advantage. There can be no doubt that more is expected of them at school and that they receive preferential treatment there, that they obtain more qualifications, higher status and better paid jobs, and that they also have power over women which they duly exercise, both individually and collectively. However, many other things happen to men.

First and foremost, in many ways males are generally treated more harshly than females. As babies, they are expected to behave independently more quickly. They are also handled more roughly and are more likely to be punished severely, often with violence. As boys grow up they are expected to behave competitively with each other in order to be valued within their peer group. They are conditioned to believe that they must be successful – accumulating money and possessions and wielding power – and that success can be achieved only through competition and struggle, mainly with other men.

Aggression becomes an important means of achievement among men and violence is generally seen as being an acceptable form of behaviour. Indeed, all men grow up with the knowledge that at some point in their lives they may be given a uniform and a gun and required to kill other men. Indeed, compulsory military service is still common throughout Europe and, although it was abolished in the UK in 1960, young men are still encouraged to join the armed forces with promises of glamour and excitement. War is assumed to 'bring out the best' in men and is used to provide examples of how men should behave.

Men also learn that they alone are responsible for running the world and doing all that is important; they are always to be in charge; only they are capable of controlling things. Men are expected to earn enough to run a household and maintain a family. They also have to do what is dangerous and life-threatening: men are, for example, miners, construction workers and oil-rig operators, as well as soldiers.

In order to cope with the harsh masculine world into which they are thrust, boys learn not to trust their subjective feelings and not to express their emotions; they are required to remain cool and composed. Boys who cry are 'cissies'; boys who tremble with fear are cowards. Boys who talk about how they feel are **127** 'wimps'. Boys who express warmth towards women are 'soppy' and boys who are intimate with other boys suffer the worst forms of homophobic derision and even violence. Men are forced to give up the expectation and hope of intimacy and closeness with each other.

Despite the privileges men enjoy as a result of the power and control they exercise over women, the impact of all these messages about masculinity leaves men feeling bad about themselves and disconnected both from their inner selves and from other men and women. They feel themselves to be carrying a huge and unrelenting burden and responsibility. They become suspicious and confused, scared of other men. For many men, life seems to be a relentless struggle between themselves – individuals on their own – and the rest of the world. At their core is a deep well of loneliness, although many men simply feel numb and unaware of what they are feeling (or even that they actually have feelings at all). As many women in relationships with men know, most men have become emotionally illiterate, unable to communicate how they really feel.

Given how men are influenced as they grow up and how they feel about themselves, whether awarely or unconsciously, it is understandable that they should attach such disproportionate importance to the sexual act. Sex has become almost the only means through which men can begin to feel intimate and close. The moments of greatest intimacy and warmth that men and women share together often occur before, during and after sexual intercourse. Although men bring to sex so many demands and needs which sex alone cannot possibly satisfy, the importance men give to sex is reflected in the way they measure themselves in terms of their sexual performance and the sense of self-validation and self-worth which they attempt to derive from it.[5]

The realities of men's power and their oppression of women must never be ignored and men must take full responsibility for their oppressive behaviour. Nevertheless, it is also clear that much of men's behaviour is profoundly influenced by their systematic mistreatment as men. Like women, men are hurt by gender conditioning, although clearly with very different results in terms of their experience of the mistreatment and their relative position of power and privilege within society. Addressing the issue of men's conditioning, Cynthia Cockburn has observed

that:

. . . our culture cruelly constrains [men] in varying degrees, to be the bearers of a gender identity that deforms and harms them as much as it damages women. After all, feminists have recognized the same in femininity and much of the energy of the women's liberation movement has been spent on breaking out of our half of the mould.[6]

Cockburn points out that it is masculinity rather than men which should be the target of women's anger and which should be challenged. This perspective provides the starting point for this analysis of men and pornography.

YOUNG MEN AND PORNOGRAPHY

In a group discussion published in the women's magazine *Company*, five men aged between twenty-two and twenty-eight discussed pornography.[7] Most were introduced to it while at school. 'Bill' remembered that there was 'an underground trade in pornography at my school. People would cut pictures out and sell them individually for 5p.' When 'David' was twelve years old he and a friend were 'really bored one afternoon and so we bought a copy of *Mayfair*, which we got an older friend to buy. I hid it in my filing cabinet.' In 'Harry's' class, the best reader had to read out the stories: 'You were very popular if you could read well. It was real motivation to improve your reading skills.' 'Tim' used to go round to see a friend 'who had a collection of magazines; he used to cut a hole in the magazine where the woman's vagina was, and would place it over his penis'. These stories are quite typical.

Young men are likely to be attracted to pornography partly because it appears mysterious, naughty and inaccessible (stacked high on the top shelf, and supposedly not for sale to people aged under eighteen). But it also exerts a more profound pull. Young people in our culture are generally denied any clear and accurate information about sex or, more basically, about what human bodies really look like. Most parents are too ill-informed or embarrassed to provide good sex education. This is also an area that most schools either do not cover or deal with badly. Therefore, at the very time in their lives when young people are becoming conscious of their sexuality and are seeking to establish their sexual identities, they are usually denied the information they require. Young people will therefore seek knowledge from wherever it appears to be available. In the *Company* discussion, **129** for example, 'Steve' said that he found pornography 'partly educational because it taught you some things about the act of sex that you'd never learn from your teachers or parents'.

Pornography also appeals to young men because its use is seen as being an important part of the establishment of an adult male identity. For a young man, acquiring pornography forms a kind of 'rite of passage' into manhood. Older brothers, older male friends, fathers or other male relatives are likely to be known to have used it. Indeed, these older men often introduce pornography to their juniors. Moreover, because the vast bulk of pornography is heterosexual and makes heterosexuality the norm, the introduction of young people to it assumes a further importance: it helps to ensure that young men are thoroughly 'male' and adopt 'normal' sexual desires and feelings.

Further, young men do not find it hard to understand what pornography is and what it means. Even before they see any pornography, young men have already received and internalized a great deal of false information about the roles and sexualities of men and women. The ways in which males and females are treated differently from the moment of birth will have instilled in boys the notion of their relative importance and superiority. This will have been reinforced by the experience of family life and the observation of mother and father and their different roles, the books and comics they have read, the television and films they have seen and much of what they have been told at school. Pornography will have the effect of buttressing this misinformation about women still further as well as adding new, false messages about women and their sexuality. Young men soon develop a perception of sex and sexuality which is very different from the romantic and cosy themes which are often the subjects of many young women's fantasies.

There can be no doubt that pornography has a particularly powerful effect on young men. As David Edwards has pointed out:

> Obviously there are many men who do not buy [pornographic] magazines or videos but the majority have seen such material, often during adolescence when there is a heightened sensitivity to images and ideas regarding sex and relationships. Through reading such material men acquire a very powerful language for sexual relationships, which ignores any emotional component and where sex becomes something that is 'done' to a woman/any woman.[8]

Describing how, as an adolescent, he often used pornography, one man, now in his early twenties, believes that it had a major impact on his attitudes, preventing him from learning about love, sex and women from real experiences and real women: 'How can you learn what women are like and what women may want, when all you look at and read about are make-believe versions invented to fit purely male fantasies?'⁹

Omar Johnson, in evidence given to the Minneapolis City Council public hearings on pornography in 1983, described how he was introduced to pornography at college.¹⁰ A friend gave him a copy of *Playboy*:

> It was so legitimate: an interview with Jimmy Carter and everything. The pictures gave me a feeling somewhere between queasiness and arousal. I didn't know what to do or think about them. But the section where readers write in to the editor detailing their exploits solved that problem . . . I had already internalized messages suggesting that women were second-class creatures . . . Violence as pleasure was something I already knew. This was just another context. By the end of the year I was stringing together long involved fantasies where women did what I wanted and loved me for it.

As young men become adult men, many (perhaps most) are likely either to continue to use pornography or to remember the pornography they have already seen. There is a range of reasons why they continue to do this. Some of the motivating factors are complementary, others may appear contradictory. Taken together, they demonstrate the complex nature of masculinity and the way pornography finds its place within it.

MEN AND POWER

Men are clearly the dominant sex in our society. However, men do not always *feel* that they are in complete control. They feel threatened by a range of social forces which are, rightly, slowly beginning to alter the position of women and the nature of their relationship to men. Women are edging their way into positions of higher status and greater power; many women are refusing to see domestic labour and childcare as their exclusive province; women are demanding to be sexually satisfied; and some have demonstrated that they can form relationships and lead complete and satisfying lives entirely independently of men. Moreover, **131** there is now legislation which attempts to prevent discrimination against women. From many men's point of view their grip on power actually seems to them to be rather fragile and tenuous. Some even believe that women are in control.

Men also feel threatened by three kinds of emotional 'power' that they feel women are able to exert over them.[11] These stem from men's conditioning and their reluctance or inability to feel or express emotions. Many men have learned to depend on women to help them express their emotions, even to express their emotions for them. Indeed, some men are unable to feel emotionally alive except through relationships with women. Men feel threatened by women's power to withhold and refuse to exercise this ability to express emotions for their benefit.

The second emotional 'power' that men feel women have is the power to validate men's masculinity. In order for men to experience themselves as masculine – as being 'real men' – women are required to play their prescribed role of doing the things that make men feel masculine and therefore all right about themselves. (For example, women often feel that they should praise their men as expert lovers or as geniuses when they perform a routine household task.) Men are aware that, should women refuse to validate them in this way, they would then feel deflated and inadequate.

The third 'power' concerns the closeness which women offer men. Because of their isolation from other men, if women were to withdraw the intimacy they offer, men know that they would become very isolated indeed. But men also fear what feels like the cloying emotional attachments that women desire: closeness comes with a package of unwelcome commitments, a very confusing and unfamiliar language concerning feelings and the threat of impending or increased domesticity and entrapment. Wanting closeness but also demanding freedom from commitment, men often end up feeling controlled and manipulated by women.

For many men, all these experiences are both confusing and threatening. Men are constantly reminded of their power and dominance, but they *feel* ceaselessly under threat from women. They do not feel powerful and, moreover, they feel as if women have power over them. Men also feel a vulnerability that comes from the knowledge that women often have a powerful insight into their emotional insecurities and inadequacies. Pornography can be seen as one way in which men attempt to deal with their confusion and fear. Through pornography, men can retreat into a simple world where they are effortlessly in command and where women are their obedient, willing and even grateful servants, providing the sex which men feel is central to their sense of worth and validation. The illusion is created that women are really in their rightful place and that there is after all no real and serious challenge to male authority.

A brief examination of some common themes in pornography clearly shows how this works. One such theme is the myth that women are all really 'desperate' for sex with men (and, in pornography, sex almost always means penetrative intercourse). Thus, there are endless apocryphal stories of men innocently delivering pizzas, repairing cars, decorating houses, cleaning windows who stumble across 'randy' women who are usually already partly or wholly naked and often openly masturbating. Sometimes, men discover women having sex with each other; of course, they do this only because no man is available and not because they prefer to. Similarly, there are stories of men offering lifts to women hitch-hikers or being in the same train compartment as women; inevitably, the women then proceed to initiate sexual activity or respond immediately to male advances.

The notion that women constantly demand sex and are always available for it is also applied by some pornography to women who are described as feminists. This pornography suggests that feminists are confused about their sexuality, perhaps are 'frigid', and merely require the sexual attention of a man to 'sort them out'. Pornography also includes representations of women in high status and powerful positions, for example, as lawyers, police officers or company executives. However, all these women are depicted to be fundamentally just like all other women; that is, sexual objects existing for the pleasure of men.

The language of much pornography also makes it clear that sex is something that men 'do' to women. In many scenarios, the men demonstrate their sexual expertise and control. The language is strongly reminiscent of that used to describe some sort of mechanical process. The descriptions could almost be of men at work, perhaps single-mindedly but emotionlessly riveting metal plates together or paint-spraying a car. No feelings of love or tenderness are expressed, just self-centred satisfaction with a job well done. Needless to say, the men always do a good job and the women are always satisfied.

Some pornography much more explicitly asserts men's power **133** over women. There are pictures and descriptions of men tying up women, gagging or blindfolding them, pretending to or actually torturing them and sometimes simulating or, in some cases, actually recording on film their rapes or deaths.[12] This is really only the sharp end of a continuum whose theme is the exercise of power over women whose only reason for existence is a sexual one.

Central to the exercise of power in and through pornography is the depiction of women as one-dimensional beings, as almost sub-human. (Indeed, one common pornographic theme is the representation of women as animals – for example, 'Playboy bunnies' or 'Penthouse Pets' – or as engaged in sexual acts with animals.) It is clear that this contempt for women has to be continually reinforced in order for men to believe that their domination of women is justifiable. After all, there would be no justification for abusing and subordinating a group of people who were seen as being equal and worthy of respect.

MEN AND THEIR ISOLATION

There are other reasons which explain men's use of pornography. One which is central is related to the deep sense of isolation experienced by men. Pornography often represents women as inviting, apparently desiring intimacy and physical closeness. In the most common form of pornography – the 'men's' magazines – there are countless photographs of naked women portrayed in positions of sexual availability. In these circumstances, it is not surprising that men are drawn to the material. It offers the illusion of intimacy with another person in the context of the only socially acceptable way for men to get close to women (that is, through sexual activity). It is also not surprising that men tend to use pornography when they are feeling worst about themselves, usually lonely.

Of course, pornography can never meet the real need that men have for close human contact. Many men therefore become caught in a vicious circle of feeling lonely, using pornography in an attempt to make themselves feel better, finding it does not meet their needs and so turning back to it as the only apparent hope for escaping from the isolation. There is something very sad and desperate about men's use of pornography as a substitute for real human contact. Pornography certainly offers no lasting solace to 'frustrated' men with 'uncontrollable urges', as is often claimed. This is perhaps most clearly reflected in the advertisements carried in many pornographic magazines for inflatable, plastic 'women' for men to cuddle and copulate with.

MEN AND 'VIRILITY'

Men are often obsessed with notions of virility and potency and strength. They are increasingly expected to look good, to be aware of style and fashion. They are supposed to be the initiators in relationships. Boys are expected to ask girls out; men are expected to take the first tentative steps towards intercourse. Men are increasingly (and rightly) being urged and required to perform well in the bedroom and to satisfy their partners sexually. And men compete with each other to be seen with the women who are considered to be the most attractive and desirable.

But men fall far short of the 'stud'-like image that has been created for them. Most men are not James Bonds and never will be; they are in fact just ordinary, often unfit, a bit paunchy, confused, scared and anxious about their responsibilities and duties at home and at work. In bed, they also do not find sex all it is cracked up to be. It is not surprising that many men become obsessed with the size of their penises: this organ is, in the context of a sexuality focused on penetrative intercourse, the symbol of their power and potency.

Pornography relieves men of the burden of doing, of taking charge. A common pornographic representation is that of the woman who initiates sex, who demands it from men and who is always satisfied by what she receives, no matter how perfunctory or phallocentric. Further, there is a sense that when men masturbate while using pornography, they are able to treat themselves to a sexual pleasure which is free of all responsibility to another person. The minefield of emotional entanglement can also be ignored. Men often go to prostitutes for similar reasons.

Men also turn to pornography in an attempt to feel better about themselves. In much pornography, the men are invisible. The models perform in front of the camera in such a way that the male viewer can feel himself to be the person for whom the image has been created. As the pornographers write, this is 'just for you'. Moreover, the image can seem much more than an image: its method of presentation (the quality of many of the photographs, the content of the accompanying text) makes it **135** very accessible to the viewer, almost tangible and real. In the context of this almost personal relationship with the image, all men have the means of feeling sexually desirable, sexually proficient, and completely strong and powerful, even if it is just for a few minutes.

Moreover, while pornography offers men the illusion that they are 'real men', it simultaneously undermines this pretence. The overemphasis on the penis and its imagined powers to satisfy women can only serve to increase men's doubts about the efficacy of their own organs. 'Men's' magazines therefore contain so-called advice and information about how to increase penis size and to delay ejaculation. The portrayal of women as essentially 'nymphomaniacal' is also double-edged for men. One of men's great fears about women is that they all have voracious and unlimited sexual appetites and that men will not be able to perform well enough and with sufficient regularity to hold on to them. Pornography attempts to assuage this fear by showing that men can satisfy women and graphically explaining how to do so. But all this actually has the effect of making men feel more inadequate, unequal to the challenge, and merely serves to push them further into the apparently safer, unreal world of porno-graphic fantasies.

MEN AND EARLY SEXUAL ABUSE

These are some of the reasons why men are pulled to use pornography. Pornography acts to bolster men's power at a time when many men feel threatened by the increasing power of women; pornography clearly reasserts the traditional order of things. It offers men the illusion of intimacy and closeness and it satisfies men's socialized needs to feel potent and virile. However, there may also be another reason why men use pornography and one which might also help to explain why different men are attracted to different forms of pornography.

It now seems clear that a large proportion of young people, boys and girls, are sexually abused, mostly by men. Current research suggests that about one in four girls and one in twelve boys are probably abused before they reach the age of sixteen.[13] (These figures are probably underestimates.) Although some of those who have been mistreated have no memory of the particular events that happened, they still almost certainly carry the after-effects of the incidents into adulthood. It has been established, for example, that there is a clear 'cycle' of sexual abuse through which many people who were themselves abused as children go on to abuse other young children, and/or become victims of abuse as adults.

From my experience of counselling men, it seems possible that men's sexual fantasies are related to early sexual abuse. In a published study of men's sexual fantasies, one man described how, when he was five or six, he was abused by his family's middle-aged housekeeper; in his adult life, this man's fantasies were focused on sexual activity which was both very similar to the form of the abuse and was with older women.[14] Another man became fixated on fantasies involving rubber clothes after being masturbated when he was a baby by his mother who wore a rubber apron. The sex of the abuser may not significantly affect the relationship between abuse and subsequent fantasy.

Pornography may also be used in a similar way, men being attracted to the form that is reminiscent of a way in which they have been hurt or mistreated. My own experiences certainly lead me to believe that this may be the case. It is possible, for example, that male children who have been raped are more likely to be attracted to pornography which depicts rape. Children who have been abused with animals may be attracted to pornography involving animals. Children whose abuse involved violence may prefer certain forms of violent pornography. If this relationship between abuse and pornography does exist, it may be that, by using particular forms of pornography that in some way mirror their own painful, past experiences, men are regularly replaying and reliving what was done to them, even if they are not consciously aware of this. It is as if their minds are trying to push the painful memory to the surface and expel it, although they are never quite succeeding.

If the term sexual abuse is used in its widest sense, it seems as if most young people are hurt and 'damaged' by the lack of clear information about sex and sexuality made available to them as they grow up. For example, it seems that men who were denied clear information about sex and sexuality retain a kind of 'frozen' curiosity about women's bodies (or particular parts of them); no matter how many naked women they see and in no matter how much 'detail', to them it feels as if they can never see enough. This may explain why some 'men's' magazines contain pictures of women that are commonly described as being almost medical in terms of the details revealed of particular organs. **137**

THE EFFECT OF PORNOGRAPHY ON MEN

Given the nature of male power and contemporary masculinity, it is not surprising that many men find no difficulty in accepting pornography's make-believe world and its false assumptions about men and women. While men's views of women are determined by far more than pornography alone, it does seem clear that pornography plays an important role in confirming, reinforcing and creating particular aspects of men's perceptions, especially those related to sex and sexuality.

Many male attitudes based on pornographic representations of female sexuality will not be spoken out loud or obviously acted out and will exist at the level of fantasy and day-dreaming. When men masturbate, for example, they often look at pornography or mentally re-view the images they have seen, perhaps imagining themselves as existing within the pornographic representation.

Men may also use pornography during sexual activity with a partner. Sometimes, men will openly use pornography, sometimes with and sometimes without the consent of their partner. More commonly, men will simply remember what they have seen and think about it during sex. Some men may 'transfer' the actual pornography that they have seen to their partners, imagining them in the representation. For many men, the use of fantasies based on pornography feels essential to the achievement of sexual satisfaction. Indeed, it is often recommended by many people who give advice on sexual problems. One 'agony aunt' in a leading women's magazine advised a man who wrote in complaining that he no longer was able to enjoy sex with his wife because he found her unattractive after she had borne his child that he should think about a 'sex star' while he made love with his wife. Pornography is also often given to people who experience sexual problems as a suggested method of improving their sex lives.

For some men pornography becomes so integrated with their sexuality that they will attempt to act it out with their partners. Indeed, many 'men's' magazines actually encourage men to send in pornographic photographs of their wives and girlfriends for publication. Men may ask (or force) women to dress in a certain way, to pose in a certain way, to behave in a certain way. Men assume that because women are depicted as enjoying these activities, that all women really enjoy them even when they say the opposite.

One result of the confusion caused by men's consumption of pornography is that men who fantasize during sexual activity with their partners actually find it very hard to achieve the intimacy and closeness they crave. This is not surprising: their attention is focused on an illusion not a human being and there is no way that a real person can meet the needs created by a fantasy.

Floyd Winecoff, a psychologist working with men, illustrated this point in his evidence to the Minneapolis hearings.[15] Arguing that it is a myth to see pornography as a means of liberated sexual expression for men, Winecoff considers that pornography is instead 'a source of bondage'. Men masturbate to pornography only to become addicted to the fantasy and an endless search ensues to capture the docile woman of fantasy.

> The more hopeless it is to find this sort of woman, the more desperate becomes the interaction between men and the women they pursue . . . ultimately, men lose because they never experience [the] true intimacy that comes from letting down and opening up with someone . . . Pornography portrays a fantasy of social communion, but in reality it leads to the desperation that leads men to abusiveness.

A similar point has been made by Michael Betzold.[16] He believes that pornography 'shackles' men – as well as oppresses women – and it makes it harder for men to meet their emotional needs.

> By providing substitute gratification, it provides an excuse for men to avoid relating to women as people. It encourages unrealistic expectations: that all women will look and act like *Playboy* bunnies, that 'good sex' can be obtained anywhere, quickly, easily, and without the hassle of expending energy on a relationship . . . The male consumer of pornography becomes deadened to his feelings. Emotional needs are denied altogether or telescoped mercilessly into the search to obtain exclusively genital satisfaction.

Pornography also has the effect of numbing men to the possibilities of social and personal change and development. In this context, pornography and the associated portrayal of women in advertisements, films and television serves to maintain the current system of economic and social organization by encouraging men to view human relationships in a limited, instrumental way. Pleasure is brief and is limited to the genitals. There is little **139** kissing, cuddling, hugging, fondling, touching. Sexual activity without penetrative intercourse almost never occurs; people are never just pleased to be close, warm and affectionate.

There is also considerable evidence that pornography has an effect which is much more damaging than simply preventing men getting close to women. Pornography so distances men from a clear perception of what women are really like that it facilitates a wide range of abusive and violent behaviour. For example, Bill Seals, who has worked with 'sex' offenders, has argued that pornography 'is often used by [them] as a stimulus to their sexually acting out. The sexual insecurity of sex offenders is reinforced by porn . . . Eventually, [it] is not satisfying enough and they end up acting out sexually.'[17] It is known that in the case of the so-called 'Vicarage rape' in London in 1986, the offenders had been watching pornographic videos immediately before the offences were committed. Further, Ted Bundy, the US 'serial' sexual killer, while taking full responsibility for his actions, described in some detail how his behaviour was influenced by pornography.

When he was twelve or thirteen, Bundy first encountered 'soft-core' pornography in local stores. He also found pornography in rubbish dumped in back roads and alleyways; some of this pornography was much 'harder', being more sexually explicit and including violence. Bundy felt that he was essentially 'a normal person' leading 'a normal life, except for this one, small but very potent and very destructive segment of it that I kept very secret and close to myself'. As he put it, the men who use pornography and go on to commit acts of sexual violence are not 'some kind of inherent monsters. We are your sons and we are your husbands and we grew up in regular families.' Like him they reach a point where they feel compelled to go beyond reading and looking and to act out what they have seen.[18]

Pornography has all these effects because it represents women merely as sexual commodities. This false representation of women is akin to a portrayal of Jews as mean and greedy and black people as intellectually inferior to white. But pornography expresses more than the view that women are mere sex objects. It tells men that women enjoy sex and are always available for it, even when they deny it. It tells men that women secretly enjoy rape. It tells men that women enjoy many different forms of physical abuse, including bondage, torture, mutilation and even death. The constant repetition of false information is a key part in the maintenance of any oppression: the more it is repeated, the larger the number of people (even in the oppressed group itself) who are likely to come to believe that it is true. This is as true of misinformation about women as it is about black people and Jews. It is in this way that pornography contributes to the maintenance of discrimination against women in all spheres of life, not merely the sexual.

HOW CAN MEN STOP USING PORNOGRAPHY?

Given the damaging effects of pornography on both men and women, it is essential that men stop using it. However, the purchase of pornography on men's minds is a strong one and it will not be easy for men to give it up.

Contemporary social changes may make it even harder for men to stop using pornography. The 1980s were and the 1990s will even more be a time of dramatic economic and social development. Britain has entered a period in which, for many people, the labour process and the organization of work will become more flexible, decentralized and individualized; in which there will be a greater emphasis on consumer choice and product differentiation, marketing, packaging and design; in which image, appearance and superficiality will be dominant; and in which people will pay more attention to the means of their individual satisfaction and achievement than to collective and social goals and objectives.[19] However, a large minority of the population remains largely untouched by these changes. For them, poverty has become entrenched as a way of life, encouraging feelings of hopelessness and powerlessness. Looked at from one perspective, all these changes may herald a deepening of men's isolation and despair, further encouraging their use of fantasy and pornography. The pornography, too, is likely to be available in a variety of new forms made possible by technological advances in communications (most significantly, cable and satellite television).

At the same time, however, the new developments do open up fresh opportunities for social change. The sheer pace of change and the social and economic dislocations it will cause may stimulate many people (men and women) to question the direction of development and to formulate alternative visions of human organization. (The 'Green' movement is one manifestation of this.) Also, feminism and the women's movement are 141 going to continue to force and encourage men to change. This process will occur through argument, persuasion and example as well as through women's changing and increasingly influential role in employment and other non-traditional spheres. The emphasis on individualism could encourage many men to rethink their socially determined roles and to aim for more intrinsically rewarding goals. The increasing role of women in the workforce will bring more men into contact with childcare and other domestic responsibilities. The continuing decline of the traditional male-dominated heavy industries could help to change the value men attach to physical strength and other traditional notions of masculinity.

A new understanding of men is emerging which examines and interprets their behaviour much more in terms of their socialization than in relation to fixed, innate characteristics. This increased awareness is being increasingly widely disseminated. There are signs, too, that it is more acceptable for men to express and talk about their feelings and emotions. The impact of AIDS and the importance of 'safe sex' has encouraged some men – heterosexual as well as gay – to try to develop new forms of sexual expression and close human contact. These changes are reflected in the recent emergence of the much maligned term, the 'new man'. While it would be wrong to exaggerate the extent to which men are changing – individually and collectively – there is nevertheless an observable trend.

To take this process further, it will be necessary for men to look at the crucial area of their relationships with other men, and, simply, to make better friendships with them. This is not as easy as it might sound; it represents a real challenge for men. They have a deep fear of getting close to each other, encouraged by a society in which homophobia is rampant. Indeed, there is a sense in which homophobia holds in place the whole edifice of men's mistreatment, gender conditioning and almost the entire social structure, based as it is on competitive and possessive individualism. However, it is possible for men to love and care for one another. Further, men have to develop a new positive image for themselves. It is vital for men to become fully aware of their innate strengths, potentialities and virtues as men. Men can learn to see themselves as strong *and* gentle, tough *and* kind, resilient *and* emotional.

Men will also have to take decisive steps to improve their relationships with women and to base them on full equality. One important way in which men can do this is to face up to the issue of pornography. The first thing that men have to do is to recognize that they have to do something about it. It is not an issue that should be left to women, just as tackling racism is not just an issue for black people. Those men who are already aware of the problems with pornography have a crucial role in communicating this to other men. After all (albeit unfortunately), most men are more likely to listen to another man than to a woman. Men can also take their own initiatives against pornography. They can tackle newsagents that sell pornography, write to newspapers, complain about advertisements and so on. Where they are invited, men can also join and support established pro-feminist anti-pornography campaigns.

Finally, men have to decide to stop using pornography. This means more than just stopping buying and looking at the material, although that in itself would be a big step. More important still is to prevent the images already seen from intruding into their minds. To tackle this, men need to meet together to try and talk through the feelings and images they have associated with pornography. Men need to do what is most hard for them: they need to get in touch with and examine their feelings and attitudes about pornography as well as their masculinity. In my experience, it is certainly possible for men to become aware that pornography does not form an inherent part of their sexuality. Men can also come to realize that they – as well as women – would be a lot better off without it.

Notes

1. *Willings Press Guide 1989* (East Grinstead: British Media Publications, 1988).
2. Nick Cohen, 'Reaping Rich Rewards from the Profits of Pornography', *Independent*, 19 December 1989.
3. Daily circulation figure from *Willings Press Guide*. Total readership from Central Statistical Office, *Social Trends 19* (London: HMSO, 1989).
4. Cohen, op. cit.
5. See A. Moye, 'Pornography', in A. Metcalf and M. Humphries (eds), *The Sexuality of Men* (London: Pluto Press, 1985).
6. C. Cockburn, 'Masculinity, the Left and Feminism', in R. Chapman and J. Rutherford (eds), *Male Order. Unwrapping Masculinity* (London: Lawrence and Wishart, 1988).
7. N. Martin, 'Loose Talk: What Men Really Think about Pornography', *Company*, August 1988.
8. D. Edwards, 'Turning over Page Three', *Guardian*, 28 July 1988.

9. Private correspondence.
10. O. Johnson, 'Men's Minds Trapped', in *Pornography and Sexual Violence: Evidence of the Links* (Minneapolis Hearings) (London: Everywoman, 1988).
11. See J. Pleck, 'Men's Power with Women, Other Men, and Society: A Men's Movement Analysis', in M. S. Kimmel and M. A. Messner (eds), *Men's Lives* (New York: Macmillan, 1989).
12. C. Corcoran, *Pornography: The New Terrorism* (Dublin: Attic Press, 1989).
13. C. Corcoran, *Take Care! Preventing Child Sexual Abuse* (Dublin: Poolbeg Press, 1987).
14. N. Friday, *Men in Love. Men's Sexual Fantasies: The Triumph of Love over Rage* (London: Arrow, 1983).
15. Quoted in M. Laslett, 'Men's Fantasies and Actions Controlled by Pornography', in Minneapolis Hearings, op. cit.
16. M. Betzold, 'How Pornography Shackles Men and Oppresses Women', in J. Snodgrass (ed.), *For Men Against Sexism. A Book of Readings* (Albion, CA: Times Change Press, 1977).
17. B. Seals, 'Controlling Sexual Assault', in Minneapolis Hearings, op. cit.
18. From an interview with Ted Bundy. Associated Press, 25 January 1989.
19. See S. Hall, 'Brave New World', *Marxism Today*, October 1988.

8 Pornography, Homophobia and Male Supremacy

JOHN STOLTENBERG

SEXUAL FREEDOM AND EROTICIZED INEQUALITY

There is a widespread belief that sexual freedom is an idea whose time has come. Many people believe that in the last few decades we have had more and more of it – that sexual freedom is something you can carve out against the forces of sexual repression, and that significant gains have been won, gains we dare not give up lest we backslide into the sexual dark ages when there wasn't sexual freedom, only repression.

Indeed, many things seem to have changed. But if you look closely at what is supposed to be sexual freedom, you can become very confused. Let's say, for instance, you understand that a basic principle of sexual freedom is that people should be free to be sexual and that one way to guarantee that freedom is to make sure that sex be free from imposed restraint. That's not a bad idea, but if you happen to look at a magazine photograph in which a woman is bound and gagged and lashed down on a plank with her genital area open to the camera, you might well wonder: where is the freedom from restraint? Where's the sexual freedom?

Let's say you understand that people should be free to be sexual and that one way to guarantee that freedom is to make sure that people can feel good about themselves and each other sexually. That's not a bad idea. But if you happen to read random passages from books such as the following, you could be quite perplexed:

> 'Baby, you're gonna get fucked tonight like you ain't never been fucked before,' he hissed evilly down at her as she struggled fruitlessly against her bonds. The man wanted only to abuse and ravish her till she was totally broken and subservient to him. He knelt between her wide-spread legs and gloated over the cringing little pussy he was about to ram his cock into.[1]

And here's another:

> He pulled his prick out of her cunt and then grabbed his belt
> from his pants. He seemed to be in a wild frenzy at that moment.
> He slapped the belt in the air and then the leather ripped through
> the girl's tender flesh.
> 'Sir, just tell me what it is you want and I'll do it.'
> 'Fuck you, you little two-bit whore! I don't need nothin' from a
> whore!'
> The belt sliced across her flesh again and then she screamed,
> 'I'm willing!'
> 'That's just it! You're willing! You're a whore and you are an
> abomination . . .'[2]

Passages such as these might well make you wonder: where
are the good feelings about each other's body? Where's the sexual
freedom?

Let's say you understand that people should be free to be
sexual and that one way to guarantee that freedom is to make
sure that people are free from sexualized hate and degradation.
But let's say you come upon a passage such as this:

> Reaching into his pocket for the knife again, Ike stepped just
> inches away from Burl's outstretched body. He slid the knife under
> Burl's cock and balls, letting the sharp edge of the blade lightly
> scrape the underside of Burl's nutsac. As if to reassert his power
> over Burl, Ike grabbed one of the bound man's tautly stretched
> pecs, clamping down hard over Burl's tit and muscle, latching on
> as tight as he could. He pushed on the knife, pressing the blade
> into Burl's skin as hard as possible without cutting him. 'Now, you
> just let us inside that tight black asshole of yours, boy, or else we're
> gonna cut this off and feed it to the cattle!'[3]

After reading that, you might well ask: where's the freedom
from hatred? Where's the freedom from degradation? Where's
the sexual freedom?

Let's say you understand people should be free to be sexual
and that one way to guarantee that freedom is to make sure
people are not punished for the individuality of their sexuality.
And then you find a magazine showing page after page of bodies
with their genitals garrotted in baling wire and leather thongs,
with their genitals tied up and tortured, with heavy weights
suspended from rings that pierce their genitals, and the surrounding text makes clear that this mutilation and punishment are
146 experienced as sex acts. And you might wonder in your mind:

why must this person suffer punishment in order to experience sexual feelings? Why must this person be humiliated and disciplined and whipped and beaten until he bleeds in order to have access to his homoerotic passion? Why have the Grand Inquisitor's most repressive and sadistic torture techniques become what people do to each other and call sex? Where's the sexual freedom?

If you look at the books and magazines and movies that have been produced in the USA in the name of sexual freedom over the past two decades, you have to wonder: *Why has sexual freedom come to look so much like sexual repression? Why has sexual freedom come to look so much like unfreedom?* The answer, I believe, has to do with the relationship between freedom and justice, and specifically the relationship between *sexual* freedom and *sexual* justice. When we think of freedom in any other sense, we think of freedom as *the result* of justice. We know that there can't truly *be* any freedom until justice has happened, until justice exists. For any people in history who have struggled for freedom, those people. have understood that their freedom exists on the future side of justice. The notion of freedom *prior* to justice is understood to be meaningless. Whenever people do not have freedom, they have understood freedom to be that which you arrive at by achieving justice. If you told them they should try to have their freedom without there being justice, they would laugh in your face. Freedom *always* exists on the far side of justice. That's perfectly understood – except when it comes to sex.

The popular concept of sexual freedom in this country has never meant sexual justice. Sexual-freedom advocates have described what they want and made happen what they want to happen only in terms of having sex that is free from suppression and restraint. Practically speaking, that has meant advocacy of sex that is free from institutional interference; sex that is free from being constrained by legal, religious and medical ideologies; sex that is free from any outside intervention. Sexual freedom on a more personal level has meant sex that is free from fear, guilt and shame – which in practical terms has meant advocacy of sex that is free from value judgements, sex that is free from responsibility, sex that is free from consequences, sex that is free from ethical distinctions, sex that is essentially free from any obligation to take into account in one's consciousness that the other person is a *person*. In order to free sex from fear, guilt and shame, it was thought that institutional restrictions on sex needed to be over- **147** thrown, but, in fact, what needed to be overthrown was any vestige of an interpersonal ethic in which people would be real to one another; for once people are real to one another, the consequences of one's acts matter deeply and personally; and particularly in the case of sex, one risks perceiving the consequences of one's acts in ways that feel *bad* because they do not feel *right*. This entire moral-feeling level of sexuality, therefore, needed to be undone. And it was undone, in the guise of an assault on institutional suppression.

Sexual freedom has never really meant that individuals should have sexual self-determination, or be free to experience the integrity of their own bodies and to act out of that integrity in a way that is totally within their own right to choose. Sexual freedom has never really meant that people should have absolute sovereignty over their own erotic being. And the reason for this is simple: sexual freedom has never really been about *sexual justice between men and women*. It has been about maintaining men's superior status, men's power over women; and it has been about sexualizing women's inferior status, men's subordination of women. Essentially, sexual freedom has been about preserving a sexuality that preserves male supremacy.

What makes male supremacy so insidious, so pervasive, such a seemingly permanent component of all our precious lives, is the fact that erection can be conditioned to it. And orgasm can be habituated to it. There's a cartoon from *Penthouse*. A man and woman are in bed. He's on top, fucking her. The caption reads: 'I can't come unless you pretend to be unconscious'. The joke could as well have taken any number of variations: 'I can't get hard unless . . .'; 'I can't fuck unless . . .'; 'I can't get turned on unless . . .'; 'I can't feel anything sexual unless . . .' Then fill in the blanks: 'Unless I am possessing you'; 'Unless I am superior to you'; 'Unless I am in control of you'; 'Unless I am humiliating you'; 'Unless I am hurting you'; 'Unless I have broken your will'.

Once sexuality is stuck in male supremacy, all the forms of unjust power at the heart of it become almost physically addictive. All the stuff of our primitive fight-or-flight reflexes – a pounding heart, a hard sweat, heaving lungs – these are all things the body does when it is in terror, when it is lashing out in rage, and these are all things it is perfectly capable of doing during sex acts that are terrifying and sex acts that are vengeful.

148 Domination and subordination – the very essence of injustice and unfreedom – have become culturally eroticized, and we are supposed to believe that giving eroticized domination and subordination free expression is the fullest flowering of sexual freedom.

Pre-pubescent boys get erections in all kinds of apparently non-sexual situations – being terrified, being in physical danger, being punished, moving perilously fast, simply being called on to recite in class. A boy's body's dilemma, as he grows older, as he learns more about the cultural power signified by the penis and how it is supposed to function in male-supremacist sex, is how to produce erections reliably in explicitly heterosexual contexts. His body gets a great deal of help. All around him is a culture in which rage and dread and hazard and aggression are made aphrodisiacs. And women's bodies are made the butt of whatever works to get it up.

The sexuality of male supremacy is viscerally committed to domination and subordination, because those are the terms on which it learned to feel, to feel anything sexual at all. Its heart pounds and its blood rushes and its autonomic nervous system surges at the thought and/or the action of forcing sex, bullying sex, violent sex, injurious sex, humiliating sex, hostile sex, murderous sex: the kind of sex that puts the other person in their place. The kind of sex that keeps the other person *other*. The kind of sex that makes you know you are in the presence of someone who is palpably a man.

Some of us know how male-supremacist sexuality feels better than do others. Some of us know how that sexuality feels inside because we do it, or we have done it, or we would like to do it, or we would like to do it more than we get a chance to. It's the sexuality that makes us feel powerful, virile, in control. Some of us have known how that sexuality feels when it is happening inside someone else, someone who is having sex with us, someone whose body is inhabited by it, someone who is experiencing its particular imperative and having male-supremacist sex against our flesh. And some of us don't really know this sexuality directly; in fact our bodies haven't adapted to male supremacy very successfully at all – it is not the sexuality that moves us, that touches us, that comes anywhere near feeling as good as we imagine we want our sexual feelings to feel. We don't recognize a longing for anything like it in our own bodies, and we have been lucky so far – very lucky – not to have experienced it *against* our bodies. None the less, we know that it exists; and the more **149** we know about pornography, the more we know what it looks like.

PORNOGRAPHY AND MALE SUPREMACY

Male-supremacist sexuality is important to pornography, and pornography is important to male supremacy. Pornography *institutionalizes* the sexuality that both embodies and enacts male supremacy. Pornography says about that sexuality, 'Here's how'. Here's how to act out male supremacy in sex. Here's how the action should go. Here are the acts that impose power over and against another body. And pornography says about that sexuality, 'Here's who'. Here's who you should do it to and here's who she is: your whore, your piece of ass, yours. Your penis is a weapon, her body is your target. And pornography says about that sexuality, 'Here's why'. Because men are masters, women are slaves; men are superior, women are subordinate; men are real, women are objects; men are sex machines, women are sluts.

Pornography institutionalizes male supremacy the way segregation institutionalizes white supremacy. It is a practice embodying an ideology of biological superiority; it is an institution that both expresses that ideology and enacts that ideology – makes it the reality that people believe is true, keeps it that way, keeps people from knowing any other possibility, keeps certain people powerful by keeping certain people *down*.

Pornography also *eroticizes* male supremacy. It makes dominance and subordination feel like sex; it makes hierarchy feel like sex; it makes force and violence feel like sex; it makes hate and terrorism feel like sex; it makes inequality feel like sex. Pornography keeps sexism sexy. It keeps sexism *necessary* for some people to have sexual feelings. It makes reciprocity make you go limp. It makes mutuality leave you cold. It makes tenderness and intimacy and caring make you feel like you're going to disappear into a void. It makes justice the opposite of erotic; it makes injustice a sexual thrill.

Pornography exploits every experience in people's lives that *imprisons* sexual feelings – pain, terrorism, punishment, dread, shame, powerlessness, self-hate – and would have you believe that it *frees* sexual feelings. In fact the sexual freedom represented by pornography is the freedom of men to act sexually in ways that keep sex a basis for inequality.

You can't have authentic sexual freedom without sexual

justice. It is freedom only for those in power; the powerless cannot be free. Their experience of sexual freedom becomes but a delusion born of complying with the demands of the powerful. Increased sexual freedom under male supremacy has had to mean an increased tolerance for sexual practices that are predicated on eroticized injustice between men and women: treating women's bodies or body parts as merely sexual objects or things; treating women as utterly submissive masochists who enjoy pain and humiliation and who, if they are raped, enjoy it; treating women's bodies to sexualized beating, mutilation, bondage, dismemberment . . . Once you have sexualized inequality, once it is a learned and internalized prerequisite for sexual arousal and sexual gratification, then anything goes. And that's what sexual freedom means on this side of sexual justice.

SEXUAL OBJECTIFICATION AND MALE SUPREMACY

How does a man's history of sexual objectifying begin? Toward whom? In what context? And why? There are doubtless as many different details as there are individual men, but all men's psychosexual histories share a set of common themes because all men's psychosexual histories occur within male supremacy.

Male supremacy is the honest term for what is sometimes hedgingly called patriarchy. It is the social system of rigid dichotomization by gender through which people born with penises maintain power in the culture over and against the sex caste of people who were born without penises. Male supremacy is not rooted in any natural order; rather, it has been socially constructed, socially created, especially through a socially con structed belief in what a sex is, how many there are, and who belongs to which.

Sexual objectification has a crucial relationship to male supremacy. Sexual objectification is not rooted in the natural order of things either; rather, sexual objectification is a habit that develops because it has an important function in creating, maintaining and expressing male supremacy. The relationship of sexual objectification to male supremacy works in two mutually reinforcing ways: (1) men's habit of sexually objectifying serves in part to construct the male supremacy of culture; and (2) the male supremacy of culture urges males to adapt by adopting the habit of sexually objectifying. This habit becomes as strong as it does in each man's lifetime precisely because the habit serves **151** most forcefully to locate his sense of himself as a peer in relation to the supremacy he perceives in other males. Once he knows that location palpably, he knows what can be called a male sexual identity – a sense of himself as having dissociated sufficiently from the inferior status of females.

Here's how the habit emerges: first, there comes a time in the life of the child-with-a-penis when it dawns on him that his world is organized into two discrete categories of people – male and female, or however he conceptualizes them at the time. Somewhat later he realizes, through social cues of varying weight, that he had better identify with one (male) and disidentify with the other (Mom). There also comes a time when he experiences this state of affairs and his own precarious relationship to it with no small measure of confusion, stress, anxiety and fear. Call this his gender-identity anxiety – his particular terror about not completely identifying as male. (Of course, boy children are not actually on record about this point, but it is an inference that can reasonably be drawn from memory and observation.) Next, there comes a time in the course of the growth of his body when various conditions of risk, peril, hazard and threat cause his penis to become erect – without his understanding why and without, as yet, any particular sexual content. (This much is not conjecture; it has been documented in interviews with prepubescent boys.)[4] Among the events or experiences that boys report as being associated with erections are accidents, anger, being scared, being in danger, big fires, fast bicycle riding, fast sled riding, hearing a gunshot, playing or watching exciting games, boxing and wrestling, fear of punishment, being called on to recite in class, and so on. Call this his basic fight-or-flight reflex, involuntarily expressed at that age as an erection. The catch is, of course, that this humble flurry of anatomical activity just happens to occur in the context of a society that prizes the penis not only as the locus of male sexual identity but also as the fundamental determinant of all sacred and secular power. Call this, therefore, feedback from the boy's body that is loaded with male-supremacist portent, to say the least.[5]

In his early years, a young male's involuntary 'non-sexual' erections (those that arise from peril, for instance, as against touch and warmth) can be so distracting and disconcerting that they trigger even more panic and anxiety, which in turn can make detumescence quite impossible. At some point in his life, if he is developing 'normally', he learns a physical and emotional

152

association between this dread and his 'desire'; this is the point when, perhaps irrevocably, his gender anxiety and his reflex erections become linked: in relation to other people's bodies, he experiences acutely his anxiety about his identification with authentic maleness – particularly in relation to those details of other people's bodies that he perceives as gender-specific. Somewhere in the moment of his perceiving what he regards as another body's unambiguous sexedness, he experiences a jolt, an instant of panic, a synapse of dread, as if reminded that his own authenticity as a man hangs in the balance. The panic, the physiological agitation, produces an automatic erection. He eventually learns to desire such erections because he experiences them as a *resolution* of his gender anxiety, at least temporarily – because while he is feeling them, he is feeling most profoundly a sensory affiliation with what he infers to be the sexedness of other men. Nevertheless, he continues to depend upon his gender anxiety as a source of the physical and emotional agitation that he knows can be counted on, if properly stimulated, to make his penis hard.[6]

SEXUAL OBJECTIFICATION AND VIOLENCE

Sexual objectifying in people born with penises is a learned response in a social context that is male-supremacist. Male sexual objectifying is not biologically ordained or genetically determined. Rather, the male supremacy of culture determines how penile sensations will be interpreted. The meaning of those sensations becomes variously encoded and imprinted over time, such that a male will develop a characteristic habit of responding with an erection to his perceiving of gender specificity in other bodies. In his quest for more reliable repetition of such erections, he may cultivate a private iconography of gender-specific bodies and body parts, particular emblems of gender dichotomy that revive his buried anxiety about whether he really belongs to the sex he is supposed to. The particular iconography may vary greatly from man to man – for example, the emblematic body images may be predominantly female, in which case his objectifying is deemed heterosexual, or the images may be predominantly male, in which case his objectifying is deemed homosexual. In any case, all male sexual objectifying originates in the common predicament of how to identify and feel real as a male in a male-supremacist culture. The predicament can be 153 resolved either in contradistinction to a female object or through assimilation of a male object. Either way, the resolution striven for is a body-bond with men.

Male sexual objectifying is not simply a response to male supremacy; it functions to enforce male supremacy as well. Everywhere one looks, whether in mass culture or high culture, there are coded expressions of male sexual objectification – primarily presentations of women and girls as objects – displayed like territorial markings that define the turf as a world to be seen through men's eyes only. There are some constraints on male sexual objectifying of other males; most men do not want done to them what men are supposed to do to women. Meanwhile most women find their economic circumstances determined to a large extent by whether and for how many years their physical appearance meets standards laid down by men – standards that both heterosexual and homosexual men conspire to decree. And for many women, male sexual objectification is a prelude to sexual violence.

Sometimes the mere regarding of another person's body as an object is not enough; it does not satisfy a man's habituated need to experience physical and emotional agitation sufficient to set off sensory feedback about his sexedness. At times like these, a man learns, he can reproduce the erectile result of feeling threat, terror and danger as a child simply by being threatening, terrifying and dangerous to his chosen sex object. It works even better now, because now he is in control. He can successfully do this in his imagination, then in his life, then again in his memory, then again in his life. It works even better now; the more dread he produces, the more 'desire' he can feel.

Before a man commits a sexual assault or a forced sex act, that man performs an act of sexual objectification: he makes a person out to be an object, a thing less real than himself, a thing with a sex; he regards that object as sexual prey, a sexual target, a sexual alien, in order that he can fully feel his own reality as a man. Not all sexual objectifying necessarily precedes sexual violence, and not all men are yet satiated by their sexual objectifying; but there is a perceptible sense in which every act of sexual objectifying occurs on a continuum of dehumanization that promises male sexual violence at its far end. The depersonalization that begins in sexual objectification is what makes violence possible, for once you have made a person out to be a thing, you can do anything to it you want.

PORNOGRAPHY AND HOMOPHOBIA

Homophobia is also absolutely integral to the system of sexualized male supremacy. Cultural homophobia expresses a whole range of anti-female revulsion: it expresses contempt for men who are sexual with men because they are believed to be 'treated like a woman' in sex. It expresses contempt for women who are sexual with women just *because* they are women and also because they are perceived to be a rebuke to the primacy of the penis.

But cultural homophobia is not merely an expression of woman-hating; it also works to protect men from the sexual aggression of other men. Homophobia keeps men doing to women what they would not want done to themselves. There's not the same sexual harassment of men that there is of women on the street or in the workplace or in the university; there's not nearly the same extent of rape; men are not a demeaned social caste that is sexualized, as women are. And that's thanks to homophobia: cultural homophobia keeps men's sexual aggression directed toward women. Homophobia keeps men acting in concert as male supremacists so that they won't be perceived as an appropriate target for male-supremacist sexual treatment. Male supremacy *requires* homophobia in order to keep men safe from the sexual aggression of men. Imagine the USA *without* homophobia: a woman raped every three minutes *and a man* raped every three minutes. Homophobia keeps that statistic at a manageable level. The system is not foolproof, of course. As many as one out of seven boys are sexually molested by men. There are men who have been brutalized in sexual relationships with their male lovers, and they too have a memory of men's sexual violence. And there are many men in prison who are subject to the same sexual terrorism that women live with almost all the time. But for the most part – happily – homophobia serves male supremacy by protecting 'real men' from sexual assault by other real men.

Pornography is one of the major enforcers of cultural homophobia. Pornography is rife with gay-baiting and effemiphobia. Portrayals of allegedly lesbian 'scenes' are a staple of heterosexual pornography: the women with each other are there for the male viewer, the male voyeur; there is not the scantest evidence that they are there for each other. Through so-called men's sophisticate magazines – the 'skin' magazines – pornographers outdo one another in their attacks against feminists, who are **155** typically derided as *lesbians* – 'sapphic' at best, 'bull dykes' at worst. The innuendo that a man is a 'fairy' or a 'faggot' is, in pornography, a kind of dare or a challenge to prove his cocksmanship. And throughout pornography, the male who is perceived to be the passive orifice in sex is tainted with the disdain that 'normally' belongs to women.

Meanwhile, gay male pornography, which often appears to present an idealized, all-male, superbutch world, also contains frequent derogatory references to women, or to feminized males. In order to give vent to male sexual aggression and sadism in homosexual pornography and also to circumvent the cultural stigma that ordinarily attaches to men who are 'treated like a woman' in sex, gay male pornography has developed several specific 'codes'. One such code is that a man who is 'capable' of withstanding 'discipline' – extremely punishing bondage, humiliation and fistfucking, for instance – is deemed to have achieved a kind of supermasculinity, almost as if the sexual violence his body ingests from another man enhances his own sexual identity as a man. (This is quite the reverse in heterosexual pornography, where sexual sadism against a woman simply confirms her in her subordinate status.) Another code common in gay male pornography, one found frequently in films, is that if a man is shown being ass-fucked, he will generally be shown ass-fucking someone else in turn – this to avoid the connotation that he is at all feminized by being fucked. Still another code in gay male pornography is that depictions of mutuality are not sustained for very long without an intimation or explicit scene of force or coercion – so you don't go limp out of boredom or anxiety that you've been suckered into a scene where there's no raw male power present.

There is, not surprisingly, an intimate connection between the male supremacy in both heterosexual and homosexual pornography and the woman-hating and effemiphobia in them both as well. That connection is male-supremacist sex – the social power of men over women acted out as eroticized domination and subordination. The difference is that gay male pornography invents a way for men to be the *objects* of male-supremacist sex without seeming to be its *victims*. In its own special fashion, gay male pornography keeps men safe from male-supremacist sex – by holding out the promise that you'll come away from it more a man.

156 For heterosexual men who don't buy this, it is repellent and a

crock. For homosexual men who *do* buy into this, it can become a really important part of one's sexual identity as a gay man. Because if you think the problem facing you is that your masculinity is in doubt because you are queer, then the promise of gay male pornography looks like forgiveness and redemption. Not to mention what it feels like: communion with true virility.

THE WORLD OF GAY MALE SEX FILMS

The typical gay male sex film is comprised of explicit sex scenes, frequently between strangers, often with a soundtrack consisting solely of music and dubbed-in groans. During these sex scenes there is almost always an erect penis filling the screen. If the camera cuts away from the penis, the camera will be back within seconds. Scenes are set up so that close-ups of penises and what they are doing and what is happening to them show off to best advantage. Most of the close-ups of penises are of penises fucking in and out of asses and mouths, being blown or being jacked off. A penis that is not erect, not being pumped up, not in action, just there feeling pretty good, is rarely to be seen: you wouldn't know it was feeling if it wasn't in action; and in the world of gay male sex films, penises do not otherwise feel anything.

Curiously, there is a great deal of repression of affect in gay male sex films – a studied impassivity that goes beyond amateur acting. The blankness of the faces in what is ostensibly the fever pitch of passion suggests an unrelatedness not only between partners but also within each partner's own body.

The sex that is had in gay male sex films is the sex that is showable. And what is shown about it is the fetishized penis. When the obligatory cum shot comes, you see it in slow motion, perhaps photographed from several angles simultaneously, the penis pulled out of its orifice just for the occasion, being pumped away at, squirting, maybe someone trying to catch it in his mouth. There's no way to show how orgasm feels, and the difference between the reality and the representation is nowhere more striking than in the cum shot – a disembodied spurt of fluid to certify the sex is 'real'. Even leaving aside the rough stuff of gay male pornography – the scenes of forced fellatio, assault and molestation, humiliation and exploitation, chaining and bondage, the violence interlarded among the allegedly non-coercive sucking and fucking as if to tip us off that in all this sex there is an undercurrent of force and domination – even leaving aside all   **157** of that, what exactly is there in the merely explicit sex scenes that recommends itself as good sex? What are we being told that sex can mean *between* people, if anything? What are we being told about what men must become in order to have what looks like blockbuster sex? What are we being told to do with the rest of ourselves? What are we being told to lop off from ourselves and the history of our relationships with one another and our responsibilities to one another in order to feel at liberty to have sex at all?

The values in the sex that is depicted in gay male sex films are very much the values in the sex that gay men tend to have. They are also, not incidentally, very much the values in the sex that straight men tend to have – because they are very much the values that male supremacists tend to have: taking, using, estranging, dominating – essentially, sexual powermongering.

I wonder sometimes: has the saturation of the gay male subculture by these values created a population completely numb to the consequences of pornography for women? Can gay men who are sexually hooked on these values ever perceive the harm that pornography does to women? Or has the world of the gay male sex film become the only world they want to know?

HOMOPHOBIA AND WOMAN-HATING

Homophobia is totally rooted in the woman-hating that male supremacy thrives on. The male-supremacist social hierarchy necessarily derogates both those who are female and those who are queer – namely, those who are male anatomically *but not male enough sociosexually*. Some of our gay male contemporaries seek safety and escape through macho, hypermasculine costumes and posturing, but the fact remains that cultural homophobia is a byproduct of cultural misogyny: the faggot is stigmatized because he is perceived to participate in the degraded status of the female – and it doesn't matter one whit whether or not that's how he perceives himself. The dyke is held in contempt already as a woman and even more so for having the gall not to flatter the phallic ego – and it doesn't matter one whit whether or not she tries to emulate the sexual sadism of men.

Those of us who are queer have a fairly obvious special interest in ending sex discrimination, because homophobia is both a consequence of sex discrimination and an enforcer of sex discrimination. The system of male supremacy requires gender polarity

– with real men as different from real women as they can be, and with men's social superiority to women expressed in public and in private in every way imaginable. Homophobia is, in part, how the system punishes those who deviate and seem to dissent from it. The threat of homophobic insult or attack not only keeps real men aimed at women as their appropriate sexual prey; it also keeps men real men. Homophobia is central to the maintenance of sex discrimination.

Homophobia is not just in the social system, it's not just in the structure, it's not just in the laws. You can feel it in the muscle power of cops when they're cracking gay heads, and you can feel it in the taunts of teenage boys who are on a rampage of gay-baiting and queer-bashing. It's a kind of sexualized contempt for someone whose mere existence – because he is smeared with female status – threatens to melt down the code of armour by which men protect themselves from other men.

To have internalized homophobia as a gay man means you too dread the degraded status of anything feminine about yourself; it means you too dread that anything about your body remind you of females in general, or perhaps your mother in particular; it means that in your own queer way, you're in a constant quest 'to be the man there'. One of the commonest ways to do that is by seizing on the masculinity of someone else whom you perceive as more of a real man than you – because you want to be like him, you want to acquire and assimilate his maleness in order to recharge your gender batteries, which seem to keep running down; because you need the jolt of some juice from a positive pole – and so you try things to interest him or you ingest him or you submit to his aggression sexually or you let him leave some violence on you, on your body, so you'll feel it in the morning. And it works; you get a heavy load of his manhood and it makes you feel as if it's in you too, purging your body of those soft and awful feelings you get from having had one of your parents be female. The patterns of subordination that go on between men help resolve internalized homophobia, momentarily, while you're having sex. Power-game, dominance-and-submission sex works because it lets someone 'be the man there'; in fact it can let *two* males be the man there if they're courteous about it, if they follow the rules. The trouble is, this kind of sexuality can escalate; and often as not it must, completely crossing the line of what is physically and emotionally safe for one partner or the other. Thoroughgoing subordination in sex is not victimless; there *must* **159** be victims, and there are – nobody really knows how many. Coroners know when someone gets killed from something that looks a lot like extreme S&M; there are boys who have been molested, gay men who have been battered and raped in sexual relationships. Nevertheless, there is a sexiness in subordination, and its sexiness for gay men in particular has a lot to do with the fact that subordination in sex helps resolve a misogynist struggle to cling to male supremacy. For a gay man who wants to have that kind of identity – a femiphobic sexual connection with other men – subordinating someone helps reinforce during the time of sex his tenuous connection to an idea of manhood that exists only because it exists over and against women.

The root of the sex-class system is an *eroticized* power structure of men over women. So long as that structure stays in place, homophobia will stay put too, because homophobia is necessary to the maintenance of men's power over women. The system of male supremacy can't tolerate queerness; it will never tolerate queerness. It needs the hatred of women and queerness in order to prevail, in order to keep men doing to women what men are supposed to do to women.

The system of gender polarity requires that people with penises treat people without as objects, as things, as empty gaping vessels waiting to be filled with turgid maleness, if necessary by force. Homophobia is, in part, how the system punishes those whose object choice is deviant. Homophobia keeps women the targets. Homophobia assures a level of safety, selfhood, self-respect and social power to men who sexually objectify correctly. Those of us who are queer cannot fully appreciate our precarious situation without understanding precisely where we stand in male supremacy. And our situation will not change until the system of male supremacy ends. A political movement trying to erode homophobia while leaving male supremacy and misogyny in place won't work. Gay liberation without sexual justice can't possibly happen. Gay rights without women's rights is a male-supremacist reform.

THE EROTICIZATION OF SEX DISCRIMINATION

Sex discrimination has been culturally eroticized – made sexy – and those of us who are stigmatized for being queer are not immune. It may be difficult to realize how completely sex discrimination has constructed the homosexuality that many of us feel. Though some of us perhaps think we know something about how male supremacy constructs the heterosexuality we have observed, or participated in, we're probably less aware of how sex discrimination has affected the way our personal homo-eroticism has taken shape in our lives.

Being a male supremacist in relation to another body is a quite commonplace mode of sexual behaving. Sometimes, though not always, the urgency to 'be the man there' gets expressed in ass-fucking – while one guy is fucking, for instance, he slaps the other guy's butt around and calls him contemptuous names, swats and insults that are sexually stimulating, which may progress to physically very brutal and estranging domination. Many gay men seem to think that there is no woman-hating in the sex that they have. Sexualized woman-hating, they believe, is the straight man's burden. So why do gay men sometimes find themselves all bent out of shape after a relationship between two lovers goes on the rocks – and it was a relationship in which one man was always objectified, or always pressured into sex, or forced, or battered, or perhaps always dominatingly ass-fucked, and in his growing unease over this arrangement of power and submission he found himself feeling 'feminized' and resenting it, meanwhile his partner just keeps fucking him over, both in and out of bed? No woman-hating in gay sex? Clap your hands if you believe. Sexualized woman-hating does not have a race or a class or a sexual orientation.[7] It does not even have a gender, as lesbian devotees of sado-masochism have shown.[8]

The political reality of the gender hierarchy in male supremacy requires that we make it resonate through our nerves, flesh and vascular system just as often as we can. We are *supposed* to respond orgasmically to power and powerlessness, to violence and violatedness; our sexuality is *supposed* to be inhabited by a reverence for supremacy, for unjust power over and against other human life. We are not supposed to experience any other erotic possibility; we are not supposed to glimpse eroticized justice. Our bodies are not supposed to abandon their sensory imprint of what male dominance and female subordination are supposed to be to each other – even if we are the same sex. Perhaps *especially* if we are the same sex. Because if you and your sex partners are not genitally different but you are emotionally and erotically attached to gender hierarchy, then you come to the point where you have to impose hierarchy on every sex act you attempt – otherwise it doesn't feel like sex.

Erotically and politically, those of us who are queer live inside **161** a bizarre double-bind. Sex discrimination and sex inequality require homophobia in order to continue. The homophobia that results is what stigmatizes our eroticism, makes us hateful for how we would love. Yet living inside this system of sex discrimination and sex inequality, we too have sexualized it, we have become sexually addicted to gender polarity, we have learned how hate and hostility can become sexual stimulants, we have learned sexualized antagonism toward the other in order to seem to be able to stand ourselves – and in order to get off. Sex discrimination has ritualized a homosexuality that dares not deviate from allegiance to gender polarity and gender hierarchy; sex discrimination has constructed a homosexuality that must stay erotically attached to the very male-supremacist social structures that produce homophobia. It's a little like having a crush on one's own worst enemy – and then moving in for life.

If indeed male supremacy simultaneously produces both a homophobia that is erotically committed to the hatred of homosexuality *and* a homosexuality that is erotically committed to sex discrimination, then it becomes easier to understand why the gay community, taken as a whole, has become almost hysterically hostile to radical-feminist anti-pornography activism. One might have thought that gay people – who are harassed, stigmatized and jeopardized on account of prejudice against their preference for same-sex sex – would want to make common cause with any radical challenge to systematized sex discrimination. One might have thought that gay people, realizing that their self-interest lies in the obliteration of homophobia, would be among the first to endorse a political movement attempting to root out sex inequality. One might have thought that gay people would be among the first to recognize that so long as society tolerates and actually celebrates the 'pornographizing' of women – so long as there is an enormous economic incentive to traffic in the sexualized subordination of women – then the same terrorism that enforces the sex-class system will surely continue to bludgeon faggots as well. One might have thought, for that matter, that gay men would not require the sexualized inequality of women in order to get a charge out of sex.

GAYS AND THE PRO-PORNOGRAPHY MOVEMENT

Once sexual sensation becomes enmeshed in sex discrimination, then how can there be sexual freedom? Once all the sexualized

violence required to shore up male supremacy becomes institutionalized in culture and internalized in human personalities,
then how can there be sexual justice?

Sex discrimination: being put down or treated in a second-
class or subhuman way on account of the social meaning of one's
anatomy. That is what the bulk of pornography is *for*, and that is
what the radical-feminist anti-pornography movement is *against*.

In many ways over the past decade, the gay community in the
USA – at least as it is reflected through most gay and lesbian
publications, commercial and advocacy organizations, leaders
and spokespeople – has been rather obviously committed to a
course of defending the rights of pornographers. Despite the
presence of many lesbians and some gay men in the radical-
feminist anti-pornography movement, most gay people believe –
some cynically but some very sincerely – that if the nation does
not impede its thriving pornography industry, it will someday
recognize the civil rights of gay people; but if in any way you
encroach on the rights of pornographers, you will surely jeopard-
ize gay liberation. People frame this point of view in many
different ways, but it basically comes down to an equation
between the future of gay civil rights – and sexual freedom for
gays – with the free-enterprise rights of pornographers.

So long as the gay-rights movement is committed to dissociat-
ing itself from the radical-feminist project to uproot sex discrimination completely and to create sex equality, gay liberation is
headed in a suicidal direction. So long as the gay community
defends the rights of pornographers to exploit and eroticize sex
discrimination, we who are queer do not stand a chance. Sex
discrimination is what we must oppose, even if it turns us on. It's
what puts queers down because it's what puts women down, and
ultimately it's what does us all in. You can't fight sex discrimination and protect the pornographers at the same time.

FREEDOM AND EQUALITY

Historically, when people have not had justice and when people
have not had freedom, they have had only the material reality of
injustice and unfreedom. When freedom and justice don't exist,
they're but a dream and a vision, an abstract idea longed for.
You can't really know what justice would be like or what freedom
would feel like. You can only know how it feels *not* to have them,
and what it feels like to hope, to imagine, to desire them with a   **163**

passion. Sexual freedom is an idea whose time has *not* come. It can't possibly be truly experienced until there is sexual justice. And sexual justice is incompatible with a definition of freedom that is based on the subordination of women.

Equality is still a radical idea. It makes some people very angry. It also gives some people hope.

When equality is an idea whose time has come, we will perhaps know sex with justice, we will perhaps know passion with compassion, we will perhaps know ardour and affection with honour. In that time, when the integrity within everyone's body and the whole personhood of each person is celebrated whenever two people touch, we will perhaps truly know the freedom to be sexual in a world of real equality.

According to pornography, you can't get there from here. According to male supremacy, you should not even want to try.

Some of us want to go there. Some of us want to be there. And we know that the struggle will be difficult and long. But we know that the passion for justice cannot be denied. And someday – *someday* – there will be both justice and freedom for each person – and thereby for us all.

Notes

This chapter includes parts of two chapters from *Refusing to be a Man* (London: Collins, 1990).

1. Edward Baker, *Tricked into White Slavery* (South Laguna, CA: Publisher's Consultants, 1978), p. 132.
2. *The Shamed Beauty* (New York: Star Distributors), p. 60.
3. Eli Robeson, 'Knife Point', *Folsom Magazine* 2, 1981, p. 27.
4. See, for instance, Glenn V. Ramsey's interviews with seventh- and eighth-grade boys in Peoria, Illinois, in 1939, cited in Alfred C. Kinsey *et al.*, *Sexual Behavior in the Human Male* (Philadelphia: W. B. Saunders, 1948), pp. 164–5.
5. It is considered 'normal' for young boys to act out antipathy for that which is female. Boys who *do not* are perceived to be developing in a way that is potentially, and alarmingly, deviant. Gender-identity specialist Robert Stoller provides a rough sketch of the standard for how boys are *supposed* to disidentify with females when he discusses a programme of treatment for boys who are deemed to be very feminine – perhaps, it is feared, pre-transsexual. After several years of treatment, Stoller says approvingly, masculine traits begin to develop in such boys. They

> start to value their penises (for instance, they now stand up to urinate where before they sat); they develop phobias; they physically attack females – dolls and girls, with pleasure more than anger the dominant affect; much more intrusive play appears,

such as throwing balls and charging into their mothers and other females; they play spontaneously for the first time using male dolls and masculine toys; in their drawings, instead of showing only beautiful women, masculine males appear; and stories of attacks with guns and swords, with violence, danger, and damage are now invented.

Robert J. Stoller, *Sex and Gender, Vol. II: The Transsexual Experiment* (New York: Jason Aronson, 1975), p. 28.

6. The elective 'forbiddenness' of homosexual encounters, as for instance in public places, and the objective physical danger of many sadistic sex practices can also be seen to preserve the role of risk, peril, hazard and threat in effectively inducing erections.

7. For a discussion of woman-hating in gay male pornography, see Andrea Dworkin, *Pornography: Men Possessing Women* (London, Women's Press, 1981), pp. 36–45.

8. See Robin Ruth Linden *et al.* (eds), *Against Sadomasochism: A Radical Feminist Analysis* (East Palo Alto, CA: Frog in the Well Press, 1983).

9 Pornography and the Politics of Lesbianism

JANICE RAYMOND

There was a time in this current wave of feminism when the words *lesbianism* and *feminism* went together – when there was a political movement of lesbian feminism. Today, one hears more about lesbian sado-masochism, lesbian pornography and every-thing lesbians need to know about sex – what has fashionably come to be called the 'politics of desire'. And so it becomes necessary to distinguish between *lesbianism as a political movement* and *lesbianism as a lifestyle* – what has, for many, come to be a sexual preference without a feminist politics.

For one thing, this lesbian lifestyle is preoccupied with sex. Not lesbian sexuality as a political statement, i.e. as a challenge to hetero-reality, but lesbian sex as fucking – how to do it, when to do it, what makes it work – in short, how to liberate lesbian libido. Lesbian lifestylers and hetero-conservatives agree on one thing: that, for women, sex is salvation – something that will get us into the promised land, the afterlife, that amazing grace. For example, Marabel Morgan in *The Total Woman* teaches right-wing Christian women how to act out the fantasies of their husbands complete with all the accoutrements and sexual pos-tures that would rival the lesbian libertarian warehouse. For the Marabel Morgans of this world, inside marriage, anything goes. A wife should act like a mistress. Samois, an American lesbian sado-masochist group, embraces whips and chains, 'pain is pleasure, enslavement by consent, freedom-through-bondage, reality-as-game, [and] equality-through-role-play'.[1] Outside marriage, in fact outside heterosexuality, anything goes. Lesbian liberation has become lesbian libertarianism.

In comparing Marabel Morgan to Samois, is this the kind of *difference* that exists between a lullaby and heavy metal? Or are we talking about the *similarities* between those bumper stickers that read 'Sea divers do it deeper', 'Sky divers do it higher', 'Conservatives do it with conscience', 'Lesbians do it with lust'? There seems to be little difference between a conservative worldview which locates women in this world sexually for men and a lesbian libertarian lifestyle that is increasingly preoccupied with fucking as the apogee of lesbian existence. For all its perpetual talk about sex, libertarian lesbian discourse is silent about the connection of sex to the rest of a woman's life and, therefore, it is silent about sex itself.

In *The Sexuality Papers*, Margaret Jackson points out that, historically, female sexuality has been defined as both different from and the same as male sexuality. As different, female sexuality has been portrayed as difficult to arouse, more emotional and less localized; as similar, it has been depicted as originating in the same biological drive. Traditionally, the *differentness* of female sexuality has been used to show how it complements male sexuality and thus legitimates heterosexuality as the natural and normative condition of sexual existence for women; its sameness to male sexuality has been used to legitimate the forms that male sexuality has taken and to proclaim those forms as transcending gender. 'To put it another way, female sexuality has been remoulded on the model of male sexuality, so that [women] are now held to equal or even surpass men in terms of our sexual capacity.' [2]

Recent lesbian lifestyle and libertarian theories of sexuality have advocated the *sameness* of female sexuality to male sexuality – evidenced by the supposed 'fact' that women act, or want to act, or should be free to act, in the same way that men have been able to act sexually. Lesbian lifestylers argue that female-female sexuality must be 'freed up' to take on the forms of the male-power model of male sexuality, i.e. the forms that have endowed males with the power of uninhibited sexuality in a patriarchal society. The various forms that male-power sex has taken – S&M, pornography, butch-femme role-playing, pederasty – will supposedly release the so-called 'repressed power' of female sexuality.

The libertarians and lesbian lifestylers might protest that male sexuality has no corner on these forms. Many would maintain that these forms of sexuality have existed repressed in the very being of women, only waiting to be called forth by a different social context in which women are encouraged to express themselves with the sexual latitude that men have enjoyed. Several years ago, in the United States, a group called FACT (Feminist Anti-Censorship Taskforce), composed of academics, lawyers, artists, literati, and many big-name feminists, joined forces with **167** the pornography industry to do battle against feminist civil rights legislation that would make pornography legally actionable. FACT defends pornography specifically citing the 'need' that lesbians have for it, and calling it 'enjoyable sexually arousing material' which women must have the freedom to choose. 'The range of feminist imagination and expression in the realm of sexuality has barely begun to find voice. Women need the socially recognized space to appropriate for themselves the robustness of what traditionally has been male language,' i.e., pornography.[3]

The sexual libertarians and lesbian lifestylers, for all their emphasis on sexual fantasy, lack real sexual imagination. There is a lot of sexy talk in the libertarian literature about the necessity for women to be freed from the chains of the 'goody-goody' concept of eroticism, from femininity posing as feminism, and from sentimental, spiritualized and soft sex. Yet nowhere do we see the forms that this vital, vigorous and robust female sexuality would take articulated as anything different from the forms of the male-power sexuality model.

The modes and manifestations of sexuality that the libertarians and lesbian lifestylers hold up as liberating range from the innocuous to the injurious. The mélange of forms that have been given equal status, and represented as rebellious sex for women, deserves analysis on these grounds alone. For example, Ellen Willis states: 'It is precisely sex as an aggressive, unladylike activity, an expression of violent and unpretty emotion, an exercise of erotic power, and a specifically genital experience that has been taboo for women.'[4] Side by side, we see Willis equating 'sex as aggressive' and as 'violent emotion', with sex as the 'exercise of erotic power' and 'genital experience'. All are represented as mere taboo.

Judith Walkowitz has termed the libertarian perspective on sexuality the 'advanced position'.[5] It is difficult to see what is so advanced or progressive about a position that locates 'desire', and that imprisons female sexual dynamism, vitality and vigour, in old forms of sexual objectification, subordination and violence, this time initiated by women and done with women's consent. The libertarians offer a supposed sexuality stripped naked of feminine taboo, but only able to dress itself in masculine garb. It is a male-constructed sexuality in drag.

But more appears in this drag show than the male-power sexual actors and activities: de-politicizing is also in drag. In the libertarian drag show, the politics of sexuality and sexual domination have been forced to exit, as well as the politics of lesbianism. For example, the editors of *Desire: The Politics of Sexuality* argue that lesbianism has been *unsexed* – by a sexual consensus between lesbians and heterosexual feminists that 'theoretically accepted each other's moderated, healthy sexual proclivities . . . in somewhat the same spirit that St Paul accepted the inevitability of marriage for those weak of flesh and soul'.[6] The 'advanced position' no longer talks about political lesbianism and compulsory heterosexuality. They have been relegated to a bit part in feminist discourse. And it is those extremist, anti-sex, repressed, puritanical radical feminists who insist on giving them even that much of a role!

There is the arrogant and patronizing assumption in libertarian arguments that those who make problematic the concept of sexual pleasure are deprived of its more vital and vigorous delights. Sexual wimps! Problematizing the concept of sexual pleasure means talking about male power. So the 'advanced position' hardly talks about male power any longer – that is simplistic and grim. And as the FACT brief so facilely phrased it, that only portrays men as vicious 'attack dogs' and women as victims.[7] Instead, the libertarian position talks a lot about social conditioning to sexuality or the role of socialization in achieving a sexuality. So that when men act in certain ways, they are merely products of their socialization, as are women. There is certainly evidence that sexuality is socially conditioned and that men and women are socialized into particular forms of masculinity and femininity. But when these theories lack a concept of power that highlights the fact that masculinity and male sexuality are bound up with power – that there are positive advantages in status, ego and authority for men in the ways they have exercised their sexuality – then they function to depoliticize both women's oppression and women's liberation. Women cannot uncritically bracket this analysis in order to revel in the joy of sex.

The scenario of sexual forms that mimic the male-power mode of sexuality is only one focus. Another, as Susanne Kappeler has pointed out with respect to pornography, is the *structure of representation* that must be taken into consideration. This means that somebody is making those representations, and somebody is looking at them, 'through a complex array of means and conventions'.[8] The libertarians and lesbian lifestylers tell us that the sexual actors who act out certain roles, such as butch/femme and master/slave, are women who can be both subjects and objects **169** in the sexual event. In other words, when lesbians, for example, take on butch/femme or master/slave roles, because they are two women – two lesbians – engaged in such sex 'play', no one is objectified, hurt, or violated. Libertarianism and lesbian lifestylism purport to level the cultural inequality of male subject and female object. Let us look more closely at this claim.

Many libertarians and lesbian lifestylers, when they engage in various sexual acts, claim that they and their acts are resolutely sequestered from anything these acts might represent 'out there'. The privacy of the bedroom and what goes on there is separated, they say, from reality, in a 'room of one's own' – the libertarian and lesbian lifestyle sphere of *fantasy*. In sado-masochism, for example, the whips, the chains, the swastikas, the military paraphernalia, the handcuffs, the dog collars, the masters, the slaves have no dimension in the real world. The master or slave roles, for example, are treated in a world apart, in a sanctuary of sexual activity where the game is played according to other rules, valid in that fantasy world. The artist insulates the aesthetic, often claiming it as a reality-free zone. The libertarian in the same insular fashion attempts to shelter the sexual sphere making her activities here independent of reality, independent of critique. The sexual actors and activities exist in a rarefied atmosphere. It is like playing in the sandbox, or more accurately in the kitty litter box.

The libertarians and lesbian lifestylers would have it that until women 'deal with' the whole issue of sexuality, no true liberation will ensue. Thus they re-create the re-sexualization of women, this time in the name of women's liberation. The sexualization of women, of course, is an old theme that is common to both old and 'new' sex reformers and sexologists, as is the theme that women need to be freed-up sexually in order to be liberated. Havelock Ellis said it, as did Kinsey, and most recently Masters and Johnson. But this time the 'new' sex reformers are women, and the theme is that the female sexual urge is enormously powerful, more so than it has been given credit for in the flaccid feminist literature that preceded this particular libertarian 'sexual revolution'.

The hidden dogmatism here is that sex is the source of power. Sex is central – not creativity, not thinking, not anything else but sex. Following a kind of Freudian line, the libertarians exert a re-conservatizing influence on feminism and lesbianism essentializing some vaguely defined 'power of desire'.

Sexuality seems to be at the base of everything in the libertarian and lesbian lifestyle literature. Here, the primacy of sex is reasserted, this time not necessarily as a biological drive, but as a propelling social force – a force that has not only influence but deterministic power. Sexuality takes on the tone of a new natural law theory in libertarian discourse, reversing the 'anatomy is destiny' theory of sexuality into a theory of social determinism. Sex as a primary biological drive reappears in sex as a primary social motor, driving itself to fulfilment by utilizing all of the male-power modes of sexual objectification, subordination and oppression. Like any motor, sex requires the assistance of tinkering and technique. The mechanistic model once more prevails.

Can women so readily believe that sex is our salvation? Haven't we heard this line before – that what really counts is the quality of our sex lives, our orgasms?

This most recent wave of feminism has spent much of its time de-sexualizing the images of women in the media, the marketplace and the cosmos in general. What the libertarian position has succeeded in doing is re-sexualizing women, using feminist and lesbian liberation rhetoric to assert that sexuality is a radical impulse. But sexuality is no more radical than anything else. There are certain forms of it that may be radical and there are certain forms of it that are not. It is ironic that the libertarians want to reassert the male-power forms of sexuality to empower women.

This was not always the case, however. Many feminists remember a lesbian feminism that stood for passion, principles and politics. Without romanticizing this period as a golden age, it can be said that this movement was the strongest challenge to hetero-reality that feminism embodied. It challenged the worldview that women exist for men and primarily in relation to them. It challenged the history of women as primarily revealed in the family – a history that often in the best of accounts rendered women only in relation to men and male-defined events. It challenged that seemingly eternal truth that 'Thou as a woman must bond with a man', forever seeking our lost halves in the complementarity of hetero-relations. It even challenged the definition of feminism itself as the equality of women with men.

This movement worked on behalf of all women. It was not afraid to define rape as sex – not just violence but sex. It criticized prostitution and pornography as sexually hip for women and was not afraid to speak out against the male sexual **171** revolutionaries who wanted to liberate all the women they could get access to in the name of this fake freedom. It established centres for battered women and led the feminist campaign against violence against women.

But then something happened. Women – often other lesbians – began to define things differently. Pornography came to be called erotica and enlisted in the service of lesbian speech and self-expression. Violence against women came to be called lesbian sado-masochism and enlisted in the service of lesbian sex, i.e. fucking. Prostitution came to be called necessary women's work and enlisted in the service of female economic need. What had changed was that instead of men, women – including women who called themselves lesbians – were endorsing these activities for other women. And other women, other lesbians, were reluctant to criticize in the name of some pseudo-feminist and lesbian unity.

Certainly many lesbians resisted these debasements of women's lives. Certainly many lesbians are still in the forefront of the anti-pornography movement. Many lesbians are fighting world-wide against international prostitution and sex slavery. And many lesbians have spoken out against lesbian sado-masochism. But whereas, formerly, one could count on a political movement of lesbian feminism to fight against these anti-feminist activities, the politics of lesbian feminism has diminished.

Lesbian feminism was a movement that had a politics – that realized that prostitution, pornography and sexual violence could not be redefined as therapeutic, economic or sexy to fit any individual woman's whim in the name of free choice. It was a movement that recognized the complexities of choice and how so-called choices for women are politically constructed.

Now I want to tell a story – about choice, because every time radical feminists point out the political construction of women's choices, we are accused of being condescending to women and of making women into victims. Thus, my story.

Once upon a time, in the beginnings of this wave of feminism, there was a feminist consensus that women's choices were constructed, burdened, framed, impaired, constrained, limited, coerced, shaped, etc., by patriarchy. No one proposed that this meant women's choices were *determined*, or that women were passive or helpless victims of the patriarchy. That was because many women believed in the power of feminism to change women's lives and obviously, women could not change if they were socially determined in their roles or pliant putty in the hands of the patriarchs. We even talked about compulsory motherhood and, yes, compulsory heterosexuality! We talked about the ways in which women and young girls were seasoned into prostitution, accommodated themselves to male battering, and were channelled into low-paying and dead-end jobs. The more moderate among us talked about sex-role socialization. The more radical wrote manifestos detailing the patriarchal construction of women's oppression. But most of us agreed that, call it what you will, women were not free just to be 'you and me'.

Time passed, and along came a more 'nuanced' view of feminism. It told us to watch our language of women as victims. More women went to graduate and professional schools, grew 'smarter', were received at the bar, went into the academy and became experts in all sorts of fields. They partook of the power that the male gods had created and 'saw that it was good'. They perceived the plethora of options available to them, and thus they projected to all women and, *voilà*, the gospel of unadulterated choice. They started saying things like '. . . great care needs to be taken not to portray women as incapable of responsible decisions'.[9]

Some women thought these words were familiar, that they had heard them before, but the feminist discourse analysts didn't seem particularly interested in tracing this back to what 'old-fashioned' feminists labelled liberal patriarchal discourse. They said this was boring and outmoded, and besides women had already heard enough of this and it was depressing. Let's not be simplistic and blame men, they said, since this analysis 'offers so few leverage points for action, so few imaginative entry points for visions of change'.[10] Instead they began to talk about the 'Happy Hookers' and the 'women who loved it' and those who would love it if they could only have 'the freedom and the socially recognized space to appropriate for themselves the robustness of what traditionally has been male language' (read pornography).

This was familiar too, but then something strange happened. Those women who had noted the thread of continuity between liberal patriarchal men and FACT feminism, for example, began to notice that instead of women mimicking male speech, men began to mimic women. Howard Kurtz, a *Washington Post* reporter who wrote about the testimony of women during the hearings of the Attorney General's Commission on Pornography, labelled these women as 'a parade of *self-described victims* who tell   **173** their *sad stories* from behind an opaque screen . . . Many experts on both sides of the question say such *anecdotal tales of woe* prove nothing about the effect of sexually explicit materials.'[11] In the same key, Carol Vance poured scorn on the testimony of these same women by quoting with approval a male reporter who would nudge her during the hearings and say 'phoney witness'.[12]

To make a long story short, the men got this language of disbelief from self-identified feminists who are now telling us that victims of pornography choose their own beds to lie in. It's women's right to choose, after all, which is at stake. Protecting pornography protects 'our' right to choose. This right to choose, this kind of liberty, is liberalism. And, unfortunately, lifestyle lesbianism is also liberalism.

The liberalism of lifestyle lesbianism means that lesbians, like the rest of the therapeutic society, have become self-referential. The language of common consent is replaced by the language of private preface and preference. Women say: 'In my opinion,' or 'For me,' or 'As I see it,' or 'I have the right to what turns me on'. So what are lesbians left with? Certainly not political lesbianism which cannot even frame a sentence in the first person plural at this point in lesbian history, and which cannot say 'we' any more, but rather an extremely self-centred lesbian world-view. And we are left with a tyranny of tolerance that passes for difference.

It is as if every individual desire has become a political or cultural difference that other women must not only tolerate but also promote. So one woman's *desire*, rationalized as a *need* to free-up her sexuality by engaging in sado-masochism, for example, must be tolerated and fostered by other women and/or lesbians in the name of promoting lesbian differences and foster-ing lesbian unity. In the name of some amorphously defined feminist and/or lesbian community, value judgements cannot be made because that is being divisive. What kind of unity can be built on an unwillingness to make judgements? And what kind of freedom or liberation can be built on sexualized violence and subordination?

For example, many women vaguely 'feel' that so-called lesbian sado-masochism is wrong but hold themselves back from trans-lating that feeling into words and action. Other women tell them that no one has the right to judge the behaviour of others or enforce one's own values. This is what I mean by a tyranny of tolerance – 'doing your own thing'. The tyranny of tolerance dissuades women from tough-minded thinking, from responsibility for disagreeing with others and from the will to act. What is defined as value freedom, i.e. not making judgements, may appear sensitive to and respectful of other women but in reality it makes women passive and uncritical since it stops both judgements and action. An active social and political life stems from values, choices and activities that are defined with clarity and exercised with commitment.

Mary Daly has outlined several elements of radical feminism.[13] In a similar fashion, I would highlight several commonly-held values of lesbian feminism that allow women to put the lesbian together with feminist again. Lesbian feminists have clear and present knowledge that the boys, and some of the girls, are not going to like us and that we just might run into trouble along the way.

Lesbian feminists act on behalf of women as women. Lesbian feminism is not a one-issue movement. It makes connections between all issues that affect women – not only what affects this particular group, class, nationality, and not only what affects lesbians.

Lesbian feminists are radically different from what the hetero-society wants us to be. It is not a fake difference, but a real difference. For example, lesbian sexuality is *different*, rooted in the lesbian imagination. It is not the same old sexuality that women must submit to in hetero-reality. It is not pornography, it is not butch and femme, and it is not bondage and domination. It is, for one thing, a sexuality that is imagination rooted in reality. As Andrea Dworkin has written: 'Imagination finds new meanings, new forms; values and acts. The person with imagination is pushed forward by it into a world of possibility and risk, a distinct world of meaning and choice.'[14]

Those who think that the objectification, subordination and violation of women is acceptable just as long as you call it lesbian erotica or lesbian sado-masochism – they are not lesbian feminists. And those who think that it is acceptable in the privacy of their own bedrooms, where they enjoy it, where they get off on it – they are not lesbian feminists either. As Mary Daly has said, they're lesbians 'from the waist down'.

And to those who say, how dare we define what feminism means, I say: if we don't define what feminism means, what does feminism mean?

For years, lesbian feminists fought against the depiction of **175** lesbians in hetero-pornography. We said: 'That's not us in those poses of butch and femme role-playing. That's not the way we make love. That's not us treating each other as sadists or as masochists. That's not us bound by those chains, with those whips, and in those male fantasies of what women do with other women. That's a male wet dream of what a lesbian is and what lesbians do.' And we didn't only say it; we fought it. So now what has happened? We have lesbian pornography appearing in US 'women's' porn magazines such as *Bad Attitude* and *On Our Backs*. And we have the FACT Brief. And all of this 'feminist and lesbian literature' tells us that straight pornography, that hetero-pornography, is right. Lesbians are butches and femmes, sadists and masochists, and lesbians do get off on doing violence to each other. We've come full circle – unfortunately back to the same negative starting point.

So I want to end with a vision and a context for lesbian sexuality. I want to suggest what sexuality might look like rooted in lesbian imagination, not in the hetero-fantasies of lesbian pornography.

This vision of sexuality includes the 'ability to touch and be touched'. But more, a touch that makes contact, as James Baldwin has phrased it. Andrea Dworkin, building on these words of Baldwin, writes about sexuality as the act, the point of connection, where touch makes contact if self-knowledge is present. It is also the act, the point of connection, where the inability of touch to make contact is revealed and where the results may be devastating. In sexuality, intimacy is always possible, as much as we say that sex is sex – i.e. simple pleasure. In sexuality, a range of emotions about life get expressed, however casual or impersonal the intercourse – feelings of betrayal, rage, isolation and bitterness as well as hope, joy, tenderness, love and communion.[15] All, although not all together, reside in this passion we call sexuality. Sexuality is where these emotions become accessible or anaesthetized. A whole human life does not stand still in sex.

Libertarian and lesbian lifestylism simplifies the complexity of that whole human life that is present in the sex act. Abandoning that totality – that history, those feelings, those thoughts – allows for 'All touch but no contact . . .'[16]

This chapter began with the assertion that, although the lesbian lifestylers talk about sex constantly, they are speechless
about its connection to a whole human life, and, therefore, they

are speechless about sex itself. The presence of a whole human life in the act of sexuality negates any reductionistic view of sex as good or bad, sheer pleasure or sheer perversion. Dworkin reminds us that when sex is getting even, when sex is hatred, when sex is utility, when sex is indifferent, then sex is the destroying of a human being, another person perhaps, assuredly one's self. Sex is a whole human life rooted in passion, in flesh. This whole human life is involved always.

Notes

This article was first published as 'Putting the Politics Back into Lesbianism' in the *Women's Studies International Forum* 12(2), 1989, pp. 149–56, and has been adapted from it. In a prior incarnation it was originally a talk given to the Lesbian Summer School at Wesley House, London, July 1988.

1. Jesse Meredith, 'A Response to Samois', in Robin Ruth Linden *et al.* (eds), *Against Sadomasochism* (East Palo Alto, CA: Frog in the Well Press, 1982), p. 97.
2. Margaret Jackson, 'Sexology and the Universalization of Male Sexuality (From Ellis to Kinsey, and Masters and Johnson)', in L. Coveney *et al.* (eds), *The Sexuality Papers* (London: Hutchinson, 1984), p. 81.
3. FACT (Feminist Anti-Censorship Taskforce *et al.*), *Brief Amici Curiae* no. 84–3147. In the US Court of Appeals, 7th Circuit, Southern District of Indiana, 1985, p.31.
4. Ellen Willis, 'Feminism, Moralism, and Pornography', in Ann Snitow *et al.* (eds), *Desire: The Politics of Sexuality* (London: Virago, 1983) p. 85
5. Diary of a Conference on Sexuality. Unpublished notes of the original Diary circulated among conference planners for the 1982 Barnard conference on 'The Scholar and the Feminist: Towards a Politics of Sexuality' (1981), p. 72.
6. Snitow *et al.*, op. cit., p. 27
7. FACT, op. cit., p. 39
8. Susanne Kappeler, *The Pornography of Representation* (Minneapolis, MN: University of Minnesota Press, 1986), p. 3.
9. Lori Andrews, 'Alternative Modes of Reproduction', in *Reproductive Laws for the 1990s: A Briefing Handbook* (Newark, NJ: Women's Rights Litigation Clinic, Rutgers Law School, 1988), pp. 257–99.
10. Snitow *et al.*, op. cit., p. 30.
11. Howard Kurtz, 'Pornography Panel's Objectivity Disputed', *Washington Post*, 15 October 1985, p. A4 (emphasis added).
12. Lal Coveney and Leslie Kaye, 'A Symposium on Feminism, Sexuality and Power', *Off Our Backs*, 1987, p. 12.
13. Mary Daly, *Pure Lust: Elemental Feminist Philosophy* (Boston: Beacon Press, 1984), pp. 397–8; in cahoots with Jane Caputi, *Webster's First New Intergalactic Wickedery* (Boston: Beacon Press, 1987), p. 75.   **177**

14. Andrea Dworkin, *Intercourse* (New York: Free Press, 1987), p. 48.
15. Ibid., pp. 47–61.
16. James Baldwin, *Giovanni's Room* (New York: Dial Press, 1962), p. 82.

10 Pornography and Addiction: A Political Issue

CORINNE SWEET

GENDER STEREOTYPES

Three heterosexual men interviewed on BBC Radio 4's *Woman's Hour* described how early exposure to pornography had influenced their lives.[1] They had all first come across it when young (seven, nine and thirteen years). They had found it through friends, home, school or public places and all still felt profoundly affected by it, although now in their thirties. One man said: 'The important thing is that the pornographic images burn themselves into your brain and they pop up or you can replay them inside your head whenever you want to. These pornographic images are so powerful that they're always filed away ready for use.'

The most difficult 'after-effects' were how the early exposure to pornography had shaped their perception of women and women's sexuality and, also, how it had impacted on their own developing sexualities and relationships. In youth they had 'innocently' imbibed these pornographic messages as the 'truth' about women, sex and sexuality. Although in adulthood they each had become 'conscious' of how sexism is constructed and perpetuated, all still experienced 'gut' responses to women and pornography which they believed came from their early exposure to it: 'I used to vehemently regret it in my early twenties, because I felt I had missed out on a whole era of innocent exploration.'

Pornography had also functioned as a form of sex education for these men and was an important building block in the edifice of their own sexism: 'Pornography gives you a sense of sex divorced from any relationship, it also treats sex as something geared towards performance – it's like football, you've got to train for it, you've got to learn to "do the business".'

Thus, boys' exposure to pornography is part of male culture, a 'rite of passage' which fully reinforces gender stereotypes. Its crude and simplistic messages encourage men to 'do it' to women, imply that women are 'desperate for it' or 'asking for it', and that women are smilingly 'available', always inviting them sexually, even when they say 'no'. '[Pornography] confused me about what women were really like. It communicated two main things: one is that women are merely sexual objects to satisfy my lust, and two, that women are insatiably sexual. So it made me contemptuous of women and it also made me feel inadequate.'

Young people are 'naturally' curious about the human body and its functions. To explore their bodies, to seek knowledge and pleasure alone or with others is completely 'normal'. But people are also socialized by the cultural context and content of what they see and experience. Along with gender, personal experience of class, race, religion, parental/sibling role models, school and peer groups are central to our later attitudes and behaviours. Pornography is not the *only* source of sexist misinformation, but given its immediacy, the power of its imagery, its direct appeal as a sexual stimulus, its message has a profound effect on the gender-role conditioning boys experience in society.

Although girls are kept largely ignorant about sex and sexuality, are fed 'romantic', heterosexist notions about love, courtship and marriage, they are none the less on the receiving end of pornography's influence – from sexist attitudes and behaviours towards their bodies, to sexual harassment, sexual abuse, sexual violence and rape. Women generally express far more outrage about pornography and its depiction of women as willing sexual slaves or insatiable sex objects once they actually see it for what it is; while men (even the 'aware' or the 'new' man) often fail to see what is truly objectionable about women being portrayed as submissive, sexually available or animalistic, because they have become inured to it over their lives. (Academic and clinical evidence about this process of 'desensitization' is discussed in Chapter 14.)

But there is a further issue to be considered regarding this socialization process. It is far too simplistic to say all men like pornography and all women do not like it. The truth is more complex. There are, of course, women who like it and men who do not and men and women who are simultaneously attracted and repelled. This is because pornography not only conveys very specific messages about the sexual nature of women and girls (and by implication, and sometimes description, men and boys), it also arouses deep, and sometimes conflicting, emotions – pleasure, fear, guilt, lust, desire, disgust, curiosity, excitement, **180** horror and prurience.

The nature and intensity of the emotions and sensations stimulated by experiencing pornography have a variety of effects: they can create a sense of intense, personal pleasure, where the consumer is in the role of voyeur or passive/active participant; they can defeat boredom and frustration by the depth of this excitement and distraction from everyday reality; they can create a thrilling illusion of personal power and/or powerlessness (people can experience sexual 'pleasure' as either aggressors or victims, as sadists and/or masochists); they can offer artificial companionship, temporarily dispelling feelings of isolation and unattractiveness; and they can be used as an adjunct to a sexual act, often masturbation or sexual intercourse, sometimes even sexual harassment, assault and rape.

These intense feelings can create a compulsive or addictive 'pull' towards using pornography repetitively. Many authors have alluded to the addictive nature of pornography without clearly defining how or why this addiction operates. According to Susan Griffin: 'were pornography not a kind of mental addiction, an enthralled fantasy, who would seriously credit its "ideas"?'[2] Indeed, few people have been able to explain adequately why millions of ordinary, intelligent men (and some women) world-wide spend their hard-earned income on a product which is primarily about selling a sexist illusion and short-term sexual satisfaction. This chapter therefore aims to set out how and why heterosexual pornography can be addictive and the implications of this.

HOW ADDICTIONS OPERATE

Everyday Life

There is a common belief that addictions are the preserve of neurotic, seedy, inadequate individuals, that there are distinctive 'addictive personalities' and/or that addiction is a sickness. Of course, there are seriously damaging cases of addiction where people's lives are at risk from substances and behaviours, such as heroin, alcohol, overeating/self-starvation and smoking. The mechanisms of addiction are, at root, the same whether a person is using crack or constantly drinking pots of tea or regularly slumping in front of videos. Addictions have their origins in early emotional experience and development. While it is true that there are some people who are relatively free from addictions, to **181** some extent addictions and addictive behaviour pervade everyone's lives. It is only a matter of kind and degree. Indeed, many people have multiple addictions which they take for granted as a 'normal' part of modern life.

Chemical and behavioural addictions are used as a way of dealing with difficult emotions, stresses and situations. They can be 'useful' in enabling people to live in conditions and circumstances which they could not otherwise endure. Reduce alcohol, sugar, junk food and drink, credit card spending, nicotine, tea and coffee intake and there would be a lot of irritable, disgruntled and exhausted citizens clamouring for better conditions and lives. Chemical and behavioural addictions have been encouraged or allowed to develop over centuries as an effective means of exerting social control. The cultural acceptance of a high level of addiction ensures social conformity.

Cultural Heritage

North-west European culture has created a heritage of confusing messages. Addictions are legitimated by religion, national health systems, education, peer groups, family life and the media. Some addictions are a ritualized part of social interaction (such as alcohol at parties, smoking behind the school shed, sharing joints). Some addictions are institutionalized in our culture and are integral to the economy (such as Christmas spending sprees, birthday parties, wedding breakfasts, funeral wakes). People are exhorted to be 'one of the crowd', to drink, smoke, spend, eat, and, yet, at the same time, are instructed to be moderate. Going 'too far' or 'over the top' or abstaining altogether leads to social ostracism. Thus, socially acceptable addictions (like credit card spending, alcohol, overwork, compulsive caring, TV, sugar, chocolate, tranquillizers) live alongside more socially unacceptable addictions (wife-battering, heroin, cannabis, tobacco-smoking, glue-sniffing, gambling). There is also a hierarchy of acceptability linked to class, race, age and culture (whisky is fine, potcheen is not).

Everyday addictions serve to numb feelings and to blot out thoughts. Tranquillizers still operate as 'Mother's little helper' for thousands of women who suffer from the exploitation of unpaid domestic labour and childcare. Alcohol, drugs and tea are used to anaesthetize the loss of the bereaved, rather than helping them experience the spectrum of emotions involved in grief and recovery. Alcohol, cigarettes and prostitutes are provided for men in the armed forces as 'rewards' for facing death and committing brutal acts. Men in prison get similar 'privileges' for good behaviour and drug addiction is widespread. Young people are given sweeties and 'treats' for being obedient and 'good'. Most popular addictions are marketed on the basis that they will make people 'feel better', help them 'cope', provide comfort in times of stress and isolation, make them more likeable, attractive and popular, increase their sexual prowess, push them faster up the class structure and enhance their status and power.

This craving for something to make people 'feel better' can be overpowering, given the stress and distress in most people's lives. The allure of addictions as 'cure-all' and 'comforter' can seem irresistible and justifiable. Advertisers know precisely how to exploit this aspect of people's emotional vulnerability and spend thousands of pounds to provoke them into behaving addictively. The fact that many addictive substances are legally available, endorsed by government and/or Crown, used by people in positions of power as well as families, friends and neighbours, gives them a social seal of approval. This leads to addictive substances and behaviours being represented as desirable and normal and those who decide to forgo them as cranks, moralists and killjoys.

Maintaining Capitalism

The use of addictions by the majority is, in fact, central to the maintenance of the 'status quo' in capitalist society as it provides the basis for industries creating much-needed employment; it maintains industries which create excess profit; it pacifies and moulds willing and adaptable employees; it develops people as consumers (i.e. creating more and more 'goals' for conspicuous consumption); it continually refines new goods to meet consumer 'needs'; and, in each case, perpetuates conformity and compliance within the class structure.

Ironically, many people working in industrialized societies actually earn their living manufacturing the goods and substances which they then spend their wages to consume in leisure time. These 'rewards' make people feel better temporarily, although much of what they consume is physically and mentally damaging, often contributing to further personal and social problems like debt, physical and mental illness, social unrest and family violence. Tobacco-smoking provides a good example of **183** how nicotine addiction interacts with the needs of profit in industrialized society. Peter Taylor explains:

> Cigarettes are not only cheap to make, they are addictive and recession-proof. Although millions have heeded the medical evidence and stopped smoking . . . cigarettes still remain one of the world's most profitable industries with annual sales of four trillion cigarettes, worth over $40 billion. Cigarettes remain the lifeblood of the tobacco multinationals and they have no intention of letting anybody cut off . . . the Smoke Ring is the ring of political and economic interests which has protected the tobacco industry for the past twenty years. [Thus] cigarettes provide governments with one of their biggest and most reliable sources of revenue [and] in purely economic terms the political benefits of cigarettes far outweigh their social cost.[3]

Thus, individuals can find themselves using addictions because they are trapped within the pressures of hard-selling advertisements, stressful, hard-working lives, misinformation disseminated by the politically, socially and economically powerful and their own unsatisfied emotional needs.

Key Emotions Underlying Addictions

My experience of counselling people on their addictions has shown me repeatedly that the addictive 'urge' is fuelled by deep-seated negative emotions. At the same time, addictions are used to quell these uncomfortable emotions, so the person becomes caught in a 'cycle' of addiction.

What are these negative emotions underlying addictions? Of course, each individual is different, but there are generic feelings, such as: fear, isolation, grief, boredom, frustration, humiliation, despair, unworthiness, incompetence, self-loathing and self-invalidation (feeling unattractive, unlovable, unlikeable, unimportant). Addictions are also used to deaden physical pain (from chronic illness, disabilities, etc.). If people were not numbed, they would have a chance to express their feelings. Society does not tolerate these emotions being expressed openly (except to a limited extent at specific ceremonies and social rituals). Repressive conditioning puts strict restraints on individual emotional expression. For instance, it is not regarded as socially desirable or acceptable to cry, shake, shout, yawn, rage, laugh at the 'wrong' time and place. Young people are trained *not* to show feelings of passion or pain, but rather to do a narrow

range of these things in a narrow range of circumstances.

Rewards are heaped on those who achieve the most self-control ('good girls don't cry').

People who cry, shake, rage or generally show 'too much' feeling are often 'controlled' with drugs issued by the medical profession. Not only is the expression of emotion undesirable, but people fear being labelled 'mad' or thought to be having a 'mental breakdown' when their feelings bubble over. The ultimate 'sanction' on emotional expression is to be 'contained' within the mental health system. Not surprisingly, a disproportionate number of women, black, disabled and working-class people have been so sanctioned because they do not fit in or refuse to comply.

Emotional Illiteracy

'Emotional illiteracy', or the inability and/or reluctance to express, understand or deal with human emotions, is a by-product of this conditioning process. Because people are discouraged from releasing their deep-seated distresses they do not have the language, skills or appropriate outlets to do so. There is a national addiction to 'soap operas' (like *EastEnders, Neighbours, Brookside, The Archers, Dallas*) and to 'agony aunts' and 'pop-psychological' articles in women's magazines, where emotions and relationships are rawly expressed and analysed. Yet the fascination of these programmes and columns for many people lies in a genuine need for information about how to handle the complexity of their emotional lives on a daily basis. In a sense people are striving to become emotionally literate in a repressed and uninformed culture through vicarious and, often, fictitious means.

Emotional illiteracy means it is seldom possible for people to describe how they really feel. Many people, especially men, learn to pride themselves on being reserved, moderate, stoical and feel mortified if they let down their 'front'. So when asked how they are, people will say 'all right', 'OK' or 'mustn't grumble', even if their worlds are falling apart. And counselling and/or therapy are still seen to be the secret and shameful preserve of 'sick', 'dysfunctional', wealthy, middle-class people with 'problems'. If people are brave enough to admit to using agencies such as the Samaritans or Relate for 'help' they risk attracting scorn, pity, even ridicule, from friends, relatives or colleagues because they are 'weak'.

So addictions can play a socially useful role maintaining the   **185** appearance or pretence of being 'in control', which is regarded as essential for 'normal' interaction and functioning. Unfortunately, this model is based largely on male, white, upper- and middle-class concepts of what constitutes 'correct' behaviour. Limited emotional expression is permitted along gender-stereotyped lines, just as long as women cry and men rage (in private, not public). Angry women and weeping men are even greater targets for ridicule.

Cycle of Addiction

There is a recognizable cycle of addiction. There are the under-lying feelings described above, such as fear, isolation, grief, boredom, frustration, humiliation, despair, unworthiness, incompetence, self-loathing, self-invalidation (feeling unattrac-tive, unlovable, unlikeable, unimportant) *and* the 'urge' or 'pull' towards an addictive substance or behaviour. If the 'pull' is acted upon there can be intense feelings of carefree euphoria, and/or physical and mental pleasure and satisfaction, which can aid emotional release and the dropping of inhibitions. This 'high' or intense pleasure is often followed by feelings of flat-ness, self-loathing and disgust, fear of being 'out of control' or 'bad', remorse or irritation as the repressed feelings resurface. This leads to a need to retake or re-enact the addiction and, over time, the 'hit' needs to get harder and harder to satisfy the urge.

Fantasies often accompany using addictions, providing a pseudo-reality, a dream-like, womb-like, imaginary state of safety and satisfaction. This cycle applies whether the addiction is cocaine or cream cakes, masturbation or gambling – the mechanisms are the same. Addictions provide people with the illusion of being alive by creating immediate sensations of pleasure like the 'high' of cocaine, the 'buzz' of nicotine, the 'fuzz' of alcohol. They are told 'things go better with Coke', 'a Mars a day helps you work, rest and play', which perpetuates passivity, in turn reinforcing feelings of individual hopelessness and powerlessness. Thus, people can end up oppressed by the very substances they are using to try to free themselves from emotional repression.

Self-abuse

Whether chemical or behavioural, addictions are basically a form
186 of self-abuse. Because numbing feelings creates a phoney illusion

of well-being, the actual abuse is seldom perceived or acknowledged. Yet, people often feel uneasy about abusing themselves with addictions, and this manifests itself as guilt about self- or over-indulgence. For example, anaesthetizing the emotions allows people to exhaust themselves without realizing it – workaholics and/or people doing boring, repetitive or dangerous jobs, often keep going on coffee, junk food including sugar, even amphetamines, and are completely out of touch with their real need to rest, exercise and relax. They will say, 'I know I shouldn't, but I just can't stop' or 'I'll just finish this, then I'll rest later'.

Addictions seem to offer people the fantasy of uncomplicated personal success and fulfilment without them having to *do* anything. But these addiction-induced illusions are temporary, superficial and unsatisfying. For instance, the unrealistic promise of instant fame, excitement and wealth portrayed in myriad car advertisements operates at the level of wish-fulfilment which, of course, can never come true. Addictions can work as an apparent means of gaining both conventional success (the 'perfect' car, girl, job, house, clothes, looks), and unconventional success (in rebellion – smoking cannabis, taking heroin, being a romantic outcast).

Another way addictions 'con' people is that they appear to meet their real emotional needs. This false promise of improving people's lives almost magically can *never* be fulfilled. The unhappy, disturbing or oppressive reality does not go away and the addiction – whether chemical or behavioural – has to be indulged repeatedly to obtain the temporary feelings of release and escape. It is common to this cycle of addiction that increasing doses or bouts of the addictive substance or behaviour are needed, and at more frequent intervals, to keep the underlying distressing feelings at bay and to maintain the superficial and illusory feelings of being close to others, successful, lovable, rich, attractive, sexy, confident, and so on.

Unfortunately, the situation which triggered the urge for an addiction will be dealt with less effectively as a result of succumbing to the addiction itself. This is because people who have anaesthetized themselves will be less, not more, capable of doing something about the situation in the long term, even if they are buoyed up on an immediate false sense of competence, power and security.

But how does pornography fit into this picture of addiction? **187**

PORNOGRAPHY ADDICTION

Habitual Use

One client described his addiction to pornography to me:

> It's like what people say about sugar, you know, that it's "trash energy" – pornography is "trash feeling". It's a short buzz, has absolutely no long-term meaning or use or purpose. It's empty. I don't feel particularly bad after it, but I just know, long-term, it gets in the way, that it's not good for me or anybody else.

On *Woman's hour*, another man described his addiction:

> On a good day I try to give it up, but it's like most things you come back to again and again, you think I'll never do that again, but it's very linked to masturbation and I think a lot of men have periods of bingeing and then they think I've got to give this up, I've got to give this up – but the day always comes when the only thing to do is to look at pornography and masturbate.

Pornography plays a particular role in men's lives, as Michael Laslett told the Minneapolis City Council public hearings on pornography in the US in 1983:

> The myth about pornography is that it frees the libido and gives men an outlet for sexual expression which liberates mind and body. This is truly a myth. I have found that pornography not only does not liberate men, but on the contrary is a source of bondage. Men masturbate to pornography only to become addicted to the fantasy. There is no liberation for men in pornography. Pornography becomes a source of addiction much like alcohol. There is temporary relief. It is mood-altering. And it is reinforcing, i.e. 'you want more' because 'you got relief'. It is this reinforcing characteristic that leads men to want the experience they have in pornographic fantasy to happen in real life.[4]

Of course, some people (especially women) have never seen it, some have limited exposure to it, some are occasional users, but many men are fully addicted and the extent of this addiction is both widespread and widely denied. Pornography operates at a wide social level and is legitimated by being sold in daily newspapers and, like 'Page 3', has become a well-established
national institution:

The *Sun* sells four million copies every day because its readers, women and men, want something to give them a buzz of excitement at work. When work crushes out any fulfilment from our lives, the Page 3 pin-up, the constant assault of salacious stories of rape and fake sexuality is the packaged drug they slip us to help us survive the monotony. The *Sun* takes our real experience and turns it against us, the mob language of the *Sun* is a denial of our sense and our experience. It offers us a caricature of the feelings that life under capitalism destroys. It gives us a fake excitement stripped of subversion, laced with violence and the refusal to face our own lives.[5]

Being surrounded by such sexist misinformation no one can grow up 'distress-free' in the area of sexuality. What is usually understood to be innate or 'normal' sexuality, just as much as what is termed bizarre or 'abnormal' sexuality, is largely conditioned. People will have had experiences during their childhood and adolescence, when their sexuality was developing, which will have shaped their sexual responses, whether heterosexual, homosexual or bisexual. Many of these experiences are distressing, hurtful and confusing. Much of this socialization is interlarded with misinformation about sex and sexuality (such as 'masturbation makes you blind' or 'gay people are perverted') through jokes and hearsay.

Sexual Abuse

Many more sexually distressing experiences are hidden, secret, often even unremembered and suppressed by people themselves. This sexual abuse refers to anything from rough and thoughtless handling of genitalia to deliberate sexual molestation and intercourse (including oral sex, buggery and rape). Sexual abuse can also include seeing something being done to someone else, or hearing something said, or seeing or reading something hurtful.

Until recently sexual abuse has been largely hidden from public view. When paediatricians in Cleveland diagnosed sexual abuse in a total of 165 girls and boys in 1987, there was a national outcry. Many people simply could not accept that ordinary, 'respectable' men could abuse children in the privacy of the home. Yet, we now know that sexual abuse is usually carried out by fathers, brothers, grandfathers, uncles, seldom by random strangers. And that women, too, can be abusers. The public's desire to refute any possibility of such widespread sexual abuse reflects the resistance which exists to acknowledging it as an enormous problem.[6]

My clinical work as an addictions counsellor has repeatedly shown the connections between child sexual abuse and sexual addiction in adult life. Many authors have already noted the link between sexual abuse and later 'sexual problems'. One client told me her story: 'I was eight years old when he buggered me first. He told me to go upstairs and brush the bedroom carpet on my hands and knees. I was scared of him, so I obeyed. He came up behind me, lifted my skirt and pushed his penis in my anus. It hurt and I was terrified.'

She was abused continually until fifteen. As an adolescent and adult she became sexually addicted, sleeping with anyone who came her way, and even today this cycle of abuse continues: 'I seem to end up with bastards who abuse me. I end up in bed a lot and have little respect for myself, all my relationships seem to go wrong.'

Through counselling, this woman began to get in touch with her outrage at her abuse, which, in turn, has enabled her to decide she no longer wants relationships with 'bastards', although she is still attracted to them. She has begun to understand that when she was small she was so starved of real affection, love and respect that she became used to sexual abuse being the only perverted form of parental care she could expect. Painfully neglected, the abuse provided her with warped physical contact, made her seem desirable, even important. The most confusing thing for her to admit in adult life was that there had been some sexual pleasure mixed in with the terror and pain. This does not mean she enjoyed or invited the abuse, but it means her emotional and physical reactions to it had been more complicated than she at first realized. As a consequence, she has become addicted to sex (and sexual abuse) as a means of getting close to and receiving attention from men. Once involved with them the cycle of addiction would start and she would be hurt all over again.

To break out of this cycle, she has now consciously decided to stop forming relationships with such men and look for people who are genuinely caring and respectful: 'I feel murderous hate right now, I'm furious I've missed out on my childhood. Inside I feel deeply sad and lonely, I feel very childish and powerless. I just hope I'll stop blaming myself one day.'

Sexual addiction deadens difficult emotions, but also releases what is usually termed 'sexual frustration', which wells up from deeply buried strata of sexual distress experiences, which can include sexual abuse. These sexual distresses are inseparable from all the other negative emotions (such as anger and self-hatred) and often have their roots in sexual mistreatment. However, being compulsive (or addicted) in sexual matters is currently regarded as normal, 'red blooded' behaviour – at least for men and increasingly for women.

Pornography and Sexual Abuse

Pornography addiction is but one manifestation, a branch of the main stem of sexual compulsion and addiction. People become addicted to pornography itself and it can become the centre of their sexual addiction. Were this not so there would be nothing to sustain such a mass market of repetitive imagery. Even more clearly, there is a cycle of addiction, where users seek out harder and harder pornography, leading, in extreme cases, to 'snuff' films where a woman's sexual murder constitutes 'entertainment'.[7] And exposure to pornography is itself one of the hurtful sexual experiences that many young people have in this culture.

Pornography may itself have been part of the sexual abuse, may have been used openly by the abuser, may also have been itself a 'trigger' for the abuse, in that the perpetrator is stimulated to the point where he 'acts out' what he has experienced, seen, read, watched. The 'desensitization' that accompanies early and continued exposure to pornographic misinformation can lead some men to feel what they are doing is 'harmless', 'natural', and as much 'fun' for the other person as themselves or as much fun as pornography distortedly depicts it to be. When people act out their sexual distress and mistreat others, they are largely operating on 'automatic', they are caught in the addictive 'cycle' which 'pulls' them to satisfy an urgent, overwhelming need. The desire for sexual pleasure (desire is largely an expression of the sexual addiction itself) dominates and usually puts all considerations of other people's feelings and consequences of their actions aside at the moment of acting.

In the US, Ted Bundy, the serial sexual murderer, volunteered a public 'confession' to a religious broadcaster the night before his execution on 25 January 1989. He explained how his addiction to pornography had operated:

> It happened in stages, gradually, it didn't necessarily . . . happen overnight. My experience with pornography generally, but with pornography that deals on a violent level with sexuality, is once **191**

you become addicted to it, and I look at this as a kind of addiction like other kinds of addiction, I would keep looking for more potent, more explicit, more graphic kinds of material. Like an addiction, you keep craving something that is harder, harder, something which gives you a greater sense of excitement. Until you reach a point where the pornography only goes so far, you reach that jumping off point where you begin to wonder if maybe actually doing it would give you that which is beyond just reading it or looking at it.[8]

Bundy described the 'cycle' of his addiction to sex and pornography just as he might have described an alcohol addiction.

Sexual addiction, including addiction to pornography, is fuelled by a whole reservoir of unacknowledged sexual distresses. The addictive substances are sex, sexual fantasies and pornography, and these can also be interconnected with other chemical and behavioural addictions. Yet, the extent to which pornography is itself a stimulus for sexual abusers has only started to surface relatively recently and is still largely unacknowledged or disputed.

Therapist Charlotte Kasl, who gave evidence to the Minneapolis City Council public hearings on pornography in 1983, described her work with adult women survivors of sexual abuse:

Basically I want to connect sexual addiction to childhood sexual abuse . . . it has been my experience that pornography is an integral part of sexual addiction and sexual addiction is an integral part of child abuse. And as these are addictions, they follow a course of escalation. They follow a course of compulsion. They are out of control. The addict using pornography is on a spiral, on a course that is getting worse, that leads to escalation of the sexual acting out whether it be peeping Tom, whether it be molesting children, exposing himself and so forth.[9]

The survey of (mainly) women readers of *Cosmopolitan* magazine in the UK showed connections between pornography and child sexual abuse. The proportion of respondents who first saw pornography as children was unexpectedly large. First contact included exposure to 'illegal' pornography. Thirteen per cent of respondents were aware of having been sexually abused as children and some wrote about their abusers' use of pornography.[10]

A client in her forties described to me how exposure to pornography had revived her own memories of being sexually abused as a child:

Playboy came out when I was in my teens. I remember being prurient about it, but also thinking "oh, it's not so bad". But I remember it was like being socked in the solar plexus when I found out *Playboy* had pictures of women with their legs open and their genitals exposed. That made me feel terror and total hopelessness. And then I suddenly thought, I wonder if whatever happened to me when I was a child actually involved magazines.

Pornography can therefore be an important link in the chain of sexual addiction and abuse. While it is not the *only* factor, its influence is often overlooked and underestimated.

Pornography Addiction and Women
Although this is seldom acknowledged, women can be addicted to pornography, too. *The Story of O* is part of the sado-masochistic tradition which caused one woman I interviewed to feel very confused about her own sexuality:

It was an eye-opener, I couldn't pretend it was anything other than undiluted sadism, masochism, the story was about a woman seeking the extremes of sexual humiliation and brutality. The idea that women could submit willingly to torture, and that I could find it horrific in every sense, but still attractive, said something pretty revolting about sexual arousal, pornography and women.

Women might well feel the same conflicting feelings watching *9½ Weeks* or reading the Marquis de Sade, works which depict women as enjoying violence and violation and which many women find at once sexually arousing and disgusting. But it is not surprising to find women's sexual arousal conditioned to passivity and sexual violence, for women themselves are conditioned to be passive and many women have survived sexual abuse as children, adolescents and/or sexual harassment, assault and rape as adults. The 'pull' to use these kind of materials, regardless of holding a feminist perspective about their exploitative and sexist nature, illustrates the ambivalence many women will have to feel when facing their own addiction to pornography.

This is connected to the prurient fascination with pornography which leads some women, including women who identify as feminists, to justify its existence and acceptability on the grounds that having and using pornography gives them equality with men or provides useful information about sex. This confuses the fact that erotica and sex education materials are completely **193** different from pornography because of the implicitly sexist messages conveyed in the latter about the nature of women's sexuality.

This is because the term 'sexually explicit' is used generically to describe erotica, sex education materials and pornography as one category. But there are distinct, unacknowledged, differences between them. Images, pictures, words, films which are erotic are largely based on mutuality and equality. Pornography, by its very nature, communicates a message about women which is based on sex discrimination and misogyny. Why would women want to consume something that subjugates them and discriminates against them? The answer lies in women's conditioning as women: how the oppression is internalized so they believe sexist misinformation is the reality about themselves. This is a basic part of the process of women's oppression. Even if women have consciously thrown off the oppressive trappings of conditioned gender roles, pornography can stimulate memories and feelings of the slavish models of sexually subordinated womanhood they experienced during childhood socialization.

But true equality does not mean taking on the oppressive role of men, and women do not need to 'equalize down' in this way. Because men exploit women's bodies, achieving equality does not mean that women have to do that too. Because men have the 'freedom' to look at pornography, equality does not mean that women have to follow. Similarly, many women are now harming themselves by smoking and drinking heavily, *like men*: leading dangerous, stressful and unhealthy lives, *like men*. Yet real equality must surely mean enabling each woman to realize her full potential while redefining the limited spheres occupied by men and women alike. While women might rightfully want much more woman-centred erotica and sex education materials (lesbian and heterosexual), why is it necessary or even desirable to promote pornography for women?

Clearly, the pornography industry has recognized that women, with increased spending power, are a large and growing market for pornography. Ex-porn star Candida Royalle saw a business opportunity and established Femme Films, producing pornographic videos aimed at women.[11] As Susanne Kappeler notes:

> Most pornographers would hasten to assure us that their intentions are of the best. They will tell us they are in the business because they love women – and they are telling us again, in the 1980s, as they are trying to capture the woman market for the

'adult business'. The pornographers [bring] a kind of porn liberation spirit to their work.[12]

Yet, if it is accepted that pornography is addictive, and/or that
there is a pornography industry specifically targeting men's, and
now women's, sexual distresses for profit, what does this mean
for the sensitive issue of personal responsibility?

PERSONAL RESPONSIBILITY

Whether or not people do to other people what they have
experienced themselves does not necessarily fall into a simple
'cause and effect' model. It is increasingly clear that while some
people seem to 'act out' obsessively their own sexual mistreatment, it is also true that there are others who decide not to do
this. But why do some people do this while others do not?

A major component of people's sexual behaviour is their
conditioned responses which operate on an unaware and
irrational level. In extreme cases, where people become 'lost' in
their past sexual distresses, they seem to mistreat others directly
out of their own early abuse. It is now increasingly understood
and acknowledged that sexual abusers will have been sexually
abused themselves. However, this picture of abuse having a root,
a cause, in early distress experiences, does not remove people's
responsibility for their own actions. While they are not personally
to blame for having been sexually abused in the past, they are
none the less responsible for what they do in the present and the
future.

An addiction to pornography does *not* make people helpless
victims of their own desires, does *not* have to remove individual
responsibility to treat fellow human beings respectfully and gives
no one the right to molest, assault or rape. On the contrary.
Acknowledging the addiction and understanding the mechanisms
enables this kind of behaviour to be eliminated consciously by
people themselves. Once the addiction is understood the person
has a choice whether or not to continue to act on the 'pulls', the
desires, the triggers, the feelings. Surprisingly, even a man as
damaged as Ted Bundy did not try to 'excuse' his actions by
putting the blame entirely on his obsession with pornography.

I tell you that I am not blaming pornography . . . I take full
responsibility for whatever I have done and all the things I have   **195**

done. I don't want to infer . . . that I was some kind of helpless victim [but] we're talking about an influence that is an influence of violent types of media, violent types of pornography, which had an indispensable [link] in the chain . . . of events that led to the behaviour . . . the assaults, the murders.[13]

Because pornography's whole atmosphere is the permissive, unbridled acting out of men's sexual 'desires' on women, its continued acceptance and use as a healthy pastime or sex aid supports implicitly a sexist culture which promotes dangerous misinformation about women's sexuality and the treatment of women.

Giving Up Pornography Addiction

But can or would regular users give it up without understanding or knowing that it is addictive? It is possible they could, but they probably would not, unless they could see that using pornography actually damaged their own and/or other people's lives. A convicted rapist wrote to me recently from a US prison in response to an article I'd written on addictions. He'd been on a counselling programme for several years and could now admit to what he'd done. Addicted to pornography and an inveterate liar and heavy drinker, he said:

> I got hooked on this kind of material [porn] because I enjoyed seeing women exposed in this sense. I started to masturbate to porn at thirteen years old, but it soon increased to the point that I started to abuse my ten-year-old female cousin because I couldn't find the sexual satisfaction that I so desperately needed.

Counselling had enabled him to own up:

> I have discovered through the group that I am the one responsible for the things I did and that just because I have these addictions doesn't mean I can use them as a scapegoat to get around my problems. The things I did to my cousin were very demeaning and damaging . . . I don't want to do this to anyone ever again and I want to find out the real reasons that I read pornography, masturbated and manipulated people with my lying so that I can help others who might have the same problem that I do.

It is also possible, although rare, for people to stop acting on their pornography addiction without fully comprehending the **196** political, social and personal implications. The stopping point can be when they realize how manipulated and demeaned they are by their addiction. There is plenty of evidence from smoking, alcohol and drug abuse of this phenomenon. One of my clients gave up drinking when she woke up after an alcoholic 'blackout' and was disgusted to find her own vomit all over her bedroom. Another client gave up hard drugs after he had been left standing in the rain, like a wet stray dog, for several hours waiting for a 'fix'. In both cases, their lack of dignity, their powerlessness and loss of control humiliated them eventually into wanting to take control of their lives and to retrieve some self-respect.

Similarly, some men are beginning to feel degraded by their addiction to pornography, which is a barbaric representation of women as pieces of meat for their sexual consumption. One of my clients, who is trying to be 'anti-sexist', has struggled long and hard to change himself, and tries to be an exemplary ally to women. But whenever his partner is away he finds himself conjuring up memories of films and magazines he has seen in order to masturbate. He now realizes he does this when he feels most lonely, disconnected and needs some quick comfort. But the fact that he uses images of women upsets him deeply as he genuinely wants to treat and see women as equals. Yet, the sexually arousing and sexist images and feelings surface in his imagination the minute he turns his mind to his pornographically influenced imagination.

However, few people have the chance to analyse or understand what has happened to them during their early sexual conditioning. Awareness about psycho-sexual distresses surface usually only when people are ready to deal with them, and even then, remembering can be very traumatic and painful. The sign that something is 'wrong' is often when they seek advice and help for sexual 'problems'. The counselling techniques I use involve helping people to understand what has occurred and giving them the choice to stop self-abusive behaviours and addictions, including compulsive sex and pornography. At each point it is, however, a very individual choice. I have observed that the conscious decision to stop behaving in an addictive way can be very empowering as it begins to break the cycle of addiction. On stopping, people usually begin to feel a mixture of relief and terror: relief at having permission to stop and terror at the feelings (such as fear, isolation, grief, boredom, frustration, loneliness, self-loathing, humiliation and physical pain) underlying the addiction. The crucial transition comes when they begin   **197** to feel better without the props, feel more alive and happy without artificial stimuli. They also begin to redefine what is pleasure and fun in their lives.

However, it is not an easy task and many people who decide to give up their addiction to pornography will still find it a struggle:

> It's left me feeling a bit dislocated, really, trying to develop a new understanding of sex and sexual relationships. In some ways that's nice because I was aware of feeling dissatisfied with the pornographic images I was carrying around, but at the same time . . . when something that's been a larger part of your life than you've realized is diminishing, what do you put in its place? It's a case of building from scratch.[14]

But as well as the fear of the unknown, giving up a sexual addiction also can bring a new sense of self-worth, confidence and self-validation, particularly *because* it offers hope of a new way of being. The 'pull' to act on the addiction will usually continue to surface, especially when people are in a sexually stimulating situation and/or feeling strong, negative emotions. But if they are able to release the painful emotions underlying the addiction itself, and understand their origins and purpose, the addictive urges and behaviours will eventually disappear.

Blaming Men

The most controversial implication of acknowledging that pornography is in any way addictive is that it appears to relieve men of blame and seems to exonerate any actions that may result from their use of pornography. Yet, to develop a viewpoint which does not blame or attack them for using or being addicted to it, but which provides information about the links between pornography, the misinformation and harm it perpetuates and its role as an addiction in their lives, is surely a way forward. The challenge is for men to take full, unequivocal responsibility for their thoughts and actions, whether they are addicted to pornography or not.

Women are rightly angry at their mistreatment, and the mistreatment of children, but the desire to blame men, to mistreat them in return, to take revenge, is actually to capitulate to another undesirable form of powerlessness which nearly always has the effect of cementing men's sexism even further. Some women channel a lot of fury into blaming men about sexual violence to women. While this anger is perfectly understandable, it usually fails to have the desired effect of ending violence to women. Acknowledging that pornography is addictive does not let men off the hook. But it does recognize that they are caught in a cycle where they are hugely exploited and demeaned by capitalism and, indeed, by patriarchy. At the same time, it is perfectly acceptable for women (and men) to demand that men give up pornography and the sexist attitudes and behaviours that it endorses and stimulates. Pornography is one of the places that the personal is political for men, where consciousness-raising and tough decision-making really can make a political difference. For women, it might well be more powerful to direct their anger at the sources of sexist misinformation and conditioning, including the pornography industry itself.

Further, as women begin to own up to their own addiction to pornography, it will become easier to see and talk about how both men and women are exploited by capitalism (which seeks to create markets and profit from these addictions) and patriarchy (which seeks to maintain gender-stereotyped roles). Understanding the addiction to pornography, in all its functions, mechanisms and manifestations, and deciding to give it up, will be a necessary, powerful, although sometimes uncomfortable, step on the road to complete sexual liberation.

Notes

1. Corinne Sweet, 'Men and Pornography' (12-minute feature), *Woman's Hour*, BBC Radio 4, 4 October 1989.
2. Susan Griffin, *Pornography and Silence* (London: Women's Press, 1981), p 20.
3. Peter Taylor, *Smoke Ring: The Politics of Tobacco* (London: Bodley Head, 1984), pp. xviii-xix.
4. Quoted in *Pornography and Sexual Violence: Evidence of the Links* (Minneapolis Hearings) (London: Everywoman, 1988), p. 127.
5. *Looks Can Kill* (Leeds: I-Spy Productions, 1988).
6. See Bea Campbell, *Unofficial Secrets: Child Sexual Abuse – The Cleveland Case* (London: Virago, 1988); E. Driver and A. Droison (eds), *Child Sexual Abuse: Feminist Perspectives* (London: Macmillan, 1989); Clodagh Cocoran, *Take Care! Preventing Child Sexual Abuse* (Dublin: Poolbeg Press, 1987).
7. Clodagh Corcoran, *Pornography: The New Terrorism* (Dublin: Attic Press), p. 4.
8. Interview with Ted Bundy. Associated Press, 25 January 1989, p. 4.
9. Minneapolis Hearing, op. cit., p. 120.
10. 'What You Feel About Pornography', *Cosmopolitan*, March 1990, pp. 8–12. See also Chapter 16 for a discussion of survey results.

11. J. Williams, 'Porn for Women', *Marie Claire*, October 1988, pp. 70–6.
12. Susanne Kappeler, *The Pornography of Representation* (Cambridge: Polity Press, 1986), p. 48.
13. Interview with Ted Bundy, op. cit.
14. Sweet, op. cit.

PART THREE
Pornography and Evidence of Harm

11 The Child Pornography Industry: International Trade in Child Sexual Abuse

TIM TATE

'Child pornography' is a misleading term. This is not the tawdry glamour of *Playboy* centrefolds, nor yet the gory gynaecology of hard-core. In fact it is not pornography in any real sense: simply the evidence – recorded on film or video tape – of serious sexual assaults on young children.

Still people choose to confuse it with adult pornography, lending it an air of spurious legitimacy and titillation, an aura of faintly harmless 'naughtiness'. When in 1988 the British government announced plans to make possession of child pornography an offence, a (woman) columnist in *The Times* opposed the legislation on the grounds that the problem was not sufficiently serious to warrant such 'censorship': 'One is revolted at the idea of children posing for pornographic pictures, but while the use to which the pictures may be put in someone's mind is abhorrent, I can't really see that simply photographing a child exploits him.'

Perhaps if child pornography was made up of innocent holiday snaps of naked children playing happily on the beach, she might have a point. But it is not, and the uses to which it is put are not merely in the mind.

Child pornography ranges from posed photographs of naked and semi-naked children, through more explicit shots of their genitalia thumbed apart to still, film and video recording of oral, vaginal and anal sex. Frequently the children are required to urinate on adults or each other. Almost invariably they are coated with semen when their abuser ejaculates over them. Occasionally they are photographed having sex with an animal.

Dealers' catalogues describe accurately the contents of child pornography videos:

> . . . Three exceptional Lolitas of 10, 10 and 11 get together on a playful base and it doesn't take long for them to get naked and start to play with each other's hairless pussies . . .

Many of us wonder what little girls of about 11 think about sex. This film gives you the answer . . .

When this little girl starts swinging with her mother and father things really happen . . . Pissing, sucking, you name it and those three are doing it . . .

Sweet 10 years old Lolita does not feel well and goes to the doctor . . . it does not take him long to get her pussy . . .

Plenty of action from the younger stuff. See small girl lowered onto giant prick and treated nasty . . .

14-year-old Lolita schoolgirl is drawn into a web of vice, including bondage and whipping. A must for Lolita fans.

Nor are teenagers or those just about to go through puberty the only victims. 'One of the most graphic pictures I have seen in a child pornography magazine is of a baby,' said Jack O'Malley, a US Customs agent specializing in child abuse and pornography. 'Her little body was almost completely engulfed by the hand of the adult male in the picture – his hands almost completely covered her body. The photo itself shows him ejaculating semen over her stomach.'

The reality of child pornography is that it cannot be produced without a child being sexually abused. Failure to grasp that essential truth – which, above all else, separates it from adult pornography – has lain behind twenty years of legislative confusion throughout the world. And in those twenty years child pornography has become established as a world-wide commodity.

Those catalogues quoted from, above, were sent to customers in Great Britain, Europe and the United States in the summer of 1987, more than a year after dealing in child pornography had finally become illegal in every Western nation. Most states had introduced statutes outlawing commercial dealing several years earlier. Holland was the last country to ban the production, sale and promotion of child pornography. It had resisted pressure from its European neighbours and the United States for several years before, grudgingly it appeared, falling into line.

The Dutch government knew then – as it knows now – that Holland is the junction-box of Europe, and that even after its prohibition, child pornography was freely available in Amsterdam, Rotterdam and The Hague. But little or no commercial child pornography was ever actually photographed in Holland. Historically, Dutch pornographers either simply published the material or sold it as part of their regular stock. The authorities took the view that so long as Dutch children were not involved it was not a matter for them.

The single largest geographical source of commercial child pornography has been Scandinavia, particularly Denmark. In 1969 Denmark removed all restrictions on the production and sale of any type of pornography. The result was a short-lived explosion in adult pornography, and the birth of commercial child pornography.

The godfathers of this birth were two existing adult pornography producers, Peter Theander and Willy Strauss. Strauss had already earned a reputation for excess by the time he launched *Bambina Sex* in 1971. Strauss claims it to have been the world's first child pornography magazine. First or not, *Bambina Sex* no. 1 featured photographs of a man having sex with a very young girl. The pictures had come from the collection of a paedophile who asked Strauss to bind and sell them. Most subsequent child pornography magazines followed this pattern of printing, and often soliciting, photographs of children from their abusers.

Theander was responsible for commercializing child pornography films. Between 1971 and 1978 his company, Colour Climax Corporation, produced a series of at least thirty-six ten-minute films, with titles such as *Sucking Daddy*, *Fucking Children* and *Little Girl Sex*. These 'shorts', marketed under the brand-name 'Lolita' were professionally made with titles, music and lighting. Without exception they show the oral, vaginal and anal abuse of (generally) pre-pubescent boys and girls. Colour Climax also produced child pornography magazines – *Children Love* and *Nymph Lovers* being typical titles.

Both Theander and Strauss – and by extension the dealers to whom they supplied child pornography – were acting quite legally under the relaxed Danish legislation. In fact, as the British *Report of the Committee on Obscenity and Film Censorship* (the Williams Committee) noted in 1979, Danish law enforcement deliberately chose not to examine too closely the origin of some of the material:

> The abolition of the prohibition of pornography is fully reflected in what is freely obtainable in Copenhagen ... A significant proportion of the publications we saw [in Danish sex shops] featured children, and although the Danish authorities told us that they do not hesitate to act where cases come to light in Denmark of children being used in the production of pornography, there are **205**

no restrictions on the material itself, and the authorities appeared to assume in the absence of evidence to the contrary that the children were photographed elsewhere than in Denmark.

Denmark finally banned the production, sale and distribution of child pornography in 1979. But by then it was too late: Theander and Strauss had been rivalled in the production of commercial child pornography by photographers and film producers across the country. Nor was the material confined to a domestic market. Danish child pornography was enthusiastically distributed throughout Europe and the United States. Strauss has claimed he sold 19,000 copies of the first issue of *Bambina Sex* alone, and went on to produce up to fifty other titles.

In Dordrecht, outside Rotterdam, a young homosexual paedophile took note. Born on 7 January 1943, Joop Wilhelmus was to become one of the most notorious producers of commercial child pornography and a distinct embarrassment to the Dutch police.

Wilhelmus, also known as Wilhelrus and occasionally as Jomannus Cornelius Christaan, is responsible for the most widely-traded child pornography magazine, *Lolita*. By 1972 Wilhelmus had acquired a criminal record for taking indecent photographs of minors; but it was not until 1987, facing a charge of procuring young boys for sex, that the Dutch authorities forced him out of business. By then he had produced fifty-five issues of *Lolita*. He is also believed to have been the publisher of a particularly unpleasant 'sister' magazine, *Incest*.

Lolita itself was A5 format with a colour cover of a naked child, frequently no more than five years old. Some of the photographs inside were of toddlers either displaying their genitalia or being sexually abused. Wilhelmus often included an editorial plea for new material, without which the magazine could not continue:

> This magazine can only exist if you help us! Send us photos from your collection. (*Lolita*, 41)

> We desperately need more photos from private files . . . (*Lolita*, 48)

These editorial pleas amounted to an incitement to its purchasers to abuse more children and mail the evidence to Wilhelmus. Typically they would receive cash or future issues of the magazine in return.

206   *Lolita* also provided a contact service for its readers, enabling them to advertise both for child pornography and child sexual partners. Issue 55 contained this, all-too-typical classified advert:

> English gentleman, 37, paedophile, wishes to meet a mother with Lolita daughter or lady with paedophile feelings with view to marriage.

Earlier issues had carried similar adverts – some giving an indication how widely distributed the magazine had become:

> Pretty mother with pretty young daughters invites enquiries from gentlemen anywhere who are interested in meeting us or in photography. (*Lolita*, 48)

> Single man, 28, wishes to meet girls and boys 9-13 years. Often travelling in Holland and Germany. Photo please. (*Lolita*, 41)

> Who can give the address of a good paedophile club, preferably in the district of Copenhagen? (*Lolita*, 29)

Perhaps we should be grateful to Wilhelmus for highlighting the symbiotic relationship between child pornography and paedophilia. Not only does the production of child pornography require the sexual abuse of a juvenile, but those who buy it more than once are paedophiles themselves. 'If a man buys child pornography he does so for one reason and one reason alone,' according to Ray Wyre, who runs Britain's only full-time clinic treating paedophiles. 'The reason is that he wants to have sex with children. The fact that he may not have done so is more likely to be a question of availability or the fear of getting caught than revulsion at the very concept.'

The United States postal service – which, like US Customs, runs an extremely successful anti-child-pornography programme – supports this view. Its statistics show that at least 80 per cent of those it identifies as purchasers of child pornography are active abusers. 'The rest either haven't had the opportunity to abuse or more probably haven't been caught yet,' one postal service special agent warned.

A study by Chicago police develops this thesis. In almost 100 per cent of their child pornography arrests during 1984 detectives found photographs, films and videos of the child pornography customers having sex with other children. The pictures had been taken by the men themselves. Frequently they would trade them with other paedophiles.

These collectors of child pornography have become the **207** industry's new producers. If the commercial production of child pornography magazines and films has ceased, its place has been taken by individual paedophiles recording themselves abusing children in photographs and on video. These are then sold, bartered or exchanged with other abusers. In effect, legislation aimed at eliminating child pornography has merely eliminated the middle man, requiring paedophiles to deal directly with each other.

The American government – the only Western administration to take the issue seriously – identifies child pornography as one of the world's largest cottage industries. The Department of Justice estimates it to be worth between $2 billion and $3 billion a year. More chillingly, the department claims producers have filmed the abuse of more than one million children in the United States alone.

Toby Tyler is a detective sergeant in San Bernardino County sheriff's department and an associate clinical professor of paediatrics at Loma Linda University, California. He is also one of the two most knowledgeable experts on child pornography in the world. (The other is Jack O'Malley of US Customs.) Tyler works for the 'Crimes Against Children' detail and has studied the way the child pornography industry works. He has also been able to identify some of the children it uses:

> Today the industry has changed and is very different from the commercial business of the 1970s and early 1980s. Now the producer is generally the abuser, and he will trade rather than sell his material – or if he does sell, he only does so within a tightly-knit group of fellow paedophiles. There are still a few commercial dealers who will charge huge prices – particularly for new material: that's where the billions of dollars come in. But it originates in little rings. Then the little rings become bigger because the paedophiles in them will be members of many rings, and will sell or exchange their material throughout. What you have to remember is that although the 'legitimate' industry is no longer operative, the abuse of children for child pornography continues, and will always continue for as long as there are paedophiles who want to buy it.

Tyler has seen the same pictures appear many times in different magazines. Although the abuse they record may have taken place years before, the industry continually recycles them. **208** Issue 48 of Joop Wilhelmus's *Lolita* magazine featured a Victorian picture spread headlined as 'exciting photos taken of Lolitas in action when photography was just starting'.

More recently, in May 1988, Jorgen Jensen, a Danish dealer, boasted to an undercover US postal inspector that he had a store of 300 mint-condition child pornography magazines, including 150 multiple copies of *Sweet Linda* and *Sweet Patty*. The photographs which made up those magazines were of two pre-pubescent Florida girls and show them being severely abused in a hotel bedroom in Orlando. The pictures were taken by Eric Cross, a US-resident British paedophile in 1974. Cross took the negatives to Denmark to be published. Fourteen years later child pornography dealers like Jensen were able to reproduce them at will. Cross was jailed in 1978 for producing and distributing child pornography throughout Florida. While in prison he managed to set up and run a new child pornography dealership before being discovered and given an extra prison term. Jorgen Jensen was sentenced to thirty-seven months in Boston's Salem gaol and fined $40,000 for selling more than 250 hours of child pornography videotapes to undercover postal service agent John Dunn.

The sheer quantity of material at Jensen's disposal surprised Dunn. By 1987 it was widely believed that major commercial child pornography dealers were a thing of the past. Yet when Dunn contacted Jensen at his Copenhagen adult pornography store he was immediately offered – and subsequently sold – nine videotapes:

> The child pornography scenes on these nine videotapes total twenty-seven hours' viewing time, and depict pre-pubescent minors engaging in sexually explicit conduct including masturbation, oral-genital intercourse, genital intercourse and the lascivious exhibition of the minors' genitals. Based on my training and experience I believe some of the children are as young as six or seven years of age.

Dunn paid approximately $950 for each of these tapes. Jensen then offered a further 250 hours of child pornography tapes, to be delivered personally in the USA, if Dunn agreed to pay a $10,000 deposit and the air fare.

When the postal service agent met the dealer on 5 May 1988, Jensen revealed he had a secret store full of child pornography near his shop in Copenhagen's red-light district. In the warehouse were master videotapes of the entire Colour Climax *Lolita* **209** film series, and the 300 mint-condition magazines. He also described thirty of the promised 250 hours of child pornography as 'new material', some of it depicting the abuse of an eleven-year-old German girl in 1987. Nor were these idle boasts: when Danish police raided the store they found the contents exactly as Jensen had claimed.

Jorgen Jensen's operation gave US agents an indication of the current state and scale of the child pornography industry. At the same time as Jensen was dealing with Dunn, an English paedophile was arrested and could have given British police their first insight into the extent of the business.

John Bulloch was convicted in 1985 for thirteen counts of indecency or indecent assault and one offence of gross indecency (buggery) with two twelve-year-old girls. He received a thirty-month prison sentence. Investigating officers either failed to look for or did not find any evidence of child pornography. None the less, Bulloch, an articulate forty-four-year-old single parent, had been running a profitable child pornography business as a by-product of his paedophilia:

> I started with a Polaroid camera and progressed from there to a videocamera, making films of the girls I was abusing. I had contacts with several men who were involved with the pornography business: they put a financial proposition to me which I agreed to, and I went into full commercial enterprise.

That 'full commercial enterprise' involved recording on videotape his oral, vaginal and anal abuse of a series of twelve-year-old girls from a local school:

> It was a pretty lucrative trade – it fetched in a fair amount of money, sometimes up to £200 per film. In the beginning I would make between three and six videos a week; in the end I was turning out two or three films a day sometimes. I had five video machines going just to copy the films. I knew that some of them were going abroad, but that didn't really concern me as I was happy with the money I was making. Also I was basically getting what I needed: sex with young girls.

In a two-year period Bulloch admits to having abused and filmed more than 200 girls aged between twelve and fifteen, before selling them to other paedophiles:

> When I started off I had about two or three dozen customers, but then it escalated and towards the end I must have had a

hundred or so customers on a regular basis. Some of those were wholesalers who took a few dozen tapes off me, and then I'd receive a cheque or cash in the post. I would say that in my town alone there are thousands of people who enjoyed the child pornography tapes I made. I couldn't really make enough copies for the people that wanted them.

Bulloch represented the new breed of child pornographers: abusers who produced their own material for sale or exchange. If commercial dealers like Jorgen Jensen will always exist, they will be outnumbered by the self-producing paedophiles.

So much for producers and dealers. Who, then, are their customers, and why do they seek out child pornography? Toby Tyler said:

A paedophile involved with a child or with several children realizes that his victims will grow older and out of his age or development preference. The paedophile also recognizes that he will have 'dry' periods in his life when he has no victims to molest. Paedophiles therefore have a compelling need to record the acts of physical molestation with their victims.

They will use whatever tools are available, ranging from memory, a simple written diary through a computer-recorded diary to photographs, films or videotapes. These are then viewed at will by the molester for self-gratification. Interviews with offenders consistently reveal that masturbation normally accompanies the recollection of past molestation.

That pattern alone should be enough to refute the 1970s Danish theory that child pornography acts in some way as a safety-valve, allowing the paedophile to indulge his fetish without abusing more children.

Ray Wyre reinforces the point:

Child pornography can never be a safety-valve both because the children in it are being abused, and because the paedophiles use it to validate their feelings, to make them feel they are normal. In that way it lowers their inhibitions about going out and abusing children rather than preventing them from doing so.

Law enforcement specialists now categorize typical consumers of child pornography as 'collectors'. The word is well-chosen: paedophiles are frequently obsessive about the mass of child pornography they accumulate, intricately filing, indexing and cross-referencing their collection. Toby Tyler said: **211**

Men who make child pornography often amass substantial private collections of the material. We have to realize that child exploiters rarely, if ever, destroy their collections of child pornography. They may exert great effort to secrete their collections when threatened with discovery, but their collections form such an important part of their lifestyle that destruction is rarely considered. I personally have discovered collections accumulated by paedophiles during a forty-year career of molestations.

In America where, unlike Britain, there is no federal statute outlawing simple possession of child pornography, some collectors have sued police departments for the return of their collections even after conviction for dealing or producing.

The importance of child pornography to paedophiles is not lost on British police. A 1988 internal policy review report from the Obscene Publications Branch (TO13) stressed the point:

As regards paedophiles and child pornography, 'collection' is the key word. Paedophiles do not merely look at or view child pornography – they hoard it and save it. It becomes their life's work in many cases and represents a focal point for their most cherished sexual fantasies. There are a number of characteristics to a 'collection' which are of particular interest to those engaged in an investigative role:

(i) *Importance*. It is normally one of the most important things in the life of a paedophile. He will spend considerable time, trouble and money on it, though normally making no profit whatsoever.

(ii) *Constant*. No matter how much pornography he has, a paedophile cannot get enough and he will never throw any away.

(iii) *Organized*. A paedophile invariably maintains detailed, neat and orderly records. Collections are carefully organized and maintained. In recent years computers have been used by paedophiles to store data.

(iv) *Permanent*. A collection will be moved or hidden by a paedophile if he believes he is under investigation, but whatever the circumstances it is most unlikely that he will destroy it. Collections have been known to be left in wills by one paedophile to another.

(v) *Concealed*. Due to the illegal nature of his activity the paedophile is concerned about the security of his collection – but even so he must have ready access to it at all times. Hiding places depend on his living arrangements. If he lives alone or with others who share or know of his preference then the collection will be less well concealed, but it will generally be concealed in his controlled space either at home or . . . work.

(vi) *Shared*. A paedophile often has the need to show or tell others about his collection. He will seek validation for his efforts and may boast and brag about the time, effort and skill which it has taken to gather the collection together. This feature may be exploited at interview.

Sadly, too few British paedophiles are interviewed by police. The TO13 report highlights the fundamental relationship between paedophilia and child pornography. Yet not only are there just six full-time child pornography specialists within the squad (and none outside London), but no Obscene Publications Branch officer is allowed to become involved in the investigation of actual 'hands-on' abuse. Their expertise in the patterns of paedophilia is excluded: time after time local police left to investigate alleged child sexual abuse simply do not know to look for the collection of child pornography. Yet if they did, and managed to locate it, the photographs and videos would provide irrefutable evidence to convict the paedophile. Case studies both in Britain and in America show that such specialists are also a key factor in identifying and counselling the victims of that abuse.

Collectors of child pornography use it for far more than validating their feelings or solo masturbation. The same Scotland Yard report lists the other uses:

> (i) *Blackmail*. The paedophile must ensure secrecy of any sexual activity with a child who has already been seduced – the existence of sexually explicit photographs can be an effective silencer and it can also be used to pressure them into continuing silence.
> (ii) *To lower the inhibitions of children*. It may convince a reluctant child to engage in sexual activity or pose for sexually explicit photographs, and that the activity is acceptable. Sex education books and manuals are also often used in the same way to lower the inhibitions of children, as is the showing of adult pornography.

Toby Tyler's experience of paedophiles confirms the TO13 report:

> When they are initiating their efforts to effect the sexual abuse of a child they exhibit pornography to the target victim, capitalizing on the natural sexual curiosity which children have. This may be done by allowing the child to 'accidentally' discover the material, after which the exploiter will ensure that he catches the child with the material to create a sense of guilt in the child. The child will then be reassured 'that it will be our secret'. This creates a very important component in child molestation cases – secrecy.

213

Len, a sixty-four-year-old British paedophile, used exactly this technique to molest several hundred boys between six and twelve years old:

> I used to leave the child pornography just lying around the house, and when the boy saw it he would naturally be interested in it. Then I'd go alongside him and cuddle him and eventually there would be a situation where I could put my hands on the parts I was interested in. From there onwards it was easy. In my case the pornography would invariably be men having sex with young boys, behaving with them as I would wish to with the boy in the room – buggering them. That's often what I ended up doing, and I used child pornography to get the boys more quickly. For that reason alone it can never be a safety-valve. But there's an even simpler reason: at the time you're looking at the pictures it's fine – but you're not going to look at them all day. So when you get out into the open you see another pretty boy you know what you want to do and you've seen it in the pornography.

Len sexually abused young boys for more than forty years without being caught. Even when he was arrested (for indecent exposure) the police never looked for his collection of child pornography. Len is a typical collector. He is also a typical active paedophile: for most of his adult life he had sought out employment involving children. For two decades he had even been a foster parent: he now admits he molested many of the 200 boys who passed through his care.

In 1985 the US Senate organized a formal series of hearings to investigate the nature, extent and organization of child pornography. As part of its inquiry on 15 February a sub-committee of senators heard evidence from a convicted long-term paedophile, Joe Henry. Henry first identified what had been a formative factor in his developing paedophilic behaviour: he had been molested and buggered at the age of twelve by a next-door neighbour. By the time he was twenty-four he himself had abused fourteen young girls. It is now almost universally accepted that an abused child is extremely likely to become an abusing adult. 'Eventually,' Henry testified, 'I put together a photograph collection of 500 pages of children in sexually explicit poses. Before long films started coming in so I bought a film projector.'

Within a year he had become involved in a classic child pornography ring, paying a fellow paedophile for sex with three **214** eight-year-old girls who were photographed throughout:

At the time this was the height of my paedophilic experiences. It was a dream come true . . . I wrote Duncan and described what the trip meant to me: 'I really don't know what I enjoyed the most of all the wonderful things that happened – there were so many to choose from. If it weren't for all the pictures here on the desk I would think it was all just a fantastic dream . . .'

I recount these letters, Senators, not to appear sensational, but only to try and convey just how deep my obsession was. I spent virtually every waking moment thinking about the children I molested. This type of letter writing is very typical of paedophiles. Paedophiles survive through explicit letters and the purchase or trading of child pornography, because live victims are not always available.

The children Henry molested with Duncan's help subsequently appeared in Joop Wilhelmus's *Lolita* magazine (issues 29, 30 and 31). The pictures show three sad-faced little blonde girls in a variety of explicit poses and having sex with unidentified adults. The man who sold the photographs to *Lolita* was the Florida-based child pornographer Eric Cross.

Henry told the inquiry:

> You might wonder what these children are really like. How do they act when they are with a group of men molesting them? Truthfully, they are manipulated psychologically to such a degree that their facial expressions are blank, as though they are thinking 'Just get it over with'. Do they cry or fight off my advances? Usually not. Remember in the child's mind they think they are as guilty as I am. They think other little boys and girls don't do this, so they must not be good children. They are overwhelmed with shame much of the time, and simply comply with the wishes of the adult. Can you imagine what must have gone through the mind of little eight-year-old Yvonne as her father would deliver her to yet another strange man who would keep her for hours at a time, molesting her whenever he got the urge to do so? One of my most vivid memories was of Lisa . . . the second time I saw her it was obvious someone in the group of men had brutalized her, possibly raped her. She told me she didn't want to be photographed, and she also said 'Please don't hurt me. Just please don't hurt me.'

People who cannot see the harm in children posing for pornographic pictures and people who are concerned about censoring the freedom of paedophiles and child pornographers might wish to consider the meaning of freedom from the point of view of the child. As child pornography is a record of child sexual

abuse and because the production of child pornography is part
of the abuse of children, criminalizing the possession of child
pornography is one of the few ways of targeting the abusers and
of tackling the abuse.

12. Images of Children in the Media: 'Soft Kiddie Porn'

MICHELE ELLIOTT

An article entitled 'My Image of Fashion', published in the *Sunday Times* magazine on 14 October 1984, featured the Japanese photographer Eiko Ishioka. One of Ishioka's specialities is posing children in what she called 'erotic, high-fashion fantasy'. The text accompanying Ishioka's photographs described one of her advertisements as a confrontation with an 'ageless child – boy or girl – gazing with knowing, sexy eyes'. The cover depicted two little girls about nine years old with bare nipples highlighted.

Apparently, the kind of advertising images fostered by Ishioka are effective. In the time that she worked for a major Tokyo store, her adverts were partly responsible for the annual turnover rising from £31 million to £576 million. Youth and sex combined in advertising are money-spinners. When sixteen-year-olds become too old, the only option left is younger and younger models.

'I hate to bother you with my little PERSONAL PROBLEM,' says the caption over a beautiful two-year-old on the front of a greeting card. Curiosity aroused, you look inside. She is sitting in her nappy, no other clothes. The caption reads, 'BUT I'M HORNY!!' The card, published by Mark 1 from the US, is readily available in stationery shops throughout the UK.

Who would you send the card to, and for what purpose? Another card shows a pin-up of a topless model with a two-year-old below. She is clad in underwear and looking inside her vest to compare herself with the model. Yet another has a baby with a birthday cake adorned with one candle. Inside, face covered with cake and icing, the baby says, 'Sex is bad for you, but a little piece never hurt any one.'

What is the concern? The messages in the adverts and cards are that children are sexy, cute and 'asking for it'. It is 'cute' to portray children looking sexy or talking sexy. These adverts and cards are not pornography in the accepted sense. But children's images are being sexualized because they sell and they are published for general consumption. Without our knowing, soft-core child pornography has crept into our everyday lives and most of us are unaware that this has happened.

Most people will never encounter hard-core child pornography. Without doubt it would disgust and horrify them. The images of small children and babies, looking helpless, being degraded and assaulted by adults are beyond the wildest imagination. Child pornography is easily condemned. Yet we are now seeing daily images of children being used as sexual objects to sell products: everything from nappies, clothes and baby foods to perfume, posters, greeting cards and records. While most advertisers are careful to portray children as children, some have stepped over the bounds.

A record release by an English pop group called Photomakers features a girl aged eight staring into the camera with made-up eyes and pouting lips. One of the songs is called 'Plaything', another 'Please Can I Have Some More'. Some more what? The double message is that children are sweet, innocent and sexy. The girl on the cover is 'asking for it' and available. The album is a paedophile's delight. Another record has a nine-year-old, again made-up and wearing a slinky dress. She is posed against a bar in a 'come-hither' manner. The title of the album is 'Naughty'. The implication is that the child is naughty in a sexual sense. A little Lolita just waiting to be taken.

Paedophiles claim that children are wicked little creatures, wanting and waiting for sex and throwing temptation in the paths of unsuspecting adults. One paedophile said that he could not be expected 'to resist the advances of children. After all, they know exactly what they are doing when they give you those knowing looks.' Perhaps he was reading the *Sunday Times* magazine in 1988 when it featured a twelve-year-old model, Milla, seductively posed with her sweater unbuttoned to the navel. She is described as having 'an erotic head on a babe's body: wanton and innocent in equal measure', as well as a 'siren's head mounted on a prenubile body'. Milla was doing well in the fashion and advertising world which is 'fascinated with beauty and with notions of gently toying with the forbidden'. She will make millions and never know the joys of childhood.

Even those who argue against such exploitation of children may make matters worse if they are not careful. A 1988 edition of *Harpers & Queen* magazine described the 'Lolita Syndrome' by saying that 'the increasingly popular notion that women peak at thirteen' is bewildering and discouraging. The entire article was against the notion of young girls being used sexually. Yet it was illustrated with a posed picture of a young model lying on a bed in a tightly-fitting, black crêpe de Chine slip with breasts prominently displayed. Why? It was prurient and unnecessary. A good article making important points was overshadowed by a 'double message'. This is often the case in women's magazines where the editorial content and the advertising images contradict each other. Articles extol women's independence while adverts portray women as sexual objects to sell everything from make-up to tea-bags.

Society cannot claim to abhor the sexual abuse and exploitation of children (or women) in pornography and yet allow the portrayal of children (or women) as sexualized objects in the popular press and in advertising.

It is alarming that we are becoming used to seeing children overly made-up and posed in provocative ways. Turning the pages of a children's clothes catalogue, it is no longer surprising when four-year-olds with red painted lips sell blue jeans or underwear. Athena, which sells millions of cards and posters in the UK, puts out a poster called 'Cool Kid'. According to a *Sunday Times* survey, it is the most popular poster sold in the UK. It shows a child about age four or five, heavily made-up, wearing fishnet tights and sunglasses, looking off into the distance.

We are becoming desensitized to these images. We buy them to adorn our walls. It becomes the norm when respectable magazines and products use children and sex to get their messages across. Chanel produced a Christmas advert in 1983 in which a young girl appeared, in make-up and naked from the waist up, holding a bottle of perfume. It was entitled 'Tiny Treasures – Fabulous Christmas Fantasies'. The copy reads, in part: 'jasmine and gardenia for seduction with just a hint of innocence . . .' The message: it is desirable to be child-like and seductive. The implication is that children are available sexually and that youth is the most desirable form of sexuality.

Paedophiles will tell you that this is true: that children are not only desirable sexually, but that children want to be sexually involved with adults. In his book about paedophilia, Tom O'Carroll argues that children have the 'right' to have sexual relationships with adults and that we are denying them that right with oppressive laws. Tom O'Carroll is the founder of the Paedophilia Information Exchange (PIE) which has proposed **219** that the laws be changed to allow children to have 'consensual' sexual relationships with anyone. The claim made in his book is that children as young as four can make 'informed decisions' about having sex with adults.

The images of children described here would please paedophiles. They would say that children pose in sexualized ways normally. However, looking at the faces of these children, it is obvious that the frozen smiles and pouty looks are not natural. Anyone who deals with children or who is a parent knows that children are active. It is *not* natural for children to be posed provocatively. The photograph in one newspaper of the newly crowned five-year-old – bright lipsticked mouth, carefully coiffured hair – sitting absolutely still with a frozen smile on her face is unreal. Children do not naturally sit or look that way. Ask any parent.

Why is it so important? And can anything be done? It is important because 'soft kiddie porn' is contributing to the problem of child sexual abuse. It is condoning the use of children in inappropriate sexual contexts. It is desensitizing the public and setting new standards for what is acceptable. It is strengthening the argument of paedophiles that children are asking for sex. It is exploiting and dehumanizing children *without* their informed consent. It is glamorizing children as sexual objects. It is saying to children that adults agree with the idea of them being sexualized. It is suggesting to other children that this is a desirable way to be portrayed. It is undermining the fabric of childhood: children should be protected, loved and nurtured, not used and abused.

There are a number of steps that can be taken to try to curb this trend to 'normalize' the sexualization and abuse of children. People can:

- write to the Advertising Standards Authority and complain about inappropriate adverts
- refuse to buy products which use children in sexualized ways
- tell manufacturers what they are doing and why
- become more aware of how children are being used
- think about things like discos for eight-year-olds – tell schools and organizations that it is not appropriate to dress up little girls like Playboy bunnies
- allow children time to be children – they have their whole lives to be 'grown up'

- write to MPs for laws forbidding children to be posed seductively or provocatively

It is possible to do something about soft kiddie porn, and get images withdrawn that offend. Recently a television programme, *Friday Now*, featured two postcards entitled 'Woman Child'. The images were of a young girl, inappropriately dressed and made-up. The manufacturers were contacted and asked their views. 'Harmless fun,' said their representative. 'What if our viewers don't agree?' replied the commentator. 'We'll remove the cards from sale,' was the reply. Within thirty minutes, the station had over 1,000 calls; 98.9 per cent of the callers disliked the cards. They were withdrawn from sale. It is possible to make a difference.

13 Women's Experience of Pornography: UK Magazine Survey Evidence

CATHERINE ITZIN AND CORINNE SWEET

In the US women had a number of opportunities during the 1980s to speak in public about the harm they have experienced in their private lives as a result of pornography. In 1983 there were the hearings held by the Minneapolis City Council when they were considering whether or not to enact civil rights legislation against pornography. In 1984 there were hearings held in four US cities by the National Organization of Women (NOW), and there have since been hearings held by the US Senate.

In addition to the public hearings there have been a number of surveys carried out in women's magazines to discover women's attitudes to and experiences of pornography. In the US in 1985 *Woman's Day* magazine published the results of a small questionnaire survey of its readers which found that 25 per cent had experienced sexual abuse linked with pornography, 80–90 per cent felt pornography encourages violence against women and 75 per cent thought pornography should be illegal. There have also been major sociological surveys of women's experience of pornography-related sexual violence funded by government agencies.[1]

In the UK, there have not as yet been any legal or public forums in which women can speak out about the harms of pornography. Nor has there been any government- or institutionally funded research on women's experience of pornography-related sexual violence, or on the effects of pornography on men. But many thousands of women have been given the opportunity to communicate their views and experiences of pornography through surveys carried out by two leading national women's magazines, *Company* and *Cosmopolitan*. There are some obvious limitations to research of this nature. The readership of these magazines is largely young, and more middle-class than working-class. Also, the samples are self-selected. But in the absence of other research, the data obtained from these surveys have provided the first large-scale source of information on women's experience of pornography in the UK. The results certainly suggest the need for further research on women's experience of pornography-related sexual violence and discrimination based on a representative sample.

There is some irony in the fact that these magazines, through the personal concern and commitment of their editors, have provided a platform for women, because the magazines themselves are not unconnected with the pornography industry. The same company, COMAG, distributes *Penthouse, Men Only* and *Forum* as well as *Cosmopolitan* and *Company* and even the feminist magazine *Spare Rib*. Furthermore, as part of their image and marketing strategy, these magazines publish advertisements which draw on, reflect and sometimes replicate the representation and treatment of women in pornography. Indeed, 14 per cent of the readers who responded to the *Cosmopolitan* survey actually categorized its ads as pornography.

THE *COMPANY* SURVEY

The *Company* survey was carried out in March 1988 and the results published in June 1988.[2] The magazine received a larger than usual response to the feature on pornography, along with many letters which expressed strong support for campaigning against pornography and telling in graphic, disturbing detail of the ways in which pornography had been used against women.[3] Many respondents prefaced remarks with comments such as, 'I am no rampant feminist, but . . .' or, 'I don't hate men, but . . .', and it is quite clear that many women feel that if they take a stand against pornography, men immediately categorize them, to quote one reader, 'as humourless, man-hating lesbians'.

There was an overwhelming consensus that pornography was 'distressing' and 'offensive'. Ten per cent admitted to finding pornography sexually arousing, despite strong negative feelings about it.

> I feel very strongly that porn belittles the role of a woman, making her a mere object of gratification to males who, whatever her qualifications as a person, are very likely to judge her by physical attributes.
>
> Seeing porn before being mentally able to deal with its implications may well frighten us into believing we have to act in a certain manner or adopt specific roles during sexual intercourse. Seeing

223

porn can feed inadequacies, highlighting hang-ups and frustrations which could follow through into our adult relationships.

I think that porn can be sexually arousing, even to someone like myself who finds it abhorrent. Sexual fantasies can often involve the exploration of things that we find most frightening/disgusting/degrading, and pornography feeds off those fears.

Forty-three per cent of respondents said they had been the victims of sexual abuse, and 98 per cent believed pornography encouraged violence against women.

My boyfriend has assaulted me several times. He was brought up in a house where porn was freely available – even all the mugs were in the shape of a woman's body with tits. He has since thrown away all his mags, taken down his topless calendars and is now writing to support your campaign.

I am a rape crisis counsellor and overheard one man say that after looking at a page 3 girl who 'appealed' to him he went home and 'didn't half give the wife one.'

I recently left my husband, a respectable middle-class medical consultant. It has taken two years to understand that I was not deserving of his need to tie me up, whip me and humiliate me in order to get sexual satisfaction. His 'ideas' came from pornography on which he spent a lot every month.

My ex constantly claimed that porn was a natural release for a man's frustration. We were both at university at the time; he was a socialist and claimed the sexes should be equal. But when it came to sex he was a totally different person. I was constantly compared with photos and expected to get into the positions shown. I was seldom allowed to say no.

Ninety-seven per cent favoured legislation against pornography. 'I know there will be a problem with black-market porn if it is banned altogether, but better that than the current situation which encourages men to regard all women in terms of sex appeal first.'

THE *COSMOPOLITAN* SURVEY

The *Cosmopolitan* survey was carried out in November 1989 and the results published in March 1990.[4]

The Data
Over 4,000 readers replied:

96 per cent were women

71 per cent were aged between nineteen and twenty-nine
48 per cent were from London and the South East
31 per cent were from the North and the Midlands
58 per cent were single
94 per cent were heterosexual
Average age of losing virginity: seventeen and a half.
20 per cent first had sex under age sixteen
21 per cent were students
25 per cent were in the clerical/secretarial/service sector
32 per cent were in professional/scientific/technical/ management and administration
61 per cent earned under £10,000 per annum

First Contact with Pornography
When?
Average age of first contact with pornography: fourteen and a half
36 per cent had seen pornography by age twelve
61 per cent had seen pornography by age sixteen

Where?
64 per cent had seen it first at home or at a friend/relative's house
16 per cent saw it first at school
20 per cent saw it first in public places (shop, street, work, college, party, public transport)

How?
49 per cent came across it 'accidentally'
45 per cent were shown it by someone
Only 7 per cent chose to see it

What?
69 per cent first saw adult/men's magazines
28 per cent first saw 'illegal' pornography (sex with children: 1 per cent; with animals: 4 per cent; rape: 4 per cent; anal/oral sex: 19 per cent)
8 per cent first saw violence to women
58 per cent first saw sexual intercourse (36 per cent heterosexual, 18 per cent lesbian, 4 per cent gay men)
17 per cent first saw group sex/orgies

Most Common Reactions

66 per cent did not enjoy seeing pornography

32 per cent felt disgusted, 32 per cent felt offended and 31 per cent felt guilty

18 per cent felt frightened

30 per cent believed it had had long-term disturbing or detrimental effects

Subsequent Contact with Pornography

81 per cent see pornography either occasionally or frequently

Of these, two-thirds do not see it by choice

Of the third who see it by choice:

　63 per cent looked at it out of curiosity

　26 per cent used it to masturbate on their own

　31 per cent felt aroused, but found it offensive

73 per cent never buy pornography

1 per cent buy pornography frequently

8 per cent buy pornography occasionally

Half of those who buy pornography are single

34 per cent have shared pornography with a partner

　Of these, one in ten were forced to do so

　51 per cent either had reservations or did not like it

　34 per cent felt sexually aroused, but guilty

Pornography in the Family

25 per cent of family members used pornography

Of these, 52 per cent were fathers, 30 per cent brothers, 2 per cent step-fathers and 12 per cent parents (gender unspecified)

78 per cent used it secretly

36 per cent were shocked, 17 per cent felt angry, 33 per cent were confused and 41 per cent were disturbed or upset to discover the use of pornography in the family

33 per cent felt it impaired and 7 per cent felt it destroyed family relations

Participation in Pornography

3 per cent had participated in making pornography

Of these, three-quarters were models, actors or strippers; a third were forced to participate in pornography by father, brother or partner; a third did it for money; a quarter felt bad about it at the time, and half felt bad about it in retrospect

Pornography and Sexual Violence
  13 per cent had been sexually abused as children
  34 per cent had been raped (10 per cent) or sexually assaulted
(24 per cent)
  60 per cent had been sexually harassed
  60 per cent had experienced verbal sexual abuse
  Pornography was known to have been used in the act in:
    14 per cent of the rapes
    14 per cent of the sexual assaults
    12 per cent of the sexual harassment incidents
  82 per cent believed pornography degrades women
  85 per cent believed pornography contributes to sexual violence against women
  72 per cent believed pornography contributes to sexual inequality

Defining Pornography

An effort was made to design the questionnaire in such a way as to enable respondents to define pornography in their own terms, and there were four different questions seeking a definition of pornography.[5] Respondents were first asked for an open-ended 'write-in' answer in response to the question: 'Briefly, how do you define pornography?' The question was non-directive and respondents answered it in a variety of ways.

Nearly one-third (32 per cent) defined pornography as sexually explicit material or sexual acts. But by far the largest proportion defined pornography in terms of the harm it does to women. Forty-one per cent defined it as degrading or humiliating or violent to women. Nearly a quarter (23 per cent) defined it as disgusting or indecent or offensive. Only 3 per cent replied that pornography was 'OK', 'not all bad' or 'fun'.

In a second question, respondents were asked to classify a number of different kinds of material which is usually regarded as pornography according to whether they regarded it as 'fun' or 'harmless' or 'offensive' or 'pornographic'. They were told they could tick one or more items in the following categories: Page 3 girls, adult magazines, 'special interest' magazines, pin-up calendars, sex phone lines, sex/blue videos, strip shows, live sex shows.[6] On average only 3 per cent classified any of these items as 'fun', presumably the same 3 per cent who had volunteered in the previous question that pornography was 'OK' or 'fun'. While Page 3 girls and pin-up calendars were 'only' classified as pornographic **227** by one-fifth of respondents, two-thirds found them offensive. This – together with the response to the previous question – suggests that women define pornography in terms of how it makes them feel.[7] Respondents could give more than one answer and the total number of responses to the categories of offensive and pornographic was very high indeed in each case: 80 per cent found Page 3 offensive and pornographic; 84 per cent found pin-up calendars offensive and pornographic; 91 per cent found adult/men's magazines offensive and pornographic; 93 per cent found strip shows offensive and pornographic; 94 per cent found sex phone lines offensive and pornographic; 96 per cent found 'special interest' (e.g. sex and violence) magazines offensive and pornographic; 97 per cent found sex/blue movies offensive and pornographic.[8]

The third question was also open-ended and requested a 'write-in' answer to the question – 'Is there anything else you consider to be pornographic?' Having answered the previous questions, 58 per cent did not answer this question and 7 per cent answered 'nothing' or 'no comment'. However, this question produced data on the 14 per cent of respondents who regarded the use of women in some advertisements as pornographic.

The fourth question was aimed at identifying how women regarded pornography. This provided thirteen categories and respondents were invited to tick more than one. Eight of the thirteen categories invited *positive* responses to pornography and most of these (five items) came first in the list: i.e. 'harmless', 'fun', 'helpful', 'educational', 'fantasy'. The positive responses that came later in the list were: 'good for couples (improves sex life)', 'good as a sexual outlet' and 'prevents sexual violence to women'. One category invited a neutral response ('not something I ever think about') and one category invited a combined positive and negative response ('offensive, but I still find it arousing'). Only three categories invited a potentially *negative* response to pornography: that it 'degrades women/men', 'contributes to sexual inequality' and 'causes sexual violence to women'. This question was therefore biased in favour of a *positive* response to pornography. However, 82 per cent of respondents said pornography degraded women/men, 74 per cent said that it causes sexual violence to women, and 72 per cent said that it contributed to sexual inequality.[9]

Discussion of the Data
The proportion of respondents who first saw pornography as children was unexpectedly large. More than a third had seen it

under the age of twelve, two-thirds had seen it under the age of sixteen and one in seven had first experienced pornography under the age of ten: evidence that existing laws to 'protect' children from the influence of pornography were failing to do so. First contact included exposure to 'illegal' pornography, including sex with children and animals, rape, anal/oral intercourse and violence to women.

Although women were curious (53 per cent), their feelings on first seeing pornography were overwhelmingly negative: a third felt disgusted, a third felt guilty, a third felt offended, one in five felt frightened, and a third said it had long-term disturbing or detrimental effects. Overall, two-thirds said they did not enjoy it. Significantly, there was evidence that those who had had early contact with pornography had become 'desensitized' to it. Those who had contact with pornography under twelve and sex under eighteen were more likely to regard pornography as 'harmless fun'.

There appeared to be a correlation between childhood exposure to pornography and sexual experience below the age of consent (sixteen). More than a quarter of those who first encountered pornography at the age of twelve or under first had sex under sixteen. And women who had sex under sixteen were more likely to have seen pornography at an early age. Early initiation had a lasting impact on later life.

> When I was ten my family was visiting my uncle and aunt's house. I was sitting next to my father when my uncle gave him a bound volume of "adult" magazines. I looked over his shoulder, but I couldn't believe what I saw. I felt everything I was going to grow up to had been made dirty and cheap, only for titillation.

There was evidence of causal links between pornography and sexual violence to women. Respondents were asked if they had ever been subject to sexual harassment, verbal sexual abuse, sexual assault, rape or child sexual abuse. They were then asked 'if yes, did the person responsible use pornography during the act?'[10] A third of the sample had been raped or sexually assaulted and in 28 per cent of these cases pornography had been used in the act:

> I was raped eleven years ago. The man who raped me was a friend of the people I shared a flat with and I knew he regularly watched pornographic videos of a very offensive nature.

I was raped by an ex-boyfriend who came to my house after we'd split up. I couldn't cope with the magazines and films he used and the things he wanted me to do. He scared me to death. After viewing this crap he'd turn into a monster and get violent if I refused what he wanted. When he raped me he was like that too, his eyes were just crazy and I was nothing more than a piece of meat.

The causal link between child sexual abuse and use of pornography was also clearly made by some women:

When I was six years old, my brother (then fourteen) was given or bought some 'adult' magazines and he used to show them to me when our parents were out. Then he began to sexually abuse me. He often used to read the magazines before he abused me. I was abused at three to four years old by my grandfather – I remember finding some 'adult' magazines at his flat once. For years I was abused by my grandfather and brother, but felt too guilty to tell anyone. If our parents went out on a Saturday night my brother would invite a few friends around. They'd bring their magazines and sit around joking about women's bodies. Then my brother would make me strip and straddle the bath while one by one they'd sit underneath me having a look at my genitals . . . consequently I find any pictures of women displaying their genitals very disturbing.

Thirteen per cent of respondents had been sexually abused as children.

I was abused, molested, insulted and frightened by my older brother when I was seven and he was thirteen. He had a waist-high stack of pornographic magazines. It is something I will never, ever forget. Pornography is about hate for women, power over women, revenge on women, ridicule and contempt of women.

Sixty per cent of respondents had been sexually harassed and pornography was known to have been used in twelve per cent of the sexual harassment incidents:

When I was nineteen I was assaulted by a man at work. I know for certain that he'd been looking at pornographic magazines before he attacked me – he was sexually turned on by them and had to relieve himself of his feelings.

Sexual harassment on the street also occurs. One reader described how she gets verbally abused when she passes building-sites because of her breasts:

My large bust presumably means I am available and an easy lay. I feel these ridiculous connections can only come from Page 3-type porn where big equals no brain.

Some models and ex-models also wrote in about their experiences:

At eighteen I modelled nude for a *Men Only*-type magazine. I did it mainly for money (which I never got), but also fun and curiosity. It was part of a sophisticated, open lifestyle (as I thought then), an outcome of the sexually-liberated sixties. Now thirty-six, I've been sexually assaulted twice, harassed verbally and offended many times by male sexuality in its most disturbing form – sexual lust cut off from emotion.

Eighty-one per cent of respondents saw pornography frequently or occasionally as adults. Two-thirds did not choose to see it. Of the third who saw pornography by choice, 63 per cent said they looked out of curiosity and 26 per cent used it to masturbate. A third said they shared pornography with a partner. Of these, over half had reservations or did not like it. Using the pornography created confused and contradictory feelings. A third found pornography sexually arousing, but they also felt guilty and found it offensive.

This letter is typical:

When my ex-partner wanted to use pornographic magazines I went along with it because I was curious. I did find it arousing, but I also felt disturbed. Was my partner going to start seeing me as one of those women when we were in bed? It drove a wedge between us.

Some partners wanted to go further and make women act out the pornography and one in ten women were forced to use it by their partners:

My partner tried to persuade me to dress up in suspenders, etc. This was such a prescriptive request I had no space to define what was sexually arousing for me.

A former boyfriend used to make me take part in threesomes and do anal sex, which I found revolting.

He often wanted me to watch 'dirty' videos with him. Then he presented me with a vibrator so he could watch me using it. He also masturbated over my face and tried repeatedly to spank me. **231**

After repeated requests I reluctantly shaved my pubic hair 'for him'.

Ninety-five per cent of all respondents believed some forms of pornography should be curbed and 60 per cent wanted curbs on *all* pornography. An overwhelming majority, 80 per cent, wanted government legislation against it. Three-quarters felt that men need to be educated because they are unaware of the effects of pornography. One teacher of twelve-year-old boys wrote:

> They 'discuss' the so-called glamour pictures which appear daily in the *Sun*. Their manner is totally degrading towards women. The fourteen-year-olds talk about the pornographic videos which give them ideas about women being "available to men", links between sex and violence and that women are sex objects rather than people.

A problem with legislation is how to define pornography. But *Cosmopolitan* readers did not seem to find it difficult to distinguish between pornography and erotica themselves:

> I'm really *not* anti-erotica, as long as the men and women enjoy the fun equally and not men the doers, women done unto.

> I find at times that erotic movies and literature can be very stimulating within a loving relationship, but I still abhor pornography in principle. I wonder if everyone is as split as I am in this regard?

Many women were able to recognize mutual, equal, erotic sex – which they liked – as distinct from oppressively dehumanizing pornography – which they didn't like:

> To me anything which degrades women's or men's bodies and the sexual act is pornographic. I don't find images of naked people offensive nor do I find many 'love-making' scenes in films to be offensive. On the other hand I find the *Sun* and similar Page 3 tabloids pornographic in their depiction of pouting girls and breasts alongside sensationalized stories of rape and violence against women and children.

Because the *Cosmopolitan* survey[11] was a self-selected sample of that magazine's readership, further research would be necessary to discover how representative its responses might be of the general female population. However the data from the UK women's magazine surveys were consistent with data collected in a household survey of 936 women in San Francisco in 1978 which found that 44 per cent of the women interviewed had been a victim of rape or attempted rape at some point in their lives. Forced sex in which pornography was significantly implicated occurred in 1.6 per cent of the total sample, or 16,000 rapes per million. Fourteen per cent reported that they had been asked to pose for pornographic pictures and 10 per cent said they had been upset by someone trying to get them to enact what had been seen in pornography. Father–daughter incest victims reported being upset by requests to enact pornography about four times as often as non-incest victims.[12]

This connection between child sexual abuse and the subsequent abuse of women as adults was demonstrated in another survey in San Francisco, of 200 street prostitutes. Sixty per cent of these prostitute women reported having been abused as children and 73 per cent reported that they had been raped. Again, pornography played a significant part in the abuse: 10 per cent of the sample had been used as children in pornographic films and magazines. In addition, 24 per cent of the women who had been raped mentioned allusions to pornographic material on the part of the rapist, and 22 per cent of juvenile sexual exploitation mentioned the use of pornographic materials by the adult prior to the sexual act.[13]

In this survey, the relationship between sexual abuse and pornography had not been expected, so there were no questions in the interview schedule that addressed it directly. All of the data on pornography were 'unsolicited' and volunteered incidentally in the course of the interviews and will therefore almost certainly be an *under*estimate of the incidence of pornography-related abuse.

The results of the UK magazine surveys were corroborated by a survey of women's attitudes to pornography carried out by Granada Television in March 1990. Interviews were conducted with 567 women in the Greater Manchester area.[14] Nearly two-thirds were either unhappy or very unhappy about the way women are portrayed in advertising and Page 3 photographs. Over three-quarters thought magazines like *Penthouse*, *Playboy*, and *Mayfair* degrade women, and two-thirds did not think newsagents should be allowed to sell these magazines. Three-quarters were either unhappy or very unhappy about 'soft' pornography being available on satellite and cable TV. Eighty- **233** three per cent thought pornography increased the level of violence towards women.

When they are given an opportunity to speak, the vast majority of women are consistent in saying that pornography is degrading and that it contributes to sexual violence and to sexual inequality. But when they speak about their experience of pornography often they are not believed: their experience is dismissed or denied or discredited. But this evidence would suggest that the lives of ordinary women of all ages and races and social class backgrounds are damaged by pornography.

Notes

1. 'How Pornography Strikes You', *Woman's Day* (New York), August 1985, p. 16; and 'No Easy Answers', *Woman's Day*, January 1986, p. 14; Diana G. H. Russell, 'The Incidence and Prevalence of Intrafamilial and Extra-familial Sexual Abuse of Female Children', *Child Abuse and Neglect* 7, 1983, pp. 133–46; 'The Prevalence and Incidence of Forcible Rape and Attempted Rape of Females', *Victimology: An International Journal* 7, 1982, pp. 81–93. The study was funded by the National Institute of Mental Health and the National Center on Child Abuse and Neglect.
2. Catherine Itzin, 'The Case Against Pornography', *Company*, March 1988, pp. 70–1.
3. 'Loose Talk: You Answer Back', *Company*, June 1988.
4. Catherine Itzin and Corinne Sweet, 'What Should We Do About Pornography?' *Cosmopolitan*, November 1989, pp 8–14; 'What You Feel About Pornography', *Cosmopolitan*, March 1990, pp. 8–12.
5. The *Cosmopolitan* survey questionnaire was designed and analysed by a market research company, Microdat. The authors acted in an advisory capacity.
6. The market research decision to use the euphemisms 'adult magazines' and 'special interest magazines' (for sexually violent pornography) will almost certainly have confused some respondents.
7. This is consistent with existing legislation which defines pornography as 'indecent and obscene' and likely to 'deprave and corrupt'. The law never uses the word pornography.
8. Although there were flaws in the design of this question, there were additional questions against which to corroborate the answers obtained here.
9. Only 8 per cent in this question classified pornography as harmless.
10. This was one of the best and most reliably designed questions in the survey.
11. This is a slightly edited version of the article originally published in *Cosmopolitan*, March 1990.
12. D. E. H. Russell, from Declaration to the Court, Bellingham, Washington, 1989, p. 5.
13. M. H. Silbert and A. M. Pines, 'Pornography and Sexual Abuse of Women', *Sex Roles* 10 (11/12), 1984, p. 862.

14. The interviewing was carried out between 26 and 28 March 1990 by sixteen students from Manchester Polytechnic. There was no attempt to obtain a sample balanced for social class or area but some attempt was made to ensure a varied distribution of ages. Because of the large sample size the sampling error will be quite small, i.e. if the survey were carried out again tomorrow, very similar results would be anticipated.

14 Pornography and Sexual Violence: Working with Sex Offenders

RAY WYRE*

I have worked with sex offenders in a number of different professional settings since the mid-1970s. In the course of my work I have developed a model which identifies the patterns that predictably operate in the cycle of sexual abuse. I have discovered that pornography can and does function at every stage in that cycle of abuse.

There are a number of characteristics that sex offenders have in common, and there are common factors to their sexual offences. Offenders always say it was a one-off. They always say it wasn't deliberate, it just happened. They always excuse, justify, explain, minimize. They always blame the victim for the experience, or they blame something or someone other than themselves. They always have fantasies as part of what they do, but they often in the early stages deny this. And they'll always reinterpret the behaviour of the victim. They will say the victim encouraged them, or seduced them, or asked for it, or wanted it, or enjoyed it. And if the victim survives the abuse they will interpret that to mean they were in no way harmed by it. They always objectify their victim, depersonalize them, see them as a type of woman, or a stereotype, representing something they can hate and hurt. They never see their victims as individuals or as human beings, and if something does happen to make them see their victims as human, they often cannot carry out their attack.[1]

One reason why pornography is incredibly dangerous is because 97 per cent of all the rape stories in pornography end with the woman changing her mind and having orgasms and being represented as enjoying rape. Sex offenders use this kind of pornography to justify and legitimate what they do. It provides them with an excuse and a reason for doing what they do.

I'd like to explain how pornography relates to what I've

* This chapter is the edited transcript of an interview with Ray Wyre conducted by the editor in April 1990.

1. Predisposition
2. Fantasy arousal
3. Distorted thinking
4. Overcoming internal inhibitors
5. Overcoming external inhibitors
6. Targeting
7. Initiating
8. Overcoming victims' resistance
9. Reinterpreting victims' behaviour
10. New set of distorted thinking/New set of distorted fantasy
11. Normalising stage
12. Maintaining stage
13. Trapped stage
14. Ending stage

Figure 1   Preconditions for abuse: 14-stage model
© Ray Wyre

discovered about sexual abuse. I initially took David Finkelhor's model of four preconditions for abuse: a predisposition, overcoming internal inhibitors, overcoming external inhibitors and overcoming victim resistance.[2] I developed this into a fourteen-stage model (see Figure 1). The stages of the cycle include: predisposition, fantasy, distorted thinking, internal inhibitors, external inhibitors, targeting, initiating, reinterpreting victim behaviour, arousal reinforcing and maintaining. When doing an assessment of a sex offender I want to explore all of these areas. It is impossible for the offender to abuse without going through the stages of this process. If you look at all the factors involved in what I call the cycle of behaviour of an offender, pornography plays a part in certain crucial points of that cycle.

The cycle of behaviour is maintained in lots of ways. The model may be useful in diagnosing men, for example, for sexually abusing a child. But it's no good just stopping there. You need to investigate all the needs that are associated with the abuser and why he does what he does. How are those needs met? You are challenging the behaviour and trying to reduce the risk of his doing it again. Group work is a way of interrupting that cycle, reducing the risk of men doing it again. At the same time you are trying to deal with the needs, and the justification and excuses he uses to go and do it. Pornography is important here.

Pornography does predispose some men to commit sexual abuse, and I have little doubt that the predisposition for some men can actually lie solely in the area of pornography. In other words, for some men it is just pornography – and nothing else –   **237** which creates the predisposition to commit sexual abuse. I have little doubt that there are men who in reading pornography, and particularly child pornography, will acquire ideas that they will put into practice. The ideas are initiated by pornography.

Here there is, in fact, a direct cause and effect connection. I have little doubt there are some men whose attitudes and behaviour, how they see women and girls, and what they do to them, are determined by pornography. They are given ideas by getting caught up in the pornography. They then masturbate to the pornography, which creates orgasm that is directly connected to the distorted thinking of pornography. The orgasm legitimizes the distorted thinking and is also a reinforcer of the ideas and the behaviour. The actual sexual arousal and the orgasm are part of the reinforcing behaviour. Pornography makes the behaviour more acceptable and right because it reinforces the nice experience of sexual arousal and orgasm to something that is wrong. Pornography predisposes some men to act out that behaviour.

Look then at the next item, at fantasy. We don't know how many men are predisposed to abuse, but don't do it. Pornography may predispose men to rape and to have sex with children, who then don't do it. We don't know about that – yet. But we have discovered that for those men who do have a predisposition, their fantasy will always show you that they do, and pornography has a direct correlation with fantasy. Where there is fantasy, that fantasy is evidence of the predisposition. For example, if I am sitting in a restaurant with other male customers, each man in the room would know if he has a problem with children because his fantasy life would tell him that. If he has fantasies about having sex with children, then he has the problem and the potential for actually having sex with children. If he doesn't have those fantasies, then he won't have sex with children. The same is true of rape. So fantasy is very real and very important to behaviour and to predicting behaviour.

I think the feminist movement has made an important contribution to understanding rape and sexual abuse by identifying its basis in power relations. I have no doubt that this is true, but I think you miss something if you don't understand that within the power relations there are still sexual fantasy components. I have worked with the most outrageous, sadistic rapists whose whole motivation is anger, domination, putting down, controlling, but they still have a sexual fantasy element, connected to sexual thoughts during the rape. So even when they come into prison, even though their motive was anger and aggression, tied to all that is their own fantasy and thoughts and sexuality. Pornography obviously plays a very significant role in creating and reinforcing both sexual fantasy and power relations – including rape and child abuse fantasies.

There is also a tendency for fantasy to escalate. It's a danger. And if you look at some of the cases I have worked with, even the material within the pornography wasn't enough to meet their fantasy needs: so that the man who raped a mother and daughter, for example, worked out and wrote down his own pornographic fantasies, influenced by the other pornography he had in his house, which included the rape of a mother and daughter which he then carried out for real.

There is then the distorted thinking. Pornography is incredibly powerful in creating and maintaining distorted thinking, the rape myths and the child abuse myths that exist in society. Any man may have the odd rape fantasy, but rapists have more. From pornography they get rape myths: women mean yes when they say no; women ask for it; women like force – all those sets of myths. Pornography reinforces those myths. They only have to look at pornography to acquire these myths. Not only does pornography reinforce rape at the level of idea, but, as I said earlier, in using pornography men learn to experience and to enjoy rape at a 'gut' level, through masturbation and orgasm to rape. And the majority of sex offenders of all types masturbate at least sometimes to images of rapes they have committed.

I recently had referred to me a social worker who had told his supervisor that he was having sexual fantasies about children. He said he didn't know where they were coming from. But I discovered that he had a big stash of pornography, a whole suitcase full, which included a pornographic magazine with one story about father–daughter incest and another about a social worker having sex with all the girls in a girls' home. Needless to say, all the girls wanted it and were asking for it and enjoyed it. Furthermore this magazine was being sold legally in sex shops because the *photographs* were of women over the age of sixteen (made to look younger) and they had put a red dot over where the penis enters the vagina – that's how they get round the law.

But the message is that it is OK, it's good to have sex with under-age girls in your care as a social worker, that incest is good. This is the distorted thinking I refer to in my model. Pornography is amazingly powerful in maintaining that distorted   **239** thinking. So pornography certainly reinforces and can also create the predisposition to carry out abuse. It feeds the fantasy. And it creates distorted thinking.

Now we come to overcoming internal inhibitors. This is like conscience, really. It's whatever it is inside of people that stops them doing things that are wrong: our own internal set of values. Those values are never set in stone, they can be influenced, they can be changed, and I know pornography has a part to play in reducing inhibitions to rape and to child abuse. It does this by legitimizing the acts that are portrayed and by making it seem as if it is not that bad because other people do it. In pornography only 2 or 3 per cent of men who rape are portrayed as suffering any negative consequences. Whereas the opposite is happening to the women who are raped. They are all portrayed as becoming orgasmic and enjoying being raped. This distorted thinking will play a part in reducing internal inhibitions to rape.

Then there are the external inhibitors: these have to do with getting round the obstacles that may be in the way of committing the sexual assault. One example of an external inhibition would be the wife who is in the home all the time. She is in the way of a child sex abuser achieving his aims. He will have to send her out of the house. Working with sex offenders has changed my whole concept of family dysfunction: of what causes abuse and what doesn't. Women are often blamed for letting it happen but I know that men are as much grooming the wife as the child. He is as much manipulating the wife so he can abuse as he is abusing the child.

Mother-blame is essential to the psychology of the sexual abuser. Family dysfunction models actually reinforce mother-blame, and this makes the sex offenders very happy. I had a man in treatment who eventually got to the point where he could admit to himself and say to his wife: 'I encouraged your friendship with Sophie so that you would be out of the house more so that I could abuse K.' She could – and did – blame herself for being with Sophie, not realizing that he had actually manipulated it all. Or Wednesday night at the Bingo: she said, 'Oh if only I hadn't gone out to Bingo on Wednesday.' But he had actually arranged all of that to give himself access. It's essential to get all this information. You will find that pornography often plays a part in reducing external inhibitors.

The next stage in the cycle of abuse is what Finkelhor called **240** 'overcoming victim resistance' and what I call 'initiating'. Pornography is used in initiating sexual abuse in a variety of ways. It is used to show children that other children do it, as a way of getting children to talk about sex. Sex offenders use ordinary 'soft' pornography to trap children and get them interested in it. So one young man who had been sexually abused – and who was then caught sexually abusing – had been taken in by a teacher who was a paedophile. He'd been taken round the teacher's house and shown 'ordinary' heterosexual pornography. There were other boys around watching pornography and they were all involved in this naughty secret: waching pornography. Then gradually, unbeknown to them, the men involved started to suggest sexual play between them – you know, masturbate while they're watching. Of course, the boys don't know that they are the object and target of all this: they don't know that the men have designs on them. The boys just think they are watching heterosexual pornography, the stuff you buy at newsagents, you know, good twelve-year-old fun, that's all.

The men create an environment where they can have discussions and talks with the boys and make it appear harmless. The soft porn is used to soften the boys up, so the men can get access and abuse them. They introduce gay literature, they start talking about homosexuality, and say that boys go through this phase, don't they, it's just normal. Pornography is used in that way too. One man made child pornography with 200 girls. He would then play games: run a so-called soft porn video and wherever it stopped, they would act out the sexual bit that was on the screen. Pornography is often instrumental in initiating sexual abuse. In fact, it plays a part at every stage in the cycle of abuse.

I'm talking here about sex offenders. Many men see pornography and don't necessarily go out and abuse: though we are now discovering that the level of rape, sexual assault and child sexual abuse is much higher than we ever knew it to be. But the men who offend are 'ordinary' men from every walk of life. What pornography does is create a climate of thought and belief which influences attitudes towards women and children which is endemic in our society. So, although the vast majority of men will say, 'Well I don't go out and abuse because I watch pornography', what they're missing is that they're still taking on the myths those stories are portraying. That's the danger of it. It maintains that climate of misogyny. I believe that pornography influences the attitudes of all men regardless of the behaviour that takes place as a result.

If a man's wife is raped, for example, or his daughter is raped, and you look at that father or that husband's attitude or response to the rape, if he has been into pornography he will be saying things like 'What did you do to ask for it?' He will be affected by the pornography. It will be very hard for him to overcome the influence. I have known fathers slap their daughters – beat them – after they have been raped, in the belief that they shouldn't have been so stupid, or they shouldn't have dressed like that, or been looking like that, and nice girls don't get raped.

The police are also influenced by those attitudes and myths, and I know the courts are influenced. In a sense it's like the Durkheim model of suicide: the more you publicize suicide the more options you give people, the more likely you are to create an environment in which suicide takes place, and the more likely that the coroner will reach a suicide verdict because he will be influenced by that cycle. The same is true of the rape myths that are promoted in pornography.

There is a tendency to want to divide the male world into those men who are deviant and those who are normal, to suggest that deviant men would have raped whether they were influenced by pornography or not. But my experience is that this is not the case. I work with every type of man, every profession, every class: sex abusers comes from all walks of life. In prison I saw that some sadistic killers that I worked with 'progressed', one from a first sex offence of indecent assault as a teenager in a public telephone box to sexual murder. I know from work with sex offenders that they do 'progress'. The 'deviancy model', which is based on the assumption that there are deviant types of individuals who for some unknown reason do the things they do, is not accurate in my view. There are identifiable patterns to behaviour. If you have sexual harassment, sexual innuendo, inappropriate sexual gesture, at one end of the continuum, and sadistic rape at the other – all men are on it. And all men have the capacity to be influenced by pornography in the way I described earlier. So pornography can effectively push men further along the continuum of sexual mistreatment of women and children.

I am talking about all men. Women experience abuse of many kinds and at different levels from all men. We have a continuum, and we have decided arbitrarily to draw a line that says certain bits of behaviour are illegal, and that other bits of abusive behaviour are not. That line in this country has moved: you can now sack men for sexual harassment. But at one time that would never have happened and indeed sexual harassment was not even recognized as abuse: it was 'slap and tickle' or a 'bit of fun'. I believe all men are on a continuum of sexism in the same way all white people are on a continuum of racism. Implicit in this view is the potential for change – and this is very important. Men can be influenced negatively by pornography, for example, but they can also change for the better. Sex offenders can be treated and 'rehabilitated'. If men are not being influenced by pornography then they have a better chance of changing their behaviour.

I agree with Diana Russell that pornography is one of the factors that contributes to rape (see Chapter 17). I do not agree with the arguments that fantasy is something that happens in your head and that behaviour is something else. In my experience fantasy and behaviour are directly connected. I am biased here. I work with men who have already put into practice some of their sexually violent fantasies. They have more fantasies that they haven't enacted, most of them, but all of them have put some of their fantasies into practice. So I know – because all of the men I have ever worked with have put into practice their fantasies of sexual abuse – that those fantasies do get put into practice. In my experience, therefore, there is a direct connection between fantasy and action. There is also a connection between an escalation in fantasy and more extreme forms of violent behaviour.

I don't know how many men actually have fantasies and don't put them into practice. But I don't care about that. What I do know is that the more they masturbate to pornography, the more likely they will be to put their fantasy into practice. Masturbating to fantasy is part of the trigger to act out the content of the fantasy. It is the masturbation itself which both reinforces and escalates the behaviour. It blurs and it disinhibits. If men have fantasies and they masturbate to those fantasies, it leads them further towards the acting out of the fantasies. The more bizarre the fantasies are, the less likely they will have a consenting partner to comply with what they want to do. Quite enough men do enact their fantasy to make me not too concerned about men who might not put their fantasy into practice yet. I know there are a lot of men who put their fantasy into practice and it is 'society's' responsibility to do what it can to reduce the likelihood that men will commit sexual crimes, to try to ensure that men don't do it.

Men's fantasies are fuelled by pornography. It gives them ideas, and they act those ideas out. I know women have said this, and that when women say they have been raped and assaulted by men who have been influenced by pornography, they are discredited and dismissed and constantly trivialized. What women say is true. I know this because I hear it from the other side. I have met a whole range of men who have told me what they have done to women, acts which have come from the ideas they have accumulated from pornography. The ideas then go way beyond pornography. Pornography is a contributing factor to the development of what they do. When you get into the fantasy world of sex offenders you will find the bizarreness of it horrific.

Pornography is one of the factors that lead men to commit sexual offences. Another predisposing factor that leads men to rape is their own abuse as children. My experience of working with sex offenders is that they frequently were sexually abused themselves as children. Take for example some of the boys that we've already got in prison, the boys who were raped and buggered while they were in the care of a local authority in London; who then went out to demonstrate to the world that they were not homosexual by raping women. They made a declaration to this world that they are not homosexual because of their own abuse. They are now serving prison sentences. One response to being sexually abused by a man is to go out to abuse a woman to prove they are heterosexual. In one study, '75% of convicted sadistic rapists had been sexually abused as children'.[3]

Likewise, a boy in Birmingham, who raped a woman, was raped himself at twelve years old. He was buggered within a satanic cult. His sexual arousal was therefore connected to fear. Within two years of his abuse, he was phoning up women saying he was going to kill them and their children, and he was going out and raping them. His sexual arousal was connected to fear, but for other men their sexual arousal may be connected to aggression, or to pain, because those things will have been happening when they were originally abused. And those things subsequently stimulate sexual arousal. When those things – fear, aggression, pain – are associated with sex, as they are in pornography, then the pornography will trigger the abusive behaviour. And, of course, as I said before, it will also legitimate it.

Pornography is not 'just' an image: it is an image that creates **244** sexual arousal and orgasm. Through pornography men *learn* to become sexually aroused by fear, aggression, pain and violence. Those things are not inherently sexual, but pornography makes them sexual. Pornography is part of an active process whereby men use it to masturbate, for sexual arousal and orgasm, and in the process internalize the experience of sexual violence as erotic.

This also can happen against their will to women who have been raped or abused. This experience can condition their sexual arousal to abuse and their sexual fantasies may be about abuse. In this sense, women survivors of rape and incest have had their fantasy life abused. If this is not recognized, and it generally is not, it can be confusing to women. Women are told not to feel guilty, not to feel responsible, not to blame themselves, but in the privacy of their own homes they may find themselves masturbating and fantasizing about their abuse. When a man abuses a woman or a child, he is also abusing the whole sexual way that that person operates or thinks. Because this happens and it is not recognized, women feel guilty and think that they are responsible for what happens. This is another thing which the man has done to them and which they may not even be aware of. A woman, now in her thirties, whom I was counselling, had had a dog introduced when she was being sexually abused as a child and she is still fantasizing about the dog. She can't share that with anybody. It's just too horrific for her to share it.

This happens with women and girls who are sexually abused; and the same thing happens with boys who are abused. One man who was raped as a boy on an allotment later re-enacted his first sexual abuse on somebody else by taking a boy to an allotment. But for boys there is another development going on as well: there is also displacement. They will blame someone, they will defend and excuse and justify and will not take responsibility. I may be angry with the person who abused me, but I am powerless – or feel powerless to deal with my anger for that person so I take it out on someone else.

I do not want to suggest that all sexually abused boys or girls grow up to abuse because I think that's another myth, which we don't want to continue to reinforce.[4] Boys who are abused have got enough to deal with, as girls have, without thinking that they are going to grow up to abuse just because they were abused. But being abused does create a tendency to re-enact the abuse, in the role (or position) either of the abuser or of the victim. We are a totally victimizing society at all levels. If I have a hard day and take it out on my kids, my response to my kids is nothing to do with them. I'm over-reacting because I'm fed up and tired and irritable and I have been conditioned to take it out on others. Everyone does this. But we have decided as a society to draw some lines: the mother hitting the kid or half killing the kid who has just asked for a packet of sweets at a check-out is somehow regarded as not abusive. But this is really just the socially sanctioned abuse of children.

There is also emotional abuse. I know, for example, that you can sexually abuse a child without ever actually touching that child. If I emotionally abuse my daughter, she'll never grow up to be the woman sexually or emotionally that she could become. This is sexual abuse but we don't acknowledge it. There is also passive sexual abuse. One boy raped his sister because his dad was sexually abusing the girl, giving her all the goodies and attention. So the boy says 'fuck you' to the sister and he rapes her. He'd never been physically sexually abused himself. But he had watched his father sexually abuse his sister and give her all the attention and he was resentful. Instead of seeing it as the father's problem he then raped his sister. He wasn't sexually abused in the usual sense. But he was still sexually abused, what I call passively sexually abused.

I do not think that men are born rapists, that they are inherently violent or aggressive. I don't know how much of our make-up is genetic or predetermined and how much is determined by parental influence. But I do believe society is a powerful influence and can change how we are. I've gone from working on submarines in the Navy to setting up a progressive clinic for treating sex offenders, a place for sensitivity and care. Had I stayed in the military, I would have destroyed the world. If I had been told to press the button, I would have done so. And I would have cheered and shouted when we sunk the *Belgrano*. My attitudes towards women were very sexist, because I had grown up in a totally sexist society. People can be influenced positively and negatively. People can change. This is where there is a very strong argument for legislation against pornography, because if pornography influences attitudes and behaviour, then, in its absence, people are not influenced and there is the potential for change. Not only that, we can have positive images of sex and sexuality: I am not against nakedness, not against sexuality and the portrayal of equality within relationships.

Notes

1. Ray Wyre and Anthony Swift, *Women, Men and Rape* (London: Hodder and Stoughton, 1990), pp. 2–7.
2. David Finkelhor, *Child Sexual Abuse: New Theory and Practice* (New York: Free Press, 1984).
3. Wyre and Swift, op. cit., p. 20
4. Ray Wyre, *Working with Sex Abuse* (Oxford: Perry Swift, 1987).

15 The Experimental Research Evidence: Effects of Pornography on the 'Average Individual'

EDNA F. EINSIEDEL*

In order to draw conclusions about whether exposure to pornography leads to or causes certain effects, one would have to look at the experimental evidence for these causal linkages.

The experimental results are presented in terms of effects in the areas of arousal, perceptions, affective states, attitudes, and behaviour. Two categories of pornographic stimuli have generally been used to sort out differential effects in these areas: non-aggressive pornography and aggressive pornography (see Malamuth and Donnerstein, 1984; Donnerstein, 1983b). Some question may be raised about whether in fact these two categories are sufficiently representative of distinctions the average consumer or the public at large might make or whether these two categories afford reasonable conceptual value. Nevertheless, these categories provide a convenient way to organize the results from the experimental studies.

THE EFFECTS OF VIOLENT SEXUALLY EXPLICIT MATERIALS

The findings from studies investigating effects of exposure to sexually violent materials appear to be fairly unequivocal: measures in the areas of attitudes and behaviours have consistently demonstrated changes in attitudes and laboratory-measured behaviours, with the nature of the effect mediated by such additional factors as message cues (e.g. whether the female victim is shown to be abhorring or enjoying the rape) and individual personality differences.

Studies on the effects of exposure to sexually violent material have been conducted primarily in the laboratories of Neal

* This chapter is an excerpt from the Report entitled 'Social and Behavioral Science Research Analysis' written by Edna F. Einsiedel for the *Attorney General's Commission on Pornography Final Report*, (Washington, DC: US Government Printing Office, vol. 1, pp. 901–1033).

Malamuth (at Manitoba, Canada, and the University of California, Los Angeles) and Edward Donnerstein at the University of Wisconsin. With their respective colleagues, they have utilized three typical approaches.

The first approach generally has subjects exposed to stimuli (usually varying consent versus force), with physiological penile tumescence and self-report measures of arousal taken during exposure, followed by questionaires incorporating dependent variable measures (e.g. likelihood of rape, acceptance of rape myths and interpersonal violence, acceptance of sexual violence against women (see e.g. Malamuth and Check, 1980a, 1981, 1983).

A second approach typified by Linz (1985) has subjects exposed to one of several types of stimulus over time (neutral, aggressive, or sexually violent of the 'slasher' variety) under the guise of a film evaluation study. Prior to this exposure, measures are generally obtained on psychoticism, in part to eliminate participation by subjects who might be especially vulnerable to this type of exposure. The second phase has subjects participate in an ostensibly different study in the law school where they are asked to take part in a mock rape trial. Measures are then obtained at this point which assess punitiveness, rape empathy, and similar attitudes.

The third approach has been to expose subjects in the laboratory to sexually violent versus comparison material and assess negative effects by utilizing surrogate measures of aggressive behaviour (e.g., shock intensities on an aggression machine. See e.g. Donnerstein, 1980a, b; Donnerstein and Berkowitz, 1981).

All three approaches have different virtues which contribute to our ability to understand various dimensions to the problem. For example, the physiological penile measures of arousal provide an independent and objective means of corroborating self-reports. Surrogate measures of aggression avoid the ethical problems of 'inducing' actual anti-social behaviours and at the same time can be validated by actual self-reports of aggression in sexual behaviour. Finally, the 'massive' exposures afford a first step toward examining the longer-term effects of exposure to sexually explicit materials.

Effects on Fantasies
Only one study has examined the effects of sexually explicit materials on fantasies. Malamuth (1981a) presented two groups **249**

of male subjects with a slide-audio show. One version depicted rape and the other showed a mutually-consenting sexual encounter. Analyses of sexual fantasies which subjects were later asked to create and write down indicated that those exposed to the rape version were more likely to create aggressive sexual fantasies.

Aggressive sexual fantasies appear to be fairly common among certain groups of offenders. Gebhard *et al.* (1965) found that 'patterned rapists', or those who raped repeatedly, were significantly more likely than incidental rapists to engage often in sadomasochistic fantasies (twenty per cent versus zero per cent). Walker and Meyer (1981) found four in five of their rapists to report primarily deviant sexual fantasies while Abel, Becker, and Skinner (1985) similarly reported aggressive sexual fantasies among their outpatient sexual assaulters. What role pornography, particularly violent pornography, plays in the construction of these fantasies remains to be answered.

Effects on Arousal, Perceptions, and Attitudes

Are there differences in effects from exposure to violent versus non-violent sexually explicit material? An early study (Malamuth, Reisin, and Spinner, 1979) had male and female subjects exposed to one of the above stimuli or a neutral one. The materials presented were pictures from *Playboy* or *Penthouse* magazines for the sexual exposure and from *National Geographic* for the neutral exposure. Sexually violent depictions included pictures of rape or sadomasochism, whereas the sexually non-violent material had no aggressive elements. After viewing the materials, subjects filled out a mood checklist. This was followed ten minutes later by an assessment of reactions to rape after the subjects had viewed a videotaped interview with an actual rape victim as well as an assessment several days later in an ostensibly different study. Both types of stimulus were found to reduce the extent to which subjects perceived that pornography may have detrimental effects but neither one affected reactions to rape. Correlational data, on the other hand, showed that sexual arousal to the sexually violent depictions were significantly related with a self-reported possibility of engaging in rape.

Another study (Malamuth, Haber, and Feshbach, 1980) examined the effects of written descriptions of a sexual interaction based on a feature from *Penthouse* magazine and modified to create a violent and non-violent version for male and female subjects. In this study, males who had been exposed to the sexually violent depiction (sadomasochism) perceived more favourably a rape depiction that was presented to subjects subsequently. Subjects were found to believe that a high percentage of men would rape if they knew they would not be punished and that many women would enjoy being victimized. Finally, of the fifty-three male subjects, seventeen per cent said they personally would be likely to act as the rapist did under similar circumstances. Fifty-three percent of these males responded similarly when asked the same question if they could be assured they would not be caught.

In order to draw out the various dimensions in the portrayals of sexual violence which might explain the exhibition or inhibition of sexual responsiveness, Malamuth, Heim, and Feshbach (1980) conducted two experiments on male and female students. The first experiment replicated earlier findings that normal subjects seem to be less aroused by sexual violence than by 'non-violent erotica'. A second experiment manipulated reactions of the rape victim, with one version showing her as experiencing an involuntary orgasm and no pain. The second version had her experiencing orgasm with pain. Both male and female subjects were aroused by these depictions, with female subjects more aroused by the orgasm-with-no-pain version while the males were most aroused by the orgasm-with-pain stimulus. The authors postulated in this case that, under certain conditions, rape depictions can be arousing, particularly when the rape victim is shown experiencing an orgasm during the assault. According to the authors, subjects may have reinterpreted the events preceding the depiction of the victim's arousal so that the rape is now viewed as one that is less coercive and less guilt-inducing.

Three additional studies (Malamuth and Check, 1980a, 1980b, 1983) provide further evidence that victim reactions have a significant impact on sexual arousal and behavioural intentions. Results from one of these studies showed that both male and female subjects exhibited higher arousal levels when portrayals showed an aroused female, regardless of whether the context was rape or a mutually consenting situation. The second study (Malamuth and Check, 1980a) similarly showed that male subjects had higher penile tumuscence scores when viewing a victim-aroused rape portrayal compared to a portrayal showing victim abhorrence. Significant correlations were also obtained between the reported possibility of engaging in similar behaviour, **251** sexual arousal to rape depictions, and callous attitudes toward rape.

The effect of sexually violent depictions on attitudes has also been demonstrated with male and female subjects reporting greater acceptance of rape myths after exposure to such material (Malamuth and Check, 1980a; 1985; Malamuth, Haber and Feshbach, 1980).

In an attempt to approximate a 'real world' situation, Malamuth and Check (1981) had male and female subjects view full-length features as part of campus cinema showings. The films – *Swept Away* and *The Getaway* – represented sexually violent films whereas control subjects viewed a non-violent feature film. Dependent measures were obtained after a week in a questionnaire presented as a separate sexual-attitudes survey. These measures included rape-myth acceptance measures, measures on the acceptance of interpersonal violence, as well as adversarial sexual beliefs, measures developed by Burt (1980). Results showed that exposure to sexual violence increased male subjects' acceptance of interpersonal violence against women. A similar trend, though statistically nonsignificant, was found for the acceptance of rape myths. There were nonsignificant tendencies for females in the opposite direction. In addition to the advantage of external validity from this field experiment, the problem of demand characteristics in some laboratory experimental situations is quite effectively dealt with in this study.

Aggressive Behaviour

Donnerstein (1980a) had male subjects provoked or treated in a neutral manner by a male or female confederate, then had them view one of three films: a sexually explicit film, a film depicting a rape, and a neutral film. Results of this study show that when the target of angered subjects was a male, there was no difference in aggressive behaviour (measured by shock intensity on an aggression machine) among males in the erotic and the aggressive-pornographic conditions. However, when the target was a female, aggressive behaviour was higher only in the aggressive-pornographic film condition, regardless of provocation.

To account for the impact of victim reactions in a rape portrayal, Donnerstein and Berkowitz (1981) had male subjects angered by a male or female confederate. Following instigation, they then watched one of four films: a neutral film, a non-aggressive pornographic film, an aggressive pornographic film with a positive outcome (where the woman is smiling and offering no resistance, becoming a willing participant in the end) and the last with a negative outcome, where the woman is shown exhibiting disgust and humiliation. Subjects who were angered by a male confederate were not significantly more aggressive towards the male instigator after viewing the pornographic or aggressive-pornographic film; those angered by a female, however, showed significantly higher levels of aggressive behaviour in both aggressive-pornographic conditions, that is, those that portrayed a negative and those showing a positive outcome.

What about the effects of positive and negative outcomes on non-angered subjects? The same study (Donnerstein and Berkowitz, 1981) examined this issue using only female confederates. Results showed that, for non-angered subjects, only the aggressive-pornographic film with a positive ending elicited higher aggression levels. Subjects exposed to this version also saw the woman portrayed as suffering less, enjoying more, and being more responsible for her situation. These findings suggest the importance of disinhibiting factors that might produce a readiness to respond (e.g. anger or frustration) and message cues (e.g. enjoyment of sexual coercion) as enhancing the likelihood of laboratory aggressive behaviour. These are also short-term effects, although with appropriate cues there might be long-term effects as well. This remains speculative at this point (Malamuth and Ceniti, 1986).

A recent study demonstrates that such laboratory aggression is not always manifested when these 'enhancing' factors are absent (Malamuth and Ceniti, 1986). Two groups of subjects were exposed to either sexually violent or sexually non-violent depictions in films, books, and magazines over several weeks and compared to a third no-exposure control group. Several days later, in what was presented as a different study on ESP, measures of laboratory aggression using aversion noise were obtained in the typical aggression paradigm. No differences were found among the three exposure conditions. The authors speculated that a more immediate measure, in combination with stimuli which 'prime' thoughts and feelings relevant to the exhibition of specific behaviours, might be more conducive to an individual's performance of such behaviours.

An important study that clarifies the interaction of motivational, message and inhibitory factors as predictors of self-reported sexual aggression (Malamuth, 1986) has demonstrated **253** that (a) such factors as hostility to women, dominance and acceptance of interpersonal violence, arousal to sexual violence, and sexual experience all correlate with sexually aggressive behaviours; (b) the occurrence of these aggressive behaviours is better 'explained' or 'predicted' by these factors in combination; (c) arousal to sexual aggression correlates with dominance and hostility to women and is also an important predictor of sexual aggression; and (d) these self-reports of sexually aggressive behaviour are also correlated with laboratory measures of aggression.

Effects of Massive Exposure

In a study designed to evaluate the effects of massive exposure to sexual violence and to explore further the components of the desensitization process, a series of four studies was conducted by Linz (1985). College males were exposed to a series of 'slasher films', all R-rated, using a formula of sexual explicitness juxtaposed with much blood and gore. A typical example is a scene from *Toolbox Murders* showing a naked woman taking a tub bath, masturbating, then being stalked and killed with a power drill by a masked male. Comparisons were also made among R-rated non-violent films and X-rated non-violent films, both of which included sexually explicit scenes (the former were of the teenage sex films variety).[1]

After viewing one film per day for five days, subjects were asked to participate in what was presented as a different study – a pretest of a law-school documentary – then completed a questionnaire assessing the defendant's intentions, the victim's resistance, responsibility, sympathy, attractiveness, injury, and worthlessness.

Among Linz's findings:

- Those who were massively exposed to depictions of violence against women came to have fewer negative emotional reactions to the films, to perceive them as significantly less violent, and to consider them significantly less degrading to women.
- This desensitization appeared to spill over into a different context when subjects were asked to judge a female victim of rape. Those massively exposed to sexual violence judged the victim of the assault to be significantly less injured and evaluated her as less worthy than did the control group.
- There were no differences between subjects exposed to the

teenage sex film or the X-rated film and the control group on either pretrial measures on objectification of women, rape myth acceptance or the acceptance of conservative sex roles, or on the post-trial measures (defendant guilt, verdict, victim responsibility).

- Two films (about three hours' viewing time, about twenty to twenty-five violent acts) were sufficient to obtain a desensitization effect similar to the effect obtained after exposure to five films suggesting that desensitization can occur fairly rapidly.
- These findings were most pronounced for those subjects rated high on psychoticism and exposed to the highly sexually violent films. These individuals were significantly more likely to endorse the use of force in sexual relations, and to evaluate the victim portrayed in the rape case as less credible, less worthy, and less attractive.

The effectiveness of debriefing procedures was assessed, and the measures were found to be generally effective in reducing negative effects observed after film exposure.

Krafka (1985) used these same R-rated 'slasher' films in a study similar to Linz's but using female subjects. Krafka also used these films as stimuli for a 'violent' condition, and contrasted this with exposure to sexual violence and to an X-rated set of films. The effects of massive exposure obtained for male subjects were absent for females.

It is clear that, for males, exposure to sexually explicit materials juxtaposed with violence directed at a female target enhances callous attitudes in similar situations involving women as victims.

THE EFFECTS OF NONVIOLENT SEXUALLY EXPLICIT MATERIALS

The importance of specifying various contingent conditions under which certain effects may or may not be obtained becomes immediately obvious when one looks at the findings in this area. It is also clear that, while there are a greater number of studies that examined the effects of nonaggressive sexually explicit materials, particularly if one includes the 1970 Commission studies, the diversity of dependent-variable measures as well as **255** experimental stimuli used is also greater than in the area of sexual violence.

A number of different effects from a variety of studies have been obtained in the areas of affect, attitudes as well as behaviour.

Affective and Perceptual Responses

Wishnoff (1978) exposed sexually inexperienced undergraduate females to explicit erotic films. He found that sexual anxiety decreased while expectations about engaging in intercourse in the near future increased significantly.

Along the same lines, Byrne (1977) and Byrne and Byrne (1977) suggested that, initially, exposure to sexually explicit materials may offend and disturb some, or produce apprehension in others. These authors then hypothesized that frequent exposure reduces negative reactions and negative appraisals of these reactions. Once tolerance increases, the stimuli lead to greater pleasurable sexual fantasies and greater enjoyment, a hypothesis generally supported by their data.

Perceptual judgements have also been demonstrably affected by exposure, particularly in the areas of comparative judgements and estimations of reality. Kenrick and Gutierres (1980) found subjects' judgments of the attractiveness of an average female were lowered by exposure to media females. Proposing that such effects could be more significant in the realm of sexually explicit materials, Gutierres, Kenrick, and Goldberg (1985) did a follow-up in which subjects were asked to assess characteristics of others after exposure to slides of *Playboy* and *Penthouse* models. In four successive experiments, target persons rated were a stranger and the subject's spouse or long-term live-in partner. Both types of target persons were more negatively rated only by male subjects. Similar results were obtained after males were exposed to 'beautiful females in sexually enticing activities' (sexually provocative poses or precoital and coital activities) in contrast to males exposed to less attractive females (Weaver, Masland, and Zillmann, 1984).

This perceptual contrasting of aesthetic appraisals is contingent on whether the rated target and the comparison target are associated (Melamed and Moss, 1975; Griffitt, 1971). For example, when an individual is presented in the context of attractive friends, that individual tends to be rated as more
256 'attractive'. In the case of comparing media models with a

significant other, on the other hand (where presumably there is no association between the target and the comparison), the comparison stimulus, or the media model in this case, 'provides an anchor or contrast point for the evaluation of the target stimulus' (Melamed and Moss, 1975, p. 129).

Hatfield and Sprecher (1983) exposed males to 'a *Playboy*-type article – a romantic seduction scene designed to be arousing'. They predicted that a sexually aroused male would exaggerate a woman's sexual desirability as well as her sexual receptivity. Male subjects were then shown a photograph of 'a potential date'. Both predictions were confirmed. Aroused men, according to the authors, were more likely to agree that their potential date was 'amorous', 'immoral', 'promiscuous', 'willing', 'unwholesome', and 'uninhibited'.

Different results were obtained by Dermer and Pyszcynski (1978) in an investigation of the effects of erotica on males' responses to women they loved. They were particularly interested in whether erotica would enhance 'loving' or 'liking' responses. Males who read an erotic story (an explicit account of sexual behaviours and fantasies of a college female) reported greater romantic involvement than those in a control condition. That is, they were more apt to report expressing 'loving' than 'liking' statements to their loved ones when sexually aroused than when not sexually aroused.

In looking at the above studies as a whole, it is quite possible that stimuli that primarily enhance arousal reactions (as in the Hatfield and Sprecher, 1983, and Dermer and Pyszcynski, 1978, studies, which used textual material) enhance more 'love-oriented' responses for loved ones and 'lust-oriented' responses in a dating situation.

Effects on Behaviour

Initial studies conducted for the 1970 Commission showed either that sexually explicit materials had no effect on sexual behaviour or, when effects were observed, these were generally slight increases in those sexual activities already in the individual's established repertoire (Amoroso *et al.*, 1970; Byrne and Lamberth, 1970; Kutchinsky, 1970*b*). These behavioural effects generally occurred within a short period after exposure. However, as one of the 1970 research investigators observed, it was also possible that the effects of erotica on behavior could have been obscured in the initial body of research because two major components of the influence process were missing from the early investigations: the extended time period necessary for change to occur and the specification of the depicted behavior as well as the relationship between the interactants. (Byrne and Kelley, 1984)

While more recent studies examined the impact of non-violent sexually explicit materials after repeated exposure, others have also examined behavioural effects after short-term exposure. It is in the latter area of behavioural effects from exposure to nonviolent sexually explicit stimuli where apparently conflicting results are found.

Baron and Bell (1977) exposed male students to stimuli that included semi-nude females, nudes, heterosexual intercourse, and some explicit erotic passages. The mild erotic stimuli (semi-nudes and nudes) inhibited aggression levels whereas the 'stronger' stimuli had no effects. A follow-up study (Baron, 1979), this time on female subjects, using the same stimulus materials, found mild stimuli inhibiting aggressive behaviour while the stronger stimuli increased aggression. Both these studies measured aggressive behaviour via 'shocks' derived on an aggression machine.

In another study, photographs variously depicting 'nonerotica', nude females and couples in sexual activities were shown to male subjects (Zillmann and Sapolsky, 1977). Additionally, subjects were either provoked or unprovoked. For the latter group, no differences in aggression levels by type of stimulus were observed. No differences were observed in aggression levels for subjects who were provoked either, although respondents in this condition also exhibited lower annoyance levels. The authors explained these findings in terms of the aggression-reducing effect of relatively non-arousing but usually pleasant sexually explicit images which act to reduce annoyance or anger and, consequently, aggressive behaviour.

Along these lines, Sapolsky (1984) has suggested that content characteristics have an impact on affective states (that is, how pleasing or displeasing the stimulus is) as well as on arousal levels. The combination of these factors appears to produce differential responses.

Situational factors such as provocation and the removal of restraints against aggression appear to mediate further the effects **258** of nonviolent pornography on viewers. Donnerstein, Donnerstein, and Evans (1975) found that 'mild erotica' (semi-nudes and nudes from *Playboy*) inhibited aggressive responses in contrast to 'stronger erotica' (frontal heterosexual nudes in simulated intercourse and oral-genital contact) which enhanced aggression, particularly for previously provoked subjects. A subsequent study similarly showed that a pornographic film (black and white 'stag' film depicting oral and anal intercourse and female homosexual intercourse) increased aggression among angered males to a significantly greater extent than a neutral film (Donnerstein and Barrett, 1978).

In comparing the effects of both aggressive and erotic films on aggressive behaviour of male subjects, Donnerstein and Hallam (1978) found both types of stimulus to increase aggressive behaviour against both a male and a female target. However, when these subjects were given a second opportunity to aggress, these responses increased in the pornographic film condition for the female but not for the male target. The second aggression opportunity, the authors suggest, acts to reduce restraints on aggression against women.

In sum, the experimental effects from exposure to non-violent pornographic material appear to be mediated by a number of conditions: the strength of the stimulus to induce arousal, the affective nature of the stimulus, and situational factors such as the removal of restraints against aggression.

Effects from Longer-Term Exposure

A number of studies, both from the 1970 Commission and more recent ones, examined the effects of 'massive' exposure to pornography. 'Massive exposure' in these studies means exposure over a duration of one to several weeks. Mann, Sidman, and Starr (1970) exposed married couples in four consecutive weekly sessions to sexually explicit films or to non-erotic films (for the control group). Sexual activities were recorded in diaries by the subjects during the exposure period and attitudes toward pornography also assessed both prior to and after exposure. Sexual activities increased in frequency during exposure days although these activities were ones these subjects normally engaged in (i.e., they were not related to specific ones portrayed in the stimulus materials). An additional finding was that the reported stimulating effect grew weaker as the weeks progressed. Whether this diminution is attributable to boredom or to habituation is not entirely clear.

Howard, Reifler, and Litpzin (1971) similarly exposed male college students to heavy doses of pornographic films, photographs, and reading material during ninety-minute sessions over a three-week period. Experimental subjects could choose from among these materials and other 'non-erotic' ones during the first ten sessions. This was followed by three sessions where the original pornographic material was replaced by new material. During the last two sessions, the non-erotic materials were taken away. Control subjects were not exposed to these types of material. The findings, based on physiological and attitudinal measures, revealed initial high interest which faded rapidly with repeated exposure. After this period of unrestricted exposure, the provision of new materials failed to revive interest. Decreased penile response was measured as well as concomitant reductions in other responsiveness measures (e.g. heart rate, respiration rate, and skin temperature). While the authors interpreted these results in terms of boredom, Zillmann and Bryant (1984) suggested that habituation is a potential alternative explanation, based on the premiss that continued exposure to emotion-inducing stimuli produces declines in the arousal component of the reaction: evidence that habituation effects might be occurring.

To test this hypothesis, Zillmann and Bryant (1984) had eighty male and female undergraduates randomly assigned to a massive, intermediate, no exposure or control group. Subjects in the three experimental groups met in six consecutive weekly sessions and watched six films of eight minutes' duration each, with varying degrees of exposure to the explicit sex films. Ostensibly, the subjects were to evaluate the aesthetic aspects of these films. All erotic films depicted heterosexual activities, mainly fellatio, cunnilingus, coition, and anal intercourse, none of which depicted infliction of pain. The non-erotic films were educational or entertaining materials, all previously judged as interesting. Experimental subjects returned to the laboratory one week after treatment and were then exposed to three films of varying degrees of explicitness (pre-coitus, oral–genital sex and intercourse, and sadomasochism and bestiality) followed by measurements of excitation levels (heart rate and blood pressure) and affective ratings.

Two weeks after initial treatment, subjects were randomly assigned within initial exposure treatments to view one of the following: (*a*) a film depicting oral–genital sex and heterosexual **260** intercourse; (*b*) a film depicting sadomasochistic activities; (*c*) a film featuring bestiality; (*d*) no film. Measures of aggressive behaviour were also obtained at this point.

The results three weeks later indicated that, with increasing exposure to various explicit stimuli, arousal responses diminished, as did aggressive behaviour. Furthermore, more unusual or 'harder' erotic fare appeared to grow increasingly more acceptable, with subject evaluations that the material was offensive, pornographic, or should be restricted progressively diminishing. Measures of sex callousness suggested further habituation effects, as did projective measures of the commonality of these behaviours. According to Zillmann and Bryant, these effects were, 'evident for both male and female subjects'. Similar habituation effects after 'massive exposure' were reported by Ceniti and Malamuth (1984) for subjects who were 'force-oriented', effects which were most pronounced with exposure to sexually violent depictions. Arousal patterns were not affected, however.

An earlier report on other aspects of the same study (Zillmann and Bryant, 1982) showed that subjects also exhibited greater sex callousness, using measures developed by Mosher (1970*a*). They also showed some cognitive distortion in terms of exaggerated estimates of the prevalence of various sexual activities as a result of massive exposure.

There is contrary evidence from Linz (1985) on the effects of massive exposure to non-violent sexually explicit materials, in a study described earlier under 'Effects of Massive Exposure to Sexual Violence'. Subjects exposed to 'teen sex' films, and 'X-rated non-violent films'[2] did not show the same effects in a rape-judgement situation as in the 'slasher' films. These perceptual changes were described as desensitization to film violence and to violence against women in the 'slasher' film condition.

Another investigation into the effects of massive exposure to non-violent sexually explicit materials tested the habituation hypothesis (Zillmann and Bryant, 1987), using both male and female students and adults from a metropolitan community, and similarly examined effects of massive exposure. This time, the 'behaviour' of interest was choice of entertainment material. Two weeks after exposure, subjects were provided an opportunity to watch videotapes in a private situation with G-rated, R-rated, and X-rated programmes available. This opportunity to view was provided during an ostensible 'waiting period' between procedures, with the subject's choice of entertainment and length of viewing unobtrusively recorded. Subjects with considerable **261** prior exposure to common, non-violent pornography showed very little interest in this type of fare, choosing instead to watch more uncommon materials that included bondage, sadomasochism, and bestiality. These effects, while observable among both males and females, were again more pronounced among the former.

While habituation is certainly a plausible explanation for these findings, choice of entertainment fare on the basis of stimulus novelty cannot be precluded entirely (see Kelley, 1986). An examination of the mean amount of time spent viewing the videotapes shows that, for those massively exposed, male students watched an average of three-and-a-half minutes of 'uncommon fare' (featuring bondage, S & M, bestiality) while female students watched an average of a minute and a half, with viewing times for their non-student counterparts only slightly higher. Keeping in mind that subjects had fifteen minutes of viewing time, the graduation to a preference for stronger fare, or habituation, does not seem to be firmly supported by the data. Furthermore, the measurement situation might also be viewed as 'permission-granting', with choice of what might normally be considered taboo material being more permissible or socially condoned. One could argue that greater availability of these materials in the real world might also be analogous to an indication of social sanctions being lifted, so to speak; and the laboratory evidence obtained here certainly merits more attention, perhaps through longitudinal studies.

Further measures were obtained from the same samples of subjects in the last study described above in the areas of 'sexual satisfaction' and 'family values', both through an extensive battery of questions (Zillmann and Bryant, 1986a, 1986b). Subjects were asked how satisfied they were with their present sexual partner, their partner's physical appearance, affectionate behaviour, commitment and so forth. Their findings showed significantly increased dissatisfaction in these various areas of sexuality after massive exposure.

In the area of 'family values', a variety of questions tapped attitudes on premarital and extramarital sex, estimations of occurrences of 'sexual faithfulness' in the population, and perceptions of the institution of marriage and divorce. Again, massive exposure appears to have increased acceptance of premarital and extramarital sex and diminished the importance of the institution of marriage. These findings have to be viewed with caution, since the large number of statistical tests conducted increases the chances of obtaining false positive conclusions. Because of the complexity of the experimental procedures, the long battery of questions asked, and the absence of a measure validating the effectiveness of the cover story, we must also view these findings as tentative and worthy of further examination.

On the basis of the above findings, it appears that short-term effects have been observed in the laboratory but under very specific conditions. These conditions should be further elaborated on in future research. Massive exposure studies varying the lengths of exposure, on the other hand, suggest that certain types of effects may occur with long-term exposure. The question arises whether this is true of all types of sexually explicit stimuli that do not have any violent elements.

A recent Canadian study has tried to address this issue (Check, 1985). Four hundred thirty-six college students and nonstudent metropolitan Toronto residents, recruited by means of advertise-ments, were exposed over three videotape viewing sessions to one of three types of material, or to no material at all. The stimulus materials were constructed (primarily because no materials could be found that exclusively contained the intended manipulations) from existing commercially available entertainment videos to represent one of the following:

1. Sexual violence – Scenes of sexual intercourse which included a woman strapped to a table and being penetrated by a large plastic penis.
2. Sexually explicit and degrading – Scenes of sexual activity which included a man masturbating into a woman's face while sitting on top of her.
3. Sexually explicit – Sex activities leading up to intercourse between a man and woman.

These categorizations were validated in preliminary question-naires assessing subjects' perceptions of these materials. Results indicated that exposure to both the sexually violent and nonvi-olent dehumanizing pornography (1) were more likely to be rated 'obscene', 'degrading', 'offensive', and 'aggressive'; (2) tended to elicit more pronounced feelings of anxiety, hostility, and depression; and (3) tended to be successfully differentiated from the materials classified as 'erotica'. The patterns were less clear on reported likelihood of rape measures and reported likelihood of engaging in coercive sex acts. While those in the violent and **263** in the degrading exposure conditions reported significantly greater likelihood of engaging in these behaviours compared to the control group, an effect more pronounced among those with high psychoticism scores, those exposed to the 'erotica' stimulus did not differ significantly from either the control or both pornography conditions. The findings also have to be viewed with caution, as the exposure conditions were not completely equivalent (i.e. the no-exposure control group came in for a single session while the experimental groups came in for four sessions), a caveat Check recognizes and discusses. Finally, it is not entirely clear what differential effects on the exposure groups the preliminary instructions to all subjects might have had, which included some reference to the study being funded by the Fraser Commission on Pornography.

Similar findings were obtained by Senn (1985) for female subjects exposed over four sessions to slides of 'erotica', 'nonviolent dehumanizing pornography', and 'violent pornography'. The first class of materials was described as mutually pleasurable sexual expression between two individuals presented as equal in power. The second category was described as having no explicit violence but portraying acts of submission (female kneeling, male standing; female naked, male clothed) while the third included acts of explicit violence in the sexual interaction (e.g., hair-pulling, whipping, rape).

Both violent and non-violent pornography resulted in greater anxiety, depression, and anger than erotica, and both were also reliably differentiated from the latter on a number of affective dimensions, with 'erotica' consistently rated more positively.

These findings on non-violent, 'degrading' pornography are by no means definitive, but they do suggest the importance of examining the effects of various content attributes.

Individual Differences

Not everyone reacts in the same way to sexually explicit materials. Researchers have examined various individual explanatory variables which might explain more fully why individuals respond in different ways. We do not intend an exhaustive summary of the variety of individual attributes examined, but merely wish to illustrate that observed effects are mediated by a number of factors. Three sets of factors will suffice for discussion.

One characteristic which has been examined is gender. It has often been asserted that females are less interested in sex than males. Some of the early studies in sexual behaviour (Kinsey, Pomeroy, Martin, and Gebhard, 1953) concluded that females were uninterested in pornography and were less aroused by it. The same sex differences were reported in the national survey of the 1970 Commission (Abelson *et al.*, 1970).

Experimental findings, however, seem to suggest otherwise. Males and females in laboratory exposure situations reported the same levels of arousal in response to sexually explicit stimuli (Sigusch *et al.*, 1970; Byrne and Lamberth, 1971; Griffitt, 1973). Females, however, are also more apt to report negative affect toward erotic stimuli, that is, they report more shock, disgust and annoyance than males (Schmidt *et al.*, 1973). These differences, not surprisingly, are even more pronounced when aggressive sexual themes such as rape portrayals are employed (Schmidt, 1974). The context of the portrayal is also significant as Stock (1983) demonstrated. Female subjects exposed to an eroticized version of a rape exhibited high arousal levels, while a version which emphasized the victim's fear and pain elicited negative affective reactions and lower arousal levels. Krafka's (1985) female subjects did not exhibit the same negative effects that Linz's (1985) males did after exposure to R-rated slasher films, which the former attributed to some emotional distancing because the victim in these films was invariably female.

Personality differences also mediate effects. One personality dimension which has been examined is 'psychoticism' (Eysenck and Eysenck, 1976) which Barnes, Mamaluth and Check, (1984*a*, 1984*b*) found to be positively related to the enjoyment of force and unconventional sexual activities. Linz (1985) and Check (1985) similarly found psychoticism scores to be highly correlated with the acceptance of rape myths.

Finally, experiential factors also help explain response differences. Those with more previous experience with sexually explicit materials also tend to be less inclined toward restrictions (*Newsweek*–Gallup Survey, 1985) and also tend to exhibit more sex-calloused attitudes (Malamuth and Check, 1985) and more self-reported sexually aggressive behaviour (Check, 1985).

SUMMARY FOR VIOLENT AND NON-VIOLENT SEXUALLY EXPLICIT MATERIALS

In evaluating the results for sexually violent material, it appears that exposure to such materials (1) leads to a greater acceptance of rape myths and violence against women; (2) has more pronounced effects when the victim is shown enjoying the use of force or violence; (3) is arousing for rapists and for some males in the general population; and (4) has resulted in sexual aggression against women in the laboratory.

Malamuth's research has further demonstrated that such attitudes as rape myth acceptance and acceptance of violence against women are correlated with arousal to such materials and with 'real-world' sexual aggression, and that subjects who have demonstrated sexual aggression in the laboratory are also more likely to report using coercion and force in their actual sexual interactions. The validation of the measures used in his studies, the use of physiological measures of arousal, and the attempt systematically to examine patterns among different populations with a variety of measures—arousal, attitudinal, and behaviourial—all tend to provide the type of convergent validation we feel is required of social science evidence.

We are less confident about the findings for non-violent sexually explicit materials, and we hasten to add that this is not necessarily because this class of materials has no effects but because the wide variety of effects obtained needs to be more systematically examined and explained. We can speculate, as have others, about potential explanations regarding some of these differences. For example, Check and Malamuth (1985) have pointed to the differences between Mosher's (1970a) lack of effects on sex callousness and Zillmann and Bryant's (1982) finding of greater sex callousness from exposure to non-violent sexually explicit stimuli (using the same scale developed by Mosher) as possibly attributable to a difference in stimulus characteristics. Mosher's film, based on his own descriptions, depicted 'more affection than is typical of much pornography', while Zillmann and Bryant's (1984) material tended to portray women as 'nondiscriminating, as hysterically euphoric in response to just about any sexual or pseudosexual stimulation, and as eager to accomodate seeemingly any and every sexual request' (p. 22). Check and Malamuth (1985) maintain that the portrayal in Zillman and Bryant's study suggests 'a dehumanized portrayal of women, which had the effect of generating disrespectful, anti-female attitudes in both male and female subjects' (p. 205).

This explanation could conceivably hold for the differences
266 between Linz's (1985) findings and those of Zillmann and Bryant

(1984). Because specific atttributes that may characterize these films (other than the fact that they contain no violence) and explain their effects either are confounded (i.e., more than one factor is emphasized, making it difficult to attribute results to a particular one) or are not clearly explicated, it is more difficult to say definitively that this particular class of materials has a particular pattern of effects. There are very tentative suggestions that the manner in which the woman is portrayed in the material (i.e., whether she is portrayed in a demeaning or degrading fashion) might be an important content factor, but this is clearly an area that should be investigated. Certainly, the theoretical (and, many will argue, the commonsensical) reasons for mediating effects on the basis of content cues are already available from social learning theory (Bandura, 1977; Bandura, Underwood, and Fromson, 1975).

SOME METHODOLOGICAL CONSIDERATIONS

It is necessary to consider certain issues that pertain to experimental studies that will help clarify our evaluation of research findings. We will consider five issues in particular which are probably most often mentioned: the problem of the ability to generalize the results outside the laboratory (what researchers call 'external validity'); the problem of 'the college student' as volunteer subject; the measures used to reflect 'anti-social behaviour'; ethical issues; and the operationalization of 'pornography'.

Ability to Generalize from Experimental Findings

The problem of the 'artificiality' of the experimental situation is not new to social psychologists (see discussions by Berkowitz and Donnerstein, 1982; Littman, 1961). While it is true that the experiment is indeed 'artificial', it is so by design. If one wanted to examine if X 'causes' Y, a necessary condition for establishing such a causal connection is the elimination or control of other factors which may also affect Y. Such a condition then obviates a 'real-world' setting in which numerous factors interact and jointly impinge on the individual. Littman (1961) maintains that systematic experimental designs are designed to test 'more universal theoretical propositions that apply to large groups of human beings'. That is, they are designed to test theorized relationships about human behaviour, making the issues of representativeness of the experimental setting and subjects of **267** lesser consequence. Berkowitz and Donnerstein (1982) offer a cogent summary of arguments on this point (see also Kruglanski, 1975).

The College Student as Experimental Subject

The issue of representativeness has also been raised with regard to the college student as experimental subject, with the implication that the college student hardly represents 'real people' in the 'real world'. To reduce the issue to one of demographics is an oversimplification. If we are interested in the question of human response to sexually explicit materials, why should being in college, or being male for that matter, be a problem? As Berkowitz and Donnerstein (1982) point out, 'The meaning the subjects assign to the situation they are in and the behaviour they are carrying out plays a greater part in determining the generalizability of an experiment's outcome than does the sample's demographic representativeness or the setting's mundane realism' (p. 249).

Having said that, we also need to point out that there are, in fact, other attributes of the subject who participates in experiments involving exposure to sexually explicit materials that might have an impact on the interpretations of experimental results. Results from various studies suggest that:

1. Males, more than females, are likely to volunteer for sex-related experiments (Kendrick, Gutierres, and Goldberg, 1980).
2. Subjects who are willing to watch sexually explicit materials also tend to be sexually liberal, more sexually experienced, less anxious about sexual performance, and to have fewer objections to pornography (Kaats and Davis, 1971; Farkas, Sine and Evans, 1978; Wolchick, Spencer, and Lisi, 1983; Wolchick, Braver, and Jensen, 1985).
3. Volunteer rates drop for both men and women the more intrusive the experimental conditions. Volunteer rates dropped by two-thirds (from thirty-eight per cent to thirteen per cent) for women and by over half for men (from sixty-seven per cent to thirty per cent) with the requirement of partial undressing to accommodate physiological arousal measurements (Wolchick, Braver, and Jensen, 1985).

If participants are in fact more liberal, more experienced, and more accepting of sexually explicit materials, then it is certainly plausible that the 'error', if there is one, might be in the direction of null findings, while observed effects, particularly in the short term, might be indicative of their robustness (Eysenck, 1984). In any case, it is apparent that these other attributes ought to at least be considered in both the design and interpretation of experimental studies involving sexually explicit materials.

Ethical Considerations

While some bias may be inherent in the volunteer subject in general (Rosenthal and Rosnow, 1969) and in the volunteers for experiments involving sexually explicit materials in particular, we are constrained even more by understandable concerns regarding the more 'vulnerable' segments of the population. Sherif's (1980) observations about the lack of evaluation procedures for the effectiveness of debriefing subjects in one particular study (see Malamuth, Heim and Feshbach, 1980 for the study in question and Malamuth, Feshbach, and Heim, 1980 for response to Sherif, 1980) have prompted researchers to measure debriefing effects (Malamuth and Check, 1984; Linz, 1985; Krafka, 1985) and also to eliminate from participation those who might be more vulnerable to the effects of exposure to materials in these studies. For example, Linz (1985) measured potential subjects on a psychoticism scale and eliminated from participation those who had high scores on this measure. Krafka (1985) excluded from her female subject pool those who were sexually inexperienced because of earlier findings (Wishnoff, 1978) that when these types of females were exposed to explicit erotic films, their sexual anxiety diminished while their expectations about engaging in sexual intercourse increased. The trade-off between ethical concerns and representativeness is evident in Krafka's observation: 'Although this restricts the population to which the present results generalize, the author was unwilling to show sexually inexperienced females degrading images of sexual behaviour and, especially, pornographic rape depictions' (p. 17).

These efforts to protect subjects from potential harm are, of course, laudable and a healthy response to concerns that have been raised. In terms of the final pool of subjects who participate in pornography experiments, however, the self-selection process described above and the researcher-imposed selection process must circumscribe our evaluation of research results.   **269**

Measures of Behavioural Effects

The range of dependent-variable measures used in these studies is reasonably diverse. The use of similar measures across studies allows for better validation, and the use of varied measures also provides the advantage of convergent validation. We will focus on behavioural measures of effects in this discussion and briefly discuss how attitude measures may or may not predict behaviour.

Four categories of behavioural measures have been used in these studies.

Measures of Aggressive Behaviour

The Buss aggression machine, sometimes known as a 'shock box', has been widely used in laboratory experimeents in the area of media violence and aggressive behaviour (see reviews by Andison, 1978; Comstock, forthcoming). Donnerstein and his colleagues have used this measure to examine similar effects of exposure to violent and non-violent pornography and aggressive behaviour (Donnerstein, *et al.*, 1975; Donnerstein and Barrett, 1978; Donnerstein, 1980; Donnerstein and Berkowtiz, 1981).

The procedure usually involves putting the subject in a 'learning' situation where the subject's task as 'teacher' is to make sure that a 'learner' (usually an experimental confederate) masters a given lesson. When the learner makes a 'correct' response, the subject is instructed to reward him or her by pressing a button illuminating a light. Whenever the learner makes an error, he is punished by means of an electric shock. The sequence of response has, of course, been preprogrammed. The subject's 'aggressive tendencies' are recorded by means of the intensity and the duration of the shock which, in reality, is not received by the confederate (see Baron, 1977*b* for discussion on this measure).

While this procedure has been criticized (see e.g. Baron and Eggleston, 1972), subsequent procedural modifications have increased its validity, and it has, in fact, been found to be highly predictive of physical aggression (Baron, 1977*b*). The question, however, of this measure's predictive validity in the areas of sexually aggressive behaviour outside the laboratory still remains open since no efforts have been directed at examining this question.

Other surrogate measures of aggressive behaviour have included the infliction of aversive noise (Cantor, Zillmann, and **270** Einsiedel, 1978; Malamuth, 1983) and infliction of 'pain' on an experimental confederate in a retaliation move where the subject has the opportunity to apply too much cuff pressure in a blood-pressure reading situation (Zillmann and Bryant, 1984). Some validation is offered by Malamuth (1983) for the use of the aversive-noise measure with evidence that attitudes about real-world aggression (such as wife-battering and rape) are clearly correlated with levels of laboratory aggression against females, suggesting some linkage betwen laboratory aggression and external responses outside the laboratory.

Judgments Toward Sexual Assailants
In numerous studies, dependent measures have been obtained by having subjects respond to a rape case by evaluating both the victim and the assailant. While perceptual measures are most often used in this instance, one could also presumably consider delivering a verdict or a sentence as 'behaviour'. In these instances, the presentation of a mock-trial situation provides an element of mundane realism to the experimental situation. The studies by Linz (1985) and Krafka (1985) are excellent attempts at further diminishing demand characteristics of the experimental situation, since the location of this phase of the experiment was conducted at the law school moot court, where subjects were asked to evaluate what is purported to be the details of an actual rape case. An earlier study, a field experiment, by Malamuth and Check (1981) provides what may be the best procedure for eliminating demand characteristics and the measurement of effects in a setting that affords both control and realism. In this study, subjects were asked to watch the experimental films which were being shown on campus as part of the regular campus film programme. Dependent measures were obtained a week later in what was presented as a public opinion survey. More studies in this area are clearly called for.

Choice and Viewing of Pornographic Fare
Zillmann and Bryant (forthcoming) utilized a unique way of measuring behavioural effects of exposure by examining subjects' choice of entertainment fare in an unobtrusively measured procedure. In their study of the effects of massive exposure, the following procedure was used to determine subjects' preferences for entertainment fare after they had been repeatedly exposed to pornography or to a neutral stimulus in the control condition: the subjects were met individually by the experimenter and   **271**

informed of a brief delay caused by equipment problems. The subject was then taken to another waiting area (ostensibly another student's office) with a television set, a video tape-recorder, and some videotape cassettes (including general interest and adult tapes ranging from 'common erotica to graphic depictions of relatively uncommon sexual practices') and invited to feel free to watch. To ensure the subject knew he could watch in privacy, the subject was told the experimenter would call him on the phone to report to the designated room. Unknown to the subject was the fact that each casette tape was programmed to emit a unique signal such that when the tape was played, an event recorder also recorded the amount of time spent watching.

The advantage of this procedure is its experimental as well as ecological realism.

Self-Reports of Aggressive Sexual Behaviour

Two types of measures have been used to describe sexually aggressive behaviour: a behavioural inclination measure operationalized by a self-reported likelihood of raping and using force in sexual interactions (see Malamuth, Haber, and Feshbach, 1980; Malamuth, 1981; Briere and Malamuth, 1983) and a self-report inventory developed by Koss and Oros (1982) and used in several studies (see Malamuth, 1982; Malamuth, forthcoming; Check, 1985). The latter includes a range of sexual-behavioural measures, from saying things one does not mean to obtain sexual access, to using various degress of physical force.

An instrument developed by Burt to measure attitude (1980) has been used in a number of studies (Koss, 1986; Linz, 1985; Krafka, 1985; Malamuth and Check, 1981; Malamuth, 1981) to tap three dimensions: the acceptance of rape myths; the acceptance of interpersonal violence; and the acceptance of violence against women. The following are examples of the rape myth acceptance measure:

> When women go around braless or wearing short skirts and tight tops, they are just asking for trouble.
>
> Women who get raped while hitch hiking get what they deserve.

In evaluating these attitudinal measures and the laboratory measures of sexual behaviour, two important questions have been raised to which we have alluded earlier. First, do attitudes predict behaviour? And second, do laboratory measures of aggressive behaviour predict actual aggressive behaviour?

On the first question, Malamuth and his colleagues have demonstrated a consistent correlation between Burt's (1980) attitudinal measures and their own measures of behavioural intentions (Briere and Malamuth, 1983; Malamuth, 1981; Malamuth, Haber, and Feshbach, 1980; see also Malamuth and Briere, 1986, for a discussion on the attitude-behaviour question in the area of sexual aggression). Koss (1986) has similarly demonstrated a high correlation between these sex-steroryped beliefs and self-reports of sexual aggression. We do not have these same attitudinal data from those members of the population who provide the more extreme measures of sexually aggressive behaviour – rapists – which might provide another means of validating the attitude–behaviour postulate. However, interviews of incarcerated rapists appear to show similar acceptance of rape myths (Scully and Marolla, 1984). A number of studies are also reviewed in Malamuth and Briere (1986) which support the correlation between attitudes and non-laboratory aggressive behaviour.

Operationalizations of Pornography
Researchers, like lay people or the courts, have had some differences in the operationalization of 'pornography'. Malamuth (1984), for instance, uses the term with the qualifier that 'no pejorative connotaton is intended', and points out the difficulty of operationalizing the distinction between 'aggressive versus positive types of pornography' (p. 29). However, he also relies on Steinem's (1980) separation of 'acceptable erotica', in Malamuth's terms emphasizing the notion of what Steinem called 'shared pleasure', as against 'objectionable pornography', or what Steinem referred to as 'sex in which there is clear force, or an unequal power', and described stimuli in his research as using material belonging to the latter. Others have similarly used the term to refer only to sexually violent material, and have used 'erotica' to refer to non-violent sexually explicit material (Abel, 1985). Still others on occasion simply use the term 'erotica', and employ subclasses of aggressive and nonaggressive 'erotica', (Donnerstein, 1983). Senn (1985) and Check (1985) have operationalized pornography to include both sexually violent and non-violent but degrading categories, and have classified all other sexually explicit portrayals as 'erotica'.

In examining the types of stimulus used in these studies, it is clear that a wide diversity of research stimuli has been employed. These have ranged from partial nudity (Baron, 1979; Baron and Bell, 1977) to various levels of sexual activity, from 'implied' to 'explicit', covering a varied range of behaviours – masturbation, homosexual and heterosexual intercourse, oral – genital and oral – anal intercourse, fellatio, cunnilingus, bondage, and bestiality. Sources of materials have also run the gamut from so-called stag films to mainstream sexually explicit magazines, 'adult' videos from the neighbourhood video store, and even sex education films (Schmidt and Sigusch, 1970; see also the earlier description of stimulus materials used in 1970 experimental studies; Check, 1985). The 1970 Commission found the term 'sexually explicit materials' to have greater utility.

Comparison among studies has become hampered by the differences in stimulus materials. A common classification system has been to make use of two subclasses: violent and non-violent pornography (see Donnerstein, 1983, 1984); and while the stimulus materials representing the former have been relatively consistent (usually a rape scene with variations on victim reactions), the same cannot be said for 'non-violent pornography'. The full range of stimuli mentioned earlier, from partial nudity to bestiality (used, for instance, by Zillmann, *et al.* 1981) falls within the 'non-aggressive' pornography category. Perhaps not surprisingly, a full range of effects (negative, no effect, and positive) has also been elicited.

Donnerstein (1983) has maintained that differential arousal levels evoke different reactions, with 'mild erotica' producing a pleasant distraction and more strongly arousing material resulting in negative effects. However, this differential-arousal attribute has not been pursued in subsequent studies. Zillmann and Sapolsky (1977) have suggested that, in addition to arousal, the stimulus's valence property – how pleasing or displeasing it is – also accounts for differential findings.

If the effects from exposure to nonaggressive sexually explicit materials are mediated in part by their affect value, a problem still remains: how do we explain the 'pleasing' or 'displeasing' character of a stimulus? Pleasing or displeasing evaluations could arise from a number of factors, including the explicitness of the material, the type of activity portrayed (see e.g. Glass's (1978) scale analysis of the 1970 Commission survey data, which clearly shows gradations in public perceptions of different activities), or the theme employed. For example, Sherif (1980) raised the possibility of power differentials to explain female subjects' arousal but high negative affect in response to a stimulus portraying a rape victim experiencing an involuntary orgasm in Malamuth, Heim, and Feshbach's 1980 study.

Two studies (Check, 1985; Senn, 1985) have attempted to reconceptualize non-aggressive sexually explicit materials into two further classes ('sexually explicit and degrading or dehumanizing' and simply 'sexually explicit'). There is theoretical justification for expecting differential effects from these subclasses. Bandura, Underwood, and Fromson (1975) have demonstrated that socially reprehensible attitudes or behaviours may be made more acceptable by dehumanization of victims. 'Inflicting harm on individuals who are subhuman and debased is less apt to arouse self-reproof than if they are seen as human beings with dignifying qualities', (p. 255). Again, this is clearly a line of research that merits further attention.

The problem of explicating stimulus attributes is complicated with examination of a class of materials categorized by their commercial label: 'R-rated slasher films' (see Linz, Donnerstein, and Penrod, 1984; Linz, 1985; Krafka, 1985), or 'X-rated films'. The former 'contain explicit scenes of violence in which the victims are nearly always female. While the films often juxtapose a violent scene with a sensual or erotic scene (e.g. a woman masturbating in the bath is suddenly and brutally attacked), there is no indication in any of the films that the victim enjoys or is sexually aroused by violence. In nearly all cases, the scene ends in the death of the victim' (Linz *et al*, 1984, p. 137). These studies using this film genre have generally found desensitizing effects among male subjects, after massive exposure.

But the question still remains: what does this class of 'R-rated slasher films' mean conceptually? If one were interested in describing potential effects from classes of sexually explicit materials, where does this set of materials fit in? This appears compounded in an examination of effects of sexually violent, violent, and sexually explicit materials on female subjects (Krafka, 1985), where these films are used to operationalize 'violent' films, despite allowing that they have 'some sexual content'.

'X-rated films' pose the same problems. While they appear to be used to represent sexually explicit material without any **275** violence, different themes may be emphasized, leading to quite different results.

The need to utilize meaningful classes that go beyond those in current use is important not just for validity requirements. After all, the question which social scientists must ultimately address – with both theoretical and pragmatic or public-policy implications – is: what types of effect have been demonstrated for what classes of material? Such investigations for some social scientists may have undesirable political or ideological implications; but ignoring the issue also hampers our ability to explain the nature of effects more fully so as to provide for nonlegal policy strategies that are firmly anchored in social science findings (see e.g. Bryne and Kelley, 1984; Kelley, 1985).

SOME THEORETICAL CONSIDERATIONS

In designing research studies to answer particular questions, social scientists do not ordinarily operate in a vacuum. Quite often, the relationships posited, the selection of variables and their operationalizations, the groups of people selected for examination, and the general research procedures are guided by 'theory'. Quite simply, this is the explanatory framework which rationalizes or justifies why a particular relationship might be expected.

We think it useful to summarize some of the theoretical reasoning that has been applied to the general question of what effects, if any, might be found from exposure to sexually explicit stimuli.

Social Learning Theory

This approach offers a perspective on human behaviour based on the notion that there is 'a continuous reciprocal interaction' between environmental factors, an individual's processing of information from his environment, and his behaviour (Bandura, 1977). This framework assigns a prominent role to the processes of vicarious and symbolic learning (i.e. learning by observing others' behaviour and one's own) and a self-regulating process whereby an individual selectively organizes and processes stimuli and regulates his other behaviours accordingly.

The generic process of modelling is a major component of social learning which many mistakenly interpret as simply imitation, or a one-to-one correspondence between some portrayed novel behaviour and the reproduction of such behaviour. While this type of effect is not precluded (and there are certainly many anecdotal media accounts of such instances), 'modelling' embraces a more complex array of processes which can be subsumed under two categories. First, modelling includes the facilitation of particular response categories ('response facilitation') which assumes that a portrayed behaviour functions as an external inducement for similar sets of responses which can be performed with little difficulty. Second, it includes the capacity to strengthen or weaken inhibitions of responses ('inhibition' or 'disinhibition') that may already be in the observer's repertoire. If there are restraints on a particular behaviour (self-restraints, as in anxiety over a particular behaviour, or external restraints, including the possibility of getting caught and punished for some socially disapproved – or illegal – action), such restraints may be lifted when an observer sees a model engage in disapproved acts without any adverse consequences (Bandura, 1973, 1977).

In Check and Malamuth's (1985) application of this theoretical framework, they discuss their findings in terms of Bandura's postulated 'antecedent' and 'consequent' determinants. The former incorporates symbolic expectancy learning principles, exemplified by the symbolic pairing of sex with violence against women, and vicarious expectancy learning, or observing others becoming aroused to sexual violence. Consequent determinants include observing seeing a male use force, not getting punished, and, furthermore, finding the experience pleasurable for himself and for his victim.

Behavioural Models
Two studies based on survey data provide additional information that certain sexually explicit materials may provide 'models' for behaviour for some individuals.

Russell (1985) reported findings from an earlier study on sexual abuse of women. A probability sample of 930 adult female residents in San Francisco were interviewed. Of this number, about four in ten (389 women) said they had seen pornography, and forty-four per cent of this group reported being upset by it. Fourteen per cent of the total sample reported they had been asked to pose for pornographic pictures and ten per cent said they had been upset by someone trying to get them to enact what had been seen in the pornographic pictures, movies, or books. An additional finding in this study was that those who **277** were upset by pornographic requests were twice as likely to be incest victims than those who were not upset by similar requests. A similar pattern was found among those who reported being upset at being asked to pose for pornographic pictures, i.e., those who were asked to pose were more than twice as likely to suffer incest abuse in their childhood (thirty-two per cent versus fourteen per cent). What this suggests, according to Russell, is that women who suffered sexual abuse are significantly more vulnerable to pornography-related victimization, a 're-victimization' syndrome.

Silbert and Pines (1986), in a similar study on sexual assault of street prostitutes, came upon unexpected information in the course of their interviews. From detailed descriptions the subjects provided to open-ended questions in regard to incidents of juvenile sexual assault in their childhood and to incidents of rape following entrance into prostitution, it became evident that violent pornography played a significant role in the sexual abuse of street prostitutes. Of the 200 prostitutes interviewed, 193 reported rape incidents, and of this number, twenty-four per cent mentioned allusions to pornographic material on the part of the rapist. Since these comments were not solicited, it is likely that this figure is a conservative estimate. The authors described the comments as following the same pattern: 'the assailant referred to pornographic materials he had seen or read and then insisted that the victims not only enjoyed the rape but also the extreme violence' (p. 12).

Positive Learning/Negative Learning

If we take the entire potential range of 'effects' which could occur as a result of exposure to sexually explicit materials, and if we take the commission of sex offences to be one extreme of that continuum, then the other might be represented by beneficial effects. Many have made an argument for such benefits (Tripp, 1985; Wilson, 1978).

Public opinion data both in 1970 and in 1985 show that a majority believe use of sexually explicit materials 'provides entertainment', relieves people of the impulse to commit crimes, and improves marital relations.

If they are any indication, the popularity of 'How-To' articles on sex in the popular media, and in bestsellers such as *The Joy of Sex* and *The Sensuous Woman*, are also testament to the learning that might occur from these materials.

There are also two areas in which sexually explicit materials have been used for positive ends: the treatment of sexual dysfunctions and the diagnosis and treatment of some paraphilias.

In the area of sexual dysfunctions, a common conceptual model views a particular goal as a new response to be learned. The reduction of sexual anxieties or the attainment of orgasm for nonorgasmic individuals might be examples of such objectives. In the process of learning a new response, two steps are implicated: the weakening of response inhibitions and the facilitation of the acquisition of new behaviour patterns that comprise the steps toward the final objective.

For instance, in teaching nonorgasmic females to achieve orgasm, therapeutic procedures might include desensitization techniques, followed by the modelling of a hierarchy of behaviours such as body exploration, genital manipulation, self-stimulation to orgasm, and the generalization of the response to a partner (Caird and Wincze, 1977; LoPiccolo and Lobitz, 1972; Heiman, LoPiccolo, and LoPiccolo, 1976).

A number of controlled experimental studies have demonstrated the efficacy of therapeutic treatments involving videotaped modelling, written instructions which implicate principles of observational learning, and information-processing. Such procedures have been successful in changing both attitudes and behaviours (Anderson, 1983; Heiby and Becker, 1980; Nemetz, Craig, and Reith, 1978; Wincze and Caird, 1976; Wish, 1975).

In the case of diagnosis and treatment of sex offenders, the identification of arousal patterns and the subsequent therapy programme (which might involve the inhibition of inappropriate arousal responses such as arousal to a photograph of a child) have involved the use of sexually explicit materials. As part of some treatment methods, the use of aversive techniques might be directed at extinguishing deviant arousal, or they might be combined with positive reinforcement for more appropriate sexual responses. In some treatment programmes, the combination of these procedures with social-skills training has been found to be effective (Abel, Becker, and Skinner, 1985; Whitman and Quinsey, 1981). However, the results have been less conclusive for narrower approaches to treatment (see Quinsey and Marshall, 1983).

On the whole, the learning principles that include vicarious learning, reinforcement, and disinhibition principles that are used in these therapeutic controlled settings are no different from **279** those which have been employed to explain the acquisition of negative attitudes and behaviours.

Arousal

Arousal has been conceived of as a 'drive' that 'energizes or intensifies behaviour that receives direction by independent means' (Zillmann, 1982, 1978). This model relies on the notion that arousal based on exposure to some communication stimulus can facilitate behaviours which could either be prosocial or antisocial, depending on situational circumstances. Such circumstances could include specific content cues which might elicit either positive or negative affect (Sapolsky, 1984). If arousal levels are minimal and the stimulus evokes pleasant responses (as might be the case when viewing mildly erotic material), the effect might be reduced aggression. If, on the other hand, the stimulus elevates arousal to high levels, then the outcome might be aggressive behaviour. This approach has been criticized for its inability to account for the predominance of one response rather than another.

Habituation

The idea of habituation is akin to drug treatment or drug dependency where, over time, one must rely on increasing doses to obtain the same effect. In the area of exposure to explicit sexual stimuli, repeated exposure has resulted in initially strong arousal reactions becoming weaker over time, leading to habituation (Zillmann, 1982, 1984). One attitudinal manifestation of this effect is callousness, either to victims of aggression or simply to the violent or anti-social behaviours themselves. While this holds promise as an explanatory framework, more research is needed, particularly longitudinal studies, to demonstrate its predictive utility.

Cue Elicitation/Disinhibition

Berkowitz (1974, 1984) has proposed a stimulus–response relational model which suggests that an individual (e.g. a film viewer) reacts impulsively to environmental stimuli, and that this reaction is determined in part by predispositions and in part by stimulus-situational characteristics which could function to 'disinhibit' such predispositions. Berkowitz has demonstrated that cues associated with aggressive responding, such as a situation depicting a female victim, when viewed by an individual predisposed to aggress (one who is provoked or angered), will more likely evoke the aggressive response as a result of the stimulus–response connection already established by previous exposure to the films. (See Donnerstein and Berkowitz, 1981, and Linz, 1985, for applications).

Catharsis Theory

These explanatory-predictive approaches may not necessarily operate independently; they could conceivably complement each other. They stand, however, in contrast and direct opposition to the catharsis theory which is still being promoted in many quarters as the explanation for why exposure to sexually explicit materials has only beneficial effects. Catharsis suggest that exposure to highly arousing material actually leads to a diminution of antisocial effects because relieving the arousal then reduces the instigation to commit any sex crimes in the future. Unfortunately, little evidence exists for this claim, and numerous research reviews (primarily in the area of media violence and aggressive behaviour) have arrived at this same conclusion (Berkowitz, 1962; Bramel, 1969; Weiss, 1969; Geen and Quanty, 1977; National Institute of Mental Health, 1982; Comstock, 1985). The following observation typifies comments made about the catharsis theory:

> The cause–effect hypothesis that we already described is not supported by the data. Little evidence for catharsis, as we have defined it, exists and much of the evidence that has been adduced in its favour is susceptible to alternative explanations that are at least parsimonious. In fact, when conditions that give rise to such alternative explanations are removed from the experimental setting, the reverse of what the catharsis hypothesis predicts is usually found, i.e., aggression begets more, not less, aggression. (p. 6)

It is instructive that some have called a moratorium on catharsis (Bandura, 1973), others have proclaimed its demise (Comstock, 1985). Even its major proponent has reformulated his position by explaining why it does not apply to situations involving media exposure (Feshbach, 1980).

AN INTEGRATION OF THE RESEARCH FINDINGS

It is clear that the conclusion of 'no negative effects' advanced by the 1970 Commission is no longer tenable. It is also clear that   **281** catharsis, as an explanatory model for the impact of pornography, is simply unwarranted by evidence in this area, nor has catharsis fared well in the general area of mass media effects and antisocial behaviour.

This is not to say, however, that the evidence as a whole is comprehensive enough or definitive enough. While we have learned much more since 1970, even more areas remain to be explored.

What do we know at this point?

- It is clear that many sexually explicit materials, particularly of the commercial variety, that are obviously designed to be arousing, *are* in fact arousing, both to offenders and to non-offenders.
- Rapists appear to be aroused by both forced as well as consenting sex depictions while non-offenders (college males) are less aroused by depictions of sexual aggression. On the other hand, when these portrayals show the victim as 'enjoying' the rape, these portrayals similarly elicit high arousal levels.
- Arousal to rape depictions appears to correlate with attitudes of acceptance of rape myths and sexual violence and both these measures likewise correlate with laboratory-observed aggresive behaviours.
- Depictions of sexual violence also increase the likelihood that rape myths are accepted and sexual violence toward women condoned. Such attitudes have further been found to be correlated with laboratory aggression toward women. Finally, there is also some evidence that laboratory aggression toward women correlates with self-reported sexually aggressive behaviours.

What we know about the effects of non-violent sexually explicit material is less clear. There are tentative indications that negative effects in the areas of attitudes might also occur, particularly from massive exposure. The mechanics of such effects need to be elaborated more fully, however, particularly in light of more recent findings that suggest that degrading themes might have effects that differ from non-violent, nondegrading, sexually explicit materials. This is clearly an area that deserves further investigation.

- There are suggestions that pornography availability may be one of a nexus of sociocultural factors that has some bearing on rape rates in the USA. Other cross-cultural data, however, offer mixed results as well, so these findings have to be viewed as tentative at best.
- We still know very little about the causes of deviancy, and it is important to examine the developmental patterns of offenders, particularly patterns of early exposure. We do have some convergence on the data from some rapists and males in the general population in the areas of arousal and attitudes, but, again, this remains to be examined more closely.

Clearly, the need for more research remains as compelling as ever. The need for more research also to examine the efficacy of strategies for dealing with various effects is as compelling. If learning – both pro-social and anti-social – occurs from various depictions, and there certainly is clear evidence of both, the need for strategies that implicate the same learning principles must be evaluated. Educational and media strategies have been discussed elsewhere and found to be effective in such disparate areas as health and media violence (see Rubinstein and Brown, 1986; Johnston and Ettema, 1982; American Psychological Association, 1985). Researchers in the area of pornography have no less a responsibility.

For References, see end of book.

Notes

1. The following films were used: R-rated nonviolent 'teen sex' films – *Porky's, Fast Times at Ridgemont High, Private Lessons, Last American Virgin, and Hots.* X-rated nonviolent films – *Debbie Does Dallas, Health Spa, The Other Side of Julie, Indecent Exposure, and Fantasy.* R-rated 'slasher' films; *Texas Chainsaw Massacre, Maniac, Toolbox Murders, Vice Squad,* and *I Spit on Your Grave.*
2. Psychoticism measures included such items as the following (Linz, 1985); (a) The idea that someone else can control your thoughts. (b) Having thoughts about sex bothers you a lot. (c) The idea that something is seriously wrong with your body. (d) Never feeling close to another person. (e) Feeling lonely when you are with other people.

16. The Social Science and Psychological Research Evidence: Perceptual and Behavioural Consequences of Exposure to Pornography

JAMES WEAVER

This chapter examines recent theory and research on the perceptual and behavioural effects of exposure to mass-media depictions of human sexual behaviour, especially sexually explicit materials consumed as entertainment (i.e. pornography). First, it outlines the basic contentions in the debate on sexually explicit materials. Next, it summarizes pertinent empirical research highlighting the perceptual and behavioural consequences of exposure to contemporary pornography. Finally, it discusses some potential implications suggested by the growing volume of investigations.*

The Controversy over Pornography

Over the last two decades the status of sexually explicit materials in the entertainment market-place has been radically transformed and substantially expanded (Weaver, forthcoming). The production and distribution of such materials have rapidly evolved from 'a seedy and illicit cottage industry to a stable and well-refined, mass-production business employing the latest know-how' and yielding annual worldwide revenues in excess of $5 billion (Hebditch and Anning, 1988, p. 3). Spurred by new communication technologies – especially the domestication of video tape recorders – the market for sexually explicit materials has been metamorphosed from one tailored to a few elite connoisseurs into a mass market providing an affordable form of entertainment to all consumers (Zillmann and Bryant, 1989).

The prolific availability and tremendous popularity of pornography has rekindled and fuelled substantial public scrutiny of and debate over such materials in the 1980s (Attorney General's Commission on Pornography, 1986; Committee on Sexual Offences Against Children and Youths, 1984; Joint Select Com-

* For References, see end of book.

mittee on Video Material, 1988; Lederer, 1980; Scott, 1985; Special Committee on Pornography and Prostitution, 1985; Zillmann and Weaver, 1989). The basic contentions in the controversy over pornography have focused on two distinct and yet inseparable concerns (Kendrick, 1987): interpretation of the content characteristics of pornography, and the potential perceptual and behavioural consequences of viewing such materials.

Theoretical Proposals

Although a variety of theories have been advanced to explain the basic interaction between the content of pornography and the consequences of exposure, three predominant theoretical perspectives have emerged (Weaver, forthcoming). Common to all three viewpoints is the tenet that 'merely observing a model engaging in sexual behaviour (on film, in written material, or wherever) may affect our sexual beliefs, expectancies, and fantasies' and, consequently, our sexual behaviours (Fisher, 1986, p. 143; also see Check and Malamuth, 1985b). However, conclusions about the nature and extent of the responses following exposure to pornography differ between the perspectives.

Sexual communication model. One theory maintains that pornographic materials are simply entertaining communications that pertain to sexual behaviour and have no negative consequences. Advocates of this viewpoint (Gagnon, 1977; Kaplan, 1984; Stoller, 1976; Wilson, 1978), which has been labelled the 'sexual communication' model (Malamuth and Billings, 1986), contend that such materials perform a positive function by serving as important educational and/or therapeutic aids that encourage 'sexual pleasure and sexual abandon' and help eradicate 'puritanical attitudes about sex that have long dominated our society' (Goldstein, 1984, p. 32). Wilson (1978) argues, for example, that pornographic presentations are 'part of a latent mechanism by which our society provides opportunities for learning sex', especially during adolescence, and that such materials 'help to prevent sexual problems' such as guilt, anxiety, and inhibition regarding sex and the enactment of deviant sexual behaviours (pp. 160–1). However, according to this perspective, the learning process is assumed to be selective in that consumers are believed to recognize readily the various themes and portrayals of pornography as fictional representations (Gagnon, 1977). As a result, exposure to all forms of sexually explicit materials is regarded as **285** producing only minimal adverse consequences (Malamuth and Billings, 1986).

Sexual callousness model. The proposition that viewing pornography produces only beneficial effects has been rejected by many analysts, however. In fact, advocates from diverse social and political orientations have identified such materials as fostering detrimental perceptions of female sexuality and a misogynous cultural climate, and promoting inter-gender violence (Weaver, 1987). Several variations of this 'sexual callousness' model (Zillmann and Weaver, 1989) have been articulated (e.g. Attorney General's Commission on Pornography, 1986; Check and Malamuth, 1985b; Kendrick, 1987), including one advanced by the Commission on Obscenity and Pornography (1970) which stated:

> It is often asserted that a distinguishing characteristic of sexually explicit materials is the degrading and demeaning portrayal of the role and status of the human female. It has been argued that erotic materials describe the female as a mere sexual object to be exploited and manipulated sexually.
>
> One presumed consequence of such portrayals is that erotica transmits [sic] an inaccurate and uninformed conception of sexuality, and that the viewer or user will (a) develop a calloused and manipulative orientation toward women and (b) engage in behavior in which affection and sexuality are not well integrated (pp. 239–40).

Although the 1970 Commission concluded, based on limited data, that such concerns were 'probably unwarranted' (Commission on Obscenity and Pornography, 1970, p. 240), this basic proposition has remained a focal point of the continuing controversy.

Feminist analysts, for example, have taken the initiative in elaborating this viewpoint (Snitow, 1985). Several commentators have noted that sexually explicit materials do typically depict women as promiscuous and sexually hyperactive. They argue that this characterization disparages and demeans women by portraying them as 'malleable, obsessed with sex, and willing to engage in any sexual act with any available partner' (Diamond, 1985, p. 42); that sexually explicit materials require 'that women be subordinate to men and mere instruments for the fulfillment of male fantasies . . . that our pleasure consists of pleasing men, and not ourselves' (Longino, 1980, pp. 45–6); and that women are consistently depicted as 'anonymous, panting playthings, adult toys, dehumanized objects to be used, abused, broken and discarded' (Brownmiller, 1975, p. 394).

Exposure to this 'dangerously distorted picture of female sexuality' (Brownmiller, 1984, p. 34), argue these writers, produces adverse perceptions of women – such as a general 'loss-of-respect' for women as persons – and, ultimately, results in asocial behavioural consequences ranging from sexual discrimination to rape (Brownmiller, 1975; Diamond, 1985; Garry, 1978; McCarthy, 1980). For example, Morgan (1980) proposes that exposure to contemporary pornography leads to 'the erosion of the (traditional) virgin/whore stereotypes to a new "all women are really whores" attitude, thus erasing the last vestige of (even corrupt) respect for women' (p. 138). Within this framework, Russell (1988) has developed an extensive rationalization for a causal connection between heightened sexual callousness towards women resulting from exposure to pornography and the enactment of rape, women-battering, and other sexually violent crimes against women (see Chapter 17).

Violence desensitization model. A third viewpoint, derived from a general 'desensitization' model (e.g. Donnerstein, Linz, and Penrod, 1987), proposes that only blatant portrayals of women as victims of coercion, aggression and violence influence asocial attitudes and behaviours towards women. Specifically, advocates of this idea (e.g. Donnerstein, 1984b; Donnerstein and Linz, 1986) argue that concerns about negative consequences of exposure to most contemporary non-violent sexually explicit materials are ill-founded. They maintain that the typical, sexually explicit presentation 'does not foster negative attitudes or behaviors *unless* it is combined with images of violence' (Donnerstein, Linz, and Penrod, 1987, jacket). In this view, only innocuous effects are regarded as resulting from exposure to pornography devoid of violence.

More recently, their research on materials which are violent and sexually suggestive, but not sexually explicit (colloquially referred to as 'slasher films'), has led advocates of this idea to argue that it is 'only violence and not sex' which has negative consequences. This has diverted attention away from the authors' own research on the negative consequences of sexually violent materials and the research of others implicating non-violent **287**

pornography with negative attitudes and behaviour. The flaws
in this research and its conclusions are discussed below.

Pertinent Research Findings

What are the predominant content themes of contemporary
pornography and what, if any, consequences result from consumption of these sexually explicit materials? This question has
stimulated the production of a large volume of investigations
utilizing a broad range of research procedures and samples. For
instance, over 145 papers dealing with some aspect of this topic
have been published in various social science periodicals during
the past eight years (American Psychological Association, 1990).

Although this research provides a rich foundation for developing an understanding of the pornography phenomenon, the
tremendously diverse nature of the data has also proven problematic. Indeed, investigators have demonstrated quite extensive
eclecticism in their examination of pornography and its uses and
effects (cf. Howitt, 1989; Zillmann, 1989b). This eclecticism is
apparent in the ways social scientists have conceptually and
operationally defined sexually explicit materials, in the responses
they have observed following exposure to such materials, and in
the interpretations they have accorded their results. This has led
some analysts to warn *caveat emptor* (i.e. 'let the buyer beware') to
consumers of this material, since an incautious or poorly
informed review of the aggregate findings can yield a complex
picture of seemingly contradictory results (e.g. Copp, 1983;
Howitt, 1989; Page, 1989; Zillmann, 1989b; Zillmann and
Bryant, 1988c).

With this in mind, and in an effort to clarify the complexities
and to promote synthesis, this summary concentrates first on
research findings relating to the content characteristics of contemporary pornography. A three-category typology for the classification of sexually explicit materials is outlined. This content-
based framework is then used to examine a number of pertinent
investigations illustrating many of the perceptual and behavioural responses resulting from exposure to pornography.

Content Characteristics of Pornography

A broad range of both critical and empirical studies has examined the content characteristics of contemporary sexually explicit
materials (e.g. Brown and Bryant, 1989; Huer, 1987; Lawrence,
1936; Lederer, 1980; Steinem, 1980; Attorney General's Commis-

sion on Pornography, 1986; Joint Select Committee on Video Material, 1988). Common to all these studies is a three-part typology which distinguishes between pornography that features (1) standard non-violent themes, (2) coercive and/or violent themes, and (3) idealized sexual themes (Zillmann, 1989a).

The bulk of the pornographic material available world-wide falls within the *standard non-violent themes* category. This standard-fare or 'mainstream' category, according to Hebditch and Anning (1988), accounts for 'more than 90 per cent of the world production of still photographs and video/film sequences of heterosexual acts of intercourse' (p. 7). These standard-fare productions – which include both men's magazines and sexually graphic videos – typically feature a narrow range of highly stylized content conventions that involve a uniquely 'macho or masculinized orientation' towards sexual behaviours (Crabbe, 1988; Day, 1988). Most notable among these is a seemingly complete 'preoccupation with sexual activity to the exclusion of all other facets of human social behavior' (Hebditch and Anning, 1988, p. 15). Many analysts (e.g. Brosius, Staab & Weaver, 1991; Brown and Bryant, 1989; Palys, 1984, 1986; Prince, 1987; Slade, 1984; Winick, 1985) have noted, for instance, that this pornography typically features all variants of heterosexual intercourse in a variety of circumstances and 'as a matter of routine – lesbianism, group sex, anal intercourse, oral-genital contact and visible ejaculation' (Hebditch and Anning, 1988, p. 7). At the same time, depictions of other basic aspects of human sexuality – such as communication between sexual partners, expressions of affection or emotion (except for fear and lust), foreplay, afterplay, or friendly cuddling, and concern about sanitation or the consequences of sexual activities – are minimized (Prince, 1987; Rimmer, 1986). Furthermore, within this context women are normatively portrayed as eagerly soliciting, and responding with hysterical euphoria to, any of a variety of sexual encounters (Abeel, 1987; Palys, 1984; Rimmer, 1986). Standard-fare pornography presents a 'somewhat tasteless celebration of a "sex is fun" mentality' (Palys, 1984, p. 61) that ignores basic social and relational aspects of sexual activity and often depicts sexual behaviours 'which degrade, debase and dehumanize women' (Check and Guloien, 1989).

The availability of sexually explicit materials involving *coercive and/or violent themes*, which were initially the focus of considerable critical attention, appears limited by comparison with the market **289** for standard-fare pornography (Brown and Bryant, 1989; Slade, 1984; Yang and Linz, 1990). Along with the content conventions presented in standard-fare pornography, productions in this category typically inject portrayals of rough or aggressive actions (i.e. biting, hitting, spanking, verbal abuse) as a component of otherwise 'normal' sexual behaviours. Research suggests that depictions of this sort dominate this category (Palys, 1984, 1986), which also include portrayals of coercion and/or violence as a successful means of initiating sexual activities. When shown in such circumstances women are, as a rule, portrayed in a manner consistent with the cultural myth that women enjoy being raped. In this 'rape-myth' scenario, the woman's initial reactions of distress during rape are quickly transformed into sexual arousal and, ultimately, enjoyment (Burt, 1980).

Only a small proportion of sexually explicit materials involve *idealized sexual themes* (Abeel, 1987). Productions in this category, which are referred to by some as 'erotica' (e.g. Lawrence, 1936; Steinem, 1980; Check and Guloien, 1989), present more com-passionate, egalitarian portrayals of sexuality by focusing on the social and relational aspects of heterosexual coital activities. Interestingly, although some analysts have projected a strong consumer demand for sexually explicit materials within this category (e.g. Rimmer, 1986), there is little evidence of such a trend (Abeel, 1987).

Although not included in the three-part content typology common to the majority of pornography research, there is a fourth category of material which has been included in some research on pornography (Donnerstein, 1984a; Linz, 1985). This is the material which is violent and 'sexually suggestive' rather than sexually explicit; the teenage 'slasher horror films', for example, which often show young women and men as victims of violence (Weaver, forthcoming).

Perceptual Consequences of Exposure to Pornography

There is considerable research evidence which shows that expo-sure to contemporary sexually explicit materials facilitates the formation and reinforcement of inappropriate or undesirable perceptions of women in both sexual and non-sexual contexts (Donnerstein, 1983a; Malamuth, 1984a; Zillmann, 1989a; Zill-mann and Weaver, 1989). Zillmann and Bryant (1982, 1984, 1988a, 1988b), for example, have observed numerous persistent changes in perceptions concerning sexuality, especially female sexuality, after repeatedly exposing research subjects to 'standard' pornography. In an initial study (Zillmann and Bryant, 1982, 1984) involving both male and female college students, exposure to 'standard' non-violent sexually explicit materials over six one-hour weekly sessions led to the trivialization of rape as a criminal offence, exaggerated perceptions of the prevalence of most sexual practices, and increased callousness towards female sexuality. Compared with control groups, for example, this 'prolonged exposure' group recommended a significantly shorter incarceration period for a convicted rapist. Interestingly, this was the case for both male and female respondents, although women prescribed much longer punishment for rape overall than men. These findings led Zillmann and Bryant (1982, 1984) to speculate that regular viewing of commonly available sexually explicit materials might foster, for many individuals, callousness towards women, dissatisfaction with existing sexual relationships and diminished caring for and trust in partners.

In a second study designed to test these considerations, Zillmann and Bryant (1988a, 1988b) recruited men and women from both a college student body and the adult population of a city to view either standard pornographic videos or innocuous television fare during one-hour sessions conducted over six consecutive weeks. In an ostensibly unrelated study one week later, subjects completed several questionnaires designed to assess their perceptions of societal institutions and personal contentment with their lives. The findings revealed that the 'prolonged exposure' to standard pornography adversely affected attitudes about sexual intimacy and numerous aspects of sexuality. Subjects in the exposure group, when compared with their control group counterparts, reported greater acceptance of pre- and extramarital sex, of non-exclusive sexual intimacy, and of sexual promiscuity as vital for emotional and physical health.

For both men and women, students and non-students, exposure to standard pornography facilitated acceptance of male dominance in intimate relationships, culminating in the 'general abandonment of the notion that women are or ought to be equals in intimate relationships' (Zillmann, 1985, p. 10). After the 'prolonged consumption' of sexually explicit materials the subjects also reported less satisfaction with their intimate partners' affection, physical appearance, sexual curiosity, and sexual performance, and they attributed greater importance to sexual   **291** activities without emotional involvement. In contrast, exposure to standard pornography did not affect perceptions of happiness and satisfaction in areas unrelated to sexuality (personal finances, professional/academic accomplishments, etc.).

Recent research has also demonstrated that exposure to sexually explicit materials can have an adverse impact on perceptions of children who are sexually abused. Buchman (1988) recruited college men and women to view either standard-fare pornographic videos, sexually suggestive videos, or non-sexual videos in four daily sessions. All videos were devoid of violence and showed the actions of consenting adults only. On the fifth day, subjects responded to several case-study descriptions detailing a wide variety of criminal and non-criminal transgressions. Among these were scenarios involving the sexual abuse of both adult and child victims. The findings revealed that exposure to pornography promoted callous perceptions of the extent of suffering experienced by child victims of sexual abuse. Equally important, exposure to pornography also significantly trivialized the sexual abuse of females, whether adults or children, as a criminal transgression.

Other research demonstrates that even brief exposure to standard pornography can produce adverse perceptions. Weaver, Masland and Zillmann (1984), for example, examined the impact of exposure to sexually explicit materials on young men's perceptions of their female sexual partners. Subjects were exposed to slides and videotapes of either (a) nature scenes, (b) conventionally attractive, nude females in provocative poses or engaged in precoital or coital behaviour, or (c) females typically not regarded as conventionally attractive engaged in these activities. After a brief project designed to disguise the purpose of the study, subjects answered a questionnaire exploring various aspects of their relationship with present girlfriends with whom they were sexually intimate. The findings showed that men exposed to pornography featuring conventionally attractive women, compared with those who viewed women conventionally regarded as unattractive, reported a significant under-appraisal of their mate's aesthetic sexual appeal. A similar pattern of results was reported by Kenrick, Gutierres and Goldberg (1989) who found that both men and women evidenced less affection for their mates after exposure to sexually explicit depictions involving conventionally attractive models. Thus, in a manner consistent with the effects of prolonged exposure (Zillmann and Bryant, 1988a,

1988b), even limited exposure to standard pornography appears sufficient to occasion dissatisfaction with one's intimate partner.

Research examining the perceptual consequences of exposure to pornography involving coercive and/or violent themes reveals that exposure to 'rape-myth' scenarios (women portrayed as enjoying rape) consistently produces adverse effects on observers' perceptions of women in general, and of rape victims in particular. Exposure to realistic rape depictions (i.e. the victim expresses abhorrence throughout her assault), on the other hand, yields essentially no negative effects. This pattern is illustrated clearly in a series of experiments reported by Malamuth and others (e.g. Malamuth, 1984a). In two studies (Malamuth and Check, 1980a; Malamuth, Haber, and Feshbach, 1980) using the same research procedures, male subjects were first presented with a brief story about a heterosexual couple engaged in either rape-myth, realistic rape, or idealized sex. All subjects were then exposed to a detailed depiction of a realistic rape and asked to indicate their perceptions of the victim's experience. Evidence from both studies showed that those first exposed to the rape-myth scenario reported significantly lower estimates of the victim's trauma, when compared to subjects exposed to realistic rape or idealized sex.

Data from several other investigations (Check and Malamuth, 1983; Malamuth and Check, 1983, 1985) provide further documentation that exposure to rape-myth depictions can adversely influence men's perceptions about the extent of enjoyment that women experience when forced to submit to unwanted sexual activities, including rape.[1] Particularly informative are the findings of a study by Malamuth and Check (1981) in which male and female college students were recruited to watch two commercially released, feature-length films on different evenings. Approximately half of the subjects viewed two sexually suggestive films that – although devoid of the close-up, graphic depiction of sexually explicit activities common to pornography – unambiguously portrayed women as responding positively to abusive sexual assaults. One film, in particular, conveyed very vivid images of female sexual promiscuity and marital disloyalty. A woman was first depicted as a willing participant in a sexual assault and then as collaborating with her rapist to taunt her husband until he committed suicide. The remainder of the subjects watched two neutral films.

A number of days later, all subjects completed scales measuring their sexual perceptions. Among male subjects, the   **293** results revealed, exposure to the rape-myth films significantly increased acceptance of and positive attitudes towards interpersonal violence against women and tended to increase endorsement of rape-myth perceptions. The 'rape-myth' film had the opposite effect on female subjects, however, who responded negatively to the presentation of women as the willing victims of sexual violence.

Recent studies comparing the perceptual consequences following consumption of both sexually explicit (X-rated) and sexually suggestive (R-rated) materials portraying the standard non-violent pornographic theme, sexual coercion and/or violence, and idealized sexuality have also been informative. Among these comparative analyses are several using elaborate designs (i.e., extended exposure and delayed assessments) that have revealed strong negative shifts in perceptions concerning sexual assaults and the victims of such crimes.

Data from an investigation[2] reported by Donnerstein (1984a) and his associates (Donnerstein and Linz, 1984; Linz, 1985; Linz, Donnerstein and Penrod, 1984) illustrate these negative perceptual shifts. After completing personality assessment questionnaires men were randomly assigned to one of three categories of film exposure groups or to a no-exposure control group. Subjects in the exposure groups viewed five films over five consecutive days. In two of these groups, subjects viewed sexually explicit material that involved either standard sexual themes or sexually explicit, coercive and/or violent themes. Subjects in the third exposure group watched graphically violent, sexually suggestive (but not sexually explicit) horror films.[3] After viewing each film, subjects exposed to these three kinds of material completed a detailed mood assessment questionnaire and evaluated the films on several dimensions (e.g. the number of violent, sexual and sexually violent actions depicted; the simultaneous occurrence of sexual and violent content; and the extent that the film degraded women). A fourth group of men was assigned to a no-exposure control group; these men viewed no films and did not participate in the repeatedly administered mood assessment and film-evaluation exercises.

On the fifth day, the three exposure group subjects were joined by the men in the control group to view a videotaped re-enactment of a trial in which a man was accused of forcefully raping a woman he had met briefly in a bar, and to report their perceptions of both the defendant and victim. The findings revealed that the repeated exposure of men to the standard pornography increased their evaluations of the victim's 'worthlessness' to a level significantly above the evaluation of men from all other exposure groups. Approximately equal increases in judgements of victim 'worthlessness' were also evident for the men in the two exposure groups involving coercive and/or violent themes. Judgements of victim worthlessness proved significantly greater for men in all three exposure groups than for those of the control group. Also, compared to the control, the men in all three exposure groups perceived the rape victim as significantly less injured by her experience. This pattern of findings has also emerged from other studies using slightly modified experimental procedures (Krafka, 1985; Linz, 1985; Linz, Donnerstein and Adams, 1989; Linz, Donnerstein and Penrod, 1988).

Although there were negative shifts in attitude towards the victim as a result of exposure to all three categories of material, dispositions towards the alleged rapist were not affected by exposure to any of the material in these studies. This was inconsistent with results of other investigations, and a re-analysis of the data revealed some shortcomings in the research that could account for the inconsistency. In particular, two aspects of the research designs and procedures employed in these studies proved to be problematic, and therefore possibly responsible for the inconsistent results.

First, all of these investigations employed either a no-exposure control group or no control group at all. This fact undermines the confidence that can be accorded the findings since this basic experimental design deficiency (the absence of a neutral-content control group with parallel experimental conditions), when combined with the complex, repeated interactions between the experimenters and subjects, leaves the data open to several alternative interpretations. One viable explanation (Weaver, 1991), for instance, is that the reported pattern of effects represents experimental artifact (i.e. bias within the experiment itself). Careful review of the procedures used in these studies indicates that the repeated administration of film-evaluation measures that suggested or 'cued' the subject to ideas associated with the sexual abuse and degradation of women produced a biased response from subjects. Even a cursory glance at the film-evaluation questionnaires used in these studies (e.g. Linz, Donnerstein and Penrod, 1984) leaves little doubt that most subjects must have recognized the experimenters' interest in the sexually violent **295** aspects of the films. In light of this, the fact that these investigations employed no-exposure control groups or no control groups at all makes it difficult to determine how much of the negative perceptual shifts were a result of the repeatedly administered female-degradation cues and how much of the negative shifts in attitude were actually a result of viewing the films. The use of a neutrally worded questionnaire and a control group would have alleviated this problem and produced more reliable results.

The second problem evident in the comparative analyses reported by Donnerstein and associates was the failure of the various sexually explicit and/or violent materials appreciably to impact on the punitive judgements allotted the rapists by the subjects. This was surprising given the repeatedly demonstrated robustness of this effect in other research (cf. Zillmann, 1989a). However, one plausible explanation for this discrepancy is suggested by consideration of the information provided in the mock jury scenarios. Unlike the scenarios used in other studies, where vicious actions by rapists were unambiguously presented, the scenarios employed in these comparative analyses were ambiguous because they involved extenuating circumstances surrounding the assaults implying that the victims asked for or deserved to be raped (e.g. the rapist met his victim in a bar, the victim became intoxicated during a social gathering, or the victim was a prostitute). This ambiguity could have strongly mitigated perceptions of the perpetrators and their actions, while at the same time fostering callous, unsympathetic perceptions of the victims.

Whether these considerations were significant in biasing the results reported by Donnerstein and associates was examined in a recent investigation conducted by Weaver (1991). Men and women were randomly assigned to one of two exposure groups (neutral, eroticized violence) where they viewed and evaluated three brief scenes from contemporary films. Half of the subjects evaluated each scene by responding to questions designed to 'cue' or suggest ideas associated with female degradation (e.g. 'how degrading to women was this scene?'). The remaining subjects answered neutral questions (e.g. 'how well produced was this scene?'). Subjects then participated in an ostensibly unrelated project where they read summaries of three legal proceedings in which men were said to have been convicted of physical and/or sexual assaults against women. The details of each case were varied so that the perpetrators' actions in two cases (incidences of domestic violence and rape) were unambiguous. The third case involved an ambiguous scenario in which the perpetrator of a sexual assault enjoys mitigating circumstances. After reading each summary, the subjects reported both punitive judgements for and perceptual dispositions towards the men and women involved in each case.

Consistent with the theory that the experimental procedures themselves influenced the results of the research by Donnerstein and associates, the findings showed that, regardless of the gender of the subjects and whether they were in the neutral group or the group exposed to eroticized violence, the use of questions suggesting female degradation resulted in subsequent judgements that reflected the disparagement of, and a loss of compassion for, female victims of physical and/or sexual assaults. Specifically, the data revealed that subjects 'cued' to female degradation reported significantly less concern for a female assault victim and more strongly endorsed the idea that a victim of rape is a 'lesser woman' when compared with those in the category without such cues. Equally important, no significant effects emerged in the punitive judgements against the perpetrator in the sexual assault scenario which was ambiguous in suggesting extenuating circumstances for the violence (i.e. 'she asked for it', in some sense). This fact suggests that the degree of ambiguity incorporated into the assault scenarios provided a reasonable explanation for the null effects obtained in the comparative analyses in which attitudes towards the alleged rapist were not affected (e.g. Krafka, 1985; Linz, 1985; Linz, Donnerstein and Penrod, 1984, 1988).

Taken together, the findings reported by Weaver (1991) demonstrate that the basic design and procedural shortcomings evident in the studies reported by Donnerstein (1984a) and his associates (Krafka, 1985; Linz, Donnerstein and Adams, 1989; Linz, Donnerstein and Penrod, 1984, 1988) probably biased the findings that have been reported. Interpretation of the evidence from this group of comparative analyses therefore requires considerable prudence. In spite of the experimental design bias, however, the range of data nevertheless suggests that – when comparing standard sexually *explicit* materials and sexually *suggestive* materials, both of which involve themes of coercion and/or violence, with the control groups – exposure to non-violent, standard-fare pornography produces the most substantial **297** adverse consequences. These effects include significantly elevated callousness towards rape victims in both male and female respondents. Exposure to materials in which sexuality and violence were juxtaposed, compared to the control groups, also yielded a similar pattern of negative perceptual shifts. But, contrary to the expectations of many, the negative influence of standard non-violent pornography was greater than the negative impact of sexually violent materials.

Substantial validation of these conclusions has been provided by other recent comparative analyses. In an investigation reported by Check and Guloien (1989), for example, significant differences in the impact of sexually explicit depictions of 'rape myths', standard pornography, and idealized sexual themes (referred to by the authors as erotica) were evident. Male students and non-students participated in three sessions of exposure to this material over a one- to two-week period. During these sessions, subjects viewed a thirty-minute videotape montage of excerpts from films that exemplified one of the three themes and, among other things, were then asked to indicate how exciting, boring, aggressive and realistic they considered each montage. Approximately five days later, the subjects exposed to this material and a no-exposure control group[4] completed a questionnaire to identify their sexually aggressive perceptions and dispositions, sexual callousness towards women, and self-reported likelihood of (a) forcing a woman to engage in unwanted sexual activities and (b) committing rape.

Compared with subjects in the control group, the likelihood of committing rape reported by those exposed to either rape-myth or standard pornography was significantly higher. This 'prolonged' consumption (three sessions over two weeks) of standard pornography also increased the reported likelihood of forced sexual acts above the control group level. Increases were also apparent for those who viewed idealized sex materials but were not statistically significant. Further, the impact of either rape-myth or standard pornography was particularly strong on men who scored comparatively high on a pre-exposure measure of psychoticism – suggesting that they tended to be solitary and hostile and to prefer impersonal sex (Eysenck, 1978). This suggests that men who are predisposed to aggression are particularly vulnerable to negative influence from pornography.

Finally, a comparative analysis conducted by Weaver (1987; also see Zillmann and Weaver, 1989) provides information about the content characteristics of depictions involving sexual and violent themes which can adversely affect perceptions of women and rape. Male and female volunteers were exposed to portrayals of either neutral, sexual or sexually coercive and/or violent themes in a study that was conducted in three phases.

In the first phase, subjects reported their perceptual reactions to narrative descriptions of women and men. The females were, by design, described as assertive or permissive and sexually discriminating or sexually promiscuous. Thus, stereotyped descriptions ranging from nice and virtuous women to wild and promiscuous women were created to provide reference points in determining the direction and magnitude of shifts in the perception of women resulting from exposure to pornography.

In the study's second phase, approximately one week later, subjects were exposed to three brief scenes taken from contemporary television programmes and films in one of five content categories. In a neutral category, subjects viewed non-sexual and non-violent inter-gender interactions. Portrayals of consenting sexual activities were divided into 'consensual sex', which presented idealized sexual themes, and 'female-instigated sex', which emphasized sexual promiscuity and infidelity by a female character. The sexually coercive and/or violent themes were also subdivided. A category labelled 'male-coerced sex' presented scenes in which males employed verbal and/or physical coercion to gain sexual access to females. The other category, labelled 'eroticized violence', included scenes common to modern 'slasher' horror films in which graphically violent acts were shown to occur within an erotic context (see note 3 for an example). Subjects responded to a neutrally worded evaluative questionnaire after viewing each scene.

In phase three, immediately following exposure to these materials, subjects participated in two ostensibly unrelated projects. The first project was a person-perception task in which subjects evaluated women and men presented on slides. The women presented in this project were subdivided into peers and non-peers (i.e. into women about the subjects' age or notably older) and were then further divided into those women perceived as sexually discriminating and sexually promiscuous. Subjects rated each person using an extensive adjective inventory.

In the second 'post-exposure' project, subjects responded to fictional summaries of two legal proceedings by providing punitive judgements for men convicted of assaulting women. The first **299** case described the attack on a young woman by her intoxicated boyfriend in which the woman was said to have sustained extensive physical injuries. Subjects were asked to recommend a monetary award against the male assailant. The second case described the knife-point rape of a woman. Subjects were asked to recommend the prison sentence for the rapist whose guilt was not in doubt.

Consistent with previous research, the findings revealed that exposure to depictions of both standard sexually explicit and coercive and/or violent themes is capable of inducing negative shifts in the general perception of women and in dispositions about the punishment of a convicted rapist. The most striking finding was that exposure to standard sexually explicit themes strongly influenced men's perceptions of the sexual availability of otherwise sexually discriminating peer females, without adversely affecting other personality assessments. Specifically, compared with those exposed to neutral materials, men who viewed the consensual and female-instigated sex perceived sexually discriminating peer women as substantially more permissive. This would suggest that men who use standard pornography (whose common theme is female-instigated sex) are likely to view women generally as sexually available.[5] The perception of increased permissiveness was not observed, however, following men's exposure to either the male-coerced sex or eroticized violence materials.

The findings concerning perceptions of rape as a criminal offence, as measured by the sentencing of a rapist, revealed that exposure to all of the sexual and/or violent categories of material trivialized the rape judgements of both men and women. Exposure to female-instigated sex (which is common to most standard pornography) actually produced the strongest overall reduction in recommended prison sentence for the rapist. There was also a significant rape-trivializing effect in the two categories involving coercion and/or violence, but it was less than for the female-instigated sex category. In this study, exposure to consensual and female-instigated sex also tended to reduce recommended prison sentences for the rapist, although not to a statistically significant extent. The findings also showed that the more strongly exposure to pornography influenced perceptions of women as sexually permissive and promiscuous, the greater the

300 trivialization of rape as a criminal offence.

Behavioural Consequences of Exposure to Pornography

The research evidence discussed above highlights the fact that exposure to many commonly available sexually explicit materials facilitates the formation and reinforcement of inappropriate or undesirable perceptions of and attitudes towards women in both sexual and non-sexual contexts. In general, these perceptual shifts, which are apparent for both male and female consumers, include the trivialization of sexual assault as a criminal offence, increased callousness towards women, and heightened dissatisfaction with one's existing sexual relationship, including diminished caring for and trust in one's partner. In short, these data show that consumers of pornography do 'develop a calloused and manipulative orientation toward women' (Commission on Obscenity and Pornography, 1970, p. 239). But the question remains whether such negative perceptual shifts and changes in attitudes bring about corresponding calloused and manipulative behaviours.

Before addressing this question, however, it is necessary to recognize that research examining the behavioural consequences of exposure to sexually explicit materials has been deemed by some critics insufficient to determine whether or not pornography is a cause of harm. Specifically, it has been argued that anything less than compelling proof of a causal connection between the consumption of pornography and the enactment of sexually violent behaviours is inadequate (Brannigan, 1987; Brannigan and Goldenberg, 1987; Byrne and Kelley, 1986; Howitt, 1989).

Despite such criticism, it must be understood that, given ethical considerations, evidence sufficiently definitive to satisfy this mandate will not be forthcoming. Obviously, any research protocol employing sexually abusive or violent behaviours as a response to viewing pornography cannot be sanctioned. Consequently, we *must* rely on the available research to develop an understanding of the behavioural consequences of exposure to pornography; realizing that such data, with several acknowledged limitations, is more informative and reliable than conventional wisdom, guessing, or ignorance (cf. Zillmann, 1989b).

Given these considerations, what can be learned from the available research evidence? Two facts are readily apparent. First, in several controlled circumstances, exposure to sexually explicit materials has been shown to cause men to target **301** aggressive and/or manipulative behaviours against women. Equally important, a substantial and robust correlation emerges between the availability of pornography and the incidence of sexually abusive behaviours across a variety of natural settings.

Evidence of the link between the availability of sexually explicit materials and the occurrence of criminal sexual offences has been provided by several investigations (cf. Baron and Straus, 1984; Court, 1984). Initially, data from a study in Denmark revealed a negative association between the availability of sexually explicit materials and the incidence of sexual offences reported to police (Kutchinsky, 1973). That is, increased circulation of such materials appeared linked to a significant drop in sexual offences, particularly rape and child molestation. This trend was interpreted as suggesting that unrestricted distribution of sexually explicit materials provided a 'safety valve' for deviant sexual behaviours. Subsequent critiques have, however, outlined shortcomings in this study that profoundly challenge this conclusion (Cline, 1974; Court, 1984). More importantly, recent investigations of this issue have demonstrated a positive relationship between the availability of sexually explicit materials and the incidence of sexual offences. In an examination of data collected from various countries, for example, Court (1984) provides substantial evidence that variations in the availability of pornography correspond positively with changes in the reported occurrences of rape. In addition, extensive data from the United States have substantiated this pattern in considerable detail (Baron and Straus, 1984, 1987; Jaffee and Straus, 1987; Scott and Schwalm, 1988). Scott and Schwalm (1988) found, for instance, a quite significant positive relationship between the incidence of rape and per capita sales of sexually explicit magazines (e.g. *Playboy* and *Penthouse*), that withstood statistical control for numerous demographic factors and for the general circulation rates of non-erotic magazines (e.g. *Newsweek*). Baron and Straus (1987) examined similar data using a structural equation model that provided substantial control for both demographic characteristics and other variables believed to mediate the incidence of rape. From this elaborate model emerged strong evidence of a very robust, direct relationship between the circulation rate of sex magazines and rape rates.

Other survey research highlights the fact that women often suffer sexually abusive treatment instigated by exposure to sexually explicit materials. Russell (1984), for example, ques-

302

tioned a representative sample of the adult females in San Francisco and found that approximately 10 per cent reported 'upsetting sexual experiences with people who tried to get them to do something sexual they'd seen in pornography' (p. 124). (See Chapter 17.) Similarly, the Committee on Sexual Offences Against Children and Youths (1984) concluded that the 'findings of two [Canadian] national surveys – population and police – indicate that for a number of persons, pornography had served as a stimulus to committing sexual assaults against children' (p. 1283).

Recent clinical research further illustrates the potential role of sexually explicit materials in the commission of sex-related criminal offences (Marshall, 1989; Silbert and Pines, 1984). Working with a sample of sex offenders in a voluntary outpatient environment, Marshall (1988) found that child-molesters and rapists frequently used sexually explicit materials both immediately prior to and during sexual assaults. In addition, Marshall discovered that, when compared with two different control groups, offenders reported substantially greater use of sexually explicit materials, and that such use was significantly related to the chronicity of sexual offenders' assaults. Other investigations highlight the pivotal impact of exposure to sexually explicit materials in the development of deviant sexual interests (e.g. Abel, 1985)—which appear to exert a strong, negative influence on subsequent sexual behaviour (Davis and Braucht, 1973; Propper, 1970).

Taken together, this recurrent pattern of results strongly implicates a direct link between exposure to sexually explicit material and the occurrence of criminal sexual offences. Correlational data has limitations, however. It is not possible to determine the causal direction of the link between exposure to sexually explicit materials and the incidence of sexually abusive and/or sexually violent behaviours. It is also possible that the observed relationships actually result from the intervention of other, as yet unidentified factors, but this is increasingly improbable given the weight of the evidence. Both of these limitations have been overcome, however, by experimental research.

Direct evidence of the adverse behavioural effects of exposure to sexually explicit materials has been provided by studies using experimental paradigms which offer considerable control over intervening factors and permit determination of causality (Malamuth and Donnerstein, 1984). It is now well established that **303** exposure to both violent and non-violent sexually explicit materials can cause aggressive behaviours under certain circumstances (Nelson, 1982; Sapolsky, 1984; Zillmann, 1984). Consistent with physiological excitation-transfer theory (Zillmann, 1978, 1979), which holds that any activity or stimulus that elevates physiological arousal can accentuate subsequent behaviour, research has repeatedly demonstrated that the 'elevated physiological excitedness' or sexual arousal induced by exposure to standard, non-violent, sexually explicit materials can intensify aggressive reactions directed at both male and female targets (Zillmann, 1984).

In a study by Leonard and Taylor (1983), for example, male subjects were paired with a female confederate and exposed to a slide presentation featuring persons engaged in explicitly depicted pre-coital and coital heterosexual behaviours or non-sexual, neutral behaviours (in a control group). The female confederate was presented in three different situations. In what was called the 'permissive cues' category, the female made apparently spontaneous positive comments such as 'that looks like fun' and 'I'd like to try that'. In a 'non-permissive cues' category the female made negative, disapproving comments such as 'this is disgusting' and 'Oh, that's awful'. And, in a 'no-cues' category, the female made no comments. Following exposure to the material, the male subjects participated in a series of aggression tests giving electric shocks to the female confederates. The shock intensity selected by the male subject served as the measure of aggression.

Leonard and Taylor found, in the absence of any provocation from the female confederates, that where the female displayed eager sexual openness (i.e. in the 'permissive cues' category) men were significantly more aggressive in their response than when the woman had made a negative response. As a common theme of all pornography is that women approve of their sexual treatment, whatever it is, this suggests that sexually explicit materials can provoke otherwise unprovoked male aggression. Leonard and Taylor also found that physical provocation from female confederates substantially enhanced the aggressive responses of males in the 'permissive cues' condition. Recognizing that these effects could not be explained entirely by excitation-transfer considerations, Leonard and Taylor speculated that, in response to the woman's sexually permissive and promiscuous behaviour, male subjects formed callous perceptions of the female confederate that disinhibited aggressive responsiveness (cf. Check and Malamuth, 1985b).

This explanation also applied to the findings of investigations exploring aggression facilitated by sexually explicit materials involving coercive and/or violent themes (Donnerstein, 1983a, 1984b; Malamuth and Donnerstein, 1982; Zillmann, 1984). This research shows, for example, that exposure to rape-myth depictions can intensify both provoked and non-provoked aggressive reactions against women, but not against male targets. This pattern of effects is illustrated by findings reported by Donnerstein and Berkowitz (1981; see also Donnerstein, 1980a).

Male subjects were either provoked or not provoked by a female peer, exposed to a rape-myth film, a realistic rape film, an idealized sex-theme film, or a neutral film, and then given an opportunity to aggress against the women by delivering electrical shocks. The rape-myth film showed a young woman being tied up, stripped, slapped around, and raped by two men; the woman exhibited no resistance and the assertion that she enjoyed the incident was clearly expressed in the film and amplified by a narrative epilogue. The incidents in the realistic rape film were parallel, except that the female's response to the rape was not positive, and the epilogue indicated that she responded with humiliation and disgust to the experience.

Confirming earlier observations, it was found that after exposure to either one of the rape films, provoked males directed stronger attacks toward their female annoyers. Furthermore, the rape-myth portrayal significantly increased non-provoked aggression against the female target above the level of the other three films. The results of this and other investigations (e.g. Donnerstein, 1984b) highlight the aggression-facilitating influence of sexually explicit materials that involve demeaning and degrading portrayals of female sexuality, and/or sexual violence.

Experimental research exploring the impact of exposure to sexually explicit materials on behaviours other than aggression is limited (Kelley, Dawson and Musialowski, 1989). However, one recent study examining behavioural interactions between opposite-gender strangers is particularly informative. Specifically, McKenzie-Mohr and Zanna (1990) exposed male college students to a standard-fare pornographic video or a non-sexual one and then subjected them to an interview by a female research assistant. The interview concerned students' transition from high school to college and did not involve questions pertaining to sexual matters. The female assistant, who did not know whether or not the man had been exposed to any sexual material, recorded the subjects' apparent sexual interest in her (How sexually motivated was he? How much did he look at her body?) and how close to her each subject placed his chair. The findings revealed that the female research assistant could readily distinguish men who had seen the pornographic video from those who had seen neutral material. Additionally, men exposed to the sexually explicit video also moved their chairs closer to the female assistant. The study also involved a free-recall test about the interview. Men who viewed the sexually explicit materials stood out in recalling physical features of the female assistant – in contrast to those who had seen neutral material and who concentrated more on the content of the interview.

Conclusions

The fact that exposure to contemporary pornography can activate sexually callous perceptions of women and promote manipulative and, in some instances, aggressive behaviours is highlighted consistently in the research evidence. Enhanced perceptual and behavioural callousness towards women is most apparent following consumption of materials that unambiguously portray women as sexually promiscuous and undiscriminating – a depiction that dominates modern pornography. Adverse consequences resulting from exposure to coercive and/or violent sexually explicit material – especially portrayals in which women are shown tolerating, if not enjoying, abusive treatment as in the rape-myth scenario – also appear to be equally substantial. Furthermore, although findings concerning idealized-sex depictions are limited, there are some that indicate that consumption of such materials may also elevate sexual callousness towards women. However, where this has been observed, the effect appears weaker (i.e. not achieving the traditional level of statistical significance) than that produced by the other two content categories.

The nature and extent of the observed responses to contemporary sexually explicit materials, taken together, appear most consistent with the sexual callousness model (Zillmann and Weaver, 1989) while contradicting the expectations of the sexual communication and violence desensitization viewpoints. For example, although it is evident that consumers can acquire

information about sexuality from pornography as suggested by the sexual communication model, it is equally apparent that they typically fail to respond to the various content themes and portrayals as fictional representations 'for enjoyment only'. In fact, the findings show that many viewers extract callousness-promoting information from pornography. The fact that exposure to pornography can produce significant asocial perceptual responses presents a serious challenge to the 'it is not sex, but violence' (Donnerstein and Linz, 1986, p. 56) proclamation espoused by advocates of the violence desensitization model.

Consideration of the pragmatic implications of the evidence suggests first that contemporary sexually explicit materials may be, as others have argued (Russell, 1988; Chapter 17), a potent catalyst for sexually abusive behaviours such as rape. Exposure to pornography, it should be remembered, resulted in both a 'loss-of-respect' for female sexual autonomy *and* the disinhibition of men in the expression of aggression against women. Extensive research evidence shows that these two factors are prominent, interwoven components in the perceptual profiles of sexually abusive and aggressive individuals (e.g. Briere, 1987; Costin, 1985; Kanin, 1969, 1985; Koss, Leonard, Beezley and Oros, 1985; Rapaport and Burkhart, 1984).

A second implication concerns the extent to which pornography induces misogynist perceptions which negatively influence the welfare of women in everyday, non-sexual circumstances. Many writers (e.g. Garry, 1978; Lederer, 1980) have suggested that the most damaging consequences of the essentially unrestricted availability of pornography are evident in the ill-treatment of women (employment discrimination, economic exploitation, etc.) simply because of their gender. Although empirical evidence addressing this issue is lacking, the occurrence of such effects seems, at least to some degree, probable given that pornographic productions typically present women as socially and sexually subordinate and inferior to men (cf. Brosius, Staab and Weaver, 1991) in a manner consistent with sexual stereotypes which permeate Western cultures (Belk and Snell, 1987; Garry, 1978; Rimmer, 1986).

Finally, there is reason to suspect that pornography – with its seemingly factual, documentary-style presentation of sexual behaviours – has usurped most other socialization agents to become a primary institution of sexual indoctrination in many societies (Zillmann and Weaver, 1989). Research shows, for example, that a substantial proportion of young people in North 307

America become consumers of sexually explicit materials during pre-adolescence (Bryant and Brown, 1989). Clearly, in light of the research findings, the desirability of pornography as a rudimentary 'educator' about sex must be contemplated.

Notes

1. The reader is cautioned, however, that the generalizability of the findings from many of these studies is compromised because neutral exposure control groups – which would have permitted comparisons between subjects exposed to pornography and those not exposed – were excluded from the experimental designs. Consequently, while we can conclude that exposure to the rape-myth is more detrimental than the other pornographic themes, it is impossible to determine the impact of all three forms of sexually explicit materials relative to innocuous material (e.g. a travelogue). Recognition of this fact is critical in the interpretation of these data, since the previously detailed research indicates that all three pornographic themes can produce undesirable perceptual shifts.

2. Some controversy has developed over this investigation (Christensen, 1987; Linz and Donnerstein, 1988; Zillmann and Bryant, 1987, 1988c). Specifically, procedural details and findings concerning the two categories involving sexually explicit materials were reported in some forums (Donnerstein, 1984a; Donnerstein and Linz, 1984) but excluded from subsequent published accounts (Linz, Donnerstein and Penrod, 1984; Linz, 1985) which only referred to the horror or 'slasher' films (i.e. the material which was violent and sexually suggestive, but not sexually explicit). The results reported here are from an integration and re-analysis of these data conducted by Weaver (1987).

3. Specifically, these investigators used commercially released 'slasher' or 'splatter' horror films. One content convention common to these films is the presentation of graphic, gory violence in otherwise eroticized circumstances (Weaver, forthcoming). An illustrative example of this 'eroticized violence', from a film entitled *The Toolbox Murders*, shows a young woman bathing when a man forcefully enters her apartment and assaults her. Failing in several attempts to escape, the woman offers herself sexually to the attacker. He is uninterested, however, and instead brutally murders the woman.

4. The reader is cautioned that Check and Guloien (1989) also used a no-exposure control group. However, these researchers employed an essentially neutral post-exposure film evaluation questionnaire. Under these circumstances, although the potential for artifact must be recognized, the impact of demand characteristics on the observed results appears minimal.

5. Women responded quite differently. They did not perceive more permissiveness in females who instigated sex or who participated in consensual sex. But they did tend to perceive greater permissiveness

in women after exposure to male-coerced sex. This would suggest that women have been influenced by rape myths: that women who are raped in some way encouraged, provoked, or asked for it. Consistent with this interpretation, judgements of innocence and pleasantness were also affected by exposure to these materials.

For References, see end of book.

17 Pornography and Rape: A Causal Model

DIANA E. H. RUSSELL

In this chapter I present my theoretical model of the causative role of pornography and describe some of the research that I believe substantiates this theory.* First, I wish to point out that, when addressing the question of whether or not pornography causes violence and sexual assault, many people fail to acknowledge that in many instances the actual *making* of pornography involves or even requires violence and sexual assault. Testimony by women and men involved in such activity provides numerous examples of this (*Public Hearings*, 1983; Attorney General's Commission, 1986). In one case, a man who said he had participated in over a hundred pornographic movies testified at the Commission hearings in Los Angeles as follows: 'I, myself, have been on a couple of sets where the young ladies have been forced to do even anal sex scenes with a guy which [sic] is rather large and I have seen them crying in pain' (1986, p. 773).

Another witness testified at the Los Angeles hearings as follows:

> Women and young girls were tortured and suffered permanent physical injuries to answer publishers' demands for photographs depicting sadomasochistic abuse. When the torturer/photographer inquired of the publisher as to the types of depictions that would sell, the torturer/photographer was instructed to get similar existing publications and use the depictions therein for instruction. The torturer/photographer followed the publisher's instructions, tortured women and girls accordingly, and then sold the photographs to the publisher. The photographs were included in magazines sold nationally in pornographic outlets. (1986, pp. 787–8)

Peter Bogdanovich writes of *Playboy* 'Playmate of the Year' Dorothy Stratten's response to her participation in a pornographic movie: 'A key sequence in *Galaxina* called for Dorothy to be spread-eagled against a cold water tower. The producers

---

* Such research is listed in the References at the end of the book.

insisted she remain bound there for several hours, day and night. In one shot of the completed film, the tears she cries are real' (1984, p. 59). This movie wasn't made for the so-called 'adult' movie houses. Nevertheless, I consider it pornography because of its sexist and degrading combination of sexuality and bondage.

A letter was sent to the United States Attorney General's Commission on Pornography reporting that: 'A mother and father in South Oklahoma City forced their four daughters, ages ten to seventeen, to engage in family sex while pornographic pictures were being filmed' (1986, p.780).

Nor should it be assumed that violence occurs only in the making of violent pornography. For example, although many people would classify the movie *Deep Throat* as non-violent pornography because it does not portray rape or other violence, we now know from Linda Marciano's two books (*Ordeal*, 1980, and *Out of Bondage*, 1986), as well as from her public testimony (for example, *Public Hearings*, 1983), that this film is in fact a documentary of her rape from beginning to end. Many people, including some of the best researchers on pornography, ignore the violence pornographers use in the manufacturing of these miso- gynist materials (for example, see Malamuth and Donnerstein, 1984). Catharine MacKinnon points out the frequently forgotten fact that 'before pornography became the pornographer's speech it was somebody's life' (1987, p. 179). Testimony presented at the hearings held on the anti-pornography civil rights ordinance in Minneapolis, Minnesota, in 1983 provides powerful evidence for the truth of this statement (*Public Hearings*, 1983).

MALES'* PROPENSITY TO RAPE AND SEXUALLY ABUSE

> Why do I want to rape women? Because I am basically, as a male, a predator and all women look to men like prey. I fantasize about the expression on a woman's face when I capture her and she realizes she cannot escape. It's like I won, I own her. (Male respondent, Hite, 1981, p. 718)

It is important to know the state of mind and proclivities of those to whom pornography is geared. Research indicates that in our current milieu, 25 to 30 per cent of the male college students

---

* I often use the term *males* rather than *men* because many rapists are juveniles. Even more victims are girls – sometimes baby girls – not women.

studied at universities in the United States and Canada report that there is some likelihood that they would rape a woman if they could get away with it.* In the first of these studies conducted at the University of California at Los Angeles, the word *rape* was not used; instead, an account of rape was read to the male subjects, of whom 53 per cent said there was some likelihood that they would behave in the same fashion as the man described in the story if they could be sure of getting away with it (Malamuth, Haber, and Feshbach, 1980). Without this assurance, only 17 per cent said they might emulate the rapist's behaviour. It is helpful to know exactly what behaviour these students said they might enact.

> Bill soon caught up with Susan and offered to escort her to her car. Susan politely refused him. Bill was enraged by the rejection. 'Who the hell does this bitch think she is, turning me down,' Bill thought to himself as he reached into his pocket and took out a Swiss army knife. With his left hand he placed the knife at her throat. 'If you try to get away, I'll cut you,' said Bill. Susan nodded her head, her eyes wild with terror.

The story then depicted the rape. There was a description of sexual acts with the victim continuously portrayed as clearly opposing the assault (Malamuth, Haber, and Feshbach, 1980, p. 124).

In another study, 356 male students were asked: 'If you could be assured that no one would know and that you could in no way be punished for engaging in the following acts, how likely, if at all, would you be to commit such acts?' (Briere and Malamuth, 1983). Among the sexual acts listed were the two of interest to these researchers: 'forcing a female to do something she really didn't want to do' and 'rape' (Briere and Malamuth, 1983). *Sixty per cent of the sample indicated that under the right circumstances, there was some likelihood that they would rape, use force, or do both.*

In a study of high school males, 50 per cent of those interviewed believed it acceptable 'for a guy to hold a girl down and force her to have sexual intercourse in instances such as when "she gets him sexually excited" or "she says she's going to have

---

* As recently as 1984 Malamuth reported that an average of about 35 per cent of male students in several studies indicated some likelihood of raping a woman (p. 22). However, he says this figure has decreased to 25 to 30 per cent since then for reasons he does not know (personal communication, July 1986).

sex with him and then changes her mind"' (Goodchilds and Zellman, 1984).

Some people dismiss the findings from these studies as 'merely attitudinal'. But this conclusion is not justifiable. Malamuth has found that male subjects' self-reported likelihood of raping is correlated with physiological measures of sexual arousal by rape depictions. Obviously, erections cannot be considered attitudes. More specifically, the male students who say they might rape a woman if they could get away with it are significantly more likely than other male students to be sexually aroused by portrayals of rape. Indeed, these men were more sexually aroused by depictions of rape than by mutually consenting depictions. And when asked if they would find committing a rape sexually arousing, they said yes (Donnerstein, 1983b, p. 7). They were also more likely than the other male subjects to admit to having used actual physical force to obtain sex with a woman. These latter data were self-reported, but because they refer to actual behaviour they too cannot be dismissed as merely attitudinal.

Looking at sexual arousal data alone as measured by penile tumescence – not its correlation with self-reported likelihood to rape – Neil Malamuth (1985) reports that:

- About 10 per cent of the population of male students are sexually aroused by 'very extreme violence' with 'a great deal of blood and gore' that 'has very little of the sexual element'. (p. 95)
- About 20 to 30 per cent show substantial sexual arousal by depictions of rape in which the woman never shows signs of arousal, only abhorrence. (Ibid.)
- About 50 to 60 per cent show some degree of sexual arousal by a rape depiction in which the victim is portrayed as becoming sexually aroused at the end. (personal communication, 18 August 1986)

Given these findings, it is hardly surprising that after reviewing a whole series of related experiments, Malamuth concluded that 'the overall pattern of the data is . . . consistent with contentions that many men have a proclivity to rape' (1981b, p. 139).

Shere Hite (1981, p. 1123) provides data from the general population outside the university laboratory on men's self-reported desire to rape women. Distinguishing between those men who answered the question anonymously and those who revealed their identities, Hite reports the following answers by **313** the anonymous group to her question 'Have you ever wanted to rape a woman?': 46 per cent answered 'yes' or 'sometimes', 47 per cent answered 'no', and 7 per cent said they had fantasies of rape, but presumably had not acted them out yet.

For reasons unknown, the non-anonymous group of men reported slightly more interest in rape: 52 per cent answered 'yes' or 'sometimes', 36 per cent answered 'no', and 11 per cent reported having rape fantasies. Although Hite's survey was not based on a random sample and therefore, like the experimental work cited above, cannot be generalized to the population at large, her finding that roughly half of the more than 7,000 men she surveyed admitted to having wanted to rape a woman one or more times suggests that men's propensity to rape is probably very widespread indeed. Interestingly, her percentages come quite close to my finding that 44 per cent of a probability sample of 930 adult women residing in San Francisco reported having been the victim of one or more rapes or attempted rapes over the course of their lives (Russell, 1984).

With regard to the proclivity of males to abuse children sexually, Malamuth found that from 10 to 15 per cent of male students reported some likelihood of sexually abusing a child if they could be assured of getting away with it (personal communication, July 1986). Although many people believe that children are abused only by mentally disturbed paedophiles, Kevin Howells points out that there is considerable agreement among researchers that 'adults sexually involved with children vary from technically paedophilic persons to those of a normal orientation' (1981, p. 77). Indeed, Howells maintains that 'there is good reason to think . . . that such persons [paedophiles] form a minority in the total population of people who become sexually involved with children' (1981, p. 62).

Kurt Freund's research demonstrates that 'children have some arousal value even for normal males' (1981, p. 162). (By 'normal' Freund and Howells mean non-paedophilic in these passages.) More specifically, Freund found that non-paedophilic heterosexual males 'respond even to very young girls' and that boys similarly have some arousal value for non-paedophilic homosexual males (1981, p. 162). 'These findings,' Howells concludes, 'would seem to imply, as Freund suggests, that normal males show sufficient penile response to children to allow the possibility that children might become "surrogate" partners when an adult partner is not available.' Furthermore, 'Freund's studies show

314

that the female child elicits stronger reactions than the male child in normals and might be regarded as a more likely surrogate' (1981, p. 80).

The studies reviewed here suggest that at this time in the history of our culture, a substantial percentage of the male population has some desire or proclivity to rape females and/or to sexually abuse children. Indeed, some men in this culture consider themselves deviant for *not* wanting to rape a woman. For example, the answer one of Hite's male respondents was: 'I have never raped a woman, or wanted to. In this I guess *I am somewhat odd*. Many of my friends talk about rape a lot and fantasize about it. The whole idea leaves me cold' (1981, p. 719; my italics). Another replied: 'I must admit a certain part of me would receive some sort of thrill at ripping the clothes from a woman and ravishing her. But I would probably collapse into tears of pity and weep with my victim, *unlike the traditional man*' (1981, p. 719; my italics).

Feminists are among the optimists who believe that males' proclivity to rape is largely a consequence of social and cultural forces, not biological ones. And, of course, having a *desire* to behave in a certain way is not the same as actually *behaving* in that way, particularly in the case of anti-social behaviour. Nevertheless, it is helpful to have this kind of baseline information on the desires and predispositions of males, who are, after all, the chief consumers of pornography.

What, then, is the content of the pornography men consume?

A DEFINITION OF PORNOGRAPHY

Like many feminists, I consider it important to distinguish between pornography and erotica. Feminist philosopher Helen Longino's definition of pornography is the best one I have come across. Pornography, is '*material that explicitly represents or describes degrading or abusive sexual behavior so as to endorse and/or recommend the behavior as described*' (Longino, 1980, p. 44).

One of the important features of this definition is that it makes a clear differentiation between representations of abusive sexual behaviour that are intended to educate and those that are not. Some mainstream movies depicting rape are clearly not pornographic by this definition, for example *The Rape of Love*, *Extremities* and the more recent 1988 award-winning but controversial *The*   315

Accused. These three movies include sexually abusive images in order to shed light on the reprehensible nature of rape.

It is true, however, that in some cases the way rape is portrayed is itself abusive for the audience, particularly the female members. Some women I know felt this to be the case with the long-drawn-out group rape bar-room scene in *The Accused.* Many women, myself included, found it excruciating to watch. On the other hand, I am one of those who think that without this scene, most of the male audience would not have found the rape victim credible. However, I have also been told by women who viewed the movie that some men delighted in being aroused by the rape scene. This sexist response has also been witnessed in audiences of the excellent Canadian-made anti-pornography documentary, *Not a Love Story.*

Although this discussion reveals that deciding when a depiction is pornographic or not can be complicated, few definitions are free of the same problem. For example, because it may sometimes be difficult to determine whether forcible rape has occurred or not (how much physical pressure constitutes force?), no one argues that therefore rape should not be considered a crime. In addition, millions of court cases have revolved round arguments as to whether a killing constitutes murder or manslaughter. (The frequent reality of womanslaughter is obliterated by this term.) Just because it takes a court case to arrive at a conclusion, no one argues that killing should therefore not be subject to legal sanction. In contrast, because it is sometimes difficult to determine if the pornographic label is appropriate, many people have argued that it is therefore ridiculous to try to outlaw it, or even to oppose it. The often-quoted statement of one judge that though he could not necessarily define pornography, he could recognize it when he saw it, is frequently cited to support the view that pornography is entirely in the eyes of the beholder, and therefore should not be subject to any legal restraints, or even opprobrium.

Longino's definition of pornography avoids the term 'sexually explicit' common to most definitions. Nevertheless, because sexual explicitness is frequently used as the criterion for differentiating pornography from other sexual materials, this term warrants some discussion. The legal definition of sexual explicitness requires that sexual scenes are not simulated, and that intercourse or other sex acts are explicitly shown. Personally, I

consider the use of female nudity to eroticize violence and/or abuse to constitute pornography, even if there are no portrayals of intercourse, genitals or semen.

For example, I see the 'slasher' movies, a genre of films featuring extreme violence against women – most involving 'teenage girls being raped or stabbed to death, usually both' (Ebert and Siskel, n.d.) – to be soft-core pornographic snuff movies. Although the original hard-core snuff movies involved footage of the actual (not simulated) torture of women culminating in their actual murder for the sexual climax of the 'actor'/hero and the male audience, I nevertheless think it appropriate to view slasher films as soft-core pornography despite the fact that they are shown to mainstream audiences, mostly teenagers, and do not involve the actual death of actresses. I find it both amusing and absurd that Edward Donnerstein and Daniel Linz (1987), whose research in recent years has focused on these slasher movies, believe that they are showing that pornography is less harmful than non-pornographic media violence.

Donnerstein and Linz's implicit message, so convenient for obtaining funding in the hysterically anti-anti-pornography climate of today, as well as for gaining approval by their male colleagues, seems to be that concerned people should be more upset about violence in the mainstream media than about pornography. They draw this conclusion despite the fact that the most frequent scenario in these movies has the nude or partially nude non-heroine-victim in some naked, seductive pose (for example, masturbating in a bath tub, breasts exposed) before the exciting climax of her gruesome murder is achieved by the hero in a long-drawn-out orgy of sexual violence. Only in a misogynist intercourse-obsessed patriarchy could this kind of material be seen as non-pornographic.

I do, however, consider a distinction between pornography and erotica to be extremely important. By erotica I mean *sexual representations that aim to be sexually arousing, but that are non-abusive and non-sexist*. These representations may or may not be sexually explicit. Interestingly, Canadian psychologists Charlene Senn and Lorraine Radtke have found this distinction between pornography and erotica to be significant and meaningful to the women subjects in their experimental research. After slides had been categorized as violent pornography, non-violent pornography (sexist and dehumanizing), or erotica (non-sexist and non-violent), Senn and Radtke found that the violent and non-violent pornographic images had a negative effect on the mood states of **317** their women subjects, whereas the erotic images had a positive effect (1986, pp. 15–16). Furthermore, the violent images had a greater negative impact than the non-violent pornographic images (these differences were significant at p less than 0.05; p. 16). This shows that our conceptual distinction between pornography and erotica is both meaningful and usable.

THE CONTENT OF PORNOGRAPHY

> I've seen some soft-porn movies, which seem to have the common theme that a great many women would really like to be raped, and after being thus "awakened to sex" will become lascivious nympho-maniacs. That . . . provides a sort of rationale for rape: "they want it, and anyway, it's really doing them a favor". (Male respondent, Hite, 1981, p. 787)

Don Smith did a content analysis of 428 'adults only' paperbacks published between 1968 and 1974. His sample was limited to books that were readily accessible to the general public in the United States, excluding paperbacks that are usually available only in so-called adult bookstores (1976). He reported the following findings:

● One-fifth of all the sex episodes involved completed rape. (p.5)
● The number of rapes increased with each year's output of newly published books. (p.12)
● Of the sex episodes, 6 per cent involved incestuous rape. (p.10)
● The focus in the rape scenes was almost always on the victim's fear and terror which became transformed by the rape into sexual passion. Over 97 per cent of the rapes portrayed in these books resulted in orgasm for the victims. In three-quarters of these rapes, multiple orgasm occurred. (p.10)
● Less than 3 per cent of the rapists experienced any negative consequences, and many were rewarded. (p.11)

A few years later, Neil Malamuth and Barry Spinner under-took a content analysis to ascertain the amount of sexual violence in cartoons and pictorials in *Penthouse* and *Playboy* magazines from June 1973 to December 1977 (1980). They found that:

● By 1977, about 5 per cent of the pictorials and 10 per cent of the cartoons were rated as sexually violent.
● Sexual violence in pictorials (but not in cartoons) increased

significantly over the five-year period, 'both in absolute numbers and as a percentage of the total number of pictorials'.

• *Penthouse* contained over twice the percentage of sexually violent cartoons as *Playboy* (13 vs 6 per cent).

In another study of 1,760 covers of heterosexual magazines published between 1971 and 1980, Park Dietz and B. Evans (1982) reported that bondage and confinement themes were evident in 17 per cent.

Finally, in a more recent content analysis of videos in Vancouver, Canada, T. S. Palys found that 19 per cent of all the scenes coded in a sample of 150 sexually-oriented home videos involved aggression, and 13 per cent involved sexual aggression (1986, pp. 26–7). A 'scene' was defined as 'a thematically uninterrupted sequence of activity in a given physical context' (1986, p. 25). Only scenes involving sex, aggression or sexual aggression were coded. Of all the sexually aggressive scenes in the 'adult' videos, 46 per cent involved bondage or confinement; 23 per cent slapping, hitting, spanking, or pulling hair; 22 per cent rape; 18 per cent sexual harassment; 4 per cent sadomasochism; and 3 per cent sexual mutilation. In comparison, 38 per cent of all the sexually aggressive scenes in the triple-X videos involved bondage or confinement; 33 per cent slapping, hitting, spanking or pulling hair; 31 per cent rape; 17 per cent sexual harassment; 14 per cent sadomasochism; and 3 per cent sexual mutilation (1986, p. 31).

While Palys's analysis focuses largely on the unexpected finding that 'adult' videos 'have a significantly greater absolute number of depictions of sexual aggression per movie than [have] triple-X videos', the more relevant point here is that violence against women in both types of pornographic videos is quite common, and that rape is one of the more prevalent forms of sexual violence depicted. Moreover, I would expect a comparable content analysis of videos in the United States to reveal more rape and other sexual violence than was found in this Canadian study, since the Canadian government has played a more active role than the US government in trying to control pornography.

In addition, Palys reported that about 60 per cent of the aggressors in the videos he studied were portrayed in a positive fashion as good people with positive attributes. And in 73 per cent of the codable cases they suffered no negative consequences for their aggressive behaviour (1986, p. 32). Interestingly, Palys **319** did not find an increase in the amount of sexual violence portrayed in these videos over time. However, as Palys points out, it was not clear whether this was because some proprietors had become sensitized to issues of sexual violence as a result of protests by Canadian women, or whether they hoped to avoid protests by selecting less violent fare in recent years (1986, p. 34).

In a comparison of the contents of sexual and non-sexual media violence, Malamuth (1986) points out the following important differences between them:

- The victim is usually female in pornography and male in non-sexual portrayals of violence on television. (p. 5)
- 'Victims of non-sexual aggression are usually shown as outraged by their experience and intent on avoiding victimization. They, and at times the perpetrators of the aggression, suffer from the violence.' (p. 6) In contrast, 'when sexual violence is portrayed, there is frequently the suggestion that, despite initial resistance, the victim secretly desired the abusive treatment and eventually derived pleasure from it'. (Ibid.)
- Unlike non-sexual violence, pornography is designed to arouse men sexually. Such arousal 'might result in subliminal conditioning and cognitive changes in the consumer by associating physical pleasure with violence. Therefore, even sexual aggression depicted negatively may have harmful effects because of the sexual arousal induced by the explicitness of the depiction.' (pp. 6–7)

In summary: experiments reveal that from 25 to 60 per cent of male student subjects admit to some likelihood of raping or forcing sex acts on a woman if they can get away with it. Other studies show that pornography has become increasingly violent over the years – at least in the non-video media – and that it presents an extremely distorted view of rape and sexuality.

A THEORY ABOUT THE CAUSATIVE ROLE OF PORNOGRAPHY

Sociologist David Finkelhor has developed a very useful multi-causal theory to explain the occurrence of child sexual abuse (1984). According to Finkelhor's model, in order for child sexual abuse to occur, four conditions have to be met. First, someone has to *want* to abuse a child sexually. Second, this person's internal inhibitions against acting out this desire have to be undermined. Third, this person's social inhibitions against acting out this desire (e.g. fear of being caught and punished) have to be undermined. Fourth, the would-be perpetrator has to undermine or overcome his or her chosen victim's capacity to avoid or resist the sexual abuse.

According to my theory, these conditions also have to be met in order for rape, battery and other forms of sexual assault on adult women to occur (Russell, 1984). Although my theory can be applied to other forms of sexual abuse and violence against women besides rape, this formulation of it will focus on rape because most of the research relevant to my theory has been on this form of sexual assault.

In *Sexual Exploitation* (1984) I suggest many factors that may predispose a large number of men in the United States to want to rape or assault women sexually. Some examples discussed in this book are biological factors, childhood experiences of sexual abuse, male sex-role socialization, exposure to mass media that encourage rape (e.g. woman-slashing films), and exposure to pornography. Here I will discuss only the role of pornography.

Although women have been known to rape both men and women, and have even more often been known to sexually abuse children, males are by far the predominant perpetrators of sexual assault as well as the biggest consumers of pornography (see, for example, Finkelhor, 1984; Russell, 1984). Hence, my theory will focus on male perpetrators.

A diagrammatic presentation of this theory appears in Fig. 1. As previously noted, in order for rape to occur, a man not only must be predisposed to rape, but his internal and social inhibitions against acting out his rape desires must be undermined. My theory, in a nutshell, is that pornography predisposes some men to want to rape women or intensifies the predisposition in other men already so predisposed; it undermines some men's internal inhibitions against acting out their desire to rape; and it undermines some men's social inhibitions against acting out their desire to rape.

Most discussions about the causative role of pornography in rape focus on whether or not pornography can create a desire to rape in someone who previously had no such desire. If a person is not convinced that this is possible, he or she frequently concludes that the causative role of pornography has not been established. I disagree with this very restricted interpretation of what the term *cause* means. According to Webster's dictionary, **321** *cause* refers to '*anything* producing an effect or result'. Hence, *anything* that transforms a desire to rape into rape behaviour should be considered a cause of rape.

To illustrate this point, it may be helpful to present a hypothetical example. Let us say that Mr A had been aware of a desire to rape women for some time but had never done so because he considered rape to be cruel and immoral. Let us suppose Mr A then goes to see a typical pornographic film in which women are depicted as getting turned on by being raped, and that Mr A becomes sexually aroused by the rape scenes. Then let us suppose that the next time Mr A is on a date, he feels a desire to rape the woman. He remembers the movie portrayal of women enjoying being raped. He reasons that if women secretly enjoy rape, it cannot be cruel or immoral as he had previously thought. So he rapes his date. Is this a case of pornography causing rape? If cause means 'anything producing an effect or result', then the answer is yes. The belief that women like to be raped would have successfully undermined Mr A's inhibitions against acting out his desire.

Since I have already presented the research on men's proclivity to rape, I will next discuss the evidence for the causal connection between pornography and rape listed on the far right side of Fig. 1. I will point out when the research findings I describe apply to violent pornography and when to pornography that appears to the viewer to be non-violent.

Earlier, I noted that research indicates that 60 per cent of the male students tested say there is some likelihood that they would rape or force sex acts on a woman if they knew they could get away with it. High as this figure is, it is likely that men's self-assessed *likelihood* of raping or sexually assaulting women is more inhibited by moral compunctions than is their self-reported *desire* to rape or sexually assault women.

1. The Role of Pornography in Predisposing Some Males to Want to Rape

> I went to a porno bookstore, put a quarter in a slot, and saw this porn movie. It was just a guy coming up from behind a girl and attacking her and raping her. That's when I started having rape fantasies. When I seen that movie, it was like somebody lit a fuse from my childhood on up . . . I just went for it, went out and raped.
> (Rapist interviewed by Beneke, 1982, pp. 73–4)

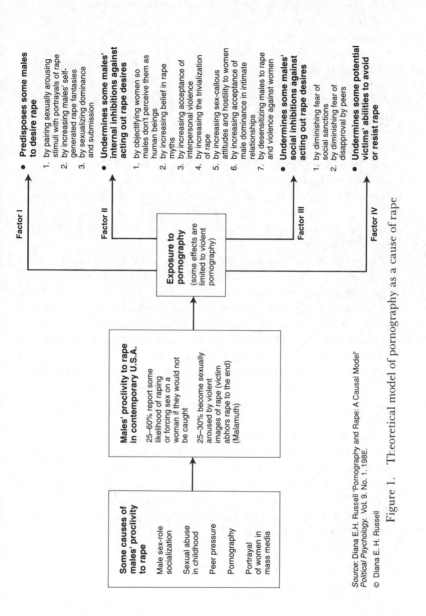

Figure 1. Theoretical model of pornography as a cause of rape

Source: Diana E.H. Russell 'Pornography and Rape: A Causal Model'
Political Psychology. Vol 9. No. 1. 1988.

Diana E. H. Russell

A simple application of the laws of social learning (e.g. classical conditioning, instrumental conditioning and social modelling), about which there is now considerable consensus among psychologists, suggests that viewers of pornography can develop arousal responses to depictions of rape, murder, child sexual abuse or other assaultive behaviour. Researcher S. Rachman of the Institute of Psychiatry, Maudsley Hospital, London, has demonstrated that male subjects can learn to become sexually aroused by seeing a picture of a woman's boot after repeatedly seeing women's boots in association with sexually arousing slides of nude females (Russell, 1984, p. 131). The laws of learning that operated in the acquisition of the boot fetish can also teach men who were not previously aroused by depictions of rape to become so. All it may take is the repeated association of rape with arousing portrayals of female nudity (or clothed females in provocative poses).

Even for men who are not sexually excited during movie portrayals of rape, masturbation subsequent to the movie reinforces the association. This constitutes what R. J. McGuire, J. M. Carlisle and B. G. Young refer to as 'masturbatory conditioning' (Cline, 1974, p. 210). The pleasurable experience of orgasm – an expected and planned-for activity in many pornography parlours – is an exceptionally potent reinforcer.

Further evidence that exposure to pornography can create in men a predisposition to rape where none existed before is provided by an experiment conducted by Malamuth. Malamuth (1981a) classified twenty-nine male students as sexually force-oriented or non-force-oriented on the basis of their responses to a questionnaire. These students were then randomly assigned to view either a rape version or a mutually consenting version of a slide-audio presentation. The presentation was based on a rape story and pictorials in a recent popular pornographic magazine.

The man in this story finds an attractive woman on a deserted road. When he approaches her, she faints with fear. In the rape version, the man ties her up and forcibly undresses her. The accompanying narrative is as follows:

> You take her into the car. Though this experience is new to you, there is a temptation too powerful to resist. When she awakens, you tell her she had better do exactly as you say or she'll be sorry. With terrified eyes she agrees. She is undressed and she is willing to succumb to whatever you want. You kiss her and she returns the kiss.

324

Portrayal of the man and woman in sexual acts follows; intercourse is implied rather than explicit.

In the mutually consenting version, there is no tying up or threats; instead, on her awakening in the car, the man tells the woman that 'she is safe and that no one will do her any harm. She seems to like you and you begin to kiss.' The rest of the story is identical to the rape version (Malamuth, 1981a, p. 38).

All subjects were then exposed to the same audio description of a rape read by a female. This rape involved threats with a knife, beatings and physical restraint. The victim was portrayed as pleading, crying, screaming and fighting against the rapist (Abel *et al.*, 1977, p. 898). Malamuth reports that measures of penile tumescence as well as self-reported arousal 'indicated that relatively high levels of sexual arousal were generated by all the experimental stimuli' (1981a, p. 33).

After the twenty-nine male students had been exposed to the rape audio tape, they were asked to try to reach as high a level of sexual arousal as possible by fantasizing about whatever they wanted but without any direct stimulation of the penis (1981a, p. 40). Self-reported sexual arousal during the fantasy period indicated that those students who had been exposed to the rape version of the first slide-audio presentation created more violent sexual fantasies than those exposed to the mutually consenting version *irrespective of whether they had been classified as force-oriented or non-force-oriented* (1981a, p. 33).

Since the rape version of the slide-audio presentation is typical of what is seen in pornography, the results of this experiment suggest that such pornographic depictions are likely to generate rape fantasies even in previously non-force-oriented consumers. And, as Edna Einsiedel points out (1986, p. 60): 'Current evidence suggests a high correlation between deviant fantasies and deviant behaviors . . . Some treatment methods are also predicated on the link between fantasies and behavior by attempting to alter fantasy patterns in order to change the deviant behaviors.'

It is important to note that this first factor in my theoretical model assumes that pornography can induce a desire to rape women in males who had no such desire previously, and that it can increase or intensify the desire to rape in males who already felt this desire. This assumption is supported by Malamuth's experimental findings (described above), since both the previously non-force-oriented male subjects and the force-oriented **325** ones became aroused by self-generated rape fantasies after viewing violent pornography. Case studies such as the rapist interviewed by Timothy Beneke (1982) and quoted at the beginning of this section, also provide dramatic examples of how pornography can generate rape fantasies in males who did not have them before.

People who are committed to the idea that pornography cannot predispose males to rape might respond to this kind of case study evidence by maintaining that the man interviewed by Beneke must have been predisposed to rape despite his lack of awareness of such a desire. This inference may be correct in this particular case. But the experimental data cited earlier indicate that at least 60 per cent of male students – not the most violent subpopulation in US culture – admit that there is some likelihood that they would rape or sexually assault a woman if they could be assured of getting away with it. This suggests that *most men have at least some predisposition to rape women*. We cannot know if the rapist quoted by Beneke became *more* predisposed or *developed* a predisposition to rape. However, if pornography can intensify the desire to rape in 60 per cent of the male population that admit harbouring such a desire, this is obviously an extremely serious state of affairs. Being totally preoccupied with whether or not pornography can predispose a male who was not previously disposed to it ignores the fact that a majority of men *are* so predisposed. Furthermore, there is no good scientific reason to assume that people cannot develop new ideas or desires from the media. Would billions of dollars be spent on advertising or propaganda if it had no effect?

Because so many people resist the idea that a desire to rape may develop as a result of viewing pornography, let us focus for a moment on behaviour other than rape. There is abundant testimonial evidence that at least some men decide they would like to try certain sex acts on women after seeing pornography portraying the same acts being performed on women. For example, one of the men who answered Shere Hite's question on pornography wrote: 'It's great for me. *It gives me new ideas to try and see,* and it's always sexually exciting' (1981, p. 780; italics mine). Of course, there's nothing wrong with getting new ideas from pornography or other media, nor with trying them out, as long as they are not actions that subordinate or violate other human beings. Unfortunately, many of the behaviours modelled in pornography *do* subordinate and violate women, sometimes viciously.

The following three quotes of respondents in my probability sample of 930 San Francisco women suggest that pornography may have played a role in their experiences of men wanting to be violent towards them or, in one case, in proposing she participate in bestiality (Russell, 1980).

Respondent 43: 'He'd read something in a pornographic book, and then he wanted to live it out. It was too violent for me to do something like that. It was basically getting dressed up and spanking. Him spanking me. I refused to do it.'

Respondent 44: 'This guy had seen a movie where a woman was being made love to by dogs. He suggested that some of his friends had a dog and we should have a party and set the dog loose on the women. He wanted me to put a muzzle on the dog and put some sort of stuff on my vagina so that the dog would lick there.'

Respondent 51: 'I was staying at this guy's house. He tried to make me have oral sex with him. He said he'd seen far-out stuff in movies, and it would be fun to mentally and physically torture a woman.' (Did he use force?) 'No, he didn't succeed.'

When someone engages in a particularly unusual act that he had previously encountered in pornography, it becomes even more plausible that the decision to do so was inspired by the pornography. For example, one woman testified to the Attorney General's Commission on Pornography about the pornography-related death of her son.

My son, Troy Daniel Dunaway, was murdered on August 6, 1981, by the greed and avarice of the publishers of *Hustler* magazine. My son read the article "Orgasm of Death," set up the sexual experiment depicted therein, followed the explicit instructions of the article, and ended up dead. He would still be alive today were he not enticed and incited into this action by *Hustler* magazine's "How to Do" August 1981 article, an article which was found at his feet and which directly caused his death. (1986, p. 797)

When children do what they see in pornography, it is more difficult than in the case of adults to attribute their behaviour **327** entirely to their predispositions. The mother of two girls testified to the Commission on Pornography as follows:

> [My daughters] also had an experience with an eleven-year-old boy neighbor . . . Porno pictures that [he] had were shown to the girls and to the other children on the block. Later that day, [he] invited [my daughters] into his house to play video games, but then tried to imitate the sex acts in the photos with [my] eleven-year-old [daughter] as his partner; [my other daughter] witnessed the incident. (1986, p. 785)

Psychologist Jennings Bryant also testified to the Pornography Commission about a survey he had conducted involving 600 telephone interviews with males and females who were evenly divided into three age groups: students in junior high school, students in high school, and adults aged nineteen to thirty-nine years (1985, p. 133). Respondents were asked if 'exposure to X-rated materials had made them want to try anything they saw' (1985, p. 140). Two-thirds of the males reported 'wanting to try some of the behavior depicted' (1985, p. 140). Bryant reports that the desire to imitate what is seen in pornography 'progressively increases as age of respondents *decreases*' (1985, p. 140; italics mine). Among the junior high school students, 72 per cent of the males reported that 'they wanted to try some sexual experiment or sexual behavior that they had seen in their initial exposure to X-rated material' (1985, p. 140).

In trying to ascertain if imitation had occurred, the respondents were asked: 'Did you actually experiment with or try any of the behaviors depicted?' within a few days of seeing the materials (1985, p. 140). A quarter of the males answered that they had. A number of men answered no but said that some years later they had experimented with the behaviours portrayed. However, only imitations within a few days of seeing the materials were counted (1985, p. 140). Male high school students were the most likely to report imitating what they had seen in pornography: 31 per cent of them reported experimenting with the behaviours portrayed (1985, p. 141).

Unfortunately, no information is available on the behaviours imitated by these males. How many imitated rape, for example? Imitating pornography is cause for concern only if the behaviour imitated is violent or abusive, or if the behaviour is not wanted by the recipient. Despite the unavailability of this information, Bryant's study is valuable in showing how common it is for males to *want* to imitate what they see in pornography, and for revealing that many *do* imitate it within a few days of viewing it. Furthermore, given the degrading and often violent content of pornography, as well as the youthfulness and presumable susceptibility of many of the viewers, how likely is it that these males only imitated or wished to imitate the non-sexist, non-degrading, and non-violent sexual behaviour?

Almost all the research on pornography to date has been conducted on men and women who were at least eighteen years old. But as Malamuth points out, there is 'a research basis for expecting that children would be more susceptible to the influences of mass media, including violent pornography if they are exposed to it' than adults (1985, p. 107). Bryant's telephone interviews show that very large numbers of children now have access to both hard-core and soft-core materials. For example:

- The average age at which male respondents saw their first issue of *Playboy* or a similar magazine was eleven years. (1985, p. 135)
- All of the high school age males surveyed reported having read or looked at *Playboy*, *Playgirl* or some other soft-core magazine. (1985, p. 134)
- High school males reported having seen an average of 16.1 issues, and junior high males said they had seen an average of 2.5 issues.
- In spite of being legally under-age, junior high students reported having seen an average of 16.3 'unedited sexy R-rated films' (1985, p. 135) (Although R-rated movies are not usually considered pornographic, many of them meet my definition of pornography cited earlier.)
- The average age of first exposure to sexually oriented R-rated films for all respondents was 12.5 years. (1985, p. 135)
- Nearly 70 per cent of the junior high students surveyed reported that they had seen their first R-rated film before they were thirteen. (1985, p. 135)
- The vast majority of all the respondents reported exposure to hard-core, X-rated, sexually explicit material (1985, p. 135). Furthermore, 'a larger proportion of high school students had seen X-rated films than any other age group, including adults': 84 per cent, with the average age of first exposure being sixteen years, eleven months. (1985, p. 136)

Clearly, more research is needed on the effects of pornography on young male viewers, particularly in view of the fact that recent studies suggest that 'over 50 percent of various categories of paraphilias [sex offenders] had developed their deviant arousal patterns prior to age 18'(Einsiedel, 1986, p. 53). Einsiedel further observes that 'it is clear that the age-of-first-exposure variable and the nature of that exposure needs to be examined more carefully. There is also evidence that the longer the duration of the paraphilia, the more significant the association with use of pornography (Abel, Mittelman, and Becker, 1985)' (Einsiedel, 1986, p. 53).

The first two items listed under Factor I in my theoretical model (some males becoming predisposed to rape women (1) by the pairing of sexually arousing stimuli with portrayals of rape, and (2) by becoming more sexually aroused by self-generated rape fantasies after viewing pornography) both relate to the viewing of *violent* pornography. But non-violent pornography can also predispose men to want to act violently. Sexualizing dominance and submission is the third way in which pornography may predispose some men to want to rape women.

Like Senn and Radtke, James Check and Ted Guloien – also Canadian psychologists – conducted an experiment in which they distinguished between degrading non-violent pornography and erotica and compared their effects (1989). Check and Guloien's experiment is rare not only for making this distinction but also for including non-students as subjects. Four hundred and thirty-six Toronto residents and college students were exposed to one of three types of sexual material over three viewing sessions, or to no material. The sexual materials were constructed from existing commercially available videos and validated by measuring subjects' perceptions of them. The contents of the sexual materials were as follows:

- The *sexual violence* material portrayed scenes of sexual intercourse involving a woman strapped to a table and being penetrated by a large plastic penis.
- The *sexually explicit dehumanizing but non-violent* material portrayed scenes of sexual activity which included a man sitting on top of a woman and masturbating into her face.
- The *sexually explicit non-degrading* material portrayed sexual activities leading up to heterosexual intercourse.

The viewing of both the violent and the non-violent dehumanizing materials resulted in male subjects reporting a significantly greater likelihood of engaging in rape or other coercive sex acts than the control group.*

Although self-reported likelihood of raping is not a proper measure of *desire* to rape, since it also indicates that the internal inhibitions against acting out rape desires have been undermined to some extent, Check and Guloien's experiment does offer tentative support for the third category in Factor I: sexualizing dominance and submission. In addition, it makes theoretical sense that sexualizing dominance and submission would likely be generalized to include eroticizing rape for some men. Further research is needed on this issue, and more researchers need to follow the lead of the Canadian researchers in going beyond the distinction between violent and non-violent pornography, and distinguishing also between non-violent degrading pornography and erotica.

In summary: Malamuth has shown that men who did not previously find rape sexually arousing generate such fantasies after being exposed to a typical example of violent pornography. Bryant found that many men and boys say they want to imitate sexual acts they have seen in pornography, and admit to having done so. And I have argued that the laws of social learning apply to pornography, just as they apply to other media. As Donnerstein testified at the hearings in Minneapolis: 'If you assume that your child can learn from "Sesame Street" how to count one, two, three, four, five, believe me, they can learn how to pick up a gun' (Donnerstein, 1983b, p. 11). Presumably, males can learn equally well how to rape, beat, sexually abuse and degrade females. However, as already stressed, learning how to do something is not the same as doing it.

Evidence will be presented in the next section to show that pornography not only contributes to the number of males who would like to rape and otherwise abuse girls and women. It also plays a role in undermining their internal inhibitions against acting on these desires.

---

* However, 'those exposed to the "erotica" stimulus did not differ significantly from either the control or both pornography conditions' (Einsiedel, 1986, p. 93). But this is not the most salient comparison for the point being made here. Another finding that relates to the broader issue of the effects of pornography, rather than the specific issue of rape, is that both the non-violent dehumanizing and the violent materials elicited stronger feelings of depression, hostility and anxiety than the non-violent non-dehumanizing material.

2. The Role of Pornography in Undermining Some Males' Internal Inhibitions Against Acting Out Their Desire to Rape

> The movie was just like a big picture stand with words on it saying, "go out and do it, everybody's doin' it, even the movies". (Rapist interviewed by Beneke, 1982, p. 74)

The first way in which pornography undermines some males' internal inhibitions against acting out their desires to rape is by objectifying women. Feminists have been emphasizing the role of objectification in the occurrence of rape for years (e.g. Medea and Thompson, 1974; Russell, 1975). Some men in this culture literally do not see women as human beings but as body parts. They are tits, cunts and arses. 'It was difficult for me to admit that I was dealing with a human being when I was talking to a woman,' one rapist reported, 'because, if you read men's magazines, you hear about your stereo, your car, your chick' (Russell, 1975, pp. 249–50). After this rapist had hit his victim several times in the face, she stopped resisting and begged, 'All right, just don't hurt me.' 'When she said that,' he reported, 'all of a sudden it came into my head, "My God, this is a human being!" I came to my senses and saw that I was hurting this person.' And another rapist said of his victim, 'I wanted this beautiful fine *thing* and I got it' (Russell, 1975, p. 245).

Dehumanizing oppressed groups or enemy nations in times of war is an important mechanism for facilitating brutal behaviour towards members of those groups. However, the dehumanization of women that occurs in pornography is often not recognized, because of its sexual guise and its pervasiveness. And it is important to note that the objectification of women is as common in non-violent pornography as it is in violent pornography.

If males believe that women enjoy rape and find it sexually exciting, this belief is likely to undermine the inhibitions of some of those who would like to rape women. Sociologists Diana Scully and Martha Burt have reported that rapists are particularly apt to believe rape myths (Scully, 1986; Burt, 1980). For example, Scully found that 65 per cent of the rapists in her study believed that 'women cause their own rape by the way they act and the clothes they wear'; and 69 per cent agreed that 'most men accused of rape are really innocent'. However, as Scully points out, it is not possible to know if their beliefs preceded their behaviour or constitute an attempt to rationalize it. Hence, findings from the experimental data are more telling for our purposes than these interviews with rapists.

Since the myth that women enjoy rape is a widely held one, the argument that consumers of pornography realize that such portrayals are false is totally unconvincing (Russell, 1975; Brownmiller, 1975; Burt, 1980). Indeed, several studies have shown that portrayals of women enjoying rape and other kinds of sexual violence can lead to increased acceptance of rape myths in both men and women. For example, in an experiment conducted by Neil Malamuth and James Check, one group of college students saw a pornographic depiction in which a woman was portrayed as sexually aroused by sexual violence, and a second group was exposed to control materials. Subsequently, all subjects were shown a second rape portrayal. The students who had been exposed to the pornographic depiction of rape were significantly more likely than the students in the control group (1) to perceive the second rape victim as suffering less trauma; (2) to believe that she actually enjoyed it; and (3) to believe that women in general enjoy rape and forced sexual acts (Check and Malamuth, 1985a, p. 419).

Other examples of the rape myths that male subjects in these studies are more apt to believe after viewing pornography are as follows: 'A woman who goes to the home or the apartment of a man on their first date implies that she is willing to have sex'; 'Any healthy woman can successfully resist a rapist if she really wants to'; 'Many women have an unconscious wish to be raped, and may then unconsciously set up a situation in which they are likely to be attacked'; 'If a girl engages in necking or petting and she lets things get out of hand, it is her own fault if her partner forces sex on her' (Briere, Malamuth, and Check, 1985, p. 400). According to Donnerstein: 'After only 10 minutes of exposure to aggressive pornography, particularly material in which women are shown being aggressed against, you find male subjects are much more willing to accept these particular myths' (1983b, p. 6). These men are also more inclined to believe that 25 per cent of the women they know would enjoy being raped.

Men's internal inhibitions against acting out their desire to rape can also be undermined if they consider male violence against women to be acceptable behaviour. Studies have shown that viewing portrayals of sexual violence as having positive consequences increases male subjects' acceptance of violence **333** against women. Examples of some of these items include 'Being roughed up is sexually stimulating to many women'; 'Sometimes the only way a man can get a cold woman turned on is to use force'; 'Many times a woman will pretend she doesn't want to have intercourse because she doesn't want to seem loose, but she's really hoping the man will force her' (Briere, Malamuth, and Check, 1985, p. 401).

Malamuth and Check conducted an experiment of particular interest because the movies shown were part of the regular campus film programme. Students were randomly assigned to view either a feature-length film that portrayed violence against women as being justifiable and having positive consequences (*Swept Away* or *The Getaway*) or a film without sexual violence. The experiment showed that exposure to the sexually violent movies increased the male subjects' acceptance of interpersonal violence against women (1981). This effect did not occur with the female subjects. These effects were measured several days after the films had been seen.

Malamuth suggests several processes 'by which media sexual violence might lead to attitudes that are more accepting of violence against women' (1986, p. 4). Some of these processes also probably facilitate the undermining of pornography consumers' internal inhibitions against acting out rape desires.

1. Labeling sexual violence more as a sexual rather than a violent act.

2. Adding to perceptions that sexual aggression is normative and culturally acceptable.

3. Changing attributions of responsibility to place more blame on the victim.

4. Elevating the positive value of sexual aggression by associating it with sexual pleasure and a sense of conquest.

5. Reducing negative emotional reactions to sexually aggressive acts. (1986, p. 5)

According to Donnerstein, in most studies 'subjects have been exposed to only a few minutes of pornographic material' (1985, p. 341). In contrast, Dolf Zillmann and Jennings Bryant have **334** studied the effects of what they refer to as 'massive exposure' to pornography (1984). In fact, it was not that massive: four hours and forty-eight minutes over a period of six weeks. These researchers, unlike Malamuth and Donnerstein, focus on trying to ascertain the effects of *non-violent* pornography and, in the study to be described, they use a sample drawn from a non-student adult population.

Subjects in the *massive exposure* condition saw thirty-six non-violent pornographic films, six per session per week; subjects in the *intermediate* condition saw eighteen such movies, three per session per week. Subjects in the control group saw thirty-six non-pornographic movies. Various measures were taken after one week, two weeks and three weeks of exposure. In the third week the subjects believed they were participating in an American Bar Association study in which they were asked to recommend the prison term they thought most fair in the case of a rape of a female hitch-hiker.

Zillmann and Bryant (1985) found that:

- 'Heavy exposure to common nonviolent pornography trivialized rape as a criminal offense' (p. 117). In addition, sexual aggression and abuse was perceived as causing less suffering for the victims, for example, an adult male having sexual intercourse with a twelve-year-old girl (p. 132).
- 'Males' sexual callousness toward women was significantly enhanced' (p. 117). For example, there was an increased acceptance of statements such as 'A woman doesn't mean "no" until she slaps you'; 'A man should find them, fool them, fuck them, and forget them'; and 'If they are old enough to bleed, they are old enough to butcher.' Judging by these items, it is difficult to distinguish sexual callousness from a general hostility to women.
- The acceptance of male dominance in intimate relationships was greatly increased (p. 121), and the notion that women are or ought to be equal in intimate relationships was more likely to be abandoned (p. 122). Support of the women's liberation movement also sharply declined (p. 134).
- An appetite for stronger material was fostered, presumably, Zillmann suggests, 'because familiar material becomes unexciting as a result of habituation' (p. 127). Hence, 'consumers graduate from common to less common forms of pornography', that is, to more violent and more degrading materials (p. 127).

All these effects – both separately and together – are likely to contribute to undermining some males' inhibitions against acting out their desires to rape.

It may be remembered that Malamuth and his colleagues found that from 25 to 30 per cent of male students admit that there is some likelihood that they would rape a woman if they could be assured of getting away with it. According to Donnerstein, after exposure to sexually violent images, particularly sexually violent images depicting women enjoying rape, up to 57 per cent of male subjects indicate some likelihood that they would commit a rape if assured they would not be caught (1983b, p. 7). This means that *as a result of one brief exposure to pornography, the number of men who are willing to consider rape as a plausible act for them to commit actually doubles.*

In an experiment specifically designed to study desensitization, Linz, Donnerstein and Penrod showed ten hours of R-rated or X-rated movies over a period of five days to male subjects (Donnerstein and Linz, 1985, p. 34A). Some students saw X-rated movies depicting sexual assault; others saw X-rated movies depicting only consenting sex; and a third group saw R-rated sexually violent movies – for example, *I Spit on Your Grave*, *Toolbox Murders*, *Texas Chainsaw Massacre*. Donnerstein describes *Toolbox Murders* as follows: there is an erotic bathtub scene in which a woman massages herself. A beautiful song is played. Then a psychotic killer enters with a nail gun. The music stops. He chases the woman around the room, then shoots her through the stomach with the nail gun. She falls across a chair. The song comes back on as he puts the nail gun to her forehead and blows her brains out. According to Donnerstein, many young males become sexually aroused by this movie (1983b, p. 10).

R-rated films are made for audiences of fifteen to eighteen-year-olds, but the subjects in Donnerstein and Linz's experiment were all at least eighteen years old and had been preselected to make sure that they were not psychotic, hostile or anxious. As Donnerstein and Linz point out: 'It has always been suggested by critics of media violence research that only those who are *already* predisposed toward violence are influenced by exposure to media violence. In this study, all those individuals have already been eliminated' (1985, p. 34F).

Donnerstein and Linz described the impact of the R-rated movies on their subjects as follows: 'Initially, after the first day of viewing, the men rated themselves as significantly above the norm for depression, anxiety, and annoyance on a mood adjective checklist. After each subsequent day of viewing, these scores dropped until, on the fourth day of viewing, the males' levels of anxiety, depression, and annoyance were indistinguishable from baseline norms' (1985, p. 34F).

By the fifth day, the subjects rated the movies as less graphic and less gory and estimated fewer violent or offensive scenes than after the first day of viewing. They also rated the films as significantly less debasing and degrading to women, more humorous and more enjoyable, and reported a greater willingness to see this type of film again (1985, p. 34F). However, their sexual arousal by this material did *not* decrease over this five-day period (Donnerstein, 1983b, p. 10).

On the last day, the subjects went to a law school where they saw a documentary re-enactment of a real rape trial. A control group of subjects who had never seen the films also participated in this part of the experiment. Subjects who had seen the R-rated movies: (1) rated the rape victim as significantly more worthless; (2) rated her injury as significantly less severe; and (3) assigned greater blame to her for being raped. In contrast, these effects were not observed for the X-rated non-violent films.* However, the results were much the same for the violent X-rated films, despite the fact that the R-rated material was 'much more graphically violent' (Donnerstein, 1985, pp. 12–13).†

In summary, I have presented a small fraction of the research evidence for seven different effects of pornography, all of which likely contribute to the undermining of some males' internal inhibitions against acting out rape desires. This list is not a comprehensive one. Some of the research reviewed here has focused on violent pornography and some on non-violent pornography.

The rapist interviewed by Timothy Beneke was cited earlier because of his claim that it was only after viewing a rape scene in a pornographic movie that he started having rape fantasies. This man's account – cited in the epigraph at the beginning of

---

* Why Donnerstein finds no effects for non-violent pornographic movies while Zillmann reports many significant effects is not known.

† In their written testimony to the Attorney General's Commission on Pornography, Donnerstein and Linz failed even to mention the effects of the violent X-rated films (1985). And Donnerstein gave this topic only a cursory mention in his spoken testimony to the commission. This is particularly odd since, by his definition, the R-rated movies do not constitute pornography and he was testifying to a commission that was evaluating pornography.

this section – also provides a dramatic example of how pornography may undermine a man's internal inhibitions against becoming a rapist.

3. The Role of Pornography in Undermining Some Males' Social Inhibitions Against Acting Out Their Desire to Rape

> I have often thought about it [rape], fantasized about it. I might like it because of having a feeling of power over a woman. But I never actually wanted to through *fear of being caught and publicly ruined*. (Hite, 1981; my italics)

A man may want to rape a woman *and* his internal inhibitions against rape may be undermined by his hostility to women or by his belief in the myths that women really enjoy being raped and/ or that they deserve it, but he may still not act out his desire to rape because of his *social* inhibitions. Fear of being caught and convicted for the crime is the most obvious example of a social inhibition. A second man's answer to Shere Hite's question on whether he had ever wanted to rape a woman illustrates this form of inhibition: 'I have never raped a woman, but have at times felt a desire to – for the struggle and final victory. I'm a person, though, who always thinks before he acts, and *the consequences wouldn't be worth it. Besides I don't want to be known as a pervert*' (1981, p. 715; my italics).

In one of his early experiments, Malamuth and his colleagues, Haber and Feshbach, reported that after reading the account of a violent stranger rape 17 per cent of their male student subjects admitted that there was some likelihood that they might behave in a similar fashion in the same circumstances (1980). However, *53 per cent* of the same male students said there was some likelihood that they might act as the rapist did *if they could be sure of getting away with it*. The difference between 17 and 53 per cent reveals the significant role that can be played by social inhibitions against acting out rape desires. My hypothesis is that pornography also plays a role in undermining some males' social inhibitions against acting out their desire to rape.

In his content analysis of 150 pornographic home videos, Palys investigated 'whether aggressive perpetrators ever received any negative consequences for their aggressive activity – if charges were laid, or the person felt personal trauma, or had some form of "just deserts"' (1986, p. 32). The answer was no in 73 per cent of the cases in which a clear-cut answer was ascertainable. As previously mentioned, Don Smith found that fewer than 3 per cent of the rapists portrayed in the 428 pornographic books he analysed experienced any negative consequences as a result of their behaviour (1976). Indeed, many of them were rewarded. The common portrayal in pornography of rape as easy to get away with likely contributes to the undermining of some males' social inhibitions against acting out their rape desires.

Fear of disapproval by one's peers is another social inhibition that may be undermined by pornography. For example, Zill-mann found that 'massive' exposure to non-violent pornography produced overestimates by the subjects of uncommon sexual practices, such as anal intercourse, group sexual activities, sadomasochism and bestiality (1985, p. 118). Rape is portrayed as a very common male practice in much violent pornography, and the actors themselves may serve as a kind of pseudo-peer group and/or role models for consumers. Further research is needed to evaluate these hypotheses.

In general, I hypothesize the following social inhibitory effects of viewing violent pornography – particularly 'massive' amounts of it:

1. Viewers' estimates of the percentage of other men who have raped women would likely increase.
2. Viewers would likely consider rape a much easier crime to commit than they had previously believed.
3. Viewers would be less likely to believe that rape victims would report their rapes to the police.
4. Viewers would be more likely to anticipate that rapists would not be prosecuted or convicted in those cases that are reported.

Since we already know that pornography results in men trivializing rape, I would also anticipate consumers becoming less disapproving of others who rape; they would also likely expect less disapproval from others if they decide to rape. I hope that future researchers will test these hypotheses.

4. The Role of Pornography in Undermining Potential Victims' Abilities to Avoid or Resist Rape

He . . . told me it was not wrong because they were doing it in the magazines and that made it OK. (Attorney General's Commission, 1986, p. 786)

Once the first three conditions of my theoretical model have been met – a male not only wants to rape a woman but is willing to do so because his inhibitions, both internal and social, have been undermined – he may use pornography to try to weaken his victim's resistance or to get her to do what he wants her to do. Obviously, this step is not necessary for rape to occur, and it is more likely to be used to rape intimates than strangers.

Most adult rape victims are not shown pornography in the course of being raped, although the testimony of some prostitutes reveals that this is quite a common experience for them when they are raped (Everywoman, 1988). Pornography is more often used to try to *persuade a woman or child to engage in certain acts, to legitimize the acts, and to undermine resistance, refusal or disclosure.* Here are some examples:

> I was sexually abused by my foster father from the time I was seven until I was thirteen. He had stacks and stacks of *Playboy*s. He would take me to his bedroom or his workshop, show me the pictures, and say, "This is what big girls do. If you want to be a big girl, you have to do this, but you can never tell anybody." Then I would have to pose like the woman in the pictures. I also remember being shown a *Playboy* cartoon of a man having sex with a child. (Attorney General's Commission, 1986, p. 783)

> He encouraged me by showing me pornographic magazines which he kept in the bathroom and told me it was not wrong because they were doing it in the magazines and that made it OK. He told me all fathers do it to their daughters and said even pastors do it to their daughters. The magazines were to help me learn more about sex. (Ibid., p. 786)

And here is the statement of an adult woman about her experience with her husband.

> Once we saw an X-rated film that showed anal intercourse. After that he insisted that I try anal intercourse. I agreed to do so, trying to be the available, willing creature that I thought I was supposed to be. I found the experience very painful, and I told him so. But he kept insisting that we try it again and again. (Ibid., p. 778).

Another woman described her husband's use of pornography as follows: 'He told me if I loved him I would do this. And that, as I could see from the things that he read me in the magazines initially, a lot of times women didn't like it, but if I tried it enough I would probably like it and I would learn to like it' (Everywoman, 1988, p. 68).

More systematic research is needed to establish how frequently males use pornography to try to undermine the ability of potential victims to avoid or resist rape and other sexual abuse, and how effective this strategy is. Even if it could be conclusively shown that pornography cannot predispose men to want to rape women if they are not previously so disposed, and that it cannot intensify the desires of men who are already predisposed, and that it cannot undermine men's internal and external inhibitions against acting out their desire to rape, if it is used to undermine potential victims' capacity to avoid the rape, this alone would be cause enough to be deeply concerned about its harmfulness.

In summary: a significant amount of research supports my theory of the causative role of pornography in rape. However, much of the research undertaken to date does not fit within its framework. For example, Malamuth's self-reported-likelihood-of-raping construct does not permit one to differentiate between a male's desire to rape and the undermining of his internal inhibitions against acting out this desire. Some of the findings from this research will be described in the next section. I hope that in future more research will be guided by the theoretical distinctions required by my model.

FURTHER EMPIRICAL FINDINGS ON THE CAUSATIVE ROLE OF PORNOGRAPHY IN RAPE

As Donnerstein points out, 'One cannot, for obvious reasons, experimentally examine the relationship between pornography and *actual* sexual aggression' (1984, p. 53). However, Donnerstein has conducted a series of experiments on the effects of pornography on aggressive behaviour in the laboratory. The delivery of a phoney electric shock to a confederate of the experimenter constituted the measure of aggressive behaviour. These experiments show that when male subjects are exposed to violent pornography in which a female is the victim, there is an increase in their aggression against females, but not against males (Donnerstein, 1984). Violent films that were non-pornographic (depicting, for example, a man hitting a woman) also increased the levels of aggression in male subjects, but not to the same extent as violent pornographic films.

Levels of aggression were higher when subjects were first **341** angered by the confederate. In fact, when the victim in the pornographic movie was portrayed as distressed throughout its duration by the sexual assault, only subjects who had been first angered by the confederate showed higher levels of aggression than those subjects who had not been exposed to the pornographic movie. However, when the victim was portrayed as becoming sexually aroused at the end of the movie, there was a marked increase in aggressive behaviour for both the angered and the non-angered male subjects (Donnerstein, 1984). To explain these findings, Malamuth suggests that 'positive victim reactions . . . may act to justify aggression and to reduce general inhibitions against aggression' (1984a, p. 36). This interpretation is consistent with my model's emphasis on the important role pornographic depictions play in undermining males' inhibitions against acting out hostile behaviour towards women.

Malamuth undertook an experiment to test whether men's attitudes and sexual arousal by depictions of rape could predict aggression in the laboratory. The attitudes of male subjects to, and sexual arousal by, rape were measured. A week later these subjects were angered by a female confederate of the experimenter. When the subjects were given an opportunity to behave aggressively towards her by administering an unpleasant noise as punishment for errors she made in an alleged extrasensory perception experiment, men who had higher levels of sexual arousal to rape and who had attitudes that condoned aggression 'were more aggressive against the woman and wanted to hurt her to a greater extent' (1986, p. 16). On the basis of this experiment, as well as two others, Malamuth concluded that 'attitudes condoning aggression against women related to objectively observable behaviour – laboratory aggression against women' (1986, p. 16). And I have shown that there is now a great deal of evidence that exposure to pornography increases acceptance of attitudes that condone aggression, with or without intervening anger.

Both Donnerstein and Malamuth emphasize that their findings relate to violent and not to non-violent pornography. For example, in contrast to the effects of aggressive pornography, Donnerstein concludes that 'non-aggressive materials only affect aggression when inhibitions to aggress are quite low, or with long-term and massive exposure. With a single exposure and normal aggressing conditions, there is little evidence that nonviolent pornography has any negative effects' (1984, pp. 78–9). However, in the real **342** world, inhibitions to aggress are often very low, and long-term and massive exposure to non-violent material is also very common. Furthermore, there is a lot of evidence of harm aside from the impact on aggressive behaviour (for example, see my earlier discussion of some of Zillmann's findings).

Finally, given how saturated our whole culture is with pornographic images and how much exposure many of the male subjects being tested have already had, the task of trying to design experiments that can show effects on the basis of one more exposure is challenging indeed. Because of this methodological problem, when no measurable effects result, it would be wrong to interpret the experiment as proving that there are no effects in general. We should therefore focus on the effects that *do* show up, rather than being equally impressed by the effects that do not.

Given the fact that even one brief exposure in an experimental situation increases male subjects' acceptance of rape myths and interpersonal violence against women, and given the hypothesis that such increased acceptance would serve to lower viewers' inhibitions against acting out violent desires, one would expect pornography consumption to be related to rape rates. This is, indeed, what one ingenious study found.

Larry Baron and Murray Straus (1984) undertook a fifty-state correlational analysis of rape rates and the circulation rates of eight pornographic magazines: *Chic, Club, Forum, Gallery, Genesis, Hustler, Oui* and *Playboy*. A highly significant correlation (+0.64) was found between rape rates and circulation rates. Baron and Straus attempted to ascertain what other factors might possibly explain this correlation. Their statistical analysis revealed that the proliferation of pornographic magazines and the level of urbanization explained more of the variance in rape rates than the other variables investigated (for example, social disorganization, economic inequality, unemployment, sexual inequality).

In another important study, Mary Koss (1986) conducted a large national survey of over 6,000 college students from a probability sample of institutions of higher education. She found that college men who reported behaviour that meets common legal definitions of rape were significantly more likely than college men who denied such behaviour to be frequent readers of at least one of the following magazines: *Playboy, Penthouse, Chic, Club, Forum, Gallery, Genesis, Oui* or *Hustler*.

Several other studies have assessed the correlation between the degree of men's exposure to pornography and attitudes supportive of violence against women. Malamuth reports that in three **343** out of four of these studies 'higher levels of reported exposure to sexually explicit media correlated with higher levels of attitudes supportive of violence against women' (1986, p. 8).

> In a sample of college men, Malamuth and Check (1985) found that higher readership of sexually explicit magazines was correlated with more beliefs that women enjoy forced sex.
>
> Similarly, Check (1985) found that the more exposure to pornography a diverse sample of Canadian men had, the higher their acceptance of rape myths, violence against women, and general sexual callousness.
>
> Briere, Corne, Runtz and Malamuth (1984) reported similar correlations in a sample of college males.

Shere Hite found that 67 per cent of the men who admitted that they had wanted to rape a woman reported reading men's magazines compared to only 19 per cent of those who said that they had never wanted to rape a woman (1981, p. 1123). With regard to the frequency of exposure to pornography of the 7,000 men she surveyed, Hite reports that only 11 per cent said that they did not look at pornography, and never had. Thirty-six per cent said they viewed it regularly; 21 per cent, sometimes, 26 per cent, infrequently; and 6 per cent simply acknowledged that they used to look at it (1981, p. 1123).

While correlation does not prove causation, and it therefore cannot be concluded from these studies that it was the consumption of the pornography that was responsible for the men's higher acceptance of violence against women, their findings are certainly consistent with a theory that a causal connection exists.

If the rape rate was very low in the USA, or if it had declined over the past few decades, these facts would likely be cited to support the view that pornography does not play a causative role in rape. While drawing such a conclusion would not be warranted, it is also of interest to note that my probability sample survey in San Francisco shows that a dramatic increase in the rape rate has occurred in the USA over the last several decades (Russell, 1984). Unlike those of Straus and Baron, most cases of rape and attempted rape described in my survey were never reported to the police. Once again, positive correlation does not prove causation, but it is highly suggestive.

Finally, it is significant that many sex offenders claim that viewing pornography affects their criminal behaviour. Ted Bundy is perhaps the most notorious of these men. Although the studies in which such testimonies are reported do not permit a distinction to be made between the first three factors in my causal theory, they are relevant to the notion that a cause-and-effect relationship exists between pornography and sex offences. For example, in one study of eighty-nine non-incarcerated sex offenders conducted by W. Marshall, 'slightly more than one-third of the child molesters and rapists reported at least occasionally being incited to commit an offense by exposure to forced or consenting pornography' (Einsiedel, 1986, p. 62). Exactly a third of the rapists who reported being incited by pornography to commit an offence said their use of pornography in their preparation for committing the offence was deliberate, and 53 per cent of the child molesters so reported (Einsiedel, 1986, p. 62). Although we do not know if pornography played a role in predisposing any of these sex offenders to desire rape or sex with children, these findings do indicate at least that pornography was used for arousal purposes. It may also have undermined the offenders' inhibitions against acting out their desires.

Gene Abel, Mary Mittleman and Judith Becker evaluated the use of pornography by 256 perpetrators of sexual offences who were undergoing assessment and treatment (Einsiedel, 1986, p. 62). Like Marshall's sample, these men were outpatients, not incarcerated offenders. This is important because there is evidence that the data provided by incarcerated and non-incarcerated offenders differ (Einsiedel, 1986, p. 47). It is also likely that incarcerated offenders might be substantially less willing to be entirely frank about their anti-social histories than non-incarcerated offenders for fear that such information might be used against them.

Abel and his colleagues reported that 56 per cent of the rapists and 42 per cent of the child molesters 'implicated pornography in the commission of their offenses' (Einsiedel, 1986, p. 62). Edna Einsiedel, in her review of the social science research for the Pornography Commission, concluded that these studies 'are suggestive of the implication of pornography in the commission of sex crimes among *some* rapists and child molesters'* (p. 63).

---

* Einsiedel also pointed out, however, that Abel, Mittelman, and Becker and his colleagues (1985) found no difference between those offenders who did use pornography and those who did not in the 'frequency of sex crimes committed, number of victims, ability to control deviant urges, and degree of violence used during commission of the sex crime. The longer the duration of paraphiliac arousal, however, the greater the use of erotica.' **345**

In another study Michael Goldstein and Harold Kant found that incarcerated rapists had been exposed to hard-core pornography at an earlier age than the men presumed to be non-rapists. Specifically, 30 per cent of the rapists in their sexual offender sample said that they had encountered hard-core pornographic photos in their pre-adolescence (i.e. before the age of eleven) (1973, p. 55). This 30 per cent figure compares with only 2 per cent of the control group of subjects obtained by a random household sample that was matched with the offender group for age, race, religion and educational level (1973, p. 50). Could it be that this early exposure of the offenders to hard-core pornography played a role in their becoming rapists? Further research should address this question.

CONCLUSION

I have amplified here for the first time a theory about how pornography – both violent and non-violent forms of it – causes rape and other sexual assault. I have drawn on the findings of recent research to support this theory. Since most of this research pertains to rape rather than to child sexual abuse or non-sexual violence against women, my discussion has focused on rape. But I believe my theory also applies to other forms of sexual and non-sexual abuse and violence.

In ending I want to note once more that I believe that the rich and varied data now available to us from all kinds of sources considered together strongly support this theory. A high percentage of non-incarcerated rapists and child molesters say that they have been incited by pornography to commit crimes; pre-selected normal healthy male students say they are more likely to rape a woman after one exposure to violent pornography; large percentages of male junior high school students, high school students, and adults in a non-laboratory survey report imitating X-rated movies within a few days of exposure; hundreds of women have testified in public about how they have been victimized by pornography; 10 per cent of a probability sample of 930 women in San Francisco and 25 per cent of female subjects who participated in experiments on pornography in Canada reported having been upset by requests to enact pornography (Russell, 1980; Senn and Radtke, 1986); and one of the most vulnerable groups in our society – prostitutes – reports abuse by pornography as almost an everyday event (Silbert and Pines, 1984). In addition, the laws of social learning must surely apply to pornography at least as much as to the mass media in general. Indeed, I – and others – have argued that sexual arousal and orgasm likely serve as unusually potent reinforcers of the messages conveyed by pornography. Finally, experimental research has shown that the viewing of violent pornography results in higher rates of aggression against women by male subjects.

Some people might wonder why I am more convinced than some of the major researchers on pornography that it plays a causative role in violent acts against women. Malamuth, for example, hypothesizes only *'indirect* causal influences of media sexual violence on antisocial behavior against women' (1986, p. 20). This is how he concluded his formal presentation to the Pornography Commission: 'Clearly, the mass media is [*sic*] certainly not just a matter of fantasy, and it can affect responses relevant to aggression against women such as attitudes. Such attitudes, finally, may in combination with other factors affect actual behavior such as aggression against women' (1985, p. 86).

Donnerstein appears to be highly inconsistent in what he says and writes about the causative role of pornography. For example, in his chapter for the book he co-edited with Malamuth, he ends the summary of his research by writing: 'We have now seen that there is a direct causal relationship between exposure to aggressive pornography and violence against women' (1984, p. 78). One and a half pages later, in the second-to-last sentence of his conclusion to the chapter, he writes: 'But more importantly, we need to be more certain as to what the causal factor is, if there is one, in the relationship between pornography and violence against women' (1984, p. 80). More recently, however, Donnerstein is downplaying the negative effects of pornography (Donnerstein, Linz, and Penrod, 1987).

What might explain our different conclusions? One difference between myself and these researchers is that they are psychologists, whereas I am a sociologist. This is significant because in drawing conclusions from the research about the causative effects of viewing pornography, it makes a great deal of difference whether one focuses on an individual or a group level of analysis. For example, on the individual level it is obvious that all viewers are not affected in the same way. It is easy to conclude from this that the effects of viewing pornography are mediated by other individual and/or social variables, and hence to argue that pornography has only indirect effects.

347

If, however, instead of trying to explain why Mr X is affected by such viewing but Mr Y is not, one focuses on whether the average aggression scores (or whatever is being measured) of those exposed to violent pornography are significantly higher than the aggression scores of those exposed to non-violent, non-abusive material, then any consistent effects that are registered are not indirect at all. It is this common difference of focus between psychologists and sociologists that may explain why Malamuth concludes from his research that sexually violent media contribute only indirectly to anti-social behaviour, while I conclude from his research that there are direct effects.*

Whereas the individual level of analysis is the more relevant one for clinicians, the group level of analysis is more relevant for social policy-makers. If researchers had insisted on being able to ascertain why Mr X died from lung cancer after twenty years of smoking but Mr Y did not, before being willing to warn the public that smoking causes lung cancer, there would have been a lot more deaths from lung cancer. Similarly, if we refused to see excessive alcohol consumption by drivers as a cause of accidents because not all drivers who are drunk have traffic accidents, there would be even more deaths than currently occur as a result of drunken drivers. Although it is important for researchers to continue to try to explain all the variables that might account for individual differences, we do not need to have all these answers before recognizing group effects.

Another factor that may help explain what seems to me an overly cautious stance by many researchers on this issue may be that they subscribe to the notion that scientists are not supposed to take a stand. When Donnerstein was asked by a commissioner about his being interviewed for a feature in *Penthouse* magazine, including whether he had been paid for the interview and whether the pornography industry had ever tried to influence him, he replied: 'I have never taken sides in this issue, and have tried to stay as objective as possible' (1985, p. 33). If he were doing research on racism rather than on aggression against women, and if he had found that media portrayals of African Americans seriously desensitize people to violence against them, would he be so proud about not taking sides? If one is doing

* Readers may be interested to know that on reading the previously published article on which this revised article is based (Russell, 1988), Malamuth told me that he 'had no quarrel with it'; indeed, he told me he thought I had done a 'very good job' (personal communication, August 1988).

research on the holocaust, is one not supposed to take sides? Is one not supposed to take sides about the effects of poverty? Or nuclear war? Or rape?

I personally take sides on all these issues. I do not believe scientists should be expected to be morally indifferent to human suffering and abuse. Yes, we need to be very clear about which of our opinions are based on data and how good the data are, which are based on theory, and which are based on hunch. But once there is very strong evidence that harm is being caused – by pornography, for example – surely it is the duty, particularly of scientists, to say so. And surely such scientists should also feel able to say that they deplore the harm done. Now *this* really *is* freedom of speech!

One of the effects of viewing non-violent pornography discovered by Zillmann is that 'the more extensive the exposure, the more accepting of pornography subjects became' (1984, p. 133). Although females expressed significantly less acceptance than males, this effect also applied to females. Pornography has expanded into a multi-billion-dollar-a-year industry. I believe we are seeing on a massive scale some of the very effects so brilliantly and carefully documented in some of the experiments by Malamuth, Donnerstein, Bryant, Zillmann and their colleagues. Donnerstein's description of the desensitization that occurred to healthy pre-selected male students after five days of viewing woman-slashing films may apply to ever-growing segments of our society.

The whole culture appears to have been affected by the very effects the research shows. The massive propaganda campaign is working; people now actually *see* differently. The stimuli keep having to be made more and more extreme for the violence to be recognized. As Zillmann shows, 'heavy consumption of common forms of pornography fosters an appetite for stronger materials' (1985, p. 127). What was considered hard-core in the past has become soft-core in the present. Where will this all end? Will we as a culture forever refuse to read the writing on the wall?

This chapter is a slightly revised version of 'Pornography and Rape: A Causal Model' published in *Political Psychology* 9(1), 1988.

The author would like to thank the following people for their helpful suggestions in the writing of this chapter: Catharine MacKinnon, Dorchen Leidholdt, Marny Hall, Sandra Butler and Helen Longino.

18 The Effects of Violent Pornography, Nonviolent Dehumanizing Pornography, and Erotica: Some Legal Implications from a Canadian Perspective

JAMES V. P. CHECK

Until about the mid-1970s, the pornography question for the most part centred around the moralistic issue of whether or not the distribution of sexually explicit materials *per se* would have a tendency to adversely affect the viewer (see e.g. Commission on Obscenity and Pornography, 1970). Moreover, the implicit assumption underlying this 'negative effects' hypothesis was that there was something immoral or antisocial about sexuality, and therefore about the public display of sexuality. In the past fifteen years, however, several important changes have taken place in various countries around the world, changes which have had a profound effect on the pornography debate. Perhaps the most important of these is the fact that contemporary researchers currently tend to focus much more on the *social content* of pornography rather than on the *sexual explicitness* of these materials. It is the purpose of this chapter to document the profound effect that this change has had on the 'pornography effects' debate, with particular reference to Canadian obscenity laws.

The Social Content of Pornography: A Typology of Sexually Explicit Materials

In 1984, I suggested that the most commonly found forms of sexually explicit materials might usefully be divided into three categories (see also Check, 1985):
    1. Sexually violent pornography;
    2. Non-violent dehumanizing pornography;
    3. Erotica.
In terms of operational definitions of these terms, Mr Justice Mel Shannon of the Alberta (Canada) Court of Queen's Bench had this to say after hearing various expert testimonies (including my

own) in his 1985 Canadian obscenity ruling (*R*. v. *Wagner*, 1985; p. 331):

> In *sexually violent pornography* one finds the overt infliction of pain and the overt use of force, or the threat of either of them.
>
> In sexually explicit pornography that is free of violence, but is *degrading or dehumanizing*, men and women are often verbally abused and portrayed as having animal characteristics. Women, particularly, are deprived of unique human character or identity and are depicted as sexual playthings, hysterically and instantly responsive to male sexual demands. They worship male genitals and their own value depends upon the quality of their genitals and breasts. Thus in such films professional women, such as nurses and secretaries, are hired solely for the purpose of sexual gratification, without regard for their professional qualifications and abilities.
>
> On the other hand, sexually explicit *erotica* portrays positive and affectionate human sexual interaction, between consenting individuals participating on a basis of equality. There is no aggression, force, rape, torture, verbal abuse or portrayal of humans as animals.

Having adopted the above classification system, Judge Shannon went on to make a number of precedent-setting decisions about pornography in the above-mentioned obscenity case, decisions which for the most part stand today. Following is a brief review of some of these decisions, and the social-scientific research evidence bearing upon them.

The Legal Issue of Obscenity

The Canadian Criminal Code (currently listed as Section 163) prohibits the production or distribution of 'obscene' materials. This prohibition applies throughout Canada. Moreover, through a series of precedents, 'obscene' materials have come to be operationally defined by the courts as materials which the Canadian contemporary community would be unwilling to *tolerate*. In this context, the term 'tolerate' refers to what Canadians would allow for distribution to others, and *not* simply what they themselves would be willing to view. Thus, the now familiar Community Standards Test has evolved, according to which sexually explicit material is deemed to be obscene if it is held that Canadians would be unwilling to tolerate its distribution.

In applying the Community Standards Test to the Wagner case, Shannon ruled that both sexually violent pornography and non-violent dehumanizing pornography would not be tolerated **351** by the Canadian contemporary community, and were therefore obscene. At the same time, however, he found that erotica would be tolerated by Canadians, and were therefore not obscene. Thus, he found that seven of the eight videotapes in question were either violent pornography or non-violent dehumanizing pornography, were intolerable, and were therefore obscene. The eighth videotape he found to be erotica, and therefore not obscene (even though it was highly sexually explicit). He described this eighth video (titled 'Greenhorn') as follows (*R* v. *Wagner*, 1985, p. 332):

> It is painfully boring, as it represents scene after scene of homosexual activities, but it is free of violence, crime, horror, and cruelty. All of the participants are willing, consenting adults. No one is degraded or dehumanized. It qualifies as erotica.

In a recent case (*R*. v. *Ross Wise*, 1990), Judge H. R. Locke used the expert testimony of social scientists (including, again, my own) to convict sexually violent and non-violent dehumanizing pornography and to acquit sexually explicit erotica. Judge Locke's descriptions of the material and his judgments in the case are reproduced in Appendix 3.

What is the empirical evidence, if any, that people are unwilling to tolerate violent or dehumanizing pornography? Unfortunately there is very little data that bears on this question in the Canadian context, and that at the same time meets the rather stringent criteria for admissible evidence that have been imposed by the Courts. In one obscenity case, for example, Justice Gale in *R*. v. *Times Square Cinema Ltd*. (1971) rejected the defence's 'survey' evidence because it was based upon a poll of people who attended one or both of two free showings of a videotape titled *Vixen*, as well as a poll of people who were selected at random from a local (Toronto) telephone directory and were invited to a free showing of a 'controversial' film. As Justice Gale observed (pp. 232–3), the problem with these data was that

> The opinions expressed came from persons who were not sufficiently objective or impartial as to be representative of the average contemporary Torontonian, and certainly not of the average contemporary Ontarian or Canadian. Neither group of persons surveyed could be objective, for they must have had some desire to see an exhibition which, at the front of the theatre, was indicated as being very sensual in nature.

In contrast, the courts have shown a willingness to consider survey data which reasonably reflects at a national level the attitudes of Canadians regarding the distribution of sexually explicit materials. For one such study, Check, Heapy, and Iwanyshyn (1985; forthcoming), surveyed a national sample of 1071 Canadians, who were reasonably representative of the average Canadian with respect to age, gender, and regional distribution. These authors found that 60 per cent of Canadians would be unwilling to allow anyone to see video cassettes showing 'sexually violent or degrading scenes (rape, torture, bondage, etc.)', while another 28 per cent wanted these scenes to be restricted to those 18 years or older. In contrast, only 25 per cent said that they would ban 'scenes of mutually consenting sexual activities, with no violent or degrading content, where the sex is "explicit" (you can see everything)'. Most respondents (57 per cent) simply wanted these latter materials restricted to those 18 years and older. Finally, these findings were more or less consistent across gender, region of the country, and community size (over or under 100,000 in population).

It seems, then, that there are at least some data consistent with Mr Justice Shannon's judgment that Canadians would be unwilling to tolerate the more abusive forms of pornography, but would indeed be willing to tolerate explicit erotica. Note as well that, in another national study conducted four years later, the data in Check, Heapy, and Iwanyshyn (1985; in press) were essentially replicated by Check (1989). Thus it seems that, at least over a four-year period, Canadians' attitudes regarding sex in the media are remarkably stable.

The Legal Question of Harm

Since the early 1980s Canada has been operating under a new Charter of Rights and Freedoms (Constitution Act, 1982), Section 2 (*b*) of which provides for 'freedom of thought, belief, opinion and expression including freedom of the press and other media of communication'. (Essentially, this is the 'Free Speech' section of the Charter). At the same time, however, this freedom is not absolute, but rather subject in Section 1 of the Charter 'only to such reasonable limits prescribed by law as can be demonstrably justified in a free and democratic society'.

In the Wagner case, the defence argued (1) that the provisions of Canada's obscenity law are 'unreasonably vague', so that a citizen of common intelligence would be unable to comprehend **353** and therefore comply with what is expected of him/her, and (2) that pornography is not harmful and therefore there is no need for the law. The importance of these two arguments stems from the fact that, if they are true, the court is bound to strike down the obscenity laws as unconstitutional, and acquit the defendant.

Mr Justice Shannon rejected the 'vagueness' argument. (As a matter of fact, although popular with pornography distributors, the vagueness argument never works in court, even to this day.) Shannon also rejected the 'no harm' argument put forward by the defence. Having heard expert testimony from social scientists on both sides of the 'harm' question, Shannon concluded that 'social harm' does in fact result from repeated exposure to both violent pornography and non-violent dehumanizing pornography.

What is the currently available evidence regarding these issues? With respect to the vagueness question, the only study comparing the three types of pornography discussed here has been reported by Check and Guloien (1989 see also Check, 1985). In this study, men who responded to newspaper advertisements for research subjects were shown 30-minute videotaped excerpts from commercially released, mainstream sexual entertainment materials and from sex education and sex therapy films. One group of men was shown excerpts of sexually violent pornography, and a second group viewed non-violent dehumanizing pornography. A third group was shown erotica. After viewing the films, and with no discussion or other input from the researchers, the men were simply asked to give their subjective ratings of the material on a series of scales. (For exampe, the men were asked to rate how obscene, offensive, degrading, affectionate, educational, etc., the materials were.) The results of this investigation were quite informative. A classification analysis of the men's subjective ratings revealed that over 90 per cent of the videos could be correctly classified as falling into the 'abusive' category (which included both violent pornography and nonviolent dehumanizing pornography) as against the erotica category. Note here again that the men were not provided with any definitions such as those delineated in the present chapter. Rather, this 90 per cent correct classification was obtained by simply examining the men's subjective ratings of the material that they were shown. Thus it seems that, at least with respect to the men who volunteered for this study, there was little confusion about what constituted erotica and what constituted violent and/

or dehumanizing pornography. (Note, however, that women were not included in this investigation, and thus caution must be exercised in generalizing from these findings.)

With respect to the legal issue of the 'harmful' effects of exposure to pornography, the research bearing upon this point has been extensively reviewed elsewhere (e.g. Check and Malamuth, 1986; Donnerstein, Linz, and Penrod, 1987; Malamuth and Donnerstein, 1984; Zillmann and Bryant, 1989), with no fewer than three excellent reviews in the present volume (see Einsiedel, Chapter 15; Weaver, Chapter 16; Russell, Chapter 17). However, the reader should be aware that there have been a number of what can only be described as polemic, 'junk' reviews of the social science and psychological research literature reviews which are biased and better serve the political ends of the reviewers than inform and educate the reader. (Two of the worst of these are D. Scott's 1985 paper damning sex in the media as causing an absolutely incredible number of evils, and the 1991 Howitt and Cumberbatch report to the British Home Office, in which the authors confused the reader and promoted their own political views regarding censorship (see Check, 1991, and Donnerstein et al., 1987 for further comments).

While all reviewers are naturally not unanimous with respect to the details of the research literature, the reasonable conclusion that can be drawn from the research (on considering all the reviews) is that sexually violent pornography has antisocial effects and non-violent dehumanizing pornography has antisocial effects, but erotica seems to be pretty much benign. As an example of findings consistent with this overall conclusion, Check and Guloien (1989) found that repeated exposure to either sexually violent pornography or non-violent dehumanizing pornography increased men's self-reported proclivity for rape and forced sex acts, whereas exposure to erotica had no significant impact (see Fig. 1).

While not belabouring the issue, we should note a number of important points concerning the pornography effect of literature as it relates to the legal issue of 'harm'. First, the social-scientific evidence reviewed by the above-mentioned reviewers is not the only evidence considered by the various courts and pornography commissions that have considered the harm issue in various countries. It is true, for example, that pornography commissions in Canada, the United States, Australia, and New Zealand have all concluded that certain types of pornography do cause harm **355**

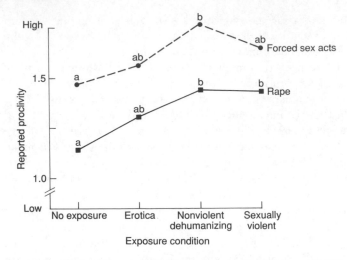

Figure 1. Reported proclivity for rape and forced sex acts following repeated exposure to pornography (3 sessions); $N = 436$ males. *Note*: Means with common lettering do not differ at $P < .05$.

in the legal sense, but they have not always considered the social-scientific research evidence to be the 'acid test' of this issue. (The importance of the work of social scientists seems sometimes to be over-rated on the world stage.) Similarly, despite the fact that both the Supreme Court of Canada and the Supreme Court of the United States have concluded that pornography can cause harm, the social science evidence is not always primary in judges' decision-making (although it is certainly carefully considered).

Another point to remember about social scientists studying pornography effects is that they are often ill-prepared to translate their findings into legally 'consumable' applied conclusions. A classic example of this problem occurs when we find null effects in one of our studies, but do not consider the possibility that we have committed a Type 2 error. (A Type 2 error occurs when research fails to uncover an effect of pornography that is really there.) Unless we have conducted the appropriate statistical 'power analysis', we must be very cautious in concluding that there are no effects of exposure to pornography just because we didn't find them in one study.

The Issue of Sexual Explicitness
Perhaps the most important ruling that Mr Justice Shannon made in the Wagner case was that the level of sexual explicitness

of the material is for the most part irrelevant in the determination of obscenity. For example, he ruled that erotica would not be obscene even if it were fully explicit, leaving absolutely nothing to the imagination. From an empirical perspective, this ruling is consistent with the results of Check, Heapy, and Iwanyshan (1985; forthcoming), who found that Canadians would be willing to tolerate non-abusive consenting sex for distribution to adults, no matter how explicit. Once again, we see that sexual explicitness becomes a less important dimension than the social content of the materials in question. (See Mahoney, forthcoming.)

The Sex Equality Issue
Finally, in generalizing from the social-science evidence discussed by the experts in *R. v. Wagner*, Mr Justice Shannon concluded that violent and dehumanizing pornography undermines men's receptiveness to women's legitimate claims for equality and respect. Although not explicitly raised as an issue in *Wagner*, Shannon's implicit reference to sex equality was a portent of things to come. To a greater and greater extent, constitutional arguments in Canadian obscenity cases have centred around Section 15(1) of the *Canadian Charter*:

> 15(1)   Every individual is equal before and under the law and has the right to the equal protection and equal benefit of the law without discrimination, and, in particular, without discrimination based on race, national or ethnic origin, colour, religion, sex, age, or physical or mental disability.

Several recent obscenity rulings in Canada have held that, notwithstanding the empirical research evidence, violent and dehumanizing pornography undermines women's right to equal treatment, and therefore as speech must 'yield' to Section 15 of the *Canadian Charter*. In other words, if pornography producers' rights to free speech impinge upon or conflict with women's rights to equal treatment, then the courts have held that the law is justified in limiting the production and distribution of the pornography.

Concluding Commentary
I have attempted here to illustrate how one country deals with the issue of pornography, and how social science evidence has been used in the legal decision-making process. At the same time, **357**

however, I would like to make it *absolutely clear* that I neither endorse these legal decisions, nor disapprove of them. It is not my purpose here to recommend policy, but rather to articulate some of the thinking behind certain decisions that have been made by the Canadian courts, and to provide some food for thought for those in other countries who are making their own legal decisions about this important topic.

References

Canadian Charter of Rights and Freedoms: pt. 1 of the Constitution Act, 1982, being Schedule B of the Canada Act, 1982 (UK), c. 11, s. 1.

Check, J. V. P. (1985). 'Evaluations and effects of violent and nonviolent pornography: Does erotica exist?', *Canadian Psychology* 26 (2a).

—— (1989). 'Changes in attitudes towards sex in the media: 1984–1988', *Canadian Psychology* 30, p. 206.

—— (1991). Review of Howitt and Cumberbatch (1990), Toronto: York Univ. Dept. of Psychology.

—— and Guloien, T. H. (1989). 'Reported proclivity for coercive sex following exposure to sexually violent pornography, nonviolent dehumanizing pornography, and erotica', in D. Zillmann and J. Bryant (eds.), *Pornography: Research Advances and Policy Considerations*, Hillsdale NJ: Erlbaum.

——, Heapy, N. A., and Iwanyshyn, O. (1985). 'A national survey of Canadians' attitudes regarding sexual content in the media', paper presented at the meeting of the Canadian Communications Association, Montreal.

—— —— —— (forthcoming). 'A survey of Canadians' attitudes regarding sexual content in the media', *Canadian Psychology*.

—— and Malamuth, N. M. (1985). 'Pornography and sexual aggression: A social learning theory analysis', *Communication Yearbook* 9, pp. 181–213.

Commission on Obscenity and Pornography (1970). *Report of the Commission of Obscenity and Pornography*, Washington, DC: Govt. Printing Office.

Donnerstein, E., Linz, D., and Penrod, S. (1987). *The Question of Pornography: Research Findings and Policy Implications*, New York: Free Press.

Howitt, D., and Cumberbatch, G. (1991). *Pornography – Impacts and Influences: A Review of Available Research Evidence on the Effects of Pornography*, London: Home Office Research and Planning Unit.

Mahoney, K. E. (forthcoming). 'An equality approach to freedom of expression', *Duke Law Journal*.

Malamuth, N., and Donnerstein, E. (eds.) (1984). *Pornography and Sexual Aggression*, Orlando. Fla.: Academic.

Scott, D. A. (1985). *Pornography: Its Effects on the Family, Community and Culture*, Washington, DC: Child and Family Protection Institute.

Zillmann, D., and Bryant, J. (eds.) (1989). *Pornography: Research Advances and Policy Considerations*, Hillsdale, NJ: Erlbaum.

19 On the Question of Pornography and Sexual Violence: Moving Beyond Cause and Effect

DEBORAH CAMERON AND ELIZABETH FRAZER

What is to be done about pornography? Whenever feminists raise this question – and they have raised it insistently, on both sides of the Atlantic – one particular issue can be counted on to dominate discussion. That issue is: does pornography actually have significant effects in terms of causing violent and misogynistic behaviour? Can we, in other words, establish a firm relationship between the sphere of representation where pornography is located, and the sphere of action in which specific individuals harm other individuals? Any feminist who objects to pornography is immediately challenged to demonstrate such a causal relationship; anyone who doubts that the relationship exists is under pressure to concede that pornography is not a problem. The entire agenda for debate is drawn up in terms of this question.

The purpose of this chapter is to show what is wrong with framing the pornography issue in this way, and to suggest how feminists can move beyond simplistic notions of cause and effect without conceding the argument altogether. Arguments that pornography 'causes' violent acts are, indeed, inadequate. But the conclusion that therefore we should not be concerned about pornography at all is equally unjustified. Representation and action may not be related in a chain of cause and effect, but one can nevertheless discover important and complex connections between them – connections which imply that feminists should indeed concern themselves with the forms of representation that exist in our culture.

The specific case with which we will be concerned here is sexual murder, an extreme form of violence whose catastrophic effects are impossible to deny or minimize; we believe, however, that our analysis can just as well be applied to less extreme instances. By examining the role that representations (primarily, but not exclusively, pornographic representations) play in the lives of sexual killers and in the cultures to which they belong, we hope to indicate new directions for the argument, producing a critique of pornography that does not depend on proving a specifically *causal* link with violence.

PORNOGRAPHY AND MURDER: CAUSE AND EFFECT?

More than any other form of sexual violence, sadistic sexual murder – killing in order to obtain sexual gratification – produces widespread unease about the health of the culture in which it occurs. Ever since the Jack the Ripper murders in 1888, one predictable response to this type of crime has been to ask what is wrong with the modern world that it has such people in it? And in addressing that question it has long been customary to cite the pervasiveness of pornography as a sign – perhaps even a cause – of social and sexual malaise.

This particular line of argument used to be associated with conservatives who saw sex-crime as indicative of a 'decline in moral values'. In recent years, though, it has also been deployed by a progressive and radical movement, namely feminism. It needs to be emphasized, of course, that the feminist and the conservative differ in their diagnoses of our moral ills as well as in the treatment they prescribe. Whereas conservatives criticize almost all expressions of sexuality as immoral and recommend a return to traditional religious and family values, feminist analysis criticizes instead the oppressive and misogynistic forms such expressions typically take in male-dominated culture. Stressing the pervasiveness of misogyny through time – that is, denying that we are witnessing a moral decline – feminists identify religion and the family as part of the problem.

From these otherwise opposed perspectives, however, there is some common support for the idea that pornography 'causes' sexual violence. This is the argument we want to take issue with here. For although we agree with the feminist contention that pornography is (1) oppressive and misogynistic and (2) connected with sexual violence, we do not believe that the idea of representations causing or leading to acts such as sexual murder is either theoretically compelling or politically progressive.

We want to rehearse the arguments for this position at greater length than we were able to do in our extended analysis of the phenomenon of sexual killing, *The Lust to Kill*.[1] It is worth elaborating on the position we sketch there if only because it is relatively unusual, differing in crucial respects from the two most familiar feminist positions on pornography and sexual violence: to put it very briefly, we disagree *both* with those anti-porn feminists who see a connection between pornography and violence, but analyse it only in causal terms, *and* with those feminists who have been critical of causal arguments, but who basically do not believe that there is any significant connection to be made between representation and action.

Causal Models and the Case of Ted Bundy

The issue of pornography and its alleged role in sexual murder has recently come to the attention of the public once again following the confession of US serial killer Ted Bundy immediately prior to his execution early in 1989. In his final account of himself, Bundy placed great emphasis on the role of pornography in his career as a sexual murderer. He represented himself as an obsessive consumer of increasingly sadistic material, and implied that pornography had been formative of desires which he was ultimately driven to act out in real life. He began with 'milder' forms of deviant behaviour, such as 'peeping Tom' activities, and worked his way up to repeated acts of killing. (See Chapters 7 and 10.)

Ted Bundy's story postulates some kind of cause and effect relation between what he read and what he did. It draws on certain familiar ideas: that images of torture, rape and murder engender (at least in some people) a compulsion to go out and do likewise; and that there is a progression – its course somehow inexorable – from less to more harmful fantasies and, by association, behaviours.

We may label these ideas about how porn affects its users the COPYCAT MODEL – you see it, then (therefore?) you do it – and the ADDICTION MODEL – initially erotic stimulation is obtained from relatively 'mild' forms of representation, but as the habit becomes established, it requires a stronger stimulus to achieve the same effect, and eventually representation itself is no longer strong enough, so that the user is impelled to act out the stimulus.

If these models are familiar, it is feminism which has made them so. For example, the copycat model is implicit in part of one of the best-known pieces of feminist writing/action against pornography: the Minneapolis ordinance devised by Andrea Dworkin and Catharine MacKinnon.[2] Among other things, the ordinance provides for victims of sexual violence to sue producers **361** of pornography on the grounds that their product directly inspired an assault.

Let us hasten to point out the uselessness of denying that some incidents of sexual violence do indeed re-enact specific scenarios from pornographic texts with a literalness that might justify the epithet 'copycat'. At the hearings which took place in Minneapolis while the ordinance was being debated, witnesses testified to such incidents.[3] The question we raise is not whether copycat incidents occur, but whether they should be treated as paradigmatic of the general relationship between pornography and sexual violence, or whether they should be analysed as a special case. If they are paradigmatic then they provide very strong evidence for a causal model (and the adherents of causal models evidently do interpret them in this way). But we shall argue later that if we treat copycat incidents as paradigmatic we leave most incidents unexplained; that even in the case of clear copycat incidents the causal model is over-deterministic; and that copycat incidents can be explained satisfactorily without treating them as paradigmatic.

The addiction model is perhaps less familiar, though it is often an implicit accompaniment to the copycat model. Lately, though, it seems to have been gaining ground in its own right; we are hearing more and more about it, especially from women and men who wish to stress the damage pornography does to *men*.[4] We label it the addiction model (and note that the word *addiction* is used explicitly by the writers we are talking about) because it trades on an analogy between the use of pornography and the use of drugs (alcohol, tobacco, narcotics, etc.): all these habits are seen as harmful both to those who indulge in them – the 'addicts' – and to the community which must cope with the anti-social behaviour they engender. Although addiction is viewed as a social problem, there is a new emphasis on the individual within this model; the addict himself can be viewed as a victim whose weakness or inadequacy is exploited by the unscrupulous. We should not be surprised, then, that men find this model appealing when applied to their use of pornography; but we might do well to be suspicious of its depoliticizing implications (since the collective power of men and the institutionalized nature of sexual violence against women are nowhere at issue in this account).

The politics of the addiction account will be examined in more **362** detail below; meanwhile, though, let us go back to the case of

Ted Bundy, who characterized himself as both copycat and junkie.

A serial sexual murderer like Bundy stretches the addiction model to its limits; here we have a habit that got totally out of control. Just as smoking a joint is sometimes depicted as the first step on a slippery slope that leads to the shooting gallery, so in Bundy's case the addiction model posits that looking at pornographic representations was the first step on the long road which led to repeated and brutal killing. Once 'hooked', he could not stop: he was compelled to increase the 'dose' to the point where his behaviour became almost unimaginably destructive.

How compelling is this account? In a society currently obsessed with the 'drug problem' it is a way of understanding deviant behaviour that carries a powerful resonance; it commands instant understanding and, given that it is a medical model, the respect accorded to scientific truths. This might be one reason why feminists find it convenient: we have very often been obliged to describe the oppression of women in terms of other, more familiar social evils in order to be understood and, beyond that, taken seriously. But what has to be remembered is that when we explain one thing in terms of another we are constructing an essentially metaphorical account. The notion of addiction to pornography is a metaphor; the mechanisms of physiological dependence that characterize, say, cocaine addiction are not directly paralleled in someone who feels a compulsion to look at porn. Feminists are usually very cautious in using 'biological' analogies which imply that aspects of sexuality are 'natural', rather than constructed or indeed chosen: it is therefore necessary to consider very carefully how apt this particular metaphor is.

Nor should we be swayed in this by the fact that Ted Bundy himself thought the metaphor apt. We make this point because it is tempting to believe that Bundy's own endorsement constitutes the strongest possible evidence for the model and for causal explanations in general. From his disinterested position as a complete misogynist, Bundy has confirmed what feminists have been saying for years, i.e. that using pornography can lead to the commission of sexual crimes. Before we turn to the theoretical shortcomings of this argument generally, it is worth pointing out why we should be wary of treating what sex murderers say about themselves as unproblematically true, even when it seems to coincide with our own analysis. **363**

Just after Bundy's execution, a feminist friend expressed the opinion that his confession, with its support for the idea of pornography as a cause of sex crime, would not be taken seriously by our generally misogynistic culture. She contrasted this apathy with the attention paid to less 'feminist' accounts produced by murderers: 'If he'd blamed it all on his mother,' she remarked, 'everyone would have believed him.' This is a revealing comment (and doubtless, an accurate prediction). But what it reveals is not that either the misogynistic, mother-blaming account of sex murder or the 'feminist', porn-blaming account is the truth of the matter; rather, it reveals that the discourse of explanation on this subject is highly contested and profoundly ideological.

Where does a sex killer's account of himself come from? Not, we suggest, from some privileged personal insight, but from a finite repertoire of cultural clichés which the murderer, like everyone else, has come across in case histories, pop-psychology, newspapers, films and ordinary gossip with family, friends and workmates. At any given time the clichés available are a heterogeneous and contradictory collection; some may carry more authority than others (for instance, we no longer think much of a killer who tells us he was possessed by the devil, though traces of this ancient supernatural account can be seen in the tabloid label 'fiend' used for sex murderers); new clichés may enter the repertoire, challenging or providing alternatives to the existing explanations. Porn-blaming is a recent example.

Let us examine how cultural clichés work by examining one that feminists are in no danger of confusing with 'the truth': the mother-blaming explanation of sexual murder. The idea that sexual killers are revenging themselves on dominating or inadequate mothers is a relatively recent cliché. Although it was found in expert discourse (i.e. forensic psychiatry, criminology) much earlier – its source, in fact, is psychoanalytic theory – it entered popular awareness only in the 1950s and 1960s, by way of cultural products like the Hitchcock movie *Psycho*. At this point, not untypically, the popularized version 'fed back' into expert pronouncements in a circular, reinforcing process. Police in the Boston Strangler case in the 1960s announced that they were looking for someone like Norman Bates, the mother-fixated character in *Psycho*.[5] The actual strangler, Albert DeSalvo, in fact bore little resemblance to this stereotype. But the perception of sexual murder as a consequence of pathological mother–son relations persisted, and during the 1970s became a theme in the testimony of some real-life killers (a striking example is Edmund Kemper, the 'Co-ed Killer' of Santa Cruz)[6] – whereupon it re-entered expert discourse in case-history form. The circle was completed once again.

By the time of Ted Bundy's confession in 1989, a new account had become culturally available: the porn-blaming explanation. This one entered popular awareness in a relatively unusual way, through organized political activity on the part of feminists during the 1970s. It did not replace earlier accounts like the mother-blaming explanation (or any number of other clichés, from the oversexed 'Beast' to the 'split personality' to the 'psychopath'), but it achieved sufficient status in the culture that Ted Bundy could invoke it where Ed Kemper (for example) could not.

That sexual offenders other than murderers use cultural clichés to construct their accounts of themselves is attested by the sociologists Diana Scully and Joseph Marolla who interviewed convicted rapists and found recurring, culturally familiar themes in their narratives.[7] Scully and Marolla call these clichés 'voca-bularies of motive' and suggest that rapists use them in order to justify their behaviour and 'negotiate a non-deviant identity' for themselves.

In the case of murderers, of course, the goal is more likely to be negotiating a *deviant* identity. It is hardly surprising to find Kenneth Bianchi, one of the 'Hillside Stranglers', claiming a multiple personality – or Ted Bundy himself asserting, as he did for a number of years, that his murders had been committed by an 'entity' inside him – when one considers that, in a murder trial, convincing the court that you are incompetent or insane may be literally a matter of life and death. But for the purposes of the argument here it does not matter whether murderers have cynical and self-interested motives in offering their stereotypical accounts, or whether they sincerely believe those accounts to be true. The crucial point is that the accounts *come from the culture*. If they did not, they would make no sense, either to the murderer or to those he seeks to convince.

When Ted Bundy tells us he was corrupted by pornography, we need to ask not whether he is lying but where he got the story. It is unsatisfactory to accept Bundy's account while rejecting Kemper's just because one is misogynist while the other appears to be feminist. Instead, we must treat both accounts *as accounts*, that is, as discourse, subjecting them to further analysis and **365** scrutiny. This is what we intend to do with the pornography-blaming explanation of sexual murder.

Before we turn to this central part of our argument, though, we want to return to a point we mentioned earlier regarding the politics of the explanation. In the discussion of cultural clichés we observed that murderers' accounts have a place within the judicial process in which their fates are decided, and this is something which feminists cannot afford to overlook.

The Politics of Addiction

Most court cases involving sexual murder do not revolve round the question of 'whodunnit'; there is usually, by this stage, agreement that the accused man did indeed commit the acts of which he stands accused. What is at issue is usually whether or not he should be held fully responsible for those acts. The accused and his counsel construct an account of the crimes in the hope of establishing a defence of what in English law is called 'diminished responsibility'. If such a defence succeeds, the offence is reduced from murder to manslaughter and the offender becomes a candidate for treatment rather than retributive punishment. (In most states of the USA, a crucial issue is whether the death penalty can be invoked.)

Feminists would presumably be reluctant to punish the mentally ill, and would therefore not object to this sort of defence *per se*. But in far too many cases, as a number of feminist scholars have demonstrated, diminished responsibility defences and their equivalents in other legal systems succeed although the grounds are flimsy and the underlying rationale systematically sexist. For instance, in several recent cases of wife-killing, the alleged infidelity or promiscuity or 'nagging' of the victim has been grounds for reducing the offence to manslaughter.[8] Sexually violent men have been defended on grounds of provocation, especially when their victims were prostitutes but even when they were children.[9] It thus appears that attributions of responsibility, however thickly cloaked in expert discourse, are fundamentally ideological and sexist in their operation. Their overall effect is to condone violence against women by repeatedly failing to punish its perpetrators.

If feminists follow through with the logic of the addiction model, they risk adding to an already depressing catalogue of defences and excuses. The truly novel thing about porn-blaming explanations may turn out to be that a feminist, as opposed to misogynist, account is being co-opted for use in the interests of violent men and against those of women.

The addiction model has political implications over and above its possible judicial uses, however. The central metaphor of drug addiction carries strong connotations of abnormality and deviance of the individual addict: drug abusers are seen as personally or socially inadequate – in some more liberal accounts, as disadvantaged and in need of help. Feminists have spent around twenty years attempting to combat the notion that sexual violence is the province of the pathological individual, arguing instead that it is structural and systemic, arising from gender hierarchy and conflict (which it also helps to maintain by intimidating women collectively). The addiction metaphor undermines that analysis, taking us back to abnormal individuals, and evacuating sexual politics from the account. Why it should be men and not women who (1) become 'addicts' and/or (2) turn to violence as a consequence of addiction remains totally mysterious in this individualized model. Surely we can agree to locate murderers at an extreme of male violence without completely losing sight of the wider social and political context: men as a group derive benefits from the institutionalized control of women, in which violence plays a major role.

BEYOND CAUSE AND EFFECT

It will not have gone unnoticed that so far we have put forward no sustained argument against causal explanations linking pornography to sexual violence; rather we have been trying to cast doubt on some of the arguments advanced in support of such explanations. But if a sex killer's endorsement of a particular explanation does not make it true, it does not necessarily make it false either. Nor is an argument automatically false just because its political implications are unpalatable. Surely the fact that Ted Bundy read pornography and attached significance to it calls for comment from a feminist?

We fully accept each of these points, and will respond to them by doing two things. First, we will put forward a general argument against causal accounts of human action. Second, we will try to construct an alternative model of the connections between pornography and sexual violence.

What Is Wrong with Causal Explanations?

The central objection we have to causal explanations of the relationship beween pornography and sexual violence can be stated very simply: causal accounts are completely inappropriate to explain any kind of human behaviour. Indeed, that very common term, human behaviour, has a certain misleading quality. Animals 'behave', impelled by instinct or simple stimuli; inanimate objects can (metaphorically) be said to 'behave', impelled by physical forces. Human beings, however, *act*.

The notion of cause is most appropriate in the physical sciences. For example, if we understand the forces acting upon them – things like gravity and inertia – and we know their physical specifications (mass, weight, etc.) – we can accurately predict the motion of two billiard balls colliding on a flat surface. The balls' 'behaviour' is determined by the laws of physics.

Humans are not like billiard balls – or indeed like animals, whose behaviour can be described in terms of a stimulus–response model. Humans have the capacity for symbolization and language, which enables us – and perhaps even obliges us – to impose meaning on the stimuli we encounter, and to respond in ways which also carry meaning. Human 'behaviour', therefore, is not determined by laws analogous to those of physics. It is not deterministically 'caused'. It needs to be explained in a different way, by interpretation of what it means and elucidation of the beliefs or understandings that make it possible and intelligible.

At this point, a sceptic might well raise two questions. First of all, is not sexual behaviour an exception to this rule? Sex is surely part of our 'natural', animal endowment, an instinctive rather than a cultural phenomenon, and therefore susceptible to less complex explanations. To this we would reply, using a formulation feminists are familiar with, that there is a conceptual distinction to be made between sex, which is a biological phenomenon, and sexuality, which is a social or cultural construct. Sexuality reflects human consciousness and the ability to impose meaning on basic bodily experience. It has to do not with instinctual need but with desire; and that the forms of desire are cultural rather than natural can be appreciated if one considers the extraordinary variety of sexual practice attested by historians, anthropologists and so on (not to speak of the blatant artificiality of many human sexual conventions: do animals wear black stockings?). In human culture sex is always overlaid with sexuality; more generally, biological phenomena (the emotions, pain, the cycle of birth, maturation and death) are always overlaid with cultural discourse.

Secondly, our sceptic might object that the actions of sex murderers are also exceptional, since they are too bizarre for us to be able to say what understandings make them 'possible and intelligible'. For most people, indeed, the acts of a sex murderer are impossible and unintelligible. But a moment's reflection will show this to be false. Of course not all of us share Ted Bundy's desires; but we are perfectly able to interpret them. We have a category for people like Bundy ('serial sexual killer') and a number of accounts are available to us to make sense of his actions (namely the cultural clichés discussed above). However repellent Bundy's acts, however distant his desires from our own, they are intelligible to us. They do not strike us as pointless and uninterpretable in the way the actions of, say, a severely autistic individual might seem pointless and uninterpretable. The difference between Ted Bundy and the autistic person is the difference between having a language (i.e. a set of socially shared meanings) and not having one. The autistic person's actions defy interpretation because only they have access to the code.

The code of sexual murder was once as uninterpretable as autistic behaviour – in some cultures, it still would be. As recently as 1888, the year of Jack the Ripper, people were at a loss to understand the motivation of someone who murdered and disembowelled prostitutes. It was seriously suggested that the killer wanted to sell his victims' reproductive organs to anatomists for profit; or that he was trying, in a grotesque way, to draw attention to the scandal of slum housing in London.[10] Nowadays we would immediately respond to a comparable set of killings by invoking the category of sexual murder. This account was given by some commentators in 1888, but it had to compete with other explanations (whereas today it would be the obvious, preferred account). And what this shows is that a certain interpretation or discourse has entered the culture and become familiar in the space of a hundred years.

The question we need to ask, then, is where that discourse came from, why it arose at the specific time and in the particular place it did, how it spread and developed subsequently and so on. These would be important questions because, from the kind of perspective advocated here, it is precisely the emergence of a discourse making sexual murder 'possible and intelligible' which **369** creates the conditions for sexual murder to exist on the scale it now does: no longer as an isolated, random aberration but as a culturally meaningful act which an individual might consciously choose to perform.

We may sum up the argument so far by asserting that sexual murder is not a piece of abnormal sexual behaviour determined by innate drives, but a cultural category with a social significance. Sex killers are not responding unthinkingly or involuntarily to a stimulus, they are adopting a role which exists in the culture, as recognizable and intelligible to us (albeit not as acceptable) as the role of 'artist' or 'feminist' or 'hippie'.

What of pornography? Feminist proponents of the copycat and addiction models may be espousing a causal account, but it is not guilty of the biological determinism that pervades many so-called 'scientific' explanations (e.g. the account of sexual deviance which postulates excessive levels of testosterone in offenders). Rather, the 'cause' here is social conditioning through exposure to sadistic representations. And is this not a somewhat different, less objectionable version of the causal model?

The answer, in our view, is ultimately no. This 'social' account too is inadequate because it leaves out the crucial area of interpretation of meaning. The whole idea of conditioning – addiction is simply an extreme form of conditioning – implies a gradual process over which the subject has no control, and in which he does not actively engage (it is done to him, it determines his subsequent behaviour). Here it seems to us there is an implicit behaviouristic (stimulus–response) model in operation. It is taken for granted, for instance, that the addict's compulsion is fuelled by need and not desire, his initial arousal when looking at pornography is rooted somehow in natural/biological responses. At the point where need erupts into action, the behaviourism becomes explicit.

But if once again we compare the use of pornography with the use of narcotics – a comparison to which the addiction model directs us – this account seems less than compelling. A person does not have to interpret a line of cocaine in order to feel certain effects when it enters the bloodstream. S/he does have to interpret the picture of a dead and mutilated female body, along fairly narrow and conventional lines, in order to find it erotic. When someone looks or reads, they are constantly engaging, interacting with the text to produce meaning from it. The meaning is not

magically, inherently 'there' in the pictures or the words: the reader has to make it. The text does not independently have effects on readers or compel them to act in particular ways, as if they were passive and unreflecting objects. They are subjects, creators of meaning; the pornographic scenario must always be mediated by their imagination. (This, incidentally, is why pornography calls forth such a variety of responses; why not only individuals, but groups derive such different meanings from it.)

Violent sexual acts, for example murders, are also works of the imagination before they are public events. Both common sense and the testimony of convicted rapists and killers suggest that these acts are conceived, planned, acted out in the imagination, in a way that is active, creative and conscious.[11] To speak of such acts as being 'caused' in the way a virus causes disease, gravity causes objects to fall or a bell caused Pavlov's famous dogs to salivate is to misunderstand their essence, their motivation, the very thing that makes them exciting and desired: in short, it is to overlook their *meaning*.

What, then, is the meaning of sexual murder for the cultures which recognize it and the men who engage in it? Let us answer this question by giving a brief account of the emergence of sex killing (drawn from Cameron and Frazer, 1987). This involves talking mainly about the forms of discourse which made sex murder 'possible and intelligible' (and continue to do so); our focus on discourse, representation, will lead into a more specific discussion of this chapter's main topic, pornography.

The Emergence of Sexual Murder

We have already indicated that there is evidence to suggest sexual murder was not widely conceived of as a type of phenomenon before the 1880s. As far as we can tell from the historical records available, the kinds of acts which we now call sexual murder, however conceived, were extraordinarily rare before that time too. Several cases were categorized as sex killings retrospectively; but the vast majority of the incidents which conform to our definition of a sex murder occurred in the late nineteenth and twentieth centuries.

Eroticized murder had however been represented in fiction before the late nineteenth century. The sadistic and necrophiliac aesthetic of the Romantic period (i.e. from the late eighteenth century) – its insistent linking of cruelty and death with eroticism and beauty – is analysed by Mario Praz in his study *The Romantic Agony*.[12] It was underpinned by an explicit philosophy, whose   **371**

most relevant exponent (for the purposes of tracing the emergence of sexual murder, at least) was the Marquis de Sade.

Sade wrote fictions which also philosophize, and the views he
espouses may be summed up as follows. The nature of 'man' is
not to be good only, but also to be evil, and there is great (erotic)
pleasure to be found in wicked acts. Indeed, it is by *transgressing*
the bounds of accepted morality, as embodied in religion, the law
and social mores, that 'man' may *transcend* all the constraints that
keep him in a state of unfreedom. Murder, the ultimate transgressive act, is both particularly pleasurable and particularly
liberating. It gives 'man' *mastery*: over another human being (an
Other), the victim whom he kills, but also and perhaps even
more importantly over nature, the universe and his own destiny.
This Sadeian theme is echoed in more recent writing; for
instance, in André Gide's characterization of murder as 'the
culminating *acte gratuite* which liberates man from the determinism of the material universe'.[13]

Sade's philosophy did not, of course, come from nowhere. It
was a product of the Western intellectual and political movement
we know as the Enlightenment. During the seventeenth and
eighteenth centuries, many questions were raised concerning the
nature of human beings, their place in the universe and their
relation to the state. The traditional feudal order, centred on
God and his appointed governor, the king, was questioned, and
in some places overthrown. Ideas about political 'liberty' were
propounded, and Sade himself was a notable supporter of the
French Revolution. This was also an era when scientific knowledge expanded considerably: indeed the sort of causal account
of natural phenomena discussed above is associated with Enlightenment philosophy and science.

The shifts and upheavals of the eighteenth century, which
focused on individual rights and liberties, but at the same time
began to understand and systematize the general forces constraining individual action, were bound to pose questions about
'man's' free will and to intensify the desire for transcendence and
mastery over the material universe so evident in Sade's writings.
The elaboration of ideas linking murder with liberty and sexual
pleasure can be seen as one specific expression of this general
current of thought.

At this point it might occur to the reader to ask what the
products of eighteenth-century intellectual culture, abstract con-
372 cepts like 'free will' and 'transcendence' could possibly have to

do with the activities of someone like Jack the Ripper a hundred years later. Is it reasonable to suppose that Ted Bundy had ever heard of the Enlightenment? Well, maybe not. But the philosophy and art of one age become the common sense and popular culture of succeeding ages. For instance, even the less educated citizens of modern democracies take for granted the concept of individual rights and freedoms. They find it hard to comprehend times and cultures in which that concept did not exist, was contested or daringly avant-garde. We need not suppose that people like this are deeply familiar with the writings of Mill and Rousseau in order to explain where their political consciousness comes from.

The discourse connecting sex, murder, mastery, liberty and transcendence no longer appears as a coherent and revolutionary philosophy, but it is nevertheless familiar enough cultural fare. Not only has it continued to inform philosophy (e.g. existentialism), 'high art' (e.g. surrealism) and critically acclaimed literature (cf. D. M. Thomas's *The White Hotel*), it is also woven into more popular representations, many of which portray the murderer as a rebel and a hero: true crime magazines and journalism, crime fictions, waxwork museums, movies, 'bodice ripper' Gothic novels and, of course, pornography.

Ted Bundy apart, there is a large body of evidence showing that those men who actually do become sexual killers have often immersed themselves in this culture of murder as transcendence and murderer as hero. In *The Lust to Kill* we have argued that the element in murder to which these men are attracted above all is the scope it offers them to become transcendent, masterful heroes who control their own destiny by sheer will. They are not primarily motivated by hatred of their victims, nor by an animal lust for blood. They are concerned with *themselves* much more than with their Others (who are needed merely to confirm the will of the self); the thrill they get from murder is the thrill of transgressing and thereby demonstrating their freedom from ordinary constraints. If we are right in reading the motivation of the sex killer in this way, it is clear that sexual murder does crucially depend on the discourse whose history has just been summarized. These ideas are exactly what makes it possible to get this kind of pleasure from killing.

In support of the idea that murderers directly manipulate the discourse of transcendence which they encounter in various cultural sources, we may consider an illustrative example, that of **373** the 'Moors Murderer' Ian Brady. Brady is now known to be responsible for the deaths of four young children and a youth in the 1960s; his trial, where he and his lover Myra Hindley were jointly accused of three murders, was probably the most sensational ever held in Britain. What did Brady read, and what did he make of it?

First of all, Brady did read pornography, and much was made of this in court. (He also produced pornographic representations of his crimes, a point whose significance we shall return to later on.) A text he particularly liked was Sade's *Justine*, a novel in which virtue is repeatedly punished while sexual violence, including murder, is described as a form of ecstasy.

But Brady did not confine himself to pornographic texts. He was also a devotee of two twentieth-century 'classics'. One of these is of doubtful respectability: Hitler's *Mein Kampf*. (It should not be hard, incidentally, to see that fascism makes use of ideas of mastery and transcendence just as sex murder does; there are good reasons why we find them frequently linked, as in Brady's case.) The other one, though, is less distasteful to the liberal mind: Dostoyevsky's novel *Crime and Punishment*.

The court which tried Brady had little to say about his reading of the Russian novel in comparison with the issue of pornography as the key to Brady's moral depravity. This suggests that the nature of that depravity was completely misunderstood: since it was taken to be connected with sex, and since Hitler and Dostoyevsky did not write about sex, the fact that Brady read their texts could not have contributed to his crimes.

But Brady himself perceived the link between *Justine, Mein Kampf* and *Crime and Punishment*. All of them have as their central theme the individual's quest for transcendence and mastery by an act of will, that act prototypically taking the form of murder. Dostoyevsky, of course, was critical of the quest, but the fact remains that his book, in which the student Raskolnikov murders an old woman to set himself free and prove he is 'a man', was about it. To say, as some commentators have, that Brady misunderstood the real point of *Crime and Punishment* (the ultimate repentance and redemption of the murderer) is once again to overlook the fact that interpreting a text is a creative process which cannot be fully controlled. Brady has said explicitly that in his career as a sexual killer he modelled himself only secondarily on Sade, but primarily on the character of Raskolnikov.

374   This is emphatically not to argue that Brady's acts had no sexual significance. Rather it is to argue that transcendence and mastery *have become sexualized*: they are part of a concept of masculine identity (for who can doubt that the transcendent Subject, the entity we have been calling 'man' is in fact a male?) and therefore an element in masculine sexuality. The representation does not have to concern sex to be available for a reading which involves erotic pleasure. Both Sade and Dostoyevsky provided Ian Brady's imagination with material, shaping his desires and the identity he chose to assume.

Other sexual murderers have been attentive readers of forensic literature: journals of criminology, psychiatry, law, police procedure, as well as quasi-forensic accounts of the exploits of their predecessors in the great tradition from Jack the Ripper on. This points to another important influence in the development of sexual murder as a cultural category: expert discourse. Indeed, it cannot be a coincidence that the sex-murderer 'type' became recognizable at just the time (the late nineteenth century) when forensically oriented writers like the sexologist Richard von Krafft-Ebing were busy codifying the forms of sexual crime and deviance.[14]

Krafft-Ebing, the most influential figure in establishing a 'scientific' category of sexual killing, was himself indebted to the artistic and philosophical tradition described above. It is to him, for instance, that we owe the clinical use of the term *sadism* to describe the eroticization of acts of cruelty. In *Psychopathia Sexualis*, his massive catalogue of sexual perversions, Krafft-Ebing redefines what for Sade was a revolutionary act of willed defiance as a disorder or pathology. The two views have coexisted in the culture ever since.

This lengthy discussion should serve to show that sexual murder is enmeshed in a web of discourse: from high art to popular culture to scientific journals to sensational true crime reports, we find a range of meanings with which the imagination of the culture, and of individuals within that culture, can engage. When someone like Ted Bundy plans to commit a murder, he is creatively reworking this whole tradition in the light of his own circumstances. The tradition itself is then reflexively affected by his acts: Ian Brady modelled himself on Raskolnikov, a future killer may model himself on Ian Brady. What needs to be emphasized here is the complexity of the tradition, its many interwoven strands, the way it is constantly being reinscribed within the culture.

Pornography

The reader may be starting to wonder whether we have wholly lost sight of the issue of pornography. So let us point out two things which seem to follow from the analysis just put forward.

First, we are suggesting that there is, indeed, a connection between representations and sexual violence. It is not, however, a cause-and-effect relation; it is a relation which turns on the construction of desire. Representations (in which category we include all the forms of discourse alluded to above) have the power not to create desire from nothing, but to shape it in particular ways. Once, there was no general eroticization of murder, no 'lust to kill'. Now, the existence of this 'meaning' is a part of the sexual understanding we grow up with. For this to happen, it was not only necessary that certain individuals should act out the lust to kill. It had first to be imagined, given a form, a set of conventions and criteria. It was discourse which accomplished this, making killing for sexual gratification possible, intelligible, part of the order of things.

Pornography is, obviously, a form of representation. Even if, as we argue here, it does not *cause* sexual violence it may be criticized for its role in shaping certain forms of desire (and not others). As we will try to show in more detail below, pornography occupies an important place in the culture of transcendence/transgression which is so important to our understanding of modern sex crime. It holds this place in virtue of several characteristics: the narratives it constructs, the form in which it renders them and the position it has in our culture as inherently a transgressive genre (though at the same time a pervasive one).

Having said that, though, our second point is that pornography is by no means the only form of representation one would want to criticize in this way, no matter how broadly or narrowly defined. (Like many other feminists, we have long since ceased to make a distinction between pornography and 'art' or 'literature'; the relationship between them has long been close and indeed symbiotic, as Susanne Kappeler argues.[15] Nevertheless it is difficult to come up with a definition that would encompass *Mein Kampf* and *Crime and Punishment*, not to speak of scientific reports.) Other types of discourse are implicated in the lust to kill. And if we want to ask how the imaginative structures which enable sexual murder can be changed, it is not self-evident that we should concentrate all our efforts on pornography while letting every other form of discourse off the hook.

Nevertheless, it is important for feminists to go on analysing and criticizing pornography, if only because it provides such a clear illustration of the themes (transcendence, transgression, mastery) that are also to be found in the other cultural products through which our sexualities and sexual imaginations are shaped. Let us therefore return to the characteristics of pornography which were briefly mentioned above.

Pornography occupies a somewhat curious position in the cultures where it is prevalent. One of the things which makes it attractive is its inherent transgressiveness: it is illicit, forbidden, a dirty secret. Men writing about the process whereby porn became part of their lives typically tell stories about a submerged, shared male culture into which the adolescent or pre-adolescent is initiated: a furtive passing around of magazines in the playground or the park; secret, snatched readings of material belonging to fathers and older brothers; clandestine visits to sex shops undertaken as a dare. On the other hand, though, pornography must be among the most open secrets our culture has. Its 'softer' forms are all-pervading in nearly all public environments (trucks, billboards, assembly lines, offices, the newspapers and the shops where you buy them).

The result of this paradox is that pornography seems to tell us what we must not do – the scenarios in it are by definition transgressive – but in practice, given that for many people it is the most familiar representation of sexuality, it effectively tells us what we should be doing. Like so-called descriptive sexology, porn has a normative aspect to it; it can be presented as a model of how to do sex, a sort of prototypical narrative or user's manual. And because it purports to be describing the forbidden, the normative model it presents is much more appealing and powerful than something presented overtly as normative, like government 'Safer Sex' guidelines. (An AIDS activist colleague made this point very clearly when he suggested that henceforth pornography should always depict condoms: 'We have to make them sexy' is what he said!)

There is plenty of evidence, especially from feminist research, that pornography is used in this way by many men in heterosexual relations, as a source of narratives whose authenticity and pleasure potential they wish their female partners to recognize. In an in-depth study of sixty women, for instance, Liz Kelly was **377**

surprised at how often her informants – most of them quite
unfamiliar with the feminist debate on porn – raised this point
unprompted. One told her: 'Whatever happened in this magazine
we used to have to do it, it was like a manual. I'd think, oh God,
I better read it to see what I've got to do tonight.'[16] The women
who made these sorts of comments did quite often object to the
specific practices and scenarios their partners pressured them to
engage in (unsurprisingly, since these most often involved
extreme male dominance and female submission). But they also
objected, perhaps even more so, to the fact that this mechanical
transfer of a scenario from the page or the screen to the bedroom
removed all mutuality and interactiveness from sex, leaving no
space for the woman to define her own form of pleasure. They
disliked being written into someone else's script – their partner's,
but also and especially the pornographer's.

It is obvious, of course, that no form of human action can be
totally unscripted: everything we do reflects a complex interaction between the cultural meanings and norms we have available
and our own individual creativity. There is, then, no culture-free
space in which people can come to some wholly authentic and
personal sexual expression. What is problematic, though, is the
stranglehold pornography seems to have on the available meanings in this particular sphere. Only a certain number of 'author-
ized versions' are given expression in pornography, and they
tend to the 'transcendence' model which feminists would want to
criticize.

That the prototypical stories told in pornographic fictions are
narratives of (male) transcendence and mastery is obvious
enough from content analyses which are available. But it has
also been argued that the form of the pornographic representation carries this meaning too. The reader or looker in pornography becomes the Subject of the representation, while the
person(s) represented is/are objectified. The Object is Other,
existing in relation to the gaze and desire of the Subject. The
Subject can project anything he likes on to the Object: fear,
acquiescence, active desire, even total dominance (as in fictions
for masochists). But whatever the content of the scenario, the
Object is written into the Subject's script and he controls her by
virtue of that fact.[17] This reassurance that one is a Subject, free
and in control, is obtained in pornography as it is in acts of
violence like rape and murder, by objectifying and imposing
one's will upon an Other.

Of course, we may wish to make a moral distinction between doing this to live individuals and doing it to fictional objects who exist only in words and pictures (though this is to leave aside the fact that models in pornography are real people, and frequently suffer real exploitation in the process of production). But what needs to be emphasized for the purposes of this argument is the similarity of the act from the point of view of the Subject who is writing the script. His perspective is essentially a solipsistic one, in which even 'real' women are rendered imaginary by objectification; it is the Self and its pleasures which become the central focus. From this perspective, looking at porn and committing a sex murder appear as two versions of the same enterprise – the enterprise Susanne Kappeler calls 'subjectification' and we call 'transcendence'. Here is the link between representation and action: a construction of pleasure as necessarily involving transcendence of the Subject's will through transgressive acts negating the will of the Object.[18]

The Marquis de Sade rhetorically asked: 'Do not all passions require victims?'[19] A feminist must surely meet this question with a question: 'Why should they?' Desire could be less solipsistic than this, and less dependent on eroticized relations of dominance and submission. But while pornographic fictions continue to shape our culture's sexual and social imagination more thoroughly and powerfully than competing discourses can, the feminist will be crying in a wilderness.

'I Am Telling the Story Now': Killers and Their Scripts

The analysis of pornography and what it means put forward here does not differ significantly from what many other feminists have written. What we have tried to do, though, is place the analysis in a different theoretical frame, yielding a different kind of account of how pornography affects our lives.

Instead of arguing that words and pictures act on individuals, causing them to behave in certain ways, we have focused on the cultural meanings in the light of which individuals produce *both* representations *and* actions. (Note that those meanings can be criticized whether or not they are 'acted upon' in obvious and sensational ways; we take it that people are always acting in the light of meanings, and it hardly takes a murder to demonstrate the ill-effects of the pervasive ways of thinking analysed here!) We have argued, too, that there is a reflexive relationship   **379** between the meanings an individual has available, that is the cultural discourse s/he inherits, and the new representations and actions s/he produces, which in turn become sources of meaning for other individuals and for the culture at large.

The process is a circular one and sex murderers are notable in that many of them complete the circle by producing copious representations of and discourse about themselves and their acts. They tell stories about themselves, as we have seen; they write letters, poems, take photographs, make drawings, even record home videos. Unlike the 'copycat', whose imagination is satisfied with someone else's script, most murderers want to create their own. Ted Bundy, for instance, created an enormous edifice of discourse about himself, including various different personas and narratives. It is interesting that he should have felt the need to produce a 'final version' just before he was executed (for by that stage he had nothing to gain in terms of deferring the sentence). His last account made more sense to the culture than the previous ones; in constructing it Bundy achieved a sort of 'narrative closure', and we may speculate that this in itself gave him some satisfaction.

Sometimes, for obvious reasons, killers design their discourse for private consumption (like Ian Brady's photographs and tape recordings of his victims begging for mercy, the discovery of which eventually convicted him). Sometimes, as in Bundy's case, they are trying to control the way their stories will be presented to the public. In a recent Japanese incident, especially interesting because Japan has no real cultural tradition of sexual murder, the killer of a child sent the parents a package containing the child's ashes, photographs of her murdered body and a letter retelling the story of the killing. The writer adopted a female persona, writing under the pseudonym 'Yuko Imada', which can be read as a pun on the Japanese phrase meaning 'I am telling the story now'.[20] It seems that the creation of fictions, the telling of stories of which one is the author as well as the hero, is experienced as a further form of mastery and transcendence.

CONCLUSION

In analysing sexual violence and its links to cultural forms such as pornography, we overlook at our peril the pre-eminent role of imaginative mediation and the creation of meaning. All humans **380** are endowed with the capacity and perhaps the need to interpret and represent their actions, their lives; our possession of consciousness, language and culture ensure that we will impose meaning on even the most fundamental bodily experience. That is not, in itself, problematic. But it does mean we need to move beyond causal accounts of human actions, and look instead at the resources humans bring to their interpretations and representations, the meanings which shape their desires and constrain the stories they can imagine for themselves. For we are clearly not free to imagine just anything; we work both with and against the grain of the cultural meanings we inherit.

In the sphere of sexuality, pornography is a significant source of ideas and narratives. It transmits to those who use it – primarily men but also women – notions of transcendence and mastery as intrinsic to sexual pleasure. These ideas are not taken up only by those who become rapists and killers. On the contrary, they pervade our everyday, unremarkable sexual encounters as surely as they do the grotesque acts of Ted Bundy and his ilk.

In the case of sex murderers (as in many other cases), the extreme, what is perceived as abnormal and deviant, throws light on the normal (of which it turns out to be a version). If we as feminists want to do something about sexual violence, it is precisely the normal and normative sexual practice of our culture that we must change. That means, among other things, that we must be critical of pornography and the other discourses which inform sexual practice, using our imagination to shape alternatives to the pleasures of transcendence and the thrills of transgression. In fact, feminists have been doing this for more than twenty years. But the recent focus of so many writers on causal models of sexual violence (which often imply that the problem is non-normal individuals and extreme sexual practices) is, at least in our view, a retreat from that radical politics of sexuality.

Notes

1. See Deborah Cameron and Elizabeth Frazer, *The Lust to Kill: A Feminist Investigation of Sexual Murder* (Cambridge: Polity Press, 1987).
2. For an account, see Catharine MacKinnon, *Feminism Unmodified: Discourses on Life and Law* (Cambridge, Mass. and London: Harvard University Press, 1987), ch. 14.
3. Cf. *Pornography and Violence: Evidence of the Links* (Minneapolis Hearings) (London: Everywoman, 1988); MacKinnon, op. cit., pp. 184–6.
4. The discourse of 'addiction' can be found in a number of very different sources, ranging from right-wing polemics (as in the Bundy

case) through clinical materials used by those who counsel sex offenders to feminist critiques of socially-constructed dependence on various types of stimulus (drugs, alcohol, cigarettes, TV) induced by people's increasing alienation within patriarchal and capitalist cultures (see e.g. Sweet, this volume, Chapter 10).

5. Gerold Frank, *The Boston Strangler* (London: Pan, 1967); also discussion in J. Caputi, *The Age of Sex Crime* (London: Women's Press, 1988).

6. For discussion of Edmund Kemper, see Cameron and Frazer, op. cit.

7. Diana Scully and Joseph Marolla, cited in L. Kelly, *Surviving Sexual Violence* (Cambridge: Polity Press, 1989), p. 47.

8. Cameron and Frazer, op. cit., p. 14. note.

9. S. Edwards, quoted in Kelly, op cit., p. 224 note 61.

10. Cameron and Frazer, op. cit., p. 125.

11. A pertinent example here is the case of Ronald Frank Cooper, discussed in Cameron and Frazer, op. cit., pp. xiii–xiv.

12. Mario Praz, *The Romantic Agony* (London: Fontana, 1960).

13. André Gide, quoted in R. Coe, *The Vision of Jean Genet* (London: Peter Owen, 1968), p. 181.

14. Richard von Krafft-Ebing, *Psychopathia Sexualis* 10th ed. (Aberdeen: Aberdeen University Press, 1901).

15. Susanne Kappeler, *The Pornography of Representation* (Cambridge: Polity Press, 1986).

16. Kelly, op. cit., p. 111.

17. The gender of the pronouns here is deliberate, reflecting the fact that men are prototypical Subjects and women generic Objects. However, men can be placed in the Object position and women (arguably) in the Subject position in relation to pornography; the analysis holds for subject–object relations irrespective of gender, but it needs to be stressed that these positions usually are not neutral in respect of gender.

18. Meryl Altman (whom we thank for her numerous helpful comments on drafts of this piece) has raised the question of whether, if this analysis is right, there can be any unobjectionable erotic representations at all – the looker/reader will always be Subject, getting pleasure by objectifying the people in the story. Altman reads Kappeler's critique of pornography, which focuses on its asymmetric and non-dialogic form rather than its objectionable (e.g. violent or stereotypical) content, as leading ultimately to a rejection of all representation, since the content could be ameliorated but the form presumably could not. She asks if anyone can imagine a world without representation, and whether such a world would not be seriously impoverished.

These are clearly questions of some importance and, as Altman points out, our inability to resolve them leads to some ambiguity or maybe even contradiction in the above argument (should we pursue a 'positive politics' of alternative representations, or stick to a 'negative politics' of criticizing existing ones?). Feminist practice over the past five years has shown dangers in both approaches:

many women are dissatisfied with the 'repressiveness' of a negative politics, but on the other hand alternative 'positive' representations are easily recuperated to prevailing sexist interpretations. There is little point in creating novel images if we do not at the same time create novel ways of reading them.

We should point out, however, that Altman's is a somewhat extreme reading of Kappeler: subjectification/transcendence is not the only actual or imaginable effect of representation, and the representations produced in a 'post-transcendence' culture might have a very different significance (as presumably the representations of 'pre-transcendence' cultures did and do). How to achieve a transformation of our culture and its subjectivities is, of course, an enormous problem for feminists. And while we don't think any culture will be without representations and narratives of some kind, it is at least worth posing the question whether it is inevitable or desirable that people should derive specifically sexual pleasure from representations.

19. Sade, quoted in Praz, op. cit.
20. Reported in the *Guardian*, 24 March 1989.

20 Pornography and Pollution: An Environmental Analogy

H. PATRICIA HYNES

ECOFEMINISM AND PORNOGRAPHY

Ten years ago ecofeminism looked like terrain where one could synthesize the liberation of women and the integrity of nature. The findings of environmental science were directly applicable to the conditions of women in patriarchy. Polluted and stressed environments are identified by their low species diversity and low occupational diversity. Species die off – often the complex ones – and the ecosystem becomes more homogeneous.[1] Similarly, many women live under severe stressful conditions of poverty, powerlessness and sexual violence. Like polluted eco-systems, women in sexist societies have low occupational diversity and few resources. Large numbers of women in industrial societies are concentrated in few, low-status occupations: housewife, secretary and the service professions, so that women have limited power and self-expression in society.[2]

In the ensuing ten years, ecofeminism has become a fast-moving current of the US women's movement. Concurrently, deep ecology[3] has developed into what some deep ecologists like to portray as a male counterpart to ecofeminism. Environmentalism has broadened with a wide range of non-profit environmental activist groups. Environmental protection has generated a profession of engineers and lawyers who enforce a burgeoning number of environmental laws.

As these currents progress, certain contradictions have emerged. One can be a successful professional environmentalist by being a good bureaucrat. One can be a deep ecologist and illiterate in feminism. One can be an ecofeminist who denounces the 'rape' of the planet but is reticent to denounce pornography, sexual violence and the traffic in women. Lawyers who would cut down a polluting industry in court, champion the legal standing of the pornography industry. Some of these contradictions form the starting point of my analysis.

For most of the past ten years I have enforced environmental laws, first as an environmental engineer and then as section chief in the US Environmental Protection Agency (EPA), and later as Chief of Environmental Management at the Massachusetts Port Authority. Many of these laws and their amendments have come into effect, caused a limited but remarkable change in consciousness, and become an established reality within a decade.[4] Simultaneously, I have worked in the anti-pornography movement, particularly for the anti-pornography civil rights law, the Dworkin–MacKinnon Ordinance, introduced into numerous US city governments. The work of organizing and educating for the ordinance has raised some consciousness; but unlike environmental law, the ordinance has a very tenuous and embattled existence.[5] At every step, liberal lawyers swarm like flies to protect the pornography industry's 'free speech', even though – in the case of pornography – a man's speech is a woman's terror. Yet the same lawyers would and do limit the freedom of industry to pollute, because – in the case of pollution – one man's freedom is another man's hazard.

My earlier analysis of women and ecosystems under extreme conditions still holds. But as the movements to end pollution and pornography mature, I find increasingly critical differences between the conditions of women under patriarchy and nature under patriarchy.

Because feminism is tangential to deep ecology (ecofeminism being regarded as a small lens that *women* bring to ecology), deep ecologists can borrow unabashedly from the 'feminine' imagery of 'male erotica' to describe nature. In some deep ecology writing, nature is sexualized with imagery – pictures and words – used in pornography. Deep ecologists do not pinpoint male dominance as the cause of alienation from nature. Rather, industrial countries develop at the expense of nature because, they explain, *people* are damaged by *human* chauvinism, egoism, abstraction, competition and domination.[6]

'People are damaged' is a passive construction. 'People are damaged' does not say *whose* chauvinism, egoism, abstraction, competition and dominance creates the damage. Women do not hold up half that sky. With few exceptions and without complete success, women are induced to be selfless, feeling, co-operative and submissive as a base of support for male chauvinism, egoism, abstraction, competition and dominance. (Using a kind of moral alchemy, some feminists are making virtues out of these **385** permitted 'feminine' behaviours.) If deep ecologists would split the responsibility of men who degrade nature, by virtue of economic, military and political power, from the responsibility of women who, for example, wear fur coats – then their often elegant treatises on *human* alienation from nature would better fit reality.[7]

Ecofeminism appeared to be the terrain where fundamental connections between women and nature could be made – for our liberation, for the integrity of nature. However, prominent eco-feminist writing, most notably what is called 'spiritual ecofeminism', is reticent about looking at the specific sexual dominance of women by men and calling it sexual violence and a violation of women's civil rights, while it is specific, detailed and clear on violence done to nature. Male dominance of women is explained by spiritual ecofeminists as originating in male 'fear and resentment of the elemental power of the female'.[8] This explanation of patriarchy emphasizes the limits and weakness of men before women, and obscures their power and dominance of women. 'Fear and resentment' is a passive description of hatred, and could almost make you feel pity for the 'fearful'. It does not describe or analyse the worst of what men do to women – encouraged by pornography – and the pleasure men find in sadistic sex. Pornography, incest, woman-battering, traffic in women: all this ugly, necrophilic degradation is 'women's nuclear winter'.[9] But ecofeminism is braver, more explicit, angrier and more effective about the threat of nuclear winter than the fact of an epidemic in male violence against women.

Why is it less threatening to talk about the dominance and death of rainforests and the unnamed species which disappear with them, than the dominance and death of women in pornography, prostitution and sex slavery? Why is the language of rape – borrowed from the worst of what men do to women and applied to what men do to nature – now used more easily, frequently and publicly about nature than about women? One effect of this uncritical use of rape is to reduce women's issues of pornography, prostitution, sexual slavery to small, domestic and individual concerns while the large, global and collective concerns of the earth are the arms race, nuclear power, global warming, the disappearing of species, etc. The ecology movement will rush off in small dinghies against nuclear-powered ships and whaling vessels; but they hold back against (and thus protect) the 'destroyer' – male dominance. The environmental movement is popular and respected, especially *when* dissenting from dominant industrial and political powers; the anti-pornography movement is controversial and embattled precisely *for* dissenting from men, male sexuality and the institutional male pimping of women. This difference makes men like George Bush want to be known as environmentalists, even when they are not. This difference makes women not want to be called feminists (the feared 'f-word'), even when they are.

Despite these points of discontinuity in the two movements, there are important connections between pornography and pollution to be explored here. Also the environmental movement has made gains in environmental consciousness and action which we can apply to our work against pornography. If the connections embolden ecofeminism and push deep ecology to confront the epidemic of male violence against women, all the better.

ANALOGIES BETWEEN CHEMICAL POISONS AND PORNOGRAPHY

About eight years ago I sat in on safety-training for engineers and scientists working in hazardous waste. The instructor, a Vietnam vet who turned to hazardous waste safety-training when the war was over, enlivened his course with stories of toxic waste dumps full of explosive and combustible chemicals, dead bodies and 'lists of prostitutes'. The implication was that all of this was equally deadly, dirty and dangerous business. I filed this away, knowing the association of prostitutes with toxic waste was a rich vein to be mined. We went different ways with the association. He saw prostitutes as agents in an underworld of hazard and crime; I saw the system of prostitution as hazardous for women caught in it.

A few months later, in the fall of 1981, Alan Dershowitz debated Andrea Dworkin on the issue of pornography at Harvard University. Dershowitz is a lawyer, who has made his fame defending the First Amendment rights of neo-Nazis and pornographers. By the time of the debate, I had worked for EPA sufficiently long to know that a law on toxic substances had been used to ban the manufacture of polychlorinated biphenyls (PCBs) and to phase out PCBs currently used in transformers and capacitors. The grounds for the ban had been the toxicity and misuse of the chemical: it had endangered some lives in a spill which contaminated cooking oil and could potentially harm **387** others. It occurred to me during the debate that environmental attorneys justify banning certain chemicals in a free market economy, even though the ban is a limitation on free enterprise, and is a threat to profit and to industrial licence. The right of society to an existence unendangered by PCBs supersedes the right of industries in a free market system to use an industrially important, toxic chemical. But industry resisted and still resists the encroaching nature of environmental regulation, saying that EPA could exercise arbitrary power in determining what constitutes endangerment to human health and the environment.

If they can ban a chemical for its toxicity, why can't they ban magazines and films which poison and destroy women's lives, I thought, as I listened to Dershowitz defend the First Amendment right of free speech and warn against the 'domino effect' of banning pornography. If they can limit 'free enterprise' without fundamental damage to a free market economy, then why can't they limit 'free speech' without fundamental damage to First Amendment rights? If EPA can define toxicity in an industrial world saturated with synthetic chemicals, then why can't we define pornography in literature, art and film? My thoughts that evening were the background to this fuller analysis of pollution and pornography: their connections, their dissimilarities, the lesson in one for the other.

'Drift' of Pollution and Pornography

Toxic chemicals cannot be restricted to where they are generated or used. Pesticides sprayed on plants are carried by wind and redeposited in soil and lakes. Residue is washed from plant and plant environment into groundwater and is drawn by the influence of a pumping well to the kitchen for drinking water. Other residue is carried in driving rain as surface runoff to nearby streams where, with stream water, it flows to a river and ultimately the sea. It is ingested by insects, which are eaten by other insects, which are eaten by a fish then eaten by a bird which is captured by a predator animal. These are the connections between local use of pollutants and global pollution. This is why bald eagles remote from where DDT was sprayed could be rendered nearly extinct by it.

A similar principle exists in pornography. Pornography reaches every corner of the world through mass media, as remote from where it was produced as is DDT in polar ice caps. It is on

newsstands, billboards and calendars in the workplace in parts per million residues of the big industry where it is concentrated in porn magazines, movies, videos, peep shows. Not only are individual women in the industry victimized, but pornography endangers all of us. Pornography encourages violence against all women by making it appear exciting for men to rape women and pleasurable for women to be raped. Men and boys who read pornography become inured to the repulsion of rape and degradation of women; pornography legitimates their doing in their private life what they see done to women in videos, movies and magazines.

These are the connections between the private use of pornography and the universal degradation of women. This is why any woman, no matter how remote from where pornography is made or used, is endangered by it. And if, for the sake of saving the bald eagle – the US national symbol – and other animal species, DDT was banned from use, then why cannot pornography be banned for the sake of stemming violence against women?

Informed Consent

Selling poisons and making pornography are justified by the argument that as long as people know what they are getting into and choose it, it is OK. The US pesticide law (FIFRA – Federal Insecticide, Rodenticide, and Fungicide Act) allows DDT and other pesticides banned from use in the United States to be exported for use in other countries, provided the country is informed what the pesticides are and accepts them. Increasingly, chemical manufacturing industries are being relocated to developing countries where labour is cheap and occupational health standards are not firmly established. Increasingly, toxic wastes from industrial countries are being shipped for disposal to the 'Third World'.[10] Debt, economic bondage, foreign aid plus pesticides, foreign aid plus waste, forgiveness of debt if waste is taken – these are the conditions which make it almost impossible for developing countries to refuse hazardous waste, toxic manufacturing facilities and pesticides.[11] Are these hazards, then, 'freely' accepted or chosen, because the recipient country is informed of their toxicity? When they are accepted within a downward spiral of poverty, famine, debt and loss of natural resources – is this 'free choice'?

An analogous system of poverty and forced dependency exists for women. It explains why women and girls enter systems of pornography and prostitution, and why they stay in situations **389** where they are battered. The moral issue at stake in prostitution and pornography is not whether a woman consents. The issue at stake is not addressed by arresting prostitutes as agents of the system of prostitution. Nor is it addressed by improving the 'working' conditions of prostitutes with health and safety measures – no more than clean, non-corrosive, well-marked containers for hazardous waste solves the problem of waste generation. The ethical issues for women are to eliminate poverty, to educate for independence, to deconstruct the eroticizing of rape, incest and battery and to name them for what they are. These are the necessary social and political conditions for women to make free choices.

Use vs Abuse

EPA regulates toxics at the waste end and, with few exceptions like PCBs and DDT, tolerates the proliferation of toxic substances, as if environmental protection is about abuse rather than *use* of toxic chemicals. Industrial accidents are blamed on human error and, in the case of accidents in 'Third World' countries, on the ignorance of unskilled workers and the backwardness of developing countries' health regulations.

Industrial accidents happen because the chemicals and processes used have a certain risk of failure and because, however remote the risk, there are always unforeseen occurrences which cannot be predicted. For this reason, even nuclear power advocates would not locate nuclear plants at the hub of a large, metropolitan area. For this reason, all nuclear power plants have emergency evacuation plans. For this reason, some of us protest against any use of nuclear power and call for the shutdown of existing plants.

Regulating access to pornography by calling it 'adult' literature and not selling to minors suggests that pornography embodies sophisticated risk which is safe for some – adults – and unsafe for others – minors. It suggests that, like high-risk technology, safety is a question of the accidental abuse of risk, not the use of risk. It suggests that adult men are moral, reasonable, not suggestible to rape and sadistic sex, not likely to do what they are entertained with in pornography, not likely to be desensitized to it and stand by and watch while someone else does it. Surveys of North American male university students found that 35 to 60 per cent of those surveyed would use force and/or rape a girl or woman if they knew they would not get caught.[12] Keeping pornography out of the hands of minors is a pseudo-control, when it has already drifted down in male culture, from men to boys, that girls and women are their property. The pervasiveness of pornography, the 'normalcy' of pornography contributes to the 'normalcy' of violence against women. The use of pornography – no matter whose hands it is in – is hazardous for women. For this reason, women against pornography want the use of pornography and the abuse of women ended.

Living with Risk: Pleasure with Danger

When the argument that the use and proliferation, not just the abuse, of hazardous chemicals challenges the toxics industry, the industry counters with the trendy philosophy of modern living, called 'living with risk'.[13] The industry has moved from denial of risk and harm in the 1950s and 1960s at the incipience of the environmental movement, to rationalistic risk–benefit calculation in support of alleged benefits of toxic substances in the 1970s and 1980s, to 'living with risk' as a modern, progressive attitude of the late 1980s. Pollution is the price we pay for living 'well'; risk is the underside of progress.

But who lives well? Not the poor who generally live closest to contamination, not the victims of pollution, not women who care for the victims, not workers in industry and industrial neighbourhoods who have higher cancer rates because of that industry, not the relocated people of Chernobyl whose town is buried, not the women of Bhopal abandoned and shunned because they cannot give birth to healthy children. Those who commit the world to living with risk are generally not the ones who suffer the risks of their actions. The risk-*makers*, calling themselves risk-*takers*, enjoy the financial and political benefits of high-risk technologies in offices and homes remote from the hazards. Some pay the price for others to live well.

Defenders of pornography use a similar progression of arguments. First, they deny that there is any connection between the use and proliferation of pornography and violence against women. Then they assert that the risks of losing speech, literature and art outweigh the benefits of banning pornography or giving women standing to sue pornographers and their merchants for their loss of civil rights from pornography. And recently, they have embraced the trendy philosophy of 'pleasure and danger'.[14] Pornography is actually being defended as necessary for **391** liberated, 'robust' sexuality. Danger is the price, the complementary underside, of sexual pleasure.

But who is endangered? Not those who finance, write, purvey, buy and use pornography. The American Civil Liberties Union (ACLU) is vigilant in protecting them from the danger of being sued by women injured by pornography.[15] Women and children are the objects of pornography, in the industry and in the home. They are the targets of male sexual fantasy, turned on by pornography, acting on it and accustomed to the degradation of women and children by the cultural normalcy of male violence.

Dressing Up the Danger

Industries cover up their toxic activities with environmentally neutral and beneficent language: thus herbicides are 'plant regulators', and herbicide spray plans are 'vegetation management plans', and incineration is 'resource recovery'.[16] Similarly, the industry dresses itself in a mantle of goodwill and progress. The DuPont Company slogan of the 1950s, when the war chemical industry and the atom bomb project were being recycled into peacetime uses, was: 'A better world through chemistry'. This has given way to the General Electric Company's motto of the 1980s, 'We bring good things to life', as major chemical companies have retooled for the age of biology and genetic engineering.

Similarly with pornography, a review in the *New York Times Book Review* exalts the 'luxuriant outcrop of Victorian pornography'.[17] Magazines which depict women gagged, bound and being beaten are called 'adult' and 'erotic' literature. And the Playboy Foundation likes to fund 'feminist' projects[18] – as phoney and morally bankrupt a gesture as a weapons-manufacturing plant garnishing itself with artificial wetlands and a childcare centre.

How Clean is 'Clean'?

Pollution is universal, in gross concentrations from direct use and disposal, in infinitesimal levels from drift and fallout. The industry blames the heightened concern that this knowledge engenders on detection instruments. Increasingly sensitive instruments enable us to find parts per trillion pollutants where once we could measure only parts per thousand, so that what used to be 'clean' no longer is. 'How clean is "clean"' nags every environmental decision because one person's 'clean' is another person's 'polluted'. Proponents of pollution blame sensitive detection for alarming people with the universality of pollution. They charge that the environment is not worsening. It only appears to be because we monitor more, we measure more, we report more, consciousness is higher, instruments are more sensitive.

The purveyors and defenders of pornography charge that it is impossible to define what is and what isn't pornography, that great art and literature and subversive, counter-cultural work and even feminist work are equally threatened by any movement to ban pornography. They thwart any attempt to define pornography by alleging that everything can be called pornography. They blame radical feminists for creating a climate of 'pollution' around sexuality when we document the extent of violence against women and the connections between male sexuality and male violence.[19]

This blaming the messenger for the message has not held environmental agencies in inaction. Environmental agencies and environmentalists have overcome the paralysis possible when you find dirt everywhere. Feminism, however, faces much more complex opposition than environmentalism. Most polluters don't pollute because they like the dirt. They like the profits of a polluting enterprise; they resent the costs of anti-pollution devices. A few are turned on by risk-laden technology, when the danger is intimately mixed with their pleasure, as in the development of the atomic bomb where male ego, male bonding and the romance of technical adventure, competition and dominance came together.[20] But *most* defenders of pornography like pornography. They are not just protecting profit and free speech; they are protecting sexuality based on dominance, degradation and humiliation. They are protecting their right to play around with misogynistic and violent sex.

The forces of opposition are much greater against those who make connections between the global traffic in women and misogynistic sex eroticized in pornography than against those who have exposed the international traffic in pollution. Feminists who oppose pornography are ridiculed as moralistic, sexless prudes.[21] Environmentalists were trivialized as quacks, Luddites, nature freaks and 'leisured'.[22] But the change in global consciousness has enabled environmentalists to break through the name-calling to convince the world that the earth is endangered. Environmentalists are now respected and admired. Two per cent **393** of the Swedish population are members of Greenpeace.[23] Would that the same per cent of any country comprised a woman-centred anti-pornography movement.

Potential Harm and Actual Harm

Proving harm is more rigorous for victims of pornography than victims of pollution. Increasingly, the presence of toxins, not proof that they caused harm, is sufficient cause for action. If organic chemicals are detected in the groundwater of a town's aquifer, the groundwater must be cleaned and the source of contamination removed, whether anyone drinking the water has been proven to be harmed or not. The presumption is that since these chemicals are toxic, they will most likely harm humans in their drinking water and they should be eliminated.

Feminists are constantly challenged to prove the connections between pornography and violence against women – that pornography harms women. Why is it that people dying from cancer due to contaminated drinking water provoke more action and more liability claims than women killed in the underworlds of prostitution, pornography and systems of sexual slavery? Why, even with the dead bodies of women, can we not put pornography on trial, when we need only detect toxic chemicals in ground-water without any evidence of harm to sue an industry?

CONCLUSION

Can we not live well, comfortably and in health without poisoning the earth? Environmentalists are urging a concept of 'sustainable' development and technology; that is, growing food, using energy, building cities and transportation systems in ways that do not deplete and erode nature's soil, reserves of water, air and species of plant and animal. 'Think globally and act locally' expresses the environmental understanding of 'the personal is political'. Environmentalists believe that pollution is not a necessary consequence of progressive living. It is a failure to respect nature, to see ourselves as part of nature, and to design our existence accordingly. It is a result of inequity, where those who benefit from pollution and exhaustion of natural resources live apart from those who suffer from it. It is a consequence of environmental protection resources being siphoned off for military weapons and defence systems.

394   Can we not produce a rich, diverse literature without pornography? Can we not enjoy a 'vigorous and robust' sexuality without rape, battery, dominance and subordination? Like pollution, eroticizing the humiliation of and violence against women is a failure of respect and equity, and a consequence of male dominance expressed in sexuality. Of how much consequence is a global environmental movement to save all other species of being, when one-half of the human race is subordinated by the other? We who oppose pornography want no less of a change in consciousness about pornography than environmentalists want about the destruction of rainforests. We want it recognized that pornography endangers women for the pleasure of men. We want it recognized that male sexuality premised on the humiliation of women is no more sustainable for women than slashing and burning rainforest is for the ecology of the Amazon basin. We want no less in law than has been gained by environmental lawyers. We want redress in law, as victims of pollution now have, based on the fact that pornography is a violation of women's civil rights. We want no less than terrestrial ecologists demand for endangered species. We want women and girls to live in a world that has respect for our existence, where women's dignity and our life cannot be snuffed out for male sexual pleasure.

Notes

1. Howard Odum, *Environment, Power, and Society* (New York: Wiley-Interscience, 1971).
2. H. Patricia Hynes, 'The Feminism of Ecology' presented to conference on 'Women and Life on Earth: Ecofeminism in the 80s' (Amherst: University of Massachusetts, 1980).
3. Bill Devall and George Sessions, *Deep Ecology* (Salt Lake City, UT: Peregrine Smith Books, 1985).
4. For example, the Superfund law, which requires EPA to identify, study and clean up hazardous waste sites and then to collect the costs from industries responsible for the waste, has had a clear impact on environmental consciousness and public expectation. People now recognize, in principle if not technically, the hazards to groundwater, drinking water and ambient air of landfilling or dumping wastes into the environment. They are much more critical of waste disposal strategies which just repackage or relocate but do not recycle or destroy it. Consequently, people are open to municipal waste recycling programmes and cities are enjoying a degree of public co-operation with recycling which is unprecedented in recent US history.
5. The anti-pornography ordinance drafted by writer Andrea Dworkin and lawyer Catharine A. MacKinnon defines pornography as sex **395**

discrimination and therefore a violation of civil rights. It would allow anyone injured by pornography to file a civil lawsuit against pornographers. For the exact text of the ordinance and those filed in Minneapolis, Minnesota and Indianapolis, Indiana, see Andrea Dworkin and Catharine A. MacKinnon, *Pornography and Civil Rights: A New Day for Women's Equality* (Minneapolis, MN: Organizing Against Pornography, 1988).

6. Devall and Sessions, op. cit.
7. Janet Biehl, 'Ecofeminism and Deep Ecology: Unresolvable Conflict?', *Our Generation* 19(2), 1988, pp 19–32. This is an excellent critique of 'patricentric' deep ecologists, showing their complete disregard of feminism while advocating an alliance with ecofeminists.
8. Charlene Spretnak, 'Ecofeminism: Our Roots and Flowering', *Woman of Power* 9, 1988, pp. 6–10.
9. Many ecologists and humanistic scientists have attempted to forecast and describe the effects of nuclear war on human life and ecosystems, so as to deter the build-up and use of nuclear weapons by the superpowers. The horrific scenarios of a ravaged earth after nuclear war, with an atmosphere and climate inhospitable to life, are paraphrased as 'nuclear winter'.
10. Steven Greenhouse, 'UN Conference Supports Curbs on Exporting of Hazardous Waste', *New York Times*, 23 March 1989, pp. A1, B11.
11. Philip Shabecoff, 'Irate and Afraid, Poor Nations Fight Efforts to Use Them as Toxic Dumps', *New York Times*, 5 July 1988, p. B1.
12. Barbara Roberts, 'The Death of Machothink: Feminist Research and the Transformation of Peace Studies', *Women's Studies International Forum* 7(4), 1984, pp. 195–200.
13. Charles Perrow, *Normal Accidents: Living with High-Risk Technologies* (New York: Basic Books, 1984).
14. Ann Snitow *et al.* (eds), *Desire: The Politics of Sexuality* (London: Virago, 1984).
15. Dworkin and MacKinnon, op. cit.
16. In the Definitions section of the federal pesticide act, FIFRA, herbicides are called 'plant regulators'. The federal hazardous waste law is entitled the Resource Conservation and Recovery Act. Massachusetts state regulations governing use of herbicides on rights-of-way call such herbicide use 'vegetation management'.
17. Lawrence Stone, Review of Walter Kendrick, *The Secret Museum: Pornography in Modern Culture* in *New York Times Book Review*, 3 May 1987, pp. 1, 50.
18. The Playboy Foundation has made grants to organizations and projects concerned with reproductive freedom and the improved legal status of women and gay and lesbian rights. See Jill R. Shellow, *Grant Seekers Guide: Funding Sourcebook* (Mt Kisco, NY: Moyer Bell, 1988).
19. Snitow *et al.*, op. cit.
20. Peter Wyden, *Day One: Before Hiroshima and After* (New York: Simon and Schuster, 1984).

21. Sheila Jeffreys, *The Spinster and Her Enemies: Feminism and Sexuality 1880–1930* (London: Pandora, 1985).
22. The many-levelled attack on Rachel Carson after the publication of *Silent Spring* by the chemical industry, research scientists, and nutritional and agricultural organizations was replete with these stereotypes. See H. Patricia Hynes, *The Recurring Silent Spring* (New York and Oxford: Pergamon Press, The Athene Series, 1989).
23. Conversation with Greenpeace, April 1989.

PART FOUR

Pornography and the Law

21 Legislating Against Pornography without Censorship

CATHERINE ITZIN

EXISTING LEGISLATION

Obscenity

There is, in fact, no legislation against pornography. Instead there is legislation against obscenity and indecency. This is criminal legislation aimed at restricting the publication, distribution and display of material which is regarded as obscene and indecent. Legal definitions of obscenity and indecency have been vague and subjective and open to interpretation, but always formulated in terms of morality and immorality. Obscenity has therefore been something to be monitored, regulated and controlled: confined to the private sphere where it has been assumed that people should have the right to see and do whatever they want without harming or offending others. This legislation has proved to be inadequate and ineffective in dealing with pornography.

Historically, it has in fact been used to censor art and literature, to suppress homosexuality and to control women's reproduction. In practice it protects pornography, permitting the increased production and circulation of increasingly 'pornographic' pornography. It will almost certainly be unable to deal with attempts by the pornography industry to exploit the UK market following the deregulation of trade in the Single European Market from 1992. With obscenity legislation, there are problems both of definition and enforcement.

Definition

According to barrister and obscenity expert Geoffrey Robertson, writing in 1979:

> Both 'obscenity' and 'indecency' are defined by reference to vague and elastic formulae, permitting forensic debates over morality which fit uneasily into the format of a criminal trial. These

periodic moral flashpoints may edify or entertain, but they provide scant control over the booming business of sexual delectation. Occasional forfeiture orders, based upon the same loose definitions, are subject to the inconsistent priorities and prejudices of local constabularies in different parts of the country, and offer no effective deterrent to publishers with access to a printing press and a ready supply of paper.[1]

The Williams Committee on Obscenity and Film Censorship, reporting in 1979, concluded that 'the law, in short, is a mess'.[2] It still is.

The Oxford English Dictionary defines 'obscene' as 'filthy', 'repulsive', 'loathsome', 'indecent and lewd',[3] but the Obscene Publications Act 1959 defines obscenity as material whose effect is to 'tend to deprave and corrupt', not just anyone, but 'persons who are likely to read, see or hear the matter'.[4] Courts have ruled that the legal, not the dictionary, definition of obscenity must apply, and for over thirty years, the judiciary has occupied itself with trying to find a workable interpretation of 'deprave and corrupt'.

Early on the courts 'established that a tendency to corrupt is a stronger concept than a tendency to shock and disgust, and implies the spread of moral perversion'.[5] An appeal court verdict that 'the essence of the matter is moral corruption'[6] was based on a definition of 'deprave' as 'to make morally bad, to pervert, to debase or corrupt morally', and on a definition of 'corrupt' as 'to render morally unsound or rotten, to destroy the moral purity or chastity of, to pervert or ruin a good quality, to debase, to defile'.[7] These decisions firmly established obscenity as a moral issue.

The courts then concluded that corruption included 'promoting the pleasures of drug taking . . . and to conditioning young children to engage in violence' as well as 'the consequences of sexual indecency'.[8] It was also determined that the definition of obscenity should be relative, depending on 'the circumstances of distribution'. Nothing therefore could be regarded as inherently obscene: it depended on who saw it, and how 'susceptible' they were 'to some corruption from its influence'. The concept of 'inherent obscenity' was thus regarded as irreconcilable with the legislative definition of obscenity, and this led to considerations of whether the 'dirty old men' who were regarded by the judiciary as the main consumers of pornography could be 'corrupted further' once they had already been depraved and corrupted.[9]

Having established that only the 'target audience' of likely readers could be considered as potentially corruptible, there was then a further requirement that a 'significant proportion of the likely readership be guided along the path of corruption'. This requirement was designed to exclude consideration of the potential corruption of a young person – the court used as an example a fourteen-year-old schoolgirl – into whose hands an item might occasionally and accidentally fall. But it was left entirely up to a jury to decide what might constitute a 'significant proportion' of the readership.[10] Yet another level of speculation and subjectivity was added to judicial judgements of obscenity.

Other tests and interpretations were developed by the courts which have made the legislation even more 'confused and confusing' and unimplementable.[11] Juries were required to define deprave and corrupt 'keeping in mind the current standards of ordinary decent people' and 'setting the standards of what is acceptable, of what is for the public good in the age in which we live'.[12] Obscenity therefore became relative not just to who buys it, and where it is bought, but to the variable and undefined moral standards or tastes of individual magistrates and jurors. Obscenity thus became even more firmly established as a matter of moral opinion: what is 'offensive to right-thinking persons'. Harm was also defined in moral terms: 'depravity may be all in the mind without ever causing anti-social behaviour'. Depravity and corruption were thus designated as conditions of the mind: 'evidence of behaviour' was not 'needed to establish their presence'.

In addition, courts made a distinction between corruption and revulsion and required evidence that obscene materials harmed the people (primarily men) who used them. Obscenity law thus required proof 'to the normal criminal standard, beyond a reasonable doubt, that the material would tend to deprave and corrupt its likely customers'. In practice therefore 'exhibits were shocking, unpleasant, and sometimes stomach-turning and jurors would undoubtedly classify them as "obscene" in the colloquial sense as soon as they saw them', but in the absence of 'evidence that it had actually harmed anyone', by which was meant whether it had 'seriously affected the moral fabric of their society', and in the absence of a definition of harm, or any concrete definition of deprave and corrupt, juries were unable to convict 'even the most desolating pornography'.[13] In the end it was up to a jury to 'make a moral judgement'[14] on questions of a **403**

'speculative nature' about which they had 'imperfect knowledge'.[15] In Robertson's view this left 'to the jury the almost
unanswerable question of whether, in the circumstances of the
particular case, erotic material may cause social, moral, psychological, or spiritual damage'.[16]

Furthermore, in their defence, people could claim they did not
know an article was obscene. They could also claim that – as
science, art or literature – it was in the public good and they
could call expert witnesses to establish its merit. For a period of
time, this 'public good defence' was abused to defend material
with 'no pretensions to artistic or literary merit' by the use of
'expert' witnesses who would argue that 'pornographic material
was psychologically beneficial'. Juries were unable 'to convict
sado-masochistic material, in even the most extreme of which
some experts were prepared to discern some merit'. As a consequence the law was eventually strengthened to exclude this
'therapeutic effect' evidence, and to prevent abuse of the law.
However, rather than arriving at a workable definition of obscenity, every judicial interpretation of 'deprave and corrupt' has
conspired to make the law increasingly unimplementable.

Enforcement

The Obscene Publications Act is enforced either through trial by
jury in a crown court (Section 2) or through 'forfeiture proceedings' in a local magistrates' court (Section 3). The 'vagueness'
and the 'subjectivity' of the definition of obscenity and the
variable meaning of 'deprave and corrupt' has meant that 'a
wide discretion is vested in prosecuting authorities'. This has
made the obscenity law 'difficult to enforce'.

Police initiate an action by applying to a magistrates' court for
a warrant to search and seize from suspected premises material
which they believe may be obscene. Before passing the material
to the Director of Public Prosecutions, who decides whether to
launch a criminal prosecution or to apply for a civil forfeiture
order, it is up to the police to decide whether the material is
likely to be suitable for prosecution. For this purpose they will
'formulate their own internal guidelines for action',[17] based on
their experience and estimation of what a jury is likely to convict.
When they start to lose cases on certain kinds of material, they
have to 'start thinking again' about whether or not to attempt
prosecution of the same or similar material in future.[18]

For obscenity is only ever what a court decides it is: nothing is illegal until a court declares it to be so. The Williams Committee observed that 'if juries are reluctant to convict, then prosecuting authorities are likely to be less keen to initiate prosecutions'.[19] Furthermore, 'the decision of one court trial is not binding on any other, so the fact that one jury has found particular material not to be obscene' – or to be obscene – 'does not necessarily rule out future proceedings involving similar material'.[20] The fact that material is found to be not obscene by one court does not necessarily mean that it is not obscene. Even when a case is won and material is judged by a court to be obscene, not a great deal is gained because distribution of the material is only prohibited within the jurisdiction of that particular court. The identical 'obscene material' can be sold legally anywhere else in the country until it is prosecuted following the same procedures and found to be obscene again – or to be found not obscene, depending on the view of the jury. The same item can, therefore, be obscene and illegal in one place, and for sale legally some-where else. The fact that material is for sale is not evidence of its legality, only that it has not been prosecuted. Enforcement of the obcenity law, like the definition of obscenity, is so 'relative' as to make prosecution virtually pointless.

In this system the Director of Public Prosecutions acts as 'custodian of public morals'[21] and the 'demarcation line between what is and what is not obscene in law becomes more obscure'. Under the present law, the 'inconsistencies and geographical variations in obscenity decisions by magistrates' demonstrates that decisions are 'essentially a matter of personal prejudice'.[22] When the publishers of *Inside Linda Lovelace* were acquitted in 1976, the view of both the trial judge and the Metropolitan Police was 'that it was difficult to imagine what written material would be regarded as obscene if that was not'.[23] The Director of Public Prosecutions told the Williams Committee in 1979 that it was 'now quite impossible' to be certain of securing a conviction by a jury of what he considered to be a grossly obscene article.[24]

The legal profession itself has thus acknowledged that the obscenity legislation is 'unworkable' and 'untenable', 'unscientific' and 'illogical',[25] providing 'unpredictable' and often 'conflicting' results. Even various Directors of Public Prosecutions, whose job it is to decide whether or not any material should proceed to prosecution, have had to admit that they 'do not know what corrupts', that they 'get no help from the Acts', and that **405** there is 'a generally recognized uncertainty in the operation of the law in this field'.

Obscenity legislation, in the words of one Law Lord, 'provides a formula which cannot in practice be applied'. In practice obscenity is overwhelmingly permitted. Obscenity law appears to be designed to have little effect on the sale of pornography and 'even determined efforts' by police 'will not avail against the wiles of determined pornographers'.[26] In spite of complaints about censorship, the pornography industry has in practice been at liberty to define the boundaries of obscenity law, in its terms going further and further in testing the 'tolerance' of the market-place and the judicial system, until that tolerance itself increases in response to the desensitizing properties of pornography. By 1979 the Williams Committee considered that given 'the number of highly explicit magazines in circulation', there were 'doubts as to whether the law could effectively control them'.[27] By 1990 the number of magazines and their 'explicitness' had increased still further, and the deregulation of trade in the European Community in 1992 would greatly increase the potential for expanding the pornography market in the UK, unchecked by obscenity law.

Home Office statistics on prosecutions under the Obscene Publications Act 1959 show a consistent and sometimes dramatic decrease in prosecutions during the 1980s. In magistrates' courts in England and Wales, prosecutions halved between 1984 and 1985 (falling from 458 to 225) and halved again between 1985 and 1986 (from 225 to 114). Crown court prosecutions remained level between 1984 (258) and 1985 (216), but there was a dramatic drop in 1986 (to 88) and then to just over 30 in 1987 and 1988. In both courts, only about half of those prosecuted were convicted in each year.

There was a similar pattern of decreasing prosecutions under the Customs Consolidation Act 1876, and prosecutions halved between 1984 and 1985 (from 65 to 30). There was also a dramatic fall in items seized, from 170,000 in 1984 to 43,400 in 1985. Prosecutions averaged 59 per year between 1986 and 1989, with gaol sentences averaging four per year. The Customs and Excise Annual Report for 1985 noted 'the significant reductions compared with last year's total', and considered it 'a consequence of the need to reflect changing standards'. The prosecution of Gay's the Word Bookshop in 1984 (see below), when the 1876 Customs and Excise Act was used to censor non-pornographic homosexual materials, generated widespread publicity against the 'obscenity legislation' generally. This may have influenced reductions in Customs and Excise seizures and prosecutions and probably also in Obscene Publications Act prosecutions of pornography after 1985.[28]

Indecency

The Indecent Displays Act 1981, which followed in the wake of the Williams Committee Report on Obscenity and Film Censorship in 1979, did nothing to improve the legal mess, and added further problems of definition and enforcement. The 1981 Act amended the Vagrancy Act 1824[29] and made it an offence to display publicly 'indecent matter' on the grounds of 'public nuisance'. The Act targeted the 'cinema club posters, bookshop and sex window displays that people cannot avoid seeing as they walk along the pavement or go into a shop to buy cigarettes or chocolates'.[30]

The Williams Committee had gone further in recommending restrictions on the availability of material which it proposed to define as 'offensive to reasonable people by reason of the manner in which it portrays, deals with or relates to violence, cruelty or horror or sexual, faecal or urinary functions or genital organs'.[31] The effect of the proposals would have been 'to ensure that those who did not want to see pornography were not forced to do so', that 'nothing to which this definition applies' would 'be able to be displayed in public places or be sold in shops to which children and young people have access'.[32]

In the event, the 1981 Act did *not* define indecency and it was apparently the deliberate intention of Parliament that the meaning of indecency should remain vague. In the debate on the Act, the need to define indecency was emphasized: 'there's a clear possibility that because different people have different standards of "indecency" the Act will not be applied consistently'.[33] It was proposed therefore to insert the formula – 'offensiveness to reasonable people' – suggested by the Williams Committee which 'felt that the word "indecency" was surrounded with such vagueness and confusion as to be useless'.

The government rejected this and pointed out that 'since there was no question of restricting the availability of indecent matter, but only its display, any uncertainty surrounding the word was not serious'. It was pointed out that as the Act was concerned with 'indecent displays', not 'displays of the indecent', it did 'not matter that material contained inside a magazine or a package is indecent, provided that the cover wrapping is not'. The deliberate ambiguity was reportedly accepted by MPs with 'equanimity' and 'even approval'.[34]

The Indecent Displays Act has been used relatively little since it was passed. In the whole of England and Wales between 1982 and 1988 there were on average twenty-one convictions per year in magistrates' courts; and in the crown court, there were only a *total* of nineteen convictions in England and Wales between 1982 and 1985.[35] Although it may have restricted the *display* of pornography, the Act has not significantly restricted the *production* and *distribution* of pornography. And while the Act restricted the *display*, for example, to the top shelf of local newsagents, with the covers overlapping in order partially to obscure the 'display of the indecent', the *availability* of 'indecent material' by the end of the 1980s was widespread in virtually every newsagent, tobacconist and sweetshop – in precisely those places children, young people and women were most likely to frequent.

Censorship

The deliberate vagueness of the definitions of obscenity and indecency has left the legislation open to abuse. It has consequently been used as an instrument to censor art and literature, to oppress gays and lesbians and to control women's fertility. This is not surprising since the original target of state censorship was not sex, but seditious and politically subversive literature.[36] For centuries, morality was a smokescreen for political suppression.[37] As recently as the 1970s, obscenity legislation was being used against the radical, counter-culture 'underground' press. There was the IT (*International Times*) trial in 1970 and the OZ trial in 1971, whose editor claimed that his 'bust' by the police, 'had turned into a search for drugs and politically subversive literature'.[38] *Last Exit to Brooklyn* was prosecuted in 1967 as obscenity because of its portrayal of homosexuality and drug-taking.[39]

Homosexuality, whether gay or lesbian, has historically been regarded as inherently obscene. In 1936 Radclyffe Hall's *The Well of Loneliness* was declared obscene because it dealt with lesbianism, and as recently as 1984 Gay's the Word Bookshop was prosecuted under the Customs Consolidation Act 1876 when Customs and Excise seized 142 titles (800 items) on the grounds that they were 'indecent and obscene'.[40] Over 100 charges were brought – but later dropped – against nine individuals on 'conspiracy' to 'fraudulently evade the prohibition of indecent and obscene material'. The material was prosecuted because it was homosexual not because it was obscene: it included 'literature which would merit no legal action if it were heterosexual, books already available in the UK, on syllabuses of respectable higher education institutions by writers such as Oscar Wilde, Kate Millett and Jean Genet'.[41] Silver Moon, the women's bookshop, reported that in their first two years of operation their imported feminist and lesbian books were regularly opened by customs officers under the guise of a search for obscenity – a form of informal unauthorized harassment.[42]

'Classic' literature has also been prosecuted as obscenity. Following the introduction of the definition of obscenity as tending to deprave and corrupt in 1868,[43] 'Victorian prosecutors proceeded to destroy many examples of fine literature and scientific speculation'.[44] In 1888 books by Zola, Flaubert, de Maupassant and Gautier were successfully prosecuted. In 1960 D. H. Lawrence's *Lady Chatterley's Lover* was used to test the new Obscene Publications Act (1959) in a famous case which ended in acquittal.[45]

Obscenity legislation has also been used to restrict women's access to contraception and abortion: 'The history of criminal obscenity legislation is, in many ways, the history of how women's reproductive self-determination and sexuality have been repressed.'[46] In 1876 *The Fruits of Philosophy: An Essay on the Population Problem* was prosecuted because it advocated birth control.[47] In Canada and Ireland, 'obscenity provisions have been used to regulate information on birth control, abortion, women's sexuality, alternative sexualities and dissident politics'.[48] In Ireland, for example, the Censorship of Publications Act 1929 prohibited the publication of a book that is 'indecent or obscene' or which 'advocates the unnatural prevention of conception or the procurement of abortion or miscarriage'.[49] Information on contraception was decriminalized in Ireland in 1979, but it is still illegal within the obscenity legislation to 'advocate' abortion in print. While obscenity legislation has functioned in these ways to censor art and literature, to restrict women's reproductive freedom and to suppress 'feminism and homosexuality',[50] the 'interpretation of obscenity provisions' has 'ensured' that 'men' have 'maintained access to women's sexuality in the form of pornography'.[51]

Pornography and Gender

Scrutiny of the obscenity legislation shows that while it poses some risk of censorship to material which is not pornography, it poses no real threat at all to pornography. Why have the courts deliberately opted for a 'vague and elastic' definition of obscenity and then proceeded to apply conditions that make it even more indefinable and less applicable to its ostensible target material – pornography? Why does the law contain enforcement procedures which guarantee the continued circulation of 'obscene material' even after it has been successfully prosecuted? Given this catalogue of legislative absurdity, why does government persist in maintaining a law which in the view of the judiciary itself is a 'formula which cannot in practice be applied'? It almost seems to be the deliberate intention of obscenity legislation – largely obscured by its vagueness and obfuscation – actually to protect pornography.

Certainly obscenity legislation obscures the fact that if we look, we see that pornography is almost entirely about women and women's bodies. In obscenity law, pornography is not only not defined, it is never even specifically mentioned, and in obscenity law's concern about morality, women are rendered entirely invisible. Is it not odd, asks Catharine A. MacKinnon, Professor of Law at Michigan University, that 'although the content and dynamic of pornography are about women – about the sexuality of women, about women as sexuality – in the same way that the vast majority of "obscenities" refer specifically to women's bodies . . . that the law of obscenity has *never even considered pornography a women's issue*?'[52]

The crucial point here – and the problem with obscenity law – is that pornography is 'not a moral issue' but a gender issue. Obscenity legislation looks at pornography and sees sex, but from the point of view of women we can look again at pornography and see sexual objectification (photographs of women's vaginas and anuses, pulled open and posed gaping for the camera, inviting penetration) or forms of technically legal child pornography (women with their pubic hair shaved and posed to look like little girls or little girls made up and sexualized to look like women) or sexual violence (women being humiliated, whipped and beaten). In the UK all of this is on sale in newsagents and, not having been challenged in court, is not illegal. And in the illegally circulating pornography we can see

women bound and gagged, raped and tortured: burnt on their
breasts and genitals with cigarettes, labia nailed to the top of a
table, hanging by their breasts from meat hooks, disembowelled
and murdered.[53]

Obscenity legislation looks at this and, because it sees nakedness and genitals (sexual explicitness) it just sees sex. But from
the point of view of women we can look at this pornography and
see sexual objectification, sexual violence, sexualized violence,
male dominance and the sexual subordination of women,
women's inequality eroticized, misogyny. Obscenity looks for
evidence of harm to men or to morals, to see if men or the moral
fabric of society is 'depraved and corrupted'. From the point of
view of women we look at the evidence of harm to women – 'to
report about who did what to whom' – and we see injury. We see
the harm that is taking place to the women in the pornography
described above. This harm – certainly the sexual objectification
and sometimes even the sexual violence – has been invisible to
the male eye. We see the harm to women that takes place daily
in society (often as invisible there as it is in pornography) and
we see the evidence that women are harmed – subject to sexual
violence and sex discrimination – by men's use of pornography.

Male Power and Morality
In this context, MacKinnon argues that 'obscenity law is concerned with morality, specifically morals from the male point of
view, meaning the standpoint of male dominance' while 'pornography is a politics, specifically politics from women's point of
view, meaning the standpoint of the subordination of women to
men . . . Morality here means good and evil; politics means
power and powerlessness.' MacKinnon argues that 'the obscenity
standard is built on what the male standpoint sees', and 'so is
pornography':

> Men are turned on by obscenity, including its suppression, the
> same way they are by sin. Animated by morality from the male
> standpoint, in which violation – of women and rules – is eroticized,
> obscenity law can be seen to proceed according to the interest of
> male power, robed in gender-neutral good and evil.[54]

What is at issue in pornography – and what obscenity legislation
protects – is maintaining male power and sexual inequality.
'Differences in the law over time – such as the liberalization of   **411**

obscenity doctrine – reflect either changes in which groups of men have power or shifts in perceptions of the best strategy for maintaining male supremacy – probably some of both. But it must be made to work.'[55] Pornography is a crucial element in making male power work.

With this new perspective on the meaning of pornography and its function in maintaining power relations, it is possible to return to obscenity legislation and to make sense of what was previously confusing: to see its irrevocable logic in relation to male power. In this context, MacKinnon sees 'the fight over a definition of obscenity as a fight among men over the best means to guarantee male power as a system'. She sees the 'indefinability of pornography, "all the one man's this is another man's that" ', as 'central to pornography's definition'. The obscenity 'standard centres upon the . . . erect penis and penetration'. The purpose of pornography is to engineer sexual arousal – 'to give a man an erection'. The real reason therefore that obscenity is undefined is that: 'Men are scared to make it possible for some men to tell other men what they can and cannot have sexual access to because men have power. If you don't let them have theirs, they might not let you have yours.'[56] ·

Idea – or Injury?

Obscenity legislation likes to pretend that the effects of pornography are all in the mind. But as MacKinnon points out, pornography is 'not harmless fantasy' or 'simulation or catharsis but sexual reality'. There is evidence that men treat women as they see women being treated in pornography. Before acts can be done, they have to be imagined. Pornography is not therefore simply an idea or an image, but a mechanism of sexual subordination, 'a means of systematizing the definition of women as a sexual class'. Women's economic subordination is engineered through the labour market and the family; women's sexual subordination is engineered through pornography.

Obscenity legislation likes to pretend that images and words are harmless: 'The idea is that words or pictures can only be harmful if they produce harm in a form that is considered an action. Words work in the province of attitudes, actions in the realm of behaviour. Words cannot constitute harm in themselves.'[57] But what about 'libel, blackmail, bribery, conspiracy or sexual harassment'? Or racial harassment? These are all examples of where, in law, words are regarded as a cause of harm. 'Which,' asks MacKinnon, 'is saying "kill" to a trained guard dog, a word or an act?' Or 'how about a sign that reads "Whites only"? Is that the idea or the practice of segregation?' The words on the sign are an act of segregation, and pornography similarly is an act of subordination. Only in so far as social reality is defined by white supremacy and racial segregation, or by male supremacy and pornography, is that harm difficult to see.

Obscenity legislation likes to pretend that harm is a matter of moral degradation and injury. For women, however, the harm of pornography is physical injury and social degradation in the form of sexual violence and subordination. Thus *Inside Linda Lovelace* was tried and acquitted of obscenity in England in 1976: it supposedly contained no 'moral' harm. But Linda 'Lovelace' Marciano herself was brutally harmed so that pornographic films could be made of her.[58]

The problem of pornography is its influence on the attitudes and behaviour of men and how this in turn harms women. Women are harmed through the manufacture and use of pornography. The harm is therefore inherent, not relative to who uses it, or where it is bought. A significant proportion of men (at least 2.25 million a month in Britain) use pornography: a significant proportion of men are therefore influenced by it – not just a few 'deviant men' or 'dirty old men'. Men who use pornography come from all walks of life.[59] Pornography is not 'therapeutic': it is damaging to men and through men it harms women. Restricting the public display and sale of pornography, keeping it out of sight of women and children does not therefore solve the problem of the use of women and children in pornography and of men's use of pornography: that women and children are injured in private because of men's access to pornography.

Obscenity legislation likes to pretend that it is hunting down, searching out and destroying pornography. But it is not really. Obscenity legislation is not concerned with what men do or don't do, but how publicly it is done or seen to be done. It used to be that pornography would be, as Catharine MacKinnon says, 'publicly repudiated while being privately consumed and actualized: do anything to women with impunity in private behind a veil of public denial and civility'. Pornography is now much more public, but this probably does not alter women's actual treatment all that much. According to MacKinnon, 'Women were sex and still are sex.'

413

Obscenity legislation pretends to protect fourteen-year-old schoolgirls from seeing pornography, but men buy it and bring it home and fourteen-year-old schoolgirls see it (two-thirds of girls under sixteen according to a recent study), and the girls are sexually abused by the men who are influenced by it (13 per cent according to the same study), and women are raped (10 per cent) and sexually assaulted (24 per cent according to the study) and pornography is known to have been used in over a quarter of these rapes and assaults.[60]

Obscenity is defined in relation to 'community standards' in a community that is saturated with pornography.[61] As exposure to pornography is known to desensitize men (and indeed women too),[62] it is not surprising therefore that juries are increasingly tolerant of increasingly violent pornography. In this perspective it is pornography itself that pushes the boundaries back further and further. Community standards are likely to reflect the damage that pornography has done. And in so far as women are excluded from positions of power, influence and speech, community standards will in any case be 'male' standards.

The Influence of Feminism

This new understanding of pornography was developed by feminism in the 1970s and '80s but others have made similar observations about pornography and the subordination of women. Geoffrey Robertson wrote in 1979 that 'a difficult problem emerges' when the pornography 'issue is viewed, not in terms of the right of the individual to dilate over pornographic fantasies, but from the perspective of a community which requires a limited social cohesion to secure equal and civilized treatment for all its members'.[63] Robertson saw freedom from prejudice and discrimination as 'challenged by propaganda designed to stir hatred against blacks, women, homosexuality, Christians or any other group defined in discriminatory terms'. He was concerned about 'propaganda against homosexuals' because it 'exploits the emotion of hatred to destroy the happiness of a particular group of law-abiding citizens'. He referred to the 'strains of pornography which glamorize the degradation and maltreatment of women, and assert their subordinate function as mere receptacles for male lust'. He mentioned the men's magazines which 'feed the traditional fantasy of the female as nympho-maniac' – saying no when she really means yes – willing to surrender, the humiliation of young models masturbating for the 'mass titillation of prurient-minded men'.[64]

> A jury which is really concerned to reflect 'progressive' thinking might find such magazines would 'tend to corrupt' by perpetrating false and degrading sexual stereotypes. What is truly corrupting is not sexual explicitness in itself, or even the suggestion that people should do whatever they like with a consenting partner, but the idea that they should overbear the will of another.[65]

Robertson argued that 'a society which wishes to tolerate minorities may be powerless to protect them against verbal or written assault by degradation, humiliation or defamation', and probably needed legislation. But what legislation? The law against moral corruption? Robertson showed this to be thoroughly discredited: 'The real problem of pornography is the problem of finding any reasonably acceptable legal alternatives to the Obscene Publications Act.'[66] The Williams Committee came to a similar conclusion about the need for a new definition of pornography: 'If there is to be a law against the kind of material against which the present definitions uncertainly work, then there has to be some other definition.'[67] The Williams Committee also believed that what was needed in relation to evidence of harm was 'not so much new facts, as new ideas'. A feminist perspective has produced answers to all of these requirements: a new idea of harm, a new way of defining pornography and an alternative to the Obscene Publications Act, which address the need for effective legislation against pornography and at the same time offer 'a way of suppressing that material and *only* that material'.[68]

NEW WAYS OF LEGISLATING

None of the existing legislation addresses the key issue of pornography: the power imbalance in society – male dominance, female subordination and sexual inequality. None of the existing legislation takes account of the evidence that exists of the harm caused to women by men's use of pornography. None of the existing legislation defines pornography specifically for what it is and what it does to women.

With the recognition of the role pornography plays in constructing and maintaining sexual inequality and the evidence of the part pornography plays in contributing to sexual **415** violence has come the opportunity to target pornography specifically for legislation on the grounds of harm to women, defining harm to include sex discrimination and subordination as well as sexual violence, using a definition of pornography which describes it objectively for what it is and what it does. By the end of the 1980s, there was activity in several countries in pursuit of such legislation, including the USA, Canada, West Germany, Norway, Australia, New Zealand and Ireland.

The USA
The Civil Rights Ordinance
In Minneapolis, Minnesota, in 1983 the city council commissioned Catharine A. MacKinnon and Andrea Dworkin to draft an 'ordinance relating the violation of women's rights in regard to pornography to civil rights'.[69] The statute they drafted – referred to as 'the Ordinance' – was based on the principles underlying the Fourteenth Amendment to the US Constitution which 'guarantees equality and freedom from discrimination to all', but which, in fact, had historically not included women's right to vote (until 1920) or equal protection under the law for women (until 1971). The intention of the Ordinance, as with prior unsuccessful attempts to legislate an Equal Rights Amendment in the USA, was to extend the equality rights to include women and to mandate 'freedom from discrimination on the basis of sex'.[70]

Dworkin and MacKinnon explained the principle of legislating against pornography on grounds of sex discrimination in the statement of policy and findings that prefaced the Minneapolis Ordinance:

> Pornography is a systematic practice of exploitation and subordination based on sex that differentially harms women. The harm of pornography includes dehumanization, sexual exploitation, forced sex, forced prostitution, physical injury, and social and sexual terrorism and inferiority presented as entertainment. The bigotry and contempt pornography promotes, with the acts of aggression it fosters, diminish opportunities for equality of rights in employment, education, property, public accommodations, and public services; create public and private harassment, persecution, and denigration; expose individuals who appear in pornography against their will to contempt, ridicule, hatred, humiliation, and embarrassment and target such women in particular for abuse and physical aggression; demean the reputations and diminish the

416

occupational opportunities of individuals and groups on the basis of sex; promote injury and degradation such as rape, battery, child sexual abuse, and prostitution and inhibit just enforcement of laws against these acts; contribute significantly to restricting women in particular from full exercise of citizenship and participation in public life, including in neighbourhoods; damage relations between the sexes; and undermine women's equal exercise of rights to speech and action guaranteed to all citizens under the Constitutions and laws of the United States.[71]

They found existing legislation ineffective in dealing with the harms of pornography:

While many of the acts that make up the distinctive harms of pornography are formally illegal, no existing laws are effective against them. If they were, pornography would not flourish as it does, and its victims would not be victimized through it as they are. Lawyers seeking to protect pornography often become extremely ingenious in inventing legal theories that they insist already cover all serious harms of pornography – legal theories they seldom intend to try to make work.[72]

The Ordinance differed from other legislation in providing civil rather than criminal relief within a legal framework in which women themselves could take action against the publishers and distributors of pornography on the grounds of harm.

In fact, no laws now permit those victimized by pornography to sue the pornographers for the pornography. So long as the pornography can be made and sold, the harms of its making and use will continue, and the incentive to make it and sell it will continue.[73]

The preface to the Ordinance was based on the results of Public Hearings held by the Minneapolis City Council where evidence for and against the proposed legislation was heard.[74] According to Dworkin and MacKinnon:

No one claimed that these things never happen without pornography. They said that sometimes it was because of pornography that these things happened. No one claimed that these are the only things that happen because of pornography. They said only that no matter what else happens, this does.[75]

As a result of the evidence presented in the Minneapolis Hearings the legislation was passed by the city council on 30 December 1983. It was vetoed by the mayor. The Bill was **417** passed again with a few revisions in July 1984 by a newly elected city council. Again it was vetoed by the mayor.

A similar Bill was presented to the Indianapolis City Council and was passed on 23 April 1984. It was signed by the mayor and became law. Almost immediately an injunction was taken by a 'coalition' of pornography and trade publishers and distributors, supported by the American Civil Liberties Union (ACLU), to stop it being used on the grounds that it was unconstitutional because it infringed the right to freedom of speech guaranteed in the First Amendment to the US Constitution.

In the resulting case, in 1985, a US Federal Court of Appeal agreed with the premise of the Indianapolis Ordinance that 'pornography is a systematic practice of exploitation and subordination based on sex' and accepted all the evidence of harm caused by pornography to women on which it was based. But the court none the less considered pornography to be speech which had to be protected. The evidence of pornography's power to harm women was taken as proof of its value as speech.[76] The freedom to publish pornography took automatic precedence over women's freedom from harm and discrimination. Two freedoms appeared to be in conflict, but pornography was valued more highly than women's equality and freedom from discrimination.

The legislation was never implemented in Indianapolis. In 1988 a similar piece of legislation was considered in Bellingham, Washington, as part of the ballot for the presidential election, giving citizens an opportunity to vote for civil rights legislation against pornography. A 62 per cent majority of the electorate voted in favour of civil rights anti-pornography legislation.[77] But, as in Indianapolis, the new legislation was again challenged successfully in the courts by the American Civil Liberties Union representing a local bookseller.[78] In this case, the judge reiterated the Indianapolis decision, accepting the evidence of harm with respect to sexual violence, subordination and sexual inequality, but giving precedence to the 'free speech' of pornography. In neither case was the issue of pornography's silencing effect on women's speech addressed, nor was any real injury of pornography placed directly before the courts.

The Pornography Victims Compensation Act (1989)

In 1989 a Pornography Victims Compensation Act was introduced in the US Senate. This was a piece of civil legislation which would enable victims of 'any sexual offence that was at least partially caused by the sexual offender's exposure to . . . sexually explicit material' to hold 'the producers, distributors, exhibitors and sellers of sexually explicit material to be . . liable for all damages'.[79] The Act affirmed that 'protecting freedom of speech is essential to the preservation of a just and free society', but that 'consistent with the Constitutional protection of freedom of speech, the State has a legitimate interest in restricting explicit material if there is a danger of harm or actual harm to individuals or society'. The Act cited a number of sources of evidence and kinds of harm caused by the use of pornography and claimed the state's legitimate interest in 'protecting its citizens' from sexual crimes, in preventing such crimes and 'in providing adequate compensation to the victims of sexual crimes'.[80] The Pornography Victims Compensation Act 1989 was endorsed by the National Organization of Women (NOW) at its national conference in 1989 because it 'empowered victims, not the State, "after the fact" of criminal offence', and therefore did not conflict with the First Amendment'. The Act did not proceed beyond committee stage.

The Pornography Victims Protection Act (1990)

A similar piece of legislation was introduced in the Senate in 1990. This also provided a remedy whereby women could hold pornographers responsible for sexual assault in which pornography was involved. The Act was still in committee at the time of writing.

The UK

The 'Page 3' Bill

Labour MP Clare Short put forward a Private Members Bill in 1986, and again in 1989, aimed at banning the scantily clad, bare-breasted, provocatively posed 'pin-ups' which are published in British tabloid newspapers such as the *Sun*, the *Star*, the *News of the World*, and the *Sport*. She used the Indecent Displays legislation which would make it unlawful to publish such pictures, and in the 1989 Bill, also unlawful to 'display indecent matter' in the workplace.

The 'Page 3 Bills', as they are known, attracted widespread support from women throughout the country (a mailbag of thousands of letters) who said they found the presentation of women on Page 3 degrading, offensive and dangerous, **419** contributing to sexual harassment and sexual assault.[81] The legislation was promoted by the grass-roots women's Campaign Against Pornography (CAP).

But there was also some debate – and not just among those who opposed the legislation – about whether 'Page 3' should be categorized as pornography. It was felt that 'pictures of naked or partially naked women in sexually provocative poses' could apply to works of art (Rodin's sculpture 'The Kiss' and paintings by Titian were mentioned by MPs opposing the Bill). While the proposed Bill solely targeted such pictures in newspapers, it was felt that the proposed legislation, taken out of that particular context, could be used to 'censor' works of art that most people would not regard as pornographic. Thus, the definition of Page 3 *as a definition of pornography* was flawed and open to potential abuse.

A further problem with the legislation was its definition of pornography in terms of indecency (rather than its influence on the attitudes and behaviour of men), with the assumption inherent in the existing Indecent Displays legislation that women's bodies themselves are indecent or obscene. The Indecent Displays legislation is also unsatisfactory from the point of view of censorship and civil liberties. As criminal legislation which simply names an object to be banned, it could be used as a precedent and a form of legislation for banning anything: not just pornography, but information about abortion or contraception, for example, or even criticism of government policy.

The Location of Pornographic Material Bill (1989)

In July 1989 another Labour MP, Dawn Primarolo, introduced a Private Members Bill on 'The Location of Pornographic Material' supported by the Campaign for Press and Broadcasting Freedom (CPBF). Under the terms of the Bill, pornographic material would only be available from licensed vendors set up solely for that purpose. As with existing legislation for the licensing of sex shops in the Local Government Act 1982, local authorities would be responsible for issuing licences and trading standards officers for enforcing the regulations.[82]

The Campaign for Press and Broadcasting Freedom was closely involved in drafting the Bill, in what they described as 'a significant effort to extend the freedom of women in society'.

Why should women be confronted by pornographic material every time they walk in a newsagents? Why should their children grow up thinking this is a normal part of everyday life? We are no longer prepared to see women's bodies sold in shops on a par with cigarettes and chewing gum. These degrading images belittle women and make the achievement of a more equal society much harder. Laws regulate the sale of cigarettes and alcohol. Surely similar legislation should apply to harmful pornographic material.[83]

One of the main aims of the CPBF has traditionally been to campaign *against* censorship and *for* freedom of speech in the press. As an organization it had come to the decision that the freedom to publish pornography no longer took precedence over women's freedom, safety and equality, and in balancing the two freedoms (of women and pornographers) put women's freedom first.

Dawn Primarolo described the Bill as avoiding censorship and accommodating a variety of currently competing civil rights claims: respecting the rights of those who worked in the pornography industry, the right of pornographers to manufacture and sell pornography, the right of men to buy it, but also 'women's rights not to be exposed to this humiliating and degrading material.'[84] She saw it as an interim strategy which enabled a continuing debate on the issues of censorship, but also 'enabled women to choose whether they wished to see pornography or not'.[85]

There are, however, some real problems as well as some positive gains with this form of legislation. Removing pornography from sale in high street newsagents and petrol stations would prevent women and children seeing pornography unwillingly in public, but it would not stop them seeing it, in private, 'at home', and it would not prevent it being 'forced' upon them against their will in private where most sexual abuse occurs. Locating pornography in licensed premises would reduce the number of outlets, but whether it would reduce the volume of sales would have to be monitored. It would probably be available to and therefore influence the attitudes and behaviour of fewer men, and while it might stop women *seeing* the degrading and humiliating material, it would not stop women from *being* humiliated and degraded by its use.

This legislative approach is flawed in several respects. It assumes that the problem of pornography is that it causes 'offence'. There is in fact evidence to suggest that pornography is **421**

'offensive' to most women, not because of prudery or fastidious-
ness but because it is frightening and women recognize it as a
threat.[86] But the real problem is the harm caused to women
because of men's use of pornography: keeping it out of sight of
women and children does not solve this problem, and continues
to disempower women by keeping them ignorant and uninformed. Experience of zoning legislation in the USA has shown
that pornography is usually 'zoned' out of white middle-class
neighbourhoods and 'located' into poor, black and working-class
neighbourhoods. Property values fall even further in these areas
because of the blight created by the sale of pornography: the
danger, the violence and the increased harassment of and assault
on women and children in these areas.

The Race Relations Model – 'Incitement to Sexual Hatred'
The Race Relations Act 1976 (by amending the Public Order
Act 1936) made 'incitement to racial hatred' unlawful. Under
this Act: 'A person who uses threatening, abusive or insulting
words or behaviour, or displays any written material which is
threatening, abusive or insulting, is guilty of an offence if (a) he
intends thereby to stir up racial hatred, or (b) having regard to
all the circumstances racial hatred is likely to be stirred up
thereby.'[87]

The Act applies to the publication and distribution of written
material, to private as well as public places and includes the
private circulation of material. The 1986 amendments to the
Public Order Act created a new offence of 'possessing racially
inflammatory material' with powers of entry, search and forfeiture. 'Racial hatred' is defined as 'hatred against a group of
persons defined by reference to colour, race, nationality (including citizenship) or ethnic or national origins . . . "Hatred" is not
defined but connotes intense dislike, animosity or enmity. It
implies sufficient dislike to be manifested in active demonstration
of ill-will.'

The incitement section of the Race Relations Act is criminal
legislation which provides a precedent for restraints on freedom
of expression which can be oppressive and harmful to a particular
group on grounds of race. It could similarly be used as a model
for restraints on freedom of expression which, as in the case of
pornography, can be oppressive and harmful to a particular
group on grounds of gender.

422   This legislation acknowledges the existence of racial hatred, that it can be 'spoken' (and published) and that it can be stimulated or incited by 'speech' (or publication). Misogyny or sexual hatred also exists: like race hatred it can be spoken (published) and incited by speech (publication). The Race Relations Act could therefore be used as a model to legislate against pornography on the grounds that it can act as an 'incitement to sexual hatred' and 'contribute to acts of violence against women in the form of sexual abuse, sexual assault, sexual harassment, rape and murder', and to sexism and sex discrimination.

In the incitement to racial hatred legislation society has agreed to restraints on freedom of expression which could cause identifiable harm to black people and Jews. This degreee of censorship is regarded as reasonable to ensure a measure of freedom from racial hatred, violence and discrimination. It is suggested that similar restraints would be appropriate on pornography which could be proved to cause identifiable harm to women in order to ensure a measure of freedom from sexual hatred, violence and discrimination (see Chapters 5 and 26).

One drawback to the incitement legislation is that, being a criminal law, it puts the power of enforcement in the hands of the police and the 'state' (the Director of Public Prosecutions). Potential for abuse in this form of legislation, however, would be rendered virtually impossible, by a concrete, specific and unambiguous definition of pornography (see Chapter 22). In favour of this form of legislation, race hatred literature is neither readily available nor mass-marketed.

The Campaign Against Pornography and Censorship (CPC) – launched in April 1989 by a group of writers, artists, lawyers and trade unionists with a long tradition of both civil liberties anticensorship *and* women's rights work – took up the campaign for legislation against pornography on the grounds of incitement to sexual hatred and violence using the UK Race Relations Act 1976 as a model.

The Sex Discrimination Model
The CPC also proposed legislation against pornography as a form of discrimination against women on the grounds of sex. There are precedents for legislating against sex discrimination. The Sex Discrimination Act 1975 made it illegal to discriminate directly or indirectly on grounds of sex in employment with respect to recruitment, promotion, dismissal and redundancy, **423**

and the Sex Discrimination Act 1986 removed differential compulsory retirement ages. The Equal Pay Act 1970 and the Equal Pay (Amendment) Regulations 1983 enabled women to claim equal pay for work of equal value. The existing sex discrimination law is civil legislation.

Civil sex discrimination legislation against pornography would enable women to take action on grounds of harm done to them by pornography. It has been argued that asking women to sue the pornography industry is to turn them into victims because women would have to prove they were harmed by – or victims of – pornography. But the reverse is true: 'the chance to challenge pornographers is the opposite of making women victims'.[88] Civil legislation would simply acknowledge that women are victimized as a result of their subordinate status in an oppressive and unequal society: that pornographers turn women into victims. Civil legislation would enable women to take a stand on their own behalf against the pornography industry, and enable them to obtain compensation for harm or injury. This is arguably a form of empowerment: of those with the least power taking on the most powerful, the poor taking on the rich, the exploited taking on the exploiters.

British law puts the burden of proof on the individual 'plaintiff' to prove harm in order to obtain redress. In the case of pornography this is arguably an unfair burden given the subordinate status of women in society. However, placing the burden of proof on the publisher or distributor of pornography to show that harm was not done is not possible, although there are currently attempts to reverse the burden of proof in European law in cases of race and sex discrimination in recognition of social power structures and the lack of power of discriminated groups. An advantage of civil legislation is the lower standard of proof required to convict. Criminal law requires proof of guilt beyond a reasonable doubt, whereas civil law requires only a balance of probabilities, sufficient evidence to show that something is more likely than not to have happened.

Economic inequality puts women at a disadvantage in the legal system and lack of financial resources could make it difficult for women to make full use of civil law. It might therefore be necessary to arrange for actions to be taken on behalf of women by an independent agency: a new agency modelled perhaps on the Health and Safety Executive or the Nuclear Inspectorate (or

Local Government Trading Standards Officers) with powers to

investigate and prosecute, or an extension of the Equal Opportunities Commission with powers both to assist individuals with civil suits and to prosecute in its own right in criminal courts.[89]

Civil legislation is a guaranteed way to legislate against pornography without censorship. It would put power into the hands of individuals, not the state. As in cases of medical negligence, individuals could take action on the grounds of harm or injury. Harm might result from coercion into pornography, pornography being forced on a person, assault or physical attack due to pornography or trafficking in pornography: i.e. producing, selling, exhibiting or distributing pornography. As with other forms of equality legislation, sex discrimination legislation against pornography would acknowledge harms that derive their 'meaning and sting from group status'.[90] Provision could therefore be made to enable an individual woman to bring a complaint against pornographers for injuries to women as a group.[91] Harm would have to be proven, and this would not necessarily be easy within an unsympathetic judicial system. But seeking remedy for injury is not censorship; there could therefore be no censorship with civil legislation: 'Only materials that can be *proven harmful* can be reached, and only by their victims, not by the government.'[92]

Civil rights or sex discrimination legislation which enables women to sue for injury is a legislative alternative to the Obscene Publications Act which would eliminate censorship. It is based on a new concept of harm in terms of subordination and sex discrimination as well as sexual violence. And it is based on a new way of defining pornography derived from an understanding of pornography as a mechanism in constructing and maintaining sexual inequality, which resolves the dilemma of how to target pornography without at the same time targeting sexually explicit material which is not pornography such as erotica, sex education materials, forensic and medical literature, information about contraception, reproduction and abortion (see Chapter 22).

WHY BOTHER WITH LEGISLATION?

A variety of criticisms are sometimes levelled against using legislation against pornography. The judicial system is a bastion of male power, and unlikely to be sympathetic either to the claims of women or to creating sexual equality. Even effective legislation will not eliminate pornography or end violence against women. There would still be violence against women, there always has been, and pornography is only one element of a sexist and misogynist culture that contributes to violence against women. There would still be pornography and it would probably go underground and be distributed illegally – like hard drugs in the UK now or bootleg liquor in the USA in the period of prohibition. Legislation on its own can never achieve its goals. Why bother, then, with legislation that might also prove to be poorly enforced?

Similar questions could be asked of the other 'equality legislation'. After fifteen years of the Sex Discrimination Act 1975, women's pay is still only three-quarters of men's pay and women are still largely located in low-status, low-paid employment. The Equal Pay Act 1970 and Equal Pay (Amendments) Regulations 1983 have proved to be a judicial nightmare, taking years to reach decisions in individual cases which have then, in the absence of class actions in the UK, had little or no effect beyond the individual remedy. Racism is still deeply entrenched in British culture and although there is a legal obligation for firms employing more than twenty people to have a 3 per cent quota of disabled employees, this rarely happens.

However, although the equality legislation has not been wholly successful so far in eliminating economic and institutionalized discrimination, it has enabled some important changes to take place, by reducing race and sex discrimination in employment and increasing representation of women and black people in senior positions in some organizations. The equality legislation has also had some considerable effect in increasing awareness and in changing attitudes. On those grounds it has fulfilled a useful function. It has also had a role to play in establishing social values, including the visible public statement that some practices are regarded as socially unacceptable and wrong. Laws against theft and murder do not stop theft and murder, but that failure is not used as an excuse to remove them from the statute book. Laws against murder or rape or race and sex discrimination have a value in setting goals and standards of behaviour in society, in deterring and therefore reducing the number of abusive acts and the amount of abusive behaviour.

Carol Smart thinks that the value of legislation 'whether criminal or civil' is 'not so much in its implementation and enforcement, as in its wider symbolic value'.

It would enable women to shift the debate away from the terrain of sex and sexual prudery, towards that of discrimination. It would open up the issue for wider debate because new positions become available and stereotyped positions could be avoided.[93]

But while sex discrimination legislation against pornography might have 'symbolic' value for some, for others – for women who now cannot do anything and with a law could – it would begin to end the abuse of pornography.

Civil legislation would not criminalize the production of pornography and would not therefore drive pornography underground. On the contrary, it would bring pornography and its injuries to women out into the open. Criminal laws create underground trade, but from the point of view of harm to women, the fact that pornography might go underground is less a problem than its legal, mass-market sales. If the problem of pornography exists because of its influence on the attitudes and behaviour of men, then the fewer men who are exposed to it, the more women will benefit in freedom from sexual violence and sex discrimination. It would obviously be better for women if thousands rather than millions of men are using pornography.

Legislating against pornography could not guarantee the elimination of sexism and sexual violence any more than the abolition of slavery ended racism and racial violence. But black slavery in the USA – once, as pornography is now, a major international profit-making industry – was ended. Lynching was ended and segregation was largely ended. Those particular practices of racism and racial violence were ended through legislation. Legislation could also be used to end the abuse of women through pornography and the practice of sex discrimination which takes the form of pornography.

Notes

1. Geoffrey Robertson, *Obscenity: An Account of Censorship Laws and Their Enforcement in England and Wales* (London: Weidenfeld and Nicolson, 1979), pp. 1–2.
2. *Report of the Committee on Obscenity and Film Censorship* (Williams Committee) (London: HMSO, 1979), p. 20.
3. Robertson, op. cit., p. 46.
4. There have been three Obscene Publications Acts. The first dates from 1857. It aimed to prevent the sale of obscene books, pictures and prints and it gave the police powers to search for obscene publications, to seize them with force if necessary and to destroy them. It contained no definition of obscenity. Over 100 years later, **427**

the Act was amended in the Obscene Publications Act 1959 specifically 'to provide for the protection of literature' and 'to strengthen the law concerning pornography'. It made it an offence to publish an obscene article. The Obscene Publications Act was subsequently amended in 1964 to create an additional offence to have an obscene article for publication or gain and to penalize possession.

There are also laws which control the movement of pornography from place to place. Customs and Excise Officers have powers within the Customs Consolidation Act 1876 and the Customs and Excise Management Act 1979 to seize and destroy material which is defined as 'indecent and obscene'. Indecent is 'usually taken to be a weaker term than "obscene". . . in addition the courts have held that the word "obscene" has its dictionary meaning rather than the meaning of "deprave and corrupt"' (Williams Committee, op. cit., p.12). The Post Office Act 1953 also makes it unlawful to 'send indecent or obscene publications'. The Video Recordings Act 1984 made it unlawful to depict: '(a) human sexual activity or acts of force or constraint associated with such activity; (b) mutilation or torture of, or other acts of gross violence towards humans or animals; (c) human genital organs or human urinary or excretory functions'.

5. Robertson, op. cit., p. 3. (R. *v.* Penguin Books, *Lady Chatterley's Lover*, 1960, Crim. L. R. 176.

6. Ibid. p. 48 (R. *v.* Calder & Boyars, *Last Exit to Brooklyn* 1967, I. Q. B. 151).

7. C. H. Rolph, *The Trial of Lady Chatterley* (Harmondsworth: Penguin, 1961), p. 229.

8. Robertson, op. cit., p. 3. (Calder *v.* Pavell 1965 and DPP *v.* A & B C Chewing Gum 1968). The Children and Young Persons (Harmful Publications) Act 1955 aimed 'to prevent the dissemination of certain pictorial publications harmful to Children and Young Persons, and likely to fall into their hands'. It referred specifically to 'stories portraying the commission of crimes, acts of violence or cruelty, or incidents of a repulsive or horrible nature'. Like obscenity legislation, however, the test of harm was what would 'tend to corrupt'.

9. Ibid., p. 10. 'We see regular customers as inadequate, pathetic, dirty-minded men, seeking cheap thrills – addicts to this type of material, whose morals were already in a state of depravity and corruption. We consequently entertained grave doubt as to whether such minds could be said to be open to any immoral influence which the said articles were capable of exerting.' When the case reached the House of Lords, it was decided that dirty-minded men *could* be depraved more than once.

10. Ibid., pp. 59, 46, 60.

11. Williams Committee, op. cit., p. 16.

12. Robertson, op. cit., p. 68.

13. Ibid., pp. 47, 49, 50.

14. I. Smith and B. Hogan, *Criminal Law* (Edinburgh: Butterworths, 1989), p. 564.

15 Ibid., p. 565.
16. Robertson, op. cit., p. 50
17. Ibid., pp. 4, 81, 87, 81.
18. Personal interview with Obscene Publications Branch Officer, 5 April 1990.
19. Williams Committee, op. cit., p. 36.
20. Ibid.
21. Robertson, op. cit., p. 85.
22. Ibid., pp. 5, 109.
23. Williams Committee, op. cit., p. 35.
24. Ibid., p. 36.
25. Robertson, op. cit., p. 7.
26. Ibid., pp. 45, 85, ?, 45, 87.
27. Williams Committee, op cit., p. 37.
28. Tables of Statistics provided by E. F. Cook, C4 Division, Home Office, 2 March 1990. See also The Comissioners of Her Majesty's Customs and Excise Report for Years Ended 1984–9. In the USA there has been a reverse pattern in the enforcement of obscenity legislation. The following information, derived from the US Attorney General Commission's Report in 1986 shows the very low level of enforcement prior to 1985: 'Under Attorney General William French Smith, there was not a single indictment brought against producers of adult pornography in 1983 . . . There were only six in 1982, but four of those were advanced by one motivated prosecutor. In 1981 there were two. Of the ninety-three United States Attorneys, only seven have devoted any effort to the prosecution of obscenity. Obviously, the multi-billion-dollar porn industry is under no serious pressure from federal prosecutors.

   'The United States Postal Service makes virtually no effort to prosecute those who send obscene material through the mail. Attorney Paul McGeady testified that there are conservatively 100,000 violations of 18 USC 1461 every day of the year. Likewise, the Federal Communications Commission and Interstate Commerce Commission do not attempt to regulate the interstate transportation of obscene material. Eighty per cent of all pornography is produced in Los Angeles County and then shipped to the rest of the country. It would not be difficult to identify and prosecute those who transport it across state lines. The Federal Communications Commission does not regulate obscenity on cable or satellite television. The Customs Service makes no effort to prevent even adult pornography from entering this country and catches only five per cent of child porn from abroad. The Internal Revenue Service permits organized crime to avoid taxes on the majority of its retail sales, especially the video booth market. The Federal Bureau of Investigation assigns only two of 8,700 special agents to obscenity investigation, even though organized crime controls the industry . . .

   'Local law enforcement agencies are equally unconcerned about obscenity. The City of Miami has assigned only two of 1,500 policemen to this area, neither of which is given a car. Chicago allocates two of 12,000 officers to obscenity control. Los Angeles assigns eight out of 6,700, even though Los Angeles is the porn capital of the country. Very few indictments have been brought against a pornographer in Los Angeles County in more than ten years, despite the glut of materials produced there . . .

'Even when rare convictions have been obtained, the penalties assessed have been pitiful. Producers of illegal materials may earn millions in profit each year, and yet serve no time in prison and pay fines of perhaps $100. One powerful entrepreneur in Miami was convicted on obscenity charges for the sixty-first time, yet received a fine of only $1,600. The judge in another case refused to even look at child pornography which the defendant had supposedly produced. He said it would prejudice him to examine the material. That judge had never sentenced a single convicted pornographer to a day in prison.' Highlights from the *Final Report of the Attorney General's Commission on Pornography* (Nashville, Tenn: Rutledge Hill Press, 1986). From 1987 there were an increasing number of obscenity prosecutions in some of the 44 states with obscenity laws. See Alan Sears, *Pornography: An Outline of Legal Approaches to Solving Community Problems in the United States*, Briefing at New Scotland Yard, 1991

29. The Vagrancy Act 1824 covered both indecent displays and indecent exposure: not only 'exposing to view obscene or indecent prints, pictures, or other exhibitions in public places, but also the lewd and obscene' indecent exposure of the male person in public with 'intent to insult females'.

30. Indecent Displays Act 1981, c. 42.

31. Williams Committee, op. cit., p. 124.

32. Ibid., p. 125.

33. Indecent Displays Act, op. cit.

34. Ibid.

35. Statistics provided by the Home Office, 2 March 1990.

36. Robertson, op. cit., p. 15 and C. Itzin, 'Sex and Censorship: The Political Implications', *Red Letters*, 1982, pp. 5–12.

37. Richard Findlater, *Banned : A Review of Theatrical Censorship in Britain* (London: MacGibbon and Kee, 1967).

38. Robertson, op. cit., p. 91. The editors of *International Times* were convicted of a conspiracy to corrupt public morals. The *Oz* editors were convicted, but the Court of Appeal quashed the obscenity conviction. (R. V. Anderson 1972 1 QP. 304.)

39. Ibid., p. 3. The Court of Appeal quashed the *Last Exit to Brooklyn* conviction because the jury might have mistaken revulsion for corruption.

40. Customs and Excise officers have powers under the Customs Consolidation Act 1876 and the Customs and Excise Management Act 1979 to seize and destroy material which is defined as obscene in the Obscene Publications Act 1959. The Post Office Act 1953 also makes it unlawful to 'send indecent or obscene publications'. However a different test – of 'indecent and obscene' – is applied in this legislation. Indecent is taken to be a weaker term than 'obscene' which has its

dictionary meaning, and not the 'deprave and corrupt' definition of the OPA (Williams Committee, op cit., p. 12). See note 4.

41. Corinne Sweet, 'Censorship, Pornography and Women's Rights', unpublished speech to a Women in Publishing Conference, 1986. The case was committed for trial, but Customs and Excise dropped the case following a European Court ruling on the importation by Conegate of German 'dolls', lifesize female mannequins for simulated sexual intercourse.

42. Personal interview, 1990. Orders from Giovanni's Room, gay literature suppliers in the USA, were regularly opened.

43. R. v. Hicklin (1868) L. R. 3. Q. B. 360.

44. Robertson, op. cit., p. 30.

45. Ibid., pp. 31, 44.

46. Susan G. Cole, *Pornography and the Sex Crisis* (Toronto: Amanita Publications, 1989), p. 70.

47. Robertson, op. cit., p. 30.

48. Cole, op. cit.

49. Censorship of Publications Act, 1929, No. 21, Dublin, p. 9.

50. Kate Ellis *et al.* (eds) *Caught Looking: Feminism, Pornography and Censorship* (Seattle, Real Comet Press, 1988), p. 58.

51. Cole, op. cit.

52. Catharine A. MacKinnon, 'Not a Moral Issue', *Yale Law and Policy Review*, Vol. II No. 2, Spring 1984, p. 333. The following discussion draws extensively on MacKinnon's essay, with permission.

53. Materials shown to the author by Obscene Publications Branch of the Metropolitan Police, April 1990.

54. MacKinnon, op. cit., pp. 323, 325, 329.

55. Ibid., p. 331.

56. Ibid., p. 333.

57. Ibid., p. 337.

58. Declaration of Defendant Intervenor Linda Marciano, in the United States District Court for the Western District of Washington, No. C88-1470, 12 January 1989, p. 2.

59. 'Studies of sex-shop patrons in America and Copenhagen coincide in describing the average customer as white, middle-aged, middle-class, married, male, wearing a business suit and shopping alone. A survey of 4,000 readers of *Forum* . . . revealed a predominantly sober, middle class and highly educated readership' (Robertson, op. cit., pp. 9–10). The Williams Committee found that 'readership spans all social classes but is . . . weakest among the highest and lowest socio-economic groups' (p. 45). Newsagents surveyed by Catherine Itzin and Corinne Sweet (*Independent*, April 1989) said their pornography customers were predominantly white middle-class males in spite of the fact that the shops were located in a mixed race, mixed class neighbourhood. However the 'National Readership Survey' (JICNARS) 1981 showed the largest percentage of readers for *Mayfair, Men Only, Penthouse, Fiesta* and *Knave* in social class grades 2 C and D.

60. C. Itzin and C. Sweet, 'What You Feel About Pornography', *Cosmopolitan*, March 1990, pp. 8–12.

61. In the UK it is estimated that at least 2.25 million men buy pornography every month. These figures are based on the published circulation rates of six major men's magazines. Most of the magazines – seventy-three different titles were purchased in four high street newsagents in April 1989 – do not publish circulation figures. This will therefore be a conservative estimate. In the USA 'six of the ten most profitable newsstand monthlies are male entertainment magazines. The combined circulation of *Playboy* and *Penthouse* is greater than that of *Time* and *Newsweek*' (*Pornography: A Practice of Inequality*, Organizing Against Pornography, Minneapolis, Minnesota, 1986).
62. See Diana Russell's survey of the evidence, Chapter 17. A tendency 'to minimize the seriousness of rape was found among female as well as male subjects', see D. Zillmann and J. Bryant, 'Effects of Massive Exposure to Pornography' in N. M. Malamuth and E. Donnerstein (eds), *Pornography and Sexual Aggression* (New York: Academic Press, 1984), p. 133. The effects of exposure to pornography on women are not well-known, but they may include seeing less harm over time.
63. Robertson, op. cit., p. 12.
64. Ibid., pp. 12–13.
65. Ibid., pp. 13.
66. Ibid., pp. 13, 7.
67. Williams Committee, op. cit., pp. 7, 13.
68. Ibid., pp. 4, 57.
69. A. Hyatt, Assistant City Attorney for Minneapolis, in *Pornography and Sexual Violence: Evidence of the Links* (London: Everywoman, 1988), p. 8.
70. Ibid. Catharine A. MacKinnon, giving evidence to the Public Hearings on Ordinances to Add Pornography as Discrimination Against Women, (Minneapolis City Council, Government Operations Committee, 12 and 13 December 1983.
71. A. Dworkin and C. A. MacKinnon, *Pornography and Civil Rights: A New Day for Women's Equality* (Minneapolis, Minnesota: Organizing Against Pornography, 1988), p. 33.
72. Ibid., p. 31.
73. Ibid.
74. See Catharine A. MacKinnon in Chapter 22 for details of the evidence presented to the Minneapolis Hearings.
75. Dworkin and MacKinnon, op. cit., p. 35.
76. Hudnut v. American Booksellers Association in the US Court of Appeals for the Seventh Circuit, August 1985, No. 84–3147, p. 12.
77. A. Nostadt, 'Porn measure had widespread support', *Bellingham Herald*, 17 November 1988.
78. ACLU News, 23 November 1988.
79. US Senate Congressional Record, 22 June 1989.
80. Ibid.

'(3) The Attorney General's Commission on Pornography in 1986 found clinical and experimental evidence of a relationship between exposure to sexually explicit materials and sexual aggression, including the commission of unlawful sexual acts.

'(4) The Attorney General's Commission on Pornography also found evidence that sexually explicit material need not be legally obscene to stimulate anti-social and potentially unlawful sexual aggression, if the material presents violent acts in a clear sexual context, or the sexual abuse of children.

'(5) Behavioral studies of serial murderers conducted by the Federal Bureau of Investigation have revealed a strong correlation between heavy exposure to violent sexual material and violent serial criminality.

'(6) Investigations conducted by the Child Pornography and Protection Unit of the United States Customs Service have revealed a nearly absolute correlation between heavy consumption of child pornography and child sexual abuse, including the use of child pornography to entrap children into the performance of sexual acts.

'(7) Recent psychological studies indicate a correlation between the growing number of children and youths who commit rape and other violent sexual offences, and the declining age of first exposure to sexually explicit materials.

'(8) Sexual crimes such as rape and child abuse usually leave life-long psychological scars that may prevent the victim and his or her family from leading normal, fulfilled lives . . .

81. Indecent Displays (Newspapers and Workplaces) 1989, Bill 30, 50/2. The letters were published in *Dear Clare*, ed. Kiri Tunks and Diana Hutchinson (London: Hutchinson Radius, 1991).

82. Location of Pornographic Material 1989, Bill, 50/2. There is existing licensing legislation in the Local Government (Miscellaneous Provisions) Act 1982 which requires that certain categories of sexual material can be sold only in shops licensed by a local authority. The Act defines a sex shop as any premises used for a business which consists to a significant degree of selling: '(a) sex articles; (b) other things intended for use in connection with or for purpose of stimulating or encouraging (i) sexual activity, (ii) acts of force or restraint that are associated with sexual activity.'

83. CPBF Press Release, 19 July 1989.

84. Speech by Dawn Primarolo MP at a conference on Women and Pornography organized by Bristol City Council Women's Committee, February 1990.

85. Location of Pornography Material Bill Briefing, 1989.

86. Itzin and Sweet, op. cit.

87. Public Order Act 1986. Part III. Racial Hatred, Section 18 C.64 17–18.

88. Cole, op. cit., p. 202.

89. Proposals developed by the Campaign Against Pornography and Censorship Legislation Working Group 1988–90.

90. Dworkin and MacKinnon, op. cit., p. 30.

91. The Civil Rights Ordinance conceived the idea of a group-based **433**

injury such that relief to the individual would provide relief to the group, enabling one woman 'to enjoin a whole pornography traffic' because it subordinates women as a group. This is a different approach to 'class action' which is not possible in the UK and is used in the USA primarily in consumer cases to get a little bit of money for a lot of people. Class action is a collective remedy. It 'enables individuals, each of whom has suffered a common wrong at the hand of the defendant but none of whom has suffered damage large enough to make separate litigation desirable or practical, to join together to enforce the goals of the law' and 'it helps to eradicate inequality of bargaining power in litigation'. David Pannick, *Sex Discrimination Law* (Oxford: Clarendon Press, 1985), pp. 285–6.

92. Dworkin and MacKinnon, op. cit., pp. 85–6.
93. Carol Smart, 'Theory into Practice: The Problem of Pornography', *Feminism and the Power of Law* (London: Routledge, 1989), p. 133.

22 A Legal Definition of Pornography

CATHERINE ITZIN

Pornography is an industry which manufactures and markets a very profitable product. The people who make it, sell it, buy it and use it know exactly what pornography is, but the belief has been fostered that it is somehow indefinable and that defining it for purposes of legislation would be difficult or impossible. 'I can't define pornography, but I know it when I see it,' said a US Supreme Court judge. The challenge certainly has been how to formulate a legal definition which includes only pornography. But once removed from the moral realm and placed in the context of structures of power, pornography is not inherently indefinable. The task – of looking and describing what exists – had just not, until recently, been undertaken, arguably because no one wanted it done.

The USA
The civil rights ordinance (see Chapter 21) provided a major breakthrough in defining pornography by conceptualizing it as *a practice of sex discrimination which sexualizes the subordination of women and which eroticizes violence against women*: as 'a political practice of power and powerlessness' which 'eroticizes dominance and submission'.[1] It then defined pornography specifically, descriptively and objectively for what it depicted and communicated about the sexualized subordination of women:

> Pornography means the graphic sexually explicit subordination of women through pictures and/or words that also includes one or more of the following: (i) women are presented dehumanized as sexual objects, things, or commodities; or (ii) women are presented as sexual objects who enjoy humiliation or pain; or (iii) women are presented as sexual objects experiencing sexual pleasure in rape, incest or other sexual assault; or (iv) women are presented as sexual objects tied up, cut up or mutilated or bruised or physically hurt; or (v) women are presented in postures or positions of sexual submission, servility, or display; or (vi) women's body parts –

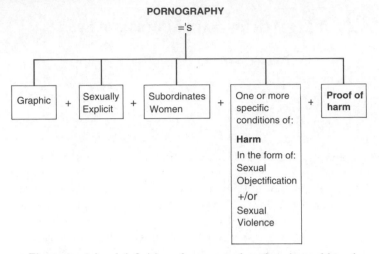

Figure 1   A legal definition of pornography – how it would work

including but not limited to vaginas, breasts, or buttocks – are
exhibited such that women are reduced to those parts; or (vii)
women are presented being penetrated by objects or animals; or
(viii) women are presented in scenarios of degradation, humiliation, injury, torture, shown as filthy or inferior, bleeding, bruised,
or hurt in a context that makes these conditions sexual.[2]

Action could only be taken against material that could be
shown to fall within this very narrow and limited definition of
pornography. Anything falling within this definition of pornography would have to be *simultaneously* graphic *and* sexually explicit
and to subordinate women; *and also* include one or more of the
specific itemized characteristics which describe the content of
pornography. It would *also* have to be proved to have harmed
someone. This definition makes a distinction between sex and
pornography. Material could not be targeted simply because it
was sexually explicit, as sexual explicitness is only one of four or
more characteristics of pornography.

Many of the items in the specified characteristics of pornography refer to violence, but some refer 'merely' to 'acts of
submission, degradation, humiliation and objectification'. The
harm, the violation, indeed the violence inherent in these acts –
and in dehumanization and exploitation – have simply not been
recognized as harm because these acts have traditionally been
regarded as 'just sex'. Also, because the consumers of pornography
436   enjoy the material sexually, and see the submission and objectifi-

cation of women as both natural and 'sexy', its harm has been obscured to them 'even though the non-violent materials are also known to be harmful . . . for instance in their use by rapists and child molesters, in increasing the acceptability of forced sex, and in diminishing men's vision of the desirability and possibility of sex equality'.[3]

Furthermore, turning women into objects and dehumanizing women is a precondition for overt violence. It is easier to hurt someone who is 'less human': the function of anti-Semitic and racist representation is to dehumanize in order to enable overt acts of violence to be done. Thus the definition would include pornography in which women are 'bound, battered, tortured, harassed, raped and sometimes killed'. But it would also include women in 'glossy men's magazines' who are '"merely" humiliated, molested, objectified and used for the entertainment and sexual pleasure of men'.[4]

In practice this definition has been drafted sometimes to include only violent pornography, sometimes both sexually violent and other violating and sexually objectifying materials. The Minneapolis Ordinance included all pornography, 'objectifying' as well as violent, for example 'women presented dehumanized as sex objects, things or commodities'. The Indianapolis Ordinance excluded that clause and restricted itself to covering violent and degrading pornography.[5] The Pornography Victims Compensation Act 1989 borrowed from this definition.[6]

Dworkin and MacKinnon based the definition on a content analysis of the materials published by the pornography industry.

> The Ordinance adopts a simple if novel strategy for definition. It looks at the existing universe of the pornography industry and simply describes what is there, including what must be there for it to work in the way that it, and only it works . . . Everything in pornography is sex to someone, or it would not be there.[7]

The lowest common denominator of pornography is that it is sexually arousing to someone. However, attempts to define pornography simply in terms of sexual arousal have been inadequate because there are so many other things that produce 'that definite stirring between the legs, including the violence against women and violation of women in R-rated movies or *Vogue* magazine or Calvin Klein commercials or Yeats' *Leda and the Swan*'.

It is true that pornography exists on a larger social continuum with other materials that objectify and demean women and set the stage for and reflect women's social devaluation. It is true that many materials (such as some religious works and sociobiology texts) express the same message as pornography and are vehicles for the same values. This does not mean either that pornography cannot be defined or that it does not operate in a distinctive way.[8]

It is also true that many things which are not pornography within this definition have become 'pornographic' because of the existence of pornography.

The same message of sexualized misogyny pervades the culture – indeed, it does so more and more because pornography exists. But that does not make 'Dallas' and 'Dynasty' into pornography, however close they come . . . in the world, a lot of people know the difference between pornography on the one hand and art, literature, mainstream media, advertisements, and sex education on the other. Such materials are not pornography – and, frankly, everyone knows they are not.[9]

Pornography is not therefore simply synonymous with sexual arousal, though 'for pornography to work sexually with its major market, which is heterosexual men, it must excite the penis'. Nor is pornography simply its misogynist message, though its message, what it communicates about women, is part of what makes pornography what it is. What distinguishes pornography from anything else is its combination of subordination and sexual explicitness.

Sexually Explicit Subordination
According to Dworkin and MacKinnon: 'To accomplish its end, it must show sex and subordinate a woman at the same time.'[10]

From the evidence of the material itself, its common denominator is the use or abuse of a woman in an expressly sexual way. Under the Ordinance, pornography *is* what pornography *does*. What it does is subordinate women through sexually explicit pictures and words.

Just as there is sexual explicitness which is not pornography, there are also materials which show women being subordinated, but which are not sexually explicit and not pornography. 'For this reason the Ordinance restricts its definition only to those sexually explicit pictures and words that actually can be proven to subordinate women in their making or use.'[11] Sexually explicit subordination is the key to the definition: 'Subordination is an active practice of placing someone in an unequal position or in a position of loss of power.'[12]

A subordinate is not an equal: 'Subordination is at the core of every systematic social inequality. It includes the practices that enforce second-class status. Subordination includes objectification, hierarchy, forced submission, and violence.'[13] Pornography is 'sexual subordination for sexual pleasure'.[14] According to Carol Smart, 'the pornographic genre succeeds by transforming the meaning of domination into (natural) sex and thereby making it invisible'. She defines pornography as 'the dominant, persuasive, and routine regime of representation which sexualizes and limits women'.[15] According to Susan Cole, 'pornography cannot exist without the subordination of women' and 'pornography is active in the subordination of women' – in the material itself and in the social sphere.

Subordination is an active practice because it is something that is done, not just thought or spoken. A person would be free to think or believe or even say (i.e. speak) that women are inferior, or subordinate and should be raped or discriminated against, but within this definition and this legislation they would not be free to do it: they would not be free to subordinate or sexually violate or discriminate in the form of pornography. Therefore, as Dworkin and MacKinnon point out, 'Anyone who brought a case under the Ordinance would have to *prove* that the challenged materials actually subordinated women in their making or use in order to show that the materials were pornography.[16] The civil rights ordinance therefore defines pornography as *a practice of sex discrimination* in two ways: in itself it is a form of subordination, hence sex discrimination, and it is also a cause of subordination, hence of sex discrimination.

A Practice of Sex Discrimination
Pornography is itself a form of sex discrimination in a number of ways. In pornography women are treated as sexual objects/sexually objectified/subordinate/sexualized/reduced to sexual parts/ as objects of sexual use and abuse/pieces of meat/objectified for male desire. This sexual objectification is an act which dehumanizes, degrades and denies women their humanity. Pornography is often described as communicating messages of misogyny, and it does. But its messages are not what make pornography discriminatory. It is what is done to women in the words and pictures and **439**

what the words and pictures do to women in society which make pornography itself a practice of sex discrimination. Pornography 'instils the values of male dominance and female subordination',[17] and sexualizes male power. Sexual subordination is what is done to women in and through pornography, and in and through pornography men learn how to do it.

Pornography is also a practice of sex discrimination in that it is a product manufactured and distributed by an industry. The product is made from real women, many of whom have been coerced or injured in its manufacture.[18] What happens in the making is real. The pictures are real, and the women in the pictures are real. The act of buying and looking is real, and whatever happens as a result is real and has real discriminatory consequences on the lives of women: whether it is a feeling or a 'fantasy', the formulation of an attitude or belief, or whether it is a behaviour or action, or some combination of all of these. As a 'real' product in which women are sexually subordinated, pornography is a practice of sex discrimination.

Pornography is also a cause of sex discrimination and subordination. The trafficking provision of the civil rights ordinance would enable women to take action against pornographers for subordinating women, to attempt to prove 'a direct connection between the pornography and harm to women as a group . . . Such harm could include being targeted for rape, sexual harassment, battery, sexual abuse as children, and forced prostitution', and 'the harm of being seen and treated as a sexual thing rather than as a human being'. But it could also include 'the harm of second-class citizenship on the basis of gender'.[19]

> By making a public spectacle and a public celebration of the worthlessness of women, by valuing women as sluts, by defining women according to our availability for sexual use, pornography makes all women's social worthlessness into a public standard. Do you think such a being is likely to become Chairman of the Board? Vice President of the United States. Would you hire a 'cunt' to represent you? Perform surgery on you? Run your university? Edit your broadcast? Would you promote one above a man? . . . In creating pervasive and invisible bigotry, in addition to constituting sex discrimination in itself, pornography is utterly inconsistent with any real progress toward sex equality for women.[20]

The new definition of pornography in terms of 'sexually explicit subordination' and harm marks a radical departure from the old moral view of obscenity:

Whatever one's moral judgements, the presentations in the definition are there because there is material evidence that they do harm, and the decision has been made that the harm they do to some people is not worth the sexual pleasure they give to other people – not because the people making the laws do not like these acts sexually or disapprove of them morally.[21]

The definition is 'closed, concrete and descriptive, not open-ended, conceptual, moral' or vague. It targets only pornography, but it also defines pornography narrowly rather than broadly and 'takes the risk that all damaging materials might not be covered in order to try to avoid misuse of the law'.[22]

The UK

In the UK there have been a number of attempts to define pornography in terms of sexually explicit subordination and sexual objectification. The National Council for Civil Liberties (Liberty) for example, in establishing its anti-pornography policy in 1989 (reversed in 1990) required that any definition of pornography should include 'three main ingredients':

1. It must be sexually explicit.
2. It must depict women as enjoying or deserving some form of physical abuse.
3. It must objectify women, that is define women in relation to men's lust and desire.

The Campaign for Press and Broadcasting Freedom (CPBF)-sponsored Location of Pornographic Material Bill (1989) defined pornographic material as 'films and videos and any printed matter which, for the purpose of sexual arousal or titillation, depicts women or parts of women's bodies as objects, things or commodities, or in sexually humiliating or degrading poses, or being subjected to violence'.[23]

The Campaign Against Pornography and Censorship (CPC) lawyers were developing a definition of pornography that could be used in both sex discrimination and incitement to sexual hatred legislation modelled on the Race Relations Act. They were considering a definition of pornography as:

the graphic sexually explicit subordination of women through pictures and/or words in any form which also includes one or more of the following: women (or parts of women's bodies) presented as sexual objects, or in positions of sexual submission, servility or

441

display; or presented as sexual objects who enjoy humiliation, pain, rape, incest or other sexual assault, or penetrated by objects or animals, or hurt and/or dehumanized or subjected to violence or degradation in a context that is sexual.

The CPC was also considering definitions of 'graphic' as 'sharply outlined or delineated with nothing vague or left for inference';[24] of 'sexual object' as the 'presentation of women as sexualized and dehumanized, turned into a thing or commodity in relation to male sexual desire and lust' (a woman can be defined in relation to male lust or desire whether or not a male is actually in the picture); and of subordination as the 'act of subordinating or subjection' or the 'state of being subordinate' or 'inferior', or of 'sexually servicing someone' (to include the apparently 'female dominant' pornography). CPC also proposed to define sexually explicit to include the conventions of sado-masochistic sex as well as the 'exploitative exhibition of genitals', and 'subordinating sexual acts'. The CPC definition did not include sexually explicit materials which were non-subordinating and premised on equality (referred to as erotica) and it did not include bona fide sex education materials or medical or forensic literature.[25]

Sometimes the *intention* of material to cause sexual arousal is included within definitions of pornography. Thus the Location of Pornographic Material Bill referred to material which has 'the purpose of sexual arousal or titillation'. While it is true that pornography is manufactured and sold specifically to engineer sexual arousal, it is difficult legally to *prove* intent in a court of law and attempts to do so have often proved unsuccessful. Pornography magazines in the UK carry disclaimers. Magazines devoted solely to sexual violence state that 'it is not the publisher's intention to encourage any of the acts portrayed', when the text and the pictures clearly associate sexual arousal with sexual violence. Pornographers have also successfully claimed artistic or educational intentions to avoid prosecution. 'Intent' has, in practice, proved to be an ineffective way of defining pornography for legal purposes.[26] In addition, from the point of view of women hurt through pornography, its consequences for them are far more relevant than the motivations of the pornographers who may not have considered their welfare at all.

Child Pornography

The civil rights ordinance included child pornography within its definition by stating that 'the use of . . . children . . . in the place of women is also pornography'. Legislation in the USA and in the UK has taken a stronger position on child pornography than on pornography involving adult women, putting the rights and freedom of children before pornographers' freedom of speech.[27] If every piece of child pornography represents an incident of child sexual abuse (see Chapters 6 and 11) then child pornography is by definition child sexual abuse.[28] Under existing federal law in the USA, any use of a child to make sex pictures is by its nature exploitative and harmful and hence unprotected by the First Amendment. To define child pornography as child sexual abuse is to define it, appropriately, in terms of the harm that it is and does. A legal definition of child pornography could be based on this.

Child pornography legislation is *criminal* legislation as befits a dependent group (i.e. children) as distinct from civil legislation for an independent group (women) which can fight for itself. 'Possession' of child pornography is a ground for criminal legal action in the UK. This was resisted by civil libertarians in the UK as an invasion of privacy (people can do what they like in their own home) and because of the precedents of police abuse with regard to the possession of drugs. But as Liz Kelly and Tim Tate explain (Chapters 6 and 11), the manufacture and distribution of child pornography is different from pornography involving adult women and criminalizing possession is one of the few ways of dealing with it effectively.[29]

Gay and Lesbian Pornography

The civil rights ordinance includes within its definition gay pornography that can be proven to subordinate by stating that the 'use of men . . . or transsexuals in the place of women is also pornography' because:

> Other people are sometimes used in similar ways, sometimes in exactly the ways women are, but always exploiting their gender. This is the reason that the definition covers everyone regardless of sex, yet covers each person as a member of their sex: that is the way the pornographers use them.[30]

The problem with trying to include gay or lesbian pornography within legislation against pornography is twofold. Traditionally, obscenity legislation has been used repressively against 'same-sex materials' and there is thus a fear that *any* legislation could **443** be used in the same way. Also, because gay men and lesbians have often defined their liberation in terms of their sexual practice as well as their sexual orientation or preference, it can easily appear that *any* sexual practice must therefore equate with liberation and that *any* restriction on *any* sexual practice must necessarily equate with oppression. Concern is therefore expressed by some gays and lesbians that pornography as defined in the civil rights ordinance would restrict their legitimate sexual practice and limit their freedom in a way that it would not restrict the freedom of heterosexuals.

Although lesbian feminists have been at the forefront of campaigns for civil rights legislation against pornography in the USA, the legislation has also come up against hostility from some lesbians and gays who are committed to defending their right to use sadistic pornography, and calling it freedom to do so. These gays and lesbians apparently believe their right to use sadistic pornography takes precedence over considerations of sexual violence to women and sex discrimination. But the same question needs to be asked of them as is asked of heterosexual men: whose freedom?

> Does *anyone* have a right to materials that are produced through coercion, that will be forced on others, that are the cause of assaults, that defame individuals, and that are integral to the second-class status of half the population? Is *anyone's* sexuality – however conventional or unconventional, however sincere – more important than the lives that must be, will be, ground up and spit out in little pieces in the making and use of the pornography so that the consumer's sexuality can be provided with what it needs, wants, or enjoys? ... Is some gay men's access to pictures of subordinating gay sex more important than the right of men or boys not to be raped or violated so that pictures can be made of them, or the desire of other gay men to shape a community free of eroticized self-hatred?[31]

That women – and particularly lesbians, and even more particularly feminists – defend sadistic pornography is used as an excuse for its continued existence: because if women want it, it must be all right, and it would be oppressive to say to women, 'No, you can't have this', even more oppressive to say 'No' to lesbians. But as Baker, Sweet and Wyre have shown in Chapters 7, 10 and 14, the desire for sadistic and masochistic sex will be conditioned through childhood socialization and abuse for

women as well as for men, for lesbians and gay men as well as for heterosexuals. Are we to accept harmful materials just because some women want them when we would not accept men's addiction to sexual violence as an argument in its favour? 'Harm is still harm when done by women to women and by men to men.'[32] If it is acceptable to equate violence with liberation for gays and lesbians, then the same 'logic' would have to equate rape and sexual violence with men's freedom to define their sexuality and masculinity as they liked. This doesn't make sense.

What does it mean for lesbian libertarians to 'identify with and defend pornographers' women-hating so-called lesbian sexuality'?

> All lesbians have necessarily suffered from the pornographers' definition of lesbian that is so central to the violence, hatred, contempt, and discrimination directed against lesbians in society. All lesbians in societies saturated with pornography must live with the fact that the pornographers have made lesbianism into a pornographic spectacle in the eyes of men.[33]

What does it mean in any case to define one's freedom and liberation in terms of violence? Is this a model of women's liberation? Or human rights?

The lesbian libertarian and lesbian pornographers' defence of sadistic pornography represents another form of internalized oppression which rationalizes oppression through denial ('I'm not oppressed') or justification ('I like it' or 'I don't mind it' or 'I need it'). The women's liberation movement has gone far beyond believing that agreeing to or liking one's own oppression is a reason for defending or maintaining it. Women have taken great risks in giving up the parts of the oppression to which they are most attached or conditioned: 'letting go' has been painful, but it has also been liberating. Lesbian and gay liberation must likewise lie *beyond* sado-masochism; letting go of it will almost certainly be part of the process of achieving freedom. Many lesbians and gays have in fact welcomed – and indeed led the campaigns for – the civil rights ordinance because they see how gay and lesbian pornography actually contributes to the continuing oppression of gays and lesbians.

The proposed civil rights definition of pornography could *only* refer to sexually explicit subordination. While this *would* include sexually explicit homosexual subordination (and John Stoltenberg and Janice Raymond argue elsewhere in this book why it should), it would not include any non-subordinating sexually **445** explicit homosexual representations. This form of legislation also 'requires proof of actual harm before any materials can be found illegal'.

> The harm cannot be a moral one – say, that someone is offended by the materials or believes they are not proper family entertainment or finds that they violate their religious beliefs. The harm proven must be a harm of coercion, assault, defamation, or trafficking in sex-based subordination. The fact that the participants in the sex acts shown are of the same sex is not itself a form of sex-based subordination.[34]

Given the history of gay and lesbian oppression, it has been suggested that legislation could be drafted 'with a special section stating explicitly that gay and lesbian materials are not pornography by definition',[35] making it clear that same-sex material was not inherently pornography just because it was same-sex material, that it would, like heterosexual pornography, have to meet all the criteria of the definition of pornography to qualify as pornography. On the other hand, civil rights legislation would acknowledge that men as well as women and children can be harmed by pornography and enable men to take action for the harm they had experienced through coercion or assault or physical attack or trafficking or having pornography forced upon them.

Erotica and Sexual Explicitness

The definition of pornography proposed by the UK Campaign Against Pornography and Censorship (CPC) makes a distinction between pornography and erotica: 'Pornography does not include erotica (defined as sexually explicit materials premised on equality) and it does not include bona fide sex education materials, or medical or forensic literature.'

In the absence of any concrete definition, the traditional interpretation of obscenity has been that sexual explicitness is synonymous with genitals and explicit sexual activity, and particularly with the erect penis, sexual intercourse and penetration of other orifices. In the obscenity formula, sexual explicitness is synonymous with pornography: sex and pornography are seen as the same thing and they are both seen as obscene. Under obscenity law, there is then a hierarchy of value which reflects the sexual hierarchy. The erect male penis is sacrosanct. Its display – through the custom and practice of obscenity law – has remained prohibited, while sex in pornography has virtually become equated with the 'lewd display' of women's genitals and anuses, inviting penetration. (That this 'double standard' should have come to operate quite 'naturally' under the aegis of obscenity law lends credence to the view that pornography and obscenity legislation operate together to maintain male power and male sexual access to women.)

Under current USA obscenity law, although sexually explicit has no single legal definition, it is used to refer to explicitly shown sex (including the 'lewd' exhibition of genitals, to distinguish pornography from erotica or sex education materials), and also sado-masochism (although not all violence). In an affidavit to the court in Bellingham, Washington in support of the civil rights ordinance, Andrea Dworkin explained the meaning of sexually explicit in commercial pornography. This included the 'conventional sex act fully realized: for instance, the penis being inserted in the vagina, or less conventionally, in the anus or in the mouth'. Sexually explicit commercial pornography also included sexual practices such as 'paedophilia, sado-masochism and fetishism'. Dworkin therefore proposed to define sexually explicit broadly enough to include the sexual practices of sado-masochism: 'A woman fully bound and wrapped in rubber with no exposed body parts at all, tied up and strung up, is sexually explicit in torture pornography, because for the sado-masochist this is a sexual presentation with the character and quality of a fully realized sex act.' She also proposed to define sexually explicit to include 'the exposure of a fetishized body part or ejaculate: for instance, the almost-to-term swollen bellies of pregnant women in *Knocked up Mamas*, the breast milk used as a sexual ejaculate in *Milky Tits*, the place of amputation (maiming) where a limb is missing in *Amputee Times*'. Sexual explicitness would also include 'the penetration and evisceration of a woman's body by a knife' in snuff films.[36]

In the sex discrimination formula, whether sexual explicitness is defined or interpreted broadly or narrowly, the definition of pornography includes not only sexual explicitness but also subordination and one or more elements of sexual objectification and/or sexual abuse. And the distinction between pornography and erotica is not whether the material is sexually explicit (which in both cases it is), but whether it subordinates women. Pornography, in this formula, ceases to be defined solely in terms of sexual explicitness, but always also by *subordination*. Neither **447** sexual explicitness nor subordination on their own is pornography.

Sexual explicitness – in this definition – thus ceases to be synonymous with pornography. Sexual explicitness, on its own, without the other constituents of pornography,[37] can be recognized as something else: as sex education or as erotica. In this definition, sex and sexual explicitness and women's bodies are freed from the taint of obscenity. Using a definition which identifies subordination as an essential constituent of pornography means that sexually explicit materials which are not based on subordination, which are premised on equality, could not be prosecuted: 'Sexual explicitness per se is not actionable under this law. This means that sex education materials are not vulnerable and neither are explorations of eroticism.'[38] The tests of pornography become: is it sexually explicit? Does it in practice subordinate women? And does it also sexually objectify women and/or subject women to violence in one or more specific ways? This is a stringent test and will certainly exclude erotica and any form of non-subordinating sex.

Over a decade ago Gloria Steinem drew what she described as the 'clear and present difference' between erotica and pornography. 'Pornography', she wrote, 'is about dominance, an imbalance of male–female power' while 'erotica is about mutuality'. She gave examples:

> Look at any photo or film of people making love; really making love. The images may be diverse, but there is usually a sensuality and touch and warmth, an acceptance of bodies and nerve endings. There is always a spontaneous sense of people who are there because they *want* to be, out of shared pleasure. Now look at any depiction of sex in which there is clear force, or an unequal power that spells coercion. It may be very blatant, with weapons of torture or bondage, wounds and bruises, some clear humiliation, or an adult's sexual power being used over a child. It may be much more subtle: a physical attitude of conqueror and victim, the use of race or class difference to imply the same thing, perhaps a very unequal nudity, with one person exposed and vulnerable while the other is clothed. In either case, there is no sense of equal choice or equal power.
>
> The first is erotic: a mutually pleasurable, sexual expression between people who have enough power to be there by positive choice. It doesn't require us to identify with a conqueror or a victim. It is truly sensuous, and may give us a contagion of pleasure.
>
> The second is pornographic: its message is violence, dominance,

and conquest. It is sex being used to reinforce some inequality, or to create one, or to tell us the lie that pain and humiliation (ours or someone else's) are really the same as pleasure. If we are to feel anything, we must identify with conqueror or victim. That means we can only experience pleasure through the adoption of some degree of sadism or masochism.[39]

John Stoltenberg (see Chapter 8) defines erotica as 'sexually explicit materials premised on equality, mutuality, reciprocity and so forth'.[40] Diana Russell defines erotica as 'sexual representations that are non-abusive and non-sexist' (Chapter 17). Janice Raymond refers to a vision of sexuality that includes the 'ability to touch and be touched', a touch that makes contact; and sex as 'a whole human life rooted in passion, in flesh' (Chapter 9).

According to Gloria Steinem, there is 'too little erotica' and 'so much pornography'. The dominance of pornography in our culture operates to suppress sexually explicit expressions which are premised on equality and to 'pornographize' (by association) presentations which are not pornography. The definition of pornography in the civil rights ordinance is based on the assumption that there could and should be sex which is premised on equality and not subordination 'even though many people apparently cannot imagine sex any other way'. Although there may be many more examples of pornography than erotica, and because people may be confused at times about what erotica is because of the association of sex with obscenity, the difference between pornography and non-pornography is not a mystery: does it create sexual inequality or doesn't it? Does it sexualize violence? Does it subordinate women? Does it sexualize women's subordination?

Sexualized Violence
There has been concern and debate about the genre of 'slasher films', largely aimed at young males in the USA and presenting extreme forms of sexualized violence (see Russell, Chapter 17). In *Toolbox Murders*, for example, a nude woman is attacked, chased, and murdered, shot in the belly and the brain by a man with a nail-gun. Because there is no sexual explicitness in these films, no portrayal of genitals or penile penetration, slasher films do not fall within obscenity legislation and are marketed legally. They would not fall, either, within the sex discrimination definition of pornography. Although they subordinate women and include sexual objectification and injury in a context that is **449**

sexual, they are not sexually explicit. To fall within either the existing obscenity legislation or the proposed sex discrimination legislation would require a broader definition of sexual explicitness.

The absence of sexual explicitness has led to the exclusion of slasher films from the category of pornography and led some researchers to argue that it is violence, not sex, which is harmful. But it is more likely that existing concepts of sexual explicitness and a certain degree of desensitization have obscured the sexual nature of the violence that takes place. These films demonstrate the extent to which subordination and violence have become sexualized in a way that is regarded as socially acceptable. The sexually explicit sexualizing of women's bodies, women's subordination, and violence to women in pornography will have contributed to legitimating the slasher films. If it were possible to act against the sado-masochistic pornography which makes violence into sex, then the sexualized subordination and violence of slasher films might cease to be regarded as acceptable forms of entertainment.

Art

A major concern about legislation against pornography will always be its potential for censoring art and literature. This is an important and legitimate concern, but there is some irony in raising censorship as an objection to civil rights or to sex discrimination legislation. As an alternative to obscenity definitions, a sex discrimination definition would greatly reduce the potential for abuse and the scope of censorship. Those who oppose defining pornography in terms of the sexually explicit subordination of women put themselves in the position of defending the demonstrably repressive obscenity legislation, or of defending pornography.

Two questions arise in relation to the issue of pornography and art. Recognizing the very limited censorship potential of defining pornography in terms of the sexually explicit subordination of women, what would it mean if some work of art or literature fell within the terms of the definition? What is the relative value of art in relation to the value of women?

In 1989 the Victoria and Albert Museum presented an exhibition entitled 'The Nude: A New Perspective'. The purpose of the exhibition was to show that some art communicated some of **450** the same messages as pornography – including some art by some of those categorized as 'the world's greatest artists' (Picasso, Matisse, Munch, Manet, Renoir, Rubens, Poussin, Tintoretto, Blake). The exhibition drew attention to 'the combination of passive display and invitation', the 'open mouth as signifier of desire in the passive female'.[41] It was instructive to be shown the similarity between some images in fine art and some of the images in pornography: the drawing by Gustav Kleist (1862–1918), for example, in which 'the woman becomes a submissive victim of male power and sexual domination', in which 'the image becomes a justification, a celebration of rape'. But in spite of the similarities and its obvious place in the spectrum of sexual objectification and sexist representation, this material would not fall within the proposed definition of pornography because it is not sexually explicit.

Susanne Kappeler has analysed art and literature in relation to pornography. She takes, for example, an academic discussion of Titian's 'Tarquin and Lucretia' (Fitzwilliam Museum, Cambridge), which 'interprets' the rape of Lucretia as a scenario of invitation and seduction, consensual sex and pleasure (hers as well as his, as she is supposedly smiling), which sees rape belonging 'to the sphere of discourses, not events' and juxtaposes it with her own description of the painting:

> Lucretia, half-sitting, half-lying on her bed, is naked bar a veil across her thigh and the jewellery around her neck and wrists. Tarquin, fully dressed, looms over her, his right knee thrust between her legs, his left arm holding off Lucretia's arm, while his right arm holds a dagger about a yard from her face and chest, extended to strike with full swing. Lucretia's face is focused with an expression of fear on her attacker. Threat and intimidation are compounded and visually supplied out of the image's internal resources, its means of visualizing the differential in power: the woman is faced by a man; she is naked while he is dressed, unarmed while he is armed; she is half-lying on her back, having lost her balance, while he is towering over her, knee firmly lodged on the edge of the bed; her one arm is made defenceless by his grip, her other cannot reach the arm that holds a knife over her, ready to strike. It is an unambiguous exhibition of force and defencelessness, of intimidation and fear, of violation of the woman's privacy, integrity, selfhood and will. We are told we are seeing her consent.[42]

Kappeler's description exposes the pornographic convention of 'the smile', how academic sophistry, just like the pornography industry, can explain rape in terms of pleasure and willing **451** participation. She also shows the extent to which the painting represents the 'subordination of women' presented as 'enjoying pain, humiliation and rape.'[43] Kappeler's point is that the same apparatus and structure of male power creates literary value and pornographic value (see Chapter 4). But although this material may be subordinating, sexually objectifying and sexually violent, it is not sexually explicit and would not fall within the proposed definition of pornography. Nor would most fine art.

If, however, a work of art did fall within the proposed definition of pornography as the 'graphic sexually explicit subordination of women' which also included one or more specific elements of sexual objectification or sexual violence, would this be inappropriate? Kappeler and others, like Cameron and Frazer (in Chapter 19), have suggested that the label or category of art might not be sacrosanct, that the 'graphic sexually explicit subordination of women which also includes women portrayed as sexual objects enjoying pain or humiliation or rape' in a novel or a painting should not be exempted as pornography because the white male literary establishment calls it art. Should the law place art above women's lives? Is the loss of a piece of pornographic 'art' a greater loss than the loss experienced by a woman who is subordinated or sexually assaulted as a result of pornography? The answer surely is 'no': 'When sexually explicit materials, even if expressed with the most impressive virtuosity, subordinate women, calling the producer an artist would not place him out of the reach of the law.'[44] The cultural debate should consider the value of women in relation to the value of art.

CONCLUSION

It is essential to protect art and literature from censorship: it is also essential to protect women from the harm of pornography. The reality is that repealing the obscenity legislation and replacing it with legislation against pornography defined in terms of sex discrimination would at least greatly reduce if not actually eliminate the censorship that has been possible with the obscenity legislation. The reality is that legislation against pornography, defined as the sexually explicit subordination of women, would effectively target the pornography industry – that's all.

Notes

1. Catharine A. MacKinnon, 'Pornography, Civil Rights and Speech', *Harvard Civil Rights – Civil Liberties Law Review* 1 (11), 1985.
2. Andrea Dworkin and Catherine A. MacKinnon, *Pornography and Civil Rights: A New Day for Women's Equality* (Minneapolis, MN: Organizing Against Pornography, 1988) op. cit., pp. 138–9.
3. Ibid., p. 40. The materials used in social science research and described as non-violent often do contain acts of force or violence which men just do not see.
4. Dworkin and MacKinnon, op. cit., p. 45.
5. The Indianapolis Ordinance defined pornography as follows:

   Pornography shall mean the graphic sexually explicit subordination of women, whether in pictures or in words, that also includes one or more of the following:

   (1) Women are presented as sexual objects who enjoy pain or humiliation; or

   (2) Women are presented as sexual objects who experience sexual pleasure in being raped; or

   (3) Women are presented as sexual objects tied up or cut up or mutilated or bruised or physically hurt, or as dismembered or truncated or fragmented or severed into body parts; or

   (4) Women are presented being penetrated by objects or animals; or

   (5) Women are presented in scenarios of degradation, injury, abasement, torture, shown as filthy or inferior, bleeding, bruised or hurt in a context that makes those conditions sexual; or

   (6) Women are presented as sexual objects for domination, conquest, violation, exploitation, possession, or use, or through postures or positions of servility or submission or display.

6. The definition in the Pornography Victims Compensation Act 1989 included some of the vocabulary of the civil rights definition, but excluded the practice of subordination as a characteristic of pornography and included sexually explicit material that was non-subordinating (i.e. masturbation and sexual intercourse).
7. Dworkin and MacKinnnon, op. cit., pp. 37 and 40.
8. Ibid., p. 37.
9. Ibid., pp. 37-8.
10. Ibid., p. 38.
11. Ibid., pp. 38–9.
12. Ibid., p. 39.
13. Ibid.
14. Susan Cole, *Pornography and the Sex Crisis* (Toronto: Amanita Publications, 1989), pp. 64, 66, 98.
15. Carol Smart, 'Theory into Practice: The Problem of Pornography', *Feminism and the Power of Law* (London: Routledge, 1989), p. 133.
16. Dworkin and MacKinnon, op. cit., p. 39.
17. Cole, op. cit., p. 102.
18. Written pornography – just words – has been shown in laboratory studies to have the same effect as pictures. Audio-taped studies **453**

have also had the same effect as pictures: see N. M. Malamuth and J. V. P. Check, 'Sexual Arousal to Rape Depictions: Individual Differences', *Journal of Abnormal Psychology*, 92(1), 1983, pp. 55–67.

19. Dworkin and MacKinnon, op. cit., p. 45.
20. Ibid., p. 48.
21. Ibid., p. 40.
22. Ibid., p. 39.
23. Dawn Primarolo MP was consulting with individuals and organizations and considering revisions to the definition at the time of publication.
24. Borrowed from Dworkin, Washington Declaration, op. cit., p. 7.
25. It would seem to be common sense to exclude medical and forensic literature from a legal definition of pornography because of their social and scientific value, and they are listed here as a category of sexually explicit exclusion. There are, however, potential problems with this. In the USA the deliberate use of pornographic pictures of women in medical textbooks occurs and it is increasingly common for pornography to be used in medical schools for sex education purposes to 'desensitize' doctors to women with 'sexual complaints'. Early pornography films managed to obtain protection in the USA under the guise of being for medical purposes (i.e. a discussion of sexual deviancy) and pornography books are specifically presented as 'medical texts' in order to get around the obscenity law in the USA.
26. Sexual arousal is a criterion under obscenity law in the USA. Child pornographers have been acquitted because the jury did not find the material sexually arousing.
27. Catharine A. MacKinnon, *Feminism Unmodified: Discourses on Life and Law* (Cambridge, Mass, and London: Harvard University Press, 1987), p. 130. In child pornography, 'the speech of pornographers was once someone else's life'.
28. Clodagh Corcoran, *Take Care: Preventing Child Sexual Abuse* (Dublin: Poolbeg Press, 1987), p. 10.
29. The Criminal Justice Act 1988 criminalized possession of child pornography.
30. Dworkin and MacKinnon, op. cit., p. 38.
31. Ibid., pp 86–7.
32. Ibid., p. 87.
33. Ibid.
34. Ibid., pp. 85–86
35. Cole, op. cit., p. 105
36. Dworkin, Washington Declaration, op. cit., pp. 7–8.
37. In order for any item to fall within the definition of pornography, it must be graphic, it must be sexually explicit, it must subordinate women and it must include at least one other specified characteristics of sexual objectification and/or sexual violence.
38. Cole, op. cit., p. 105
39. Gloria Steinem, 'Erotica and Pornography: A Clear and Present Difference', *MS* magazine, November 1978 in Laura Lederer, ed.

Take Back the Night: Women on Pornography (New York: William Morrow and Company, 1980).

40. John Stoltenberg, 'Gays and the Pornography Movement: Having the Hots for Sex Discrimination', in Michael S. Kimmel (ed.), *Men Confront Pornography* (New York: Crown Publishers, Inc., 1990) pp. 259–60.

41. Caption to painting in Victoria & Albert Exhibition, 'The Nude: A New Perspective', Summer 1989.

42. Susanne Kappeler, 'No Matter How Unreasonable', *Art History*, II, (1), March 1988, p. 121.

43. Susanne Kappeler, *The Pornography of Representation* (Cambridge: Polity Press, 1986), pp. 85, 87.

44. Cole, op. cit., p. 105.

23 Pornography, Civil Rights and Speech

CATHARINE A. MACKINNON

I.

Substantively considered, the situation of women is *not really like anything else*. Its specificity is due not only to our numbers – we are half the human race – and our diversity, which at times has obscured that we are a group with an interest at all. It is, in part, that our status as a group relative to men has almost never, if ever, been much changed from what it is. Women's roles do vary enough that gender, the social form sex takes, cannot be said to be biologically determined. Different things are valued in different cultures, but whatever is valued, women are not that. If bottom is bottom, look across time and space and women are who you will find there. Together with this, you will find in as varied forms as there are cultures, the belief that women's social inferiority to men is not that at all, but is merely the sex difference.

Doing something legal about something that is not really like anything else is hard enough in a legal system that prides itself methodologically on reasoning by analogy.[1] Add to this the specific exclusion or absence of women and women's concerns from the definition and design of this legal system since its founding, combined with its determined adherence to precedent, and you have a problem of systemic dimension. The best attempt at grasping women's situation in order to change it by law has centred on an analogy between sex and race in the discrimination context. This gets a lot, since inequalities are alike on some levels, but it also misses a lot. It gets the stigmatization and exploitation and denigration of a group of people on the basis of a condition of birth. It gets that difference, made an issue of, is an excuse for dominance, and that if forced separation is allowed to mean equality in a society where the line of separation also divides top from bottom in a hierarchy, the harm of that separation is thereby made invisible. It also gets that defining neutrality as principle, when reality is not neutral, prevents change in the guise of promoting it. But segregation is not the central practice of the inequality of the sexes. Women are as often forcibly integrated with men, if not on an equal basis. And it did help the struggle against white supremacy that blacks had not always been in bondage to white people.

Most importantly, I think it never was a central part of the ideology of racism that the system of chattel slavery of Africans really was designed for their enjoyment and benefit. The system *was* defended as an expression of their true nature and worth. They *were* told to be grateful for good treatment and kind masters. Their successful struggle to organize resistance and avoid complicity while still surviving is instructive to all of us. But although racism *has* been defended by institutionalizing it in law, and then calling that legal; although it *has* been cherished not just as a system of exploitation of labour but as a way of life; and although it *is* based on force, changes in its practices are opposed by implying that they are really only a matter of choice of personal values, for instance: 'You can't legislate morality.'[2] And slave owners *did* say they couldn't be racist – they loved their slaves. None the less, few people pretended that the entire system existed *because* of its basis in love and mutual respect and veneration, that white supremacy really treated blacks in many cases *better* than whites, and that the primary intent and effect of their special status was and is their protection, pleasure, fulfilment and liberation. Crucially, many have believed, and some actually still do, that black people were not the equals of whites. But, at least since Brown vs Board of Education,[3] few have pretended, much less authoritatively, that the social system, as it was, *was equality for them.*

There is a belief that this is a society in which women and men are basically equals. Room for marginal corrections is conceded, flaws are known to exist, attempts are made to correct what are conceived as occasional lapses from the basic condition of sex equality. Sex discrimination law has centred most of its focus on these occasional lapses.[4] It is difficult to overestimate the extent to which this belief in equality is an article of faith to most people, including most women, who wish to live in self-respect in an internal universe, even (perhaps especially) if not in the world. It is also partly an expression of natural law thinking: if we are inalienably equal, we can't 'really' be degraded.

This is a world in which it is worth trying. In this world of **457** presumptive equality, people make money based on their training or abilities or diligence or qualifications. They are employed and advanced on the basis of merit. In this world of just deserts, if someone is abused, it is thought to violate the basic rules of the community. If it doesn't, that person is seen to have done something she could have chosen to do differently, by exercise of will or better judgement. Maybe such people have placed themselves in a situation of vulnerability to physical abuse. Maybe they have done something provocative. Or maybe they were just unusually unlucky. In such a world, if such a person has an experience, there are words for it. When they speak and say it, they are listened to. If they write about it, they will be published. If there are certain experiences that are never spoken, or certain people or issues seldom heard from, it is supposed that silence has been chosen. The law, including much of the law of sex discrimination and the first amendment, operates largely within the realm of these beliefs.

Feminism is the discovery that women do not live in this world, that the person occupying this realm is a man, so much more a man if he is white and wealthy. This world of potential credibility, authority, security, and just rewards, recognition of one's identity and capacity, is a world that some people do inhabit as a condition of birth, with variations *among them*. It is not a basic condition accorded humanity in this society, but a prerogative of status, a privilege, among other things, of gender.

I call this a discovery because it has not been an assumption. Feminism is the first theory, the first practice, the first movement, to take seriously the situation of all women from the point of view of all women, both on our situation and on social life as a whole. The discovery has therefore been made that the implicit social content of humanism, as well as the standpoint from which legal method has been designed and injuries have been defined, has not been women's standpoint. Defining feminism in a way that connects epistemology with power as the politics of women's point of view, this discovery can be summed up by saying that women live in another world: specifically, a world of *not* equality, a world of inequality.

Looking at the world from this point of view, a whole shadow world of previously invisible silent abuse has been discerned. Rape, battery, sexual harassment, forced prostitution, and the sexual abuse of children emerge as common and systematic.[5] We find rape happens to women in all contexts, from the family,

458

including rape of girls and babies, to students and women in the workplace, on the streets, at home, in their own bedrooms by men that they do not know, and by men that they do know, by men they are married to, men they have had a social conversation with, or, least often, men they have never seen before.[6] Overwhelmingly, rape is something that men do or attempt to do to women (44 per cent according to a recent study)[7] at some point in our lives. Sexual harassment of women by men is common in workplaces and educational institutions.[8] Up to 85 per cent of women in one study report it, many in physical forms.[9] Between a quarter and a third of women are battered in their homes by men.[10] Thirty-eight per cent of little girls are sexually molested inside or outside the family.[11] Until women listened to women, this world of sexual abuse was *not spoken* of. It was the unspeakable. What I am saying is, if you *are* the tree falling in the epistemological forest, your demise doesn't make a sound if no one is listening. Women did not 'report' these events, and overwhelmingly do not today, because no one is listening, because no one believes us. This silence does not mean nothing happened, and it does not mean consent. It is the silence of women of which Adrienne Rich has written, 'Do not confuse it with any kind of absence.'[12]

Believing women who say we are sexually violated has been a radical departure, both methodologically and legally. The extent and nature of rape, marital rape, and sexual harassment itself, were discovered in this way. Domestic battery as a syndrome, almost a habit, was discovered through refusing to believe that when a woman is assaulted by a man to whom she is connected, that is not an assault. The sexual abuse of children was uncovered, Freud notwithstanding, by believing that children were not making up all this sexual abuse.[13] Now what is striking is that when each discovery is made, and somehow made real in the world, the response has been: it happens to men too. If women are hurt, men are hurt. If women are raped, men are raped. If women are sexually harassed, men are sexually harassed. If women are battered, men are battered. Symmetry must be reasserted. Neutrality must be reclaimed. Equality must be re-established.

The only places where the available evidence supports this, where anything like what happens to women also happens to men, are with children – little boys are sexually abused – and in prison.[14] The liberty of prisoners is restricted, their freedom **459** restrained, their humanity systematically diminished, their bodies and emotions confined, defined and regulated. If paid at all, they are paid starvation wages. They can be tortured at will, and it is passed off as discipline or as means to an end. They become compliant. They can be raped at will, at any moment, and nothing will be done about it. When they scream, nobody hears. To be a prisoner means to be defined as a member of a group for whom the rules of what can be done to you, of what is seen as abuse of you, are reduced as part of the definition of your status. To be a woman is also that kind of definition and has that kind of meaning.

Men *are* damaged by sexism. (By men, I am referring to the status of masculinity which is accorded to males on the basis of their biology, but is not itself biological.) But whatever the damage of sexism is to men, the condition of being a man is not defined as subordinate to women by force. Looking at the facts of the abuses of women all at once, you see that a woman is socially defined as a person who, whether or not she is or has been, *can at any time* be treated in these ways by men, and little, if anything, will be done about it. This is what it means when feminists say that maleness is a form of power and femaleness is a form of powerlessness.

In this context, what all of this 'men too' stuff is about, is that people don't really seem to believe that the things I have just said are true, though there really is little question about their empirical accuracy. The data are extremely simple, like women's fifty-nine cent on the dollar pay figure.[15] People don't really seem to believe that either. Yet there is no question of its empirical validity. This is the workplace story: what women do is seen as not worth much or what is not worth much is seen as something for women to do. *Women* are not seen as worth much, is the thing. Now why are these basic realities of the subordination of women to men, such that for example only 7.8 per cent of women have never been sexually assaulted,[16] not effectively believed, not perceived as real in the face of all this evidence? Why don't *women* believe our own experiences? In the face of all this evidence, especially of systematic sexual abuse – subjection to violence with impunity is one extreme expression, although not the only expression, of a degraded status – the view that basically the sexes are equal in this society remains unchallenged and unchanged. The day I got this was the day I understood its real message, its real coherence: *this is equality for us.*

I could describe this but I couldn't explain it until I started studying a lot of pornography. In pornography, there it is, in one place, all of the abuses that women had to struggle so long even to begin to articulate, all the *unspeakable* abuse: the rape, the battery, the sexual harassment, the prostitution and the sexual abuse of children. Only in the pornography it is called something else: sex, sex, sex, sex and sex, respectively. Pornography sexualizes rape, battery, sexual harassment, prostitution and child sexual abuse; it thereby celebrates, promotes, authorizes and legitimizes them. More generally, it eroticizes the dominance and submission that is the dynamic common to them all. It makes hierarchy sexy and calls that 'the truth about sex[17] or just a mirror of reality. Through this process, pornography constructs what a woman is as what men want from sex. This is what the pornography means.

Pornography constructs what a woman is in terms of its view of what men want sexually, such that acts of rape, battery, sexual harassment, prostitution and sexual abuse of children become acts of sexual equality. Pornography's world of equality is a harmonious and balanced place.[18] Men and women are perfectly complementary and perfectly bipolar. Women's desire to be fucked by men is equal to men's desire to fuck women. All the ways men love to take and violate women, women love to be taken and violated. The women who most love this are most men's equals, the most liberated; the most participatory child is the most grown-up, the most equal to an adult. Their consent merely expresses or ratifies these pre-existing facts.

The content of pornography is one thing. There, women substantively desire dispossession and cruelty. We desperately want to be bound, battered, tortured, humiliated and killed. Or, to be fair to the soft core, merely taken and used. This is erotic to the male point of view. Subjection itself with self-determination ecstatically relinquished is the content of women's sexual desire and desirability. Women are there to be violated and possessed, men to violate and possess us either on screen or by camera or pen on behalf of the consumer. On a simple descriptive level, the inequality of hierarchy, of which gender is the primary one, seems necessary for the sexual arousal to work. Other added inequalities identify various pornographic genres or sub-themes, although they are always added through gender: age, disability, homosexuality, animals, objects, race (including anti-Semitism) and so on. Gender is never irrelevant. **461**

What pornography *does* goes beyond its content: it eroticizes hierarchy, it sexualizes inequality. It makes dominance and submission sex. Inequality is its central dynamic; the illusion of freedom coming together with the reality of force is central to its working. Perhaps because this is a bourgeois culture, the victim must look free, appear to be freely acting. Choice is how she got there. Willing is what she is when she is being equal. It seems equally important that then and there she actually be forced and that forcing be communicated on some level, even if only through still photos of her in postures of receptivity and access, available for penetration. Pornography in this view is a form of forced sex, a practice of sexual politics, an institution of gender inequality.

From this perspective, pornography is neither harmless fantasy nor a corrupt and confused misrepresentation of an otherwise natural and healthy sexual situation. It institutionalizes the sexuality of male supremacy, fusing the eroticization of dominance and submission with the social construction of male and female. To the extent that gender is sexual, pornography is part of constituting the meaning of that sexuality. Men treat women as who they see women as being. Pornography constructs who that is. Men's power over women means that the way men see women defines who women can be. Pornography is that way. Pornography is not imagery in some relation to a reality elsewhere constructed. It is not a distortion, reflection, projection, expression, fantasy, representation or symbol either. It is a sexual reality.

In Andrea Dworkin's definitive work on pornography, sexuality itself is a social construct gendered to the ground. Male dominance here is not an artificial overlay upon an underlying inalterable substratum of uncorrupted essential sexual being. Dworkin's *Pornography: Men Possessing Women*[19] presents a sexual theory of gender inequality of which pornography is a constitutive practice. The way in which pornography produces its meaning constructs and defines men and women as such. Gender has no basis in anything other than the social reality its hegemony constructs. Gender is what gender means. The process that gives sexuality its male supremacist meaning is the same process through which gender inequality becomes socially real.

In this approach, the experience of the (overwhelmingly) male audiences who consume pornography is therefore not fantasy or simulation or catharsis but sexual reality, the level of reality on which sex itself largely operates. Understanding this dimension of the problem does not require noticing that pornography models are real women to whom, in most cases, something real is being done; nor does it even require inquiring into the systematic infliction of pornography and its sexuality upon women, although it helps. The way in which the pornography itself provides what those who consume it want matters. Pornography *participates* in its audience's eroticism through creating an accessible sexual object, the possession and consumption of which *is* male sexuality, as socially constructed; to be consumed and possessed as which, *is* female sexuality, as socially constructed; and pornography is a process that constructs it that way.

The object world is constructed according to how it looks with respect to its possible uses. Pornography defines women by how we look according to how we can be sexually used. Pornography codes how to look at women, so you know what you can do with one when you see one. Gender is an assignment made visually, both originally and in everyday life. A sex object is defined on the basis of its looks, in terms of its usability for sexual pleasure, such that both the looking – the quality of the gaze, including its point of view – and the definition according to use become eroticized as part of the sex itself. This is what the feminist concept 'sex object' means. In this sense, sex in life is no less mediated than it is in art. One could say men have sex with *their image* of a woman. It is not that life and art imitate each other; in this sexuality, they *are* each other.

To give a set of rough epistemological translations, to defend pornography as consistent with the equality of the sexes is to defend the subordination of women to men as sexual equality. What in the pornographic view is love and romance looks a great deal like hatred and torture to the feminist. Pleasure and eroticism become violation. Desire appears as lust for dominance and submission. The vulnerability of women's projected sexual availability, that acting we are allowed (i.e. asking to be acted upon), is victimization. Play conforms to scripted roles. Fantasy expresses ideology, is not exempt from it. Admiration of natural physical beauty becomes objectification. Harmlessness becomes harm. Pornography is a harm of male supremacy made difficult to see because of its pervasiveness, potency, and principally, because of its success in making the world a pornographic place. Specifically, its harm cannot be discerned, and will not be addressed, if viewed and approached neutrally, because it *is* so **463** much of 'what is'. In other words, to the extent pornography succeeds in constructing social reality, it becomes invisible as harm. If we live in a world that pornography creates through the power of men in a male-dominated situation the issue is not what the harm of pornography is, but how that harm is to become visible.

II

Obscenity law provides a very different analysis and conception of the problem.[20] In 1973, the legal definition of obscenity became that which

> the average person, applying contemporary community standards, would find that, taken as a whole, appeals to the prurient interest; that which depicts and describes in a patently offensive way . . . sexual conduct as defined by the applicable state law; and that which, taken as a whole, lacks serious literary, artistic, political or scientific value.[21]

Feminism doubts whether the average gender-neutral person exists; has more questions about the content and process of defining what community standards are than it does about deviations from them; wonders why prurience counts but powerlessness does not, and why sensibilities are better protected from offence than women are from exploitation; defines sexuality, and thus its violation and expropriation, more broadly than does state law; and questions why a body of law which has not in practice been able to tell rape from intercourse should, without further guidance, be entrusted with telling pornography from anything less. Taking the work 'as a whole' ignores that which the victims of pornography have long known: legitimate settings diminish the injury perceived to be done to those whose trivialization and objectification it contextualizes. Besides, and this is a heavy one, if a woman is subjected, why should it matter that the work has other value? Maybe what redeems the work's value is what enhances its injury to women, not to mention that existing standards of literature, art, science and politics, examined in a feminist light, are remarkably consonant with pornography's mode, meaning and message. And finally – first and foremost, actually – although the subject of these materials is overwhelmingly women, their contents almost entirely comprised **464** of women's bodies, our invisibility has been such, our equation as a sex *with* sex has been such, that the law of obscenity has never even considered pornography a women's issue.

Obscenity, in this light, is a moral idea; an idea about judgements of good and bad. Pornography, by contrast, is a political practice, a practice of power and powerlessness. Obscenity is ideational and abstract; pornography is concrete and substantive. The two concepts represent two entirely different things. Nudity, excess of candour, arousal or excitement, prurient appeal, illegality of the acts depicted and unnaturalness or perversion are all qualities that bother obscenity law when sex is depicted or portrayed. Sex forced on real women so that it can be sold at a profit to be forced on other real women; women's bodies trussed and maimed and raped and made into things to be hurt and obtained and accessed and this presented as the nature of women in a way that is acted on and acted out over and over; the coercion that is visible and the coercion that has become invisible – this and more bothers feminists about pornography. Obscenity as such probably does little harm.[22] Pornography is integral to attitudes and behaviours of violence and discrimination which define the treatment and status of half the population.

III

At the request of the city of Minneapolis, Andrea Dworkin and I conceived and designed a local human rights ordinance in accordance with our approach to the pornography issue. We define pornography as a practice of sex discrimination, a violation of women's civil rights, the opposite of sexual equality. Its point is to hold accountable, to those who are injured, those who profit from and benefit from that injury. It means that women's injury – our damage, our pain, our enforced inferiority – should outweigh their pleasure and their profits, or sex equality is meaningless.

We define pornography as the graphic sexually explicit subordination of women through pictures or words that also includes women dehumanized as sexual objects, things or commodities, enjoying pain or humiliation or rape, being tied up, cut up, mutilated, bruised or physically hurt, in postures of sexual submission or servility or display, reduced to body parts, penetrated by objects or animals, or presented in scenarios of degradation, injury, torture, shown as filthy or inferior, bleeding, bruised or hurt in a context that makes these conditions sexual.[23]   **465**

Erotica, defined by distinction as not this, might be sexually explicit materials premised on equality.[24] We also provide that the use of men, children or transsexuals in the place of women is pornography.[25] The definition is substantive in that it is sex-specific, but it covers everyone in a sex-specific way, so is gender-neutral in overall design.

There is a buried issue within sex discrimination law about what sex, meaning gender, is. If sex is a *difference*, social or biological, one looks to see if a challenged practice occurs along the same lines; if it does, or if it is done to both sexes, the practice is not discrimination, not inequality. If, by contrast, sex inequality is a matter of *dominance*, the issue is not the gender difference but the difference gender makes. In this more substantive, less abstract approach, the concern is whether a practice *subordinates* on the basis of sex. The first approach implies that marginal correction is needed; the second suggests social change. Equality to the first centres on abstract symmetry between equivalent categories; the asymmetry that occurs when categories are not equivalent is not inequality, it is treating unlikes differently. To the second approach, inequality centres on the substantive, cumulative disadvantagement of social hierarchy. Equality to the first is non-differentiation; to the second, equality is non-subordination.[26] Although it is consonant with both approaches, our anti-pornography statute emerges largely from an analysis of the problem under the second approach.

To define pornography as a practice of sex discrimination combines a mode of portrayal that has a legal history – the sexually explicit – with an active term central to the inequality of the sexes – subordination. Among other things, subordination means to be placed in a position of inferiority or loss of power, or to be demeaned or denigrated.[27] To be someone's subordinate is the opposite of being their equal. The definition does not include all sexually explicit depictions *of* the subordination of women. That is not what it says. It says, this which *does* that: the sexually explicit which subordinates women. To these active terms to capture what the pornography *does*, the definition adds a list of what it must also contain. This list, from our analysis, is an exhaustive description of what must be in the pornography for it to do what it does behaviourally. Each item in the definition is supported by experimental, testimonial, social, and clinical evidence. We made a legislative choice to be exhaustive and specific and concrete rather than conceptual and general, to minimize problems of chilling effect, making it hard to guess wrong, thus making self-censorship less likely, but encouraging (to use a phrase from discrimination law) voluntary compliance, knowing that if something turns up that is not on the list, the law will not be expansively interpreted.

The second half of the definition, by itself, would be a content regulation.[28] But together with the first part, the definition is not simply a content regulation. It is a medium-message combination that resembles many other such exceptions to first amendment guarantees.[29]

In order to focus upon what our law is, I will say what it is not. It is not a prior restraint. It does not go to possession. It does not turn on offensiveness. It is not a ban, unless relief for a proven injury is a 'ban' on doing that injury again. Its principal enforcement mechanism is the civil rights commission, although it contains an option for direct access to court as well as de novo judicial review of administrative determinations, to ensure that no case will escape full judicial scrutiny and full due process. I will also not discuss various threshold issues, such as the sources of municipal authority, pre-emption, or abstention, or even issues of overbreadth or vagueness, nor will I defend the ordinance from views which never have been law, such as first amendment absolutism. I will discuss the merits: how pornography by this definition is a harm, specifically how it is a harm of gender inequality, and how that harm outweighs any social interest in its protection by recognized first amendment standards.[30]

This law aspires to guarantee women's rights consistent with the first amendment by making visible a conflict of rights between the equality guaranteed to all women and what, in some legal sense, is now the freedom of the pornographers to make and sell, and their consumers to have access to, the materials this ordinance defines. Judicial resolution of this conflict, if they do for women what they have done for others, is likely to entail a balancing of the rights of women arguing that our lives and opportunities, including our freedom of speech and action, are constrained by – and in many cases flatly precluded by, in and through – pornography, against those who argue that the pornography is harmless, or harmful only in part but not in the whole of the definition; or that it is more important to preserve the pornography than it is to prevent or remedy whatever harm it does.

In predicting how a court would balance these interests, it is **467** important to understand that this ordinance cannot now be said to be either conclusively legal or illegal under existing law or precedent,[31] although I think the weight of authority is on our side. This ordinance enunciates a new form of the previously recognized governmental interest in sex equality. Many laws make sex equality a governmental interest.[32] Our law is designed to further the equality of the sexes, to help make sex equality real. Pornography is a practice of discrimination on the basis of sex, on one level because of its role in creating and maintaining sex as a basis for discrimination. It harms many women one at a time and helps keep all women in an inferior status by defining our subordination as our sexuality and equating that with our gender. It is also sex discrimination because its victims, including men, are selected for victimization on the basis of their gender. But for their sex, they would not be so treated.[33]

The harm of pornography, broadly speaking, is the harm of the civil inequality of the sexes made invisible as harm because it has become accepted as the sex difference. Consider this analogy with race: if you see black people as different, there is no harm to segregation; it is merely a recognition of that difference. To neutral principles, separate but equal was equal. The injury of racial separation to blacks arises 'solely because [they] choose to put that construction upon it'.[34] Epistemologically translated: how you see it is not the way it is. Similarly, if you see women as just different, even or especially if you don't know that you do, subordination will not look like subordination at all, much less like harm. It will merely look like an appropriate recognition of the sex difference.

Pornography does treat the sexes differently, so the case for sex differentiation can be made here. Men as a group do not tend to be (although some individuals may be) treated like women are treated in pornography. But as a social group, men are not hurt by pornography the way women as a social group are. Their social status is not defined as *less* by it. So the major argument does not turn on mistaken differentiation, particularly since women's treatment according to pornography's dictates makes it all too often accurate. The salient quality of a distinction between the top and the bottom in a hierarchy is not difference, although top is certainly different from bottom; it is power. So the major argument is: subordinate but equal is not equal.

Particularly since this is a new legal theory, a new law, and **468** 'new' facts, perhaps the situation of women it newly exposes deserves to be considered on its own terms. Not to mention, why the problems of 53 per cent of the population have to look like somebody else's problems before they can be recognized as existing, but then can't be addressed if they do look like other people's problems, about which something might have to be done if something is done about these, is a construction of things that truly deserves inquiry. Limiting the justification for this law to the situation of women would serve to limit the precedential value of a favourable ruling. Its particularity to one side, the *approach* to the injury is supported by a whole array of prior decisions that have justified exceptions to first amendment guarantees, when something that matters is seen to be directly at stake. What unites many cases where speech interests are raised and implicated but not, on balance, protected, is harm,[35] harm that counts. In some existing exceptions, the definitions are much more open-ended than ours.[36] In some, the sanctions are more severe, or potentially more so. For instance, ours is a civil law; most others are criminal, although not all.[37] Almost none shows as many people directly affected. Evidence of harm in other cases tends to be vastly less concrete and more conjectural, which is not to say that there is necessarily less of it.[38] None of the previous cases addresses a problem of this scope or magnitude – for instance, an $8 billion a year industry.[39] Nor do other cases address an abuse the practice of which has such widespread legitimacy. Courts have seen harm in other cases. The question is, will they see it here, especially given that the pornographers got there first? I will confine myself here to arguing from cases on harm to people, on the supposition that, the pornographers notwithstanding, women are not flags.[40]

I will discuss the four injuries we make actionable with as much evidence as time permits. I want you to hear the voices of the women and men who spoke at our hearing.

A.

The first victims of pornography are the ones in it. To date, it has only been with children, and male children at that, that the Supreme Court has understood that before the pornography became the pornographer's speech, it was somebody's life.[41] This is particularly true in visual media, where it takes a real person doing each act to make what you see. This is the double meaning in a statement one ex-prostitute made at our hearing: '[E]very single thing you see in pornography is happening to a real **469** woman right now.'[42] Linda Marciano, in her book *Ordeal*,[43] recounts being coerced as 'Linda Lovelace' into performing for *Deep Throat*, a fabulously profitable film,[44] by abduction, systematic beating, being kept prisoner, watched every minute, threatened with her life and the lives of her family if she left, tortured and kept under constant psychological intimidation and duress. Not all pornography models are, to our knowledge, coerced so expressly; but the fact that some are not does not mean that those who are, aren't. It only means that coercion into pornography cannot be said to be biologically female. The further fact that prostitution and modelling are structurally women's best economic options should give pause to those who would consider women's presence there a true act of free choice. In the case of other inequalities, it is sometimes understood that people do degrading work out of a lack of options caused by, say, poverty. The work is not seen as *not* degrading 'for them' because they do it. With women, it just proves that this is what we are really for, this is our true nature. I will leave you wondering, with me, why it is that when a woman spreads her legs for a camera, what she is assumed to be exercising is free will. Women's freedom is rather substantively defined here. And as you think about the assumption of consent that follows women into pornography, look closely some time for the skinned knees, the bruises, the welts from the whippings, the scratches, the gashes. Many of them are not simulated. One relatively soft-core pornography model said, 'I knew the pose was right when it hurt.'[45] It certainly seems important to the audiences that the events in the pornography be real. For this reason, pornography becomes a motive for murder, as in 'snuff' films in which someone is tortured to death to make a sex film. They exist.[46]

Coerced pornography models encounter devastating problems of lack of credibility because of a cycle of forced acts in which coercion into pornography is central. For example, children are typically forced to perform the acts in the pornography that is forced on them; photographs are taken of these rapes, photographs which are used to coerce the children into prostitution or into staying in prostitution, telling them that if they try to leave, the pictures will be shown to the authorities, their parents, their teachers (whoever is *not* coercing them at the time) and no one will believe them. This gets them into prostitution and keeps them there.[47] Understand, the documentation of the harm as it is being done is taken as evidence that no harm was done. Partly, desire for the abuse is attributed to the victim's nature from the fact of the abuse: she's a natural born whore; see, there she is chained to a bed. Too, the victims are often forced to act as though they are enjoying the abuse. One pornographer said to a woman he abducted and was photographing while bound: 'Smile or I'll kill you. I can get lots of money for pictures of women who smile when they're tied up like you.'[48] When women say they were forced, they are not believed, in part because, as Linda Marciano says, 'What people remember is the smile on my face.'[49]

Pornography defines what a woman is through conditioning the male sexual response to that definition, to the unilateral sexuality pornography is part of and provides. Its power can be illustrated by considering the credibility problems Linda Marciano encounters when she says that the presentation of her in *Deep Throat* is not true, in the sense that she does not and did not feel or enjoy what the character she was forced to portray felt and enjoyed. Most concretely, before 'Linda Lovelace' was seen performing deep throat, no one had ever seen it being done in that way, largely because it cannot be done without hypnosis to repress the natural gag response. *Yet it was believed.* Men proceeded to demand it of women, causing the distress of many, and the death of some.[50] Yet when Linda Marciano now tells that it took kidnapping and death threats and hypnosis to put her there, that is found *difficult to believe.*[51] The point is not only that when women can be coerced with impunity the results, when mass-produced, set standards that are devastating and dangerous for all women. The point is also that the assumptions that the law of the first amendment makes about adults – that adults are autonomous, self-defining, freely-acting, *equal* individuals – are exactly those qualities which pornography systematically denies and undermines for women.[52] Some of the same reasons children are granted some specific legal avenues for redress – relative lack of power, inability to command respect for their consent and self-determination, in some cases less physical strength or lowered legitimacy in using it, specific credibility problems, and lack of access to resources for meaningful self-expression – also hold true for women's comparative social position to men. It is therefore vicious to suggest, as many have, that women like Linda Marciano should remedy their situations through the exercise of more speech. Pornography makes their speech impossible and where possible, worthless. Pornography makes women into objects. **471**

Objects do not speak. When they do, they are by then regarded as objects, not as humans, which is what it means to have no credibility. Besides, how Ms Marciano's speech is supposed to redress her injury, except by producing this legal remedy, is unclear since no amount of saying anything remedies what is being *done* to her in theatres and on home videos all over the world, where she is repeatedly raped for public entertainment and private profit.

What would justice look like for these women?[53] Linda Marciano said, 'Virtually every time someone watches that film, they are watching me being raped.'[54] Nancy Holmes, who was forced to perform for pornography by her father and who, like many such victims, has been searching for the film for years, says:

> You wonder who might have seen the film. In some back-alley adult book shop someone has dropped a quarter and maybe it might be you they are looking at. You would not ordinarily mix company with this person under these circumstances . . . [b]ut in some back alley, in someone's dark mind you are worth 25 cents. Someone has just paid 25 cents to see you being brutally raped and beaten. And some total stranger gets to gain sadistic and voyeuristic pleasure from your pain. It costs you your sanity and years of suffering and psychological turmoil. It cost him only a quarter, and he gained tremendous pleasure. It robbed you of your childhood; it gave him satisfaction.[55]

Now think about his freedom and her powerlessness, and think about what it means to call that 'just the construction she chooses to put upon it'.

As part of the relief for people who can prove this was done to them, our law provides an injunction to remove these materials from public view. The best authority we have for this is the Ferber case, which permits criminal prohibitions on child pornography.[56] That case recognized that child pornography need not be obscene to be child abuse. The court found such pornography harmful in part because it constituted 'a permanent record of children's participation and the harm to the child is exacerbated by circulation'.[57] This was a film, by the way, largely of two boys masturbating.[58] The sensitivities of obscenity law, the court noted, were inapt because 'a work which, taken on the whole, contains value may nevertheless embody the hardest core of child pornography'.[59] Whether a work appeals to the prurient interest is not the same as whether a child is physically or psychologically harmed to make it.[60]

Both of these reasons apply to coerced women. Women are not children, but coerced women are effectively deprived of power over the expressive products of their coercion. Coerced pornography should meet the test that 'the evil to be restricted . . . overwhelmingly outweighs the expressive interests, if any, at stake'.[61] Unless one wishes to retain the incentive structure that has introduced a profit motive into rape, pornography made this way should be able to be eliminated.[62]

B.

We also make it actionable to force pornography on a person in employment, education, in a home or in any public place.[63] The person who was forced cannot, under this part of the law, reach the pornography, but they can reach the perpetrator or institution that does the forcing. In our hearings we heard the ways in which pornography is forced on people. Children, it is used to show how to perform sex acts, to duplicate exactly these so-called natural childish acts,[64] women in men's jobs, to intimidate them into leaving,[65] women in women's jobs, to have or set up a sexual encounter,[66] prostitutes or wives, so they will know what a natural woman is supposed to do.[67] In therapy, it is seen as aiding in transference, i.e. submitting to the therapist,[68] in medical school, it desensitizes doctors so that when patients say they are masturbating with a chicken or wondering if intercourse with a cow will give them exotic diseases, the doctor does not react.[69] In language classes, it becomes material to be worked over meticulously for translation.[70] It is used to terrorize children in homes, so they will keep still about its use in the rape of their mothers and sisters: look at this, if you tell, here's what I'll do to you.[71] Sometimes it ends there; some children 'only' have the pornography forced on them. Some of them later develop psychological difficulties that are identical to children who had the *acts* forced on them.[72] Do a thought–act distinction on that one.

Women who live in neighbourhoods where pornography is concentrated, much of it through state and local legal action called 'zoning', report similar effects on a broad scale.[73] Because prostitutes know what others seem to have a lot staked on denying, which is that pornography makes men want the real thing, they sometimes locate around it. This means that any woman there can be taken as prostitute, which is dangerous enough if you are a prostitute, but becomes particularly dangerous if you do not mean to deliver. The threat of sexual **473** harassment is constant. The presence of the pornography conditions women's physical environment. Women have no place to go to avoid it, no place to avert their eyes *to*.[74] Certainly not home, where the presence of the pornography is so sanctified[75] that we don't even challenge it in this law. One woman who as a child was a victim of incest and now lives in a community saturated with pornography, relates a Skokie-type injury.[76] She relives the incest every time she walks by the pornography she cannot avoid. '[L]ooking at the women in those pictures, I saw myself at fourteen, at fifteen, at sixteen. I felt the weight of that man's body, the pain, the disgust . . . I don't need studies and statistics to tell me that there is a relationship between pornography and real violence against women. My body remembers.'[77] Now recall that over a third of all women are victims of child sexual abuse; about the same proportion are victims of domestic battery; just under half are victims of rape or attempted rape. I am not saying that every such presence of the pornography is legally force, but what does it mean for targeted survivors to live in a society in which the rehearsal and celebration and ritual re-enactment of our victimization is enjoyed, is an entertainment industry, is arguably a constitutional right?

C.

Specific pornography directly causes some assaults.[78] Some rapes are performed by men with paperback books in their pockets.[79] One young woman testified in our hearings about walking through a forest at thirteen and coming across a group of armed hunters reading pornography. As they looked up and saw her, one said, 'There is a live one.'[80] They gang-raped her at gunpoint for several hours. One Native American woman told us about being gang-raped in a re-enactment of a videogame on her.

> [T]hat's what they screamed in my face as they threw me to the ground, 'This is more fun than Custer's Last Stand.' They held me down and as one was running the tip of his knife across my face and throat he said, 'Do you want to play Custer's Last Stand? It's great, you lose but you don't care, do you? You like a little pain, don't you, squaw? . . . Maybe we will tie you to a tree and start a fire around you.'[81]

Received wisdom seems to be that because there is so little difference between convicted rapists and the rest of the male **474** population in levels and patterns of exposure, response to, and consumption of pornography, pornography's role in rape is insignificant.[82] A more parsimonious explanation of this data is that knowing exposure to, response to, or consumption of pornography will not tell you who will be reported, apprehended and convicted for rape. But the commonalities such data reveal between convicted rapists and other men are certainly consistent with the fact that only a tiny fraction of rapes ever come to the attention of authorities.[83] It does not make sense to assume that pornography has no role in rape simply because little about its use or effects distinguishes convicted rapists from other men, when we know that a lot of those other men *do* rape women; they just never get caught. In other words, the significance of pornography in acts of forced sex is one thing if sex offenders are considered deviants and another if they are considered relatively non-exceptional except for the fact of their apprehension and incarceration. Professionals who work with that tiny percentage of men who get reported and convicted for such offences, a group made special only by our ability to assume they once had sex by force in a way that someone (in addition to their victim) eventually regarded as serious, made the following observations about the population they work with. 'Pornography is the permission and direction and rehearsal for sexual violence.'[84] '[P]ornography is often used by sex offenders as a stimulus to their sexually acting out.' It is the 'tools of sexual assault',[85] 'a way in which they practice' their crimes, 'like a loaded gun',[86] 'like drinking salt water',[87] 'the chemical of sexual addiction'.[88] They hypothesize that pornography leads some men to abusiveness out of fear of loss of control that has come to mean masculinity when real women won't accept sex on the one sided terms that pornography gives and from which they have learned what sex is. '[Because pornography] is reinforcing, [and leads to sexual release, it] leads men to want the experience which they have in photographic fantasy to happen in "real" life.'[89] 'They live vicariously through the pictures. Eventually, that is not satisfying enough and they end up acting out sexually.'[90] '[S]exual fantasy represents the hope for reality.'[91] These professionals are referring to what others are fond of terming 'just an idea'.

Although police have known it for years, reported cases are increasingly noting the causal role of pornography in some sexual abuse.[92] In a recent Minnesota case, a fourteen-year-old girl on a bicycle was stopped with a knife and forced into a car. Her hands **475** were tied with a belt, she was pushed to the floor and covered with a blanket. The knife was then used to cut off her clothes, and fingers and a knife were inserted into her vagina. Then the man had her dress, drove her to a gravel pit, ordered her to stick a safety pin into the nipple of her left breast, and forced her to ask him to hit her. After hitting her, he forced her to commit fellatio and to submit to anal penetration, and made her use a cigarette to burn herself on her breast and near her pubic area. Then he defecated and urinated on her face, forced her to ingest some of the excrement and urine and made her urinate into a cup and drink it. He took a string from her blouse and choked her to the point of unconsciousness, leaving burn marks on her neck, and after cutting her with his knife in a couple of places, drove her back to where he had gotten her and let her go. The books that were found with this man were: *Violent Stories of Kinky Humiliation*, *Violent Stories of Dominance and Submission* – you think feminists made up these words? – *Bizarre Sex Crimes*, *Shamed Victims* and *Water Sports Fetish*, *Enemas and Golden Showers*. The Minnesota Supreme Court said, 'It appears that in committing these various acts, the defendant was giving life to some stories he had read in various pornographic books.'[93]

D.

To reach the magnitude of this problem on the scale it exists, our law makes trafficking in pornography – production, sale, exhibition, or distribution – actionable.[94] Under the obscenity rubric, much legal and psychological scholarship has centred on a search for the elusive link between pornography defined as obscenity and harm.[95] They have looked high and low – in the mind of the male consumer,[96] in society or in its 'moral fabric',[97] in correlations between variations in levels of anti-social acts and liberalization of obscenity laws.[98] The only harm they have found has been one they have attributed to 'the social interest in order and morality'.[99] Until recently, no one looked very persistently for harm to women, particularly harm to women through men. The rather obvious fact that the sexes *relate* has been overlooked in the inquiry into the male consumer and his mind. The pornography doesn't just drop out of the sky, go into his head and stop there. Specifically, men rape, batter, prostitute, molest, and sexually harass women. Under conditions of inequality, they also hire, fire, promote, and grade women, decide how much or whether or not we are worth paying and for what, define and approve and disapprove of women in ways that count, that determine our lives.

If women are not just born to be sexually used, the fact that we are seen and treated as though that is what we are born for becomes something in need of explanation. If we see that men relate to women in a pattern of who they see women as being, and that forms a pattern of inequality, it becomes important to ask where that view came from or, minimally, how it is perpetuated or escalated. Asking this requires asking different questions about pornography from the ones obscenity law made salient.

Now I'm going to talk about causality in its narrowest sense.[100] Recent experimental research on pornography[101] shows that the materials covered by our definition cause measurable harm to women through increasing men's attitudes and behaviours of discrimination in both violent and non-violent forms. Exposure to some of the pornography in our definition increases normal men's immediately subsequent willingness to aggress against women under laboratory conditions.[102] It makes normal men more closely resemble convicted rapists attitudinally, although as a group they don't look all that different from them to start with.[103] It also significantly increases attitudinal measures known to correlate with rape and self-reports of aggressive acts, measures such as hostility towards women, propensity to rape, condoning rape, and predicting that one would rape or force sex on a woman if one knew one would not get caught.[104] This latter measure, by the way, begins with rape at about a third of all men and moves to half with 'forced sex'.[105]

As to that pornography covered by our definition in which normal research subjects seldom perceive violence, long-term exposure still makes them see women as more worthless, trivial, non-human and object-like,[106] i.e. the way those who are discriminated against are seen by those who discriminate against them. Crucially, all pornography by our definition acts dynamically over time to diminish one's ability to distinguish sex from violence. The materials work behaviourally to diminish the capacity of both men and women to perceive that an account of a rape is an account of a rape.[107] X-only materials, in which subjects perceive no force, also increase perceptions that a rape victim is worthless and decrease the perception she was harmed.[108] The overall direction of current research suggests that the more expressly violent materials accomplish on less exposure what the less overtly violent – that is, the so-called 'sex only   **477** materials' – accomplish over the longer term. Women are rendered fit for use and targeted for abuse. The only thing that the research cannot document is which individual women will be next on the list. (This cannot be documented experimentally because of ethics constraints on the researchers – constraints which do not operate in life.) Although the targeting is systematic on the basis of sex, it targets individuals at random. They are selected on the basis of roulette. Pornography can no longer be said to be just a mirror. It does not just reflect the world or some people's perceptions. It *moves* them. It increases attitudes that are lived out, circumscribing the status of half the population.

What the experimental data predict would happen, actually does happen in women's real lives. You know, it's fairly frustrating that women have known that these things do happen for some time. As Ed Donnerstein, an experimental researcher in this area, often puts it, 'we just quantify the obvious'.[109] It is women, primarily, to whom the research results have been the obvious, because we live them. But not until a laboratory study predicts that these things *would* happen, do people begin to believe you when you say they *did* happen to you. There is no – *not any* – inconsistency between the patterns the laboratory studies predict and the data on what actually happens to real women. Show me an abuse of women in society, I'll show it to you made sex in the pornography. If you want to know who is being hurt in this society, go see what is being done and to whom in pornography and then go look for them other places in the world. You will find them being hurt in just that way. We did in our hearings.

In our hearings, women spoke, to my knowledge for the first time in history in public, about the damage pornography does to them. We learned that pornography is used to break women, to train women to sexual submission, to season women, to terrorize women and to silence their dissent. It is this that has previously been termed 'having no effect'. Men inflict on women the sex that they experience through the pornography in a way that gives women no choice about seeing the pornography or doing the sex. Asked if anyone ever tried to inflict sex acts on them they did not want that they knew came from pornography, 10 per cent of women in a recent random study said yes.[110] Twenty-four per cent of married women said yes.[111] That is a lot of women. A lot more don't know. Some of those who do testified in Minneapolis. One wife said of her ex-husband: 'He would read from the pornography like a textbook, like a journal. In fact when he asked me to be bound, when he finally convinced me to do it, he read in the magazine how to tie the knots.'[112] Another woman said of her boyfriend: '[H]e went to this party, saw pornography, got an erection, got me . . . to inflict his erection on . . . There is a direct causal relationship there.'[113] One woman who said her husband had rape and bondage magazines all over the house, discovered two suitcases full of Barbie dolls with rope tied on their arms and legs and with tape across their mouths.[114] Now think about the silence of women. She said, 'He used to tie me up and he tried those things on me.'[115] A therapist in private practice reported:

> Presently or recently I have worked with clients who have been sodomized by broom handles, forced to have sex with over twenty dogs in the backseat of their car, tied up and then electrocuted on their genitals. These are children, [all] in the ages of fourteen to eighteen, all of whom [have been directly affected by pornography,] [e]ither where the perpetrator has read the manuals and manuscripts at night and used these as recipe books by day or had the pornography present at the time of the sexual violence.[116]

One woman, testifying that all the women in a group of ex-prostitutes were brought into prostitution as children through pornography, characterized their collective experience: '[I]n my experience there was not one situation where a client was not using pornography while he was using me or that he had not just watched pornography or that it was verbally referred to and directed me to pornography.'[117] 'Men,' she continued, 'witness the abuse of women in pornography constantly and if they can't engage in that behaviour with their wives, girlfriends or children, they force a whore to do it.'[118]

Men also testified about how pornography hurts them. One young gay man who had seen *Playboy* and *Penthouse* as a child said of heterosexual pornography:

> It was one of the places I learned about sex and it showed me that sex was violence. What I saw there was a specific relationship between men and women . . . [T]he woman was to be used, objectified, humiliated and hurt; the man was in a superior position, a position to be violent. In pornography I learned that what it meant to be sexual with a man or to be loved by a man was to accept his violence.[119]

For this reason, when he was battered by his first lover, which he described as 'one of the most profoundly destructive experiences of my life',[120] he accepted it.

Pornography also hurts men's capacity to relate to women. One young man spoke about this in a way that connects pornography – not the prohibition on pornography – with fascism. He spoke of his struggle to repudiate the thrill of dominance, of his difficulty finding connection with a woman to whom he is close. He said:

> My point is that if women in a society filled by pornography must be wary for their physical selves, a man, even a man of good intentions, must be wary for his mind . . . I do not want to be a mechanical, goose-stepping follower of the Playboy bunny, because that is what I think it is . . . [T]hese are the experiments a master race perpetuates on those slated for extinction.[121]

The woman he lives with is Jewish. There was a very brutal rape near their house. She was afraid; she tried to joke. It didn't work. 'She was still afraid. And just as a well-meaning German was afraid in 1933, I am also very much afraid.'[122]

Pornography stimulates and reinforces, it does not cathect or mirror, the connection between one-sided freely available sexual access to women and masculine sexual excitement and sexual satisfaction. The catharsis hypothesis is fantasy. The fantasy theory is fantasy. Reality is: pornography conditions male orgasm to female subordination. It tells men what sex means, what a real woman is, and codes them together in a way that is behaviourally reinforcing. This is a real five-dollar sentence but I'm going to say it anyway: pornography is a set of hermeneutical equivalences that work on the epistemological level. Substantively, pornography defines the meaning of what a woman is by connecting access to her sexuality with masculinity through orgasm. The behavioural data show that what pornography means *is* what it does.

So far, opposition to our ordinance centres on the trafficking provision. This means not only that it is difficult to comprehend a group injury in a liberal culture – that what it *means* to be a woman is defined by this and that it is an injury for all women, even if not for all women equally. It is not only that the pornography has got to be accessible, which is the bottom line of virtually every objection to this law. It is also that power, as I said, is when you say something, it is taken for reality.[123] If you talk about rape, it will be agreed that rape is awful. But rape is a conclusion. If a victim describes the facts of a rape, maybe she was asking for it, or enjoyed it, or at least consented to it, or the man might have thought she did, or maybe she had had sex before. It is now agreed that there is something wrong with sexual harassment. But describe what happened to you, and it may be trivial or personal or paranoid, or maybe you should have worn a bra that day. People are against discrimination. But describe the situation of a real woman, and they are not so sure she wasn't just unqualified. In law, all these disjunctions between women's perspective on our injuries and the standards we have to meet go under dignified legal rubrics like burdens of proof, credibility, defences, elements of the crime and so on. These standards all contain a definition of what a woman is in terms of what sex is and the low value placed on us through it. They reduce injuries done to us to authentic expressions of who we are. Our silence is written all over them. So is the pornography.

By contrast, we have as yet encountered comparatively little objection to the coercion, force or assault provisions of our ordinance. I think that's partly because the people who make and approve laws may not yet see what they do as that. They *know* they use the pornography as we have described it in this law, and our law defines that, the reality of pornography, as a harm to women. If they suspect that they might on occasion engage in or benefit from coercion or force or assault, they may think that the victims won't be able to prove it – and they're right. Women who charge men with sexual abuse are not believed. The pornographic view of them is: they want it; they all want it.[124] When women bring charges of sexual assault, motives such as veniality or sexual repression must be invented, because we cannot really have been hurt. Under the trafficking provision, women's lack of credibility cannot be relied upon to negate the harm. There's no woman's story to destroy,[125] no credibility-based decision on what happened. The hearings establish the harm. The definition sets the standard. The grounds of reality definition are authoritatively shifted. Pornography is bigotry, *period*. We are now – *in* the world pornography has decisively defined – having to meet the burden of proving, once and for all, for all of the rape and torture and battery, all of the sexual harassment, all of the child sexual abuse, all of the forced prostitution, *all* of it that the pornography is part of and that is part of the pornography, that the harm *does happen* and that when it happens it looks like this. Which may be why all this evidence never seems to be enough.

E.

It is worth considering what evidence has been enough when other harms involving other purported speech interests have been allowed to be legislated against. By comparison to our trafficking section, analytically similar restrictions have been allowed under the first amendment, with a legislative basis far less massive, detailed, concrete and conclusive. Our statutory language is more ordinary, objective and precise, and covers a harm far narrower than its legislative record substantiates. Under Miller, obscenity was allowed to be made criminal in the name of the 'danger of offending the sensibilities of unwilling recipients, or exposure to juveniles'.[126] Under our law, we have direct evidence of harm, not just a conjectural danger, that unwilling women in considerable numbers are not simply offended in their sensibilities, but are violated in their persons and restricted in their options. Obscenity law also suggests that the applicable standard for legal adequacy in measuring such connections may not be statistical certainty. The Supreme Court has said that it is not their job to resolve empirical uncertainties that underlie state obscenity legislation.[127] Rather, it is for them to determine whether a legislature could reasonably have determined that a connection might exist between the prohibited material and harm of a kind in which the state has legitimate interest. Equality should be such an area. The Supreme Court recently recognized that prevention of sexual exploitation and abuse of children is, in their words, 'a governmental objective of surpassing importance'.[128] This might also be the case for sexual exploitation and abuse of women, although I think a civil remedy is initially more appropriate to the goal of empowering adult women than a criminal prohibition would be.[129]

Other rubrics provide further support for the argument that this law is narrowly tailored to further a legitimate governmental interest consistent with the interests underlying the first amendment. Exceptions to the first amendment – you may have gathered from this – exist. The reason they exist is that the harm done by some speech outweighs its expressive value, if any. In our law, a legislature recognizes that pornography, as defined and made actionable, undermines sex equality. One can

say – and I have – that pornography is a causal factor in

violations of women; one can also say that women will be violated so long as pornography exists; but one can also say simply that pornography violates women. Perhaps this is what the woman had in mind who testified at our hearings that whether or not pornography causes violent acts to be perpetrated against some women is not her only issue: 'Porn is already a violent act against women. It is our mothers, our daughters, our sisters, and our wives that are for sale for pocket change at the newsstands in this country.'[130] Chaplinsky v New Hampshire recognizes the ability to restrict as 'fighting words' speech which, 'by [its] very utterance inflicts injury'.[131] Perhaps the only reason that pornography has not been 'fighting words' – in the sense of words which by their utterance tend to incite immediate breach of the peace – is that women have seldom fought back, yet.[132]

Some concerns close to those of this ordinance underlie group libel laws, although the differences are equally important. In group libel law, as Justice Frankfurter's opinion in Beauharnais illustrates, it has been understood that individuals' treatment and alternatives in life may depend as much on the reputation of the group to which such a person belongs as on their own merit.[133] Not even a partial analogy can be made to group libel doctrine without examining the point made by Justice Brandeis,[134] and recently underlined by Larry Tribe:[135] would more speech, rather than less, remedy the harm? In the end the answer may be yes, but not under the abstract system of free speech, which only enhances the power of the pornographers while doing nothing substantively to guarantee the free speech of women, for which we need civil equality. The situation in which women presently find themselves with respect to the pornography is one in which more *pornography* is inconsistent with rectifying or even counterbalancing its damage through speech, because so long as the pornography exists in the way it does there *will not be more speech by women*. Pornography strips and devastates women of credibility, from our accounts of sexual assault to our everyday reality of sexual subordination. We are deauthoritized and reduced and devalidated and silenced. Silenced here means that the purposes of the first amendment, premised upon conditions presumed and promoted by protecting free speech, do not pertain to women because they are not our conditions. Consider them: individual self-fulfilment[136] – how does pornography promote our individual self-fulfilment? How does sexual inequality even permit it? Even if she can form words, who listens to a woman **483** with a penis in her mouth? Facilitating consensus – to the extent pornography does so, it does so one-sidedly by silencing protest over the injustice of sexual subordination. Participation in civic life – central to Professor Meiklejohn's theory[137] – how does pornography enhance women's participation in civic life? Anyone who cannot walk down the street or even lie down in her own bed without keeping her eyes cast down and her body clenched against assault is unlikely to have much to say about the issues of the day, still less will she become Tolstoy. Facilitating change[138] – *this law* facilitates the change the existing first amendment theory has been used to throttle. Any system of freedom of expression that does not address a problem where the free speech of men silences the free speech of women, a real conflict between speech interests as well as between people, is not serious about securing freedom of expression in this country.[139]

For those of you who still think pornography is only an idea, consider the possibility that obscenity law got one thing right. Pornography is more act-like than thought-like. The fact that pornography, in a feminist view, furthers the idea of the sexual inferiority of women, which is a political idea, doesn't make the pornography itself into a political idea. One can express the idea a practice embodies. That does not make that practice into an idea. Segregation expresses the idea of the inferiority of one group to another on the basis of race. That does not make segregation an idea. A sign that says 'Whites Only' is only words. Is it therefore protected by the first amendment? Is it not an act, a practice, of segregation because of the inseparability of what it means from what it does?[140] *Law* is only words.

The issue here is whether the fact that the central link in the cycle of abuse that I have connected is words and pictures will immunize that entire cycle, about which we cannot do anything without doing something about the pornography. As Justice Stewart said in Ginsberg: 'When expression occurs in a setting where the capacity to make a choice is absent, government regulation of that expression may coexist with and *even implement* first amendment guarantees.'[141] I would even go so far as to say that the pattern of evidence we have closely approaches Justice Douglas's requirement that 'freedom of expression can be suppressed if, and to the extent that, it is so closely brigaded with illegal action as to be an inseparable part of it'.[142] Those of you who have been trying to separate the acts from the speech –

that's an act, that's an act, there's a law against that act, regulate that act, don't touch the speech – *notice here* that the fact that the acts involved are illegal doesn't mean that the speech that is 'brigaded with' it, *cannot* be regulated. It is when it *can* be.[143]

I take one of two penultimate points from Andrea Dworkin, who has often said that pornography is not speech for women, it is the silence of women.[144] Remember the mouth taped, the woman gagged, 'Smile, I can get a lot of money for that.' The smile is not her expression. It is her silence, and it is not her expression not because it didn't happen, but because it *did* happen. The screams of the women in pornography are silence, like Kitty Genovese's screams, whose plight was misinterpreted by some onlookers as a lovers' quarrel. The flat expressionless voice of the woman in the New Bedford gang-rape, testifying, is the silence of women. She was raped as men cheered and watched like they do in and with the pornography. When women resist and men say, 'Like this you stupid bitch, here is how to do it' and shove their faces into the pornography,[145] this 'truth of sex'[146] is the silence of women. When they say, 'If you love me, you'll try,'[147] the enjoyment we fake, the enjoyment we learn, is silence. Women who submit because there is more dignity in it than in losing the fight over and over [148] live in silence. Having to sleep with your publisher or director to get access to what men call speech is silence. Being humiliated on the basis of your appearance, whether by approval or disapproval, because you have to look a certain way for a certain job, whether you get the job or not, is silence. The absence of a woman's voice, everywhere that it cannot be heard, is silence. And anyone who thinks that what women say in pornography is women's speech – the 'Fuck me, do it to me, harder,' all of that – has never heard the sound of a woman's voice.[149]

The most basic assumption underlying first amendment adjudication is that, socially, speech is free. The first amendment says Congress shall not abridge the freedom of speech.[150] Free speech, get it, *exists*. Those who wrote the first amendment *had* speech – they wrote the Constitution. *Their* problem was to keep it free from the only power that realistically threatened it: the federal government. They designed the first amendment to prevent government from constraining that which if unconstrained by government was free, meaning *accessible to them*. At the same time, we can't tell much about the intent of the framers with regard to the question of women's speech, because I don't think we crossed their minds. It 485 is consistent with this analysis that their posture to freedom of speech tends to presuppose that whole segments of the population are not systematically silenced, socially, prior to government action. If everyone's power were equal to theirs, if this were a non-hierarchical society, that might make sense. But the place of pornography in the inequality of the sexes makes the assumption of equal power untrue.

This is a hard question. It involves risks. Classically, opposition to censorship has involved keeping government off the backs of other people. The risks that it will be misused have to be measured against the risks of the status quo. Women will never have that dignity, security, compensation that is the promise of equality so long as the pornography exists as it does now. The situation of women suggests that the urgent issue of our freedom of speech is not primarily the avoidance of state intervention as such, but getting affirmative access to speech for those to whom it has been denied.

Notes

1. See Levi, *An Introduction to Legal Reasoning*, 15 U. Chi. L. Rev. 501 (1948).
2. See, e.g., D. Bell, *Race, Racism and American Law*, 1–85 (1972).
3. 347 US 483 (1954).
4. On my analysis, the combined effect of Texas Dep't of Community Affairs vs Burdine, 450 US 248 (1981) and Furnco Constr. Corp. vs Waters, 438 US 567 (1978), both purporting to follow the standard first announced in McDonnell Douglas Corp. vs Green, 411 US 792 (1973), is that anyone who has been discriminated against is assumed exceptional and living in that sex-discrimination-free universe that the burdens of proof are allocated to presuppose. The difficulty arises in the attempt to assume neither that discrimination because of sex exists nor that it does not exist in assessing facts such as those in *Burdine*, in which two persons are equally qualified, the man gets the job, and the woman sues. The Fifth Circuit in *Burdine* had required the employer to prove that the man who got the job was more qualified, but its decision was reversed. Facing the impossibility of neutrality here makes one wonder if there is any difference between non-discrimination and affirmative action.
5. Selected publications are listed from the large body of work that exists.
   On rape: S. Brownmiller, Against Our Will: Men, Women and Rape (1975); L. Clark & D. Lewis, Rape: The Price of Coercive Sexuality (1977); N. Gager & C. Schurr, Sexual Assault: Confronting Rape in America (1976); A. Medea & K. Thompson, Against Rape (1974); D. Russell, Rape in Marriage (1982); D. Russell, The Politics of Rape (1975); Burt, *Cultural Myths and Supports for Rape*, 38

J. Personality & Soc. Psychology 219 (1980); Frieze, *Investigating the Causes and Consequences of Marital Rape*, 8 Signs: J. Women Culture & Soc'y 532 (1983); LaFree, *Male Power and Female Victimization: Towards a Theory of Interracial Rape*, 88 Am. J. Soc. 311 (1982); Russell & Howell, *The Prevalence of Rape in the United States Revisited*, 8 Signs: J. Women Culture & Soc'y 688 (1983).

On battery: R. Dobash & R. Dobash, Violence Against Wives: A Case Against the Patriarchy (1979); R. Langley & R. Levy, Wife Beating: The Silent Crisis (1977); D. Martin, Battered Wives (rev. ed. 1981); S. Steinmetz, The Cycle of Violence: Assertive, Aggressive, and Abusive Family Interaction (1977)(referenced in E. Stanko, *infra* note 20, at 73); L. Walker, The Battered Woman (1979); Stark, Flitcraft & Frazier, *Medicine and Patriarchal Violence: The Social Construction of a 'Private' Event*, 3 Int'l J. Health Services 461 (1979).

On sexual harassment: C. MacKinnon, Sexual Harassment of Working Women: A Case of Sex Discrimination (1979); Benson & Thompson, *Sexual Harassment on a University Campus: The Confluence of Authority Relations, Sexual Interest and Gender Stratification*, 29 Soc. Probs. 236 (1982); Crocker & Simon, *Sexual Harassment in Education*, 10 Cap. UL Rev. 3 (1981); US Merit Systems Protection Board, Sexual Harassment in the Federal Workplace: Is It a Problem? (1981).

On incest and child sexual abuse: L. Armstrong, Kiss Daddy Goodnight (1978); K. Brady, Father's Days: A True Story of Incest (1979); A. Burgess, N. Groth, L. Holmstrom & S. Sgroi, Sexual Assault of Children and Adolescents (1978); S. Butler, Conspiracy of Silence: The Trauma of Incest (1978); D. Finkelhor, Child Sexual Abuse: New Theory and Research (1984); D. Finkelhor, Sexually Victimized Children (1979); J. Herman, Father-Daughter Incest (1981); F. Rush, The Best-Kept Secret: Sexual Abuse of Children (1980); D. Russell, The Incestuous Abuse of Females (manuscript in progress); Jaffe, Dynneson & TenBensel, *Sexual Abuse: An Epidemiological Study*, 6 Am. J. Diseases Children 689 (1975); Russell, *The Prevalence and Seriousness of Incestuous Abuse: Stepfathers vs Biological Fathers*, 8 Child Abuse & Neglect: The Int. J. 15 (1984); Russell, *The Incidence and Prevalence of Intrafamilial and Extrafamilial Sexual Abuse of Female Children*, 7 Child Abuse & Neglect: The Int. J. 2 (1983).

On prostitution: K. Barry, Female Sexual Slavery (1979); J. James, The Politics of Prostitution (2d ed. 1975); Griffin, *Wives, Hookers and the Law: The Case for Decriminalizing Prostitution*, 10 Student Law. 13 (1982); James & Meyerding, *Early Sexual Experience as a Factor in Prostitution*, 7 Archives of Sexual Behav. 31 (1977); *Report of Jean Fernand-Laurent, Special Rapporteur on the Suppression of the Traffic in Persons and the Exploitation of the Prostitution of Others* (a United Nations report), in International Feminism: Networking Against Female Sexual Slavery 130 (K. Barry, C. Bunch, S. Castley eds. 1984)(Report of the Global Feminist Workshop to Organize Against Traffic in Women, Rotterdam, Neth., Apr. 6–15, 1983).

On pornography: A. Dworkin, Pornography: Men Possessing Women (1981); L. Lovelace & M. McGrady, Ordeal (1980); P. Bogdanovich, The Killing of the Unicorn: Dorothy Stratten, **487**

1960–1980 (1984); Take Back the Night: Women on Pornography (L. Lederer ed. 1980); Donnerstein, *Pornography: Its Effects on Violence Against Women*, in Pornography and Sexual Aggression (N. Malamuth & E. Donnerstein eds. 1984); Langelan, *The Political Economy of Pornography*, Aegis: Mag. on Ending Violence Against Women 5 (1981); Leidholdt, *Where Pornography Meets Fascism*, Women's International News (WIN), March 15, 1983, at 18; D. Linz, E. Donnerstein & S. Penrod, The Effects of Long-Term Exposure to Filmed Violence Against Women (March 22, 1984) (unpublished manuscript).

See generally: J. Long & P. Schwartz, Sexual Scripts: The Social Construction of Female Sexuality (1976); E. Morgan, The Erotization of Male Dominance/Female Submission (1975); D. Russell, Sexual Exploitation: Rape, Child Sexual Abuse & Workplace Harassment (1984); D. Russell & N. Van de Ven, Crimes Against Women: Proceedings of the International Tribunal (1976); E. Schur, Labeling Women Deviant: Gender, Stigma, and Social Control (1984); Phelps, *Female Sexual Alienation*, in Women: A Feminist Perspective 16 (J. Freeman ed. 1975); Rich, *Compulsory Heterosexuality and Lesbian Existence*, 5 Signs: J. Women Culture & Soc'y 4 (1980); E. Stanko, No Complaints: Silencing Male Violence to Women (1984)(unpublished manuscript).

6. See M. Amir, Patterns in Forcible Rape 229–52 (1971); See also N. Gager & C. Schurr, Sexual Assault: Confronting Rape in America (1976); D. Russell, Sexual Exploitation: supra note 5.

7. See D. Russell, *The Prevalence of Rape in the United States Revisited*, 8, Signs: J. Women Culture & Soc'y, 689 (1983).

8. See 'sexual harassment' references, *supra* note 5.

9. US Merit Systems Protection Board, *supra* note 5.

10. See 'battery' references, *supra* note 5.

11. See 'child sexual abuse' references, *supra* note 5, especially D. Russell, *The Incidence and Prevalence of Intrafamilial and Extrafamilial Sexual Abuse of Female Children*, 7 Child Abuse and Neglect: The Int. 2, 1983.

12. A Rich, *Cartographies of Silence*, in The Dream of a Common Language 16, 17 (1978).

13. See F. Rush, The Best-Kept Secret: Sexual Abuse of Children (1980). See also J. Masson, The Assault on Truth: Freud's Suppression of the Seduction Theory, (1983).

14. See D. Finkelhor, Child Sexual Abuse: Theory and Research (1984); D. Lockwood, Prison Sexual Violence 117 (1980):

> For the player [the pimp-type prison rapist] to operate his game, however, he must 'feminize' his object of interest. We must remember that prisoners consider queens to be women, not men. As a consequence, the one who dominates the queen is a 'man'. Players live according to norms that place men who play female roles in submissive positions ... The happy conclusion ... is for the target to become a 'girl' under his domination, a receptacle for his penis, and a female companion to accentuate his masculinity.

See also J. Timmerman, Prisoner without a Name, Cell without a Number (1981).

15. See Employment Standards Admin., US Dep't of Labor, Handbook on Women Workers (1975); US Dep't of Labor, Women's Bureau Bulletin 297 (1975 and 1982 update).
16. This figure was calculated at my request by D. Russell on the random sample data base discussed in D. Russell, Rape in Marriage (1982). The figure includes all the forms of rape or other sexual abuse or harassment surveyed, non-contact as well as contact, from gang-rape by strangers to obscene phone calls, unwanted sexual advances on the street, unwelcome requests to pose for pornography, and subjection to 'Peeping Toms' and sexual exhibitionists.
17. Foucault, *The West and the Truth of Sex*, 20 Sub-Stance 5 (1978).
18. This became a lot clearer to me after reading Baldwin, *The Sexuality of Inequality: The Minneapolis Pornography Ordinance*, 2 L. & Inequality: J. Theory & Practice 629 (1984). This paragraph is directly indebted to her insight and language there.
19. A. Dworkin, Pornography: Men Possessing Women (1981).
20. For a fuller development of this critique, see my discussion in MacKinnon, *Not a Moral Issue*, 2 Yale Rev. L. & Pol'y 321 (1984). See Chapter 20.
21. Miller v California, 413 US 15, 24 (1973).
22. See The Report of the Presidential Commission on Obscenity and Pornography (1970).
23. For the specific statutory language, see Chapter 18.
24. See, e.g., G. Steinem, *Erotica v Pornography*, in Outrageous Acts and Everyday Rebellions 219 (1983).
25. See Indianapolis Ordinance, Chapter 18, note 96.
26. See C. MacKinnon, Sexual Harassment of Working Women 101–41 (1979).
27. For a lucid discussion of subordination, see Dworkin, *Against the Male Flood: Censorship, Pornography, and Equality*, 8 Harv. Women's L. J. (1985). See Chapter 20.
28. If this part stood alone, it would along with its support, among other things, have to be equally imposed – an interesting requirement for an equality law, but arguably met by this one. See Carey v Brown, 447 US 455 (1980); Police Department of Chicago v Mosley, 408 US 92 (1972); Karst, *Equality as a Central Principle in the First Amendment*, 43 U. Chi. L. Rev. 20 (1975).
29. See KPNX Broadcasting Co. v Arizona Superior Court, 459 US 1302 (1982)(Rehnquist as Circuit Justice denied application to stay Arizona judge's order that those involved with heavily covered criminal trial avoid direct contact with press; mere potential confusion from unrestrained contact with press held to justify order); New York v Ferber, 458 US 747 (1982)(child pornography, defined as promoting sexual performance by a child, can be criminally banned as a form of child abuse); FCC v Pacifica Found., 438 US 726 (1978)('indecent' but not obscene radio broadcasts may be regulated by FCC through licensing); Young v American Mini

Theatres, Inc., 427 US 50 (1976)(exhibition of sexually explicit 'adult movies' may be restricted through zoning ordinances); Gertz v Robert Welch, Inc., 418 US 323, 347 (1974)(state statute may allow private persons to recover for libel without proving actual malice so long as liability is not found without fault); Pittsburgh Press Co. v Human Relations Comm'n, 413 US 376 (1973)(sex-designated help-wanted columns conceived as commercial speech may be prohibited under local sex discrimination ordinance); Miller v California, 413 US 15, 18 (1973)(obscenity unprotected by first amendment in case in which it was 'thrust by aggressive sales action upon unwilling [viewers] . . .'); Red Lion Broadcasting Co. v FCC, 395 US, 367 387 (1969)(FCC may require broadcasters to allow reply time to vindicate speech interests of the public: 'The right of free speech of a broadcaster, the user of a sound truck, or any other individual does not embrace a right to snuff out the free speech of others.'); Ginzburg v United States, 383 US 463, 470 (1966)(upholding conviction for mailing obscene material on 'pandering' theory: '[T]he purveyor's sole emphasis [is] on the sexually provocative aspects of his publications.'); Roth v United States, 354 US 476, 487 (1957)(federal obscenity statute found valid; obscene defined as 'material which deals with sex in a manner appealing to prurient interest'); Beauharnais v Illinois, 343 US 250 (1952)(upholding group libel statute); Chaplinsky v New Hampshire, 315 US 568 (1942)(a state statute outlawing 'fighting words' likely to cause a breach of peace is not unconstitutional under first amendment); Near v Minnesota, 283 US 697 (1931)(Minnesota statute permitting prior restraint of publishers who regularly engage in publication of defamatory material held unconstitutional; press freedom outweighs prior restraints in all but exceptional cases, i.e. national security or obscenity);[for one such exceptional case, see United States v Progressive, Inc., 486 F. Supp. 5 (W.D. Wis. 1979)(prior restraint allowed against publication of information on how to make hydrogen bomb partially under 'troop movements' exception)]; Schenck v United States, 249 US 47, 52 (1919)('clear and present dangers' excepted from first amendment: 'The most stringent protection of free speech would not protect a man in falsely shouting fire in a theatre and causing a panic.').

30. See Young v American Mini Theatres, Inc., 427 US 50 (1976); Pittsburgh Press Co v Human Relations Comm'n, 413 US 376 (1973); Konigsberg v State Bar of California, 366 US 36, 49–51 (1961).

31. I stand by this statement not withstanding American Booksellers, Inc. v Hudnut, 11 Media L. Rep. 1105 (S.D. Ind. Nov. 19, 1984) overturning the Indianapolis Ordinance. In the decision there, the ordinance is repeatedly misquoted, the misquotations underscored to illustrate its legal errors. Arguments not made in support of the law are invented and attributed to the city and found legally inadequate. Evidence of harm before the legislature is given no weight at all, while purportedly being undisturbed, as an absolutist approach is implicitly adopted, unlike any existing Supreme Court

precedent. To the extent existing law overlaps with the ordinance, even it would be invalidated under this ruling. And clear law on sex equality is flatly misstated. The opinion permits a ludicrous suit by mostly legitimate trade publishers, parties whose interests are at most tenuously and remotely implicated under the ordinance, to test a law that directly and importantly would affect others, such as pornographers and their victims. In my opinion, the decision is also far more permissive towards racism than would be allowed in a concrete case even under existing law, and it displays blame-the-victim misogyny: 'Adult women generally have the capacity to protect themselves from participating in and being personally victimized by pornography . . .' *Id.* at 1119.

32. See, e.g., Title IX of the Educ. amends. of 1972, 20 USC 1681–1686 (1972); Equal Pay Act, 29 USC 206(d) (1963); Title VII of the Civil Rights Act of 1964, 42 USC 2000e to 2000e–17 (1976). Many states have equal rights amendments to their constitutions. See Brown & Freedman, *Equal Rights Amendment: Growing Impact on the States.* 1 Women L. Rep. 1.63, 1.63–1.64 (1974); many states and cities, including Minneapolis and Indianapolis, prohibit discrimination on the basis of sex. See also Roberts v United States Jaycees, 104 S. Ct. 3244 (1984)(recently recognizing that sex equality is a compelling state interest); Frontiero v Richardson, 411 US 677 (1973); Reed v Reed, 404 US 71 (1971); US Const. amend. XIV.

33. See City of Los Angeles v Manhart, 435 US 702, 711 (1978)(City water department's pension plan was found discriminatory in its 'treatment of a person in a manner which but for that person's sex would be different.'). See also Orr v Orr, 440 US 268 (1979); Barnes v Costle, 561 F.2d 983 (D.C. Cir. 1977).

34. See Plessy v Ferguson, 163 US at 551; Wechsler, *Toward Neutral Principles of Constitutional Law*, 73 Harv. L. Rev. 1 (1959) at 33.

35. In each case cited *supra* note 29 (except *Near*), a recognized harm was held to be more important than the speech interest also at stake. The Supreme Court has also recognized, if not always in holdings, that the right to privacy or fair trial can outweigh the right to freedom of the press. See Zacchini v Scripps-Howard Broadcasting Co., 433 US 562 (1977)(performer has proprietary interest in his act that outweighs press interest in publishing it); Nebraska Press Ass'n v Stuart, 427 US 539 (1976)(restraint on press unconstitutional); Cox Broadcasting Corp. v Cohn, 420 US 469, 491 (1975)(no civil liability for privacy violations against broadcaster for truthfully publishing court records in which daughter of plaintiff was rape victim, but: 'In this sphere of collision between claims of privacy and those of the free press, the interests on both sides are plainly rooted in the traditions and significant concerns of our society.'); Time, Inc. v Hill, 385 US 374 (1967)(magazine has no liability for inaccurate portrayal of private life unless knowingly or recklessly false). But see KPNX Broadcasting Co., 459 US 1302 (1982)(Rehnquist, J., as Circuit Justice denying stay on limitations in finding that trial judge exercised his discretion in seeking prior restraints to protect defendant's right to a fair trial). See also Globe **491**

Newspaper Co. v Superior Court, 457 US 596 (1982)(state may not require exclusion of press and public from courtroom during testimony of minor victim of sex offence); Richmond Newspapers, Inc. v Virginia, 448 US 555 (1980).

The harm of defamatory speech to personal reputation is also the reason libel is actionable notwithstanding first amendment protections of speech. See, e.g., Gertz v Robert Welch, Inc., 418 US 323 (1974); '[D]efamation has long been regarded as a form of "psychic mayhem", not very different in kind, and in some ways more wounding, than physical mutilation.' L. Tribe, American Constitutional Law 576–77 (1978) at 649 (discussing issues raised by *Gertz*). In Los Angeles v Taxpayers for Vincent, 104 S. Ct. 2118 (1984), the City of Los Angeles' *aesthetic* interests outweighed a political candidate's speech right to post signs on public property.

36. Under the standard in *Miller*, 413 US 15 (1973), obscenity prohibits materials that, inter alia, are 'patently offensive' and appeal to the 'prurient interest', 413 US at 24, terms with no apparent determinate meaning. Offensiveness is subjective. Prurience is a code word for that which produces sexual arousal. See Schauer, *Response: Pornography and the First Amendment*, 40 U. Pitt. L. Rev. 605, 607 (1979). See also Justice Brennan's discussion of the vagueness of terms like 'lewd' and 'ultimate', in Paris Adult Theatre I, 413 US at 86 (Brennan, J., dissenting). 'Community standards', also part of the *Miller* test, is a standard that is open-ended by design. In FCC v Pacifica Found., 438 US 726 (1978), the Supreme Court allowed a regulatory body to construe the meaning of the term 'indecent', which represents a social value judgement. In *Ferber*, 458 US 747 (1982), the Supreme Court did not seem at all bothered by the fact that 'lewd', as in 'lewd exhibition of the genitals' in the statute's definition of sexual performance, was statutorily undefined, 458 US at 765. *Beauharnais*, 343 US 250 (1952), sustained a law that prohibited the publishing, selling, or exhibiting in any public place of any publication that 'portrays depravity, criminality, unchastity, or lack of virtue of a class of citizens of any race, color, creed or religion . . .' 343 US at 251. Although there has been doubt cast on the vitality of *Beauharnais*, see, e.g., Collin v Smith, 578 F.2d 1197, 1205 (7th Cir. 1978), '*Beauharnais* has never been overruled or formally limited in any way.' Smith v Collin, 436 US 953 (1978)(Blackmun J., joined by Rehnquist, J., dissenting from denial of stay of Court of Appeals order).

37. Most obscenity laws provide criminal sanctions, with the appropriate procedural requirements. *Roth*, 354 US at 478 n.1; *Miller*, 413 US at 16 n.1. However, the injunction proceeding in *Paris Adult Theatre 1*, 413 US 49 (1973), was civil, and the statutory scheme discussed in Freedman v Maryland, 380 US 51 (1964)(under which prior restraints imposed by a censorship board were legal only if certain procedural requirements were met) was non-criminal. Of course, all a civil injunction can do under our ordinance is stop future profit-making or assault. A potential award of civil damages under our ordinance is not a negligible sanction; it is designed to

deter victimization, but differently than potential incarceration does. A major purpose of pornography is to make money. Depriving the pornographers of profits by empowering those whom they exploit to make them, directly counteracts one reason pornographers engage in the exploitation at all, in a way that potential incarceration does not. Another not inconsiderable benefit of a civil rather than criminal approach to pornography is that criminal prohibitions, as well as eroticizing that which they prohibit, tend to create underground markets wherein the prohibited commodity is sold at inflated prices, passed hand to hand in secret settings, and elevated in value. If it is not possible to make or use pornography as it now is without exploiting its victims as they are exploited now, a civil prohibition would create no underground. This approach does not solve the problems of terror and intimidation that keep victims from suing, or give them resources for suit. It does define who is hurt directly (versus the amorphous 'community' that is considered hurt on the criminal side), gives the victims (and lawyers) the incentive of a potential civil recovery, and leaves control over the legal actions as much as possible in the hands of the victims rather than the state. For further views on civil as opposed to criminal approaches to this area, see the opinions of Justice Stevens in FCC v Pacifica Found., 438 US 726 (1978); Young v American Mini Theatres, Inc., 427 US 50 (1976); and most fully, his dissent in Smith v United States, 431 US 291, 317 (1977)(criticizing community standards in a criminal context, but approving their 'flexibility [as] a desirable feature of a civil rule designed to protect the individual's right to select the kind of environment in which he wants to live'). Some who oppose or are critical of obscenity restrictions have found first adjudicating pornographic materials obscene in a civil or administrative proceeding preferable. See Miller v California, 413 US 15, 41 (1973)(Douglas, J., dissenting); Z. Chafee, 1 Government and Mass Communications 228–31 (1947); Lockhart, *Escape from the Chill of Uncertainty: Explicit Sex and the First Amendment*, 9 Ga. L. Rev. 533, 569–86 (1975); Lockhart & McClure, *Censorship of Obscenity*, 45 Minn. L. Rev. 5, 105–07 (1960); ACLU, Policy No. 4(c)(2)(Feb. 11, 1970)(civil proceeding seen as the least restrictive method of censorship).

38. The harm of obscenity recognized in *Miller*, 413 US 15 (1973), was the 'danger of offending the sensibilities of unwilling recipients or of exposure to juveniles'. 413 US at 19. This statement was adduced from the Presidential Commission on Obscenity finding that it could not be concluded that obscenity causes harm. '[The] Commission cannot conclude that exposure to erotic materials is a factor in the causation of sex crime or sex delinquency.' Report of the Presidential Commission on Obscenity and Pornography 27 (1970). The harm in FCC v Pacifica Found., 438 US 726 (1978), was the possible overhearing of indecent speech by children, since radio intrudes into the home. 438 US at 748–50. In United States v Orito, 413 US 139, 143 (1973), a federal ban on interstate transportation of obscene materials for private use was sustained on 'a legislatively determined risk of ultimate exposure to juveniles or to the public'. Throughout, **493**

exposure of juveniles to obscenity is assumed to be a risk, but the harm that exposure does per se is unspecified, not to say unsubstantiated and not in evidence. The harm recognized in *Ferber*, 458 US 747 (1982), appears to be that done to a minor male be being seen having sex. The prosecuted film depicted two boys masturbating, and the Court concluded that 'a permanent record of children's participation and the harm to the child is exacerbated by [its] circulation'. 458 US at 759. This same harm is at times characterized by the Court as 'psychological', *id.* at 759 n.10, but is otherwise unspecified and in evidence only in the form of the film. In *Chaplinsky*, 315 US 568 (1942), the harm apparently combined the offence given by the speech itself with the risk of imminent breach of the peace occasioned by its utterance. As to group libel, the harm of the racist leaflet to the group as a whole recognized in *Beauharnais*, 343 US 250 (1952), was *inferred* from observed racial inequality and racial unrest. 343 US at 258–61.

39. See Galloway & Thornton, *Crackdown on Pornography – A No-Win Battle*, US News & World Rep., June 4, 1984, at 84; see also Cook, *The X-Rated Economy*, Forbes, Sept. 18, 1978, at 81 ($4 billion per year); Langelan, *The Political Economy of Pornography*, Aegis: Mag. on Ending Violence Against Women 5 (1981)($7 billion per year); *The Place of Pornography*, Harper's, Nov. 1984, at 31 ($7 billion per year).

40. Flags, seen as symbols for the nation rather than mere pieces of brightly-coloured cloth or even as personal property, receive special solicitude by legislatures and courts, both as to the patriotic value of their protection and the expressive value of their desecration. See, e.g., Spence v Washington, 418 US 405 (1974); Street v New York, 394 US 576 (1969). I have not considered the applicability of this line of cases here, in light of my view that women in pornography are not simply symbols of all women but also *are* women. Of course, under male supremacy, each woman represents all women to one degree or another, whether in pornography or in bed or walking down the street, because of the stereotyping intrinsic to gender inequality. But that does not mean that, in a feminist perspective, each woman, including those in pornography, can be treated solely in terms of her representative or symbolic qualities, as if she is not at the same time alive and human. An underlying issue has to do with the extent to which women's bodies must be freely available as vocabulary and imagery for the expression of others, such that once they are so converted, whatever the means, women retain no rights in their use or abuse, in the face of evidence of the harm from such expropriation and exposure ranging from the individual so used to anonymous women subsequently used or treated or seen in light of their availability for such use. (Given the extent to which women now must be men's speech, one might rather be a flag.)

41. *Ferber*, 458 US 747 (1982).

42. II *Hearings* 75 (testimony of a named former prostitute).

43. L. Lovelace and M. McGrady, *Ordeal* (1980).

44. As of September, 1978, *Deep Throat* had grossed a known $50 million worldwide. See Cook, *supra* note 39. Many of its profits are

untraceable. The film has also recently been made into a home video cassette.

45. Priscilla Alexander, co-ordinator for the National Organization for Women's Task Force on Prostitution, said that she was told this by a woman pornography model. Panel on Pornography, National Association of Women and the Law, Los Angeles, California, April 1, 1984.

46. 'In the movies known as snuff films, victims sometimes are actually murdered.' 130 Cong. Rec. S13192 (daily ed. Oct. 3, 1984)(statement of Senator Specter introducing the Pornography Victims Protection Act). Information on the subject is understandably hard to get. See People v Douglas, Felony Complaint No. NF 8300382 (Municipal Court, Orange County, Cal. Aug. 5, 1983); 'Slain Teens Needed Jobs, Tried Porn' and 'Two Accused of Murder in "Snuff Films"', Oakland Tribune, Aug. 6, 1983 (on file with Harvard Civil Rights-Civil Liberties Law Review); L. Smith, The Chicken Hawks (1975)(unpublished manuscript)(on file with Harvard Civil Rights-Civil Liberties Law Review).

47. '[W]e were all introduced to prostitution through pornography, there were no exceptions in our group, and we were all under 18 . . . There were stacks of films all over the house, which my pimp used to blackmail people with.' II *Hearings* 70, 79 (testimony of a named former prostitute). Kathleen Barry, author of Female Sexual Slavery (1979), refers to 'season[ing]' to prostitution by 'blackmailing the victim by threatening to send [photographs of coerced sex] to her family, and selling them to the pornographers for mass production.' 1 *Hearings* 59 (letter of Kathleen Barry). A worker with adolescent prostitutes reports:

> These rapes are often either taped or have photographs taken of the event. The young woman when she tries to escape or leaves is told that either she continues in her involvement in prostitution or those pictures will be sent to her parents, will be sent to the juvenile court, will be used against her. And out of fear she will continue her involvement in prostitution.

III *Hearings* 77 (testimony of Sue Santa).

48. Speech by Andrea Dworkin, in Toronto, Canada (Feb. 1984)(account told to Ms. Dworkin), reprinted in Healthsharing, Summer 1984, at 25.

49. L. Marciano, Panel on Pornography, Stanford University (Apr. 2, 1982).

50. 'When *Deep Throat* was released, we [prostitutes] experienced men joking and demanding oral sex.' II *Hearings* 74 (testimony of a named former prostitute). Increasing reports of throat rape in emergency rooms followed the exhibition of *Deep Throat*. One woman told Flora Colao, CSW, an emergency room nurse in New York City at the time, that the men who raped her said, as she was becoming unconscious, 'Let's deep throat her before she passes out.' I *Hearings* 60 (Exhibit 13 [letter], Nov. 10, 1983). One woman wrote the Minneapolis City Council the day after Ms Marciano's **495**

testimony before it, in a letter typical of the accounts received by Ms Marciano since the publication of *Ordeal*:

> I read about Linda Lovelace in our morning paper which said that she testified for women's civil rights. I only hope that she is able to undo some of the terrible damage that was done by making her movie. Those years started days of misery for me and a lot of my friends. Linda was so convincing that she enjoyed what she was doing that our husbands began to think they were cheated in life with us upper-middle-class wives. 'I'm not satisfied!' 'You don't know how to be a woman.' And every young girl in town was brainwashed to show our husbands that they could be a better 'Linda Lovelace' than the wife they had at home. I saw a lot of heartbreaks, nervous breakdowns to women that were being coerced in sex – many tranquilizers taken because they had to keep up with the times or else. Being forced to do something they don't enjoy or 'someone else will gladly go out with me!' I even saw a business fail because the husband was so preoccupied with this type of sex. Why do you think women's lib evolved – women became tired of being exploited, brainwashed and now Linda says she didn't enjoy it. It's too late for us 50-year-olds but help the young girls not to wreck their lives by letting boyfriends and husbands force them to be recepticals [sic] instead of cherished wives . . .

Letter from 'a bitter wife' to the Minneapolis City Council (Dec. 14, 1983).

51. The credibility of the pornography, as compared with that of the women in it, is underlined by the following: Vanessa Williams, formerly Miss America, lost her title when pornographic pictures of her were published by *Penthouse*. Ms Williams says she posed for the sexually explicit pictures under the representation that they were for private use, at most for silhouettes, and that she did not consent to their publication. Brian DePalma, director of *Dressed to Kill* and *Body Double*, both 'splatter' films of sexualized violence against women, who should know what it takes for a director to create an image of an interaction so that it *looks* like sex, was interviewed concerning the Williams episode. Asked about her version of the events, DePalma said: 'I believed her until I saw the pictures.' *'Double' Trouble: Brian DePalma Interviewed by Marcia Pally*. 20 Film Comment, Sept.–Oct. 1984, at 13, 16.

52. I am indebted for this argument's development to Baldwin, *Pornography: More Than a Fantasy*, The Hennepin Lawyer. Mar.–Apr. 1984, at 8, 25.

53. This question and the paragraph that follows draw directly on Andrea Dworkin's speech, *supra* note 48.

54. I *Hearings* 56.

55. The National Task Force on Child Pornography, *Let's Protect Our Children* 17 (1983)(on file with Harvard Civil Rights-Civil Liberties Law Review).

56. 458 US 747 (1982).

57. *Id*. at 759

58. *Id*. at 747

59. *Id.* at 761
60. *Id.*
61. *Id.* at 763–64
62. The harm of child pornography cannot be stopped effectively without also addressing the pornography of adult women. Adult pornography has been found commonly used 'to show, teach or induce the children into the sexual activity or pornographic modeling' by child sex rings. See Burgess, Hartman, McCausland & Powers, *Response Patterns in Children and Adolescents Exploited Through Sex Rings and Pornography*, 141 Am. J. Psychiatry 656, 657–58 (1984). Given what is done in pornography, it is even more difficult than usual to tell the difference between adults and children. Adult women are infantilized in pornography; children are dressed and used as if they were adult women. The resulting materials are then used against both, and target both for abuse relatively interchangeably. For instance, the 'shaved pussy' genre, in which adult women's genitals are made to resemble those of young girls, converges with the 'Lolita' or 'cherry tarts' genre, in which young girls are presented resembling the pornographers' image of adult female sexuality. It also seems worth observing that a law that has the abuse disappear legally when its victims get one day older is difficult to administer effectively.
63. 'The forcing of pornography on any woman, man, child or transsexual in any place of employment, in education, in a home, or in any public place.' Code of Indianapolis and Marion County, *supra* note 25. See Chapter 21, note 96.

    Section 16–17(a) states: 'A complaint charging that any person has engaged in or is engaging in a discriminatory practice . . . may be filed . . . in any of the following circumstances: . . . (7) in the case of forcing pornography on a person, against the perpetrator(s) and/ or institution.'
64. III *Hearings* 71, 76 (testimony of Charlotte K. & Sue Santa).
65. II *Hearings* 85–90 (testimony of Jackie B.)
66. Along with events like those described in the text accompanying notes 65 & 66, *supra*, these often arise under the rubric of sexual harassment. See, e.g., C. MacKinnon, Sexual Harassment of Working Women, *supra* note 5, at 29. Although not providing the same range of relief, sexual harassment cases recognize concerns related to those underlying the Minneapolis ordinance:

    > The . . . workplace was pervaded with sexual slur, insult and innuendo, and [the plaintiff] Katz was personally the object of verbal sexual harassment by her fellow controllers. This harassment took the form of extremely vulgar and offensive sexually related epithets addressed to and employed about Katz by supervisory personnel as well as by other controllers. The words used were ones widely recognized as not only improper but as intensely degrading, deriving their power to wound not only from their meaning but also from 'the disgust and violence they express phonetically'.

Katz v Dole, 709 F.2d 251, 254 (4th Cir. 1983)(quoting C. Miller & K. Swift, Words and Women 109 [1977]).

Do such words become *not* injurious by virtue of appearing in print? To an extent, Professor Tribe's observation about the words whose regulation was allowed in *Chaplinsky* applies here: '[S]uch provocations are not part of human discourse but weapons hurled in anger to inflict injury or invite retaliation.' L. Tribe, *supra* note 35, at 605. The fact that in the case of pornography, the projectiles hurled at women are other women, or constructions of one's own gendered anatomy, puts them on a slightly different plane, and also helps to explain why pornography's injury has neither been seen by its perpetrators nor retaliated against by its victims: the injury it inflicts, it inflicts in such a humiliating and undermining way that it disables retaliation. Silence has been the usual response.

67. 'Women were forced constantly to enact specific scenes that men had witnessed in pornography. They would direct women to copy postures and poses of things they had seen in magazines . . .' II *Hearings* 73 (testimony of a named former prostitute).

68. Letter from Marvin Lewis, Esq., to Catharine MacKinnon (Dec. 7, 1983)(on file with Harvard Civil Rights-Civil Liberties Law Review). Attorney Lewis described to me situations in which therapists had women patients act out scenes from *The Story of O*.

69.

> The pornographic view of women is one that is prevalent within the medical community unfortunately. This is expressed by the kinds of jokes that are made about women and their bodies, especially when they are under anesthesia and undergoing surgical procedures. This view includes seeing women as not worthy of respect and also seeing them primarily in terms of their sexual functioning. Several years ago when I was teaching at the Rutgers Medical School there was a week-long sexuality program planned annually for students. The first day of this program consisted of all-day viewing of pornographic movies. The intent was to 'de-sensitize' the students to sex.

Letter from Michelle Harrison, MD, to the Minneapolis City Council (Dec. 9, 1983)(on file with Harvard Civil Rights-Civil Liberties Law Review).

See also P. Bart, From Those Wonderful People Who Brought You the Vaginal Orgasm: Sex Education for Medical Students 2 (1976)(paper presented at the Meetings of the Am. Soc. Ass'n in New York)(on file with Harvard Civil Rights-Civil Liberties Law Review):

> When I was asked to participate in the sex education program at the University of Illinois 6 years ago it was a joint venture of Gynecology and Psychiatry and its primary purpose was to 'desensitize' the medical students. My first thought was 'Aren't they insensitive enough as it is?' The term, however, has a technical meaning. It means that the subject will not react emotionally when presented with certain stimuli that previously she/he had such reactions to . . . In order to achieve this purpose the students were shown porno films.

The specifics in the text accompanying this note are drawn from examples many people have recounted to me as a standard part of the program customarily used in medical schools.

70. Students and clients reported this to me in the course of my research into sexual harassment in education.

71. See III *Hearings* 13–16 (testimony of Susan G.)(discussing sexual abuse of an adult woman with whom she lived).

72. See, e.g., III *Hearings* 69–74 (testimony of Charlotte K.). Now tell me no girl was ever ruined by a book. See also United States v Roth, 237 F.2d 796, 812 (2d Cir. 1957)(Frank, J., appendix to concurring opinion)('Echoing Macaulay, Jimmy Walker remarked that he had never heard of a woman seduced by a book.') Seduction here is the term that attributes consent or acquiescence or enjoyment of rape to the rape victim.

73. See II *Hearings* 90–100 (testimony of Shannon M.). If you still think pornography is harmless, 'you move into my neighborhood and I will move into yours'. *Id.* at 99.

74. Averting eyes is supposed to be an alternative to the injury, as it may well have been in Cohen v California, 403 US 15, 21 (1971)('Those in the Los Angeles courthouse could effectively avoid further bombardment of their sensibilities simply by averting their eyes'), or, less so but still arguably, in Erznoznik v City of Jacksonville, 422 US 205, 212 (1975)(the screen was not 'so obtrusive as to make it impossible for an unwilling individual to avoid exposure to it')(quoting Redrup v New York, 386 US 767, 769 [1967]). The situations that our ordinance is premised upon, and is designed to address directly, are more like the woman who was tied to a chair in front of a videoscreen in her home and forced to watch pornography, see e.g., III *Hearings* 24.

75. See Stanley v Georgia, 394 US 557 (1969)(right to privacy protects possession of obscenity at home). The *Stanley* Court seems to assume that Mr Stanley is at home *alone*.

76. Many Jewish citizens, survivors of the Nazi extermination, live in Skokie, Illinois. The town's attempts to keep Nazis from demonstrating there produced years of local ordinances, all ultimately held unconstitutional. Dissenting from a denial of certiorari, Justice Blackmun said: 'On the one hand, we have precious First Amendment rights vigorously asserted . . . On the other hand, we are presented with evidence of a potentially explosive and dangerous situation, inflamed by unforgettable recollections of traumatic experiences in the second world conflict.' Smith v Collin, 439 US 916, 918 (1968). Observing that citizens had asserted 'that the proposed demonstration is scheduled at a place and in a manner that is taunting and overwhelmingly offensive to the citizens of that place', he thought their claim deserved to be heard, 'for "the character of every act depends upon the circumstances in which it is done."' *Id.* at 919 (quoting Schenck v United States, 249 US 47, 52 [1919]).

77. II *Hearings* 112 (testimony of Mags D.).

78. Code of Indianapolis and Marion County, ch.16, 16–3(g)(as **499**

amended, June 11, 1984) provides: 'Assault or physical attack due to pornography: The assault, physical attack, or injury of any woman, man, child, or transsexual in a way that is directly caused by specific pornography.' No damages or compensation for loss is recoverable under this section 'unless the complainant proves that the respondent knew or had reason to know that the materials were pornography'. *Id.* at 16–3(g)(8). Pornography that caused the acts can be reached under this provision, although it would be very difficult to prove 'direct cause'.

79. 'The First Amendment demands more than a horrible example or two of the perpetrator of a crime of sexual violence, in whose pocket is found a pornographic book, before it allows the Nation to be saddled with a regime of censorship.' Memoirs v Massachusetts, 383 US 413, 432 (1966)(Douglas, J., concurring). One wonders how many bodies must pile up before individual victims will be allowed to enjoin the proven cause, simply because that cause is a book. See also *Memoirs, id.* at 452 (Clark, J., dissenting)(noting repeated reports 'that pornography is associated with an overwhelmingly large number of sex crimes'.)

80. II *Hearings* 43 (testimony of Rita M.).

81. III *Hearings* 18–19 (testimony of Carol L.).

82. On-going research on Hennepin County, Minn. sex offenders that documents these similarities was presented by Candace Kruttschnitt to the City of Minneapolis Task Force on Pornography (Mar. 13, 1984). The data are consistent with that of all researchers who find it difficult to document differences between sex offenders and populations of normal men on virtually any dimension. See *infra* note 103. My analysis of the few measurable differences between these populations is that they involve the likelihood of getting caught for sex offences more than the likelihood of committing them.

83. Nine and one-half per cent of all rapes and rape attempts are reported. Russell, Sexual Exploitation: Rape, Child Sexual Abuse, and Workplace Harassment 31 (1984). The reporting rate of most sexual violations is as low or lower. Six per cent of extra-familial child sexual assault and two per cent of incestuous assault are reported to authorities. *Id.* at 172. See also J. Herman, Father-Daughter Incest 12–15 (1981). Another study estimates that only one of every 270 incidents of wife abuse is ever reported to authorities. See S. Steinmetz, The Cycle of Violence: Assertive, Aggressive, and Abusive Family Interaction (1977)(referenced in E. Stanko, *supra* note 5, at 73). This is probably a low figure. Although 42 per cent of federal employees had been subjected to sexual harassment in the two years prior to one survey, 29 per cent in severe forms, most had not reported the behaviour. US Merit System Protection Board *supra* note 5, at 35, 71.

84. III *Hearings* 36 (testimony of Barbara Chester, Director of the Rape and Sexual Assault Center, Hennepin County, Minn.).

85. III *Hearings* 44–45 (testimony of Bill Seals, Director of Sexual Assault Services, Center for Behavior Therapy, Minneapolis, Minn.).

86. III *Hearings* 64 (testimony of Nancy Steele, therapist with sex offenders).
87. *Id.*
88. III *Hearings* 88 (testimony of Michael Laslett [reading statement by Floyd Winecoff, psychotherapist specializing in services for men]).
89. *Id.* at 86.
90. III *Hearings* 44, *supra* note 100 (testimony of Bill Seals).
91. III *Hearings* 59 (testimony of Gerry Kaplan, Executive Director of Alpha Human Services [inpatient programme for sex offenders]).
92. Examples exist that range from the seemingly correlational to the integral to the causal. See, e.g., Hoggard v State, 277 Ark. 117, 640 S.W.2d 102 (1982), *cert. denied*, 460 US 1022 (1983), in which the court, in ruling on a challenge that the prejudicial effect of pornography outweighed its probative value in allegation of rape of six-year-old boy, stated:

> We readily agree the material was prejudicial, it could hardly be otherwise. But the argument that its probative value was lacking fades under scrutiny. This pornography and the offense being tried had a clear correlation: the pornography depicted deviate sexual acts by young males and the crime charged was deviate sexual acts of a forty-two-year-old man and a six-year-old boy. More importantly, the pornography was used as the instrument by which the crime itself was solicited – the child was encouraged to look at the pictures and then encouraged to engage in it. The value of the evidence as proof of the crime is obvious.

Id., 277 Ark. at 124–25, 640 S.W.2d at 106.

See these other situations: in an action for statutory rape, the defendant cared for two children, seven and six, 'and while they were there had the children perform various sexual acts with him and each other while he took photographs, some of which he sent to foreign publishers of pornographic magazines'. Qualle v State, 652 P.2d 481, 483 (Alaska Ct. App. 1982). As to his own children:

> Documents, photographs, and films seized from Qualle's home in 1979 showed that he had taken sexually explicit films and photographs of his children and had tried to sell at least two rolls of such pictures to European companies. He asked for money or pornographic magazines in exchange for his pictures. One magazine ('Lolita') published a series of pictures of one of his daughters.

Id. at 484; State v Natzke, 25 Ariz. App. 520, 522, 544 P.2d 1121, 1123 (1976)(pornography admissible in rape case in which defendant's daughter 'expressed a reluctance to perform the requested sexual acts . . . appellant told her that these acts were all right and that "everybody does it", and that as proof of this fact, appellant showed his daughter pictures and magazines showing sexual activities'). In People v Reynolds, 55 Cal. App. 3d 357, 127 Cal. Rptr. 561 (1976), the defendant sought to suppress pornographic pictures of victims in a prosecution for kidnapping and rape. **501**

> According to Tracy, the suspect forced her to take some yellow
> capsules with a can of cola, and she became groggy; he gave her
> pornography to read, and at one point stopped the car to make a
> telephone call and she heard him say: 'I have got the girl.' . . . When
> the officers searched his room they discovered pornographic negatives
> and photographs, some of which depicted the Konoske girls . . . More
> photographs were [later] found which were pornographic . . .

Id., 55 Cal. App. 3d at 362, 365, 127 Cal. Rptr. at 564, 566. In
another case, the defendant was charged, inter alia, with encouraging minors to participate in pornographic films and to engage in
sexual intercourse with him:

> Defendant showed pornographic films to two boys, and defendant
> was an actor in one of them. He also showed a pornographic film of
> two of the girls . . . He suggested to two of the girls that they become
> prostitutes. Defendant had a movie camera set up to photograph his
> bed so that, 'in case some of these young girls tried to say that he
> raped them, he would have this as proof that he did not'.

State v Dobbs, 665 P.2d 1151, 1155, 1159 (N.M. Ct.App. 1983). In
one case, the defendant was an Episcopal priest who ran a Boys'
Farm, which was supposedly for the benefit of wayward and
homeless boys, but was

> maintained largely from funds raised . . . from the sale of photographs
> and slides of the children to some 200 or more 'sponsors'. These
> photographs depicted the boys (most of whom were eleven to sixteen
> years of age when photographed) posed in the nude and engaged in
> various acts of simulated or actual fellatio and sodomy.

Vermilye v State, 584 S.W.2d 226, 228 (Tenn. Crim. App. 1979).
   See also People v Cramer, 67 Cal. 2d 126, 127, 429 P.2d 582, 583,
60 Cal. Rptr. 230, 231 (1967)('At the house, they swam, and
defendant served Phillip vodka and 7-Up and showed him some
Playboy magazines.'); People v Hunt, 72 Cal. App. 3d 190, 195–196,
139 Cal. Rptr. 675, 677 (1977)(rape case in which the '[d]efendant
told her his name was John and that he was a "porno" photographer
. . . This time the defendant took a polaroid picture of Chris [the
victim] performing the act [oral copulation].'); People v Mendoza,
37 Cal. App. 3d 717, 721, 112 Cal. Rptr. 565, 567 (1974)('He then
invited Tad and Jim into his apartment, where he gave the boys
candy and pointed out a Playboy magazine centerfold photograph
of a nude girl on the wall.'); Whiteman v State, 343 So. 2d 1340
(Fla. Dist. Ct. App.)(admissibility of pornography in sexual battery
of niece), *cert. denied*, 353 So. 2d 681 (Fla. 1977); Brames v State, 273
Ind. 565, 406 N.E.2d 252 (1980)(attempt to introduce evidence of
rape defendant's prior visit to pornographic movie house rejected as
part of insanity plea); Allan v State, 92 Nev. 318, 321, 549 P.2d
1402, 1404 (1976)(minor's testimony concerning defendant's past
advances admissible as 'tending to show proof of a motive . . .
wherein minors were lured to appellant's quarters and, after being

"conditioned" by the showing of his pornographic movies, subjected to his sexual desires.'); Stein v Beta Rho Alumni Ass'n, 49 Or. App. 965, 968, 621 P.2d 632, 634 (1980)(personal injury suffered to a burlesque dancer who performed for a fraternity after 'a pornographic movie had been shown'). Finally, in Padgett v State, 49 Ala. App. 130, 133, 269 So. 2d 147, 149 (Crim.)(reversing and remanding to trial court on other grounds), *cert. denied*, 289 Ala. 749, 269 So. 2d 154 (1972), a husband was convicted for shooting his wife, allegedly accidentally, after he admittedly '"nagged" [her] about the girls in the Playboy magazine "to try to irritate her"'.

California's new spousal rape law, effective January, 1980, has produced many relevant reports of sexual violence in intimate contexts visible in courts for the first time. 'Beglin was watching an X-rated movie [on cable TV] in the family room. Beglin allegedly entered the bedroom, threw her [his wife] on the bed and bound her. Beglin also ripped off her clothing and began taking nude photos of her, [Prosecutor Alphonsus C.] Novick said. He then sexually assaulted her . . .' Brown, *Man on Trial Again on Wife Rape Count*, L.A. Times, May 19, 1981 (this newspaper article, and the other articles cited in this note, are on file with Harvard Civil Rights-Civil Liberties Law Review). The husband was acquitted after claiming his wife consented. See Kutzmann, *Beglin Innocent of Wife Rape*, Costa Mesa Daily Pilot, May 29, 1981. Evidence included testimony of crisis center workers and an emergency room doctor, both of whom had seen and talked with Mrs Beglin after the incident, and photos of her wrists and ankles, 'allegedly marked from being tied to a bed with ropes'. The prosecutor said, 'The case couldn't have been any better . . . Unfortunately, we may have to wait until some wife is severely mutilated or murdered until they'll see.' LaGuire, *Spousal-rape Trial: Husband Cleared, Prosecutor Angered*, L.A. Herald Examiner, May 30, 1981, at A-1. In Merced, California, Victor Burnham was convicted of spousal rape for forcing his wife to have sex with neighbours and strangers (a total of 68, see Wharton, *Sex Torture Charges Unveiled in Burnham Trial*, Sun-Star [Merced, Cal.] May 29, 1981) while he took photographs. She was also forced, through assault and holding their child hostage, to stand on the corner and invite men in for sex, and to have sex with a dog. See *Burnham Pleads No Contest on Charge of Possession of Automatic Rifle*, Sun-Star (Merced, Cal.) May 27, 1981; *Man Found Guilty of Spousal Rape*, Times-Delta (Tulare County, Cal.) June 6, 1981. She testified to 'episodes of torture with a battery-charged cattle prod and an electric egg beater'. Wharton, *supra*. The defence attorney 'attempting to show the jury there was no force used by the defendant, quizzed Mrs Burnham about photographs in the albums showing her smiling during the sexual encounters. Mrs Burnham said her husband threatened her with violence if she did not smile when the pictures were taken.' *Wife Testifies in Burnham Sex Case*, Sun-Star (Merced, Cal.) May 28, 1981. Two of Mr Burnham's previous wives testified that he had forced them to commit similar acts during their marriages. *Id*. Burnham said Mrs Burnham agreed **503** to the acts, and his lawyer showed the photos to the jury so they could 'see for themselves that the pictures were in complete conformity with Becky's morals'. See Wharton, *Guilty Verdict in Sex Trial*, Sun-Star (Merced, Cal.) June 5, 1981.

My general impression from rape and sexual harassment cases is that it takes a minimum of three women testifying to the same or similar treatment to create a chance of overcoming the man's credibility when he defends against an accusation of sexual force by saying that the woman consented to the act. (For example, some educational institutions have a covert policy of not moving to investigate claims of sexual harassment of students by teachers until they receive complaints from three different women about the same man. They also do not keep reports over time except by memory.) In another such case,

> the woman testified that her husband tortured her on several occasions, including 'sewing her to the bed, burning her with a lamp until she blistered, cutting her with a razor blade and raping her with objects ranging from a coat hanger to a hair brush . . . [He] used duct tape to keep her from screaming . . .' When Deputy Attorney Lela Henke asked the woman where her husband got the idea to rape her with a coat hanger, the woman replied they had seen it in a movie on cable television.

Wife Tells of Assault, Torture, Press Courier (Oxnard, Cal.) May 9, 1984; similarly, a woman told of her husband 'sewing her sexual organs with needle and yarn . . .' Greene, *Wife Describes Brutal Attacks by Mate as He Listens in Court*, Star Free Press (Ventura, Cal.) May 10, 1984.

Apparently 500 to 1,000 deaths occur each year from 'autoerotic asphyxia', in which young men asphyxiate usually from a noose around the neck, something presented in pornography as producing intense erections. Usually 'pornographic material is nearby'. Brody, *'Autoerotic Death' of Youths Causes Widening Concern*, N.Y. Times, Mar. 27, 1984, at C3.

93. State v Herberg, 324 N.W.2d 346, 347 (Minn. 1982).
94. Code of Indianapolis and Marion County, see Chapter 19, 16–3(4) states:

> Trafficking in pornography: the production, sale, exhibition, or distribution of pornography.
>
> (A) City, state and federally funded public libraries or private and public university and college libraries in which pornography is available for study, including on open shelves, shall not be construed to be trafficking in pornography, but special display presentations of pornography in said places is sex discrimination.
>
> (B) The formation of private clubs or associations for purposes of trafficking in pornography is illegal and shall be considered a conspiracy to violate the civil rights of women.
>
> (C) This paragraph (4) shall not be construed to make isolated passages or isolated parts actionable.

Section 16–17(b) states:

In the case of trafficking in pornography, any woman may file a complaint as a woman acting against the subordination of women and any man, child, or transsexual may file a complaint but must prove injury in the same way that a woman is injured in order to obtain relief under this chapter.

95. See, e.g., US Comm'n on Obscenity & Pornography, Comm'n Report (1970); Comm. on Obscenity and Film Censorship, Report, Cmd. No. 7772 (1979)(United Kingdom).

96. Regina v Hicklin, 3 L.R.-Q.B. 360, 370 (1868)(obscene meaning 'calculated to produce a pernicious effect in depraving and debauching the minds of the persons into whose hands it might come').

97. Roth v United States, 354 US 476, 501–02 (1956)(Harlan, J., concurring in companion case of Alberts v California); see also Jacobellis v Ohio, 378 US 184, 202 (1964)(Warren, C.J., dissenting)('[p]rotection of society's right to maintain its moral fiber').

98. The data of Court and of Kutchinsky, both correlational, reach contradictory conclusions on the relation between the availability of pornography and the level of crime. *Compare* Kutchinsky, *The Effect of Easy Availability of Pornography on the Incidence of Sex Crimes: The Danish Experience*, J. Soc. Issues 1973, No. 3, at 163; Kutchinsky, *Towards an Explanation of the Decrease in Registered Sex Crime in Copenhagen*, 7 US Comm'n on Obscenity and Pornography, Technical Report 263 (1971) *with* Court, *Pornography and Sex-Crimes: A Re-Evaluation in the Light of Recent Trends Around the World*, 5 Int'l J. Criminology & Penology 129 (1977). More recent investigations into the relationship between the circulation rates of popular men's sex magazines and the rate of reported rape establish a correlation between them in the United States. L. Baron & M. Straus, *Sexual Stratification, Pornography, and Rape in the United States* in Pornography and Sexual Aggression 185 (N. Malamuth and E. Donnerstein eds. 1984).

99. Roth v United States, 354 US 476, 485 (1957)(quoting Chaplinsky v New Hampshire, 315 US 568, 572 [1942]). See also Paris Adult Theatre I v Slaton, 413 US 49, 57–58 (1973)('[T]here are legitimate state interests at stake . . . [T]hese include the interest of the public in the quality of life . . .')

100. Positive causality – linear, exclusive, unidirectional – has become the implicit standard for the validity of connection between pornography and harm. This standard requires the kind of control that can only be achieved, if at all, in laboratory settings. When it is then found there, as it has been, that pornography causes harm, see *infra* note 102, the objection is heard that laboratory settings are artificial. But their artificiality is what makes a conclusion about causality possible under this causal model. In real-world settings, a relation of linear consequentiality between pornography and harm is seldom sufficiently isolable or uncontaminated – indeed, seldom even sufficiently separable, the pornography and its impact being as pervasive and intertwined as they are – to satisfy this standard. I am suggesting that the positivistic model of causation may be inappropriate to the social reality of pornography. **505**

See also W. Heisenberg, The Physical Principles of the Quantum Theory 63 (1930); Horowitz, *The Doctrine of Objective Causation*, in The Politics of Law 201 (D. Kairys ed. 1982).

101. Major sources are: Pornography and Sexual Agression, *supra* note 98; D. Zillmann, Connections Between Sex and Aggression (1984); Donnerstein & Berkowitz, *Victim Reactions in Aggressive Erotic Films as a Factor in Violence Against Women*, 41 J. Personality & Soc. Psychology 710–24 (1981); Malamuth & Check, *The Effects of Mass Media Exposure on Acceptance of Violence Against Women: A Field Experiment*, 15 J. Research Personality 436–46 (1981); Malamuth & Donnerstein, *The Effects of Aggressive-Pornographic Mass Media Stimuli*, 15 Advances Experimental Soc. Psychology 103 (1982); Russell, *Pornography and Violence: What Does the New Research Say?*, in Take Back the Night 216 (L. Lederer ed. 1983); Zillmann & Bryant, *Pornography, Sexual Callousness, and the Trivialization of Rape*, 32 J. Com. 16–18 (1982); I *Hearings* 13–45 (testimony of E. Donnerstein); Linz, Donnerstein & Penrod, The Effects of Long-Term Exposure to Filmed Violence Against Women (Mar. 22, 1984).

102. In addition to the references listed *supra* note 101, see: Donnerstein & Hallam, *The Facilitating Effects of Erotica on Aggression Toward Females*, J. Personality & Soc. Psychology 1270 (1978); Geen, Stonner & Shope, *The Facilitation of Aggression by Aggression: Evidences Against the Catharsis Hypothesis*, 31 J. Personality & Soc. Psychology 721 (1975); Zapolsky & Zillmann, *The Effect of Soft-Core and Hard-Core Erotica on Provoked and Unprovoked Hostile Behavior*, 17 J. Sex Research 319 (1981); Zillmann, Hoyt & Day, *Strength and Duration of the Effect of Aggressive, Violent, and Erotic Communications on Subsequent Aggressive Behavior*, 1 Com. Research 286 (1974). See also Malamuth, *Factors Associated with Rape as Predictors of Laboratory Aggression Against Women*, 45 J. Personality & Soc. Psychology 432 (1983)(valid relation between factors associated with real-world aggression against women and laboratory aggression).

103. Malamuth & Check, *Penile Tumescence and Perceptual Responses to Rape as a Function of Victim's Perceived Reactions*, 10 J. Applied Soc. Psychology 528 (1980); Malamuth, Haber & Feshbach, *Testing Hypotheses Regarding Rape: Exposure to Sexual Violence, Sex Difference, and the 'Normality' of Rapists*, 14 J. Research Personality 121 (1980). The lack of distinction between convicted rapists and control groups may be the reason many people have concluded that pornography does not do anything. When all the unreported, undetected, not to mention unconscious or potential rapists in the control groups are considered, this conclusion stops being mysterious. See *supra* text accompanying note 83. See also Abel, Becker & Skinner, *Aggressive Behavior and Sex*, 3 Psychiatric Clinics North America 133, 140 (1980)(fewer than 5 per cent of rapists are psychotic while raping); Malamuth, *Rape Proclivity Among Males*, 37 J. Soc. Issues 4 (1981); Malamuth & Check, *The Effects of Mass Media Exposure on Acceptance of Violence Against Women: A Field Experiment*, 15 J. Research Personality 4 (1981); Malamuth, Heim

& Feshbach, *Sexual Responsiveness of College Students to Rape Depictions: Inhibitory and Disinhibitory Effects*, 38 Soc. Psychology 399 (1980).

On the general subject of men's attitudes towards rape, see T. Beneke, Men on Rape (1982); Burt, *Cultural Myths and Supports for Rape*, 38 J. Personality & Soc. Psychology 217 (1980); Scully & Marolla, *Riding the Bull at Gilley's: Convicted Rapists Describe the Pleasures of Raping*, J. Soc. Issues (1985)(forthcoming); S. D. Smithyman, The Undetected Rapist (PhD Diss., Claremont Graduate School 1978). A currently unknown number of incidents originally reported as rapes are now considered by police to be unfounded, meaning 'the police established that no forcible rape offense or attempt occurred'. In 1976, the last year the FBI reported its 'unfounding' rate, it was 19 per cent of reports. Federal Bureau of Investigation, Crime in America 16 (1976).

This note is dedicated to those members of the Biddle Lecture audience who hissed when I made the statement in the accompanying text on the supposition that it was not the truth of the statement that they were protesting.

104. See *supra* notes 101 and 103. It is perhaps worth noting that there is no experimental research to the contrary.
105. See Briere & Malamuth, *Self-Reported Likelihood of Sexually Aggressive Behavior: Attitudinal Versus Sexual Explanations*, 37 J. Res. Personality 315, 318 (1983) (58 per cent of college males in survey report some likelihood of forcing sex on woman if they knew they would not get caught). See also Koss & Oros, *Sexual Experiences Survey: A Research Instrument Investigating Sexual Aggression and Victimization*, 50 J. Consulting & Clinical Psychology 455 (1982).
106. See I *Hearings* 21–38 (testimony of E. Donnerstein discussing supporting data submitted in the record. See also Zillmann & Bryant, *supra* note 101 (normal males exposed to films like *Debbie Does Dallas* see rape victims as five times more worthless than men who had not seen the films, and also saw less than half the amount of injury to the victim). In spite of this factual support, it is likely that the Indianapolis version of the ordinance would not apply to trafficking in such materials. See Section 16–3(8) of the Indianapolis Ordinance which states: 'Defenses: [I]t shall be a defense to a complaint under paragraph (g)(4) . . . that the materials complained of are those covered only by paragraph (q)(6) . . .'
107. See *supra* note 106. See also Linz, Donnerstein & Penrod, *supra* note 101. I have the reports on female subjects orally from Carol Krafka, a researcher at the University of Wisconsin.
108. See I *Hearings* 37–38 (testimony of E. Donnerstein)('Subjects who have seen violent material or X-rated material see less injury to a rape victim than people who haven't seen these films. Furthermore, they consider the woman to be more worthless . . .'); See also Zillmann & Bryant, *supra* note 101.
109. Dr Donnerstein says this in most of his talks.
110. D. Russell, Rape in Marriage 228 (1984).
111. *Id.* at 84.

112. See II *Hearings* 68 (testimony of Ruth M.).
113. II *Hearings* 55 (testimony of Nancy C.).
114. III *Hearings* 29 (testimony of Sharon Rice Vaughn [reading statement by Donna Dunn of Women's Shelter, Inc., in Rochester, Minnesota, which describes events reported by a woman at the shelter]).
115. *Id.*
116. III *Hearings* 83 (testimony of Sue Schafer).
117. II *Hearings* 74 (testimony of a named former prostitute). The use of pornography in sexual abuse of prostitutes, and its use in getting them into prostitution, is documented by Silbert & Pines, *Pornography & Sexual Abuse of Women*, 10 Sex Roles: J. Research 857 (1984). Even though no specific questions were asked about pornography, 24 per cent of the subjects (current and former prostitutes) mentioned references to pornography by the men who raped them, often references to specific materials in which prostitutes were presented as loving and wanting violent abuse and death. Ten per cent mentioned being used as children in pornography, again in unsolicited open-ended accounts of their lives. Had they been directly asked, 'it is assumed that the actual response to this question would be notably higher'. *Id.* at 865.
118. II *Hearings* 74–75 (testimony of a named former prostitute).
119. I *Hearings* 56 (testimony of Gordon C.).
120. *Id.*
121. III *Hearings* 94–95 (testimony of Omar J.).
122. *Id.* at 95.
123. See Dworkin, *The Bruise That Doesn't Heal*, 3 Mother Jones 31, 35 (1978)('Reality is when something is happening to you and you know it and you say it and when you say it, other people understand what you mean and believe you.')
124. See A. Dworkin, *Pornography: Men Possessisng Women* 149 (1981) ('She wants it, they all do.').
125. I think it is important that when the *actual object*, for example the pornography, is present, finding facts about it is thought to become *more* rather than less difficult – compared, for example, with finding facts about a rape. This suggests that the usual process of proof amounts to a credibility contest between conflicting stories, which come to court in personae. Pornography has pervasively written women's side of the story as not a rape. When there is no story about reality to provide a proxy for simplifying it to a question of whose version one believes, but the reality itself is there, perhaps – if it is measured against standards devised to describe it – women will have a chance.
126. See Miller v California, 413 US 15, 19 (1973).
127. See Kaplan v California, 413 US 115, 120 (1973); Paris Adult Theatre I v Slaton, 413 US 49, 60 (1973); Roth v United States, 354 US 476, 501 (1957)(Harlan, J., concurring).
128. New York v Ferber, 458 US 742, 757 (1982).
129. See consideration of civil as opposed to criminal procedures and remedies *supra* note 37. It does seem to me that criminal civil rights

legislation might be worth considering at the federal level, but only in addition to providing access to court to private civil claimants.

130. III *Hearings* 53 (testimony of Cheryl Champion, member, Sexual Abuse Unit, Washington County [Minn.] Human Services).

131. 315 US 568, 572 (1941).

132. Actually, some have. See Hansen, *Direct Action: Sentencing Statements*, 17 Open Road, Winter 1984(Vancounver, BC), at 11–12 (on receiving a life sentence for firebombing the Red Hot Video store, among other actions). Nikki Craft, with the Preying Mantis Women's Brigade, engages in disruptive and exemplary acts against pornography from staging the Myth California Pageant (in opposition to the Miss California Pageant) to destroying copies of *Hustler*, for which she served time. See Linda Hooper, *Preying on Porn Propaganda*, City on a Hill 5–7 (Apr. 5, 1984)(Santa Cruz, California)(on file with Harvard Civil Rights-Civil Liberties Law Review). Women in Europe have also engaged in destruction of property to express their dissent against pornography, and to attempt to destroy some of it. See Dworan, *Review*, Off Our Backs, May 6, 1984, at 18–19 (reviewing Breaching the Peace: A Collection of Radical Feminist Papers [1983])(1984)(on file with Harvard Civil Rights-Civil Liberties Law Review).

133. See Beauharnais v Illinois, 343 US 250, 263 (1952)('[T]he dignity accorded him may depend as much on the reputation of the racial and religious group to which he willy-nilly belongs as on his own merits.')

134. See Whitney v California, 274 US 357, 377 (1927) (Brandeis, J., concurring).

135. See L. Tribe, *supra* note 35, at 731.

136. See Emerson, *Toward a General Theory of the First Amendment*, 72 Yale L. J. 877 879–81 (1963); Baker, *Scope of the First Amendment Freedom of Speech*, 25 UCLA L. Rev. 964, 990–1005 (1978).

137. See A. Meiklejohn, Political Freedom, 24–28 (1960). The importance of participation in civic life is also recognized by Emerson: '[M]an in his capacity as a member of society has a right to share in the common decisions that affect him.' T. Emerson, The System of Freedom of Expression 6 (1970).

138. See T. Emerson, *supra* note 137. Emerson is entirely aware that some groups lack power in a way that the political process does not accommodate, but simply considers this a risk posed principally to 'the nonbelonging individual', *id.* at 37, rather than advancing any substantive analysis of who does and does not have power and thus access to the means of speech. In the absence of such a substantive analysis, pornographers can cast themselves as outsiders when they are actually paradigmatic. See also Clark, *Liberalism and Pornography*, in Pornography and Censorship 57 (D. Copp & S. Wendell eds. 1983).

139. One case has squarely balanced a municipal ordinance prohibiting sex discrimination in advertising against the first amendment. Noting that commercial speech is not the highest order of speech – a position with strong parallels to the plurality's treatment of the **509**

'sexually explicit' in Young v American Mini Theatres, 427 US 50 (1976) – the *presumptive* connection between sex segregation in job advertisements and sex segregation in the workplace stated a harm that outweighed freedom of the press. Further the Supreme Court recently held that the compelling state interest in eradicating discrimination against women justified the impact of Minnesota's Human Rights Act on first amendment rights of expressive association. See Roberts v United States Jaycees, 104 S. Ct. 3244 (1984). Holding that the state's interest in sex equality outweighed the first amendment interests implicated, the Court stated that the equality interest is not 'limited to the provision of purely tangible goods and services', *id.* at 3254, but also includes steps to remove 'the barriers to economic advancement and political and social integration that have historically plagued certain disadvantaged groups, including women'. *Id.* In a formulation strikingly apposite to the anti-pornography ordinance, the Court said:

> [A]cts of invidious discrimination in the distribution of publicly available goods, services, and other advantages cause unique evils that government has a compelling interest to prevent – wholly apart from the point of view such conduct may transmit. Accordingly, like violence or other types of potentially expressive activities that produce special harms distinct from their communicative impact, such practices are entitled to no constitutional protection.

Id. at 3255.

140. In one obscenity case, the Supreme Court stated: 'Appellant was not prosecuted here for anything he said or believed, but for what he did, for his dominant role in several enterprises engaged in producing and selling allegedly obscene books.' Mishkin v New York, 383 US 502, 504–05 (1966). The statute upheld in *Ferber*, 458 US 747 (1982), defined publication of child pornography as 'promoting a sexual performance by a child', NY Penal Law 263 (McKinney 1980), logic that extended to support the law against the pornography's distribution. It is arguable that a major reason obscenity was defined as 'nonspeech' is because speech was considered to communicate ideas and obscenity was understood to function physically rather than ideationally. For some further thoughts on this subject, see my discussion in *Not a Moral Issue*, *supra* note 20. To state the obvious, I do not argue that pornography is 'conduct' in the first amendment doctrinal sense.

141. Ginsberg v New York, 390 US 629, 649 (1968)(Stewart, J., concurring in result)(emphasis added).

142. Roth v United States, 354 US 476, 514 (Douglas, J., dissenting)(citing Giboney v Empire Storage & Ice Co., 336 US 490, 498 [1949]); Labor Board v Virginia Power Co., 314 US 469, 477–78 (1941). See also Memoirs v Massachusetts, 383 US 413, 426 (1966)(Douglas J., concurring)(first amendment does not permit the censorship of expression not brigaded with illegal action); Pittsburgh Press Co. v Human Relations Comm'n, 413 US 376,

398 (1973)(Douglas, J., dissenting)(speech and action not so closely brigaded as to be one).

143. Rape, battery, assault, kidnapping, and prostitution are all crimes and they are absolutely integral to pornography as we define and make it actionable. Compare with *Ferber*, 458 US 747 (1982): masturbating is not a crime, nor is watching it; yet making and distributing a film of two boys masturbating is.

144. Speech by A. Dworkin, *supra* note 48.

145. This example is from an interview with a victim done in preparation for the Minneapolis *Hearings*.

146. See Foucault, *supra* note 17.

147.
> He [her husband] told me if I loved him I would do this. And that, as I could see from the things he read me in the magazines initially, a lot of times women didn't like it but if I tried it enough I would probably like it and I would learn to like it. And he would read me stories where women learned to like it.

II *Hearings* 63 (testimony of Ruth M.).

148. See Simson, *The Afro-American Female: The Historical Context of the Construction of Sexual Identity* in Powers of Desire: The Politics of Sexuality 231 (A. Snitow, C. Stansell & S. Thompson eds. 1983)(quoting Harriet Jacobs: 'It seems less demeaning to give one's self, than to submit to compulsion,' writes a black slave of rape by her white master, speaking for many women under circumstances of compulsion). Jacobs subsequently resisted by hiding in an attic cubbyhole 'almost deprived of light and air, and with no space to move my limbs, for nearly seven years' to avoid him.

149. This paraphrases a portion of Andrea Dworkin's speech. See *supra* note 48.

150. See US Const. Amend. I.

PART FIVE

Pornography, Censorship and Civil Liberties

24 Against the Male Flood: Censorship, Pornography and Equality

ANDREA DWORKIN

To say what one thought – that was my little problem – against the prodigious Current; to find a sentence that could hold its own against the male flood.

Virginia Woolf

I want to say right here, that those well-meaning friends on the outside who say that we have suffered these horrors of prison, of hunger strikes and forcible feeding, because we desired to martyrise ourselves for the cause, are absolutely and entirely mistaken. We never went to prison in order to be martyrs. We went there in order that we might obtain the rights of citizenship. We were willing to break laws that we might force men to give us the right to make laws.

Emmeline Pankhurst

CENSORSHIP

Censorship is a real thing, not an abstract idea or a word that can be used to mean anything at all.

In ancient Rome, a censor was a magistrate who took the census (a count of the male population and an evaluation of property for the purpose of taxation done every fifth year), assessed taxes, and inspected morals and conduct. His power over conduct came from his power to tax. For instance, in 403 B.C., the censors Camillus and Postimius heavily fined elderly bachelors for not marrying. The power to tax, then as now, was the power to destroy. The censor, using the police and judicial powers of the state, regulated social behaviour.

At its origins, then, censorship had nothing to do with striking down ideas as such; it had to do with acts. In my view, real state censorship still does. In South Africa, and the Soviet Union, for instance, writing is treated entirely as an act and writers are viewed as persons who engage in an act (writing) that by its very nature is dangerous to the continued existence of the state. The police do not try to suppress ideas. They are more specific, more concrete, more realistic. They go after books and manuscripts (writing) and destroy them. They go after writers as persons who have done something that they will do again and they persecute, punish, or kill them. They do not worry about what people think – not, at least, as we use the word *think*: a mental event, entirely internal, abstract. They worry about what people do: and writing, speaking, even as evidence that thinking is going on, are seen as things people *do*. There is a quality of immediacy and reality in what writing is taken to be. Where police power is used against writers systematically, writers are seen as people who by writing do something socially real and significant, not contemplative or dithering. Therefore, writing is never peripheral or beside the point. It is serious and easily seditious. I am offering no brief for police states when I say that virtually all great writers, cross-culturally and trans-historically, share this view of what writing is. In countries like the USA, controlled by a bourgeoisie to whom the police are accountable, writing is easier to do and valued less. It has less impact. It is more abundant and cheaper. Less is at stake for reader and writer both. The writer may hold writing to be a life-or-death matter, but the police and society do not. Writing is seen to be a personal choice, not a social, political, or aesthetic necessity fraught with danger and meaning. The general view in these pleasant places* is that writers think up ideas or words and then other people read them and all this happens in the head, a vast cavern somewhere north of the eyes. It is all air, except for the paper and ink, which are simply banal. Nothing happens.

Police in police states and most great writers throughout time see writing as act, not air – as act, not idea; concrete, specific, real, not insubstantial blather on a dead page. Censorship goes after the act and the actor: the book and the writer. It needs to destroy both. The cost in human lives is staggering, and it is perhaps essential to say that human lives destroyed must count more in the weighing of horror than books burned. This is my personal view, and I love books more than I love people.

---

* 'Well, you know, it amazes me . . .', says dissident South African writer Nadine Gordimer in an interview. 'I come to America, I go to England, I go to France . . . nobody's at risk. They're afraid of getting cancer, losing a lover, losing their jobs, being insecure . . . It's only in my own country that I find people who voluntarily choose to put everything at risk – in their personal life' Nadine Gordimer, *Writers at Work: The Paris Review Interviews* 261 (G. Plimpton ed., 6th ser., 1984).

Censorship is deeply misunderstood in the United States, because the fairly spoiled, privileged, frivolous people who are the literate citizens of this country think that censorship is some foggy effort to suppress ideas. For them, censorship is not something in itself – an act of police power with discernible consequences to hunted people; instead, it is about something abstract – the suppressing or controlling of ideas. Censorship, like writing itself, is no longer an act. Because it is no longer the blatant exercise of police power against writers or books because of what they do, what they accomplish in the real world, it becomes vague, hard to find, except perhaps as an attitude. It gets used to mean unpleasant, even angry frowns of disapproval or critiques delivered in harsh tones; it means social disapproval or small retaliations by outraged citizens where the book is still available and the writer is entirely unharmed, even if insulted. It hangs in the air, ominous, like the threat of drizzle. It gets to be, in silly countries like this one, whatever people say it is, separate from any material definition, separate from police power, separate from state repression (jail, banning, exile, death), separate from devastating consequences to real people (jail, banning, exile, death). It is something that people who eat fine food and wear fine clothes worry about frenetically, trying to find it, anticipating it with great anxiety, arguing it down as if – if it were real – an argument would make it go away; not knowing that it has a clear, simple, unavoidable momentum and meaning in a cruel world of police power that their privilege cannot comprehend.

OBSCENITY

In the nineteenth and twentieth centuries, in most of Western Europe, England, and the United States, more often than not (time-out for Franco, for instance), writing has been most consistently viewed as an act warranting prosecution when the writing is construed to be obscene.

The republics, democracies, and constitutional monarchies of the West, now and then, do not smother writers in police violence; they prefer to pick off writers who annoy and irritate selectively with fairly token prosecutions. The list of writers so harassed is elegant, white, male (therefore the pronoun 'he' is used throughout this discussion), and remarkably small. Being **517** among them is more than a ceremonial honour. As Flaubert wrote his brother in 1857:

> My persecution has brought me widespread sympathy. If my book is bad, that will serve to make it seem better. If, on the other hand, it has lasting qualities, that will build a foundation for it. There you are!
>
> I am hourly awaiting the official document which will name the day when I am to take my seat (for the crime of having written in French) in the dock in the company of thieves and homosexuals.[1]

A few months later that same year, Baudelaire was fined 300 francs for publishing six obscene poems. They also had to be removed from future editions of his book. In harder, earlier days, Jean-Jacques Rousseau spent eight years as a fugitive after his *Émile* was banned and a warrant was issued for his arrest. English censors criminally prosecuted Swinburne's *Poems and Ballads* in 1866. They were particularly piqued at Zola, even in translation, so his English publisher, seventy years old, went to jail for three months. In 1898, a bookseller was arrested for selling Havelock Ellis' work and received a suspended sentence. This list is representative, not exhaustive. While prosecutions of writers under obscenity laws have created great difficulties for writers already plagued with them (as most writers are), criminal prosecutions under obscenity law in Europe and the United States are notable for how narrowly they reach writers, how sanguine writers tend to be about the consequences to themselves, and how little is paid in the writer's life-blood to what D. H. Lawrence (who paid more than most modern Western writers) called the 'censor-moron'.[2] In South Africa, one would hardly be so flip. In our world, the writer gets harassed, as Lawrence did; the writer may be poor or not – the injury is considerably worse if he is; but the writer is not terrorized or tortured, and writers do not live under a reign of terror as writers, because of what they *do*. The potshot application of criminal law for writing is not good, nice, or right; but it is important to recognize the relatively narrow scope and marginal character of criminal prosecution under obscenity law in particular – especially compared with the scope and character of police-state censorship. Resisting obscenity law does not require hyperbolic renderings of what it is and how it has been used. It can be fought or repudiated on its own terms.

The use of obscenity laws against writers, however haphazard or insistent, is censorship and it does hold writing to be an act. This is a unique perception of what writing is, taking place, as it does, in a liberal context in which writing is held to be ideas. It is the obscene quality of the writing, the obscenity itself, that is seen to turn writing from idea into act. Writing of any kind or quality is idea, except for obscene writing, which is act. Writing is censored, even in our own happy little land of Oz, as act, not idea.

What is obscenity, such that it turns writing, when obscene, into something that actually happens – changes it from internal wind somewhere in the elevated mind into a genuinely offensive and utterly real fart, noticed, rude, occasioning pinched fingers on the nose?

There is the legal answer and the artistic answer. Artists have been consistently pushing on the boundaries of obscenity because great writers see writing as an act, and in liberal culture, only obscene writing has that social standing, that quality of dynamism and heroism. Great writers tend to experience writing as an intense and disruptive act; in the West, it is only recognized as such when the writing itself is experienced as obscene. In liberal culture, the writer has needed obscenity to be perceived as socially real.

What is it that obscenity does? The writer uses what the society deems to be obscene because the society then reacts to the writing the way the writer values the writing: as if it does something. But obscenity itself is socially constructed; the writer does not invent it or in any sense originate it. He finds it, knowing that it is what society hides. He looks under rocks and in dark corners.

There are two possible derivations of the word *obscenity*: the discredited one, *what is concealed*; and the accepted one, *filth*. Animals bury their filth, hide it, cover it, leave it behind, separate it from themselves: so do we, going way way back. Filth is excrement; from down there. We bury it or hide it; also, we hide where it comes from. Under male rule, menstrual blood is also filth, so women are twice dirty. Filth is where the sexual organs are and because women are seen primarily as sex, existing to provide sex, women have to be covered: our naked bodies being obscene.

Obscenity law uses both possible root meanings of *obscene* intertwined: it typically condemns nudity, public display, lewd exhibition, exposed genitals or buttocks or pubic areas, sodomy, **519** masturbation, sexual intercourse, excretion. Obscenity law is applied to pictures and words: the artefact itself exposes what should be hidden; it shows dirt. The human body and all sex and excretory acts are the domain of obscenity law.

But being in the domain of obscenity law is not enough. One must feel alive there. To be obscene, the representations must arouse prurient interest. *Prurient* means *itching* or *itch*; it is related to the Sanskrit for *he burns*. It means sexual arousal. Judges, law-makers, and juries have been, until very recently, entirely male: empirically, *prurient* means *causes erection*. Theologians have called this same quality of obscenity 'venereal pleasure,' holding that

> if a work is to be called obscene it must, of its nature, be such as actually to arouse or calculated to arouse in the viewer or reader such venereal pleasure. If the work is *not* of such a kind, it may, indeed, be vulgar, disgusting, crude, unpleasant, what you will – but it will *not* be, in the strict sense which Canon Law obliges us to apply, obscene.[3]

A secular philosopher of pornography isolated the same quality when he wrote: 'Obscenity is our name for the uneasiness which upsets the physical state associated with self-possession.'[4]

Throughout history, the male has been the standard for obscenity law: erection is his venereal pleasure or the uneasiness which upsets the physical state associated with his self-possession. It is not surprising, then, that in the same period when women became jurors, lawyers, and judges – but especially jurors, women having been summarily excluded from most juries until perhaps a decade ago – obscenity law fell into disuse and disregard. In order for obscenity law to have retained social and legal coherence, it would have had to recognize as part of its standard women's sexual arousal, a more subjective standard than erection. It would also have had to use the standard of penile erection in a social environment that was no longer sex-segregated, an environment in which male sexual arousal would be subjected to female scrutiny. In my view, the presence of women in the public sphere of legal decision-making has done more to undermine the efficacy of obscenity law than any self-conscious movement against it.

The act that obscenity recognizes is erection, and whatever writing produces erection is seen to be obscene – act, not idea – because of what it makes happen. The male sexual response is seen to be involuntary, so there is no experientially explicable division between the material that causes erection and the erection itself. That is the logic of obscenity law used against important writers who have pushed against the borders of the socially defined obscene, because they wanted writing to have that very quality of being a socially recognized act. They wanted the inevitability of the response – the social response. The erection makes the writing socially real from the society's point of view, not from the writer's. What the writer needs is to be taken seriously, by any means necessary. In liberal societies, only obscenity law comprehends writing as an act. It defines the nature and quality of the act narrowly – not writing itself, but producing erections. Flaubert apparently did produce them; so did Baudelaire, Zola, Rousseau, Lawrence, Joyce, and Nabokov. It's that simple.

What is at stake in obscenity law is always erection: under what conditions, in what circumstances, how, by whom, by what materials men want it produced in themselves. Men have made this public policy. Why they want to regulate their own erections through law is a question of endless interest and importance to feminists. Nevertheless, that they do persist in this regulation is simple fact. There are civil and social conflicts over how best to regulate erection through law, especially when caused by words or pictures. Arguments among men notwithstanding, high culture is phallocentric. It is also, using the civilized criteria of jurisprudence, not infrequently obscene.

Most important writers have insisted that their own uses of the obscene as socially defined are not pornography. As D. H. Lawrence wrote: 'But even I would censor genuine pornography rigorously. It would not be very difficult . . . [Y]ou can recognize it by the insult it offers, invariably, to sex, and to the human spirit.'[5] It was also, he pointed out, produced by the underworld. Nabokov saw in pornography 'mediocrity, commercialism, and certain strict rules of narration . . . [A]ction has to be limited to the copulation of clichés. Style, structure, imagery should never distract the reader from his tepid lust.'[6] They knew that what they did was different from pornography, but they did not entirely know what the difference was. They missed the heart of an empirical distinction because writing was indeed real to them but women were not.

The insult pornography offers, invariably, to sex is accomplished in the active subordination of women: the creation of a sexual dynamic in which the putting-down of women, the   **521** suppression of women, and ultimately the brutalization of women, *is* what sex is taken to be. Obscenity in law, and in what it does socially, is erection. Law recognizes the act in this. Pornography, however, is a broader, more comprehensive act, because it crushes a whole class of people through violence and subjugation: and sex is the vehicle that does the crushing. The penis is not the test, as it is in obscenity. Instead, the status of women is the issue. Erection is implicated in the subordinating, but who it reaches and how are the pressing legal and social questions. Pornography, unlike obscenity, is a discrete, identifiable system of sexual exploitation that hurts women as a class by creating inequality and abuse. This is a new legal idea, but it is the recognition and naming of an old and cruel injury to a dispossessed and coerced underclass. It is the sound of women's words breaking the longest silence.

PORNOGRAPHY

In the United States, it is an $8 billion trade in sexual exploitation.

It is women turned into subhumans, beaver, pussy, body parts, genitals exposed, buttocks, breasts, mouths opened and throats penetrated, covered in semen, pissed on, shitted on, hung from light fixtures, tortured, maimed, bleeding, disembowelled, killed.

It is some creature called female, used.

It is scissors poised at the vagina and objects stuck in it, a smile on the woman's face, her tongue hanging out.

It is a woman being fucked by dogs, horses, snakes.

It is every torture in every prison cell in the world, done to women and sold as sexual entertainment.

It is rape and gang rape and anal rape and throat rape: and it is the woman raped, asking for more.

It is the woman in the picture to whom it is really happening and the women against whom the picture is used, to make them do what the woman in the picture is doing.

It is the power men have over women turned into sexual acts men do to women, because pornography is the power and the act.

It is the conditioning of erection and orgasm in men to the powerlessness of women; our inferiority, humiliation, pain, torment; to us as objects, things, or commodities for use in sex as
servants.

It sexualizes inequality and in doing so creates discrimination as a sex-based practice.

It permeates the political condition of women in society by being the substance of our inequality however located – in jobs, in education, in marriage, *in life*.

It is women, kept a sexual underclass, kept available for rape and battery and incest and prostitution.

It is what we are under male domination; it is what we are for under male domination.

It is the heretofore hidden (from us) system of subordination that women have been told is just life.

Under male supremacy, it is the synonym for what being a woman is.

It is access to our bodies as a birthright to men: the grant, the gift, the permission, the licence, the proof, the promise, the method, how-to; it is us accessible, no matter what the law pretends to say, no matter what we pretend to say.

It is physical injury and physical humiliation and physical pain: to the women against whom it is used after it is made; to the women used to make it.

As words alone, or words and pictures, moving or still, it creates systematic harm to women in the form of discrimination and physical hurt. It creates harm inevitably by its nature because of what it is and what it does. The harm will occur as long as it is made and used. The name of the next victim is unknown, but everything else is known.

Because of it – because it is the subordination of women perfectly achieved – the abuse done to us by any human standard is perceived as using us for what we are by nature: women are whores; women want to be raped; she provoked it; women like to be hurt; she says no but means yes because she wants to be taken against her will which is not really her will because what she wants underneath is to have anything done to her that violates or humiliates or hurts her; she wants it, because she is a woman, no matter what it is, because she is a woman; that is how women are, what women are, what women are for. This view is institutionally expressed in law. So much for equal protection.

If it were being done to human beings, it would be reckoned an atrocity. It is being done to women. It is reckoned fun, pleasure, entertainment, sex, somebody's (not something's) civil liberty no less.

What do you want to be when you grow up? *Doggie Girl?* **523**

Gestapo Sex Slave? Black Bitch in Bondage? Pet, bunny, beaver? In dreams begin responsibilities,[7] whether one is the dreamer or the dreamed.

PORNOGRAPHERS

Most of them are small-time pimps or big-time pimps. They sell women: the real flesh-and-blood women in the pictures. They like the excitement of domination; they are greedy for profit; they are sadistic in their exploitation of women; they hate women, and the pornography they make is the distillation of that hate. The photographs are what they have created live, for themselves, for their own enjoyment. The exchanges of women among them are part of the fun, too: so that the fictional creature 'Linda Lovelace', who was the real woman Linda Marciano, was forced to 'deep-throat' every pornographer her owner-pornographer wanted to impress. Of course, it was the woman, not the fiction, who had to be hypnotized so that the men could penetrate to the bottom of her throat, and who had to be beaten and terrorized to get her compliance at all. The finding of new and terrible things to do to women is part of the challenge of the vocation: so the inventor of 'Linda Lovelace' and 'deep-throating' is a genius in the field, a pioneer. Or, as Al Goldstein, a colleague, referred to him in an interview with him in *Screw* several years ago: a pimp's pimp.

Even with written pornography, there has never been the distinction between making pornography and the sexual abuse of live women that is taken as a truism by those who approach pornography as if it were an intellectual phenomenon. The Marquis de Sade, as the world's foremost literary pornographer, is archetypal. His sexual practice was the persistent sexual abuse of women and girls, with occasional excursions into the abuse of boys. As an aristocrat in a feudal society, he preyed with near impunity on prostitutes and servants. The pornography he wrote was an urgent part of the sexual abuse he practised: not only because he did what he wrote, but also because the intense hatred of women that fuelled the one also fuelled the other: not two separate engines, but one engine running on the same tank. The acts of pornography and the acts of rape were waves on the same sea: that sea, becoming for its victims however it reached them, a tidal wave of destruction. Pornographers who use words know that what they are doing is both aggressive and destructive:

sometimes they philosophize about how sex inevitably ends in death, the death of a woman being a thing of sexual beauty as well as excitement. Pornography, even when written, is sex because of the dynamism of the sexual hatred in it; and for pornographers, the sexual abuse of women as commonly understood and pornography are both acts of sexual predation, which is how they live.

One reason that stopping pornographers and pornography is not censorship is that pornographers are more like the police in police states than they are like the writers in police states. They are the instruments of terror, not its victims. What police do to the powerless in police states is what pornographers do to women, except that it is entertainment for the masses, not dignified as political. Writers do not do what pornographers do. Secret police do. Torturers do. What pornographers do to women is more like what police do to political prisoners than it is like anything else: except for the fact that it is watched with so much pleasure by so many. Intervening in a system of terror where it is vulnerable to public scrutiny to stop it is not censorship; it is the system of terror that stops speech and creates abuse and despair. The pornographers are the secret police of male supremacy: keeping women subordinate through intimidation and assault.

SUBORDINATION

In the amendment to the Human Rights Ordinance of the City of Minneapolis written by Catharine A. MacKinnon and myself, (see Chapters 21 and 22), pornography is defined as the graphic, sexually explicit subordination of women whether in pictures or in words that also includes one or more of the following: women are presented dehumanized as sexual objects, things, or commodities; or women are presented as sexual objects who enjoy pain or humiliation; or women are presented as sexual objects who experience sexual pleasure in being raped; or women are presented as sexual objects tied up or cut up or mutilated or bruised or physically hurt; or women are presented in postures of sexual submission; or women's body parts are exhibited, such that women are reduced to those parts; or women are presented being penetrated by objects or animals; or women are presented in scenarios of degradation, injury, abasement, torture, shown as filthy or inferior, bleeding, bruised, or hurt in a context that makes these conditions sexual.

This statutory definition is an objectively accurate definition of what pornography is, based on an analysis of the material produced by the $8 billion-a-year industry, and also on extensive study of the whole range of pornography extant from other eras and other cultures. Given the fact that women's oppression has an ahistorical character – a sameness across time and cultures expressed in rape, battery, incest and prostitution – it is no surprise that pornography, a central phenomenon in that oppression, has precisely that quality of sameness. It does not significantly change in what it is, what it does, what is in it, or how it works, whether it is, for instance, classical or feudal or modern, Western or Asian; whether the method of manufacture is words, photographs or video. What has changed is the public availability of pornography and the numbers of live women used in it because of new technologies: not its nature. Many people note what seems to them a qualitative change in pornography – that it has become more violent, even grotesquely violent, over the last two decades. The change is only in what is publicly visible: not in the range or preponderance of violent pornography (e.g. the place of rape in pornography stays constant and central, no matter where, when, or how the pornography is produced); not in the character, quality, or content of what the pornographers actually produce; not in the harm caused; not in the valuation of women in it, or the metaphysical definition of what women are; not in the sexual abuse promoted, including rape, battery, and incest; not in the centrality of its role in subordinating women. Until recently, pornography operated in private, where most abuse of women takes place.

The oppression of women occurs through sexual subordination. It is the use of sex as the medium of oppression that makes the subordination of women so distinct from racism or prejudice against a group based on religion or national origin. Social inequality is created in many different ways. In my view, the radical responsibility is to isolate the material means of creating the inequality so that material remedies can be found for it.

This is particularly difficult with respect to women's inequality because that inequality is achieved through sex. Sex as desired by the class that dominates women is held by that class to be elemental, urgent, necessary, even if or even though it appears to *require* the repudiation of any claim women might have to full human standing. In the subordination of women, inequality itself is sexualized: made into the experience of sexual pleasure, essential to sexual desire. Pornography is the material means of sexualizing inequality; and that is why pornography is a central practice in the subordination of women.

Subordination itself is a broad, deep, systematic dynamic discernible in any persecution based on race or sex. Social subordination has four main parts. First, there is *hierarchy*, a group on top and a group on the bottom. For women, this hierarchy is experienced both socially and sexually, publicly and privately. Women are physically integrated into the society in which we are held to be inferior, and our low status is both put in place and maintained in the sexual usage of us by men; and so women's experience of hierarchy is incredibly intimate and wounding.

Second, subordination is *objectification*. Objectification occurs when a human being, through social means, is made less than human, turned into a thing or commodity, bought and sold. When objectification occurs, a person is depersonalized, so that no individuality or integrity is available socially or in what is an extremely circumscribed privacy (because those who dominate determine its boundaries). Objectification is an injury right at the heart of discrimination: those who can be used as if they are not fully human are no longer fully human in social terms; their humanity is hurt by being diminished.

Third, subordination is *submission*. A person is at the bottom of a hierarchy because of a condition of birth; a person on the bottom is dehumanized, an object or commodity; inevitably, the situation of that person requires obedience and compliance. That diminished person is expected to be submissive; there is no longer any right to self-determination, because there is no basis in equality for any such right to exist. In a condition of inferiority and objectification, submission is usually essential for survival. Oppressed groups are known for their abilities to anticipate the orders and desires of those who have power over them, to comply with an obsequiousness that is then used by the dominant group to justify its own dominance: the master, not able to imagine a human like himself in such degrading servility, thinks the servility is proof that the hierarchy is natural and that the objectification simply amounts to seeing these lesser creatures for what they are. The submission forced on inferior, objectified groups precisely   **527** by hierarchy and objectification is taken to be the proof of inherent inferiority and subhuman capacities.

Fourth, subordination is *violence*. The violence is systematic, endemic enough to be unremarkable and normative, usually taken as an implicit right of the one committing the violence. In my view, hierarchy, objectification, and submission are the preconditions for systematic social violence against any group targeted because of a condition of birth. If violence against a group is both socially pervasive and socially normal, then hierarchy, objectification, and submission are already solidly in place.

The role of violence in subordinating women has one special characteristic congruent with sex as the instrumentality of subordination: the violence is supposed to be sex for the woman too – what women want and like as part of our sexual nature; it is supposed to give women pleasure (as in rape); it is supposed to mean love to a woman from her point of view (as in battery). The violence against women is seen to be done not just in accord with something compliant in women, but in response to something active in and basic to women's nature.

Pornography uses each component of social subordination. Its particular medium is sex. Hierarchy, objectification, submission, and violence all become alive with sexual energy and sexual meaning. A hierarchy, for instance, can have a static quality; but pornography, by sexualizing it, makes it dynamic, almost carnivorous, so that men keep imposing it for the sake of their own sexual pleasure – for the sexual pleasure it gives them to impose it. In pornography, each element of subordination is conveyed through the sexually explicit usage of women: pornography in fact is what women are and what women are for and how women are used in a society premised on the inferiority of women. It is a metaphysics of women's subjugation: our existence delineated in a definition of our nature; our status in society predetermined by the uses to which we are put. The woman's body is what is materially subordinated. Sex is the material means through which the subordination is accomplished. Pornography is the institution of male dominance that sexualizes hierarchy, objectification, submission, and violence. As such, pornography creates inequality, not as artefact but as a system of social reality; it creates the necessity for and the actual behaviours that constitute
sex inequality.

SPEECH

Subordination can be so deep that those who are hurt by it are utterly silent. Subordination can create a silence quieter than death. The women flattened out on the page are deathly still, except for *hurt me*. *Hurt me* is not women's speech. It is the speech imposed on women by pimps to cover the awful, condemning silence. The Three Marias of Portugal went to jail for writing this: 'Let no one tell me that silence gives consent, because whoever is silent dissents.'[8] The women say the pimps' words: the language is another element of the rape; the language is part of the humiliation; the language is part of the forced sex. Real silence might signify dissent, for those reared to understand its sad discourse. The pimps cannot tolerate literal silence – it is too eloquent as testimony – so they force the words out of the woman's mouth. The women say pimps' words: which is worse than silence. The silence of the women not in the picture, outside the pages, hurt but silent, used but silent, is staggering in how deep and wide it goes. It is a silence over centuries: an exile into speechlessness. One is shut up by the inferiority and the abuse. One is shut up by the threat and the injury. In her memoir of the Stalin period, *Hope Against Hope*, Nadezhda Mandelstam wrote that screaming

> is a man's way of leaving a trace, of telling people how he lived and died. By his screams he asserts his right to live, sends a message to the outside world demanding help and calling for resistance. If nothing else is left, one must scream. Silence is the real crime against humanity.[9]

Screaming is a man's way of leaving a trace. The scream of a man is never misunderstood as a scream of pleasure by passersby or politicians or historians, nor by the tormentor. A man's scream is a call for resistance. A man's scream asserts his right to live, sends a message; he leaves a trace. A woman's scream is the sound of her female will and her female pleasure in doing what the pornographers say she is for. Her scream is a sound of celebration to those who overhear. Women's way of leaving a trace is the silence, centuries' worth: the entirely inhuman silence that surely one day will be noticed, someone will say that something is wrong, some sound is missing, some voice is lost; the entirely inhuman silence that will be a clue to human hope **529** denied, a shard of evidence that a crime has occurred, the crime that created the silence; the entirely inhuman silence that is a cold, cold condemnation of hurt sustained in speechlessness, a cold, cold condemnation of what those who speak have done to those who do not.

But there is more than the *hurt me* forced out of us, and the silence in which it lies. The pornographers actually use our bodies as their language. Our bodies are the building blocks of their sentences. What they do to us, called speech, is not unlike what Kafka's Harrow machine – ' "The needles are set in like the teeth of a harrow and the whole thing works something like a harrow, although its action is limited to one place and contrived with much more artistic skill" '[10] – did to the condemned in 'In the Penal Colony':

> 'Our sentence does not sound severe. Whatever commandment the prisoner has disobeyed is written upon his body by the Harrow. This prisoner, for instance' – the officer indicated the man – 'will have written on his body: HONOUR THY SUPERIORS!'[11]

> '. . . The Harrow is beginning to write; when it finishes the first draft of the inscription on the man's back, the layer of cotton wool begins to roll and slowly turns the body over, to give the Harrow fresh space for writing . . . So it keeps on writing deeper and deeper.'[12]

Asked if the prisoner knows his sentence, the officer replies: 'There would be no point in telling him. He'll learn it on his body.'[13]

This is the so-called speech of the pornographers, protected now by law.

Protecting what they 'say' means protecting what they do to us, how they do it. It means protecting their sadism on our bodies, because that is how they write: not like a writer at all; like a torturer. Protecting what they 'say' means protecting sexual exploitation, because they cannot 'say' anything without diminishing, hurting, or destroying us. Their rights of speech express their rights over us. Their rights of speech require our inferiority: and that we be powerless in relation to them. Their rights of speech mean that *hurt me* is accepted as the real speech of women, not speech forced on us as part of the sex forced on us but originating with us because we are what the pornographers 'say' we are.

If what we want to say is not *hurt me*, we have the real social power only to use silence as eloquent dissent. Silence is what women have instead of speech. Silence is our dissent during rape unless the rapist, like the pornographer, prefers *hurt me*, in which case we have no dissent. Silence is our moving persuasive dissent during battery unless the batterer, like the pornographer, prefers *hurt me*. Silence is a fine dissent during incest and for all the long years after.

Silence is not speech. We have silence, not speech. We fight rape, battery, incest, and prostitution with it. We lose. But someday someone will notice: that people called women were buried in a long silence that meant dissent and that the pornographers – with needles set in like the teeth of a harrow – chattered on.

EQUALITY

To get that word, male, out of the Constitution cost the women of this country 52 years of pauseless campaign; 56 state referendum campaigns; 480 legislative campaigns to get state suffrage amendments submitted; 47 state constitutional convention campaigns; 277 state party convention campaigns; 30 national party convention campaigns to get suffrage planks in the party platforms; 19 campaigns with 19 successive Congresses to get the federal amendment submitted, and the final ratification campaign.

Millions of dollars were raised, mostly in small sums, and spent with economic care. Hundreds of women gave the accumulated possibilities of an entire lifetime, thousands gave years of their lives, hundreds of thousands gave constant interest and such aid as they could. It was a continuous and seemingly endless chain of activity. Young suffragists who helped forge the last links of that chain were not born when it began. Old suffragists who helped forge the first links were dead when it ended.

– CARRIE CHAPMAN CATT

Feminists have wanted equality. Radicals and reformists have different ideas of what equality would be, but it has been the wisdom of feminism to value equality as a political goal with social integrity and complex meaning. The Jacobins also wanted equality, and the French Revolution was fought to accomplish it. Conservatism as a modern political movement actually developed to resist social and political movements for equality, beginning with the egalitarian imperatives of the French Revolution.

Women have had to prove human status, before having any claim to equality. But equality has been impossible to achieve, perhaps because, really, women have not been able to prove human status. The burden of proof is on the victim.

Not one inch of change has been easy or cheap. We have fought so hard and so long for so little. The vote did not change the status of women. The changes in women's lives that we can see on the surface do not change the status of women. By the year 2000, women are expected to be 100 per cent of this nation's poor. We are raped, battered, and prostituted: these acts against us are in the fabric of social life. As children, we are raped, physically abused, and prostituted. The country enjoys the injuries done to us, and spends $8 billion a year on the pleasure of watching us being hurt (exploitation as well as torture constituting substantive harm). The subordination gets deeper: we keep getting pushed down further. Rape is an entertainment. The contempt for us in that fact is immeasurable; yet we live under the weight of it. Discrimination is a euphemism for what happens to us.

It has plagued us to try to understand why the status of women does not change. Those who hate the politics of equality say they know: we are biologically destined for rape; God made us to be submissive unto our husbands. We change, but our status does not change. Laws change, but our status stays fixed. We move into the marketplace, only to face there classic sexual exploitation, now called sexual harassment. Rape, battery, prostitution, and incest stay the same in that they keep happening to us as part of what life is: even though we name the crimes against us as such and try to keep the victims from being destroyed by what we cannot stop from happening to them. And the silence stays in place too, however much we try to dislodge it with our truths. We say what has happened to us, but newspapers, governments, the culture that excludes us as fully human participants, wipe us out, wipe out our speech: by refusing to hear it. We are the tree falling in the desert. Should it matter: they are the desert.

The cost of trying to shatter the silence is astonishing to those who do it: the women, raped, battered, prostituted, who have something to say and say it. They stand there, even as they are erased. Governments turn from them; courts ignore them; this country disavows and dispossesses them. Men ridicule, threaten, or hurt them. Women jeopardized by them – silence being safer than speech – betray them. It is ugly to watch the complacent destroy the brave. It is horrible to watch power win.

Still, equality is what we want, and we are going to get it. What we understand about it now is that it cannot be proclaimed; it must be created. It has to take the place of subordination in human experience: physically replace it. Equality does not co-exist with subordination, as if it were a little pocket located somewhere within it. Equality has to win. Subordination has to lose. The subordination of women has not even been knocked loose, and equality has not materially advanced, at least in part because the pornography has been creating sexualized inequality in hiding, in private, where the abuses occur on a massive scale.

Equality for women requires material remedies for pornography, whether pornography is central to the inequality of women or only one cause of it. Pornography's antagonism to civil equality, integrity, and self-determination for women is absolute; and it is effective in making that antagonism socially real and socially determining.

The law that Catharine A. MacKinnon and I wrote making pornography a violation of women's civil rights recognizes the injury that pornography does: how it hurts women's rights of citizenship through sexual exploitation and sexual torture both.

The civil rights law empowers women by allowing women to civilly sue those who hurt us through pornography by trafficking in it, coercing people into it, forcing it on people, and assaulting people directly because of a specific piece of it.

The civil rights law does not force the pornography back underground. There is no prior restraint or police power to make arrests, which would then result in a revivified black market. This respects the reach of the first amendment, but it also keeps the pornography from getting sexier – hidden, forbidden, dirty, happily back in the land of the obscene, sexy slime oozing on great books. Wanting to cover the pornography up, hide it, is the first response of those who need pornography to the civil rights law. If pornography is hidden, it is still accessible to men as a male right of access to women; its injuries to the status of women are safe and secure in those hidden rooms, behind those opaque covers; the abuses of women are sustained as a private right supported by public policy. The civil rights law puts a flood of light on the pornography, what it is, how it is used, what it does, those who are hurt by it.

The civil rights law changes the power relationship between pornographers and women: it stops the pornographers from producing discrimination with the total impunity they now enjoy, and gives women a legal standing resembling equality from which to repudiate the subordination itself. The secret-police power of the pornographers suddenly has to confront a modest amount of due process.

The civil rights law undermines the subordination of women in society by confronting the pornography, which is the systematic sexualization of that subordination. Pornography is inequality. The civil rights law would allow women to advance equality by removing this concrete discrimination and hurting economically those who make, sell, distribute, or exhibit it. The pornography, being power, has a right to exist that we are not allowed to challenge under this system of law. After it hurts us by being what it is and doing what it does, the civil rights law would allow us to hurt it back. Women, not being power, do not have a right to exist equal to the right the pornography has. If we did, the pornographers would be precluded from exercising their rights at the expense of ours, and since they cannot exercise them any other way, they would be precluded period. We come to the legal system beggars: though in the public dialogue around the passage of this civil rights law we have the satisfaction of being regarded as thieves.

The civil rights law is women's speech. It defines an injury to us from our point of view. It is premised on a repudiation of sexual subordination which is born of our experience of it. It breaks the silence. It is a sentence that can hold its own against the male flood. It is a sentence on which we can build a paragraph, then a page.

It is my view, learned largely from Catharine MacKinnon, that women have a right to be effective. The pornographers, of course, do not think so, nor do other male supremacists; and it is hard for women to think so. We have been told to educate people on the evils of pornography: before the development of this civil rights law, we were told just to keep quiet about pornography altogether; but now that we have a law we want to use, we are encouraged to educate and stop there. Law educates. This law educates. It also allows women to *do* something. In hurting the pornography back, we gain ground in making equality more likely, more possible – someday it will be real. We have a means to fight the pornographers' trade in women. We have a means to get at the torture and the terror. We have a means with which to challenge the pornography's efficacy in making exploitation and inferiority the bedrock of women's social status. The civil rights law introduces into the public consciousness an analysis: of what pornography is, what sexual subordination is, what equality might be. The civil rights law introduces a new legal standard: these things are not done to citizens of this country. The civil rights law introduces a new political standard: these things are not done to human beings. The civil rights law provides a new mode of action for women through which we can pursue equality and because of which *our* speech will have social meaning. The civil rights law gives us back what the pornographers have taken from us: hope rooted in real possibility.

Notes

1. Gustave Flaubert, *Letters*, trans. J. M. Cohen (London: George Weidenfeld & Nicolson, 1950), p. 94.
2. D. H. Lawrence, *Sex, Literature and Censorship* (New York: Twayne Publishers, 1953), p. 9.
3. Harold Gardiner (S. J.), *Catholic Viewpoint on Censorship* (Garden City: Hanover House, 1958), p. 65.
4. Georges Bataille, *Death and Sensuality* (New York: Ballantine Books, Inc., 1969), p. 12.
5. Lawrence, op. cit., p. 74.
6. Vladimir Nabokov, 'Afterward', *Lolita* (New York: Berkeley Publishing Corporation, 1977), p. 284.
7. The actual line is 'In dreams begins responsibility', quoted by Yeats as an epigram to his collection, *Responsibilities*.
8. Maria Isabel Barreno, Maria Teresa Horta, and Maria Velho da Costa, *The Three Marias: New Portuguese Letters*, trans. Helen R. Lane (New York: Bantam Books, 1976), p. 291.
9. Nadezhda Mandelstam, *Hope Against Hope*, trans. Max Hayward (New York: Atheneum, 1978), pp. 42–3.
10. Franz Kafka, 'In the Penal Colony', *The Penal Colony*, trans. Willa and Edwin Muir (New York: Schocken Books, 1965), p. 194.
11. Ibid., p. 197.
12. Ibid., p. 203.
13. Ibid., p. 197.

25 Working in the Ministry of Truth: Pornography and Censorship in Contemporary Britain

MICHAEL MOORCOCK*

> Pornography turns sex inequality into sexuality and turns male
> dominance into the sex difference. Put another way, pornography
> makes inequality into sex, which makes it enjoyable, and into
> gender, which makes it seem natural. By packaging the resulting
> product as pictures and words, pornography turns gendered and
> sexualized inequality into 'speech', which has made it a right. Thus
> does pornography, cloaked as the essence of nature and the index
> of freedom, turn the inequality between women and men into those
> twin icons of male supremacy, sex and speech, and a practice of
> sex discrimination into a legal entitlement.
>
> Catharine A. MacKinnon, *Feminism Unmodified*

KEEPING THE PROLES CONFUSED

> The Yugoslav erotic press is the freest in the world, both in content
> and, even more, in its promotion and distribution . . . All you have
> to do is stroll to the nearest kiosk, which will openly offer you . . .
> domestic pornographic magazines, which multiply every day like
> mushrooms after rain.
>
> Bogdan Tirnanic, Yugoslav critic

In Orwell's *Nineteen Eighty-Four* state censorship was universal
and omniscient. At the Ministry of Truth Winston Smith was
employed in censoring and rewriting the news, altering history,
while elsewhere Julia was turning out pornography with titles
like *Spanking Stories* and *One Night in a Girls' School*, produced by
the state to divert the proletariat and preserve the status quo.

Not a lot, it seems, has changed in Airstrip One.

In today's Little England, our liberty and free speech are
under attack almost daily. The old notion of rights of citizenship
gave way to 'consumers' rights' – the rights of those with
spending power: a good citizen is a wealthy citizen. Still, post-
Thatcher, the geriatric war-horses of the Tory and Labour

* Part of this chapter was commissioned by the *Sunday Telegraph* magazine,
who decided not to use it.

parties creak into a diversionary pantomime of conflict while a few powerful men help themselves to what's left of the nation's resources. Increasingly, they alone determine what issues in society are 'important' and what are not. Press barons pontificate on the nobility of their purpose, the glory of their fights for freedom and liberty, their value to society, while publishing the newspapers and magazines which, increasingly, represent only their interests and the interests of the power élite to which they belong. Pornography proliferates, endorsed by the state, to divert the proletariat and preserve the status quo. More sophisticated than the chaps at the Ministry of Truth, these chaps have combined the propaganda with the pornography and saved considerably on staff costs. A model of Thatcherism, efficient, privatized and, in Thatcher newspeak, 'free'.

It is in this climate that the pornography issue has frequently been diverted into endless debates on the subject of what is and what is not 'obscene', of what should or should not be 'banned', and so on. Liberal socialists, who appear cheerfully to support the monarchy, the class system and the status quo in general, write in the *New Statesman* about the dangers of the anti-pornography campaign, the threat to society as we know it if an anti-pornography law based on sex equality were to be passed by Parliament, and dismiss as 'nonsense' the statements of those who declare themselves opposed to both censorship and por-nography and who work to produce a legal formula which would empower people to fight pornography while attacking the state's powers of censorship. The measure of their acceptance of the status quo, it seems to me, is revealed in their simple inability to argue the issue in any terms but those of thirty years ago and is a graphic example of today's Labour Party's ideological bank-ruptcy and failure of social perception.

To suggest, as the line goes, that a sex-discrimination por-nography law would enable any lunatic to bring charges against, for instance, *Woman's Own* for running an underwear ad or cause *Romeo and Juliet* to be banned is clearly nonsense. That isn't, for one thing, how the law operates. Courts are not only antagonistic to people trying to use the law frivolously or inappropriately, they are, as we all know, presently constituted so that it is difficult enough for the ordinary person to use them seriously or appropriately. Suggesting that a law enabling a woman to challenge the image of herself that pornography promotes is 'censorship' echoes, somewhat unpleasantly, those very similar **537** arguments predicting that once our Race Relations Act became law it would be impossible for a writer to have a West Indian villain and *Uncle Tom's Cabin* or *Othello* would vanish from the public library shelves. We all know that this is not what happens in real life.

What does happen in real life is that pornography desensitizes sexuality and promotes an image of women as sex objects, as subhuman, as second-class citizens, as willing (biologically determined) victims. This is how pornography is defined by those feminists who are trying, by a variety of strategies, to get rid of it. We all know what that is and we all know who, in the main, buys it and who profits from it. I do not believe that sexually specific fiction (like some of my own, for instance) or photographs of naked people, or drawings of people fucking, or educational material are, by definition, pornographic. I do believe, however, that pornography contaminates such things and frequently makes them seem pornographic because the spirit and intention of material found in, say, *Playboy* or *Whitehouse* is so prevalent in British society.

I believe that only in a 'pornographic climate' could anyone find *Lady Chatterley's Lover*, for instance, pornographic. If we could, somehow, eliminate or even seriously reduce the amount of pornography in our society, I believe it would be possible to increase and enjoy sexually specific representations of all kinds. The vocabulary of pornography (both visual and verbal) has come to infect every aspect of the media, offering innuendo and 'sub-texts' which, when porn was a 'secret' and minority industry, simply did not exist for the majority of us. I do not believe pornography can be 'eliminated' by law but it might, with the right laws, be made socially unacceptable again, *not* because it is 'dirty' but because it represents a kind of attitude towards human beings which, like racism, should be anathema to a modern state founded on the ideals of the Enlightenment. Such a law would free us to celebrate our sexuality in all its variety and allow us to publish work which is the very antithesis of pornography.

Only in a society which tolerates and even celebrates the continuing subjection of women as a class could books like *Lolita*, *The Blue Angel*, *Lady Chatterley's Lover*, *Ulysses*, *Nana*, *Manon Lescaut* or other books about sexual obsession seem pornographic. They would in no way be threatened by a law designed to attack material which objectifies and fetishizes adults and children as usable property, as sexual toys, as animals who enjoy being hurt.

By substituting such legislation for the existing obscenity laws we would also strengthen society's power to identify and attack material which clearly infects the lives of the majority of citizens.

By getting rid of the Obscene Publications Act (OPA) and replacing it with an Act recognizing pornography as discriminatory we would at last be allowed to see, for instance, an erect male penis, sexual penetration, acts of love-making between adults of the same sex and so on. Such a law would help the police. It would curtail random raids and would remove the excuse police forces presently have for raiding shops selling 'obscene' material when they are actually seizing political, gay and drug-related material, all covered by the vague 'deprave and corrupt' wording of the OPA. It would clarify Customs regulations. It would enable me, as a writer who has experienced quite a bit of suppression and attempted suppression over the past twenty-five years, to feel more secure about writing and publishing what I like. A 'porn as sex discrimination' law would, in other words, be a powerful weapon against attempted censorship.

In common with some of my critics I believe we are living in dangerously repressive times. All around us political censorship is increasing. At the end of the 1980s I experienced more 'editing' or 'spiking' of my political material (in a variety of well-known and respected publications) than I have ever known before. There's a mood of brutal cynicism in Britain reminiscent of the Second Empire (which also sought to attack the ideals of the Enlightenment and reinflate its economy by unjust, simplistic, ultimately disastrous, financial policies) which not only permits but which appears to celebrate the abuse of power by the privileged. If I believed a sex-discrimination anti-pornography law to be in any way a means of increasing that abuse I would do everything I could to fight it. As it is, I believe such a law, carefully formulated, to be an important means of attacking the fundamental inequalities in British society. It would be a law based firmly and clearly on egalitarian principles. It would not be a mere reaction to so-called obscenity or immorality. It would, I think, reflect the wishes of the majority of women, if the opinion polls conducted by popular women's magazines are anything to go by or, indeed, if the quantity of letters received by anti-pornography groups from women, who feel abused and threatened by the pornography this proposed law would attack, are an accurate gauge.

Alternatively, I suppose, we could learn to love Big Brother **539** and suck his cock whenever he feels the urge. We might even learn, in time, to believe it's the best and most natural thing in the world and insist to others that there's nothing sweeter or more beautiful.

TEACH YOURSELF NEWSPEAK

What I remember most about Carl taking photographs of me is that I was not allowed to do 'certain things' while the pictures were being taken. I could and in fact had to do those same 'certain things' when pictures were not being taken. I recall thinking, how come Carl does not want my mouth touching his cock while pictures are being taken? Today I know why: because actual physical contact was considered hard-core porn and hard-core was not as easily sold as soft-core porn was. I was 14 years old and Carl was 28. It was just a month or two ago – nineteen years after the fact – that I came to remember and acknowledge that my stepbrother involved me in child pornography.

I remember Carl saying he couldn't wait for me to become 18 years old because then he would put me on drugs. Carl had me in training for a life of violent sexual abuse. As I now think about porn, I realize that Carl's intent was to use me and to use my body for money and for sex. Carl's intent is socially sanctioned, protected, and accepted in our society.

Valerie Heller, WAP News Report

From the age of seventeen I have actively attacked and challenged censorship in Britain and the US, working for and financing publications constantly threatened by someone's attempts to silence them. Sometimes those attempts were successful.

I have been threatened by the Special Branch, by W. H. Smith, by 'morality groups' and other arms of the Establishment and have devoted a lot of my resources into fighting back. I am angered by the way the Official Secrets Act is used to control the press. I am angered by the way in which the large-circulation newspapers almost invariably promote the interests of a white male power élite. Profoundly opposed to the OPA, I believe life would be enormously improved in Britain by a Freedom of Information Act allowing us access to all official records.

My anti-censorship activities, from the late 1950s on, are a matter of history. I have published articles in a variety of recent journals, including *Time Out* and *Index on Censorship*, attacking the

very real abuses by the police of powers granted them under the

OPA. I have also, over the years, avoided association with pornography publishers (some of whom have offered me help) and have come to identify my confusion and distress around pornography as a reaction to its denigration and sexual objectification of women. One of the reasons I refused, for instance, Bob Guccione's assistance for my beleaguered magazine *New Worlds* in the 1960s was because I saw no connection between his commercial exploitation of women's bodies and my own distinctly non-commercial attempts to break down the taboos then existing on what you could and could not say in print. With Guccione's help I might have kept my magazine alive much longer, but somehow the terms didn't look attractive. Equally, I have refused to be published in the *Penthouse* spin-off *Omni*, as well as *Playboy*, though I was once published in *Penthouse* (who asked me to play up the 'female dominant' angle – i.e. I had an active woman as a central character – in a story, but when I refused, published the story anyway).

Before that I had also edited and produced soft-core pornography magazines and it was this experience which helped me identify why, over the past twenty years or so, I believe the stuff to be deeply pernicious and a strong contributing factor to continuing inequalities in our society. I had direct evidence of all kinds of the harm pornography causes both those who use it and the women who so often become its victims, and as a result was faced with a problem shared by many who believe that personal liberty within the law is the most important concern of a democratic society: how do you attack pornography while decreasing censorship? It was feminism which provided me not only with that answer but with an analysis of many of the other political problems puzzling me as a younger man. The formulation, by MacKinnon and Dworkin, of sex-discrimination legislation in the USA was the answer I had been looking for.

During the mid-1960s *New Worlds* had, in fact, been taken over by a porn publisher (the infamous and now infinitely more powerful Gold family). In those days I shared a common belief that 'soft' porn, at any rate, generally acted as a release mechanism rather than a stimulant to violence. After a few weeks' exposure to daily life at the porn publishers, however, I learned that this simply wasn't the reality.

Two things helped change my mind. The first was the manipulative cynicism of magazine staff towards their subject matter. During photo-sessions, for instance, photographers were cajoling,   **541** 'egalitarian', friendly. After the sessions, however, they talked about the women in terms that were to me shockingly crude and brutal, joking about how they had tricked the 'girls' into lewd poses, sometimes by seducing them first. The 'girls', flattered, usually not very bright, frequently confused, were manipulated not just by the photographers into certain poses but also into signing release forms before they had seen the pictures. The second, and perhaps most persuasive, was the letters sent in by readers.

The letters which the magazines were prepared to publish were the usual cleaned-up equivalent of what most men have seen, from time to time, in lavatory cubicles. The letters which the magazine could not publish were often horrifying. Usually written in response to particular photo-features, they would name the pictures they liked best, sometimes discussing in clinical detail how the photos could be 'improved' or 'made stronger'. Frequently revealing a psychopathic hatred of women, the writers would describe what they did to their wives and lovers in scenarios directly borrowed from the magazine features. They could also be accusatory, complaining that women they knew were 'holding back' by refusing to take part in 'fun' clearly enjoyed by the smiling sirens of the photos. ('Fun books' is a familiar trade term for porn magazines.) *Why won't she do it for me?* was a frequent theme. Then we had: *I made her do it and now she likes it.* Or: *I know she'll like it once she tries it.* Or: *I showed her the pictures so she could see what I wanted. She loves to look at the pictures with me and then we . . .* etc.

Many of the real letters were too blatant for the magazine to print. They ranged from detailed fantasies of rape, seduction and group orgies, to astonishing admissions of incest, child abuse and complicated seductions of teenage girls. Instead of publishing them, editorial members wrote fictitious letters purporting to come from women who liked nothing better than to act out the stories and poses that were published. Mild S&M was a particular favourite of these invented women.

A small percentage of the genuine writers (none of them women) expressed a strong interest in 'kiddies' and wrote of their own and neighbours' children lusting after sex and being stimulated by the pictures. They, of course, wanted 'stronger' material, especially involving women dressed up as schoolgirls and being spanked (echoes of *Nineteen Eighty-Four* again . . .). The only candidates *for* spanking we ever heard from of course were men, most of those clearly middle-aged. Larger numbers of letters described an interest in bondage, leather and rubber, rape (never called that), sadistic anal sex and forced sex of every variety. There were also, of course, the Nazi fantasies, the racist fantasies, the transference fantasies (some of these writers pretended to be women but usually revealed their actual gender in some way). They saw the editorial people as fellow aficionados and addressed them in the confidential, knowing tones of one club-member to another. They wanted more bestiality, more 'discipline' and more (usually minor) mutilation. In common with most prostitutes, the staff encouraged this sense of security. Readers were told their desires were 'natural' and nothing to be ashamed of. Only off duty did they allow themselves to express contempt for the punters. Laughter was rarely permitted in 'fun books'. Once, I was thrown out of a Soho porn temple for chuckling at one of the more bizarre titles.

The editorial staff responded with amusement to the letters, passed the detailed and unusual ones around and then used them to plan future issues, angling their features and photo-sessions, as well as their fictitious letters, to meet readers' demands. In those days bondage, sadism (Nazi scenarios, for instance) and 'schoolgirl' themes were the commonest because these actually fell more easily within the guidelines about the degree of nudity and intercourse tolerated by the authorities. Erotic or educational pictures showing ordinary sex between men and women were deemed obscene, while pictures of women hanging by their ankles from poles, chained to chairs, struck by flails and canes or encased in bizarre bondage paraphernalia were 'acceptable'. These subjects met with considerable reader approval.

In letters neither markedly illiterate nor mentally subnormal, men would write in offering suggestions about how to improve future issues. They wanted more shots, say, of 'Suzie' tied up with ropes but needed clearer shots of the knots to copy. They complained that the welts on 'schoolgirl Sharon's buttocks' looked as if they had been emphasized by lipstick. There was a tone to the majority of these letters which I can only describe as a dull, psychopathic drone – the appalling banality of the mental ward, the concentration camp, the massage parlour.

I think that once you have been exposed to pornography and its users you are infected for life, whether your response is one of fascination or disgust. I came to believe that pornography was a drug at least as harmful to society as heroin and far more widely **543** used. I think it is folly to minimize its effect or the extent of its distribution. One of the differences nowadays, of course, is that society frowns far more readily on the users of hard drugs than it does on the users of hard pornography. People who will happily see heroin as a contributing factor to serious crime refuse to accept that *Hustler* could be an equally important factor.

In spite of this conviction of the social harm done by pornography I remain opposed to Mary Whitehouse and have refused to endorse, for instance, Clare Short's strategy (which offers a feminist analysis, I think, but an authoritarian answer). I believe that the OPA, with its vague wording about the tendency to deprave and corrupt, is both ineffectual at 'controlling' pornography and socially dangerous. Depravity and corruption are, after all, a matter of opinion. Whoever happens to be in power can define what constitutes these tendencies and therefore it is a bad law. A good law is one which is, as it were, 'above' such abuse, in keeping with the spirit and ideals of those who founded our modern system of democratic parliamentary politics. Thus Joyce's *Ulysses*, Hall's *The Well of Loneliness*, Forster's *Maurice*, Miller's *Tropic of Cancer*, Burroughs's *The Naked Lunch* can and have been prosecuted or suppressed under such legislation while all kinds of political, social and sexual material can and have been defined as 'harmful'. The activities of people like James Anderton in Manchester, whose police force was responsible for jailing a bookseller friend of mine for selling novels which had been on public sale in England for ten years, is a case in point. The OPA is a law which is rife with examples of abuse at every level. Courts permit out-of-context extracts of books to be presented to juries who are then asked to judge if they are likely to 'deprave and corrupt'. These extracts can be from political books, books about drugs, books about safe sex for gay men or, indeed, erotic books of all sorts. For this reason even people who understand the damage pornography can do to women have in the past been reluctant to see the Act employed.

I can only think that the English critics of those feminists proposing sex-discrimination legislation against pornography are responding so negatively because they still confuse such legislation with the OPA and its abuses. This can be the only reason why they use words like 'dangerous' and 'pernicious' when referring to such proposed legislation. Unlike anarchist groups or groups such as the US Citizens for Media Responsibility

Without Law who hold the view that pretty much all legislation is bad (my own ideals for the long term), such critics do not seem particularly upset by other forms of legislation designed to protect the interest of those with little or no real power in the community, so it is hard to understand what they see as 'dangerous' here. I've yet to read a coherent examination of, say, Dworkin's or MacKinnon's published arguments which are, after all, easily available to feminists. I'd like to read one, especially if it raised the level of the current debate. So far the only criticisms have been vaguely perturbed or have resorted to name-calling (Dworkin – ex-battered wife, Jew and civil rights activist from the 1960s to the present – was recently called a Nazi by a *Nation* feature-writer, echoing the words of *Hustler* proprietor Larry Flynt, and making me, for one, wonder who in fact was leaguing themselves with 'the Right'). The anti-porn feminist argument is that since the bulk of pornography depicts women as fetishised sex objects, since much of it represents them as enjoying humiliation and degradation, it encourages men in their tra-ditional attitudes towards women as second-class citizens or worse, and therefore, like racist propaganda (happy niggers, greedy Jews, degenerate Indians), it constitutes an ongoing threat to a woman's civil rights, her rights to quiet enjoyment of her life, her rights to a life free from sudden and random attack. The pornography question then becomes one that does not have to define what is 'obscene' but what promotes the continuing subjugation of women as a class.

Since the law already agrees, for instance, that publications promoting the degradation and pernicious stereotyping of people of colour can be an incitement to racial hatred which threatens their civil rights, and since we have sex equality legislation allowing people to bring cases of sexual harassment and discrim-ination before the courts, it should be possible to prosecute material which blatantly promotes the myth that most women 'secretly' enjoy being hurt and/or degraded. Obviously a clear definition of such pornography is required and a blueprint for such a definition and the legislation itself exists in the bill proposed by MacKinnon and Dworkin in the USA. Others evidently found this blueprint useful. In the US at least two liberal city councils, with good records on sex equality, asked MacKinnon and Dworkin to help them gather evidence of the links between pornography and sexual violence with a view to passing legislation on the lines proposed. They felt that, while they agreed that pornography was discriminatory to women,   **545** they had to produce a case for direct links between porn and violence if they were to persuade people to accept discrimination-based porn legislation. The evidence given was enough to convince the majority of voters. It was given over a period of two days and came from academics, public servants (including police and prison workers) and, perhaps most tellingly, from those who were the victims of pornographers. Psychologists, sociologists and academics described studies proving over and over again links between pornography and sexual violence.

Soon after the evidence was heard, the multi-million-dollar porn industry began marshalling its forces in attempts to block the legislation which followed. So far – with the active help of the American Civil Liberties Union – they have been successful. In magazines like *Playboy*, *Penthouse* and *Hustler* pictures of women being beaten, fucked by animals, brutalized and physically injured have so far been accepted as examples of free speech by the US courts, as have pornographic cartoons of well-known feminists. *Pornography and Sexual Violence*, the complete record of the public hearings in Minneapolis, has yet, however, to find a US publisher. Free speech, it seems, is, as ever, the domain of those powerful enough to define it. The book eventually appeared, with a somewhat misleading introduction, in Britain, published by Everywoman with help from the Barrow Cadbury Fund.

In spite of this, and other, published evidence, people continue to argue that there is nothing to prove the case against pornography as 'incitement to sexual hatred'. They continue to speak of anti-porn feminists' 'links' with 'the Right', when it has been liberal politicians who have supported the Dworkin/MacKinnon proposed legislation and it has been their attackers who have had the support of 'the Left' (such as the ACLU). Such continuing myths, presented as fact by people whom I otherwise respect, make me feel when I open the *New Statesman*, for instance, that I've fallen down a political rabbit hole. What, I wonder, are my own 'links with the Right'?

For me, *Pornography and Sexual Violence* provides the evidence that pornography directly leads to sexual violence, that it is a drug requiring stronger and stronger doses if it is to continue stimulating the user, that many men are encouraged by pornography to commit sexual crimes, including incest, child molestation and rape, and that they in turn use the pornography as a means of 'seasoning' – of teaching their victims what to do. Yet, in common with Andrea Dworkin, for instance, I still refuse to accept the need for any law increasing the state's powers to prosecute such material or censor or ban it as 'obscene'. The only acceptable legislation is that which empowers the victim to fight back, which enables an ordinary individual to fight a billion-pound industry. For this reason any offers of assistance by repressive or authoritarian groups or individuals have to be refused. And have been refused. I resigned from one committee, for instance, after another member asked what was wrong with censoring pornography and received support from a significant number of others who shared her view. Clearly we were not on the same wavelength.

I am certain, too, that thousands of women will welcome the evidence presented by publications like *Pornography and Sexual Violence* as confirmation of their own experience or, at least, suspicions – 'ordinary' women as well as the photographic models, prostitutes and molested girls whose experience has proven only too frequently how little 'release' and how much incitement is contained in the magazines regularly displayed by newsagents and booksellers in every British high street.

In my view, the widespread acceptance of pornography over the past twenty-five years (including the increasingly blatant stuff printed in our tabloids) has led directly to the great rise in sexual crime. None the less, even this direct connection is only an example in support of the main argument – that pornography is a pervasive propaganda weapon helping maintain a status quo which favours the male and maintains the female as a source of cheap labour, as a confused and therefore more easily manipulated second-class citizen, as a sex object conditioned to serve men's continuing needs for confirmation of their power as well as immediate gratification of sexual desire, and so on. As one of the mainstays of this status quo, pornography, it seems to me, has come to pervade society, almost in direct relation to the successes of the women's movement.

Could something be bothering Big Brother?

WHY BIG BROTHER LOVES YOU

By chance we came across your sexy newspaper *Suck*. My wife who is very open-minded suggested that we show it to the children when we got back to the hotel ... I had always fancied my daughter ... But I had up to then resisted the temptation to fuck

her especially as a close neighbour of ours, a Jamaican fellow with
a white wife, has just started a two-year prison sentence for doing
it to his twelve-year-old daughter. The daughter didn't complain
. . . However, after a few drinks in the evening we plucked up
enough courage and showed them *Suck*. Our children were both
thrilled by the pictures and stories and after promises of strict
secrecy always we undressed after locking the hotel room door . . .
We are now even a more closely knit family sworn to secrecy about
this. We are definitely more happy and healthy. Elizabeth enjoys
sucking my cock. She now calls me her 'gorgeous Daddy'. She
keeps asking me to fuck her, but up to today I haven't done her.
My wife wants me to have it with Elizabeth as she enjoys it from
Peter so much. I expect before the holiday is over I shall have her
. . . I think all families will be like this in years to come. Until the
law is changed in (England) and in others it will have to be done
secretly.

'Mr Freeman', letter to *Suck* magazine, Amsterdam, *c.* 1970

For me, censorship has a pretty precise meaning, based on my
direct experience as its not infrequent victim. It is one of the
chief methods by which those with power try to ensure that they
are never threatened by those with little or no power. They take
the simple and familiar steps (like the Chinese government over
the student massacres) of lying and rewriting history in order to
maintain control, but they cannot have those lies challenged so
they refuse to allow the truth to be spoken and punish anyone
who tries to speak it.

Censorship is a tool of authoritarianism and the degree of
authoritarianism in a society can be measured fairly accurately
by the degree of censorship it exercises. I believe that pornography (as blatant and grotesque as racism once was) is a
crucial factor in the power élite's maintenance of control over
those it exploits, by reminding the exploited of their proper place
in the social scheme, by reinforcing the belief of the exploiter in
the rightness of his position.

Because most of us are nervous of change – especially radical
change – we would all rather be reassured that what we have is
the best we are likely to get. That is what most black slaves in
America at one time came to think, it is what German Jews
thought, it is what, at least until recently, most women thought.
If we unconsciously accept the status quo we never feel called
upon to challenge it. The liberal Left, represented by the majority
of Labour Party members and MPs, reflects in almost all its
statements a fairly cheerful contentment with the status quo. As
548 I began by saying, it does not actively challenge the class system,

our monarchy (probably that system's linchpin) or the innumerable unexamined cultural assumptions which now make England the least democratic of the 'developed' nations.

Challenge this 'Left' and it falls back on a bankrupt vocabulary of tired buzz-words of which 'fascist' and 'censorship' are two of the commonest. No matter that our liberty is being eroded daily in the name of consumerism (of which the Green Movement *could* become the most sophisticated example), that the rights of minorities are under serious attack and that a large part of Britain (the poorest) is disenfranchised, that a British man can still get five years for a failed fraud and a suspended sentence for a successful rape, most British socialists remain locked in attitudes that had lost any relevance to reality forty years ago. Clearly therefore this status quo suits them. They may add the word 'feminist' to their self-description and thus gain further easy peer approval, but they remain as entrenched as any Old Guard Tory in their commitment to those attitudes and prejudices with which England established and justified its empire.

I believe some questions have to be asked and debated if 'the Left' is not to divide itself further than it is already divided. These questions are not rhetorical. I want to know what people believe is in danger of being 'censored'. Free speech?

At present it is illegal in Britain to publish bestiality magazines. By 1992 this could change. Is a picture of a woman being fucked by an Alsatian dog 'free speech' and, if so, how does this 'free speech' benefit society? What does it make 'better'? What principle is being defended? Whose freedom is the picture representing? The woman's? The dog's? The photographer's? The publisher's? Let us say it represents that particular woman's sexual preference. Who buys the picture? Is it women who like being fucked by dogs or who are at least turned on by the idea? Is it men who enjoy seeing women fucked by dogs? Given that such a picture is produced for financial gain, does a large enough public exist among women sexually stimulated by bestiality to make that publication financially viable? Or what about magazines specializing in torture, rape, bondage, child or 'lesbian' sex? Do they represent the speech of the women in the pictures? Whose *speech* are we talking about? Is *Men Only* full of pictures of men as *Woman's Own* is full of pictures of women? Does *Men Only* sell mainly to housewives? Whose freedom does it represent? Whose sexuality? If, under the present law, that bestiality image is illegal, 'obscene', subject to censorship, what freedoms are **549** being threatened by its continuing repression? What freedoms have been gained, for instance, in Germany, where such images are, indeed, legal? Is the press in Germany significantly freer than that in Britain? Are people freer, for instance, in Yugoslavia which, at time of writing, has the least-controlled pornography in the world? Have sex crimes dropped in Serbia?* Do people feel more liberated, sexually or otherwise, in those countries? Are people less 'repressed' in the USA where hard-core porn is freely available? Is there less sexual crime? Whose quality of life has been improved? What principles are involved?

How, if a law were introduced making pornography a civil rights rather than an obscenity issue, would our liberty be further endangered (as writer after writer for the *New Statesman* or *The Nation* tells us it will)? What liberties is the American Civil Liberties Union defending when it defends commercial pornographers like Heffner, Guccione and Flynt against under-financed feminist activists? The liberty to make money? The liberty to preserve male power? Why did the Minneapolis Ordinance attack civilization as we know it? What is the principle involved?

What is 'free speech'? Why, according to their critics, do anti-pornography feminists 'have to' define pornography when their critics feel no obligation to define 'free speech' or 'censorship'? If 'censorship' is the legal silencing of an individual's right to self-expression, why do we have libel laws, anti-racist laws, laws against child pornography and so on? Why are anti-porn feminists guilty of wanting more 'censorship' when so many of them have declared themselves in word and deed against the existing obscenity legislation (which is repressive, anti-female, anti-erotic and open to considerable on-going official abuse) and for a law which, after all, would simply enable individuals to bring suits against people they can prove have harmed them? How would a government be able to use such a law to 'repress free speech'? What court would allow such a law to be used frivolously, especially since such laws would take the power out of police hands and put it into private hands?

Who and what is really being threatened by proposed sex-discrimination legislation? After all, the lawyers putting it

---

* There is a prevalent myth, quoted in the wildly inaccurate 'investigation' of the porn trade *Porn Gold*, that sex crimes went down in Scandinavia as hard-core porn was deregulated. Actually sex crimes went down because at the same time sexual acts between adults were decriminalized. Rape and incest statistics have kept pace with the rise elsewhere in the West.

together are neither right-wing nor careless of any potential authoritarian use of such legislation. Indeed, all the feminist lawyers I know who are working on the problem have excellent track records as civil libertarians.

'The Left' claims that such feminists have made an unholy alliance with 'the Right' in order to attack pornography – yet there is no evidence of this in the UK or the US. One of the reasons, for instance, that I and a number of others, who had co-founded CAP, left that group was because Clare Short's proposed Indecent Displays (Newspaper and Workplace) Bill was in our view neither feminist nor anti-authoritarian. It seemed a mere riff on the OPA theme and moreover none of us thinks female bodies are 'indecent'.

I can only repeat that we are interested *only* in legislation which emphasizes our understanding that pornography is an attack on women's right to liberty and peace of mind.

I can only repeat that, while I believe there is a clear link between pornography and sexual violence at every level, this is still not my main argument for attacking it. My main argument is that *pornography plays a central role in the persistent repression of women as a class*.

This is an argument rarely addressed by critics who continue to be bound by the notion that we are somehow allying ourselves with Mary Whitehouse and the 'moral majority' to attack 'obscenity'. They talk of dangerous consequences. They display with every statement the fact that they have *not* examined our arguments, that they are primed *only* to repeat and work variations on the arguments of twenty or more years ago. What can 'socialism' and 'feminism' really mean to them? It is as if the great radical feminists had never written a word.

Who is actually allying themselves with the authoritarian 'Right', with the existing power élite? Who has the approval of that élite – or, if not its approval, its tolerance? Who feels the most comfortable within this society? The editor of the *New Statesman*, the editor of the *Nation*, Neil Kinnock or Andrea Dworkin? Who is the most directly familiar with the experience of being 'censored', of being silenced?*

---

* Since this was written we've seen the persecution of Mapplethorpe, of tattooing and piercing magazines, of the booksellers, publishers and others associated with them, of a socially harmless group of self-mutilators, and so on. Their only crime seems to be that they attacked 'masculinity'. Crimes Against Manhood are severely prosecuted in the current political climate. With the Gulf **551**

I think it is time the Left urgently re-examined its political vocabulary, its assumptions and, indeed, its very experience – on every level and relating to every major issue, including pornography.

What is pornography's function? What is censorship?

Big Brother knows.

War, Manhood is supreme. The Gulf War also tested our media and found its 'free speech' satisfactorily untroublesome . . . Our democracy could be in bad shape.

26 Pornography and Civil Liberties: Freedom, Harm and Human Rights

CATHERINE ITZIN

FREEDOM

Some of the fiercest resistance to campaigns against pornography as a women's issue has come from civil libertarians who express concern about censorship. Free speech is certainly a fundamental human right, and political and sexual censorship is a genuine concern. During ten years of Conservative government in the UK, for example, 'civil liberties have not just been eroded; they have been deliberately attacked and undermined'. According to Peter Thornton, writing on behalf of the National Council for Civil Liberties: 'The state has increased its own power at the expense of individual freedom ... the government has taken away basic rights in order to stifle legitimate protest ... has strengthened the power of servants of the state and reduced their accountability ... has created a climate of intolerance with institutional prejudice and discrimination', and has imposed the greatest ever peacetime controls on broadcasting.[1]

Some recent examples illustrate the exercise of censorship in Thatcher's (and subsequently Major's) Britain. In 1987 a BBC television programme about the Zircon spy satellite was banned. Publication of the memoirs of the former MI5 agent Peter Wright (*Spycatcher*) was banned on grounds of national security. Elected leaders of Sinn Fein are banned from speaking in the media, and since 1990 senior local government officers have been banned from holding political office, from participation in political parties, and from speaking and writing on political issues. Section 28 of the Local Government Act 1988 made it illegal to 'intentionally promote homosexuality', and Section 29 of the Criminal Justice Bill 1991 proposed to recriminalize certain consenting homosexual acts. In this climate, anyone interested in freedom of information, free speech and civil liberties will be genuinely concerned about censorship and the erosion of civil liberties. But what do we mean by 'freedom' and what do we mean by 'censorship'?

Ironically, while all these freedoms have been under attack, there has at the same time been a barrage of government-orchestrated rhetoric about freedom. The erosion of all these freedoms has often been undertaken in the name of freedom and 'free choice'. People are exhorted constantly to demand their freedom to choose: their choice, for example, of education, of health and social services, of medical care, of consumer goods. The allure of this 'freedom' has been a very powerful weapon in the government's declared war on public ownership and public services. But what this freedom really – and only – means is the freedom to buy and to spend: the freedom of the marketplace. 'Freedom' here is equated with free enterprise: money is the main value. This is a very limited and shallow freedom: those with money have it, those without do not.

FREEDOM vs. EQUALITY

This freedom is based on the narrowest concept of individualism. Whatever the individual wants and can get is good. The only valued human commonality is consumerism. Human need and human rights are alien concepts. In this formula, in this degraded, degenerated language of liberty, freedom certainly does not equate with equality or equal rights or civil rights or civil liberties.

The traditional view of civil liberties derives from the ideology that each individual has certain rights which the law should protect and uphold. This is fine as far as it goes, and historically civil libertarians in the USA and UK have sought to protect the rights and privacy of individuals from illegitimate interference and control by government. They have defended the right of the individual to religious and political freedom, and freedom of expression and movement. Civil libertarians have represented the liberal response to totalitarianism, and have provided a necessary and valuable resistance to the powers of the state.

But this is a narrow view of civil liberties which ignores the fact that the state is not the only form of power operating in society, that individuals do not exist in a vacuum, but within a variety of social power structures. The rights of individuals are constantly in conflict with one another. If, for example, one person has a right to hold parties in their home and their neighbours have a right to sleep in peace in theirs, whose right should prevail? This form of liberalism assumes that conflicts can be resolved by the adjudication of a neutral authority deciding between equal parties. But often, in fact, the parties are not equal and the authorities are not neutral.

In practice the rights of the powerful prevail. Where there is unequal power, there cannot be equal rights. Historically the law has protected the rights of men while denying the most basic freedom to women. Free speech, for example, is a fundamental human right that the majority of women do not enjoy, because women's access to publication, to positions of power and platforms of speech, is limited by their second-class economic and sexual status. The traditional view of civil liberties has failed to take into account male power and the unequal position of women in society.[2] It has also failed to take into account white supremacy: the structural inequality of black people in Western society and Western imperialist exploitation of black people in the Third World.

Within these structures of inequality, there are many situations in which there will be a conflict of interests, and someone's rights will be infringed. Whose rights take precedence? Who decides? Are the rights which apply to men more important than rights which apply to women? Do the rights of whites take precedence over the rights of blacks? In practice this has usually been the case because men (and white people) are the more powerful interest group, and their interests prevail. The interests of the powerful then masquerade as 'human rights' or 'individual freedom', when in fact the 'individual human' is gendered and male (or white); women (or blacks) – rendered invisible in the category of 'individual' – do not share the same rights or freedoms. This is a view of civil liberties which is inherently non-egalitarian and ignores the position and interests of the oppressed. Those with power have civil liberties, those without do not. Civil liberties here is reduced to individual libertarianism.

THE LIBERTARIAN FALLACY

In the USA the policy of the American Civil Liberties Union is based on this narrow individualist libertarian view of freedom. This has led the ACLU to defend as free speech the rights of racists (including the Ku Klux Klan) and Nazis to incite racial hatred through forms of verbal violence which, if they were physical, would be illegal. The same libertarianism has also led the ACLU to defend the free speech rights of pornographers and accept financial subsidy from the pornography industry:

> The ACLU's economic ties with the pornographers take many different forms, ranging from taking money from the Playboy Foundation to being housed for a nominal rent ($1 per year) in a building owned by pornographers. Sometimes lawyers represent the ACLU in public debate and as individuals work for pornographers in private. For instance, one such lawyer represented the ACLU in many debates with feminists on pornography. He talked about the importance of free speech with serious elegance and would brook no exceptions to what must be protected because, he said repeatedly, if any exceptions were made, 'feminist and gay' speech would suffer. Then, as the private lawyer for a pornographer, he sued Women Against Pornography for libel because on television a member denounced the pornographer for publishing cartoons that pornographized children. The ACLU itself also has a record of defending child pornography by opposing any laws against it as constitutionally prohibited incursions on free speech.[3]

These associations between the ACLU and the pornography industry raise fundamental questions about what is really meant by freedom and censorship.

In this liberal libertarian view, freedom is demeaned and debased: it has lost its meaning. If civil liberties are to have any value at all, they must have a social as well as an individual meaning. If civil liberties are to have anything to do with *freedom* and *liberty* for all, they must address the issue of power, and attempt to redress the imbalance of power. They must equate with equality and justice: with civil rights, with human rights.

The policy of the National Council for Civil Liberties in the UK is different from that of the American Civil Liberties Union, and civil liberties here do in *theory* equate with equality. The NCCL's Charter of Civil Rights and Liberties states: 'We are committed to the defence and extension of civil liberties in the United Kingdom and to the rights and freedoms recognized by international law.' The Charter then lists ten essential rights the NCCL is pledged to safeguard. One of these is 'the right to freedom of speech and publication'. It is the seventh item out of the ten. The first three rights the NCCL is committed to protect are:

1. To live in freedom and safe from personal harm.
2. To protection from ill-treatment or punishment that is inhuman or degrading.

3. To equality before the law and to freedom from discrimination on such grounds as disability, political or other opinion, race, religion, sex or sexual orientation.

The ninth item is the right 'to move freely within one's own country'.

In the case of pornography, the rights which the NCCL is committed to protect are in conflict. In considering the 'right to freedom of speech and publication' it is claimed that individuals have the right to produce and consume pornography. But these 'individuals' are largely men and pornography represents the interests of men. Women, because of sexual and social inequality, largely do not have the same access to 'free speech'. In considering the right 'to live in freedom and safe from personal harm . . . to protection from ill-treatment that is inhuman or degrading, to equality before the law and to freedom from discrimination on grounds of sex, and to move freely within one's own country', women largely do not have these freedoms. Instead women are raped and sexually assaulted and discriminated against in employment and cannot move freely in safety on the streets. Women do not have these freedoms, and on the basis of the evidence in this book, one of the reasons they do not is pornography. There is a conflict therefore between the 'free speech' right of some to publish pornography and a whole range of freedoms which are denied to women. Does the right to 'free speech' in this case (if indeed 'speech' is what pornography is) take precedence over women's freedom of movement and safety in public and in private; over women's right to live free from objectification, abuse, assault, over women's freedom from discrimination on grounds of sex?

HARM

In the UK, the right of the individual to free speech has not been regarded as absolute, either by the NCCL or by government. Exceptions have been made in the case of identifiable harm: the NCCL, for example, 'recognizes that a distinction must be drawn between speech or literature which is deeply offensive, and that which causes identifiable harm to those individuals against whom it is directed'.[4] The grounds therefore on which liberals and civil libertarians have agreed to limitations on freedom of speech have been in cases of *identifiable harm*: as in the case of race hatred **557** literature and incitement to racial hatred. The grounds on which some of them would be prepared to accept restrictions on pornography would be on evidence of identifiable harm. But the evidence of harm caused by pornography is denied or dismissed or discredited, often misquoted, misrepresented and misunderstood. 'Evidence' and 'harm' are as narrowly defined by these libertarians as freedom.

The reality is that there are different kinds of evidence of different kinds of harm. Harm includes sexual murder, sexual violence (sexual assault, rape), child sexual abuse, sexual harassment. It includes sexual objectification which is harmful to women. And it includes sex discrimination and sexual inequality which are also harmful to women. Evidence includes research and clinical work with sex offenders, social science and psychological research, victim testimony from women and perpetrator testimony from men, legal decisions, the findings of criminal justice and goverment inquiries, and the theory and analysis which explains women's subordinate status in society. There is now a substantial body of different kinds of consistently concurrent and corroborative evidence of different kinds of harm caused to women and children as a result of the use of pornography.

Causality and Correlation

A major point of contention is whether there are *causal* links between pornography and sexual violence. This appears to arise out of confusion about what is meant by 'causal'. There *is* evidence of *causal* links between pornography and rape. This evidence, presented in this book, comes from social science and psychological research, from studies of sex offenders, and from the personal testimony of both the perpetrators of sexual violence and their victims. There *are* cases of copy-cat crimes, where men act out on women the scenarios they have seen depicted in pornography and actually use pornography during the assaults.[5]

The evidence consistently shows pornography to be *one* of the factors that contributes to and causes sexual violence, one of several factors, for example, which predispose men to rape. The evidence that pornography directly contributes to acts of violence is important. But it is also important, as Deborah Cameron and Elizabeth Frazer explain in Chapter 19, to expose the fallacy of an argument which defines harm so narrowly in terms of causality as to require proof that a particular piece of pornography caused a particular man to rape a particular woman, or which requires proof that only pornography causes sexual crime.

In the case of pornography, there is often an attempt to apply causality as a standard of proof in a way that would be considered naïve and impossible in any other area of scientific research. When evaluating scientific evidence it is also necessary to distinguish between causality and correlation. Although there is evidence of causal links between pornography and rape, there is an even greater body of research which consistently establishes correlations between pornography and sexual violence and other negative effects. Correlation does not prove causality. It never can. Causality is a standard of proof that rarely, if ever, can be achieved, and is rarely, if ever, required. However, correlation is itself evidence.

Correlation demonstrates a relationship between one thing and another, it establishes a *connection*. Thus, while there is no proof that smoking causes lung cancer (because there are also other variables and factors affecting the health of an individual over a lifetime), the correlation between smoking and lung cancer has been established repeatedly in different research over a long period of time. In the case of smoking, the correlations have been regarded as sufficient evidence to suggest that it is highly likely that a link exists between smoking and lung cancer. The medical profession has long been convinced by this evidence, and more recently the government; only the tobacco industry still argues that there is no proof of harm, and it is motivated by profit to maintain this position. Edward Donnerstein, a leading researcher in the field of pornography, has said that the 'relationship between ... sexually violent images in the media and subsequent aggression and changes in or towards callous attitudes towards women, is much stronger statistically than the relationship between smoking and cancer'.[6] As with smoking and lung cancer, there will be other variables and factors in addition to pornography which lead to acts of sexual violence. But there is certainly sufficient evidence to say that it is highly likely that pornography is one of the factors that contributes to sexual violence.[7]

Furthermore, causality is only one of many ways that pornography influences attitudes and behaviour. Contributors to this book also demonstrate pornography's influence on culture, cultural discourse and ideology (on ideas and the imagination), in conditioning attitudes, beliefs and behaviour (including the conditioning of male orgasm to sexual violence and women's sub- **559** ordination), and on inequality and discrimination. Pornography is rarely the sole cause of sexual violence. Nor is pornography the only factor in cultural discourse or social construction or conditioning or sexual inequality; but it is one of the factors that, on the basis of the evidence in this book, operates as a cause of harm to women, and one that has not, until now, been satisfactorily addressed or redressed. What then is this consistently concurrent and corroborative evidence, and what is its status and value?

Social Science and Psychological Research Evidence

The social science and psychological research consistently shows that pornography desensitizes men, increases attitudes of callousness towards women, makes men less sympathetic to rape victims and more sympathetic to rapists, increases rape myths and the self-reported likelihood of men to commit rape, and increases aggressive behaviour to women (see Chapters 15–18). This research is sometimes said to be inconclusive. But this claim appears to have been made as a result of applying a confused and contentious standard of causality, or on the basis of partial or selective readings of the research data.

The Williams Committee's Report on Obscenity and Film Censorship, for example, came to the conclusion in 1979 that 'there does not appear to be any strong evidence that exposure to sexually explicit material triggers off anti-social sexual behaviour'.[8] The Williams Committee's conclusion was based on a review of the research literature on pornography which was subsequently described by experienced researchers in the field as 'selective' and incomplete and in which 'significant research remained unconsidered'.[9] The review omitted to refer at all to over a dozen pieces of major research from the 1970s which had 'led to a variety of theoretical models to explain the linkage between exposure to sexual and violent themes and an increased probability of sexually aggressive behaviour'.[10] What had in fact emerged from the research which had not been included in the Williams Committee review was a 'strong case for postulating a positive enhancement of sexually aggressive behaviour without adequate evidence for a decline in such behaviour'. The Williams Committee therefore came to its conclusions based on a partial and incomplete review of the research evidence.

In 1979, Guy Cumberbatch and Dennis Howitt gave evidence to the Williams Committee that the 'mass media – as far as it is

possible to tell using social scientific methodologies – do not serve to amplify the level of violence in society'. In a review commissioned by the Broadcasting Standards Council (BSC) ten years later on the effects of pornography, they concluded that 'there does not seem to be compelling and unequivocal evidence that allows any strong conclusions about pornography based on research'.[11] Their conclusion, however, was based both on a selective sample and a selective interpretation of the research. Only a very small part of the available research was considered. The research showing links between rape and male sexual aggression was dismissed as 'ideological', by which the authors apparently meant 'feminist', and therefore discreditable (feminism having been equated in their 'background to the review' with a 'moral army' of 'the most reactionary conservative anti-pornographers'). But for reasons, perhaps, of their own unacknowledged ideology and general antipathy to the research showing connections between pornography and sexual violence, their discourse obscured the fact that virtually all of the research on male aggression has been conducted by male academics located at different universities in the USA and Canada, none of whom is in any way associated with feminism or right-wing moral factions.[12]

Shortly after the publication of their views in the BSC Report, and following an interview in the *Independent* (18 December 1989) in which they were quoted as saying 'the experiments usually failed to find a link between pornography and violence', Cumberbatch and Howitt were again commissioned, this time by the Home Office, to carry out a review of the research on the effects of pornography. This report (*Pornography: Impacts and Influences*), published in December 1990, again dismissed the research evidence on pornography and sexual violence as 'inconsistent', 'equivocal', 'scant', 'far from robust', 'far from clear', showing 'little or no effects' and failing 'to establish causal links'.[13]

This report was, however, subsequently criticized by a number of leading pornography researchers in the USA and Canada in a submission to the Home Office made by Members of Parliament and experts in the field in the UK.[14] In his submission, James Check, Associate Professor of Psychology and Director of the LaMarsh Research Programme on Violence and Conflict Resolution at York University in Toronto, whose own work was reviewed in the report, considered it to be 'clearly biased and . . . at best . . . seen as a polemic for those who wish to promote political views at the expense of scholarship and scientific objectivity'. The authors, he wrote, 'mis-cite, misrepresent, and misunderstand a number of **561** studies, either deliberately or through an inability to comprehend the work (particularly when it comes to statistical analyses), and they omit a great deal of the important literature as well as important findings in the studies that they do cite'. In his judgement, the authors were 'uncomfortable with any study which reveals negative effects of exposure to pornography, and also for some reason particularly uncomfortable with feminist theory and writing'.[15]

The scientific evidence has sometimes been criticized on methodological grounds. In their BSC report, Cumberbatch and Howitt were critical of methods used for testing aggressive behaviour (electric shocks) and attitude change (attitude scales). But these are the most basic and standard of experimental psychology research methods and their methodological validity would be unlikely to be questioned when applied to subjects other than pornography. In Chapter 15 Edna Einsiedel explains what each of these measures means and how it has been used in the experimental research. She believes not only that the measures are valid, but that the variety of measures used provides an opportunity for convergent validation of the results of the different research.

Another methodological concern has been what Einsiedel calls the 'operationalization of pornography': how it is defined, and the failure in some of the experimental research to distinguish sufficiently between the kinds of material shown to subjects. In reviewing the research before 1986, Einsiedel could identify two categories of pornography – aggressive and non-aggressive. With regard to the sexually violent material, she found that the experimental research was conclusive in its evidence of harm. With regard to the very broad and undifferentiated category of 'non-aggressive' pornography, she found a mixture of results. This was, she suggested, because the non-aggressive category contained a mixture of different kinds of material: it was not that there were no effects, but that there were so many effects that further research was needed.

In subsequent and more sophisticated research, distinctions have been made between material which is sexually explicit and violent, sexually explicit material which is non-violent but degrading and dehumanizing, and erotica (sexually explicit but egalitarian sex). There are now research results on each of these categories of material which confirm the 'harm results' of sexually violent pornography and also show evidence of harm from non-violent dehumanizing pornography. This research (evaluated by Einsiedel, Weaver, Russell, and Check in Chapters 15–18) shows consistent correlations between both sexually violent material *and* nonviolent material depicting degradation, domination, subordination and humiliation, and harm to women. On the other hand, as James Check points out, this research has not produced the same evidence of links between erotica (i.e. non-violent, non-subordinating, but sexually explicit material) and harm to women.[16]

Not only have definitional distinctions been effectively made in the experimental research, they have now also been effectively operationalized in the courts. Check (Chapter 18) provides examples of prosecutions of pornography under obscenity law in Canada, where social science research evidence of harm has been used to distinguish between these three categories of material: to convict violent and dehumanizing material and to acquit erotica.

Appendix 3 includes excerpts from the judgment of one recent Canadian obscenity case which shows how these distinctions have been successfully applied to convict 'depictions of sexual cruelty and violence', magazines with 'blatant invitations to have sexual relations with children' and a collection of incest novels. But the judgment also shows the desensitising effects of pornography and the extent to which violence and dehumanisation are rendered invisible in pornography and seen as 'just sex'. Thus, for example, a magazine of pregnant women in sexually provocative poses' is judged to contain 'no depictions of dehumanising content', to be 'at most, erotica.' And although another magazine sexualizes the inequality of the boss/secretary relationship, it is judged to be 'consensual' and 'purely erotic'. The connection between the sexual 'consent' of the woman in this scenario and her economic subordination is not made, nor its legitimation of and possible incitement to sexual harassment.

Einsiedel (Chapter 15) addresses other genuine questions that have been raised about research methodology: the extent to which laboratory results can be generalized to real life, and whether college student subjects are typical or representative of the general population. Carrying out experiments in the laboratory is, she argues, the only way to test hypotheses based on real-life observations and to get controlled results with respect to causal tendencies. Research with college students, if it is unrepresentative, is likely to be biased against negative effects and in favour of pornography. These subjects, Einsiedel argues, are likely to be more sexually liberal than the general population: they would therefore be less likely to be influenced negatively, and any negative results are therefore likely to be more rather than less significant.

Einsiedel also discusses some of the theories which explain and account for the results produced by pornography research. Social learning theory, for example, explains the interaction between environment and behaviour. And habituation theory explains the process of desensitization to stimuli over time, and accounts for the acquisition of callous attitudes towards women as a result of pornography use.

In Chapter 16, James Weaver explains why there are apparently contradictory results in some of the research, and why, when most of the research consistently shows evidence of harm, the discrepancies do not invalidate the scientific evidence overall. He deals in particular with the controversy concerning the work of the US academic Edward Donnerstein, whose research was prominent in the early and mid-1980s in showing the adverse effects of both standard and sexually violent pornography on the attitudes and behaviour of men. Donnerstein found, for example, that portrayals of women enjoying rape or other forms of sexual violence increased acceptance of rape myths (after 'only 10 minutes' exposure'), incresed aggressive behaviour towards women in the laboratory, increased reported willingness to rape, and decreased perceptions of rape victim suffering. 'We are talking about an incredible amount of potential harm to women', he said, giving testimony to the Minneapolis Hearings, where he also talked about making 'quite accurate predictions of potential aggressive behavior' weeks and even months after 'normal healthy males' became sexually aroused to sexual violence.[17] Donnerstein also found strong negative effects 'to standard hard-core pornography which does not contain overtly physical violence'. In response to this material he found that men 'became more callous towards women . . . less likely to convict for a rape, less likely to give a harsh sentence to a rapist'.[18]

Later in the 1980s, Donnerstein's research on the violent, sexually suggestive, but not sexually explicit 'slasher' films apparently led him to argue that 'violence not sex' is the problem. Weaver, however, reviews Donnerstein's research and reanalyses the data to show that the research itself consistently shows evidence of links between both sexually violent and non-violent pornography and harm to women. Weaver thoroughly dismantles

564

the scientific basis of the 'violence only' theories that have appeared to exonerate standard nonviolent pornography of responsibility for adverse male attitudes and behaviour towards women.

It has been suggested that there is very little academic research and that it is out of date.[19] Clearly this is not the case. A report prepared for the Home Office in 1991 (*Pornography-Related Sexual Violence: A Review of the Evidence*) summarized the results of over 100 pieces of research showing sexual violence and other negative effects of pornography.[20] The reviews of the research by Einsiedel, Weaver, and Russell in Chapters 15–17 cover over 300 items of research (see References at the end of this book). The research is still being conducted and published,[21] and the results of recently published work by leading (male) academics in this field confirm the results of the earlier work.[22] The social science and psychological research on pornography is as valid as any other research of this nature. Inevitably there will be some inconsistencies in the experimental evidence (it would be unnatural for this not to be the case) and also occasional pieces of research which appear to contradict the results. But, as Mike Baxter pointed out in a *New Scientist* review of this research in 1990, every conclusion 'is supported by at least one significant experimental result and these have greater scientific crediblity than the inconsistencies'.[23]

Cumberbatch and Howitt concluded in their BSC report that there was not 'one jot of evidence which links this type of research finding with real-life sexual violence'.[24] This quite simply is not true. The consistent correlations between pornography and sexual violence in the scientific research are confirmed from a number of 'real-life' sources: in clinical work with sex offenders in the USA and UK, in the personal experience of victims and perpetrators of pornography-related sexual violence, and in surveys of women reporting pornography-related sexual assaults. Indeed, each category of evidence corroborates the other, and there is a pattern of concurrence in the evidence which cannot be ignored.

Research and Clinical Work with Sex Offenders
Clinical work and research with sex offenders consistently shows the prevalence of pornography among offenders and provides evidence of the direct links between pornography and sexual violence. In Chapter 14, Ray Wyre describes the model he has developed from working with sex offenders identifying a predictable cycle of sexual abuse in which pornography is implicated at **565**

every stage: in predisposing men to abuse, in legitimating abuse, in reducing internal and external inhibitions, and in initiating and carrying out abuse. Quite independently, Diana Russell (Chapter 17) arrived at similar conclusions and a similar model from her review of the scientific research. And both concluded that pornography was one of a number of factors that contribute to sexual violence.

It is sometimes suggested that pornography is beneficial, that it acts as a safety valve enabling men to obtain sexual release through 'fantasy' rather than through committing acts of sexual violence against women and children. Again the clinical evidence would appear to disprove this theory. The director of a rape and sexual assault centre in the USA questioned the very logic of the 'catharsis theory' which suggests that if men . . .

> look at pictures of women being slashed and humiliated, then they won't have to do this in real life. Yet no one would suggest that we look at films of parents beating children in order to end child abuse or to watch films of Blacks, Indians, and Hispanics being hand-cuffed and humiliated in order to end racism. There is no reason then to suspect that pictures of bound and mutilated women will decrease misogyny. Indeed, as many offenders in my experience have noted, masturbating to fantasies of these images is extremely reinforcing and in many cases led to their acts of sexual violence.[25]

As long ago as 1986, Einsiedel concluded that there was little evidence for the catharsis claims, noting that numerous research reviews had arrived at the same conclusion, and that even its major proponent had reformulated his position.

In the USA, Marshall's research with non-incarcerated sex offenders found that over a third reported occasionally being incited to commit an offence, and a third of the rapists and over half of those who commited child sexual abuse said they deliberately used pornography in preparation for committing the offence. Ray Wyre's work with sex offenders has demonstrated that fantasy is always a prerequisite to carrying out sexual offences against women and children, and that masturbating to pornography conditions sexual arousal and orgasm to the content of pornography (e.g. to rape, to child sexual abuse and to the sexual objectification and degradation of women). He has also found that sex offenders use the rape myths of pornography to rationalize, justify and validate their behaviour.

Victim Testimony

Women's experience of pornography-related sexual assault confirms the experimental and clinical data linking pornography and sexual violence. This book includes evidence of harm from women, of child sexual abuse, rape, sexual assault, sexual harassment and sex discrimination. Catharine A. MacKinnon refers to the testimony of women at the Minneapolis hearings in the USA in 1983 (Chapter 23) and Chapter 15 contains the results of the *Cosmopolitan* survey carried out in the UK in 1990. But this evidence is often trivialized and dismissed as 'anecdotal' or 'unproveable'.

Howitt and Cumberbatch, for example, in their report to the Home Office, referred to the case of a woman 'whose husband had the house filled with his collections of pornography' and left her 'hanging upside down in the bedroom', and concluded that 'it is difficult to know whether or not pornography was a cause of the man's sexual activities or merely an adjunct or a tool of existing proclivities'. 'Copy-cat crimes' are dismissed as 'cases in which pornography defines the detailed form of sexual assault, rather than stimulate the initial desire to carry out such activities'. They avoided the obvious conclusion that pornography in both cases was a contributing factor in the sexual violence. The case of a woman gang-raped at the age of thirteen by men who had been 'reading pornographic magazines' immediately prior to the rape was dismissed by Howitt and Cumberbatch with the claim that 'one cannot totally eliminate the competing possibilities that the reading of the magazines was merely a coincidence or even just part of a lust to exploit women sexually'.[26] Would they argue that it is coincidence when a driver who kills someone while jumping a red light is drunk? That it is coincidence when a heavy smoker dies of lung cancer?

The definition of causality they wish to apply to evidence of pornography-related sexual violence is unnecessarily – and bizarrely – narrow, and the standard of causality is impossibly – and also unnecessarily – high. It is utterly inappropriate to base evidence of causality on proof of whether pornography produces a desire to rape in someone who previously had no such desire, though there is evidence in this book to suggest that this is indeed the case. And it is utterly to miss the point of the influence of pornography on the mind and the imagination: on the construction and the direction and form of desire as described by Cameron **567** and Frazer in Chapter 19. If as Russell suggests (Chapter 17) 'cause' is defined as 'anything producing an effect or result', then the examples cited by Howitt and Cumberbatch do indeed provide evidence which implicates pornography in the acts of sexual violence: as 'an adjunct or a tool', in 'defining the detailed form of sexual assault', and in stimulating the 'lust to exploit women sexually'.

The *Cosmopolitan* survey asked: 'Have you ever been subject to: sexual harassment, verbal sexual abuse, sexual assault, rape, child sexual abuse?' It then asked: 'If yes, did the person responsible use pornography during the act?' Over 4,000 women responded. Thirty-four per cent had either been raped (10 per cent) or sexually assaulted (24 per cent). Sixty per cent had been sexually harassed and 13 per cent had been sexually abused as children. Pornography had been used in the act in 14 per cent of the rapes, 14 per cent of sexual assaults and 12 per cent of sexual harassment incidents.[27]

A civil libertarian response to the results of this survey was that 'victims of sexual abuse often sincerely think, and report, in interviews or questionnaires, that pornography incited the men who abused them', but that 'judgements made under stress of sexual trauma cannot be relied on'. The women were then patronized: 'Of course the victim's feelings are entirely real', and the causal connections (pornography used in the act) were trivialized to 'causal intuitions' and deemed not to be real.[28]

The status of this survey data has also been trivialized because it was obtained from a women's magazine. Yet the readers of women's magazines are as legitimate as any of the other many unrepresentative samples used in social research. The denigration of this kind of data is really gender-based. The low status accorded to this category of evidence reflects the low status and value of women in society generally. The fact that this evidence is not valued is itself a function and symptom of sexism and of the part that pornography plays in creating and maintaining women's second-class status. Victim testimony in other circumstances is respected, heeded and acted upon. The work of Amnesty International, for example, is based on personal testimony of torture. Civil libertarians will accept the personal testimony of prisoners tortured in Northern Ireland, but not the personal testimony of women harmed and sometimes tortured in and through

pornography.

Perpetrator Testimony

There is also evidence of harm in this book from the personal testimony of perpetrators about how pornography has contributed to the crimes of violence they have committed. At one extreme is the part pornography plays in serial sexual murder: 'the case histories and personal testimonies of sex killers almost universally reveal not only a regular use of pornography but also the enactment of a fantasy of making and participating in pornography itself'.[29]

A 1980s US National Institute of Justice study on sexual murder 'revealed that the murderers, in categorizing their highest sexual interest, ranked pornography as number one'[30]. Serial sexual murderer Ted Bundy, in an interview shortly before he was executed, described how pornography, and particularly sexually violent pornography, was instrumental in creating his fantasies and triggering the sexual hatred that led to his crimes (see Chapters 7, 10 and 19). There is also evidence from rapists and child sexual abusers (in Chapters 10, 11, 14 and 17) on their use of pornography in connection with their crimes.

Sexual Violence in the Production of Pornography

There is evidence that sexual violence occurs in the production of pornography.[31] Women have reported being coerced through physical and psychological threats to participate in pornography. Participation in pornography is also used to coerce women and children into prostitution.[32] In pornography women are raped and beaten and sometimes tortured. The Obscene Publications Branch at Scotland Yard have seized material which includes a woman having her labia nailed to the top of a table and needles being inserted into nipples and genitals. In the USA rapes are filmed and then sold legally and protected as 'free speech'. Sometimes women are sexually murdered in 'snuff films'. This has been reliably documented in the courts in the USA, and in Ireland where a snuff video was obtained without difficulty.[33]

Pornography and Child Sexual Abuse

Child pornography is always the record of child sexual abuse: 'the evidence – recorded on film or videotape – of serious sexual assaults on young children'.[34] (See Chapters 6 and 11.) Adult pornography, however, is also frequently used in the sexual abuse of children. In the household survey of 934 women in San **569**

Francisco, Russell found that father–daughter incest victims were requested to enact pornography four times as often as non-incest victims.[35] In Silbert and Pines's study, 60 per cent of the prostitute women reported having been abused as children, and 22 per cent of these cases of juvenile sexual exploitation mentioned the use of pornographic materials by the adult prior to the sexual act. Ten per cent of this sample had been used as children in pornographic films and magazines.[36] Another US study shows that child pornography is a core part of most sex rings, where an individual or group of adults abuse large numbers of children,[37] and adult pornography may be used to ' "normalize" the abuse and/or as a form of instruction'. (See Chapter 6.) The Canadian Government Committee on sexual offences against children concluded that the 'findings of two [Canadian] national surveys – population and police – indicate that for a number of persons, pornography had served as a stimulus to committing sexual assaults against children'.[38]

Crime Reports

Newspaper reports of court cases frequently indicate that pornography was implicated in the crimes. The 'Putney Rapist' was 'obsessed with bondage and the degradation of women. He was said by police to have copied ideas for rape from illustrations in a bondage magazine called *The Trap*' (*Independent*, 19 July 1988). An 'American airman' stationed in England had 'attempted to live out hard-core pornographic stories' when he raped a mother and teenage daughter (*Daily Mail*, 9 February 1989). A thirty-one-year-old man sexually abused an eight-year-old 'after showing her a pornographic magazine' (*Leicester Mercury*, 28 January 1989). Two convent schoolgirls were abducted and gang-raped by men 'acting out a sex magazine fantasy' (*Daily Mail*, 31 October 1989).

This is yet another category of 'real-life' evidence of links between pornography and sexual violence that confirms the social science and psychological research evidence. But again it is often dismissed by civil libertarians as merely 'anecdotal'. Information about the use of pornography by convicted offenders is not systematically or scientifically recorded. Although the police do not specifically look for evidence of pornography when making arrests, it is frequently found incidentally:

In cases involving adult ... female victims, pornographic materials are often found in a substantial percent of cases. Those materials are found in or near where the person lives, or say the motor vehicle which was used to transport the assailant to the place of the sexual assault.[39]

There is a need not to dismiss this evidence but to ensure that the police are required to look for evidence of pornography in relation to sexual crime and systematically to record their findings, and that courts are required to keep systematic records of cases which involve pornography.

The Influence of Pornography on 'Ordinary Men'
The men who carried out the rapes and assaults in the cases reported above were to all appearances 'ordinary men'. The Putney rapist was a chef, married to a policewoman he met at a Baptist Church prayer meeting. The US airman was married with two children. The eight-year-old victim was the daughter of the man's girlfriend. There has been a mistaken assumption that there are normal men who are not 'influenced' by pornography and deviant men who are. This led researchers for the 1970 US Presidential Commission on Pornography to misinterpret their data and come to the wrong conclusion about the harm of pornography.

A retrospective survey involving sex offenders, sexual deviants and non-offender adults 'inquired into the degree to which they *wished* to imitate and the degree to which they *did* imitate highly salient erotic depictions'.[40] The results of this study showed that 'reports of sex offenders did not differ significantly from the reports of the non-offender controls'.[41] In other words, 'normal' men (30 per cent) were almost as likely as 'rapists' (35 per cent) to wish to try to imitate acts they'd seen in pornography; 'normal' men (13 per cent) were almost as likely as 'rapists' (15 per cent) to have tried to imitate the acts they'd seen in pornography; and 'normal' men (65 per cent) were much *more* likely than 'rapists' (40 per cent) to *wish* to try *other* sex after exposure to pornography and to *actually* try *other* sex after seeing pornography ('normal' men 35 per cent, rapists 20 per cent). Normal men (i.e. non-offenders) were as likely or even likelier to have had their sexual behaviour influenced by pornography. In Chapters 7 and 10, there are accounts from 'ordinary' men who have not committed sexual crimes, but who believe pornography has negatively affected their attitudes towards and relationships with women.

571

The Incidence of Rape

Another category of evidence which could indicate whether the correlation between pornography and rape in social science and psychological research is confirmed by social behaviour is the correlation between an increase in the sale of pornography and an increase in the rate of rape. This is the one area in which statistics are less reliable: because it has been difficult to measure and to monitor growth in the pornography market,[42] and because of difficulties in interpreting crime statistics. However, it is often said that there is no evidence to indicate that restricting pornography will decrease the incidence of rape. This is not true.

Statistics from Denmark are quoted to suggest that when the laws were liberalized and pornography made more accessible, the incidence of sexual violence actually decreased. The research of Kutchinsky is often quoted to justify less restrictive legislation because it reported a decrease in 'sexual offences' between 1959 and 1969. But the sexual offences included in this study were 'minor' rather then 'major' offences: peeping and exhibitionism.[43] These offences were also decriminalized at that time, and this would naturally have produced a decrease in the number of incidents reported.

Subsequent analysis of the evidence from Denmark has shown it 'to have serious flaws': 'It provides no evidence that serious sex offences, like rape, decreased or could be expected to decrease.'[44] Geis and Geis found a steep increase in rape reports to the police in Stockholm throughout the 1970s,[45] and Court, 'using the same measure' found a 'closely similar trend' in Copenhagen.[46] According to Tate, lifting restrictions on pornography in Denmark 'gave birth to commercial child pornography' which flourished until it was made illegal ten years later in 1979.[47] (See Chapter 11)

Statistics, when they have been available elsewhere, have shown a correlation between an increased availability of pornography and an increase in rape. According to Court, there was 'a notable increase in rape reports over the decade 1964 to 1974', in the USA, Scandinavia, Britain, New Zealand and Australia following either 'legislative or administrative liberalization'.[47] In Australia, Queensland has the strictest controls on pornography and a 'comparatively low rate of rape reports', while South Australia, 'the most liberal state in relation to pornography, has seen escalating reports of rape since the early 1970s'.[48] In Hawaii, there was a steep rise in reported rape from 1965 when pornography became increasingly available throughout the USA. Then between 1974 and 1976 restraints were imposed on pornography and reported rape fell dramatically. When the laws were liberalized again in 1977 there was an immediate increase in reported rape.[49] Baron and Strauss found a high correlation between pornography magazine sales and the rate of reported rape in a fifty-state study in the USA: 'on average, every increase of 2 per cent in the circulation of pornography was linked to a 1 per cent increase in the incidence of rape reports'.[50]

The United States is a culture which is saturated with both violent and non-violent but degrading and dehumanizing pornography, and the USA has the highest rate of rape of any industrialized nation. According to FBI statistics a woman is beaten every eight seconds, a woman is raped every three minutes, 26 per cent of all women will be raped at least once during their lives, and one in four children will be sexually abused.[51] The rate of rape has been rising steadily since 1950 when the growth in the pornography industry first began.

In the UK the Williams Committee identified in the 1970s a 'considerable increase in the publication of British magazines with an explicit sexual content which, particularly in the years 1975 to 1977, moved very quickly to adopt a character much less restrained than had previously been acceptable'. Between 1964 and 1974 the number of reported offences of rape and attempted rape rose by 103 per cent, and the Williams Committee concluded that 'this period of ten years was clearly a bad one for offences of rape'.[52] Metropolitan police statistics on rape and attempted rape showed a steady increase from the 1950s, rising in the 1960s, and rising steeply from 1975 to 1977. The increase continued in 1978.[53]

There was a continued growth in the pornography industry in the 1980s, with over seventy different titles published and on sale in local newsagents in 1989.[54] Home Office statistics from this period for England and Wales show a steady rise in reported rape. In 1982 and 1983 there was a 25 per cent increase in reported rape; in 1985 there was an increase of 29 per cent, and in 1986 24 per cent. Between 1987 and 1989 there was a smaller increase (8 per cent 1987, 16 per cent 1988 and 16 per cent 1989). In 1990 the increase was 21 per cent and in 1991, 18 per cent.[55] Often, while reported rape was increasing, other reported crime was falling.

These statistics cannot be dismissed (as they often are), but **573** they are also of limited value in determining the actual relationship between pornography and rape. It is not possible to know, for example, whether there is an increase in the *reporting* of rapes (as the police have claimed, implying that there may be no real increase in the rate of rape) or whether there is an increase in the actual rate of rape in relation to demographic changes and population growth, or both. The statistics suggest that there *may* be connections between the increased availability of pornography and an increase in rape: there is a need for research and more reliable data in this area.

Sexual Objectification and Sexual Inequality

In addition to all of this evidence of links between pornography and sexual violence, there are also connections between pornography and sex discrimination, sexual inequality and the subordination of women to be considered. Another category of evidence of harm included in this book is the writing from the women's movement – the theory and analysis of women's oppression – which enables an understanding of the part pornography plays in sexual inequality, and which identifies sex discrimination itself as harm.

It is this work that has also begun to reveal the damage which sexual objectification does to women by dehumanizing and thus enabling women to be treated as less than human (therefore more easily harmed) and less than equal. 'Cunt' is a term of contempt and abuse, most degrading when used by men against men. It is the language of misogyny. In pornography, women are 'cunts', literally cunts, only cunts: reduced to their genitals and anuses, posed open and gaping, inviting sexual access. In society, women are located at the bottom economically and institutionally. Is it coincidence, or does pornography make it difficult for woman to be accepted as peers and people of power and influence? The social status of a 'cunt' is not high.

Government Inquiries

Governments in the USA, Canada and Australia have reviewed the social science and psychological research. They have also considered victim testimony, the clinical evidence and the role of adult pornography in child sexual abuse. On the basis of reviewing the full range of evidence, the US Attorney General's Commission on Pornography in 1985 was unanimous in its findings of a causal link between both violent and non-violent pornography and harm to women.[56] The Fraser Committee on

Pornography and Prostitution in Canada in 1985 concluded that pornography had a negative influence on the fundamental values of society and on women's legitimate pursuit of equal treatment under the law.[57] At local government level, the Minneapolis City Council held hearings in 1983 when considering whether to enact civil rights legislation against pornography. On the basis of evidence presented from social science and pscyhological research, from clinical work with sex offenders and survivors of pornography-related violence, the Council voted in favour of the legislation.

Judicial Evidence

Finally, there is evidence from the courts themselves. In 1985 the Federal Court decided in favour of pornography as free speech, when the legality of the Indianapolis civil rights ordinance was challenged. It nevertheless accepted all of the evidence of harm linking pornography with attitudes of bigotry and contempt, acts of aggression and social inequality. The following is an excerpt from the decision of the US Court of Appeals:

> Indianapolis justifies the ordinance on the ground that pornography affects thoughts. Men who see women depicted as subordinate are more likely to treat them so. Pornography is an aspect of dominance. It does not persuade people so much as change them. It works by socializing, by establishing the expected and the permissible. In this view pornography is not an idea: pornography is the injury.
>
> There is much to this perspective. Beliefs are also facts. People often act in accordance with the images and patterns they find around them. People raised in a religion tend to accept the tenets of that religion, often without independent examination. People taught from birth that black people are fit only for slavery rarely rebelled against that creed: beliefs coupled with the self-interest of the masters established a social structure that inflicted great harm while enduring for centuries. Words and images act at the level of the subconscious before they persuade at the level of the conscious. Even the truth has little chance unless a statement fits within the framework of beliefs that may never have been subjected to rational study.
>
> Therefore we accept the premises of this legislation. Depictions of subordination tend to perpetuate subordination. The subordinate status of women in turn leads to affront and lower pay at work, insult and injury at home, battery and rape on the streets. In the language of the legislation, 'pornography is central in creating and maintaining sex as a basis of discrimination. Pornography is a systematic practice of exploitation and subordination based on sex which differentially harms women. The bigotry and

575

contempt it produces, with the acts of aggression it fosters, harm women's opportunities for equality and rights [of all kinds].' Yet this simply demonstrates the power of pornography as speech.[58]

In Canada, the courts have accepted the evidence of harm established by the social science and psychological research (see Chapter 18). Recently, the Supreme Court of Canada formally recognized the links between certain kinds of pornography and violence against women. In a unanimous ruling in a judgment rendered 27 February 1992 the Canadian Supreme Court held that depictions of degrading and dehumanizing sex and sex with violence harms women. Courts in the USA and Australia have also accepted evidence of pornography-related harm.

HUMAN RIGHTS

It is not therefore a question of *whether* there is evidence of harm caused to women and children by the use of pornography. There is clearly an abundance of evidence of harm: different kinds of evidence and different kinds of harm, evidence which is consistently concurrent and corroborative. The issue is how to make the harm visible and how to make it matter: how to make women matter.[59] The question really is how much evidence is required before some action is taken.

In 1987 a motion was put to the AGM of the NCCL affirming the organization's 'commitment to free speech and expression and its opposition to censorship', but pointing out that the NCCL's opposition to censorship had not been absolute and that 'the NCCL had quite correctly accepted restrictions directed at avoiding identifiable harm'. The motion asked the NCCL 'to adopt a policy of opposing pornography which depicts violence to women or involves violence or criminal offence in its manufacture, on the grounds that it may cause identifiable harm by inciting sexual hatred and violence: and to campaign for legislation using the Race Relations Act 1976 as a precedent and a model'. The meeting voted to 'remit' the motion to the NCCL's executive committee for further consideration.

This resulted, in 1989, in a landmark decision by the NCCL to adopt an anti-pornography policy on the basis that there was 'sufficient evidence to say that it is highly likely that a link exists between pornography and harm to women both in terms of the aggregate increase of sexual violence against women, some individual attacks against women and the subordinate unequal status of women'. The policy had been formulated and agreed by the executive committee in response to a discussion paper prepared by the NCCL's legal officer, and was agreed by the membership at its AGM. Pornography was narrowly defined to include only sexually violent materials, but the policy called on the NCCL to support legal campaigns against pornography on the grounds of sex discrimination as a civil liberties issue for women, and 'to consider the kind of specific legislation (both civil and criminal) which could be enacted to curb the production and distribution of pornographic material'.[60]

The anti-pornography policy was overturned by a narrow vote the following year at the 1990 AGM, but it marked the beginning of a shift from the narrow libertarian view of freedom defined in terms of 'individuals' (typically white, male and in positions of social power) to an understanding of freedom defined in terms of justice and equality for members of groups who experience sexual, as well as social, discrimination.

The Public and the Private Spheres

Civil libertarians who also care about women's freedom sometimes defend pornography on the grounds that exercising controls over what happens in the privacy of one's own home is unacceptable, and that whatever happens between consenting adults must be permissible. But the distinction between the public and the private spheres is fallacious in this case. This idea says that while 'public' acts should be regulated by the state and its laws, 'private life' is sacrosanct and the law should not interfere with the activities of 'consenting adults in private'. This account ignores the structures of power, and especially of men's power over women. It is not possible to talk about 'consenting adults' when women are in a position of economic and sexual subordination to men. How free are subordinate groups to 'consent' or choose freely their activities? In the case of women it is particularly fatuous to talk about 'private life' (i.e. the family, sexual relationships, etc.) as a haven of individual liberty. An 'Englishman's home is his castle'; but statistics have shown that an English woman's home is the place where she is most vulnerable to exploitation and abuse.[61]

Civil libertarians also argue that exercising controls over what takes place in the privacy of the mind is unacceptable, and that 'fantasy' is in any case either harmless or liberating. But the Cartesian body/mind dichotomy is also fallacious. As this book   **577** shows, what's in the mind doesn't stay there or end there: it materializes in oppressive and injurious behaviour.

The power of pornography consumed in private to influence public behaviour is acknowledged and exploited by the military. Sado-pornographic videos were shown in the ships carrying troops to the Falklands in 1982 and to US troops in training for Vietnam in the 1960s. The military authorities obviously realize that 'private' forms of masculine aggression can be harnessed through the viewing of pornography for the purposes of 'public' acts of violence. The Nazis used anti-Semitic stereotypes as propaganda to condition both the German public and the Jews themselves to their extermination. The Nazis also disseminated pornography in Poland to facilitate its invasion and conquest.[62] The use of sado-masochistic pornography was widespread in Nazi Germany, and the Nazis knew the value of both pornographic and anti-Semitic propaganda as an exercise and an instrument of power: in inciting hatred and violence among the oppressors, and in reinforcing passivity and subjugation among the oppressed. The privacy arguments in defence of pornography cannot be justified. To defend pornography is quite simply to defend male power and privilege, sexual violence, sex discrimination and sexual inequality.

The National Council for Civil Liberties actually came into existence in the 1930s in response to the British fascist Black Shirt movement, to defend the rights of Jews to be free of anti-Semitism.[63] In 1976 the NCCL supported the Race Relations Act, limiting the freedom to publish race-hatred and anti-Semitic literature and making the incitement of hatred against black people and Jews illegal. Civil libertarians have agreed to the censorship of race-hatred literature, because of the identifiable harm it does to black people in contributing to racial hatred, racial violence and race discrimination. Black people, as Aminatta Forna points out in Chapter 5, do not regard the banning of race-hatred literature as censorship, but as guaranteeing a basic measure of freedom; or they regard it as justifiable censorship. Race-hatred legislation acknowledges that racism and race hatred silences black people, that it censors their freedom.

The Greatest Freedom

There are certain 'freedoms' that people have agreed to forgo because of the damage and harm they do to other people. These

include the freedom to steal, to assault, to rape, to murder, to incite racial hatred and race discrimination and to discriminate in employment on the grounds of race or sex. The freedom to incite sexual hatred, sexual violence and sex discrimination through pornography is another freedom people should arguably agree to forgo in order to ensure and safeguard the civil liberties and essential rights of women: so that, according to the NCCL's own charter:

1. Women can live in freedom and safe from personal harm;
2. Women can be protected from ill treatment or punishment that is inhuman or degrading;
3. Women can have equality and freedom from sex discrimination;
4. Women can move freely within their own country.

And indeed within their own homes. The right of women to be free of the misrepresentation and mistreatment of pornography is arguably a fundamental human right.[64] The evidence in this book suggests that the human rights of women should take precedence over the rights of some to publish and consume pornography and to treat women like pornography for their entertainment and pleasure.

Sincerely motivated and well-intentioned people who are opposed to pornography hold the view that it is better to have pornography than to risk any possibility of censorship. But defending pornography as free speech is no longer tenable, given the range and scale of identifiable harm it causes to women and children. And it is no longer necessary given the possibilities which now exist for taking effective legislative action against pornography without risk of censoring political free speech and non-pornographic sexually explicit materials (erotica, sex education, sex). It is now possible, as this book has demonstrated, to legislate against pornography without censorship and to introduce legislation that would greatly reduce if not eliminate the censorship which currently exists. Given the evidence of harm to women caused by the use of pornography – sufficient evidence certainly to meet the civil liberties standards for limiting 'free speech' – any liberal or civil libertarian who continues to defend the freedom to publish pornography has got to abandon any pretence of defending women's freedom: to accept that they are defending pornography-related sexual violence and sex discrimination, and that they are not therefore concerned with the civil liberties of women in any meaningful sense.

579

From a civil liberties perspective the greatest freedom would be achieved by repealing the obscenity legislation (which is censorship legislation, and ineffective in dealing with pornography) and replacing it with a Bill of Rights (guaranteeing the human rights of women), a Freedom of Information Act (guaranteeing political free speech), and effective sex discrimination legislation against pornography. This would define pornography in terms of what it is and what it does to women, using the legal definition described in Chapter 22. It would make incitement to sexual hatred and violence illegal and it would enable women who could prove they were injured by pornography to sue and to seek compensation.

Using civil legislation to seek remedy for harm is not censorship. And in the case of incitement legislation, would free speech really be threatened by restrictions on the publication of pornography? As Patricia Hynes points out in Chapter 20, it is possible to ban dangerous chemicals and to impose restrictions on free enterprise without posing a threat to the free market. It is also possible to limit freedom of expression in the case of pornography on grounds of harm without any fundamental threat to freedom of speech. It is even possible to envisage an increase in sexual freedom for everyone, and especially for women, in the absence of sex defined by pornography in terms of the subordination of women.

If women are harmed by pornography and if that harm matters – if women matter, and if women have the status of humans with rights – then taking action against pornography will not be regarded as censorship, or it will be regarded as justifiable censorship. Censorship is about the limitation of freedom. Eliminating pornography is about promoting the freedom of women, and providing women with basic human rights and civil liberties.

Notes

1. Peter Thornton, *Decade of Decline: Civil Liberties in the Thatcher Years* (London: NCCL, 1989), pp. 1–3.
2. I would like to acknowledge my indebtedness to the WAVAW Sexual Violence and the Law Group for developing the discussion of power and civil liberties.
3. Andrea Dworkin and Catharine A. MacKinnon, *Pornography and Civil Rights: A New Day for Women's Equality* (Minneapolis, MN: Organizing Against Pornography, 1988), pp. 83–4. According to the US Attorney General's Commission on Pornography, the ACLU position on child pornography has been that it should not be

produced, but once in existence there should be no restrictions on sale or distribution.

4. NCCL General Secretary, letter to the *Guardian*, 26 August 1988.

5. *Pornography and Sexual Violence: Evidence of the Links* (Minneapolis Hearings) (London: Everywoman, 1986).

6. Ibid., p. 18.

7. See Appendix 1, the NCCL's policy on pornography, 1989–90.

8. *Report of the Committee on Obscenity and Film Censorship* (Williams Committee)(London: HMSO, 1979), p. 66.

9. John H. Court, *Pornography and the Harm Condition* (Adelaide: Flinders University, 1980), p. 59.

10. John H. Court, 'Sex and Violence: A Ripple Effect' in Neil M. Malamuth and Edward Donnerstein (eds), *Pornography and Sexual Aggression* (New York: Academic Press, 1984), p. 144. Research which Yaffe did not discuss included: 'Those research studies during the past decade by Baron (1974a, b, 1978; Baron & Bell, 1977), Donnerstein (Donnerstein & Barrett, 1978; Donnerstein, Donnerstein, & Evans, 1975), Malamuth (Feshbach & Malamuth, 1978; Malamuth & Check, 1981; Malamuth, Feshbach, & Jaffe, 1977), and Zillmann (Cantor, Zillmann, & Eisiedel, 1978; Zillmann, Hoyt & Day, 1974; Zillmann & Sapolsky, 1977). Such experimental studies have been extended more recently to include further work in more naturalistic settings (e.g. Malamuth, Heim, & Feshbach, 1980) and complement the clinical work on sexual arousal of rapists in response to specific sexual stimuli (Abel, Barlow, Blanchard, & Guild, 1977, Barbaree, Marshall & Lanthier, 1979).'

11. Guy Cumberbatch and Dennis Howitt, *A Measure of Uncertainty: The Effects of the Mass Media* (London: John Libbey, 1989), p. 77; Williams Committee, op. cit., p. 67.

12. Ibid., p. 65:

> Major steps in the women's movement's visibility and acceptance had been made. While many of these were to do with work and education issues, male aggression, including male sexual aggression, was represented as a major weapon in maintaining male social power. This ideological stance has elements which provide a common purpose with the most reactionary conservative anti-pornographers, since pornography is seen by many feminists as a key cultural mechanism for encouraging sexual aggression against women . . . Furthermore, the liberal conscience has to be troubled by the notion that male power has pornography at its roots, so that the freedom of women is partly limited because of the freedom to produce and distribute pornography. Several value systems thereby share a common objective – the attack on pornography. This lead [*sic*] to an ill-assorted moral army against pornography which includes in its ranks otherwise bitterly-opposed forces.

The authors' own (again unacknowledged) ideology leads them to 'euphemize' their language: for example, they redefine what psychologists call men's 'desensitization' to rape as 'emotional adjustment'.   **581**

13. Dennis Howitt and Guy Cumberbatch, *Pornography Impacts and Influence*, Home Office Research and Planning Unit, 1990, pp. 84–5.

14. An independent report – *Pornography-Related Sexual Violence: A Review of the Evidence*, by Catherine Itzin – was submitted to the Home Office at a press conference at the House of Commons on 20 February 1990 by Dawn Primarolo, MP, Jo Richardson MP, Ray Wyre (Director, Gracewell Clinic), Trevor Price (Director, Gracewell Institute), Dr Liz Kelly, Tim Tate, the Campaign for Press and Broadcasting Freedom, the Campaign Against Pornography, the Campaign Against Pornography and Censorship and the Irish Campaign Against Pornography and Censorship.

15. James Check, 'Review of *Pornography: Impacts and Influence*', January 1991 (commissioned by Dawn Primarolo, MP).

16. A recent study by Check and Guloien found that 'exposure to both sexually violent pornography and to non-violent dehumanizing pornography fostered the perception in subjects' minds that they might rape and force women into unwanted sex acts'. But they also found that 'exposure to the non-violent erotica materials did not have any demonstrated antisocial impact . . .' James V. P. Check and Ted. H. Guloein, 'Reported Proclivity for Coercive Sex Following Repeated Exposure to Sexually Violent Pornography, Non-violent Dehumanizing Pornography and Erotica', in D. Zillmann and J. Bryant (eds), *Pornography: Research Advances and Policy Considerations* (Erlbaum, Hillsdale, N.: 1989), pp. 177–8. Edward Donnerstein also found that 'erotic films have no effect': 'there are no effects in the short term for erotica . . . material which is sexually explicit and does not show power orientation between males and females'. Donnerstein also found that 'a film that ends with intercourse between sexually consenting adults . . . does not lead to violence'. *Pornography and Sexual Violence: Evidence of the Links* (1988: Everywoman, London), pp. 13 and 19.

17. Donnerstein was, in fact, the expert who testified at the Minneapolis Hearings that the scientific evidence of links between pornography and sexual violence was stronger even than the evidence linking smoking and lung cancer. *Pornography and Sexual Violence: Evidence of the Links*, op. cit. p.18.

18. Ibid., p. 19.

19. Moore, S. (1989) 'Carry on Petting', *New Statesman*, May.

20. Catherine Itzin, *Pornography-Related Sexual Violence: A Review of the Evidence* (Colchester: University of Essex, 1991).

21. In addition to the many articles published in academic journals, there are several volumes published by leading male academics in this field. In Malamuth and Donnerstein, op. cit., there is evidence to show that pornography which represented 'negative affect, coercive imagery and rape myths' can result in 'an increase in aggressive sexual fantasies, aggressive behaviour, acceptance of anti-female attitudes and specifically a male aggression against females' (p. 9). The contents of *The Question of Pornography: Research Findings and Policy Implications* edited by Edward Donnerstein, Daniel Linz and Steven Penrod (New York: The Free Press, 1987) documented the

'. . . subtle yet profound effects violent sexual images have been shown to have in laboratory experiments, including desensitizing a viewer to the pain of victims, increasing feelings of aggression, and reinforcing the myths about rape. The authors show how repeated exposure to these images may actually increase a viewer's willingness to do harm. Further, they examine research which suggests that violent pornography not only sexually arouses men but plays a part in changing the way they think about women too.'

22. D. Linz, E. Donnerstein and S. Penrod, 'Effects of Long-Term Exposure to Violent and Sexually Degrading Depictions of Women', *Journal of Personality and Social Psychology* 55(5), 1988, p. 758, Dolf Zillmann, 'Effects of Prolonged Consumption of Pornography' in D. Zillmann and J. Bryant (eds), *Pornography: Research Advances and Policy Considerations* (New Jersey: Erlbaum, 1989); James V. P. Check and Ted. H. Guloien, 'Reported Proclivity for Coercive Sex Following Repeated Exposure to Sexually Violent Pornography, Non-Violent Dehumanizing Pornography, and Erotica', in Zillmann and Bryant, op. cit., p. 170.

23. Mike Baxter, 'Flesh and Blood: Does Pornography Lead to Sexual Violence?', *New Scientist*, 5 May 1990, p. 41.

24. Cumberbatch and Howitt, 1989, op. cit., p. 72.

25. Minneapolis Hearings, op. cit., p. 106.

26. Howitt and Cumberbatch, 1990, op. cit., pp. 76–7.

27. Catherine Itzin and Corinne Sweet, 'What You Feel About Pornography', *Cosmopolitan*, March 1990, pp. 8–12.

28. Ian Vine, unpublished paper distributed too NCCL AGM 1990.

29. Jane Caputi, *The Age of Sex Crime* (London: Women's Press, 1988), p. 164. Caputi quotes from the case studies and personal testimony of serial sexual murderers to illustrate how pornography was involved in their sex killings. See also D. Cameron and E. Frazer, *The Lust to Kill* (Cambridge: Polity Press, 1987) for a discussion of pornography and sexual murder.

30. Caputi, op. cit., p. 232.

31. Liz Kelly and Maureen O'Hara, 'The Making of Pornography: An Act of Sexual Violence,' *Spare Rib*, Issue 213, June 1990.

32. Linda Lovelace with Mike McGrady, *Ordeal* (Secacus, New Jersey: Citadel press, 1990). See also Hearings of the Minneapolis City Council 1983 in *Pornography and Sexual Violence: Evidence of the Links* (London: Everywoman, 1988).

33. Larry J. Johnson, Anaheim Police Department, Deposition in the Municipal Court, North Orange Judicial District, State of California, 5 August 1983. Clodaugh Corcoran, *Pornography: The New Terrorism* (Dublin: Attic Press, 1989).

34. Tim Tate, *Child Pornography: An Investigation* (London: Methuen, 1990); *Children of the Devil: Ritual Abuse and Satanic Crime* (London: Methuen, 1991).

35. Diana E. H. Russell, 'The Incidence and Prevalence of Intrafamilial and Extrafamilial Sexual Abuse of Female Children', *Child Abuse and Neglect*, Vol. 7, 1983, pp. 133–46.

36. M. H. Silbert and A. M. Pines, 'Pornography and Sexual Abuse of Women', *Sex Roles*, 10 (11/12), 1984, p. 862.
37. A. Burgess *et al*, 'Response Patterns in Children and Adolescents Exploited Through Sex Rings and Pornography', *American Journal of Psychiatry*, 141 (5), 1984, pp. 656–62; T. Tate, op. cit, 1991.
38. Committee on Sexual Offences Against Children and Youths, *Sexual Offences Against Children* (Ottawa, Canada: Canadian Government Publishing Center, 1984).
39. Minneapolis Hearings, op. cit., p. 96.
40. M. J. Goldstein *et al.*, 'Exposure to Pornography and Sexual Behaviour in Deviant and Normal Groups', *Technical Reports of the Commission on Obscenity and Pornography*, Vol. 7, 1970.
41. *US Commission on Obscenity and Pornography* (1970) p. 240.
42. Much of the pornography market is illegal and the magazines do not always publish audited circulation figures.
43. Kutchinsky's research also included the more serious offence of physical indecency with girls. This was defined by the following survey question: 'Imagine that a five-year-old girl comes home and says that a strange gentleman has made her touch his penis. Apart from that nothing has happened and the girl is not frightened. What would you do if that was your child?' Court, 'Sex and Violence', op. cit., p. 147.
44. Ibid. Kutchinsky appeared on Thames TV's *This Week* programme in May 1990 claiming that rape rates had decreased after liberalization of pornography in Denmark. This needs further investigation.
45. G. Geis and R. Geis, 'Rape in Stockholm: Is Permissiveness Relevant?' *Criminology*, 17 (3), pp. 311–22.
46. Court, *Pornography and the Harm Condition*, op. cit.
47. Court, 'Sex and Violence', op. cit. p. 158.
48. Baxter, op. cit.
49. Court, 'Sex and Violence', op. cit. pp. 162–3.
50. Baxter, op. cit. See L. Baron and H. A. Strauss, 'Sexual Stratification, Pornography and Rape in the US', in Malamuth and Donnerstein, op. cit.
51. Robert Brannon, 'Methodological Improvements in Research on Pornography and Rape', (unpublished, 1989).
52. Williams Committee, op. cit., pp. 72, 76.
53. Ibid., p. 78.
54. C. Itzin and C. Sweet, 'Tackling the Monsters on the Top Shelf', *Independent*, 17 April 1989. There are no statistics on the growth of the illegal market in pornography. However, both Scotland Yard Obscene Publications Branch and Customs and Excise officers said that there had been a liberalization in the *administration* of the law in the 1980s and particularly from 1984.
55. *Criminal Statistics: England and Wales* (1982–1988 CM 847) (London: HMSO). Additional figures provided by Home Office Press Officer, November 1990.
56. US Attorney General's Commission on Pornography, 1986.
57. *Pornography and Prostitution in Canada* (Fraser Commission) Report of

the Special Committee on Pornography and Prostitution, Vol. 1 (Ottowa, 1985).

58. *American Booksellers Inc. v. William H. Hudnut*, 771 F. 2d 323, 328-29 (7th civ. 1985).

59. Catharine A. MacKinnon, 'Not a Moral Issue', *Yale Law and Policy Review* 11 (2) Spring (1984), p. 335.

60. For the full text of the 1987 NCCL resolution on pornography, see Appendix 1. For the full text of the 1989 resolution see Appendix 1.

61. In 1989 there were over one million incidents of domestic violence reported to the police. There was a 54 per cent increase in domestic violence reported to the police in 1991. This will only be the tip of the iceberg given the reluctance of women to report their husbands or partners to the police and the fact that, until recently, the police would not, as a matter of policy, become involved when women were victims of violence in personal relationships. The majority of rapes are committed by men known to women rather than by strangers. In March 1991 the Appeal Court ruled that rape in marriage was a crime, and a Law Commission Report recommended a change in the law on marital rape.

62. R. Amy Elman, 'Sexual Subordination and State Intervention: Lessons for Feminists from the Nazi State', *Trivia*, 1989 p. 59. Also see Williams Committee, op. cit., p. 94.

63. Sylvia Scattardi, *Fire under the Carpet: Working for Civil Liberties in the 1930s* (London: Lawrence and Wishart, 1986).

64. The Fraser Commission on Pornography and Prostitution in Canada, reporting in 1985 (op. cit.), regarded pornography as a human rights violation. They recommended 'that jurisdictions enact by legislation a civil cause of action focusing on the violation of civil rights inherent in pornography'. They recommended extending existing legislation in Canada 'to cover the promotion of hatred by way of pornography against a person or a class of person,' in recognition that the harm 'derives its meaning and sting from group status' (see Dworkin and MacKinnon, op. cit., p. 30).

APPENDICES

1. Chronology of Anti-Pornography Initiatives in the UK

By June 1990 there were an increasing number of organizations committed to free speech and freedom of expression which also recognized that in so far as pornography contributes to sexual violence and sexual inequality its publication is incompatible with the civil liberties of women, or with women's safety and freedom of movement.

1970s

From the early 1970s Women Against Violence Against Women (WAVAW) took the lead in campaigning against pornography and violence against women. WAVAW produced newsletters, distributed leaflets, lobbied and made formal complaints about advertisements, organized meetings and workshops, and mobilized women generally on the issue of pornography. They organized pickets and direct actions against sex shops. They organized the 'Reclaim the Night Marches', produced and presented to women's groups and organizations the first 'slide show' in England (illustrating what pornography is and what it means), and published the book *Women Against Violence Against Women*, edited by Dusty Rhodes and Sandra McNeill (London: Only Women Press, 1985).

1980–86

The Women's Media Action Group (WMAG) campaigned against pornography as part of their wider campaign for fairer representation of women in the media. They published a bi-monthly bulletin, drawing attention to the influence of pornography and advertisements, and forced the Advertising Standards Authority to improve its code on sexist advertising. WMAG also produced special reports on women's representation in the media: e.g. Report No. 2, *Women as Sex Objects*, and Report No. 5,

Sugar and Spice, showing the links between pornography and the mainstream media in the sexualizing of women and little girls.

1982

The Association of Cinematograph Television and Allied Technicians (ACTT) formulated a policy on pornography:

> In view of the growing concern of union members at:
> 1. Widespread violence against women and the representation of women in pornography as passive victims of humiliation and violence for the gratification of men;
> 2. The increasing commercial success of pornographic films and videos portraying gratuitous violence against women, including rape, and murder;

This Conference resolves:

> 1. To campaign widely against the production and distribution of such films and videos; and
> 2. To offer every practical support to union members who wish to refuse to work on such material, without fear of victimization or adverse employment conditions.

1986

Labour MP Clare Short introduced the Indecent Displays (Newspapers) Act 1986 'to make illegal the display of pictures of naked or partially naked women in sexually provocative poses in newspapers', known as the 'Page 3 Bill' after the page in the tabloid press where these pictures are regularly published.

1987

April

The following resolution was debated at the National Council for Civil Liberties, and 'remitted' for further consultation and consideration:

> This AGM reaffirms its commitment to and support for freedom of speech and expression, and its opposition to censorship as fundamental aims of the NCCL. This AGM notes:
> 1. That the NCCL's opposition to all forms of censorship has not been absolute.

2. That the NCCL has quite correctly accepted restrictions directed at avoiding an identifiable harm, the prevention of which overrides the fundamental aim of free communication and expression of ideas, and where the restriction has been capable of enforcement in a way that is likely to achieve the desired end;

3. That in the Race Relations Act (1976) 'incitement to racial hatred' is deemed unlawful and it is made an offence to publish or distribute written matter (defined as 'any writing, sign or visual representation') which is 'threatening, abusive or insulting . . . in a case where, having regard to all circumstances, hatred is likely to be stirred up against any racial group in Great Britain by the matter or words in question'.

4. That pornography is a form of communication (in words and visual representations) which, at the very least, is threatening, abusive and insulting to women, and which also perpetuates the discrimination experienced by women.

5. Attempts have therefore been made in the past to legislate its control and/or restriction.

6. That there has previously been an unresolved difficulty: how to formulate legislation against pornography in a way that it can be effectively defined and enforced without:

(a) legislating against acceptable sex and sexuality, and discriminating against homosexuals

(b) handing over powers of social control that can be abused by state or church or repressive 'morality' factions, and

(c) eroding the rights of freedom of speech or expression.

7. That in the Race Relations Act (1976) the NCCL now has a precedent for restraints on freedom of expression which can be oppressive and harmful to a particular group (a racial group, or in the case of pornography, of women), and a model for the definition of the offence and its enforcement.

8. That pornography which is 'threatening, abusive and insulting' or demeaning, degrading and damaging to women can be defined or interpreted as that which 'depicts violence or involves violence or criminal offence in its manufacture'. Where 'pornography' has been difficult to define, 'violence' is and can be defined precisely in law.

9. That pornography which depicts violence against women or involves violence or criminal offences to women in its manufacture can and should be legislated against on the grounds that it can be an 'incitement to sexual hatred' and contribute to acts of violence against women in the form of sexual abuse, sexual assault, sexual harassment, rape and murder, the evidence of which has now been accepted (including by the US Supreme Court [1985]).

10. That 'freedom to' publish material which may incite racial or sexual hatred and/or violence is a 'false freedom' posited on 'freedom denied to' its victims (persons defined by reference to colour, race, nationality or ethnic or national origins – or gender) and results in identifiable harm and damage to its victims.

This AGM therefore calls on the NCCL:

1. To adopt a policy of opposing pornography which depicts violence to women or involves sexual violence or criminal offence in its manufacture, on the grounds that it may cause identifiable harm by inciting sexual hatred and violence;
2. To campaign for legislation making unlawful the manufacture and distribution of pornography of this nature, using the Race Relations Act 1976 as a precedent and a model, with offences punishable by substantial fines and imprisonment, and ensuring that prosecutions can be brought equally by the police and by women themselves.

Proposed by: Catherine Itzin.

September

The ACTT organized a conference of its women members on the issue of pornography. Speakers included Jo Richardson MP (Shadow Minister for Women), Andrea Dworkin, Catherine Itzin and Sadie Roberts (ACTT Equality Officer).

1988

January

The Campaign Against Pornography (CAP) was formally launched at the House of Commons by Clare Short MP and Barbara Rogers, editor of *Everywoman* magazine, with the publication of the complete transcript of the public hearings held in Minneapolis, Minnesota, in 1983 to consider whether to include pornography in the existing municipal civil rights legislation (entitled *Pornography and Sexual Violence: Evidence of the Links*).

1989

March

Clare Short MP presented a Private Members' Bill 'to remove pornography from the press and the workplace' (Indecent Displays Newspapers and Workplaces Bill 1989). This was supported by MPs Jo Richardson, Dawn Primarolo, Margaret Beckett, Alice Mahon, Joyce Quin, Maria Fyfe, Joan Ruddock, Diane Abbott, Audrey Wise, Marjorie Mowlam and Ann Taylor.

March

The National Union of Journalists (NUJ) at its ADM adopted a resolution supporting efforts to promote legislation against pornography on grounds of sex discrimination:

This ADM notes with alarm the increase in semi-pornographic publications, e.g. *Sunday Sport*, *The Sport* and the possibility of a *Daily Sport*, masquerading as newspapers.

In the light of the above, this ADM welcomes the debate that is now beginning to take place within the union about what is or what is not pornography and whether journalists working for pornographic magazines should be union members.

This ADM further supports efforts being made by both the Campaign Against Pornography and Censorship and the Campaign Against Pornography to produce a definition of pornography and to promote legislation which will provide for pornography being unlawful on grounds of sex discrimination.

April

At its AGM the National Council for Civil Liberties' members voted in favour of a new policy on pornography:

Pornography
24. This AGM, whilst appreciating the methodological difficulties in producing scientific evidence and therefore the ability to say the exact nature and extent of a causal link between certain kinds of pornography and harm to women, considers that there is sufficient evidence to say that it is highly likely that such a link exists both in terms of the aggregate increase of sexual violence against women, some individual sexual attacks against women and the subordinate unequal status of women.

This AGM therefore supports lawful campaigns against certain kinds of pornography as defined below, on the grounds of sex discrimination as a civil liberties issue for women, where such campaigns are aimed at changing public attitudes towards such material.

Conference notes that, in any definition of pornography, there must be three main ingredients:
1. It must be sexually explicit;
2. It must depict women as enjoying or deserving some form of physical abuse; and
3. It must objectify women, that is, define women in terms of their relationship to men's lust and desire.

This AGM recognizes that, because pornography represents deep-seated sexism, and because of the nature of the power of the pornography industry itself, the campaign against pornography is unlikely to be successful through public debate alone. It therefore resolves that NCCL should consider the kinds of specific legislation (both civil and criminal) which could be enacted to curb the production and distribution of pornographic material; material which should be narrowly defined as that which sexualizes violence and the subordination of women.

Proposed by: The Executive Committee   **593**

April

A new national organization, the Campaign Against Pornography and Censorship (CPC) was formally launched by a group of writers, artists, lawyers and trade unionists, all long-standing civil libertarians and women's rights campaigners, with a conference on 'Pornography and Civil Liberties' jointly organized with the Fawcett Society, and with a survey of pornography for sale in high street newsagents published in the *Independent*.

July

With the support of the Campaign for Press and Broadcasting Freedom (CPBF) Labour MP Dawn Primarolo presented a Private Members' Bill on 'The Location of Pornographic Material 1989' which defined pornography as 'films and videos and any printed matter which, for the purposes of sexual arousal or titillation, depicts women or parts of women's bodies as objects, things or commodities, or in sexually humiliating or degrading poses, or being subjected to violence'. Under the terms of the Bill, pornographic material would be available only from licensed vendors set up solely for that purpose, and local authorities would be responsible for issuing licences and trading standards officers for enforcing the regulations.

October

The new Irish Campaign Against Pornography and Censorship (ICPC) was launched by Clodagh Corcoran, a former treasurer of the Irish Civil Liberties Union, at a conference at Trinity College, Dublin, chaired by Irish parliamentarian Monica Barnes. The Irish Dail was considering a definition of pornography for its Video Recordings Bill based on the NCCL model.

November

A major survey of women's experiences of and attitudes to pornography was published in the women's magazine *Cosmopolitan*. Over 4,000 women replied, providing further evidence of the links between pornography and violence to women and children. The results of the survey were published in the March 1990 issue of *Cosmopolitan*.

November
The Campaign Against Pornography (CAP) launched its 'Off the Shelf' Campaign to mobilize the grassroots support of women to lobby W. H. Smith to stop distributing pornography. CAP also organized a national conference on pornography and sexual violence in Nottingham.

December
The Home Office announced that it was going to carry out an investigation into links between pornography and sexual violence. The review of existing research material was carried out by Guy Cumberbatch of Aston University and Dennis Howitt of Loughborough University and a report was produced in 1990.

1990

March
The National Union of Journalists passed the following resolutions at its annual meeting:

> This ADM instructs the NEC to convene a one-day conference for NUJ members in 1990 on the problematic issue of censorship and pornography, to be paid for from central funds and organized by the Equality Organizer in consultation with the Equality Council and the Ethics Council. The conference should be held in time for ideas it may generate to be embodied in motions to tabling bodies for the 1991 ADM.
>
> This ADM gives full support to the 'Off the Shelf' campaign being run by the National Union of Students and Campaign Against Pornography.
>
> This ADM welcomes the establishment of a Campaign Against Pornography and Censorship in Ireland, and formally pledges its support to the campaign in line with similar support given to the sister organization in Britain.

March
The Women's Trades Union Congress (TUC) agreed the following resolution submitted by the Manufacturing Science Finance (MSF) Union amended in debate to refer to positive (i.e. sex **595**

discrimination) legislation and not obscenity or other forms of repressive legislation:

> Conference, whilst acknowledging the forward thinking of the labour and trade union movement's policies on equal rights, is concerned that to date little attention has been given to the increasing pervasive incidence of pornography and violence toward women in society today.
>
> Conference recognizes, therefore, that equal rights in its fullest meaning will never be truly attained whilst we allow pornographers to portray women in a degrading, oppressive and dehumanizing manner.
>
> Further, Conference agrees that the statement adopted at the Minneapolis hearings in 1983 is the truest definition to date, and should be adopted by this conference, namely, 'pornography is the graphic, sexually explicit subordination of women through pictures or words, that also includes women de-humanized as sexual objects, things or commodities, enjoying pain or humiliation or rape, or being tied up, cut up, or mutilated, bruised or physically hurt, in postures of sexual submission or servility or display, reduced to body parts, penetrated by objects or animals, or presented in scenes of degradation, injury, torture, shown as filthy or inferior, bleeding, bruised or hurt in the context that makes these conditions sexual'.
>
> Conference therefore is of the opinion pornography is a crime against women and calls on the Women's Committee to:
>
> (a) Actively campaign against all forms of pornography with organizations already involved in this area, such as the Campaign Against Pornography, the Rape Crisis centres, Women's Aid and other similar groups;
>
> (b) encourage regional Women's Committees and affiliated organizations to include on appropriate equal rights courses, sessions on the problems of pornography within society; and
>
> (c) campaign for, and support any Parliamentary Bill which aims to outlaw pornography in the media and in the workplace.

April

The AGM of the National Council for Civil Liberties voted (123 to 102) to overturn the anti-pornography policy.

September

The Campaign Against Pornography and Censorship (CPC) organized a national conference on 'Men and Pornography' to coincide with the publication of *Refusing to be a Man* by John Stoltenberg (Fontana).

December
The Home Office published its report, *Pornography: Impacts and Influences* by Dennis Howitt and Guy Cumberbatch.

1991

February
A press conference at the House of Commons submitted to the Home Office an alternative report *Pornography-Related Sexual Violence: Evidence of the Links* and responses highly critical of the Home Office Report from leading international pornography researchers.

1992

May
The National Association of Women's Organisations (NAWO) at its annual conference, representing over two hundred women's organisations, agreed the following motion by an overwhelming majority (with only three abstentions and no votes against), proposed by the Campaign Against Pornography and Censorship and seconded by the Campaign Against Pornography:

> This conference considers that there is sufficient evidence – in survivor and in perpetrator testimony, in cases of child sexual abuse, in clinical research and work with sex offenders, and in the social science and psychological research – to say that it is highly likely that a link exists between the use of sexually violent pornography, the use of non-violent, but subordinating and dehumanising pornography, and the general level of sexual violence against women and children and the subordinate unequal status of women in society. Pornography is also implicated in some specific sexual attacks against women and children.
>
> This conference therefore supports lawful campaigns against these kinds of pornography on the grounds of sex discrimination and as a civil liberties issue for women.
>
> This conference recognises that because of the deep-seated sexism in society (to which pornography contributes, together with the many practices of economic discrimination and other forms of sexual violence and subordination), and because of the nature and the power of the ponography industry, the campaign against pornography is unlikely to be successful through public debate alone, important though it is to inform people about the effects of pornography.
>
> This conference therefore resolves that NAWO should support legislation to enable people who can prove they are victims of pornography-related harm to take civil action against the manufacturers and distributors of pornography.

2. Extracts from Letter to the Council for Periodical Distributors Associations from Gray and Co., 5 June 1986

GRAY AND COMPANY
Stephen M. Johnson
Senior Vice President

June 5, 1986

Mr John M. Harrington
Executive Vice-President
Council for Periodical Distributors Associations
60 East 42nd Street
Suite 2134
New York, NY 10165

Dear Mr Harrington:

Frank Mankiewicz, Ray Argyle and I are grateful for the opportunity to meet last week with you and other members of the Media Coalition to discuss the problems raised by the work of the Attorney General's Commission on Pornography and the threat posed by self-styled 'anti-pornography' activists.

We at Gray and Company believe we can assist the Coalition deal with the short-term challenge presented by the Commission on Pornography and the long-term challenge presented by the religious fundamentalists. This letter will set forth strategy recommendations for dealing with both these challenges . . . The Commission on Pornography plans to formally issue its final report in early July, although a draft of the introduction to the report and a list of 26 proposed recommendations have been made public. The Commission's work has already had a serious impact on selected periodical publishers, distributors and retailers . . .

Short-term Strategy

In the short term, we propose a strategy designed to further discredit the Commission on Pornography, the manner in which its members were chosen, the way in which it has conducted its deliberations, the highly political and biased way in which it has organized its findings and recommendations, and the deeper motives of those who have been its most enthusiastic proponents . . .

Yet despite this growing controversy, the Commission's findings and recommendations will likely find widespread public acceptance. Politicians and civic and community leaders will be reluctant to openly criticize the Commission lest they be branded as 'soft on pornography.' Clearly, publishers, distributors and retailers face the prospect of trying to conduct their legitimate and constitutionally-protected business in a hostile environment.

Criticism of the Commission needs to be more sharply defined and clearly focused. This can be accomplished by creation of a broad coalition of individuals and organizations opposed to the Commission's findings and recommendations. This new group – broader than the industry-based Media Coalition – would include academicians, civil libertarians, religious leaders, civic and community leaders, politicians, business and foundation executives, authors and editors, columnists, commentators and entertainers. This new group might be called 'Americans for the Right to Read' or 'The First Amendment Coalition.'

Creation of such a broad, issue-oriented group and selection of a national spokesperson would help dispel the notion that opponents of the Commission's work are only interested in protecting their own financial interests or are somehow 'pro-pornography.' Selection of a national spokesperson not directly involved in publishing would help opinion leaders, policy makers and the general public understand that the issue here is not 'pornography' but rather First Amendment freedoms . . .

Since time is short, formation of this new coalition and recruitment of a chairman and spokesperson should be undertaken at once. As soon as this task is accomplished, the new coalition should hold a news conference in Washington to announce its formation, membership, objectives and program. The new coalition should move quickly to establish state and local chapters, seeking to enlist the broadest possible support.

Quiet efforts should be undertaken to persuade the Attorney **599**

General, the White House and the leaders of both political parties that the forthcoming report of the work of the Commission is so flawed, so controversial, so contested and so biased that they should shy away from publicly endorsing the document. The more doubts that can be created about the objectivity and validity of the Commission's findings and recommendations, the more difficult it will be for anti-pornography crusaders to use the report as an effective tool for achieving their objectives.

The new coalition should launch a series of pre-emptive strikes against the Commission's report, using advertorials in major national newspapers and magazines, placing spokespersons on national and local television and radio news, public affairs and talk shows, holding a series of news conferences in major cities across the country, and meeting with government leaders and politicians to discuss the biases, misrepresentations and factual errors contained in the report.

The coalition should hold a second news conference in Washington immediately following the release of the Commission's report in July, providing the media, Members of Congress and other interested groups with a 'white paper' refuting the findings and recommendations of the Commission's report . . .

A way must be found of discrediting the organizations and individuals who have begun to seriously disrupt the legitimate business activities of publishers, distributors and sellers of legal, non-obscene books and magazines. This effort must be spearheaded by the broad new coalition of industry and non-industry forces created to deal with the more immediate and pressing problem of the Commission on Pornography.

Any long-term effort launched without such strategic positioning will fail because publishers, distributors and sellers will be thought to have no motive or justification other than economic self-interest, for their stance. Forced into a position of defending 'pornography', they are certain to find themselves in a 'no-win' situation.

Themes

A successful effort to relieve publishers, distributors and retailers from harassment will involve communicating several broad themes with which most Americans agree. They include the following:

1. There is no factual or scientific basis for the exaggerated and unfounded allegations that sexually-oriented content in

contemporary media is in any way a cause of violent or criminal behavior.

2. It makes no sense to expend the energies of community groups, law enforcement agencies or the courts in the pursuit of such allegations. In fact, it is socially harmful to direct our energies in such channels, because it diverts our attention from real economic and social problems.

3. The campaign to infringe on all our rights by attacking the rights of publishers, distributors and retailers is being orchestrated by a group of religious extremists whose tactics and goals are clearly not representative of mainstream American public opinion.

4. If this campaign against one segment of publishing is successful, it will be extended to other areas of American life; small, extremist pressure groups will step up their efforts to impose their narrow moral and social agenda on the majority . . .

5. One need not admire, agree with, purchase or read certain publications to support their constitutional right to be published, distributed and sold . . . and the right of other people to purchase and read them.

We believe these broad themes have the support of the majority of the American people. Further, we believe we can help create a coalition of prominent individuals and institutions who would lend their names and their support to the effort to communicate these themes.

Our long-term strategy is both national and local in scope. We believe a program of print and broadcast activities, creation of a national information center and speakers' bureau, development of a grass roots membership base, publication of a newsletter and a special book or collection of essays on the subject, an annual national conference and regional seminars and symposia on the First Amendment, and an effort to link the bi-centennial of the Constitution in 1987 to the current controversy will strengthen support for 'the right to read.'

About Our Capabilities

As the largest public affairs firm in Washington, Gray and Company is well qualified to assist the Media Coalition in designing and implementing short- and long-term strategies to defeat efforts by the Commission on Pornography . . .

Budget

The complex nature of the challenge facing the Media Coalition – to devise and implement short- and long-term public affairs and public relations strategies at the national and local levels – will require a substantial commitment of time and resources. This is to be expected, for the opposition is well organized and well funded and the stakes are extremely high.

Gray and Company customarily charges a client a standard monthly retainer plus the total of hourly staff time charges incurred on the client's behalf. Out of pocket expenses are billed separately. In this case, we propose a monthly retainer of $5,000, plus staff time charges and expenses. Given the magnitude of the task at hand, you should be prepared to incur charges – at least initially – in the range of $50,000–$75,000 per month. Thus, the total cost of this effort could range from $600,000 to $900,000 during the first year . . .

We look forward to hearing from you.

Sincerely,

Steve Johnson

3. District Court of Ontario, *R.* v. *Ross Wise*, before the Hon. Judge H. R. Locke, 22 June 1990: Reasons for Judgment

Editor's Introduction

I have chosen to include these excerpts from a recent Canadian obscenity case because they are useful in illustrating a number of key issues that have been discussed in this book. This case shows how the social science and psychological research evidence of harm can be used successfully to make distinctions between different kinds of sexually explicit material, to convict violent and dehumanising material and to acquit erotica. It demonstrates how these distinctions can in fact be used to protect gay and lesbian sex. It shows how the morality standards of obscenity law persist, though when set against the gendered harm standards, as they are in this case, the morality standards are more easily seen to be irrelevant and obsolete. But it also illustrates the progress that still needs to be made in recognising gendered harm when it exists, for there are examples of dehumanising material in this case which were not convicted.

Specifically, this case demonstrates that it is possible not only to define pornography, but to operationalise a definition in courts of law. It furthermore shows that the distinctions between different kinds of sexually explicit material can be operationalised in a way that protects non-violent, non-subordinating gay and lesbian sex from prosecution. Thus, for example, it does not matter in the examples below whether it is same sex or opposite sex material. Explicit lesbian and gay sex is not prosecuted.

The judgments in this case illustrate the fact that the problem is not sexual explicitness *per se*, but the sexualised and sexually explicit dominance, subordination and violence of pornography. Nor is the problem the kind of sexual act that is portrayed. Thus oral and anal sexual acts as well as vaginal intercourse are acquitted in these examples.

But the judgments in this case also illustrate the desensitising properties of pornography, and the extent to which violent and dehumanising sexual subordination is not recognised or is still seen as 'just sex'. Thus there are sexually explicit magazines which sexualize and pornographize pregnant women which are regarded as 'just erotic'. There are sexually explicit magazines which sexualize the inequality of the boss/secretary relationship which are judged to be consensual and 'just erotic.' The material depicting heterosexual buggery as consensual is also problematic. Anal intercourse is the standard sexual practice between gay males who each have the same social and sexual power status. This is not true of heterosexual relationships: in which the anus is not the standard orifice of intercourse and in which the participants do not enjoy the same social and sexual status. The extent to which anal sex is a consensual act for women must be questioned and consideration given in this, as in other contexts, to the extent to which this pornography operates to impose male sexual dominance and female subordination to sexual acts which are dehumanising for women.

This case also shows the extent to which moral obscenity standards are still operating alongside the gendered standards and judgments made here. So ejaculation from an erect male penis is judged to be 'obscene', although there is no evidence that this is a cause of gendered harm. And although ejaculation into the face of a woman is arguably dehumanising (and is judged to be so in the example of *Big Tits for a Hard Boss* below), it is penile ejaculation and not the male power relations in this and in *Big Tit Secretaries* which is judged to be 'obscene' In reality, the harm factor in both of these scenarios is the sexually explicit and sexualized inequality.

Editor

The Magazines

(Exhibit 10) Counts 1, 2, and 5: 'Hot Cameron'
This 39-page publication depicts an adult male and an adult female in multiple photographs contained in the publication. The subjects are on a bed. Both are naked. She is seen to perform fellatio upon him. Both are shown throughout engaged in acts of sexual intercourse from various angles with the camera lens viewing it all from a close to zero range to that of five or six feet. He is seen to perform cunnilingus upon her. He ejaculates on her mid body. She appears to enjoy it. There is no depiction of threatened violence in any of these scenes. The printed dialogue,

however puerile and crude it may be, does not state or allude to anything but an apparent mutual consent by the two subjects to the acts they are seen to perform.

(Exhibit 11) Counts 4 and 6: a videotape cassette entitled 'Double Penetration'
Ninety minutes in length, it opens with a motel room scene. A greedy young adult male is depicted in a crude soliloquy planning to produce a pornographic film. He decides how and where and with whom as actors the film will be made. He verbally fantasizes about all the money he hopes to make from the film. The following scenes show the results of his efforts in bringing a team of actors together who, in a further motel room setting, engage with one another as apparent consenting adults in a heterosexual series of sexual acts including simultaneous acts of buggery and sexual intercourse.

There is one scene where a naked woman slaps the bare buttocks of her consenting female adult participating partner who asks to be spanked harder. This film explicitly portrays various conventional sexual acts and some not so conventional sexual activity. The object of the film is to explicitly depict simultaneous oral, anal and normal, if I can use that term, sexual intercourse.

(Exhibit 12) Counts 7 and 8: nine magazines, titles – 'Young and Lonely' (No. 26), 'Young and Lonely' (No. 30), 'Peach Fuzz Pussies' (No. 25), 'Peach Fuzz Pussies' (No. 29), 'Baby Dolls' (No. 34), 'Baby Dolls' (No. 36), 'Young Girls' (No. 1), 'Young Girls' (No. 6), '300 Cotton Panties And Bare Bottoms' (No. 22).
These magazines all contains photographs of young females in a sexually provocative series of poses. Each is shown either totally naked or nearly so. Some of the models are mature women. The printer disclaimer in each magazine says each is over the age of 18 years. Some obviously are. Many are barely post-pubescent. In fact, the first coloured photograph past the front cover of the publication '300 Cotton Panties and Bare Bottoms' depicts a female girl who notwithstanding the mild suggestion of some pubic hair is obviously pre-pubescent. The centrefold of the magazine 'Young Girls' (No. 6). depicts a very young female, totally naked except for her running shoes and socks, lying on a child's bed with head on a teddy bear while she displays a very close-up explicit photograph of her total lower genital area. The first seven pages including the front cover of another magazine entitled 'Young Girls' depicts a very young female person dressed **605**

in childish clothes explicitly showing her genitals and wearing a childlike ribbon in her hair.

The magazine 'Young and Lonely', page 13, depicts a very young female person sitting on a chesterfield with her legs spread apart. She has a childlike haircut, there is a bow prominently displayed in her hair. She has lace at each wrist and is holding a curling iron in her left hand with its tongs encompassing the nipple of her right breast as if in self-mutilation.

The magazine entitled 'Baby Dolls' discloses a totally naked female obviously barely pubescent, displaying bare breasts under a pulled-up pink jersey. She has a pink ribbon in her hair tied in a childish hairstyle. The lower left hand corner of the front cover discloses the same female totally naked again displaying her genitals. She, in that photograph, is dressed only in shoes and socks and the same pink ribbon is in her hair.

These magazines all display young females. Each is in a sexually provocate pose. No male persons are depicted. Some of the models are shown holding a dildo which is protruding from the lower orifice.

There is a persistent common theme disclosed in all of the nine publications. The reader is obviously by the whole context of the photographic scenerio which includes the use of such props as stuffed toys, dolls, childlike bedroom decorations and the clothing worn by the models, to have a physical sexual encounter with each young girl. Each model is dressed and posed to resemble not a baby, but rather a female child. Each wears the clothes of a child. The clothing includes hair ribbons. Many wear saddle shoes. All have young female child's haircuts. Many models cuddle teddy bears and the like.

(Exhibit 13) Counts 9 and 10: entitled 'Big Tit Secretaries', 'Big Tits For A Hard Boss', 'Roly-Poly', 'Hot Lust No. 5'
The first two publications depict an adult male and female. The setting in both publications would appear to be in a business type of office. Desks, a padded swivel chair, a chesterfield, and in at least one photograph what appears to be a fax machine stand are all used as platforms upon which sexual intercourse and fellatio occur between the two people involved.

The dominant theme displayed in the many photographs in both magazines is the sexual performance of the secretary with the male person who is dressed up to appear to be her employer.

The publication 'Big Tits For A Hard Boss', the last five

photographs, excluding the one on the back cover, clearly depicts the male person ejaculating into the face and neck of the female.

The publication 'Hot Lust No. 5' is in essentially the same format. Three mature adults are involved. Two are female. The other is male. The intention is to depict one of the females in the position as a housemaid. The other plays the wife of the husband. Both women appear to be either competing with one another or cooperating with each other in conferring such sexual favours as fellatio, buggery and sexual-intercourse on the man. There are also very explicit acts of a combination of fellatio on the male and lesbianism with respect to the two women all at the same time.

The publication 'Roly-Poly' involves a series of photographs in its 62-odd pages. Each involves the sexual interaction between a mature male and a mature female. In all the photographs the female is obese and is seen performing fellatio on the male. The male is depicted as having sexual intercourse with her from various angles by the employment of many methods. Dildos are employed by the female on the genitals and in the anal orifice of the male. In a similar fashion the same thing occurs with respect to the female by the male. There are two sets of photographs of the male penis in the process of ejaculation into the face at the mouth of the female.

Other photographs at about the centre of the periodical depict a male in the process of repairing his bicycle. He is approached by the female who seduces him by partially removing her own clothes and removing his genitals from his trousers. She is then depicted holding a pair of pliers to the head of his penis. Her words are, 'I really enjoy having sex with smaller men because fat women can get men to let them do anything they want, even squeezing their cocks with pliers'. The second to last page in the publication depicts the female pushing the head of the male's penis which she has gripped in pliers through the spokes of a bicycle wheel.

Counts 11 and 12: 1. 'Those Bad, Bad Boys', 2. 'Sweet Cocks' (No. 9); 3. 'Slaves Of Anal Sex'
The first publication is 'Sweet Cocks No. 9'. The allied publication is 'Those Bad, Bad Boys'. Both magazines display male homosexual themes. They do not contain physical violence. They involve buggery and fellatio between two obvious adult consenting males.

The back covers of both magazines contain a number of ads for sexually violent magazines involving whipping, violence by one male toward another male who is hung upside down by his ankles while being assaulted. One of the ads is called 'Master's Degree'. It discloses a naked man wearing a belt and a leather neckpiece going around his neck and down to his navel beating another man who is tied up against a wall by his wrists and a whip is used. The back cover of 'Those Bad Boys' depicts a female naked from the waist up wearing leather to her knees and holding a whip.

The other magazine is entitled 'Glamour in Bondage'. It shows a female naked from the navel up. Her mouth is gagged. She is held attached to something with a number of straps both over and under her two bare breasts with another strap lashing her diagonally in the area of her navel. The third shows a virtually naked female tied up on the front cover of a magazine called 'Captured'. The fourth is entitled 'Hogtie'. It depicts a naked female whose mouth is gagged and she is tied to a chair with ropes binding her arms and holding her knees together.

The third publication entitled 'Slaves of Anal Sex' contains 66 pages of coloured photographs each depicting a male and a female in the act of various sexual manoeuvers. The first 33 pages feature the act of buggery or what is known in some circles as anal sex. Those pages include pictures of a female handcuffing a male with handcuffs behind his back. It shows her holding a whip before the partially naked male who wears a dog collar. Other photographs disclose the female in the process of taking out the male's penis with one hand while in the other hand she holds a whip ready to hit it. In yet others, she is teaching him submissions while he performs acts of buggery upon her.

The last 33 pages disclose a female conferring a birthday present upon the man in her life by offering him sex with her and then by importing a second female so that they can both engage him (and incidentally themselves) and with one another in various acts of fellatio, sexual intercourse, and buggery. The publication clearly depicts bondage. The imagery for simulated sexual violence is clearly shown.

Counts 15 and 16: 1. 'The Best Of All Male Cum'; 2. 'Lady Lovers'; 3. 'Lesbians', Volume 2, No. 4

608 'Lesbians' No. 4 depicts two adult women in sexual acts with one another. The poses struck by those photographed are explicit and otherwise unremarkable.

Under the title of 'Slim and Slinky', being two lesbian women, the printed dialogue in part states as follows: 'When Syble backs her sweet behind into Kelly's pussy, it's all Kelly can do to keep from throwing her down on the bed and raping her with a dildo.' At another point, the printed dialogue when describing the sexual antics of two blonde women has the following to say: 'One game they play is when Miranda pretends to be a man and attacks Candy sexually. She uses a plastic dildo to complete the act of fucking.' Other than these two excerpts, the publication is exclusively female homosexual lesbian disclosing sexual activity between two women.

The publication 'Lady Lovers' retailing for $45 per magazine discloses photographs of essentially consenting adult homosexual lesbian women and contains no dialogue of the type I have mentioned that pertains to the other publication.

The magazine 'The Best Of All Male Cum' depicts adult consenting males in the main one on one with the exception of certain elements of the photographs which depict three males all engaged in fellatio and buggery on one another.

Approximately five of the photographs in the publication depict acts of fellatio occuring through a hole in the partition of what is obviously a male toilet. All photographs in the publication are very explicit including the depiction of a close-up photograph of the head of a male penis in the process of ejaculation.

Counts 17 and 18: 3 Magazines – 1. 'Back Door Beginners' (No. 8); 2. 'An Anal Arrangement' (Volume 1, No. 1); 'Rear Ended' (Volume 1 No. 2)

All three of these magazines depict anal intercourse being committed in many ways. The male and female shown in each pair are obviously consenting adults. There is no sexually violent content in either the photos themselves or in any advertisements that appear. 'Anal Arrangement' is not entirely anal intercourse in nature. Some words in that publication accompany the photographs. No sexually violent images are indicated by either the words or the photos themselves.

The publication 'Back Door Beginners' features anal inter-course as its theme. It is heterosexual in context. There is one **609** quote in the written narrative such as it is and it is as follows: 'His huge cock was tearing her asshole apart, but she loved it.'

Counts 19 and 20: Magazine, 'Sinful Pleasures Annual' (No. 2)
This magazine appears to contain essentially conventional heterosexual sexual activities. A substantial portion of the publication at the beginning contains photographic scenarios wherein an adult female dressed to resemble a nurse in a medical office performs fellatio upon a male model dressed to resemble a doctor. In other photographs another female appears to be conferring sexual favours on the male.

Counts 21 and 22: Magazine, 'Poppin Mamas' (No. 2)
This publication is devoted entirely to pregnant women. All of the photographs depict pregnant women in sexually provocative postures. There is no violent content and no depiction of dehumanizing content.

Exhibits 23 and 24 are so-called novels: 1. 'Ram Rodded Daughter'; 2. 'Wife In Bondage'; 3. 'Mother in Bondage'; 4. 'Rape Bitch'; 5. 'Manacled Maiden'; 6. 'Hung Nigger'.
Exhibit 20 refers to these six paperback 'novels'. I did not read the entire set of these publications. I have read enough of each to confirm the opinion of Dr Check and the admission of Mr McCombs, counsel for the accused, again subject to the constitutional challenge.

All of them are obscene within the meaning of that term under the *Criminal Code* of Canada. The content of all of them is all about bondage. The obvious racist slur in 'Hung Nigger' is on the title of the publication itself. These publications portray in unacceptable graphic detail brutal sexual violence quite similiar in Dr Check's unchallenged opinion to the eight-millimetre films on the same subject (Exhibit 13).

'Ram Rodded Daughter' deals almost exclusively with incest. 'Mother In Bondage' describes physical cruelty for sexual gratification and the same thing applies to the other titles. . . .

[*The Judge continues with a summary of the testimony of expert witnesses, and a discussion of case law concerning free speech, and then concludes with a verdict on each exhibit based on Dr Check's three-tier classification of (a) sexually violent pornography, (b) nonviolent but dehumanizing pornography, (c) erotica.*]

. . . I find the publication 'Hot Cameron', Exhibit No. 10, to be totally explicit, totally sexual in its content but, for the reasons given prior in this judgment, to be erotic only. It is not obscene. The accused will be found not guilty on Counts 1, 2 and 5. Counts 3, 4 and 6 concern a motion picture recorded on videocassette tape entitled 'Double Penetration'. However explicitly conventional and unconventional acts of sexual intercourse and buggery may be, bearing in mind that portion whch shows one woman slapping the backside of another, I am in some doubt concerning that latter display of mild physical violence. I find that the total film discloses consenting adults indulging in sexual acts essentially devoid of physical violence or other dehumanizing content regarding either the male sex or the female sex. I hold the cassette to be not obscene. The accused is acquitted with respect to these counts.

Counts 7 and 8 include nine magazines. Every one of them from cover to cover by the photographs shown in a childlike context are nothing more than a series of blatant invitations to anyone who reads these publications to have sexual relations with children. Each publication is obscene. No average Canadian regardless of what part of the country he or she comes from, even remotely, would permit his or her fellow Canadian neighbour to view any of these publications for that reason. They are all obscene as a matter of law. The accused will be convicted on Counts 7 and 8.

There are four publications involved in Counts 9 and 10. The first two, entitled 'Big Tits Secretaries' and 'Big Tits For A Hard Boss', disclose adults engaging in consensual sexual acts that I have previously described. In my view. 'Big Tits Secretaries' depicts two mature adults, one male and one female, engaging with one another in a series of acts of sexual intercourse, fellatio and cunnilingus. It is purely erotic. It does not dehumanize anyone. It is not obscene. The publication 'Big Tits For A Hard Boss' falls into partially the category I have just described. It, however, discloses ejaculation into someone's face and that exceeds community standards, and for that reason that publication is obscene. The publication 'Roly-Poly' fails to pass the community standards test. It contains scenes depicting clear sexual violence by a female upon a male and vice versa. In addition, it is sexually explicit to a point which exceeds community standards. For example, it discloses male semen being ejaculated into the face of the female. The publication 'Hot Lust' discloses even more graphically the same type of depiction. It involves not one but two female recipients of the semen. Both publications are dehumanizing. Both grossly exceed community standards. Each is in law obscene. The accused will be convicted on Counts 9 and 10.

Counts 11 and 12 deal with three magazines – 'Those Bad, Bad Boys', 'Sweet Cocks No. 9' and 'Slaves of Anal Sex'. For the reasons I have already given, each of these publications exceeds public standards because each, in my view, unduly exploits sex. In addition, they combine that exploitation either in content or in the advertisements surrounding that content with depictions of sexual cruelty and violence. The accused will be convicted on Counts 11 and 12.

I have already found those publications described in Counts 13 and 14 to be obscene and on those counts the accused will be convicted.

Counts 15 and 16 include three publications – 'The Best of All Male Cum', 'Lady Lovers', and 'Lesbians, Volume 2, No. 4'. 'Lesbians' is totally erotic and in my view not obscene. The same result occurs with respect to 'Lady Lovers'.

However tempted I may be to label the magazine 'Lesbians, Volume 2, No. 4' as obscene by reason of the unacceptable dialogue that I have already described, I entertain a reasonable doubt as to whether or not those two pieces of dialogue alone are capable of achieving that result. I give the benefit to the accused.

'The Best Of All Male Cum' is obscene. It graphically depicts throughout the publication the male penis in the process of ejaculation. The degree of explicitness portrayed by the photographs clearly exceeds contemporary standards. In addition, as I have already stated, it depicts fellatio occurring between strangers through a hole in the partition of a male toilet in such a way that it leaves absolutely no doubt that the participants are totally unknown to one another. They are seen to be engaging in fellatio with no protection of any kind being taken. On even the most liberal interpretation of the community standard test, such a publication is obscene. No Canadian coast-to-coast in this country would ever tolerate his or her neighbour in viewing such a publication with this content. The accused will be convicted on Counts 15 and 16.

In Counts 17 and 18, three magazines entitled 'An Anal Arrangement', 'Rear Ended' and 'Back Door Beginners' all depict two consenting adults, a man and a woman, engaging with one another in acts of buggery. I do not find that the Crown has proven beyond a reasonable doubt that these publications are obscene within s. 163 of the *Criminal Code*. The verdict of not guilty is entered on these counts.

'Sinful Pleasure Annual (No. 2)' (Counts 19 and 20) in my view in its totality does not exceed what is acceptable under the comunity standards test. The accused are acquitted with respect to those counts.

There will be an acquittal with respect to Counts 21 and 22 – 'Poppin Mamas'. There is no violent content. Nor does any part of the publication dehumanize sexually or otherwise. At most, it is erotic. . . .

Mr McCombs, using careful phraseology, essentially admits that Exhibit 7 constituting four movie films entitled 'Stalked', 'MMMPH', 'Rope Dream' and 'Sceptre' all depict what is called hard-core pornography and, more specifically, bondage combined with depictions of sexually oriented violence by one or more human beings against one or more other human beings. In these exhibits the depiction is dehumanizing violence toward women. I find them all obscene within the meaning of the *Criminal Code*, along with the coloured catalogue contained in a box which holds one of the films (Exhibit 15). It shows scenes which vividly depict women tied up with ropes and being subjected to the infliction of pain upon them by other women. The victims' breasts are being pinched and twisted. Women are shown dominating men by riding on their backs as if they were animals, and pulling their hair. In yet others, a near naked woman is shown assaulting by slapping the buttocks of her female victim. . . .

SELECT BIBLIOGRAPHY

Abeel, E. (1987). 'Bedroom eyes: Erotic movies come home', *Mademoiselle*, Oct., pp. 194–5, 234, 238.

Abel, G. G. (1985). 'Use of pornography and erotica by sex offenders', paper presented to the Attorney General's Commission on Pornography, Houston, T.

——, Barlow, D. H., Blanchard, E. B., and Guild, D. (1977). 'The components of rapists' sexual arousal', *Archives of General Psychiatry* 34, pp. 895–903.

——, Becker, J., Murphey, W., and Flanigan, B. (1981). 'Identifying dangerous child molesters', in R. Stuard (ed.), *Violent Behavior: Social Learning Approaches to Prediction, Management and Treatment*, New York: Brunner/Mazel.

—— —— and Skinner, L. (1980). 'Aggressive behavior and sex', *Psychiatric Clinics of North America* 3, pp. 133–51.

—— and Blanchard, E. (1974). 'The role of fantasy in the treatment of sexual deviation', *Archives of General Psychiatry* 30, pp. 467–75.

—— —— and Becker, J. V. (1976). 'Psychological treatment of rapists', in M. Walker and S. Brodsky (eds.), *Sexual Assault: The Victim and the Rapist*, Lexington, Mass.: Lexington Books.

——, Mittelman, M., and Becker, J. (1985). 'Sexual offenders: Results of assessment and recommendations for treatment', in M. H. Ben-Aron, S. J. Hucker, and C. D. Webster (eds.), *Clinical Criminology*, Toronto: Clarke Institute of Psychiatry.

——, Rouleau, J., and Cunningham-Rathner, J. (1985). 'Sexually aggressive behavior', in W. Curran, A. McGarry, and S. Shah (eds.), *Modern Legal Psychiatry and Psychology*, Philadelphia: F. A. Davis.

Abelson, H., Cohen, R., Heaton, E., and Suder, C. (1970). 'National survey of public attitudes toward and experience with erotic materials', *Technical Report of the Commission on Obscenity and Pornography*, vi, Washington, DC: Govt. Printing Office.

Abramson, P., and Hayashi, H. (1984). 'Pornography in Japan: Cross-cultural and theoretical considerations', in Malamuth and Donnerstein (1984).

——, Perry, L., Seeley, T., Seeley, D., and Rothblatt, A. (1981). 'Thermographic measurement of sexual arousal: A discriminant validity analysis', *Archives of Sexual Behavior* 10(2), pp. 175–6.

American Psychological Association (1990). *PsychLIT Database*, Washington, DC (June).

Bandura, A. (1965). 'Influence of models: Reinforcement, contingency conditions on the acquisition of imitative responses', *Journal of Personality and Social Psychology* 1, pp. 589–95.

—— (1973). *Aggression: A Social Learning Analysis*, New York: Prentice-Hall.

—— (1977). *Social Learning Theory*, New York: Prentice-Hall.

——, Blanchard, E., and Ritter, B. (1969). 'Relative efficacy of desensitization and modeling approaches for inducing behavioral, affective, and attitudinal changes', *Journal of Personality and Social Psychology* 13, pp. 173–99.

——, Ross, D., and Ross, S. (1963). 'Vicarious reinforcement and imitative learning', *Journal of Abnormal and Social Psychology* 67, pp. 601–7.

——, Underwood, W., and Fromson, M. (1975). 'Disinhibition of aggression through diffusion of responsibility and dehumanization of victims', *Journal of Research in Personality* 9, pp. 253–69.

Barlow, D. H. (1977). 'Assessment of sexual behavior', in A. Ciminero, K. Calhoun, and H. Adams (eds.), *Handbok of Behavioral Assessment*, New York: Wiley.

Barnes, G. E., Malamuth, N. M., and Check, J. V. P. (1984*a*). 'Psychoticism and sexual arousal to rape depictions', *Personal and Individual Difference* 5, pp. 273–9.

—— —— —— (1984*b*). 'Personality and sexuality', *Personal and Individual Difference* 5, 159–72.

Baron, L., and Straus, M. A. (1984). 'Sexual stratification, pornography, and rape in the United States', in Malamuth and Donnerstein (1984).

—— —— (1985). 'Legitimate violence and rape: A test of the cultural spillover theory', paper presented at the Eastern Sociological Society meeting, Philadelphia.

—— —— (1986). 'Rape and its relation to social disorganization, pornography, and sexual inequality', paper presented at the International Congress on Rape, Israel, Apr.

—— —— (1987). 'Four theories of rape: A macrosociological analysis', *Social Problems* 34, pp. 467–89.

Baron, R. A. (1974*a*). 'Aggrression as a function of victim's pain cues, level of prior anger arousal, and exposure to an aggressive model', *Journal of Personality and Social Psychology* 29, pp. 117–24.

—— (1974*b*). 'The aggression-inhibiting influence of heightened sexual arousal', *Journal of Personality and Social Psychology* 30, pp. 318–22.

—— (1977). *Human Aggression*, New York: Plenum.

—— and Bell, P. A. (1977). 'Sexual arousal and aggression by males: Effects of type of erotic stimuli and prior provocation', *Journal of Personality and Social Psychology* 35, pp. 79–87.

Barry, K. (1979). *Female Sexual Slavery*, New York: Avon.

Belk, S. S., and Snell, W. W. Jr. (1986). 'Beliefs about women: Components and correlates', *Personality and Social Psychology Bulletin* 2, pp. 403–13.

Ben-Veniste, R. (1970). 'Pornography and sex crime: The Danish experience', *Technical Report of the Commission on Obscenity and Pornography*, vii, Washington, DC: Govt. Printing Office.

Beneke, T. (1982). *Men on Rape*, New York: St Martin's Press.

Berkowitz, L. (1971). 'Sex and violence: We can't have it both ways', *Psychology Today*, May, pp. 14–23.

—— (1974). 'Some determinants of impulsive aggression: Role of mediated associations with reinforcements for aggression', *Psychological Review* 81, pp. 165–76.

—— (1984). 'Some effects of thoughts on anti- and pro-social influences of media events: A cognitive-neoassociation analysis', *Psychological Bulletin* 95, pp. 410–27.

—— and Donnerstein, E. (1982). 'External validity is more than skin deep: Some answers to criticisms of laboratory experiments (with special reference to research on aggression)', *American Psychologist* 37, pp. 245–57.

Berlin, F. (1983). 'Sex offenders: A biomedical perspective and a status report on biomedical treatment', in J. Greer and I. Stuart (eds.), *The Sexual Aggressor: Current Perspectives on Treatment*, New York: Van Nostrand Reinhold.

Blader, J., and Marshall, W. (1984). 'The relationship between cognitive and erectile measures of sexual arousal in nonrapist males as a function of depicted aggression', *Behavioral Research and Therapy* 17, pp. 215–22.

Bogdanovich, P. (1984). *The Killing of the Unicorn: Dorothy Stratten 1960–1980*, New York: Morrow.

Bohmer, C. (1983). 'Legal and ethical issues in mandatory treatment: The patient's rights versus society's rights', in J. Greer and I. Stuart (eds.), *The Sexual Aggressor: Current Perspectives on Treatment*, New York: Van Nostrand Reinhold.

Bramel, D. (1969). 'The arousal and reduction of hostility', in J. Mills (ed.), *Experimental Social Psychology*, New York: Macmillan.

Brannigan, A. (1987). 'Pornography and behaviour: Alternative explanations', *Journal of Communication* 37(3), pp. 185–92.

—— and Goldenberg, S. (1987). 'The study of aggressive pornography: The vicissitudes of relevance', *Critical Studies in Mass Communication* 4, pp. 262–83.

Briere, J. (1987). 'Predicting self-reported likelihood of battering: Attitudes and childhood experiences', *Journal of Research in Personality* 21, pp. 61–9.

——, Corne, S. Runtz, M., and Malamuth, N. (1984). 'The rape arousal inventory: Predicting actual and potential sexual aggression in a university population', paper presented at the American Psychological Association meeting, Toronto.

—— and Malamuth, N. (1983). 'Self-reported likelihood of sexually aggressive behavior: Attitudinal versus sexual explanations', *Journal of Research in Personality* 17, pp. 315–23.

—— —— and Check, J. (1985). 'Sexuality and rape-supportive beliefs', *International Journal of Women's Studies* 8, pp. 398–403.

Brody, S. (1977). *Screen Violence and Film Censorship: A Review of Research*, Home Office Research Study No. 40, London: HMSO.

Brosius, H., Staab, J., and Weaver, J. (1991). 'Exploring the "reality" of contemporary pornography', paper presented at the International Communication Association meeting, Chicago.

Brown, D., and Bryant, J. (1989). 'The manifest content of pornography', in Zillmann and Bryant (1989).

Brownmiller, S. (1984). 'The place of pornography: Packaging Eros for a violent age', comments to a forum held at the New School for Social Research, New York, reported in *Harper's* (November), pp. 31–9, 42–5.

—— (1985). *Against Our Will: Men, Women, and Rape*, New York: Simon and Schuster.

Bryant, J. (1985). Testimony to the Attorney General's Commission on Pornography Hearings, Houston, Tx.; unpublished transcript, pp. 128–57.

—— and Brown, D. (1989). 'Uses of Pornography', in Zillmann and Bryant (1989).

Buchman, J. G. (1988). 'Effects of Repeated Exposure to Nonviolent Erotica on Attitudes about Sexual Child Abuse', doctoral dissertation, Indiana Univ., Bloomington.

Burgess, A. (1985). *Rape and Sexual Assault*, New York: Garland.

Burt, M. R. (1980). 'Cultural myths and supports for rape', *Journal of Personality and Social Psychology* 38, pp. 217–30.

Byrne, D. (1977). 'The imagery of sex', in J. Money and H. Musaph (eds.), *Handbook of Sexology*, Amsterdam: Excerpta Media.

—— and Byrne, L. A. (eds.) (1977). *Exploring Human Sexuality*, New York: Harper and Row.

—— and Kelley, K. (1986). 'Psychological research and public policy: Taking a long, hard look before we leap', in E. P. Mulvey and J. L. Haugaard (eds.), *Report of the Surgeon General's Workshop on Pornography and Public Health*, Washington, DC: Dept. of Health and Human Services, Office of the Surgeon General.

—— and Lamberth, J. (1970). 'The effect of erotic stimuli on sex arousal, evaluative responses, and subsequent behavior', in *Technical Report of the Commission on Obscenity and Pornography*, viii, Washington, DC: Govt. Printing Office.

—— and Sheffield, J. (1965). 'Response to sexually arousing stimuli as a function of repressing and sensitizing defenses', *Journal of Abnormal Psychology* 70, pp. 114–18.

Caird, W., and Wincze, J. P. (1977). *Sex Therapy: A Behavioral Approach*, New York: Harper and Row.

Cairns, R. B., Paul, J. C. N., and Wisner, J. (1962). 'Sex censorship: The assumptions of anti-obscenity laws and the empirical evidence', *Minnesota Law Review* 46, pp. 1009–41.

—— —— (1970). 'Psychological assumptions in sex censorship: An evaluation review of recent research (1961–1968)', in *Technical Report of the Commission on Obscenity and Pornography*, i, Washington, DC: US Govt. Printing Office.

Cameron, D., and Frazer, E. (1987). *The Lust to Kill*, Cambridge: Polity.

Cantor, J. R., Zillmann, D., and Einsiedel, E. F. (1978). 'Female responses to provocation after exposure to aggressive and erotic films', *Communication Research* 5(4), pp. 395–411.

Caputi, J. (1989). *The Age of Sex Crime*, London: Virago.

Carter, D. L., Prentky, R., Knight, R., Vanderveer, P., and Boucher, R.

(1985). *Use of Pornography in the Criminal and Developmental Histories of Sexual Offenders*, Report to the National Institute of Justice and National Institute of Mental Health.

Ceniti, J., and Malamuth, N. M. (1985). 'Effects of repeated exposure to sexually violent or sexually nonviolent stimuli on sexual arousal to rape and nonrape depictions', *Behavior Research and Therapy*.

Check, J. (1985). *The Effects of Violent and Nonviolent Pornography*, Ottawa: Canadian Dept. of Justice.

Check, J. V. P. (1985). *A Survey of Canadians' Attitudes regarding Sexual Content in Media*, Report to the Lamarsh Research Programme on Violence and Conflict Resolution and the Canadian Broadcasting Corporation, Ontario.

—— and Guloien, T. H. (1989). 'Reported proclivity for coercive sex following repeated exposure to sexually violent pornography, nonviolent pornography, and erotica', in Zillmann and Bryant (1989).

—— and Malamuth, N. M. (1983). 'Sex role stereotyping and reactions to depictions of stranger versus acquaintance rape', *Journal of Personality and Social Psychology* 45, pp. 344–56.

—— —— (1985*a*). 'An empirical assessment of some feminist hypotheses about rape', *International Journal of Women's Studies* 8, pp. 414–23.

—— —— (1985*b*). 'Pornography and sexual aggression: A social learning theory analysis', in M. L. McLaughlin (ed.), *Communication Yearbook*, ix, Beverly Hills, Calif.: Sage.

Chester, G., and Dickey, J. (1989). *Feminism and Censorship*, Dorset, Prism Press for the Campaign for Press and Broadcasting Freedom.

Christensen, F. (1987). 'Effects of pornography: The debate continues', *Journal of Communication* 37(1), pp. 186–8.

Cline, V. B. (1974). 'Another view: Pornography effects, the state of the art', in V. B. Cline (ed.), *Where Do You Draw the Line?*, Provo, Utah: Brigham Young Univ. Press.

Cochrane, P. (1978). 'Sex crimes and pornography revisited', *International Journal of Criminology and Penology* 6, pp. 307–17.

Commission on Obscenity and Pornography (1970). *Report of the Commission on Obscenity and Pornography*, Washington, DC: Govt. Printing Office.

Committee on Sexual Offences Against Children and Youths (1984). *Sexual Offences Against Children*, Ottawa: Canadian Govt. Printing Centre.

Comstock, G. C. (forthcoming). 'Television and film violence', in S. J. Apter and A. P. Goldstein (eds.), *Youth Violence: Programs and Prospects*, New York: Pergamon.

Cook, R., and Fosen, R. (1970). 'Pornography and the sex offender: Patterns of exposure and immediate arousal effects of pornographic stimuli', *Technical Report of the Commission on Obscenity and Pornography*, vii, Washington, DC: Govt. Printing Office.

Copp, D. (1983). 'Pornography and censorship: An introductory essay', in D. Copp and S. Wendell (eds.), *Pornography and Censorship*, Buffalo, NY: Prometheus.

Corcoran, C. (1987). *Take Care! Preventing Child Sexual Abuse*, Dublin: Poolbeg.

—— (1989). *Pornography: The New Terrorism*, Dublin: Attic.

Costin, F. (1985). 'Beliefs about rape and women's social roles', *Archives of Sexual Behavior* 14, pp. 319–25.

Court, J. H. (1977). 'Pornography and sex crimes: A reevaluation in light of recent trends around the world', *International Journal of Criminology and Penology* 5, pp. 129–57.

—— (1981). 'Pornography update', *British Journal of Sexual Medicine*, May, pp. 28–30.

—— (1982). 'Rape trends in New South Wales: A discussion of conflicting evidence', *Australian Journal of Social Issues* 17(3), 202–6.

—— (1984). 'Sex and violence: A ripple effect', in Malamuth and Donnerstein (1984).

Coveney, L. *et al.* (1984). *The Sexuality Papers: Male Sexuality and the Social Control of Women*, London: Hutchinson.

Crabbe, A. (1988). 'Feature-length sex films', in G. Day and C. Bloom (eds.), *Perspectives on Pornography: Sexuality in Film and Literature*, London: Macmillan.

Daniels, S. (1984). *Masterpieces*, London: Methuen.

Davis, K. E., and Braucht, G. N. (1973). 'Exposure to pornography, character, and sexual deviance: A retrospective survey', *Journal of Social Issues* 29, pp. 183–96.

Day, G. (1988). 'Looking at women: Notes toward a theory of porn', in G. Day and C. Bloom (eds.), *Perspectives on Pornography: Sexuality in Film and Literature*, London: Macmillan.

Dermer, M., and Pyszcynski, T. A. (1978). 'Effects of erotica on men's loving and liking responses for women they love', *Journal of Personality and Social Psychology* 36, pp. 1302–10.

Diamond, S. (1985). 'Pornography: Image and reality', in V. Burstyn (ed.), *Women Against Censorship*, Vancouver, BC: Douglas and McIntyre.

Dientsbier, R. A. (1977). 'Sex and violence: Can research have it both ways?', *Journal of Communication* 27, pp. 176–88.

Dietz, P. E. (1978). 'Social factors in rapists' behavior', in R. J. Rada (ed.), *Clinical Aspects of the Rapist*, New York: Grune and Stratton.

—— and Evans, B. (1982). 'Pornographic imagery and prevalence of paraphilia', *American Journal of Psychiatry* 139, pp. 1493-5.

——, Harry, B., and Hazelwood, R. R. (1986). 'Detective magazines: Pornography for the sexual sadist?', *Journal of Forensic Science* 31, pp. 197–211.

Donnerstein, E. (1980*a*). 'Aggressive erotica and violence against women', *Journal of Personality and Social Psychology* 39, pp. 269–77.

—— (1980*b*). 'Pornography and violence against women', *Annals of the New York Academy of Sciences* 347, pp. 277–88.

—— (1983*a*). 'Erotica and human aggression', in R. Green and E. Donnerstein (eds.), *Aggression: Theoretical and Empirical Reviews*, ii, New York: Academic.

—— (1983*b*). Public Hearings on Ordinances to Add Pornography as

Discrimination Against Women, Committee on Government Operations, City Council, Minneapolis.

—— (1983*c*). 'Aggressive pornography: Can it influence aggression against women?', in G. Albee, S. Gordon, and H. Leitenberg (eds.), *Promoting Sexual Responsibility and Preventing Sexual Problems*, Hanover, NH: Univ. of New England Press.

—— (1984*a*). 'Pornography: Its content, its effects, and its harm', in D. Scott (ed.), *Proceedings of Symposium on Media Violence and Pornography*, Toronto: Media Action Group.

—— (1984*b*). 'Pornography: Its effects on violence against women', in Malamuth and Donnerstein (1984).

—— (1985). Testimony to the Attorney General's Commission on Pornography Hearings, Houston, Tx.; unpublished transcript, pp. 5–33.

—— and Barrett, G. (1978). 'The effects of erotic stimuli on male aggression towards females', *Journal of Personality and Social Psychology* 36, pp. 180–8.

—— and Berkowitz, L. (1981). 'Victim reactions in aggressive erotic films as a factor in violence against women', *Journal of Personality and Social Psychology* 36, pp. 710–24.

——, Donnerstein, M., and Evans, R. (1975). 'Erotic stimuli and aggression: Facilitation or inhibition?', *Journal of Personality and Social Psychology* 32, pp. 237–44.

—— and Hallam, J. (1978). 'The facilitating effects of erotica on aggression toward females', *Journal of Personality and Social Psychology* 36, pp. 1270–7.

—— and Linz, D. (1984). 'Sexual violence in the media: A warning', *Psychology Today*, Jan., pp. 14–15.

—— (1985). Unpublished paper prepared for the Attorney General's Commission on Pornography Hearings, Houston, Tx.

—— —— (1986). 'The question of pornography', *Psychology Today*, Dec., pp. 56–9.

—— —— and Penrod, S. (1987). *The Question of Pornography: Research Findings and Policy Implications*, New York: Free Press.

Dowdeswell, J. (1986). *Women on Rape*, Northampton: Thorsons.

Driver, E., and Droisen, A. (1989). *Child Sexual Abuse: Feminist Perspectives*, London: Macmillan.

Dworkin, A. (1981). *Pornography: Men Possessing Women*, London: Women's Press.

—— (1988). *Letters from a War Zone*, London: Secker and Warburg.

—— and MacKinnon, C. (1988). *Pornography and Civil Rights: A New Day for Women's Equality*. Available from Organizing Against Pornography, PO Box 3000–76 Minneapolis, Minn. 55403, USA.

Ebert, R., and Siskel, G. (n. d.), Transcript, *Sneak Previews* 304.

Einsiedel, E. F. (1986). Social science report, prepared for the Attorney General's Commission on Pornography, Washington, DC: Dept. of Justice.

Eron, L. D. (1980). 'Prescription for the reduction of aggression', *American Psychologist* 35, pp. 244–52.

Evans, D. R. (1968). 'Masturbatory fantasy and sexual deviation', *Behavioral Research and Therapy* 6, p. 17.

Everywoman (1988). *Pornography and Sexual Violence: Evidence of the Links*, London: Everywoman.

Eysenck, H. J. (1978). *Sex and Personality*, London: Sphere.

—— (1984). 'Afterword: Sex, violence and the media', in Malamuth and Donnerstein (1984).

—— and Eysenck, S. B. G. (1976). *Psychoticism as a Dimension of Personality*, London: Hodder and Stoughton.

—— and Nias, D. K. (1978). *Sex, Violence and the Media*, New York: Harper and Row.

Farkas, G. M., Sine, L. F., and Evans, I. M. (1978). 'Personality, sexuality, and demographic differences between volunteers and non-volunteers for a laboratory study of male sexual behavior', *Archive of Sexual Behavior* 7, pp. 513–20.

Finkelhor, D. (1984). *Child Sexual Abuse: New Theory and Practice*, New York: Free Press.

Fisher, G., and Rivlin, E. (1971). 'Psychological needs of rapists', *British Journal of Criminology* 11, pp. 182–5.

Fisher, W. A. (1986). 'A psychological approach to human sexuality: The sexual behavior sequence', in D. Byrne and K. Kelley (eds.), *Alternative Approaches to the Study of Sexual Behavior*, Hillsdale, NJ: Erlbaum.

—— and Byrne, D. (1978*a*). 'Individual differences in affective, evaluative, and behavioral responses to an erotic film', *Journal of Applied Social Psychology* 8, pp. 355–65.

—— —— (1978*b*). 'Sex differences in response to erotica: Love versus lust', *Journal of Personality and Social Psychology* 36, pp. 119–25.

Freund, K. (1981). 'Assessment of pedophilia', in M. Cook and K. Howells (eds.), *Adult Sexual Interest in Children*, New York: Academic.

Frodi, A. (1977). 'Sexual arousal, situational restrictiveness, and aggressive behavior', *Journal of Research in Personality* 11, pp. 48–58.

Gagnon, J. H. (1977). *Human Sexualities*, Glenview, Ill.: Scott, Foresman.

Garry, A. (1978). 'Pornography and respect for women', *Social Theory and Practice* 4, pp. 395–422.

Gebhard, P. (1977). 'The acquisition of basic sex information', *Journal of Sexual Research*, 13, pp. 148–69.

——, Gagnon, J., Pomeroy, W., and Christenson, C. 1965). *Sex Offenders: An Analysis of Types*, New York: Harper and Row.

Geen, R., and Quanty, M. B. (1977). 'The catharsis of aggression: an evaluation of a hypothesis', in L. Berkowitz (ed.), *Advances in Experimental Social Psychology*, x, New York: Academic.

Gerbner, G. (1980). 'Sex on television and what viewers learn from it', paper presented at the annual conference of the National Association of Television Program Executives, San Francisco.

——, Gross, L., Eleey, M. F., Jackson-Beeck, M., Jeffries-Fox, S., and Signorelli, N. (1977). 'TV violence profile No. 8: The highlights', *Journal of Communications* 32, pp. 100–26.

—— ——, Morgan, M., and Signorelli, N. (1980). 'The mainstreaming **621** of America: Violence profile No 11', *Journal of Communications* 30(3), pp. 10–29.

Glassman, M. B. (1978). 'Community standards of patent offensiveness: Public opinion data and obscenity law', *Public Opinion Research*, pp. 161–70.

Goldstein, A. (1984). 'The place of pornography: Packaging Eros for a violent age', comments to a forum at the New School for Social Research in New York City, reported in *Harper's*, Nov., pp. 31–9, 42–5.

Goldstein, M. J., Kant, H. S., and Hartman, J. J. (1974). *Pornography and Sexual Deviance*, Berkeley: Univ. of California Press.

—— ——, Judd, L., Rice, C., and Green, R. (1970). 'Exposure to pornography and sexual behavior in deviant and normal groups', *Technical Report of the Commission on Obscenity and Pornography*, vii, Washington, DC: Govt. Printing Office.

Goldstein, S., and Ibaraki, T. (1978). 'Japan: Aggression and aggression control in Japanese society', in A. Goldsten and M. Segall (eds.), *Aggression in Global Perspective*, New York: Pergamon.

Goodchilds, J., and Zellmann, G. (1984). 'Sexual signaling and sexual aggression in adolescent relationships', in Malamuth and Donnerstein (1984).

Green, S. E., and Mosher, D. L. (1985). 'A causal model of sexual arousal to erotic fantasies', *Journal of Sex Research* 21, pp. 1–23.

Griffin, S. (1981). *Pornography and Silence*, London: Women's Press.

Griffitt, W. (1973). 'Response to erotica and the projection of response to erotica in the opposite sex', *Journal of Experimental Research in Personality* 6, pp. 330–8.

—— (1975). 'Sexual experience and sexual responsiveness: Sex differences', *Archives of Sexual Behavior* 4, pp. 529–40.

—— and Jackson, T. (1970). 'Context effects in impression formation as a function of context source', *Psychonomic Science* 20, pp. 321–2.

—— and Kaiser, D. L. (1978). 'Affect, sex guilt, gender and the reward–punishing effects of erotic stimuli', *Journal of Personality and Social Psychology* 36, pp. 850–8.

Gutierres, S., Kenrick, D. T., and Goldberg, L. (1985). 'Adverse influence on exposure to popular erotica: Effects on judgments of others and judgments of one's spouse', paper presented at the annual meeting of the Midwestern Psychological Association, Chicago.

Hanmer, J., and Saunders, S. (1984). *Well-Founded Fear: A Community Study of Violence to Women*, London: Hutchinson.

Hebditch, D., and Anning, N. (1988). *Porn Gold: Inside the Pornography Business*, London: Faber and Faber.

Hearn, J., and Morgan, David H. J. (1990). *Men, Masculinities and Social Theory* London: Unwin Hyman.

Heiby, E., and Becker, J. D. (1980). 'Effect of filmed modeling on the self-reported frequency of masturbation', *Archives of Sexual Behavior* 9, pp. 115–21.

Heiman, J. (1977). 'A psychophysiological exploration of sexual arousal patterns in females and males', *Psychophysiology* 14, pp. 266–74.

—— , LoPiccolo, L., and LoPiccolo, J. (1976). *Becoming Orgasmic: A Sexual Growth Program for Women*, Englewood Cliffs, NJ: Prentice-Hall.

Hite, S. (1981). *The Hite Report on Male Sexuality*, New York: Knopf.

Howard, J., Reifler, C., and Liptzin, M. (1970). 'Effects of exposure to pornography', in *Technical Report of the Commission on Obscenity and Pornography*, viii, Washington, DC: Govt. Printing Office.

Howard, J. L., Liptzin, M., and Reifler, C. (1973). 'Is pornography a problem?', *Journal of Social Issues* 29, pp. 163–81.

—— , Reifler, C., and Liptzin, M. (1971). 'Effects of exposure to pornography', *Technical Report of the Commission on Obscenity and Pornography*, viii, Washington, DC: Govt. Printing Office.

Howells, K. (1981). 'Adult sexual interest in children: Considerations relevant to theories of aetiology', in M. Cook and K. Howells (eds.), *Adult Sexual Interest in Children*, New York: Academic.

Howitt, D. (1989). 'Pornography: The recent debate', in D. Cumberbatch and D. Howitt (eds.), *A Measure of Uncertainty: The Effects of Mass Media*, London: Libbey.

Huer, J. (1987). *Art, Beauty, and Pornography: A Journey through American Culture*, Buffalo, NJ: Prometheus.

I-Spy Productions (1988). *Looks Can Kill: Pornographic Business*. Available from Box 60, 52 Call Lane, Leeds LS1 6DT.

Jaffe, Y., Malamuth, N. M., Feingold, J., and Feshbach, S. (1974). 'Sexual arousal and behavioral aggression', *Journal of Personality and Social Psychology* 30, pp. 759–64.

Jaffee, D., and Straus, M. A. (1987). 'Sexual climate and reported rape: A state-level analysis', *Archives of Sexual Behavior* 16, pp. 107–23.

Jeffreys, S. (1990). *Anticlimax: A Feminist Perspective on the Sexual Revolution*, London: Women's Press.

Johnson, P., and Goodchilds, J. (1973). 'Pornography, sexuality, and social psychology', *Journal of Social Issues* 29, 231–8.

Johnson, W., Kupperstein, L., and Peters, J. (1970). 'Sex offenders' experience with erotica', in *Technical Report of the Commission on Obscenity and Pornography*, vii, Washington, DC: Govt. Printing Office.

Johnston, J., and Ettema, J. S. (1982). *Positive Images: Breaking Stereotypes with Children's Television*, Beverly Hills, Calif.: Sage.

Joint Select Committee on Video Material (1988). *Report of the Joint Select Committee on Video Material*, Canberra: Australian Govt. Publishing Service.

Kanin, E. J. (1969). 'Selected dyadic aspects of male sex aggression', *Journal of Sex Research* 5, pp. 12–28.

—— (1985). 'Date rapists: Differential sexual socialization and relative deprivation', *Archives of Sexual Behavior* 14, pp. 219–31.

Kaplan, H. S. (1984). 'Have more fun making love', *Redbook*, July, pp. 88–9, 166.

Kappeler, S. (1986). *The Pornography of Representation*, Cambridge: Polity.

Kelley, K. (1985). 'Sex, sex guilt, and authoritarian differences in responses to explicit heterosexual and masturbatory slides', *Journal of Sex Research* 21, pp. 68–85.

—— (forthcoming *a*). 'Variety is the spice of erotica: Repeated exposure, novelty, sex, and sexual attitudes', *Archives of Sexual Behavior*.

—— (forthcoming *b*). 'Sexual attitudes as determinants of the motivational properties of exposure to erotica', *Personality and Individual Differences*.

—— and Byrne, D. (1983). 'Assessment of sexual responding: Arousal, affect, and behavior', in J. Cacioppo and R. Petty (eds.), *Social Psychophysiology*, New York: Guilford.

——, Dawson, L., and Musialowski, D. M. (1989). 'Three faces of sexual explicitness: The good, the bad, and the useful', in Zillmann and Bryant (1989).

Kendrick, W. (1987). *The Secret Museum: Pornography in Modern Culture*, New York: Viking.

Kenrick, D. T., Gutierres, S. E., and Goldberg, L. L. (1980). 'Influence of popular erotica on judgments of strangers and mates', *Journal of Experimental Social Psychology* 25, pp. 159–67.

Koss, M. (1986). *Hidden Rape: Survey of Psychopathological Consequences*, report to the National Institute of Mental Health, Bethesda, Md.

——, Leonard, K. E., Beezley, D. A., and Oros, C. J. (1985). 'Nonstranger sexual aggression: A discriminant analysis of the psychological characteristics of undetected offenders', *Sex Roles* 12, pp. 981–92.

Krafka, C. L. (1985). 'Sexually explicit, sexually violent, and violent media: Effects of multiple naturalistic exposures and debriefing on female viewers', doctoral dissertation, Univ. of Wisconsin, Madison.

Kruylanski, A. W. (1975). 'The human subject in the psychology experiment: Fact and artifact', in L. Berkowitz (ed.), *Advances in Experimental Social Psychology*, viii, New York: Academic.

Kupperstein, L., and Wilson, W. C. (1970). 'Erotica and antisocial behavior: An analysis of selected social indicator statistics', in *Technical Report of the Commission on Obscenity and Pornography*, vii, Washington, DC: Govt. Printing Office.

Kutchinsky, B. (1970*a*). 'Towards an explanation of the decrease in registered sex crimes in Copenhagen', in *Technical Report of the Commission on Obscenity and Pornography*, vii, Washington, DC: Govt. Printing Office.

—— (1970b). 'The effect of pornography: A pilot experiment on perception, behavior, and attitudes', in *Technical Report of the Commission on Obscenity and Pornography*, viii, Washington, DC: Govt. Printing Office.

—— (1973). 'Eroticism without censorship', *International Journal of Criminology and Penology*, pp. 217–25.

—— (1985). in R. F. Tomasson (ed.), *Comparative Social Research*, viii, Connecticut: JAI.

Lawrence, D. H. (1936). 'Pornography and obscenity', in E. D. McDonald (ed.), *Phoenix: The Posthumous Papers of D. H. Lawrence*, New York: Viking.

Lederer, L. (1980). *Take Back the Night: Women on Pornography*, New York: Morrow.

Leidholt, D., and Raymond, J. G. (1990). *The Sexual Liberals and the Attack on Feminism*, New York: Pergamon.

624 Leonard, K. E., and Taylor, S. P. (1983). 'Exposure to pornography, permissive and nonpermissive cues, and male aggression towards females', *Motivation and Emotion* 7, pp. 291–9.

Lettman, R. (1961). 'Psychology: The socially indifferent science', *American Psychologist* 16, pp. 232–6.

Liebert, R., and Schwartzberg, N. S. (1977). 'Effects of mass media', *Annual Review of Psychology* 28, pp. 141–73.

Linz, D. G. (1985). 'Sexual Violence in the Media: Effects on Male Viewers and Implications for Society', doctoral dissertation, Univ. of Wisconsin, Madison.

—— and Donnerstein, E. (1988). 'The methods and merits of pornography research', *Journal of Communication* 38(2), pp. 180–4.

—— —— and Adams, S. M. (1989). 'Physiological desensitization and judgments about female victims of violence', *Human Communication Research* 15, pp. 509–22.

—— —— and Penrod, S. (1984). 'The effects of multiple exposures to filmed violence against women', *Journal of Communication* 34(3), pp. 130–47.

—— —— —— (1988). 'Effects of long-term exposure to violent and sexually degrading depictions of women', *Journal of Personality and Social Psychology* 55, pp. 758–68.

London Rape Crisis Centre (1984). *Sexual Violence: The Reality for Women*, London: Women's Press.

Longino, H. E. (1980). 'Pornography, oppression, and freedom: A closer look', in Lederer (1980).

Lovelace, L. (1981). *Ordeal*, New York: Berkeley.

—— (1986). *Out of Bondage*, Secaucus, NJ: Lyle Stuart.

McCarthy, S. J. (1980). 'Pornography, rape, and the cult of macho', *The Humanist*, Sept./Oct., pp. 11–20, 56.

McKay, H. B., and Dolff, D. J. (1985). *The impact of pornography: An analysis of research and summary of findings*, Working Papers on Pornography and Prostitution, Report No. 13, Ottawa, Ont.: Ministry of Supply and Services.

McKenzie-Mohr, D., and Zanna, M. P. (1990). 'Treating women as sexual objects: Look to the (gender schematic) male who has viewed pornography', *Personality and Social Psychology Bulletin* 16, pp. 296–308.

MacKinnon, C. A. (1979). *Sexual Harassment of Working Women: A Case of Sex Discrimination*, New Haven, Conn.: Yale Univ. Press.

—— (1987). *Feminism Unmodified: Discourses on Life and Law*, Cambridge, Mass.: Harvard Univ. Press.

Malamuth, N. (1981a). 'Rape fantasies as a function of exposure to violent sexual stimuli', *Archive of Sexual Behavior* 10.

—— (1981b). 'Rape proclivity among males', *Journal of Social Issues* 37, pp. 138–57.

—— (1983). 'Factors associated with rape as predictors of laboratory agression against women', *Journal of Personality and Social Psychology* 45, pp. 432–42.

—— (1984a). 'Aggression against women: Cultural and individual causes', in Malamuth and Donnerstein (1984).

—— (1984b). 'The mass media and aggression against women: Research findings and prevention', in A. Burgess (ed.), *Handbook of Research on Pornography and Sexual Assault*, New York: Garland.

—— (1985). Testimony to the Attorney General's Commission on Pornography Hearings, Houston, Tx.; unpublished transcript, pp. 68–110.

—— (1986). 'Do sexually violent media indirectly contribute to antisocial behaviour?', paper prepared for the Surgeon General Workshop on Pornography and Public Health, Arlington, Va.

—— and Billings, V. (1986). 'The functions and effects of pornography: Sexual communications versus the feminist models in light of research findings', in J. Bryant and D. Zillmann (eds.), *Perspectives on Media Effects*, Hillsdale, NJ: Erlbaum.

—— and Briere, J. (forthcoming). 'Sexually violent media: Indirect effects on aggression against women', *Journal of Social Issues*.

—— and Check, J. V. P. (1980*a*). 'Penile tumescence and perceptual responses to rape as a function of victim's perceived reactions', *Journal of Applied Social Psychology* 10, pp. 528–47.

—— —— (1980*b*). 'Sexual arousal to rape and consenting depictions: The importance of the woman's arousal', *Journal of Abnormal Psychology* 89, pp. 763–6.

—— —— (1981). 'The effects of mass media exposure on acceptance of violence against women: A field experiment', *Journal of Research in Personality* 15, pp. 436–46.

—— —— (1983). 'Sexual arousal to rape depictions: Individual differences', *Journal of Abnormal Psychology* 92, pp. 55–67.

—— —— (1985). 'The effects of aggressive pornography on beliefs in rape myths: Individual differences', *Journal of Research in Personality* 19, pp. 299–320.

—— —— and Briere, J. (1986). 'Sexual arousal in response to aggression: Ideological, aggressive and sexual correlates', *Journal of Personality and Social Psychology* 50, pp. 330–40.

—— and Donnerstein, E. (1982). 'The effects of aggressive-pornographic mass media stimuli', in L. Berkowitz (ed.), *Advances in Experimental Social Psychology*, xv, New York: Academic.

—— —— (eds.) (1984). *Pornography and Sexual Aggression*, Orlando, Fla.: Academic.

——, Haber, S., and Feshbach, S. (1980). 'Testing hypotheses regarding rape: Exposure to sexual violence, sex differences, and the "normality" of rapists', *Journal of Research in Personality* 14, pp. 121–37.

——, Heim, M., and Feshbach, S. (1980). 'Sexual responsiveness of college students to rape depictions: Inhibitory and disinhibitory effects', *Journal of Personality and Social Psychology* 38, pp. 399–408.

——, Reisin, I., and Spinner, B. (1979). 'Exposure to pornography and reactions to rape', paper presented to the 86th annual convention of the American Psychological Association, New York.

—— and Spinner, B. (1980). 'A longitudinal content analysis of sexual violence in the best-selling erotic magazines', *Journal of Sex Research* 16, pp. 226–37.

626 Mann, J., Berkowitz, L., Sidman, J., Starr, S., and West, S. (1974).

'Satiation of the transient stimulating effect of erotic films', *Journal of Personality and Social Psychology* 30, pp. 729–35.

——, Sidman, J., and Starr, S. (1970). 'Effects of erotic films on the sexual behavior of married couples', in *Technical Report of the Commission on Obscenity and Pornography*, viii, Washington, DC: Govt. Printing Office.

—— —— —— (1973). 'Evaluating social consequences of erotic films: An experimental approach', *Journal of Social Issues* 29, 113–31.

Marshall, L. L. (1988). 'The use of sexually explicit stimuli by rapists, child molesters, and nonoffenders', *Journal of Sex Research* 25, pp. 267–88.

—— (1989). 'Pornography and sex offenders', in Zillmann and Byrant (1989).

Marshall, W. (1973). 'The modification of sexual fantasies: A combined treatment approach to the reduction of deviant sexual behavior', *Behavior Research and Therapy* 11, pp. 557–64.

—— (1984). 'Report on the use of pornography by sexual offenders', report to the Federal Dept. of Justice, Ottawa, Ont.

—— and Barbaree, H. E. (1978). 'The reduction of deviant arousal: Satiation treatment for sexual aggressors', *Criminal Justice Behavior* 5, pp. 294–303.

—— (1984). 'Disorders of personality, impulse and adjustment', in S. Tuiner and M. Herson (eds.), *Adult Psychopathology: A Behavioral Perspective*, New York: Academic.

—— and Christie, M. (1981). 'Pedophilia and aggression', *Criminal Justice and Behavior* 8, pp. 145–58.

——, Earls, C., Segal, Z., and Darke, J. (1983). 'A behavioral program for the assessment and treatment of sexual aggressors', in K. Craig and R. McMahon (eds.), *Advances in Clinical Behavior Therapy*, New York: Brunner/Mazel.

Medea, A., and Thompson, K. (1974). *Against Rape*, New York: Farrar, Straus and Giroux.

Melamed, L., and Moss, M. (1975). 'Effect of context on ratings of attractiveness of photographs', *Journal of Psychology* 90, pp. 129–36.

Merritt, C. G., Gerstl, J. E., and Lo Sciuto, L. A. (1975). 'Age and perceived effects of erotica-pornography: A national sample study', *Archives of Sexual Behavior* 4, pp. 605–21.

Metcalf, A., and Humphries, M. (eds.) (1985). *The Sexuality of Men*, London: Pluto.

Meyer, T. P. (1972). 'The effects of sexually arousing and violent films on aggressive behavior', *Journal of Sex Research* 8, pp. 324–33.

Morgan, R. (1980). 'Theory and practice of pornography and rape', in Lederer (1980).

Money, J. (1972). 'Pornography in the home', in J. Zubin and J. Money (eds.), *Contemporary Sexual Behavior: Critical Issues in 1970s*, Baltimore: Johns Hopkins Univ. Press.

—— (1979). 'Sexual dictatorship, dissidence and democracy', *International Journal of Medicine and Law* 1, pp. 11–20.

—— (1981). 'The development of sexuality and eroticism in human-kind', *Quarterly Review of Biology* 56 (Dec.), pp. 379–404.

—— (1982). 'Sexosophy and sexology, philosophy and science: Two halves, one whole', in Z. Hoch and H. I. Lief (eds.), *Sexology: Sexual Biology, Behavior and Therapy*, Amsterdam, Excerpta Medica.

—— (1985). 'The conceptual neutering of gender and the criminalization of sex', *Archives of Sexual Behavior* 14, pp. 279–89.

Mooney, B. (1987). *The Fourth of July*, London: Penguin.

Moreland, R. L., and Zajonc, R. B. (1976). 'A strong test of exposure effects', *Journal of Experimental Social Psychology* 12, pp. 170–79.

Mosher, D. (1970a). 'Sex callousness toward women', *Technical Report of the Commission on Obscenity and Pornography*, viii, Washington, DC: Govt. Printing Office.

—— (1970b). 'Psychological reactions to pornographic films', *Technical Report of the Commission on Obscenity and Pornography*, viii, Washington, DC: Govt. Printing Office.

—— (1970c). 'Pornographic films, male verbal aggression against women, and guilt', *Technical Report of the Commission on Obscenity and Pornography*, viii, Washington DC: Govt. Printing Office.

Mosher, D. L., and O Grady, K. E. (1979). 'Sex guilt, trait, anxiety, and females' subjective sexual arousal to erotica', *Motivation and Emotion* 3, pp. 235–49.

National Institute of Mental Health (1982). *Television and Behavior: Ten Years of Scientific Progress and Implications for the Eighties*, Bethesda, Md.

Nelson, E. C. (1982). 'Pornography and sexual aggression', in M. Yaffe and E. C. Nelson (eds.), *The Influence of Pornography on Behavior*, London: Academic.

Osgood, C. E., Suci, G. J., and Tannenbaum, P. H. (1957). *The Measurement of Meaning*, Urbana: Univ. of Illinois Press.

Page, S. (1989). 'Misrepresentation of pornography research: Psychology's role', *American Psychologist* 44, pp. 578–80.

Palys, T. S. (1984). *A content analysis of sexually explicit videos in British Columbia*, Working Papers on Pornography and Prostitution, Research Report No. 15, Ottawa, Ont.: Dept. of Justice.

—— (1986). 'Testing the common wisdom: The social content of video pornography', *Canadian Psychology* 27(1), pp. 22–35.

Prince, S. R. (1987). 'Power, Pain, and Pleasure in Pornography: A Content Analysis of Pornographic Feature Films, 1972–1985', doctoral dissertation, Univ. of Pennsylvania, Philadelphia.

Propper, M. (1970). 'Exposure to sexually oriented materials among young male prison offenders', in *Technical Report of the Commission on Obscenity and Pornography*, ix, Washington, DC: Govt. Printing Office.

Public Hearings on Ordinances to Add Pornography as Discrimination Against Women, Committee on Govt. Operations, City Council, Minneapolis, Minn.

Quinsey, V. L. (1983). 'Prediction of recidivism and the evaluation of treatment programs for sex offenders', in S. N. Verdun-Jones and A. A. Keltner (eds.), *Sexual Aggression and the Law*, : Simon Fraser Univ. Criminology Research Center.

—— (1984). 'Sexual aggression: Studies of offenders against women', in D. Weisstub (ed.), *Law and Mental Health: International Perspectives*, i, New York: Pergamon.

——— and Chaplin, T. C. (1982). 'Penile responses to nonsexual violence among rapists', *Criminal Justice and Behavior* 9 (Sept.), pp. 372–81.

——— (1984). 'Stimulus control of rapists' and non-sex offenders' sexual arousal', *Behavioral Assessment* 6, pp. 169–76.

——— ——— and Carrigan, W. (1980). 'Biofeedback and signalled punishment in the modification of inappropriate sexual age preference', *Behavior Therapy* 11, pp. 567–76.

——— ——— and Upfold, D. (1984). 'Sexual arousal to nonsexual violence and sadomasochistic themes among rapists and non-sexual offenders', *Journal of Consulting and Clinical Psychology* 52, pp. 651–7.

——— ——— and Varney, G. (1981). 'A comparison of rapist' and non-sex offenders' sexual preferences for mutually consenting sex, rape, and physical abuse of women', *Behavioral Assessment* 3, pp. 127–35.

——— and Marshall, W. (1983). 'Procedures for reducing inappropriate sexual arousal: An evaluation review', in J. G. Greer and I. Stuart (eds.), *The Sexual Aggressor: Current Perspectives on Treatment*, New York: Van Nostrand Reinhold.

———, Steinman, C. M., Bergerson, S. G., and Holmes, T. (1975). 'Penile circumference, skin conductance, and ranking responses of child molesters and "normals" to sexual and nonsexual visual stimui', *Behavior Therapy* 6, pp. 213–19.

Rada, R. T. (1978). 'Psychological factors in rapist behavior', in R. T. Rada (ed.), *Clinical Aspects of the Rapist*, New York: Grune and Stratton.

Rapaport, R., and Burkhart, B. R. (1984). 'Personality and attitudinal characteristics of sexually coercive college males', *Journal of Abnormal Psychology* 93, pp. 216–21.

Reifler, C. B., Howard, J., Lipton, M. A., Liptzin, M. B., and Widman, D. E. (1971). 'Pornography: An experimental study of effects', *American Journal of Psychiatry* 128, pp. 575–82.

Rhodes, D., and McNeill, S. (1985). *Women Against Violence Against Women*, London: Only Women Press

Rimmer, R. H. (1986). *The X-Rated Videotape Guide*, New York: Harmony.

Roberts, N. (1986). *The Front Line: Women in the Sex Industry Speak*, London: Grafton.

Root, J. (1985). *Pictures of Women: Sexuality*, London: Pandora Press.

Rosenthal, R., and Rosnow, R. (1969). *Artifact in Behavioral Research*, New York: Academic.

Rubinstein, E., and Brown, J. (1985). *The Media, Social Science, and Social Policy for Children*, Norwood, NJ: Ablex.

Russell, D. E. H. (1975). *The Politics of Rape: The Victim's Perspective*, Chelsea, Mich.: Scarborough House.

——— (1980). 'Pornography and violence: What does the new research say?', in Lederer (1980).

——— (1984). *Sexual Exploitation: Rape, Child Sexual Abuse, and Workplace Harassment*, Beverly Hills, Calif.: Sage.

——— (1988). 'Pornography and rape: A causal model', *Political Psychology* 9, pp. 41–73.

Sapolsky, B. S. (1984). 'Arousal, affect, and the aggression-moderating effect of erotica', in Malamuth and Donnerstein (1984).

—— and Zillmann, D. (1981). 'The effect of soft-core and hard-core erotica on provoked and unprovoked hostile behavior', *Journal of Sex Research* 17, pp. 319–43.

Schill, T., Van Tuinen, M., and Doty, D. (1980). 'Repeated exposure to pornography and arousal levels of subjects varying in guilt', *Psychological Reports* 46(2), pp. 467–71.

Schmidt, G. (1975). 'Male–female differences in sexual arousal and behavior during and after exposure to sexually explicit stimuli', *Archives of Sexual Behavior* 4, pp. 353–64.

—— and Sigusch, V. (1973). 'Women's sexual arousal', in J. Zubin and J. Money (eds.), *Contemporary Sexual Behavior: Critical Issues in the 1970s*, Baltimore: Johns Hopkins Univ. Press.

Scott, D. A. (1985). *Pornography: Its Effects on the Family, Community and Culture*, Washington, DC: Child and Family Protection Institute.

Scott, J. E. (1972). 'The changing nature of sex references in mass circulation magazines', *Public Opinion Quarterly* 36, pp. 80–6.

—— (1973). 'Sex references in the mass media', *Journal of Sex Research* 9 (Aug.), pp. 196–209.

—— (1974). 'A reexamination of the public's perception of sexual deviance', *Western Sociological Review* 5 (summer), pp. 82–6.

—— (forthcoming). 'A longitudinal content analysis of sex references in mass circulation magazines', *Journal of Sex Research.*

—— and Schwalm, L. A. (1988). 'Rape rates and the circulation of adult magazines', *Journal of Sex Research* 24, pp. 241–50.

Scully, D. (1985). 'The role of violent pornography in justifying rape', paper prepared for the Attorney General's Commission on Pornography Hearings, Houston, Tx.

—— and Marolla, J. (1983). *Convicted rapists: Exploring a sociological model*, final report to the National Institute of Mental Health, Bethesda, Md.

—— —— (1984). 'Convicted rapists' vocabulary of motive: Excuses and justifications', *Social Problems* 31, pp. 531–44.

—— —— (1985). 'Riding the bull at Gilley's: Rapists describe the rewards of rape', *Social Problems* (Feb.).

Senn, C. (forthcoming). 'Women's responses to pornography', in D. E. H. Russell (ed.), *Making Violence Sexy: The Politics of Pornography*, New York: Pergamon.

Senn, C. Y., and Radtke, H. L. (1986). 'Women's evaluations of and effective reactions to mainstream violent pornography, non-violent pornography, and erotica', *Violence and Victims* 5(3).

Silbert, M. (1980). *Sexual Assault of Prostitutes*, Bethesda, Md.: National Institute of Mental Health, National Center for the Prevention and Control of Rape.

Silbert, M. H., and Pines, A. M. (1984). 'Pornography and sexual abuse of women', *Sex Roles* 10, pp. 857–68.

Simpson, M., and Schill, T. (1977). 'Patrons of massage parlors: Some facts and figures', *Archives of Sexual Behavior* 6, pp. 521–5.

Sintchak, G., and Geer, J. (1975). 'A vaginal plethysmograph system', *Psychophysiology* 12, pp. 113–15.

Slade, J. W. (1984). 'Violence in the hard-core pornographic film: A historical survey', *Journal of Communication* 34(3), pp. 148–63.

Smith, D. (1976). 'Sexual aggression in American pornography: The stereotype of rape', paper presented at the American Sociological Association meeting.

Smith, D. G. (1976). 'The social content of pornography', *Journal of Communication* 26, pp. 16–33.

Smith, J. (1989). *Misogynies*, London: Faber and Faber.

Snitow, A. (1985). 'Retrenchment versus transformation: The politics of the antipornography movement', in V. Burstyn (ed.), *Women Against Censorship*, Vancouver, BC: Douglas and McIntyre.

Special Committee on Pornography and Prostitution (1985). *Report of the Special Committee on Pornography and Prostitution*, Ottawa, Ont.: Canadian Govt. Publishing Centre.

Steinem, G. (1980). 'Erotica and pornography: A clear and present difference', in Lederer (1980).

Stock, W. (1983). 'The effects of violent pornography on women', paper presented at the American Psychological Association meeting, Anaheim, Calif.

Stoller, R. (1976). 'Sexual excitement', *Archives of General Psychiatry* 33, pp. 899–909.

Stoltenberg, J. (1990). *Refusing to Be a Man: Essays on Sex and Justice*, London: Fontana.

Surgeon General's Scientific Advisory Committee on Television and Social Behavior (1972). *Television and Growing Up: The Impact of Televised Violence*, report to the Surgeon General, US Public Health Service, Washington, DC: Govt. Printing Office.

Swart, C., and Berkowitz, L. (1976). 'Effects of a stimulus associated with a victim's pain on later aggression', *Journal of Personality and Social Psychology* 33, pp. 623–31.

Tannenbaum, P. H. (1970). 'Emotional arousal as a mediator of erotic communication effects', in *Technical Report of the Commission on Obscenity and Pornography*, viii, Washington, DC: Govt. Printing Office.

Tate, T. (1990). *Child Pornography: An Investigation*, London: Methuen.

—— (1991). *Children for the Devil: Ritual Abuse and Satanic Crime*, London: Methuen.

Tieger, T. (1981). 'Self-reported likelihood of raping and the social perception of rape', *Journal of Research in Personality* 15, pp. 147–58.

Tversky, A., and Kahneman, D. (1973). 'Availability: A heuristic for judging frequency and probability', *Cognitive Psychology* 5, pp. 207–32.

Walker, C. E. (1970). 'Erotic stimuli and the aggressive sexual offender', in *Technical Report of the Commission on Obscenity and Pornography*, v Washington, DC: Govt. Printing Office.

Wallace, D. H. (1973). 'Obscenity and contemporary community standards: A survey', *Journal of Social Issues* 29, pp. 53–68.

Weaver, J. B. (1987). 'Effects of Portrayals of Female Sexuality and Violence against Women on Perceptions of Women', doctoral dissertation, Indiana Univ., Bloomington.

—— (1991a). 'The impact of exposure to horror film violence on perceptions of women: Is it the violence or an artifact?', in B. Austin (ed.), *Current Research in Film*, v Norwood, NJ: Ablex.

—— (1991*b*). 'Responding to erotica: Perceptual processes and dispositional implications', in J. Bryant and D. Zillmann (eds.), *Responding to the Screen: Reception and Reaction Processes*, Hillsdale, NJ: Erlbaum.

——, Masland, J. L., and Zillman, D. (1984). 'Effect of erotica on young men's aesthetic perception of their female sexual partners', *Perceptual and Motor Skills* 58, pp. 929–30.

Weiss, W. (1969). 'Effects of the mass media on communication', in G. Lindzey and E. Aronson (eds.), *Handbook of Social Psychology*, Reading, Mass.: Addison-Wesley.

White, L. A. (1979). 'Erotica and aggression: The influence of sexual arousal, positive affect, and negative affect on aggressive behavior', *Journal of Personality and Social Psychology* 37, pp. 591–601.

Whitman, W., and Quinsey, V. L. (1981). 'Heterosocial skills training for institutionalized rapists and child molesters', *Canadian Journal of Behavioral Science* 13, pp. 105–14.

Williams, B. (1981). *Obscenity and Film Censorship: An Abridgement of the Williams Report*, Cambridge: Cambridge Univ. Press.

Wilson, W. C. (1978). 'Can pornography contribute to the prevention of sexual problems?', in C. B. Qualls, J. P. Wincze, and D. H. Barlow (eds.), *The Prevention of Sexual Disorders: Issues and Approaches*, New York: Plenum.

—— and Abelson, H. I. (1973). 'Experience with and attitudes toward explicit sexual materials', *Journal of Social Issues* 29(3), pp. 19–39.

Winick, C. (1985). 'A content analysis of sexually explicit magazines sold in an adult bookstore', *Journal of Sex Research* 21, pp. 206–10.

Wolchik, S. A., Braver, S. L., and Jensen, K. (1985). 'Volunteer bias in erotica research: Effects of intrusiveness of measure and sexual background', *Archive of Sexual Behavior* 14, pp. 93–107.

——, Spencer, S. L., and Lisi, I. (1983). 'Volunteer bias in research employing vaginal measures of sexual arousal: Demographic, sexual and personality characteristics', *Archive of Sexual Behavior* 12, pp. 339–408.

Yaffe, M., and Nelson, E. (eds.) *The Influence of Pornography on Behavior*, New York: Academic.

Yang, N., and Linz, D. (1990). 'Sex and violence in adult videos', *Journal of Communication* 40(2), pp. 28–42.

Zajonc, R. B. (1968). 'Attitudinal effects of mere exposure', *Journal of Personality and Social Psychology Monograph Supplement* 9, pp. 1–27.

—— and Rajecki, D. W. (1969). 'Exposure and affect: A field experiment', *Psychonomic Science* 17, pp. 216–17.

Zillmann, D. (1978). 'Attribution and misattribution of excitatory reactions', in J. H. Harvey, W. J. Ickes, and R. F. Kidd (eds.), *New Directions in Attribution Research*, ii, Hillsdale, NJ: Erlbaum.

—— (1979). *Hostility and Aggression*, Hillsdale, NJ: Erlbaum.

—— (1982). 'Television viewing and arousal', in D. Pearl, L. Bouthilet, and J. Lazar, *Television and Behavior: Ten Years of Scientific Progress and Implications for the Eighties*, ii. Bethesda, Md.: National Institute of Mental Health.

—— (1984). *Connections between Sex and Aggression*, Hillsdale, NJ: Erlbaum.

—— (1985). 'Effects of repeated exposure to nonviolent pornography', paper presented to the US Attorney General's Commission on Pornography Hearing, Houston, Tx.

—— (1989*a*). 'Effects of prolonged consumption of pornography', in Zillmann and Bryant (1989).

—— (1989*b*). 'Pornography research and public policy', in Zillmann and Bryant (1989).

—— and Bryant, J. (1982). 'Pornography, sexual callousness and the trivialization of rape', *Journal of Communication* 32(4), pp. 10–21.

—— —— (1984). 'Effects of massive exposure to pornography', in Malamuth and Donnerstein (1984).

—— —— [1986]. 'Pornography's impact on sexual satisfaction', unpublished paper.

—— —— (1987). 'Pornography and behavior: Alternative explanations – A reply', *Journal of Communication* 37(3), pp. 189–92.

—— ©(1988*a*). 'Effects of prolonged consumption of pornography on family values', *Journal of Family Issues* 9, pp. 518–44.

—— —— (1988*b*). 'Pornography's impact on sexual satisfaction', *Journal of Applied Social Psychology* 18, pp. 438–53.

—— —— (1988*c*). 'The methods and merits of pornography research: A response', *Journal of Communication* 38(2), pp. 185–92.

—— —— (eds.) (1989). *Pornography: Research Advances and Policy Considerations*, Hillsdale, NJ: Erlbaum.

—— —— (forthcoming). 'Shifting preferences in pornography consumption', *Communication Research*.

—— —— and Carveth, R. A. (1981). 'The effect of erotica featuring sadomasochism and bestiality on motivated intermale aggression', *Personality and Social Psychology Bulletin* 7, pp. 153–9.

—— —— , Comisky, P. W., and Medoff, N. J. (1981). 'Excitation and hedonic valence in the effect of erotica on motivated intermale aggression', *European Journal of Social Psychology* 11, pp. 233–52.

—— , Hoyt, J. L., and Day, K. D. (1974). 'Strength and duration of the effect of aggressive, violent, and erotic communications on subsequent aggressive behavior', *Communication Research* 1, pp. 286–306.

—— and Sapolsky, B. S. (1977). 'What mediates the effect of mild erotica on annoyance and hostile behavior in males?', *Journal of Personality and Social Psychology* 35, pp. 587–96.

—— and Weaver, J. B. (1989). 'Pornography and men's sexual callousness toward women', in Zillmann and Bryant (1989).

Zuckerman, M. (1971). 'Physiological measures of sexual arousal in the human', *Psychology Bulletin* 75, pp. 297–328.

ORGANIZATIONS CONCERNED ABOUT OR ACTIVE AGAINST PORNOGRAPHY

UK

The Anti-Pornography Trust, 9 Poland Street, London, W1V 3DG.

Association of Cinematograph Television and Allied Technicians (ACTT), 111 Wardour Street, London, W1V 4AY.

Broadcasting Standards Council, The Sanctuary, London, SW1P 3JS.

Campaign Against Pornography (CAP), 96 Dalston Lane, Unity Club, London E8 1NE.

Campaign Against Pornography and Censorship (CPC), PO Box 844, London, SE5 9QP.

Campaign for Press and Broadcasting Freedom (CPBF), 96 Dalston Lane, Unity Club, London E8 1NE.

The Children's Legal Centre, 20 Compton Terrace, London, N1 2UN.

Ethical Investment Research Service (EIRIS) Services Ltd, 401 Bondway Business Centre, 71 Bondway, London, SW8 1SQ.

The Fawcett Society, 46 Harleyford Road, London, SE11 5AY.

London Rape Crisis Centre, PO Box 69, London, WC1X 9NJ. (There are also dozens of Rape Crisis Centres in cities all over the country.)

National Alliance of Women's Organisations (NAWO), 279/281 Whitechapel Road, London E1 1BY

National Union of Journalists (NUJ), 314 Grays Inn Road, London, WC1.

Women Against Violence Against Women (WAVAW), Hungerford House, Victoria Embankment, London, WC2.

IRELAND

Irish Campaign Against Pornography and Censorship (ICPC), 22 Pimlico, Dublin 8, Ireland.

USA

Men Against Pornography, PO Box 150–786, Van Brunt Station, Brooklyn, NY 11215.

National Anti-Pornography Civil Rights Organization, PO Box 140, Brooklyn, NY 11217.

Organizing Against Pornography, PO Box 3000–76, Minneapolis, MN 55403.

Women Against Pornography, 358 West 47th Street, New York, New York 10036.

COPYRIGHT CREDITS

and Corinne Sweet, 'What Should We Do About Pornography?', *Cosmopolitan*, November 1989. Published with permission.

Copyright © 1989 Michael Moorcock. First published by the Campaign Against Pornography and Censorship. Published with permission.

Chapter 2
Copyright © 1992 Catherine Itzin.

Chapter 3
Copyright © 1992 I Spy Productions.

Chapter 4
Copyright © 1992 Susanne Kappeler.

Chapter 5
Copyright © Aminatta Forna 1992.

Chapter 6
Copyright © Liz Kelly 1992.

Chapter 7
Copyright © Peter Baker 1992.

Chapter 8
Copyright © 1981, 1985, 1989, 1990, 1992 John Stoltenberg. Adapted from 'Pornography and Freedom', first published in *Changing Men* (formerly *M: Gentle Men for Gender Justice*) No. 15, Spring 1985, reprinted in *Refusing to be a Man: Essays and Discourses on Sex and Justice* by John Stoltenberg (Portland, Oregon: Breitenbush Books, 1989 and London: Fontana, 1990); 'Sexual Objectification and Male Supremacy', first published in *M: Gentle Men for Gender Justice*, No. 5, Spring 1981, reprinted in *Refusing to be a Man*; and 'Gays and the Pornography Movement: Having the Hots for Sex Discrimination', first published in *Men Confront Pornography*, ed. Michael S. Kimmel (New York: Crown Publishers, Inc., 1990).

Chapter 9
Copyright © Janice Raymond 1992. This chapter is adapted from an article first published as 'Putting the Politics Back into   **637**

Chapter 19
Copyright © Deborah Cameron and Elizabeth Frazer 1992.

Chapter 20
Copyright © H. Patricia Hynes 1992. First published in *Women's Studies International Forum*. Published with permission. An earlier version was published in *Trouble and Strife*, 15, Spring 1989.

Chapter 21
Copyright © Catherine Itzin 1992.

Chapter 22
Copyright © Catherine Itzin 1992.

Chapter 23
Copyright © 1985 Catharine A. MacKinnon. First published in the United States in *Harvard Civil Rights – Civil Liberties Law Review*, Vol. 20, No. 1, Winter 1985. Reprinted in Catharine A. MacKinnon, *Feminism Unmodified* (Cambridge, Massachusetts: Harvard University Press, 1987). Published with the kind permission of the author and Harvard University Press.

Chapter 24
Copyright © 1985 Andrea Dworkin. First published in the United States in *Harvard Women's Law Journal*, Vol. 8, Spring 1985. First published in the United Kingdom in *Letters from a War Zone*, Martin Secker & Warburg, 1987. Published with the kind permission of the author and Secker & Warburg.

Chapter 25
Copyright © Michael Moorcock 1992.

Chapter 26
Copyright © Catherine Itzin 1992.

ABOUT THE CONTRIBUTORS

Peter Baker works as a research officer on social policy issues for a local government research organization in London, and as a freelance journalist writing on men's issues for the *Guardian*, *Cosmopolitan* and *Company* magazines. He is a trained counsellor who has worked with men on their use of pornography, a member of the Campaign Against Pornography and Censorship Steering Group. In September 1990 he organized Britain's first national conference for men opposed to pornography.

Deborah Cameron has taught English Language and Women's Studies in Britain and the USA, currently at the University of Strathclyde in Scotland. She has been active in feminist politics since the late 1970s, working with Women's Aid, the Rape Crisis movement, WAVAW (Women Against Violence Against Women) and in campaigns against sexual harassment in higher education. She is co-author with Elizabeth Frazer of *The Lust to Kill: A Feminist Investigation of Sexual Murder* (Cambridge: Polity Press, 1987).

James V. P. Check is Associate Professor of Psychology and Director of the LaMarsh Research Programme on Conflict Resolution at York University, Toronto. He has published 28 journal articles and book chapters, and 29 published abstracts, and given 91 conference papers on pornography, rape, child sexual abuse, and woman abuse such as battering. He provides legal consultation and gives expert testimony in obscenity cases and other court cases related to media violence and the abuse of women.

Andrea Dworkin is a writer and a radical feminist activist. She is the author of the novels *Mercy* and *Ice and Fire*, the non-fiction books *Letters from a War Zone*, *Intercourse*, *Right-Wing Women*, *Pornography: Men Possessing Women*, *Our Blood: Prophecies and*

Discourses on Sexual Politics, and *Woman Hating*, and a collection of short stories, *the new womans broken heart*. With Catharine A. MacKinnon, she drafted sex discrimination legislation for the City of Minneapolis that recognized pornography as a violation of the civil rights of women.

Edna F. Einsiedel is Professor and Director of the Graduate Program in Communication Studies at the University of Calgary in Alberta, Canada. She served as Staff Social Scientist for the 1986 US Attorney General's Commission on Pornography while teaching at the School of Communications at Syracuse University in New York before she moved to Canada. She has published in the area of social science and public policy, examining the experiences of pornography commissions in England, Canada and the USA. Her current research interests are in the areas of science and health communications and science literacy.

Michele Elliott is the founder and Director of Kidscape, the campaign for children's safety and the prevention of child abuse. She has chaired World Health Organization and Home Office Working Groups on the prevention of child abuse. She is on the advisory councils of the National Association for the Prevention of Cruelty to Children and Child Line. She is the author of several books including *Keeping Safe: A Practical Guide to Talking with Children* (London: Hodder and Stoughton, 1988), and *Dealing with Child Abuse: A Training Guide* (London: Kidscape, 1989).

Aminatta Forna is a television journalist with the BBC, working first as a presenter on the BBC's flagship black programme 'Ebony' and then with BBC News and Current Affairs. She has a law degree from the University of London and has contributed as a feature writer and reporter to a variety of newspapers and magazines, covering the pornography debate from the perspective of a black woman.

Elizabeth Frazer is a sociologist and Fellow of New College, Oxford. She is the co-author, with Deborah Cameron, of *The Lust to Kill* (see above).

H. Patricia Hynes is Director of the Institute on Women and Technology and teaches in the Department of Urban Studies and Planning at the Massachusetts Institute of Technology. An **641**

environmental engineer, she served as Section Chief in the Hazardous Waste Division of the US Environmental Protection Agency and Chief of Environment Management of the Massachusetts Port Authority. She is author of *The Recurring Silent Spring* (Oxford: Pergamon, 1989) and *Earthright: Every Citizen's Guide* (New York: Prima/St Martin's, 1990), and editor of *Reconstructing Babylon: Women and Technology* (Earthscan and Indiana University, 1990).

I Spy Productions is a mixed-sex research collective. They are the authors of *Looks Can Kill: Pornographic Business*, 1988. Price £3. Available from I Spy Productions, Box 60, 52 Call Lane, Leeds LS1 LDT.

Catherine Itzin is a Research Fellow in the Violence, Abuse and Gender Relations Research Unit at the University of Bradford. She was a Senior Research Officer and subsequently Research Fellow in the Department of Sociology at the University of Essex from 1985. She is a member of the Executive Committee of the National Council for Civil Liberties and co-founder of the Campaign Against Pornography and Censorship (CPC). She is author, co-author and editor of many books and articles on gender and other issues, including *Stages in the Revolution* (London: Methuen, 1980), *Splitting Up* (London: Virago, 1980) and *I Don't Feel Old* (Oxford University Press, 1990).

Susanne Kappeler is a feminist activist and theorist who has taught feminist studies in universities and in other contexts. Based at the University of East Anglia's Centre for Creative and Performing Arts, she works as a freelance teacher and writer in England and West Germany. She is author of *The Pornography of Representation* (Cambridge: Polity Press, 1986).

Liz Kelly is a white feminist activist, currently Research Fellow at the Child Abuse Studies Unit, Polytechnic of North London, working on a prevalence study of child sexual abuse in Britain. She is a member of the Feminist Coalition Against Child Sexual Abuse, Women Against International Sex Trafficking and the editorial collective of *Trouble and Strife*. She is author of *Surviving Sexual Violence* (Cambridge: Polity Press, 1988), and a recently completed study (with Alison McGibbon and Libby Cooper) of services for women experiencing domestic violence in a London borough.

Catharine A. MacKinnon is Professor of Law at the University of Michigan School of Law and co-author with Andrea Dworkin of the civil rights anti-pornography ordinance. She is author of *Sexual Harassment of Working Women: A Case of Sex Discrimination* (Yale University Press, 1979), *Feminism Unmodified* (Harvard University Press, 1987), *Toward a Feminist Theory of the State* (Harvard University Press, 1989), and co-author with Andrea Dworkin of *Pornography and Civil Rights: A New Day for Women's Equality* from Organizing Against Pornography (Minneapolis, 1988).

Michael Moorcock is the author of some sixty novels. From the age of fifteen he has been a professional writer and editor and involved in radical politics, working on various 'underground publications'. He has worked for the women's liberation movement since the mid-1970s, and been the subject of much attempted censorship and suppression, especially as editor of *New Worlds* and when writing on feminist issues. In 1983 his book *The Retreat from Liberty* described feminism as the main hope for progressive politics in the future.

Janice Raymond is Professor of Women's Studies and Medical Ethics at the University of Massachusetts, Amherst. She is the author of *The Transsexual Empire* (London: The Women's Press 1980) and *A Passion for Friends* (London: The Women's Press, 1986) and the co-editor of *The Sexual Liberals and the Attack on Feminism* (New York: Pergamon, 1990). As the consulting editor of *Issues in Reproductive and Genetic Engineering: Journal of International Feminist Analysis*, she writes a regular column on reproductive and genetic issues. She is associate director of the Institute on Women and Technology, a public policy and research institute based at MIT. Her new book will be called *Technological Justice: Women and the New Reproductive Medicine* (Beacon Press, 1991).

Diana E. H. Russell is Professor of Sociology at Mills College, in California. She is the author or editor of nine books, including *The Politics of Rape*, 1975; *Rape in Marriage*, 1982, *Against Sado Masochism: A Radical Feminist Analysis*, 1982; *Sexual Exploitation: Rape, Child Sexual Abuse and Workplace Harassment*, 1984; *The Secret* **643**

Trauma: Incest in the Lives of Girls and Women, 1986: and *Lives of Courage: Women for a New South Africa,* 1990. She was a founding member of the San Francisco-based Women Against Violence in Pornography and Media in 1976. She is currently editing *Making Violence Sexy: The Politics of Pornography* to be published by Pergamon Press in 1991 and co-editing *Femicide: The Politics of Woman Killing* for Open University Press in 1991.

John Stoltenberg is a writer, editor, and anti-pornography activist living in New York City. His book, *Refusing to be a Man,* was published in September 1990 by Collins/Fontana. He is chair of the Task Group on Pornography of the National Organization for Men Against Sexism (NOMAS) and co-founder of Men Against Pornography in New York City. He conceived and co-founded BrotherPeace: An International Day of Actions to End Men's Violence, a project of NOMAS that takes place in scores of cities in the US and abroad on the third Saturday of October. He has also spoken frequently about, and lobbied for passage of, the Dworkin–MacKinnon civil-rights anti-pornography ordinance.

Corinne Sweet is a freelance writer and broadcaster, specializing in women's issues, for outlets such as *Company, Cosmopolitan, New Woman, Good Housekeeping, Spare Rib,* the *The Independent* and 'Woman's Hour' on BBC Radio 4. She also works as a counsellor and trainer in the fields of addictions and women's rights. She has a long history as a women's activist, having co-founded Women Against Sexual Harassment (WASH) and Campaign Against Pornography and Censorship (CPC). She was Women's Rights Officer for the National Council for Civil Liberties from 1984–1987, and a Woman's Officer in local government before entering journalism in 1989.

Tim Tate is a freelance investigative journalist and television producer, specializing in children's issues. He has researched and produced programmes for the BBC series 'Checkpoint' and Central Televisions's 'The Cook Report', as well as independent productions for Channel 4 and ITV. In 1987 he was responsible for the 'Cook Report' investigation into child pornography. He has been responsible for television and radio documentaries on the rights of children in care, trafficking in babies for adoption and ritualized child sexual abuse. He is the author of *Child Pornography: An Investigation* (London: Methuen, 1990) and *Chil-*

dren for the Devil: Ritual Abuse and Satanic Crime (London: Methuen, 1991).

James Weaver is an Associate Professor of Mass Communication and Director of the Behavioral Research Laboratory at Auburn University, Alabama, USA. His research interests focus on exploration of the social and psychological uses and effects of mass communication. He has written on pornography for a number of books and journals, including *Pornography: Recent Research, Interpretations, and Policy Considerations*, D. Zillmann and J. Bryant (eds) 1989, *Sex Roles: A Journal of Research* and *Journal of Broadcasting and Electronic Media.*

Ray Wyre is the Director of the Gracewell Clinic, the first residential clinic for child sex abusers in the UK, and well known for his pioneering work in promoting the treatment of male sex offenders. He is the author of *Working with Sex Abuse* (Oxford: Swift, 1987) and co-author, with Anthony Swift, of *Women, Men and Rape* (London: Hodder and Stoughton, 1990).